PARAGON
ISSUES IN
PHILOSOPHY

PARAGON ISSUES IN PHILOSOPHY

THE PARAGON ISSUES IN PHILOSOPHY SERIES

At colleges and universities, interest in the traditional areas of philosophy remains strong. Many new currents flow within them, too, but until recently many of these—the rise of cognitive science, for example, or feminist philosophy—often went largely unnoticed in undergraduate philosophy courses. The Paragon Issues in Philosophy Series responds to both perennial and newly influential concerns by bringing together a team of able philosophers to address the fundamental issues in philosophy today and to outline the state of contemporary discussion about them.

More than twenty volumes are scheduled; they are organized into three major categories. The first covers the standard topics—metaphysics, theory of knowledge, ethics, and political philosophy—stressing innovative developments in those disciplines. The second focuses on more specialized but still vital concerns in the philosophies of science, religion, history, sport, and other areas. The third category explores new work that relates philosophy and fields such as feminist criticism, medicine, economics, technology, and literature.

The level of writing is aimed at undergraduate students who have little previous experience studying philosophy. The books provide brief but accurate introductions that appraise the state of the art in their fields and show how the history of thought about their topics has developed. Each volume is complete in itself but also aims to complement others in the series.

Traumatic change characterized the twentieth century and the twenty-first will be no different in that regard. All of its pivotal issues will involve philosophical questions. As the editors at Paragon House continue to work with us, we hope that this series will help to encourage the understanding needed in a new millennium whose times will be as complicated and problematic as they are promising.

John K. Roth
Claremont McKenna College

Frederick Sontag
Pomona College

GLOBAL ETHICS: SEMINAL ESSAYS

THOMAS POGGE
KEITH HORTON

GLOBAL ETHICS: SEMINAL ESSAYS

Global Responsibilities
Volume II

PARAGON
ISSUES IN
PHILOSOPHY

PARAGON HOUSE ✦ ST. PAUL

First Edition 2008

Published in the United States by
Paragon House
1925 Oakcrest Avenue Ste 7
St. Paul, MN 55113-2619

Paragon Issues in Philosophy Series
    Global Responsibilities
        Volume I: Global Justice: Seminal Essays
        Volume II: Global Ethics: Seminal Essays

Library of Congress Cataloging-in-Publication Data

Pogge, Thomas Winfried Menko.
  Global ethics : seminal essays / Thomas Pogge, Keith Horton. -- 1st ed.
    p. cm. -- (Paragon issues in philosophy series)
  Summary: "Carefully selected papers of fundamental and philosophical
essays, written by distinguished moral and political theorists, addressing
the global ethical issues of our time"--Provided by publisher.
  Includes bibliographical references and index.
  ISBN 978-1-55778-870-2 (pbk. : alk. paper)
  1. Ethics. 2. Globalization--Moral and ethical aspects. I. Horton,
Keith, 1961- II. Title.
  BJ1031.P64 2008
  172--dc22
                            2007043692

The paper used in this publication meets the minimum requirements of American National
Standard for Information--Permanence of Paper for Printed Library Materials, AN-
SIZ39.48-1984.

Manufactured in the United States of America

10 9 8 7 6 5 4 3 2 1

For current information about all releases from Paragon House,
visit the web site at http://www.paragonhouse.com

CONTENTS

VOLUME II: GLOBAL ETHICS

VOLUME I: GLOBAL JUSTICE

Preface:

INTRODUCTION TO THE
TWO-VOLUME COLLECTION

For centuries, moral reflection on international relations was focused on matters of war and peace. These issues are still important and much discussed. Since World War II, however, other themes have become more prominent due to increasing global interdependence and an erosion of sovereignty. The United Nations and the Universal Declaration of Human Rights reflect efforts to establish globally uniform minimum standards for the treatment of citizens within their own countries. The Bretton Woods institutions and later the World Trade Organization powerfully shape the economic prospects of countries and their citizens. Global and regional organizations, most notably the UN Security Council and the European Union, have acquired political functions and powers that were traditionally thought to belong to national governments.

These developments are in part a response to the horrors of World War II. But they are also fueled by technological innovations that limit the control governments can exert within their jurisdictions. Thus, industrialization has massive transnational effects that no country can avoid—effects on culture and expectations, on biodiversity, climate, oceans, and atmosphere. New communications technologies make it much harder to control the information available to a national population. And many of the goods demanded by more affluent consumers everywhere require ingredients imported from many foreign lands. The traditional concerns with the just internal organization of societies and the moral rules governing warfare leave out some highly consequential features of the modern world.

After some delay, academic moral reflection has responded to these developments. Beginning in the early 1970s, philosophers and others have asked probing questions about how the emergence of a post-Westphalian world modifies and enlarges the moral responsibilities of governments, corporations, and individuals. These debates were driven also by the realization that world poverty has overtaken war as the greatest source of avoidable human misery. Many more people—some 300 million—have died from hunger and remediable diseases in peacetime in the seventeen years since the end of the Cold War than have perished from wars, civil wars, and government repression over the entire twentieth century. And poverty continues unabated, with some 830 million human beings chronically undernourished, 1100 million lacking access to safe water, and 2600 million lacking access to basic sanitation;[1] 2000 million lacking access to essential drugs;[2] 1000 million lacking adequate shelter and 2000 million lacking electricity;[3] 774 million adults being illiterate,[4] and 218 million children between five and seventeen doing wage work outside their household.[5] Such severe deficits in the fulfillment of social and economic human rights also bring further deficits in civil and political human rights in their wake. Very poor people—often physically and mentally stunted due to malnutrition in infancy, illiterate due to lack of schooling, and much preoccupied with their family's survival—can cause little harm or benefit to the politicians and officials who rule them. Such rulers have far greater incentive to attend to the interests of agents more capable of reciprocation: the interests of affluent compatriots and foreigners, of domestic and multinational corporations, and of foreign governments.

The great catastrophe of human poverty is ongoing, as is the annual toll of 18 million deaths from poverty-related causes, roughly one-third of all human deaths.[6] Three facts make such poverty deeply problematic,

1. UNDP (United Nations Development Program), *Human Development Report 2006* (Houndsmills: Palgrave Macmillan, 2006), 33 and 174. Also at hdr.undp.org/hdr2006.
2. See www.fic.nih.gov/about/plan/exec_summary.htm.
3. UNDP, *Human Development Report 1998* (New York: Oxford University Press, 1998), 49, http://hdr.undp.org/reports/global/1998/en/pdf/hdr_1998_ch3.pdf.
4. See www.uis.unesco.org.
5. See ILO (International Labour Office), *The End of Child Labour: Within Reach* (Geneva: ILO 2006), Table 1.1. Also at www.ilo.org/public/english/standards/relm/ilc/ilc95/pdf/rep-i-b.pdf.
6. See WHO (World Health Organisation), *The World Health Report 2004* (Geneva: WHO Publications 2004), 120-25. Also at www.who.int/whr/2004.

morally. First, it occurs in the context of unprecedented global affluence that is easily sufficient to eradicate all life-threatening poverty. Although 2735 million human beings are reported to be living below the World Bank's $2/day poverty line,[7] and 42 percent below it on average,[8] their collective shortfall from this line amounts to less than 1 percent of the national incomes of the high-income countries with their 1 billion people.[9] A shift in the global income distribution involving only 0.7 percent of global income would wholly eradicate the severe poverty that currently blights the lives of over 40 percent of the human population. While the income inequality between the top and bottom tenth of the human population is a staggering 320:1,[10] the wealth inequality is nine times greater still. In 2000 the bottom 50 percent of the world's adults together had 1.1 percent of global wealth with the bottom 10 percent having only 0.03 percent, while the top 10 percent had 85.1 percent and the top 1 percent had 39.9 percent.[11] Severe poverty today is avoidable at a cost that is tiny in relation to the incomes and fortunes of the

---

7. See Shaohua Chen and Martin Ravallion, "How Have the World's Poorest Fared since the Early 1980s?" *World Bank Research Observer* 19 (2004), 141–69, 153. Also at wbro.oupjournals.org/cgi/content/abstract/19/2/141.

8. Ibid., 152 and 158, dividing the poverty gap index by the headcount index.

9. To count as poor by the $2/day standard, a person in the US must in 2007 live on less than $1120. (This figure is based on the official definition of the poverty line in terms of the purchasing power that $2.15 had in the US in 1993 as updated via the US consumer price index at www.bls.gov/cpi/home.htm). Ascribing much greater purchasing power to the currencies of poor countries than market exchange rates would suggest, the World Bank assumes that about one-quarter of this amount, $280 per person per year, is sufficient to escape poverty in typical poor countries. The 2735 million global poor live, then, on approximately $444 billion annually and lack roughly $322 billion annually relative to the $2/day poverty line. This $322 billion is less than one percent of the gross national incomes of the high-income countries which, in 2005, summed to $35,529 billion. See World Bank, *World Development Report, 2007* (New York: Oxford University Press, 2006), 289.

10. Branko Milanovic, *Worlds Apart: Measuring International and Global Inequality* (Princeton: Princeton University Press, 2005), 108.

11. James B. Davies, Susanna Sandstrom, Anthony Shorrocks, and Edward N. Wolff, *The World Distribution of Household Wealth*, World Institute for Development Economics Research (WIDER), December 5, 2006 (www.wider.unu.edu/research/2006-2007/2006-2007-1/wider-wdhw-launch-5-12-2006/wider-wdhw-report-5-12-2006.pdf), Table 10a.

affluent—very much smaller, for instance, than the Allies' sacrifice in blood and treasure for victory in World War II.

Second, the enormous global inequalities just described are increasing relentlessly. Branko Milanovic reports that real incomes of the poorest 5 percent of world population declined 20 percent in the 1988–93 period and another 23 percent during 1993–98, while real global per capita income increased by 5.2 percent and 4.8 percent respectively.[12] For the 1988–98 period he finds that, assessed in terms of purchasing power parities (PPPs), the Gini measure of inequality among persons worldwide increased from 62.2 to 64.1, and the Theil from 72.7 to 78.9.[13] We can confirm and update his findings with other, more intuitive data. The World Bank reports that, in the high-income Organisation for Economic Co-operation and Development (OECD) countries, household final consumption expenditure per capita (constant 2000 US Dollars) rose 56.3 percent in real terms over the 1984-2004 globalization period: from $11,582 in 1984 to $18,103 in 2004.[14] World Bank interactive software can be used to calculate how the poorer half of humankind have fared, in terms of their real (inflation/PPP adjusted) consumption expenditure, during this same period.[15] Here are the gains for various percentiles of world population labeled from poorest to richest:

48.62%	gain for the	50th	percentile (median)
47.18%	gain for the	40th	percentile
42.20%	gain for the	30th	percentile
36.16%	gain for the	20th	percentile
33.72%	gain for the	15th	percentile
32.61%	gain for the	10th	percentile
31.92%	gain for the	7th	percentile
30.86%	gain for the	5th	percentile
30.44%	gain for the	3rd	percentile
22.87%	gain for the	2nd	percentile
9.64%	gain for the	1st	percentile

12. Milanovic, *Worlds Apart*, 108.
13. Ibid.
14. See devdata.worldbank.org/dataonline; last accessed 10 June 2007
15. See iresearch.worldbank.org/PovcalNet/jsp/index.jsp. Full calculations are on file with the author. Unfortunately, this database excludes the populations of the high-income countries and therefore permits no similarly detailed calculations for the top half of the human population.

Because economic inequality is increasing also within the high-income countries—in the US, for example, households in the top one percent of the income hierarchy have expanded their share of national pre-tax income from 9 percent to 16 percent since 1979[16]—we can conclude that global inequality is rising across the entire income spectrum. The shares of the most affluent percentiles of the human population are growing faster than the average, the shares of poorer percentiles are growing slower, and the shares of the poorest percentiles are growing the least.

Third, conditions of life anywhere on earth are today deeply affected by international interactions of many kinds and by the rules that shape such interactions. In the modern world, the traffic of international and even intranational economic transactions is profoundly influenced by an elaborate system of treaties and conventions about trade, investments, loans, patents, copyrights, trademarks, double taxation, labor standards, environmental protection, use of seabed resources, and much else. Insofar as we participate in this system and share some responsibility for its design, we are morally implicated in any contribution it makes to ever-increasing global economic inequality and to the consequent persistence of severe poverty.

These plain facts about the contemporary world render obsolete the traditional sharp distinction between *intra*national and *inter*national relations. Until the twentieth century, these were seen as constituting distinct worlds, the former inhabited by persons, households, corporations and associations within one territorially bounded society, the latter inhabited by a small number of actors: sovereign states. National governments provided the link between these two worlds. On the inside such a government was a uniquely important actor within the state, interacting with persons, households, corporations and associations, and dominating these other actors by virtue of its special power and authority—its *internal sovereignty*. On the outside, the government *was* the state, recognized as entitled to act in its name, to make binding agreements on its behalf, and so on—its *external sovereignty*. Though linked in this way, the two worlds were seen as separate, and normative assessments unquestioningly took this separation for granted, sharply distinguishing two separate domains of moral theorizing.

16. David Leonhardt: "Larry Summers's Evolution," *New York Times Magazine*, 10 June 2007.

Today, very much more is happening across national borders than merely interactions and relations among governments. For one thing, there are many additional important actors on the international scene: international agencies, such as the United Nations, the European Union, the World Trade Organization, the World Bank, and the International Monetary Fund, as well as multinational corporations and international non-governmental organizations (NGOs). Interactions and relations among states and these new actors are structured through highly complex systems of rules and practices, some with associated adjudication and enforcement mechanisms. Those actors and these rules powerfully influence the domestic life of national societies: through their impact on pollution and climate change, invasive diseases, culture, and information technology, and (most profoundly) through market forces that condition access to capital and raw materials, export opportunities, domestic tax bases and tax rates, prices, wages, labor standards, and much else.

This double transformation of the traditional realm of international relations—the proliferation of transnational actors and the profound influence of the systematic activities of these actors deep into the domestic life of national societies—is part of what is often meant by the vague term *globalization*. It helps explain why "global" is displacing "international" in both explanatory and moral theorizing. This terminological shift reflects that much more is happening across national borders than merely interactions and relations among states. It also reflects that the very distinction between the national and international realms is dissolving. With national borders losing their causal and explanatory significance, it appears increasingly incongruous and dogmatic to insist on their traditional role as moral watersheds.

To complete the picture, let us now attend to the distinction that underlies the division of this work into two volumes. There are distinct ways of looking at the events of our social world. On the one hand, we can see such events interactionally: as actions, and effects of actions performed by individual and collective agents. On the other hand, we can see them institutionally: as effects of how our social world is structured and organized—of our laws and conventions, practices and social institutions. These two ways of viewing entail different descriptions and explanations of social phenomena, and they also lead to two distinct kinds of moral analysis or moral diagnostics.

Take some morally salient event, for example the fact that some particular child suffers from malnutrition, that some woman is unemployed, or that a man was hurt in a traffic accident. We can causally trace such events back to the conduct of individual and collective agents, including the person who is suffering the harm. Doing so involves making counterfactual statements about how things would or might have gone differently if this or that agent had acted in some other way. We can then sort through these counterfactual statements in order to determine whether any of the causally relevant agents ought to have acted differently and thus is partly or wholly at fault for the regrettable event. This will involve us in examining whether any such agents could have foreseen that their conduct would lead to the regrettable event and could also reasonably have averted the harm without causing substantial costs to themselves or third parties. Inquiries of this kind might be referred to as *interactional* moral analysis or *interactional* moral diagnostics.

Often, regrettable events can also be traced back to standing features of the social system in which they occur: to its culture, for example, or to its institutional order. In this vein, one might causally trace child malnutrition back to high import duties on foodstuffs, unemployment to a restrictive monetary policy, and traffic accidents to the lack of regular motor vehicle safety inspections. Doing so involves making counterfactual statements about how things would or might have gone differently if this or that set of social rules had been different. We can then sort through these counterfactual statements in order to determine whether the causally relevant rules ought to have been different and whether anyone is responsible for defects in these rules that are partly or wholly to blame for the regrettable events. This will involve us in examining whether those responsible for the design of the relevant rules—for instance, members of parliament—could have foreseen that they would lead to harm and could reasonably have reformulated the rules without causing substantial harm elsewhere. We might refer to inquiries of this kind as *institutional* moral analysis or *institutional* moral diagnostics.

Interactional moral analysis emerged quite early in the evolution of moral thought. Institutional moral analysis is more demanding, presupposing an understanding of the conventional (rather than natural or divine) nature of social rules as well as of their, often statistical, comparative effects. Even a mere eighty years ago, the poor and unemployed were still often seen as lazy and delinquent merely on the ground that others of equally humble origins had risen from dishwasher to millionaire. Many people then did not understand the *structural* constraints on social mobility: that the pathways to riches are limited and that the structure of prevailing markets for capital and labor unavoidably produce certain basic rates of ("structural") unemployment and poverty. Nor did they understand that existing rates of unemployment and poverty could be influenced through intelligent redesign of the rules. Today, after Keynes, the US New Deal, and various similar national transformations, these matters are well understood, and governments are held responsible for their decisions regarding institutional design and for the effects of such decisions on the fulfillment or frustration of human needs. This understanding has been—belatedly, yet very admirably—articulated in philosophy through John Rawls's classic *A Theory of Justice.* Through this grand work, Rawls has firmly established social institutions as a distinct domain of moral assessment and has marked this domain terminologically by associating it with the term *(social) justice.* This terminological innovation has taken hold, by and large, at least in Anglophone philosophy. So the term *justice* is now predominant in the moral assessment of social rules (laws, practices, social conventions, and institutions) and used only rarely in the moral assessment of the conduct and character of individual and collective agents. In the wake of Rawls the distinction between institutional and interactional moral analysis has come to be marked as a distinction between *justice* and *ethics.*

We are quite familiar today with the focus of Rawls's book: with institutional moral analysis applied to the internal organization of one state. Still in its infancy, however, is institutional moral analysis applied beyond the state. This time lag is hardly surprising, seeing that the realm of international relations is traditionally conceived as so much smaller and more surveyable than the vast and highly complex inner workings of a modern national society. We don't need institutional moral analysis, it seems, for a world of a few dozen relevant actors in which, when bad things happen, it is usually pretty clear whose conduct is at fault. And Rawls himself, in his late work *The Law of Peoples*, explicitly shunned such analysis and confined himself to developing and defending a set of rules of good conduct for states.

The phenomena of globalization, described above, show such an account to be deeply inadequate to the world in which we live. It ignores the increasingly important transnational actors other than states as well as the increasingly profound effects transnational rules, practices, and actors have on the domestic life of national societies. Shaping the environment (e.g., global markets) in which national societies exist, such transnational rules and practices deeply shape these societies themselves: how they govern and tax themselves, how they organize education, health care, agriculture, and defense, and how they regulate foreign investment, intellectual property rights, foreign trade. Some of this influence is due to competitive pressures and transnational bargaining. Some of it works by affecting domestic incentives and power distributions: International rules that recognize any person or group exercising effective power in a less developed country as entitled to sell its natural resources, to borrow, and to import weapons in its name make it extremely tempting in resource-rich such countries to attempt to take power by force. These countries are therefore very likely to experience coup attempts, civil wars, and repressive (often military) rule. Such foreseeable effects of transnational institutional arrangements are surely relevant to their moral assessment, but other factors may be relevant as well: the way such arrangements were created or emerged, for example, and the judgments and interests of present participants in these institutional arrangements. The discourse about global justice is about this question, how to assess transnational institutional arrangements.

Justice assessment of transnational institutional arrangements can have important implications for the conduct of individual and collective actors participating in such arrangements: for governments, corporations, associations, and individuals. Insofar as transnational arrangements are just, their participants have moral reason to support them and to comply with them. Insofar as such arrangements are unjust, their participants have moral reason to seek their reform and possibly also to help protect some of their victims. Such duties must, however, be integrated into a larger account of moral responsibilities. Victims of unjust transnational arrangements in which we are participants are not the only ones who have a claim to our moral attention as individuals. We also face victims of natural calamities, victims of historical or contemporary wrongs (wrongs of colonialism, slavery, and genocide, some perhaps committed by our own country), and victims of domestic injustice (associated with race, gender, ethnic identity, religion or social class). We confront global threats and dangers (proliferation of weapons of mass destruction, climate change, new infectious diseases) as well as personal responsibilities toward our family, friends, and professional associates. And we have projects, ambitions, needs, and desires of our own that militate against devoting our whole lives to our various moral responsibilities. The situation of collective agents is characterized by a similarly diverse and confusing array of conflicting claims. Governments must balance their special responsibilities toward their own citizens against their general responsibilities toward foreign nationals who may need refuge, protection, or assistance. A corporation must analogously balance its special responsibilities toward its shareholders, customers, and those who work for it directly or indirectly against its more general responsibilities toward the communities in which it operates and toward outsiders who may be affected by its activities in multifarious ways. Religious organizations and NGOs must similarly integrate such more general and increasingly global responsibilities with their special responsibilities toward members and contributors as well as with their defining missions. For all these actors, gaining a clear moral orientation is becoming more difficult as the world in which they operate becomes larger and more interdependent. The discourse about global ethics is about how such actors should take into account and fulfill their increasingly complex and increasingly transnational moral responsibilities.

The two-volume collection before you brings together a representative sampling of the most significant, most original, most influential writings moral thinkers have composed on these issues in the three decades following 1971. These essays are of continuing importance because they have developed the terms in which these issues are debated today. These essays have sharpened the concepts that dominate our current discussions, have created the fault lines dividing present intellectual camps, and have inspired or revolted thousands of later writers, students, and ordinary citizens.

To be sure, there is other work from these three decades that could plausibly have been included, as additions or substitutions. But we wanted a manageable and affordable collection of uncut essays and have worked hard to put together a set of writings that, together, optimally reflect the formative debates. The division of the essays into two volumes follows the distinction just drawn between the two moral responsibilities of governments, corporations, and individuals. The *Global Justice* volume features essays about their political responsibilities relating to institutional design. The *Global Ethics* volume features essays about their ethical responsibilities within the context of the international order as it is. Evidently, not all the selected writings fall squarely on one or the other side of this divide. In hard cases, we were guided by the aim of making each volume as unified and self-contained as possible.

After much experimentation, we concluded that, within each volume, the essays are best presented in straight chronological order of their first publication. This ordering causes thematic leaps occasionally, but the essays do not display sufficient uniformities of scope to sustain any other arrangement. Moreover, a chronological reading is surprisingly illuminating about how the moral debate about international relations gradually took on its present shape and structure. In any case, readers and teachers will find their own selection and ordering of the materials.

For ease of use, we have inserted, in brackets, cross references within and across the two volumes. Cross references within a volume use "herein" and cross references to the companion volume use its full title or its acronym (*GJSE* or *GESE*).

From the beginning, it has been a central concern of the editors to make these texts available at an affordable price. We want our collection to be widely accessible—not merely in the affluent regions, but especially also to students in the poorer countries who are hugely interested in these issues and all too often lack electronic access to journals. It has not been easy. But in the end we have achieved an incredibly low sales price for volumes of this size. For this, the editors and readers have to thank, first and foremost, the Centre for Applied Philosophy and Public Ethics which, funded by the Australian Research Council, spans three institutions: Charles Sturt University, the University of Melbourne, and the Australian National University. CAPPE has absorbed all the permission fees as an ethical and highly cost-effective way of promoting its own mission and has also funded the crucial assistance we received from David Mollica, Matt Peterson, Tamara Shanley, and Ling Tong who competently and cheerfully converted our tables of contents into two neatly formatted volumes of text with introductory summaries and index. We must further thank Gordon Anderson and Rosemary Yokoi of Paragon House who were ready to share our vision and work with us while other publishers declared the project economically unviable. While some publishers have made extortionate demands for their copyrights, forcing us to make substitutions for some essays (though not authors), most copyright holders have been willing to waive, or greatly to reduce, their usual commercial reprinting rates. We have gratefully received cost-free permissions from Bilingual Press, from Mary Malin (Elsevier), from the *Journal of Philosophy* with authors Charles Beitz, Avishai Margalit and Joseph Raz, from the *New York Review of Books*, from Erica Wetter (New York University Press), from Peter Ohlin (Oxford University Press, US), from Dennis Moran *(Review of Politics)*, from Richard Rorty, from Springer, from the United Nations University's World Institute for Development Economics Research (UNU-WIDER), and from Utah University Press. To underscore the noncommercial character of this collection, the editors have assigned all royalties to Oxfam.

Thomas Pogge

INTRODUCTION

Global Ethics is the second part of a two-volume collection of essays on global justice and ethics. As explained in the Common Introduction to that collection, the division between the two volumes reflects a certain way of distinguishing between (social) justice and ethics. On this understanding, justice concerns the moral assessment of social institutions, and the moral responsibilities of individuals, governments, and other agents with respect to such institutions, while ethics concerns the other moral responsibilities of such agents, taking the institutional background as given. *Global* ethics, then, on this understanding, focuses on the moral responsibilities of individuals, governments, and other agents with respect to issues that have global dimensions, taking the global institutional background as given.

So understood, the field of global ethics is very broad. Indeed, given the various developments often grouped together under the heading of *globalization*, it can easily appear that there is hardly an important ethical issue that does *not* have significant global dimensions. Issues discussed in this collection, in particular, include whether individuals and governments in rich countries should give more aid to people in poor countries, and what the nature of any such obligations might be; the causes of persistent poverty in certain countries; the conditions under which military action aimed at protecting human rights in foreign countries might be morally justified; the moral basis for the right to self-determination; whether attitudes such as patriotism and nationalism are morally justified, and if so, what justifies them; what *development* is; whether there could be a genuinely universal consensus on human rights; whether the theories developed by feminists from affluent states are relevant to the situation of women in poor countries; and the moral implications of global problems such as population growth and climate change.

As noted in the Common Introduction, the task of finding a definitive classification of the pieces defeated our ingenuity, and so we have opted to present them in chronological order. For those who want to follow up particular themes, however, the following grouping of chapters according to theme may offer some guidance.[1] (Some pieces are relevant to more than one category and so appear on more than one list.)

Foreign Aid[2]
Peter Singer, "Famine, Affluence, and Morality"
Garrett Hardin, "Lifeboat Ethics: The Case Against Helping the Poor"
Peter Unger, *Living High and Letting Die* (excerpt)
Richard Rorty, "Who Are We?"
Richard Miller, "Moral Closeness and World Community"
John Rawls, *The Law of Peoples* (excerpt)

Nationalism and Patriotism[3]
Charles Beitz, "Cosmopolitan Ideals and National Sentiment"
Alasdair MacIntyre, "Is Patriotism a Virtue?"
Thomas Hurka, "The Justification of National Partiality"
Richard Miller, "Moral Closeness and World Community"

Broader Questions Concerning the Distribution of Responsibilities for Global Problems[4]
Onora O'Neill, "Rights, Obligations, and World Hunger"
Samuel Scheffler, "Individual Responsibility in a Global Age"
David Miller, "Distributing Responsibilities"
Thomas Pogge, "'Assisting' the Global Poor"

War
David Luban, "Just War and Human Rights"
Michael Walzer, "The Moral Standing of States: A Response to Four Critics"
Michael Doyle, "Kant, Liberal Legacies, and Foreign Affairs, Part I"

Rights[5]
David Luban, "Just War and Human Rights"
Onora O'Neill, "Rights, Obligations, and World Hunger"

Charles Taylor, "Conditions of an Unforced Consensus on Human Rights"

Self-Determination[6]
Michael Walzer, "The Moral Standing of States: A Response to Four Critics"
Avishai Margalit and Joseph Raz, "National Self-Determination"

Gender[7]
Susan Moller Okin, "Gender Inequality and Cultural Differences"
Amartya Sen, "Population: Delusion and Reality"
Alison M. Jaggar, "'Saving Amina': Global Justice for Women and Intercultural Dialogue"

Population and the Environment
Garrett Hardin, "Lifeboat Ethics: The Case Against Helping the Poor"
Henry Shue, "Subsistence Emissions and Luxury Emissions"
Amartya Sen, "Population: Delusion and Reality"
Stephen Gardiner, "The Real Tragedy of the Commons"

We hope that this volume will help to stimulate more work on these and other themes in the emerging field of global ethics.

NOTES

1. Some of these themes are also discussed in certain chapters of *Global Justice: Seminal Essays*, Volume 1 of this Collection; where this is so we provide references to the relevent chapters in endnotes.

2. See also *Global Justice: Seminal Essays*, chapters 1, 3, and 7.

3. See also *Global Justice: Seminal Essays*, chapters 9, 10, 11, 14, and 22.

4. See also *Global Justice: Seminal Essays*, chapters 2, 5, 10, 12, 14, 15, 16, 21, and 22.

5. See also *Global Justice: Seminal Essays*, chapter 5.

6. See also *Global Justice: Seminal Essays*, chapters 6, 8, and 19.

7. See also *Global Justice: Seminal Essays*, chapters 17.

1. PETER SINGER

Singer, writing at a time (1971) when large numbers of deaths were occurring in East Bengal due to lack of food and other essentials, argues that the affluent have a moral obligation to give a large part of their wealth to those who are suffering for want of basic necessities. He derives this conclusion from the premises that (1) "suffering and death from lack of food, shelter, and medical care are bad," and (2) "if it is in our power to prevent something bad from happening, without thereby sacrificing anything of comparable moral importance, we ought, morally, to do it," and further argues that the moral obligation of the affluent is not diminished either by the physical distance between rich and poor, or by the fact that there are many other people similarly able to help. Singer claims that the effect of his argument is to upset traditional moral categories: Giving to the distant poor is widely considered to be an act of charity and/or supererogatory, but if Singer is correct it becomes a matter of duty or obligation.

Famine, Affluence, and Morality

First published in Philosophy and Public Affairs 1: 3 (spring 1972): 229-43.

As I write this, in November 1971, people are dying in East Bengal from lack of food, shelter, and medical care. The suffering and death that are occurring there now are not inevitable, not unavoidable in any fatalistic sense of the term. Constant poverty, a cyclone, and a civil war have turned at least 9 million people into destitute refugees; nevertheless, it is not beyond the capacity of the richer nations to give enough assistance to reduce any further suffering to very small proportions. The decisions and actions of human beings can prevent this kind of suffering. Unfortunately, human beings have not made the necessary decisions. At the individual level, people have, with very few exceptions, not responded to the situation in any significant way. Generally speaking, people have not given large sums to relief funds; they have not written to their parliamentary representatives demanding increased government assistance; they have not demonstrated in the streets, held symbolic fasts, or done anything else directed toward providing the refugees with the means to satisfy their essential needs. At the government level, no government has given the sort of massive aid that would enable the refugees to survive for more than a few days. Britain, for instance, has given rather more than most countries. It has, to date, given £14,750,000. For comparative purposes, Britain's share of the nonrecoverable development costs of the Anglo-French Concorde project is already in excess of £275,000,000, and on present estimates will reach £440,000,000. The implication is that the British government values a supersonic transport more than thirty times as highly as it values the lives of the 9 million refugees. Australia is another country which, on a per capita basis, is well up in the "aid to Bengal" table. Australia's aid, however, amounts to less than one-twelfth of the cost of Sydney's new opera house. The total amount given, from all sources, now stands at about £65,000,000. The estimated cost of keeping the refugees alive for one year is £464,000,000. Most of the refugees have now been in the camps for more than six months. The World Bank has said that India needs a minimum of £300,000,000 in assistance from other countries before the end of the year. It seems obvious that assistance on this scale will not be forthcoming. India will be forced to choose between letting the refugees starve or diverting funds from its own development program, which will mean that more of its own people will starve in the future.[1]

These are the essential facts about the present situation in Bengal. So far as it concerns us here, there is nothing unique about this situation except its magnitude. The Bengal emergency is just the latest and most acute of a series of major emergencies in various parts of the world, arising both from natural and from man-made causes. There are also many parts of the world in which people die from malnutrition and lack of food independent of any special emergency. I take Bengal as my example only because it is the present concern, and because the size of the problem has ensured that it has been given adequate publicity. Neither individuals nor governments can claim to be unaware of what is happening there.

What are the moral implications of a situation like this? In what follows, I shall argue that the way people in relatively affluent countries react to a situation like that in Bengal cannot be justified; indeed, the whole way we look at moral issues—our moral conceptual scheme—needs to be altered, and with it, the way of life that has come to be taken for granted in our society.

In arguing for this conclusion I will not, of course, claim to be morally neutral. I shall, however, try to argue for the moral position that I take, so that anyone who accepts certain assumptions, to be made explicit, will, I hope, accept my conclusion.

I begin with the assumption that suffering and death from lack of food, shelter, and medical care are bad. I think most people will agree about this, although one may reach the same view by different routes. I shall not argue for this view. People can hold all sorts of eccentric positions, and perhaps from some of them it would not follow that death by starvation is in itself bad. It is difficult, perhaps impossible, to refute such positions, and so for brevity I will henceforth take this assumption as accepted. Those who disagree need read no further.

My next point is this: If it is in our power to prevent something bad from happening, without thereby sacrificing anything of comparable moral importance, we ought, morally, to do it. By "without sacrificing anything of comparable moral importance" I mean without causing anything else comparably bad to happen, or doing something that is wrong in itself, or failing to promote some moral good, comparable in significance to the bad thing that we can prevent. This principle seems almost as uncontroversial as the last one. It requires us only to prevent what is bad, and not to promote what is good, and it requires this of us only when we can do it without sacrificing anything that is, from the moral point of view, comparably important. I could even, as far as the application of my argument to the Bengal emergency is concerned, qualify the point so as to make it: If it is in our power to prevent something very bad from happening, without thereby sacrificing anything morally significant, we ought, morally, to do it. An application of this principle would be as follows: If I am walking past a shallow pond and see a child drowning in it, I ought to wade in and pull the child out. This will mean getting my clothes muddy, but this is insignificant, while the death of the child would presumably be a very bad thing.

The uncontroversial appearance of the principle just stated is deceptive. If it were acted upon, even in its qualified form, our lives, our society, and our world would be fundamentally changed. For the principle takes, first, no account of proximity or distance. It makes no moral difference whether the person I can help is a neighbor's child ten yards from me or a Bengali whose name I shall never know, ten thousand miles away. Second, the principle makes no distinction between cases in which I am the only person who could possibly do anything and cases in which I am just one among millions in the same position.

I do not think I need to say much in defense of the refusal to take proximity and distance into account. The fact that a person is physically near to us, so that we have personal contact with him, may make it more likely that we *shall* assist him, but this does not show that we *ought* to help him rather than another who happens to be farther away. If we accept any principle of impartiality, universalizability, equality, or whatever, we cannot discriminate against someone merely because he is far away from us (or we are far away from him). Admittedly, it is possible that we are in a better position to judge what needs to be done to help a person near to us than one far away, and perhaps also to provide the assistance we judge to be necessary. If this were the case, it would be a reason for helping those near to us first. This may once have been a justification for being more concerned with the poor in one's own town than with famine victims in India. Unfortunately for those who like to keep their moral responsibilities limited, instant communication and swift transportation have changed the situation. From the moral point of view, the development of the world into a "global village" has made an important, though still unrecognized, difference to our moral situation. Expert observers and supervisors, sent out by famine relief organizations or permanently stationed in famine-prone areas, can direct our aid to a refugee in Bengal almost as effectively as we could get it to someone in our own block. There would seem, therefore, to be no possible justification for discriminating on geographical grounds.

There may be a greater need to defend the second implication of my principle—that the fact that there are millions of other people in the same position, in respect to the Bengali refugees, as I am, does not make the situation significantly different from a situation in which I am the only person who can prevent something very bad from occurring.

Again, of course, I admit that there is a psychological difference between the cases; one feels less guilty about doing nothing if one can point to others, similarly placed, who have also done nothing. Yet this can make no real difference to our moral obligations.[2] Should I consider that I am less obliged to pull the drowning child out of the pond if on looking around I see other people, no farther away than I am, who have also noticed the child but are doing nothing? One has only to ask this question to see the absurdity of the view that numbers lessen obligation. It is a view that is an ideal excuse for inactivity; unfortunately most of the major evils—poverty, overpopulation, pollution—are problems in which everyone is almost equally involved.

The view that numbers do make a difference can be made plausible if stated in this way: If everyone in circumstances like mine gave £5 to the Bengal Relief Fund, there would be enough to provide food, shelter, and medical care for the refugees; there is no reason why I should give more than anyone else in the same circumstances as I am; therefore I have no obligation to give more than £5. Each premise in this argument is true, and the argument looks sound. It may convince us, unless we notice that it is based on a hypothetical premise, although the conclusion is not stated hypothetically. The argument would be sound if the conclusion were: If everyone in circumstances like mine were to give £5, I would have no obligation to give more than £5. If the conclusion were so stated, however, it would be obvious that the argument has no bearing on a situation in which it is not the case that everyone else gives £5. This, of course, is the actual situation. It is more or less certain that not everyone in circumstances like mine will give £5. So there will not be enough to provide the needed food, shelter, and medical care. Therefore by giving more than £5, I will prevent more suffering than I would if I gave just £5.

It might be thought that this argument has an absurd consequence. Since the situation appears to be that very few people are likely to give substantial amounts, it follows that I and everyone else in similar circumstances ought to give as much as possible, that is, at least up to the point at which by giving more one would begin to cause serious suffering for oneself and one's dependents—perhaps even beyond this point to the point of marginal utility, at which by giving more one would cause oneself and one's dependents as much suffering as one would prevent in Bengal. If everyone does this, however, there will be more than can be used for the benefit of the refugees, and some of the sacrifice will have been unnecessary. Thus, if everyone does what he ought to do, the result will not be as good as it would be if everyone did a little less than he ought to do, or if only some do all that they ought to do.

The paradox here arises only if we assume that the actions in question—sending money to the relief funds—are performed more or less simultaneously, and are also unexpected. For if it is to be expected that everyone is going to contribute something, then clearly each is not obliged to give as much as he would have been obliged to had others not been giving, too. And if everyone is not acting more or less simultaneously, then those giving later will know how much more is needed, and will have no obligation to give more than is necessary to reach this amount. To say this is not to deny the principle that people in the same circumstances have the same obligations, but to point out that the fact that others have given, or may be expected to give, is a relevant circumstance: Those giving after it has become known that many others are giving and those giving before are not in the same circumstances. So the seemingly absurd consequence of the principle I have put forward can occur only if people are in error about the actual circumstances—that is, if they think they are giving when others are not, but in fact they are giving when others are. The result of everyone doing what he really ought to do cannot be worse than the result of everyone doing less than he ought to do, although the result of everyone doing what he reasonably believes he ought to do could be.

If my argument so far has been sound, neither our distance from a preventable evil nor the number of other people who, in respect to that evil, are in the same situation as we are, lessens our obligation to mitigate or prevent that evil. I shall therefore take as established the principle I asserted earlier. As I have already said, I need to assert it only in its qualified form: If it is in our power to prevent something very bad from happening, without thereby sacrificing anything else morally significant, we ought, morally, to do it.

The outcome of this argument is that our traditional moral categories are upset. The traditional distinction between duty and charity cannot be drawn, or at least, not in the place we normally draw it. Giving money to the Bengal Relief Fund is regarded as an act of charity in our society. The bodies that collect money are known as "charities." These organizations see themselves in this way—if you send them a check, you will be thanked for your "generosity." Because giving money is regarded as an act of charity, it is not thought that there is anything wrong with not giving. The charitable man may be praised, but the man who is not charitable is not condemned. People do not feel in any way ashamed or guilty about spending money on new clothes or a new car instead of giving it to famine relief. (Indeed, the alternative does not occur to them.) This way of looking at the matter cannot be justified. When we buy new clothes not to keep ourselves warm but to look "well dressed," we are not providing for any important need. We would not be sacrificing anything significant if we were to continue to wear our old clothes, and give the money to famine relief. By doing so, we would be preventing another person from starving. It follows from what I have said earlier that we ought to give money away, rather than spend it on clothes we do not need to keep us warm. To do so is not charitable, or generous. Nor is it the kind of act that philosophers and theologians have called "supererogatory"—an act that it would be good to do, but not wrong not to do. On the contrary, we ought to give the money away, and it is wrong not to do so.

I am not maintaining that there are no acts that are charitable, or that there are no acts that it would be good to do but not wrong not to do. It may be possible to redraw the distinction between duty and charity in some other place. All I am arguing here is that the present way of drawing the distinction, which makes it an act of charity for a man living at the level of affluence that most people in the "developed nations" enjoy to give money to save someone else from starvation, cannot be supported. It is beyond the scope of my argument to consider whether the distinction should be redrawn or abolished altogether. There would be many other possible ways of drawing the distinction—for instance, one might decide that it is good to make other people as happy as possible, but not wrong not to do so.

Despite the limited nature of the revision in our moral conceptual scheme which I am proposing, the revision would, given the extent of both affluence and famine in the world today, have radical implications. These implications may lead to further objections, distinct from those I have already considered. I shall discuss two of these.

One objection to the position I have taken might be simply that it is too drastic a revision of our moral scheme. People do not ordinarily judge in the way I have suggested they should. Most people reserve their moral condemnation for those who violate some moral norm, such as the norm against taking another person's property. They do not condemn those who indulge in luxury instead of giving to famine relief. But given that I did not set out to present a morally neutral description of the way people make moral judgments, the way people do in fact judge has nothing to do with the validity of my conclusion. My conclusion follows from the principle I advanced earlier, and unless that principle is rejected, or the arguments shown to be unsound, I think the conclusion must stand, however strange it appears.

It might, nevertheless, be interesting to consider why our society, and most other societies, do judge differently from the way I have suggested they should. In a well-known article, J. O. Urmson suggests that the imperatives of duty, which tell us what we must do, as distinct from what it would be good to do but not wrong not to do, function so as to prohibit behavior that is intolerable if men are to live together in society.[3] This may explain the origin and continued existence of the present division between acts of duty and acts of charity. Moral attitudes are shaped by the needs of society, and no doubt society needs people who will observe the rules that make social existence tolerable. From the point of view of a particular society, it is essential to prevent violations of norms against killing, stealing, and so on. It is quite inessential, however, to help people outside one's own society.

If this is an explanation of our common distinction between duty and supererogation, however, it is not a justification of it. The moral point of view requires us to look beyond the interests of our own society. Previously, as I have already mentioned, this may hardly have been feasible, but it is quite feasible now. From the moral point of view, the prevention of the starvation of millions of people outside our society must be considered at least as pressing as the upholding of property norms within our society.

It has been argued by some writers, among them Sidgwick and Urmson, that we need to have a basic moral code that is not too far beyond the capacities of the ordinary man, for otherwise there will be a general breakdown of compliance with the moral code. Crudely stated, this argument suggests that if we tell people that they ought to refrain from murder and give everything they do not really need to famine relief, they will do neither, whereas if we tell them that they ought to refrain from murder and that it is good to give to famine relief but not wrong not to do so, they will at least refrain from murder. The issue here is: Where should we draw the line between conduct that is required and conduct that is good although not required, so as to get the best possible result? This would seem to be an empirical question, although a very difficult one. One objection to the Sidgwick-Urmson line of argument is that it takes insufficient account of the effect that moral standards can have on the decisions we make. Given a society in which a wealthy man who gives 5 percent of his income to famine relief is regarded as most generous, it is not surprising that a proposal that we all ought to give away half our incomes will be thought to be absurdly unrealistic. In a society which held that no man should have more than enough while others have less than they need, such a proposal might seem narrow-minded. What it is possible for a man to do and what he is likely to do are both, I think, very greatly influenced by what people around him are doing and expecting him to do. In any case, the possibility that by spreading the idea that we ought to be doing very much more than we are to relieve famine we shall bring about a general breakdown of moral behavior seems remote. If the stakes are an end to widespread starvation, it is worth the risk. Finally, it should be emphasized that these considerations are relevant only to the issue of what we should require from others, and not to what we ourselves ought to do.

The second objection to my attack on the present distinction between duty and charity is one that has from time to time been made against utilitarianism. It follows from some forms of utilitarian theory that we all ought, morally, to be working full-time to increase the balance of happiness over misery. The position I have taken here would not lead to this conclusion in all circumstances, for if there were no bad occurrences that we could prevent without sacrificing something of comparable moral importance, my argument would have no application. Given the present conditions in many parts of the world, however, it does follow from my argument that we ought, morally, to be working full-time to relieve great suffering of the sort that occurs as a result of famine or other disasters. Of course, mitigating circumstances can be adduced—for instance, that if we wear ourselves out through overwork, we shall be less effective than we would otherwise have been. Nevertheless, when all considerations of this sort have been taken into account, the conclusion remains: We ought to be preventing as much suffering as we can without sacrificing something else of comparable moral importance. This conclusion is one that we may be reluctant to face. I cannot see, though, why it should be regarded as a criticism of the position for which I have argued, rather than a criticism of our ordinary standards of behavior. Since most people are self-interested to some degree, very few of us are likely to do everything that we ought to do. It would, however, hardly be honest to take this as evidence that it is not the case that we ought to do it.

It may still be thought that my conclusions are so wildly out of line with what everyone else thinks and has always thought that there must be something wrong with the argument somewhere. In order to show that my conclusions, while certainly contrary to contemporary Western moral standards, would not have seemed so extraordinary at other times and in other places, I would like to quote a passage from a writer not normally thought of as a way-out radical, Thomas Aquinas.

> Now, according to the natural order instituted by divine provi-dence, material goods are provided for the satisfaction of human needs. Therefore the division and appropriation of property, which proceeds from human law, must not hinder the satisfaction of man's necessity from such goods. Equally, whatever a man has in superabundance is owed, of natural right, to the poor for their sustenance. So Ambrosius says, and it is also to be found in the *Decretum Gratiani*: "The bread which you withhold belongs to the hungry; the clothing you shut away, to the naked; and the money you bury in the earth is the redemption and freedom of the penniless."[4]

I now want to consider a number of points, more practical than philosophical, that are relevant to the application of the moral conclusion we have reached. These points challenge not the idea that we ought to be doing all we can to prevent starvation, but the idea that giving away a great deal of money is the best means to this end.

It is sometimes said that overseas aid should be a government responsibility, and that therefore one ought not to give to privately run charities. Giving privately, it is said, allows the government and the noncontributing members of society to escape their responsibilities.

This argument seems to assume that the more people there are who give to privately organized famine relief funds, the less likely it is that the government will take over full responsibility for such aid. This assumption is unsupported, and does not strike me as at all plausible. The opposite view—that if no one gives voluntarily, a government will assume that its citizens are uninterested in famine relief and would not wish to be forced into giving aid—seems more plausible. In any case, unless there were a definite probability that by refusing to give one would be helping to bring about massive government assistance, people who do refuse to make voluntary contributions are refusing to prevent a certain amount of suffering without being able to point to any tangible beneficial consequence of their refusal. So the onus of showing how their refusal will bring about government action is on those who refuse to give.

I do not, of course, want to dispute the contention that governments of affluent nations should be giving many times the amount of genuine, no-strings-attached aid that they are giving now. I agree, too, that giving privately is not enough, and that we ought to be campaigning actively for entirely new standards for both public and private contributions to famine relief. Indeed, I would sympathize with someone who thought that campaigning was more important than giving oneself, although I doubt whether preaching what one does not practice would be very effective. Unfortunately, for many people the idea that "It's the government's responsibility" is a reason for not giving that does not appear to entail any political action, either.

Another, more serious reason for not giving to famine relief funds is that until there is effective population control, relieving famine merely postpones starvation. If we save the Bengal refugees now, others, perhaps the children of these refugees, will face starvation in a few years' time. In support of this, one may cite the now-well-known facts about the population explosion and the relatively limited scope for expanded production.

This point, like the previous one, is an argument against relieving suffering that is happening now, because of a belief about what might happen in the future; it is unlike the previous point in that very good evidence can be adduced in support of this belief about the future. I will not go into the evidence here. I accept that the earth cannot support indefinitely a population rising at the present rate. This certainly poses a problem for anyone who thinks it important to prevent famine. Again, however, one could accept this argument without drawing the conclusion that it absolves one from any obligation to do anything to prevent famine. The conclusion that should be drawn is that the best means of preventing famine, in the long run, is population control. It would then follow from the position reached earlier that one ought to be doing all one can to promote population control (unless one held that all forms of population control were wrong in themselves, or would have significantly bad consequences). Since there are organizations working specifically for population control, one would then support them rather than more orthodox methods of preventing famine.

A third point raised by the conclusion reached earlier relates to the question of just how much we all ought to be giving away. One possibility, which has already been mentioned, is that we ought to give until we reach the level of marginal utility—that is, the level at which, by giving more, I would cause as much suffering to myself or my dependents as I would relieve by my gift. This would mean, of course, that one would reduce oneself to very near the material circumstances of a Bengali refugee. It will be recalled that earlier I put forward both a strong and a moderate version of the principle of preventing bad occurrences. The strong version, which required us to prevent bad things from happening unless in doing so we would be sacrificing something of comparable moral significance, does seem to require reducing ourselves to the level of marginal utility. I should also say that the strong version seems to me to be the correct one. I proposed the more moderate version—that we should prevent bad occurrences unless, to do so, we had to sacrifice something morally significant—only in order to show that even on this surely undeniable principle a great change in our way of life is required. On the more moderate principle, it may not follow that we ought to reduce ourselves to the level of marginal utility, for one might hold that to reduce oneself and one's family to this level is to cause something significantly bad to happen. Whether this is so I shall not discuss, since, as I have said, I can see no good reason for holding the moderate version of the principle rather than the strong version. Even if we accepted the principle only in its moderate form, however, it should be clear that we would have to give away enough to ensure that the consumer society, dependent as it is on people spending on trivia rather than giving to famine relief, would slow down and perhaps disappear entirely. There are several reasons why this would be desirable in itself. The value and necessity of economic growth are now being questioned not only by conservationists, but by economists as well.[5] There is no doubt, too, that the consumer society has had a distorting effect on the goals and purposes of its members. Yet looking at the matter purely from the point of view of overseas aid, there must be a limit to the extent to which we should deliberately slow down our economy; for it might be the case that if we gave away, say, 40 percent of our gross national product, we would slow down the economy so much that in absolute terms we would be giving less than if we gave 25 percent of the much larger GNP that we would have if we limited our contribution to this smaller percentage.

I mention this only as an indication of the sort of factor that one would have to take into account in working out an ideal. Since Western societies generally consider 1 percent of the GNP an acceptable level for overseas aid, the matter is entirely academic. Nor does it affect the question of how much an individual should give in a society in which very few are giving substantial amounts.

It is sometimes said, though less often now than it used to be, that philosophers have no special role to play in public affairs, since most public issues depend primarily on an assessment of facts. On questions of fact, it is said, philosophers as such have no special expertise, and so it has been possible to engage in philosophy without committing oneself to any position on major public issues. No doubt there are some issues of social policy and foreign policy about which it can truly be said that a really expert assessment of the facts is required before taking sides or acting, but the issue of famine is surely not one of these. The facts about the existence of suffering are beyond dispute. Nor, I think, is it disputed that we can do something about it, either through orthodox methods of famine relief or through population control or both. This is therefore an issue on which philosophers are competent to take a position. The issue is one that faces everyone who has more money than he needs to support himself and his dependents, or who is in a position to take some sort of political action. These categories must include practically every teacher and student of philosophy in the universities of the Western world. If philosophy is to deal with matters that are relevant to both teachers and students, this is an issue that philosophers should discuss.

Discussion, though, is not enough. What is the point of relating philosophy to public (and personal) affairs if we do not take our conclusions seriously? In this instance, taking our conclusion seriously means acting upon it. The philosopher will not find it any easier than anyone else to alter his attitudes and way of life to the extent that, if I am right, is involved in doing everything that we ought to be doing. At the very least, though, one can make a start. The philosopher who does so will have to sacrifice some of the benefits of the consumer society, but he can find compensation in the satisfaction of a way of life in which theory and practice, if not yet in harmony, are at least coming together.

NOTES

1. There was also a third possibility: that India would go to war to enable the refugees to return to their lands. Since I wrote this paper, India has taken this way out. The situation is no longer that described above, but this does not affect my argument, as the next paragraph indicates.

2. In view of the special sense philosophers often give to the term, I should say that I use "obligation" simply as the abstract noun derived from "ought," so that "I have an obligation to" means no more, and no less, than "I ought to." This usage is in accordance with the definition of "ought" given by the *Shorter Oxford English Dictionary*: "the general verb to express duty or obligation." I do not think any issue of substance hangs on the way the term is used; sentences in which I use "obligation" could all be rewritten, although somewhat clumsily, as sentences in which a clause containing "ought" replaces the term "obligation."

3. J. O. Urmson, "Saints and Heroes," in *Essays in Moral Philosophy*, ed. Abraham I. Melden (Seattle and London, 1958), p. 214. For a related but significantly different view see also Henry Sidgwick, *The Methods of Ethics*, 7th ed. (London, 1907), pp. 220–21, 492–93.

4. *Summa Theologica*, II-II, Question 66, Article 7, in *Aquinas: Selected Political Writings*, ed. A. P. d'Entreves, trans. J. G. Dawson (Oxford, 1948), p. 171.

5. See, for instance, John Kenneth Galbraith, *The New Industrial State* (Boston, 1967); and E. J. Mishan, *The Costs of Economic Growth* (London, 1967).

2. GARRETT HARDIN

Rich countries, argues Hardin, can be seen as lifeboats, full of relatively affluent people and floating through seas dotted with the world's poor, struggling to stay afloat. The poor, naturally, would like to clamber aboard the lifeboat, and this raises the question of how those aboard should react. Hardin argues for a totally exclusionary policy on the grounds that this represents the only chance for the survival of humanity as a whole. If the affluent countries open their doors and let everyone in who wants to get in, Hardin argues, the effect will be that the lifeboat is swamped and everyone drowns, rich and poor alike. Even a less generous policy will be disastrous—allowing some poor people aboard will reduce the boat's "safety factor" to the point where adverse conditions would result in catastrophe, otherwise avoided. The potential for disaster, according to Hardin, stems partly from rapid human population growth, particularly in the poor countries, and the increasing demands this places on the earth's finite environment. Another problem is what he calls "the tragedy of the commons"—Earth's environment is being degraded because those who have a right to its resources aren't held to a corresponding duty to protect it.

Lifeboat Ethics:
The Case Against Helping the Poor

First published in Psychology Today *8: 4 (September 1974): 38, 40–43, 123–124, 126.*

Environmentalists use the metaphor of the earth as a "spaceship" in trying to persuade countries, industries and people to stop wasting and polluting our natural resources. Since we all share life on this planet, they argue, no single person or institution has the right to destroy, waste, or use more than a fair share of its resources.

But does everyone on earth have an equal right to an equal share of its resources? The spaceship metaphor can be dangerous when used by misguided idealists to justify suicidal policies for sharing our resources through uncontrolled immigration and foreign aid. In their enthusiastic but unrealistic generosity, they confuse the ethics of a spaceship with those of a lifeboat.

A true spaceship would have to be under the control of a captain, since no ship could possibly survive if its course were determined by committee. Spaceship Earth certainly has no captain; the United Nations is merely a toothless tiger, with little power to enforce any policy upon its bickering members.

If we divide the world crudely into rich nations and poor nations, two-thirds of them are desperately poor, and only one-third comparatively rich, with the United States the wealthiest of all. Metaphorically each rich nation can be seen as a lifeboat full of comparatively rich people. In the ocean outside each lifeboat swim the poor of the world, who would like to get in, or at least to share some of the wealth. What should the lifeboat passengers do?

First, we must recognize the limited capacity of any lifeboat. For example, a nation's land has a limited capacity to support a population and as the current energy crisis has shown us, in some ways we have already exceeded the carrying capacity of our land.

ADRIFT IN A MORAL SEA

So here we sit, say 50 people in our lifeboat. To be generous, let us assume it has room for 10 more, making a total capacity of 60. Suppose the 50 of us in the lifeboat see 100 others swimming in the water outside, begging for admission to our boat or for handouts. We have several options: We may be tempted to try to live by the Christian ideal of being "our brother's keeper," or by the Marxist ideal of "to each according to his needs." Since the needs of all in the water are the same, and since they can all be seen as "our brothers," we could take them all into our boat, making a total of 150 in a boat designed for 60. The boat swamps, everyone drowns. Complete justice, complete catastrophe.

Since the boat has an unused excess capacity of 10 more passengers, we could admit just 10 more to it. But which 10 do we let in? How do we choose? Do we pick the best 10, the neediest 10, "first come, first served"? And what do we say to the 90 we exclude? If we do let an extra 10 into our lifeboat, we will have lost our "safety factor," an engineering principle of critical importance. For example, if we don't leave room for excess capacity as a safety factor in our country's agriculture, a new plant disease or a bad change in the weather could have disastrous consequences.

Suppose we decide to preserve our small safety factor and admit no more to the lifeboat. Our survival is then possible, although we shall have to be constantly on guard against boarding parties.

While this last solution clearly offers the only means of our survival, it is morally abhorrent to many people. Some say they feel guilty about their good luck. My reply is simple: "Get out and yield your place to others." This may solve the problem of the guilt-ridden person's conscience, but it does not change the ethics of the lifeboat. The needy person to whom the guilt-ridden person yields his place will not himself feel guilty about his good luck. If he did, he would not climb aboard. The net result of conscience-stricken people giving up their unjustly held seats is the elimination of that sort of conscience from the lifeboat.

This is the basic metaphor within which we must work out our solutions. Let us now enrich the image, step by step, with substantive additions from the real world, a world that must solve real and pressing problems of overpopulation and hunger.

The harsh ethics of the lifeboat become even harsher when we consider the reproductive differences between the rich nations and the poor nations. The people inside the lifeboats are doubling in numbers every 87 years; those swimming around outside are doubling, on the average, every 35 years, more than twice as fast as the rich. And since the world's resources are dwindling, the difference in prosperity between the rich and the poor can only increase.

As of 1973, the US had a population of 210 million people, who were increasing by 0.8 percent per year. Outside our lifeboat, let us imagine another 210 million people (say, the combined populations of Colombia, Ecuador, Venezuela, Morocco, Pakistan, Thailand, and the Philippines) who are increasing at a rate of 3.3 percent per year. Put differently, the doubling time for this aggregate population is 21 years, compared to 87 years for the US.

MULTIPLYING THE RICH AND THE POOR

Now suppose the US agreed to pool its resources with those seven countries, with everyone receiving an equal share. Initially the ratio of Americans to non-Americans in this model would be one-to-one. But consider what the ratio would be after 87 years, by which time the Americans would have doubled to a population of 420 million. By then, doubling every 21 years, the other group would have swollen to 354 billion. Each American would have to share the available resources with more than eight people.

But, one could argue, this discussion assumes that current population trends will continue, and they may not. Quite so. Most likely the rate of population increase will decline much faster in the US than it will in the other countries, and there does not seem to be much we can do about it. In sharing with "each according to his needs," we must recognize that needs are determined by population size, which is determined by the rate of reproduction, which at present is regarded as a sovereign right of every nation, poor or not. This being so, the philanthropic load created by the sharing ethic of the spaceship can only increase.

THE TRAGEDY OF THE COMMONS

The fundamental error of spaceship ethics, and the sharing it requires, is that it leads to what I call "the tragedy of the commons." Under a system of private property, the men who own property recognize their responsibility to care for it, for if they don't they will eventually suffer. A farmer, for instance, will allow no more cattle in a pasture than its carrying capacity justifies. If he overloads it, erosion sets in, weeds take over, and he loses the use of the pasture.

If a pasture becomes a commons open to all, the right of each to use it may not be matched by a corresponding responsibility to protect it. Asking everyone to use it with discretion will hardly do, for the considerate herdsman who refrains from overloading the commons suffers more than a selfish one who says his needs are greater. If everyone would restrain himself, all would be well; but it takes only one less than everyone to ruin a system of voluntary restraint. In a crowded world of less-than-perfect human beings, mutual ruin is inevitable if there are no controls. This is the tragedy of the commons.

One of the major tasks of education today should be the creation of such an acute awareness of the dangers of the commons that people will recognize its many varieties. For example, the air and water have become polluted because they are treated as commons. Further growth in the population or per-capita conversion of natural resources into pollutants will only make the problem worse. The same holds true for the fish of the oceans. Fishing fleets have nearly disappeared in many parts of the world, technological improvements in the art of fishing are hastening the day of complete ruin. Only the replacement of the system of the commons with a responsible system of control will save the land, air, water, and oceanic fisheries.

THE WORLD FOOD BANK

In recent years there has been a push to create a new commons called a World Food Bank, an international depository of food reserves to which nations would contribute according to their abilities and from which they would draw according to their needs. This humanitarian proposal has received support from many liberal international groups, and from such prominent citizens as Margaret Mead, UN Secretary-General Kurt Waldheim, and Senators Edward Kennedy and George McGovern.

A world food bank appeals powerfully to our humanitarian impulses. But before we rush ahead with such a plan, let us recognize where the greatest political push comes from, lest we be disillusioned later. Our experience with the Food for Peace program, or Public Law 480, gives us the answer. This program moved billions of dollars worth of US surplus grain to food-short, population-long countries during the past two decades. But when PL 480 first became law, a headline in the business magazine *Forbes* revealed the real power behind it: "Feeding the World's Hungry Millions: How It Will Mean Billions for U.S. Business."

And indeed it did. In the years 1960 to 1970, US taxpayers spent a total of $7.9 billion on the Food for Peace program. Between 1948 and 1970, they also paid an additional $50 billion for other economic-aid programs, some of which went for food and food-producing machinery and technology. Though all US taxpayers were forced to contribute to the cost of PL 480, certain special interest groups gained handsomely under the program. Farmers did not have to contribute the grain; the

Government, or rather the taxpayers, bought it from them at full market prices. The increased demand raised prices of farm products generally. The manufacturers of farm machinery, fertilizers, and pesticides benefited by the farmers' extra efforts to grow more food. Grain elevators profited from storing the surplus until it could be shipped. Railroads made money hauling it to ports, and shipping lines profited from carrying it overseas. The implementation of PL 480 required the creation of a vast Government bureaucracy, which then acquired its own vested interest in continuing the program regardless of its merits.

EXTRACTING DOLLARS

Those who proposed and defended the Food for Peace program in public rarely mentioned its importance to any of these special interests. The public emphasis was always on its humanitarian effects. The combination of silent selfish interests and highly vocal humanitarian apologists made a powerful and successful lobby for extracting money from taxpayers. We can expect the same lobby to push now for the creation of a world food bank.

However great the potential benefit to selfish interests, it should not be a decisive argument against a truly humanitarian program. We must ask if such a program would actually do more good than harm, not only momentarily but also in the long run. Those who propose the food bank usually refer to a current "emergency" or "crisis" in terms of world food supply. But what is an emergency? Although they may be infrequent and sudden, everyone knows that emergencies will occur from time to time. A well-run family, company, organization, or country prepares for the likelihood of accidents and emergencies. It expects them, it budgets for them, it saves for them.

LEARNING THE HARD WAY

What happens if some organizations or countries budget for accidents and others do not? If each country is solely responsible for its own well-being, poorly managed ones will suffer. But they can learn from experience. They may mend their ways, and learn to budget for infrequent but certain emergencies. For example, the weather varies from year to year, and periodic crop failures are certain. A wise and competent government saves out of the production of the good years in anticipation of bad years to come. Joseph taught this policy to Pharaoh in Egypt more than two thousand years ago. Yet the great majority of the governments in the world today do not follow such a policy. They lack either the wisdom or the competence, or both. Should those nations that do manage to put something aside be forced to come to the rescue each time an emergency occurs among the poor nations?

"But it isn't their fault!" Some kindhearted liberals argue. "How can we blame the poor people who are caught in an emergency? Why must they suffer for the sins of their governments?" The concept of blame is simply not relevant here. The real question is, what are the operational consequences of establishing a world food bank? If it is open to every country every time a need develops, slovenly rulers will not be motivated to take Joseph's advice. Someone will always come to their aid. Some countries will deposit food in the world food bank, and others will withdraw it. There will be almost no overlap. As a result of such solutions to food shortage emergencies, the poor countries will not learn to mend their ways, and will suffer progressively greater emergencies as their populations grow.

POPULATION CONTROL THE CRUDE WAY

On the average, poor countries undergo a 2.5 percent increase in population each year; rich countries, about 0.8 percent. Only rich countries have anything in the way of food reserves set aside, and even they do not have as much as they should. Poor countries have none. If poor countries received no food from the outside, the rate of their population growth would be periodically checked by crop failures and famines. But if they can always draw on a world food bank in time of need, their population can continue to grow unchecked, and so will their "need" for aid. In the short run, a world food bank may diminish that need, but in the long run it actually increases the need without limit.

Without some system of worldwide food sharing, the proportion of people in the rich and poor nations might eventually stabilize. The overpopulated poor countries would decrease in numbers, while the rich countries that had room for more people would increase. But with a well-meaning system of sharing, such as a world food bank, the growth differential between the rich and the poor countries will not only persist, it will increase. Because of the higher rate of population growth in the poor countries of the world, 88 percent of today's children are born poor, and only 12 percent rich. Year by year the ratio becomes worse, as the fast-reproducing poor outnumber the slow-reproducing rich.

A world food bank is thus a commons in disguise. People will have more motivation to draw from it than to add to any common store. The less provident and less able will multiply at the expense of the abler and more provident, bringing eventual ruin upon all who share in the commons. Besides, any system of "sharing" that amounts to foreign aid from the rich nations to the poor nations will carry the taint of charity, which will contribute little to the world peace so devoutly desired by those who support the idea of a world food bank.

As past US foreign-aid programs have amply and depressingly demonstrated, international charity frequently inspires mistrust and antagonism rather than gratitude on the part of the recipient nation.

CHINESE FISH AND MIRACLE RICE

The modern approach to foreign aid stresses the export of technology and advice rather than money and food. As an ancient Chinese proverb goes: "Give a man a fish and he will eat for a day; teach him how to fish and he will eat for the rest of his days." Acting on this advice, the Rockefeller and Ford Foundations have financed a number of programs for improving agriculture in the hungry nations. Known as the "Green Revolution," these programs have led to the development of "miracle rice" and "miracle wheat," new strains that offer bigger harvests and greater resistance to crop damage. Norman Borlaug, the Nobel Prize-winning agronomist who, supported by the Rockefeller Foundation, developed "miracle wheat," is one of the most prominent advocates of a world food bank.

Whether or not the Green Revolution can increase food production as much as its champions claim is a debatable but possibly irrelevant point. Those who support this well-intended humanitarian effort should first consider some of the fundamentals of human ecology. Ironically, one man who did was the late Alan Gregg, a vice president of the Rockefeller

Foundation. Two decades ago he expressed strong doubts about the wisdom of such attempts to increase food production. He likened the growth and spread of humanity over the surface of the earth to the spread of cancer in the human body, remarking that "cancerous growths demand food; but, as far as I know, they have never been cured by getting it."

OVERLOADING THE ENVIRONMENT

Every human born constitutes a draft on all aspects of the environment: food, air, water, forests, beaches, wildlife, scenery, and solitude. Food can, perhaps, be significantly increased to meet a growing demand. But what about clean beaches, unspoiled forests, and solitude? If we satisfy a growing population's need for food, we necessarily decrease its per capita supply of the other resources needed by men.

India, for example, now has a population of 600 million, which increases by 15 million each year. This population already puts a huge load on a relatively impoverished environment. The country's forests are now only a small fraction of what they were three centuries ago, and floods and erosion continually destroy the insufficient farmland that remains. Every one of the 15 million new lives added to India's population puts an additional burden on the environment, and increases the economic and social costs of crowding. However humanitarian our intent, every Indian life saved through medical or nutritional assistance from abroad diminishes the quality of life for those who remain, and for subsequent generations. If rich countries make it possible, through foreign aid, for 600 million Indians to swell to 1.2 billion in a mere twenty-eight years, as their current growth rate threatens, will future generations of Indians thank us for hastening the destruction of their environment? Will our good intentions be sufficient excuse for the consequences of our actions?

My final example of a commons in action is one for which the public has the least desire for rational discussion—immigration. Anyone who publicly questions the wisdom of current US immigration policy is promptly charged with bigotry, prejudice, ethnocentrism, chauvinism, isolationism, or selfishness. Rather than encounter such accusations, one would rather talk about other matters, leaving immigration policy to wallow in the crosscurrents of special interests that take no account of the good of the whole, or the interests of posterity.

Perhaps we still feel guilty about things we said in the past. Two generations ago the popular press frequently referred to Dagos, Wops, Polacks, Chinks, and Krauts in articles about how America was being "overrun" by foreigners of supposedly inferior genetic stock. But because the implied inferiority of foreigners was used then as justification for keeping them out, people now assume that restrictive policies could only be based on such misguided notions. There are other grounds.

A NATION OF IMMIGRANTS

Just consider the numbers involved. Our Government acknowledges a net inflow of 400,000 immigrants a year. While we have no hard data on the extent of illegal entries, educated guesses put the figure at about 600,000 a year. Since the natural increase (excess of births over deaths) of the resident population now runs about 1.7 million per year, the yearly gain from immigration amounts to at least 19 percent of the total annual increase, and may be as much as 37 percent if we include the estimate for illegal immigrants. Considering the growing use of birth-control devices, the potential effect of educational campaigns by such organizations as Planned Parenthood Federation of America and Zero Population Growth, and the influence of inflation and the housing shortage, the fertility rate of American women may decline so much that immigration could account for all the yearly increase in population. Should we not at least ask if that is what we want?

For the sake of those who worry about whether the "quality" of the average immigrant compares favorably with the quality of the average resident, let us assume that immigrants and native-born citizens are of exactly equal quality, however one defines that term. We will focus here only on quantity; and since our conclusions will depend on nothing else, all charges of bigotry and chauvinism become irrelevant.

IMMIGRATION VS. FOOD SUPPLY

World food banks move food to the people, hastening the exhaustion of the environment of the poor countries. Unrestricted immigration, on the other hand, moves people to the food, thus speeding up the destruction of the environment of the rich countries. We can easily understand why poor people should want to make this latter transfer, but why should rich hosts encourage it?

As in the case of foreign-aid programs, immigration receives support from selfish interests and humanitarian impulses. The primary selfish interest in unimpeded immigration is the desire of employers for cheap labor, particularly in industries and trades that offer degrading work. In the past, one wave of foreigners after another was brought into the US to work at wretched jobs for wretched wages. In recent years the Cubans, Puerto Ricans, and Mexicans have had this dubious honor. The interests of the employers of cheap labor mesh well with the guilty silence of the country's liberal intelligentsia. White Anglo-Saxon Protestants are particularly reluctant to call for a closing of the doors to immigration for fear of being called bigots.

But not all countries have such reluctant leadership. Most educated Hawaiians, for example, are keenly aware of the limits of their environment, particularly in terms of population growth. There is only so much room on the islands, and the islanders know it. To Hawaiians, immigrants from the other forty-nine states present as great a threat as those from other nations. At a recent meeting of Hawaiian government officials in Honolulu, I had the ironic delight of hearing a speaker, who like most of his audience, was of Japanese ancestry, ask how the country might practically and constitutionally close its doors to further immigration. One member of the audience countered: "How can we shut the doors now? We have many friends and relatives in Japan that we'd like to bring here someday so that they can enjoy Hawaii, too." The Japanese-American speaker smiled sympathetically and answered: "Yes, but we have children now, and someday we'll have grandchildren, too. We can bring more people here from Japan only by giving away some of the land that we hope to pass on to our grandchildren someday. What right do we have to do that?"

At this point, I can hear US liberals asking: "How can you justify slamming the door once you're inside? You say that immigrants should be kept out. But aren't we all immigrants, or the descendants of immigrants? If we insist on staying, must we not admit all others?" Our craving for intellectual order leads us to seek and prefer symmetrical rules and morals: a single rule for me and everybody else; the same rule yesterday, today, and tomorrow. Justice, we feel, should not change with time and place.

We Americans of non-Indian ancestry can look upon ourselves as the descendants of thieves who are guilty morally, if not legally, of stealing this land from its Indian owners. Should we then give back the land to the now-living American descendants of those Indians? However morally or logically sound this proposal may be, I, for one, am unwilling to live by it and I know no one else who is. Besides, the logical consequence would be absurd. Suppose that, intoxicated with a sense of pure justice, we should decide to turn our land over to the Indians. Since all our other wealth has also been derived from the land, wouldn't we be morally obliged to give that back to the Indians, too?

PURE JUSTICE VS. REALITY

Clearly, the concept of pure justice produces an infinite regression to absurdity. Centuries ago, wise men invented statutes of limitations to justify the rejection of such pure justice, in the interest of preventing continual disorder. The law zealously defends property rights, but only relatively recent property rights. Drawing a line after an arbitrary time has elapsed may be unjust, but the alternatives are worse.

We are all the descendants of thieves, and the world's resources are inequitably distributed. But we must begin the journey to tomorrow from the point where we are today. We cannot remake the past. We cannot safely divide the wealth equitably among all peoples so long as people reproduce at different rates. To do so would guarantee that our grandchildren, and everyone else's grandchildren, would have only a ruined world to inhabit.

To be generous with one's own possessions is quite different from being generous with those of posterity. We should call this point to the attention of those who, from a commendable love of justice and equality, would institute a system of the commons, either in the form of a world food bank, or of unrestricted immigration. We must convince them if we wish to save at least some parts of the world from environmental ruin.

Without a true world government to control reproduction and the use of available resources, the sharing ethic of the spaceship is impossible. For the foreseeable future, our survival demands that we govern our actions by the ethics of a lifeboat, harsh though they may be. Posterity will be satisfied with nothing less.

REFERENCES

Borlaug, Norman (October 1973) "Civilization's Future: A Call for International Granaries." *Bulletin of the Atomic Scientists* 29: 8, 7–15.

Hardin, Garrett, (1972) *Exploring New Ethics for Survival: The Voyage of the Spaceship Beagle.* New York: Viking Press.

Hardin, Garrett (December 13, 1968) "The Tragedy of the Commons." *Science* 162: 3859, 1243–48.

Ophuls, William (April 1974) "The Scarcity Society." *Harper's* 248: 1487, 47–52.

Paddock, William, and Elizabeth Paddock (1973) *We Don't Know How: An Independent Audit of What They Call Success in Foreign Assistance.* Ames: Iowa State University Press.

Paddock, William, and Paul Paddock (1967) *Famine, 1975! America's Decision: Who Will Survive?* Boston: Little, Brown and Company.

3. DAVID LUBAN

Luban argues that the traditional concepts employed in the theory of just war are an inappropriate starting point for evaluating related moral issues, as their moral content has been attenuated or distorted by political and diplomatic usage. This can be seen in how the justice of wars is commonly assessed (*jus ad bellum*) and especially in the United Nation's definition of just war as contained in its charter. Luban criticizes that, focusing on state rights rather than individual rights, the UN definition takes aggressive war to be a wrongful transgression against the sovereignty of an autonomous state, rather than against the human rights of its citizens. This focus mistakenly disregards whether a government exercising sovereign power is legitimate or not and thereby implausibly forbids interventions seeking to free citizens brutally oppressed by their own governments.

Just War and Human Rights

First published in Philosophy and Public Affairs 9: 2 (winter 1980): 160–81.

Doctrines of just war have been formulated mainly by theologians and jurists in order to provide a canon applicable to a variety of practical situations. No doubt these doctrines originate in a moral understanding of violent conflict. The danger exists, however, that when the concepts of the theory are adopted into the usage of politics and diplomacy, their moral content is replaced by definitions that are merely convenient. If that is so, the concepts of the traditional theory of just war could be exactly the wrong starting point for an attempt to come to grips with the relevant moral issues.

This is the case, I wish to argue, with the moral assessment of the justice of war (*jus ad bellum*).[1] My argument is in four parts. First I show that the dominant definition in international law is insensitive to one morally crucial dimension of politics. Second, I connect this argument with classical social contract theory. Third, I propose an alternative definition that attempts to base itself more firmly on the moral theory of human rights. And finally, I apply this definition to two hard cases.

I

JUST WAR AS DEFENSE AGAINST AGGRESSION

International law does not speak of just or unjust war as such, but rather of legal or illegal war. For the purpose of the present discussion I shall assume that the latter distinction expresses a theory of just war and treat the two distinctions as equivalent. The alternative would be to claim that international law is simply irrelevant to the theory of just war, a claim that is both implausible and question-begging.

Several characterizations of illegal war exist in international law. The Kellogg-Briand Pact of 1928, for example, condemns any use of war as an instrument of national policy except in the case of self-defense; and Brierly maintained that it did not lapse among its signers.[2] It is a very wide criterion for unjust war—wider, it may at first appear, than the United Nations Charter, which reads:

> All members shall refrain in their international relations from the threat or use of force against the territorial integrity or political independence of any State, or in any other manner inconsistent with the purposes of the United Nations.[3]

Presumably an act of war could exist that violated neither the political independence nor the territorial integrity of any state—say, a limited sea war. Or, to take another example, two states could agree to settle an issue by fighting a series of prearranged battles, with prior agreements protecting their political independence and territorial integrity. Such acts would be barred by the Kellogg-Briand Pact; whether they are prohibited by Article 2(4) depends on how one reads the phrase "inconsistent with the purposes of the United Nations." I believe that on the most plausible reading, they would be prohibited.[4] Moreover, they would most likely constitute violations of the *jus cogens*, the overriding principles of general international law.[5] Thus, Article 2(4) is in fact roughly equivalent to the Kellogg-Briand Pact.

In any case, the provisions of Article 2(4) are subsumed under the definition of aggression adopted by the UN General Assembly in 1974. It includes the clause:

> Aggression is the use of armed force by a State against the sovereignty, territorial integrity or political independence of another State, or in any other manner inconsistent with the Charter of the United Nations.[6]

Aggression, in other words, is *armed intervention* in a state's affairs. That this is a characterization of unjust war may be seen from the fact that it terms aggression "the most serious and dangerous form of the illegal use of force."[7] The definition of aggression differs from Article 2(4) in that it includes a reference to sovereignty not present in the latter. This does not, however, mean that it is a wider characterization of unjust war than Article 2(4), for an armed attack on a state's sovereignty would be barred by the latter's catchall phrase "inconsistent with the purposes of the United Nations." Thus, the definition of aggression is not really an emendation of Article 2(4). Rather, it should be viewed as an attempt to conceptualize and label the offense at issue in Article 2(4). It attempts to give a sharp statement of principle.

Matters are further complicated by the fact that the General Assembly in 1946 adopted the Charter of the Nuremberg Tribunal as UN policy. Article 6 of this Charter includes among the crimes against peace "waging of a war of aggression or a war in violation of international treaties, agreements, or assurances. . ."[8] This appears to be wider in scope than the definition of aggression, in that a war of aggression is only one type of criminal war. However, an argument similar to the one just given can be made here. Wars in violation of international treaties, agreements, or assurances are without question "inconsistent with the Charter of the United Nations," and hence fall under the definition of aggression; the Nuremberg Charter and the definition of aggression are thus extensionally equivalent.

It appears, then, that the definition of aggression captures what is essential in the Kellogg-Briand Pact, Article 2(4) of the UN Charter, and the relevant clause in the Nuremberg Charter. Thus, we may say that the UN position boils down to this:

(1)   A war is unjust if and only if it is aggressive.

This gives us a characterization of unjust war, which is half of what we want. The other half emerges from Article 51 of the UN Charter:

> Nothing in the present Charter shall impair the inherent right of individual or collective self-defense if an armed attack occurs against a member of the United Nations. . . .[9]

This tells us, at least in part, what a just war is. Thus, we have

(2)   A war is just if it is a war of self-defense (against aggression).

We note that "just" and "unjust" do not, logically speaking, exhaust the possibilities, since it is (just barely) possible that a war which is not fought in self-defense also does not threaten the sovereignty, territorial integrity, or political independence of any state, nor violate international treaties, agreements, or assurances. Now the expression "just war" suggests "permissible war" rather than "righteous war"; if so, then any war that is not specifically proscribed should be just. It is perhaps better, then, to make the two characterizations exhaustive of the possibilities. This can be done in two ways. The first is to permit wars that are not fought in self-defense against aggression, provided that they are not themselves aggressive wars—and we have just seen that it is in theory possible for a war to be neither defensive nor aggressive.

A definition more in the spirit of the UN Charter, however, would ban every war except wars of self-defense. To do this, we must modify (2) to

(2′)   A war is just if and only if it is a war of self-defense (against aggression).

Then we must expand (1) to

(1′)   A war is unjust if and only if it is not just.

Finally, we conjoin (1′) to (2′).

Thus, (1´) and (2´) capture pretty much what we want, namely the extant conception of *jus ad bellum*. In what follows I will refer to the conjunction of (1´) and (2´) as "the UN definition," although it must be emphasized that it is not formulated in these words in any United Nations document.

THE UN DEFINITION AND THE DOCTRINE OF SOVEREIGNTY: A CRITIQUE

As it is formulated in the UN definition, the crime of aggressive war is a crime of state against state. Each state, according to international law, has a duty of nonintervention into the affairs of other states: indeed, this includes not just military intervention, but, in Lauterpacht's widely accepted definition, any "dictatorial interference in the sense of action amounting to the denial of the independence of the State."[10] At the basis of this duty lies the concept of state sovereignty, of which in fact the duty of nonintervention is considered a "corollary."[11] Now the concept of sovereignty has been interpreted in a multitude of ways, and has at different times covered a multitude of sins (in such forms as the notorious doctrine that sovereign states are above the law and entitled to do anything); but in its original use by Bodin, it meant that there can be only one ultimate source of law in a nation, namely the sovereign.[12] This doctrine suffices to explain why intervention is a crime, for "dictatorial interference" of one state in another's affairs in effect establishes a second legislator.

The doctrine does not, however, explain why the duty of nonintervention is a moral duty. For the recognition of a state as sovereign means in international law only that it in fact exercises sovereign power,[13] and it is hard to see how that fact could confer moral rights on it. Might, or so we are told, does not make right. Rather, one should distinguish mere de facto exercise of sovereign power from legitimate exercise of it. The natural argument would then be that the duty of nonintervention exists only toward states that are legitimate (in the sense of the term employed in normative political theory).

Before accepting this argument, however, we must consider another possibility, namely that the duty of nonintervention in a state's affairs is not a duty owed to that state, but to the community of nations as a whole. This, in fact, seems to be one idea behind the United Nations Charter. The experience of World War II showed the disastrous nature of escalating international violence, and an absolute ban on the initiation of warfare is justified on what we would now call rule-utilitarian grounds: Regardless of the moral stature of a state, or the empirical likelihood of escalation in a given case, military intervention in the state's affairs is forbidden for the sake of international security.

I want to reject this argument as the basis for a theory of just war, however. For by giving absolute primacy to the world community's interest in peace, it does not really answer the question of when a war is or can be just; rather, it simply refuses to consider it. Obviously, the dangers posed by a war in the volatile political configuration of the nuclear era must weigh heavily into the question of *jus ad bellum*. But to make this the only factor is to refuse a priori to consider the merits of particular issues, and this is simply to beg the question of *jus ad bellum*.

Thus, I return to the claim that a state must be legitimate in order for a moral duty of nonintervention in its affairs to exist. If this is so, it pulls the rug out from under the UN definition, which is simply indifferent to the question of legitimacy, and thus to the whole moral dimension of the issue. We may put this in more graphic terms. When State A recognizes State B's sovereignty, it accepts a duty of nonintervention in B's internal affairs. In other words, it commits itself to pass over what B actually does to its own people unless B has entered into international agreements regulating its domestic behavior; and even in this case A cannot intervene militarily to enforce these agreements.[14] No matter if B is repulsively tyrannical; no matter if it consists of the most brutal torturers or sinister secret police; no matter if its ruling generals make its primary export bullion shipped to Swiss banks. If A recognizes B's sovereignty, it recognizes B's right to enjoy its excesses without "dictatorial interference" from outside.

Really, however, the point retains its force no matter what the character of B. The concept of sovereignty is morally flaccid, not because it applies to illegitimate regimes, but because it is insensitive to the entire dimension of legitimacy.

Can the UN definition be repaired, then, by restricting the concepts of sovereignty and aggression to legitimate states? This would certainly be a step in the right direction; but the attempt underlines a puzzle about the whole strategy of defining *jus ad bellum* as a crime against states. Wars are not fought by states, but by men and women. There is, therefore, a conceptual lacuna in such a definition. It can be bridged only by explaining how a crime against a state is also a crime against its citizens, that is, by relating men and women to their states in a morally cogent fashion. This, I take it, is what the concept of legitimacy is supposed to do. A legitimate state has a right against aggression because people have a right to their legitimate state. But if so we should be able to define *jus ad bellum* directly in terms of human rights, without the needless detour of talk about states. Nor is this simply a question of which terms are logically more basic. If the rights of states are derived from the rights of humans, and are thus in a sense one kind of human rights, it will be important to consider their possible conflicts with other human rights. Thus, a doctrine of *jus ad bellum* formulated in terms of human rights may turn out not to consider aggression the sole crime of war. Indeed, this is what I shall argue in Section III.

First, however, it will be helpful to consider more closely the connection between a state's rights and those of its citizens. For I have criticized the UN definition (and the doctrine of sovereignty) by suggesting that its focus on the former shows indifference to the latter.

II

CONTRACT, NATION, AND STATE

This argument may be clarified by examining social contract theory, the canonical modern account of legitimacy. The key feature of contract theory for our present discussion is its conception of the rights of political communities, particularly their right against aggression. According to contract theory, a political community is made legitimate by the consent (tacit or explicit) of its members; it thereby acquires rights that derive from the rights of its members. Thus the rights of political communities are explained by two rather harmless assumptions: that people have rights, and that those rights may be transferred through freely given consent. Contract theory, then, appears to offer a particularly clear account of how aggression against a political community is a crime against its members.

However, it is important to note that the term "political community" has two radically distinct meanings, corresponding to two very different conceptions of the social contract. The seventeenth-century theorists distinguished between a contract by which people bind themselves into a community prior to any state—Locke's version—and a contract by which people set a sovereign over them—Hobbes's version. Let us call the former a "horizontal" and the latter a "vertical" contract.[15]

A horizontal contract may be explicit: Arendt, in introducing the terms, suggests the Mayflower Compact as a paradigm case of a horizontal contract to which consent was explicitly rendered. More often, however, the consent is given tacitly through the process of everyday living itself. In Walzer's words:

> Over a long period of time, shared experiences and cooperative activity of many different kinds shape a common life. "Contract" is a metaphor for a process of association and mutuality. . . .[16]

Such a contract gives rise to a *people* or, as I shall say in order to emphasize the people's existence as a political community, to a *nation*. But only the vertical contract can legitimate a *state*. A state is an ongoing institution of rule over, or government of, its nation. It is a drastic error to confuse the two; for while every government loudly asserts, "Le peuple, c'est moi!" it is clear that this is never literally true and seldom plausible even as a figure of speech. And it is equally obvious what ulterior motives and interests lie behind the assertion.

A state's rights can be established only through a vertical contract, which according to social-contract theory means nothing more or less than that the state is legitimate. This, too, requires consent, and this will be consent over and above that which establishes the horizontal contract. For the nation is prior to the state. Political communities, not sets of atomic individuals, consent to be governed. Of course it is the typical argument of totalitarianism, with its idolatry of the state, to deny this. For example, Giovanni Gentile, the "philosopher of fascism," says:

> For it is not nationality that creates the State, but the State which creates nationality, by setting the seal of actual existence on it. It is through the *conquest* of unity and independence that the nation gives proof of its political will, and establishes its existence as a State.[17]

Gentile had in mind Italy's struggle for unity in the Risorgimento; evidently, he believed that until the Italian state was established, the nation as such did not exist. But what, then, gave "proof of its political will"? Gentile calls it the nation, and he is right, although this is inconsistent with his original contention that before the state, the nation did not exist. A national liberation movement comes about when a people acts as a political community, that is, as a nation; its state comes later if it comes at all. The nation is the more-or-less permanent social basis of any state that governs it.

The relevance of these distinctions for just-war theory is this: clearly, aggression violates a state's rights only when the state possesses these rights. According to contract theory, this entails that the state has been legitimated by the consent of its citizens. An illegitimate state, that is, one governing without the consent of the governed is, therefore, morally if not legally estopped from asserting a right against aggression. The *nation* possesses such a right, to be sure, but the state does not. Thus we have returned to the argument of the preceding section, which in our present terminology amounts to the claim that the concept of sovereignty systematically and fallaciously confuses a nation and its state, granting illegitimate states a right to which they are not entitled.

Curiously, Walzer himself falls prey to this confusion in his theory of just war. He attempts to give a contractarian justification of the UN definition, grounding the rights of states in a social contract based on tacit consent as characterized above ("shared experiences and cooperative activity of many kinds shape a common life"). This form of consent, however, can only refer to the horizontal contract, and can thus ground only the rights of nations, not of states. As Gerald Doppelt points out, "Walzer's theory seems to operate on two levels: on the *first* level, he implicitly identifies the state with the established government . . .; on the *second* level, he identifies the state with the people, nation, or political community—not its *de facto* government. . . ."[18] This is precisely a confusion of vertical with horizontal contracts. Doppelt goes on to criticize Walzer on grounds quite similar to those suggested by my argument: An illegitimate and tyrannical state cannot derive sovereign rights against aggression from the rights of its own oppressed citizens, when it itself is denying them those same rights.

The question we are facing is this: What sort of evidence shows that consent to a state has indeed been rendered? I shall not attempt to give a general answer here, since the issue is quite complex. Two things, however, are clear. The first is that the mere existence of the nation cannot be sufficient evidence of the required sort: It would then legitimate any pretender. This is why Walzer's contract in no way establishes a state's rights, contrary to his claim. The second is that clear evidence can exist that a state is *not* based on consent and hence *not* legitimate.

An example drawn from the recent Nicaraguan revolution will illustrate this. On August 22, 1978, a band of Sandinista guerrillas took over the National Palace in Nicaragua, holding virtually the entire parliament hostage. They demanded and received the release of political prisoners, a large ransom, and free passage to Panama. Newspapers reported that as the guerrillas drove to the airport, the streets were lined with cheering Nicaraguans. Within two days a general strike against the government of Anastasio Somoza Debayle had shut down the country; it was unusual in that it had the support of Nicaragua's largest business association, and thus seemed to voice a virtually unanimous rejection of the Somoza regime. Soon armed insurrection began. In the city of Matagalpa the barricades were manned mainly by high school students and other youths. Somoza responded by ordering the air force to bomb Matagalpa; the Matagalpans sent delegates to the bishopric to ask the church to intervene on their behalf with the government. The rebellion spread; at this point American newspapers were routinely referring to the Nicaraguan events as a struggle between the Nicaraguan people and the National Guard (the army). In a press statement strongly reminiscent of Woody Allen's *Bananas*, Somoza stated that his was the cause of Nicaraguan freedom, since he enjoyed the support of virtually the entire National Guard. By October the uprising was crushed—albeit temporarily—by sheer force of arms.

I do not pretend to possess a detailed understanding of Nicaraguan politics. However, it does not take a detailed understanding to realize that when the populace of a capital city cheers the guerrillas who have taken their own parliament hostage, when labor unions and business associations are able to unite in a general strike, and when a large city's residents must ask for third-party intervention to prevent their own government from bombing them to rubble, the government in question enjoys neither consent nor legitimacy. The evidence, I submit, is more than sufficient to back this claim.

It might be objected that this example shows only that the Somoza regime was illegitimate, not the Nicaraguan state as such. The distinction between regime and state, however, is simply this: The regime is a particular distribution of men and women over the leadership posts that the state institutionalizes. (I shall ignore the complication that replacements can be made in some posts without the regime changing.) If this is so, then the objection amounts to the claim that the Nicaraguan people might consent to an institutional structure involving a leadership position with Somoza's powers—that is, that they might consent to a dictatorial structure that they could change only through armed struggle. It is clear that this claim possesses vanishingly small plausibility; ultimately, I believe it rests on the question-begging assumption that a nation always consents to some state or other.

This example underlines the moral impotence of the concept of sovereignty. For other states continued to recognize the sovereignty of the Somoza regime and thus committed themselves to a policy of nonintervention in the state's war against its nation. No doubt such decisions were discreet; they were certainly not moral.[19]

Other examples are—unfortunately—not hard to find. One thinks of the Organization of African Unity's frosty reception of Tanzania's "aggression" in Uganda, despite the notorious illegitimacy of Idi Amin's regime.[20] The point is graphically illustrated as well by the United States government's response to the conquest of Cambodia by Vietnam in January 1979. The Carter administration had frequently pinpointed the regime of Pol Pot and Ieng Sary as the worst human rights violator in the world, and some reports suggested that the "auto-genocide" in Cambodia was the most awful since the Holocaust.[21] Nevertheless, the State Department denounced Vietnam for aggression and violation of Cambodia's territorial integrity and sovereignty; and this despite the fact that the Vietnamese-installed regime's first announcement concerned the restoration of human rights in Cambodia.[22] I shall discuss this issue more fully in Section IV.

THE MODERN MORAL REALITY OF WAR

Modern international law is coeval with the rise of the European nation-state in the seventeenth and eighteenth centuries. As the term suggests, it is within the historical context of nation-states that a theory will work whose tendency is to equate the rights of nations with the rights of states. It is plausible to suggest that an attack on the French state amounts to an attack on the French nation (although even here some doubts are possible: a Paris Communard in 1871 would hardly have agreed). But when nations and states do not characteristically coincide, a theory of *jus ad bellum* that equates unjust war with aggression, and aggression with violations of state sovereignty, removes itself from the historical reality of war.

World politics in our era is marked by two phenomena: a breakup of European hegemony in the Third World, which is the heritage of nineteenth-century imperialism; and maneuvering for hegemony by the (neo-imperialist) superpowers, perhaps including China. The result of this process is a political configuration in the Third World in which states and state boundaries are to an unprecedented extent the result of historical accident (how the European colonial powers parceled up their holdings) and political convenience (how the contending superpowers come to terms with each other). In the Third World the nation-state is the exception rather than the rule. Moreover, a large number of governments possess little or no claim to legitimacy. As a result of these phenomena, war in our time seems most often to be revolutionary war, war of liberation, civil war, border war between newly established states, or even tribal war, which is in fact a war of nations provoked largely by the noncongruence of nation and state.

In such circumstances a conception of *jus ad bellum* like the one embodied in the UN definition fails to address the moral reality of war. It reflects a theory that speaks to the realities of a bygone era. The result is predictable. United Nations debates—mostly ineffectual in resolving conflicts—and discussions couched in terms of aggression and defense, have deteriorated into cynical and hypocritical rhetoric and are widely recognized as such. Nor is this simply one more instance of the well-known fact that politicians lie in order to dress up their crimes in sanctimonious language. For frequently these wars are fought for reasons that are recognizably moral. It is just that their morality cannot be assessed in terms of the categories of the UN definition; it must be twisted and distorted to fit a conceptual Procrustes' bed.

III

HUMAN RIGHTS AND THE NEW DEFINITION

What, then, are the terms according to which the morality of war is to be assessed? In order to answer this question, let me return to my criticism of the contractarian derivation of the rights of states from the rights of individuals. States—patriots and Rousseau to the contrary—are not to be loved, and seldom to be trusted. They are, by and large, composed of men and women enamored of the exercise of power, men and women whose interests are consequently at least slightly at variance with those of the rest of us. When we talk of the rights of a state, we are talking of rights—"privileges" is a more accurate word—that those men and women possess over and above the general rights of man; and this is why they demand a special justification.

I have not, however, questioned the framework of individual rights as an adequate language for moral discourse. It is from this framework that we may hope to discover the answer to our question. Although I accept the vocabulary of individual rights for the purpose of the present discussion, I do not mean to suggest that its propriety cannot be questioned. Nevertheless, talk of individual rights does capture much of the moral reality of contemporary politics, as talk of sovereignty and states' rights does not. This is a powerful pragmatic reason for adopting the framework.

To begin, let me draw a few elementary distinctions. Although rights do not necessarily derive from social relations, we do not have rights apart from them, for rights are always claims on other people. If I catch pneumonia and die, my right to life has not been violated unless other humans were directly or indirectly responsible for my infection or death. To put this point in syntactic terms, a right is not to be thought of as a one-place predicate, but rather a two-place predicate whose arguments range over the class of beneficiaries and the class of obligors. A human right, then, will be a right whose beneficiaries are all humans and whose obligors are all humans in a position to effect the right. (The extension of this latter class will vary depending on the particular beneficiary.)[23] Human rights are the demands of all of humanity on all of humanity. This distinguishes human rights from, for example, civil rights, where the beneficiaries and obligors are specified by law.

By a *socially basic human right* I mean a right whose satisfaction is necessary to the enjoyment of any other rights.[24] Such rights deserve to be called "basic" because, while they are neither intrinsically more valuable nor more enjoyable than other human rights, they are means to the satisfaction of all rights, and thus they must be satisfied even at the expense of socially nonbasic human rights if that is necessary. In Shue's words, "Socially basic human rights are everyone's minimum reasonable demands upon the rest of humanity." He goes on to argue that socially basic human rights include security rights—the right not to be subject to killing, torture, assault, and so on—and subsistence rights, which include the rights to healthy air and water, and adequate food, clothing, and shelter.[25]

Such rights are worth fighting for. They are worth fighting for not only by those to whom they are denied but, if we take seriously the obligation that is indicated when we speak of human rights, by the rest of us as well (although how strictly this obligation is binding on "neutrals" is open to dispute). This does not mean that any infringement of socially basic human rights is a *casus belli*: Here as elsewhere in the theory of just war the doctrine of proportionality applies. But keeping this reservation in mind, we may formulate the following, to be referred to henceforth as the "new definition":

(3) A just war is (i) a war in defense of socially basic human rights (subject to proportionality); or (ii) a war of self-defense against an unjust war.

(4) An unjust war is (i) a war subversive of human rights, whether socially basic or not, which is also (ii) not a war in defense of socially basic human rights.

I shall explain. The intuition here is that any proportional struggle for socially basic human rights is justified, even one that attacks the nonbasic rights of others. An attack on human rights is an unjust war *unless* it is such a struggle. This is why clause (4) (ii) is necessary:

Without it a war could be both just and unjust. Clause (3) (ii) is meant to capture the moral core of the principle of self-defense, formulated above as (2). And it is worth noting that clause (4) (i) is an attempt to reformulate the concept of aggression as a crime against people rather than states; an aggressive war is a war against human rights. Since the rights of nations may be human rights (I shall not argue the pros or cons of this here), this notion of aggression may cover ordinary cases of aggression against nations.

Let me emphasize that (3) and (4) refer to *jus ad bellum*, not *jus in bello*. When we consider the *manner* in which wars are fought, of course, we shall always find violations of socially basic human rights. One might well wonder, in that case, whether a war can ever be justified. Nor is this wonder misplaced, for it addresses the fundamental horror of war. The answer, if there is to be one, must emerge from the doctrine of proportionality; and here I wish to suggest that the new definition is able to make sense of this doctrine in a way that the UN definition is not.[26] For the UN definition would have us measure the rights of states against socially basic human rights, and this may well be a comparison of incommensurables. Under the new definition, on the other hand, we are asked only to compare the violations of socially basic human rights likely to result from the fighting of a war with those it intends to rectify. Now this comparison, like the calculus of utilities, might be Benthamite pie-in-the-sky; but if it is nonsense, then proportionality under the UN definition is what Bentham once called the theory of human rights: "nonsense on stilts."

IV

TWO HARD CASES

The new definition differs in extension from the UN definition in two ways: on the one hand, an aggressive war may be intended to defend socially basic human rights, and thus be just according to (3); on the other, a war of self-defense may be fought in order to preserve a status quo that subverts human rights, and thus be unjust according to (4). But, I suggest, this is no objection, because (3) and (4) accord more with the moral reality of war in our time than (1) and (2) or (1′) and (2′).

Two situations are of particular interest for the theory of *jus ad bellum* because they exhibit marked differences between the UN definition and the new definition. The first concerns a type of economic war, the second an armed intervention in a state's internal affairs.

What I have in mind in the first case is a war for subsistence. Consider this example: *A* and *B* are neighboring countries of approximately the same military capability, separated by a mountain range. *A* is bordered by the ocean and receives plentiful rainfall; however, the mountains prevent rain clouds from crossing over to *B*, which is consequently semi-arid. One year the lack of rain causes a famine in *B*, which threatens millions of lives. *A*, on the other hand, has a large food surplus; but for a variety of cultural, historical, and economic reasons it makes none of this food available to *B*. Can *B* go to war with *A* to procure food?

According to the UN definition, such a war would constitute an aggression and consequently be unjust; but according to (3), since the war would be an attempt to procure socially basic human rights for *B*'s people, it would be just. Indeed, *A* is morally obligated to give food to *B*, and assuming that *B*'s sole purpose in fighting is to procure food, a defense by *A* would be an unjust war.

This, I suggest, is a position fully in accord with moral decency. Indeed, it is interesting to note that Walzer adopts a similar position, despite the fact that it runs counter to his basic argument concerning the criminality of aggression. Discussing the case of barbarian tribes who, driven west by invaders, demanded land from the Roman Empire on which to settle, Walzer quotes Hobbes with approval: "He that shall oppose himself against [those doing what they must do to preserve their own lives], for things superfluous, is guilty of the war that thereupon is to follow."[27] A fight for life is a just fight.

An important qualification must be made to this argument, however. If *A* itself has a food shortage, it cannot be obligated to provide food to *B*, for its own socially basic human rights are in jeopardy. Thus *B* loses its claim against *A*. And if a third nation, *C*, can supply food to *A* or *B* but not both, it is unclear who has a right to it. Socially basic human rights can conflict, and in such cases the new definition of just war will not yield clear-cut answers. Nor, however, do we have reason to expect that clear-cut answers might exist.

There are less clear examples. What about a fight against impoverishment? In the 1960s and 1970s, Great Britain and Iceland were repeatedly embroiled in a conflict over fishing grounds. This resulted in an act of war on the part of Iceland, namely, a sea attack on British ships. Of course, Iceland's belligerence may have been merely theatrical; moreover, on Iceland's interpretation of the limits of fisheries jurisdiction, she was simply defending her own right, since the British vessels were within the two-hundred-mile fisheries zone claimed by Iceland. But the moral issue had to do with the fact that Iceland's economy is built around the fishing industry, and thus a threat to this industry presented a threat of impoverishment. Now no socially basic human rights are at issue here: Impoverishment is not starvation. Nevertheless, there is a certain moral plausibility to the Icelanders' position, and it clearly resembles the position of country *B* in our previous example. But if we weaken the definition of unjust war to include struggles against economic collapse, the door is opened to allowing any economic war. For example, do industrialized countries have a right to go to war for OPEC oil?

One way to handle this would be to claim that while nations have no socially basic right to any given economic level beyond subsistence, they do possess a socially basic right not to have their economic position worsened at a catastrophic rate. There is a certain plausibility to this suggestion, inasmuch as a collapsing economy will undoubtedly cause social disruption sufficient to prevent the enjoyment of other rights. The point is nevertheless debatable. Without pretending to settle it, I would, however, claim that we are now on the right moral ground for carrying out the debate, whereas a discussion couched in terms of aggression and sovereignty would miss the point completely.

The other case I wish to discuss concerns foreign intervention into a country's internal affairs. The point is that if such an intervention is on behalf of socially basic human rights, it is justified according to the new definition.

Here again it will be useful to look at Walzer's position. He begins by endorsing an argument of Mill's, which is based on the right of national self-determination. Mill's point is that this is a right of nations to set their own house in order *or fail to* without outside interference. If a people struggles against a dictatorship but loses, it is still self-determining; whereas if it wins due to the intervention of an outside power, its right to self-determination has been violated. Walzer admits only three exceptions: (i) a secession, when there are two or more distinct political communities contending within the same national boundary; (ii) a situation in which another foreign power has already intervened; and (iii) a situation in which human rights violations of great magnitude—massacres or enslavements—are occurring. Only in these cases may intervention be justified.[28]

Now Mill's argument employs a somewhat Pickwickian conception of self-determination. A self-determining people, it suggests, fights its own battles, even if it loses them. But then one might infer that a self-determining people fights its own wars as well, even if it loses them. Thus, a nation's conquest by a foreign power would become an instance of its self-determination.[29] Surely the fact that it is a foreign rather than a domestic oppressor is not a morally relevant factor, for that would imply that oppressions can be sorted on moral grounds according to the race or nationality of the oppressor. Yet something is clearly wrong with an argument that leads to this doublethink concept of self-determination.[30]

The problem with Mill's position is that it takes the legitimacy of states too much at face value. "Mill generally writes as if he believes that citizens get the government they deserve...."[31] That is, somehow oppression of domestic vintage carries a prima facie claim to legitimacy which is not there in the case of foreign conquest. It seems that Mill suspects that the state would not be there if the people did not secretly want it. This seems to me to be an absurd, and at times even obscene view, uncomfortably reminiscent of the view that women are raped because secretly they want to be. The only argument for Mill's case, I believe, is the improbable claim that the fact that people are not engaged in active struggle against their state shows tacit consent. Even granting this, however, there remains one case in which Mill's position is unacceptable on its own terms. That is when there is overwhelming evidence that the state enjoys no legitimacy—when there is active and virtually universal struggle against it. Such struggles do not always succeed, and after each bloody suppression the possibility of another uprising grows less. Heart and flesh can bear only so much. In such a case an argument against intervention based on the people's right of self-determination is merely perverse. It makes the "self" in "self-determination" mean "other";

it reverses the role of people and state. One thinks of Brecht's poem "Die Lösung," written after the rebellion of East German workers in 1953: "After the rebellion of the seventeenth of June . . . one could read that the people had forfeited the government's confidence and could regain it only by redoubling their work efforts. Would it not be simpler for the government to dissolve the people and elect another one?"[32] I might add that in fact Walzer grants the point: "a state (or government) established against the will of its own people, ruling violently, may well forfeit its right to defend itself even against a foreign invasion."[33] Thus, it would appear that in such a case intervention is morally justified, even in the absence of massacres and slavery.

And, to make a long story short, the new definition will endorse this view. For the kind of evidence that demonstrates a government's illegitimacy must consist of highly visible signs that it does not enjoy consent, for example, open insurrection or plain repression. And this necessitates violations of security rights, which are socially basic human rights. Obedience that is not based on consent is based on coercion; thus the more obvious it is that a government is illegitimate, the more gross and widespread will its violations of security rights be, reaching even those who do not actively oppose it. This is akin to a law of nature. And thus an intervention becomes morally justified, or even morally urgent.

No definition of just war is likely to address all of the difficult cases adequately—and there is no realm of human affairs in which difficult cases are more common. Seat-of-the-pants practical judgment is a necessary supplement to one's principles in such matters: in this respect I fully agree with Walzer that "The proper method of practical morality is casuistic in character."[34] Thus, while I do not doubt that troubling examples may be brought against the new definition, it seems to me that if it corresponds with our moral judgments in a large number of actual cases, and can be casuistically stretched to address others, it serves its purpose. My claim is that, whatever its deficiencies, the new definition of *jus ad bellum* offered in (3) and (4) is superior to the existing one in this respect.

NOTES

1. I follow the traditional distinction between the justice of war, that is, which side is in the right with respect to the issues over which they are fighting, and justice in war *(jus in bello)*, which pertains to the way the war is fought.

2. J. L. Brierly, *The Law of Nations*, 6th ed., ed. Humphrey Waldock (Oxford: Oxford University Press, 1963), p. 409.

3. Article 2(4), quoted in Brierly, p. 415.

4. This is Brierly's claim, p. 409. The relevant Article of the Charter is 1(1).

5. This point was suggested to me by Professor Boleslaw Boczek.

6. Quoted in Yehuda Melzer, *Concepts of Just War* (Leyden: A. W. Sijthoff, 1975), pp. 28–29.

7. Ibid.

8. Quoted in Ian Brownlie, *Principles of Public International Law*, 2nd ed. (Oxford: Clarendon Press, 1973), p. 545.

9. Quoted in Melzer, *Concepts of Just War*, p. 18. I have omitted a clause that does not bear on the present argument.

10. Hersch Lauterpacht, *International Law and Human Rights* (London: Stevens, 1950), p. 167.

11. The term is used in Brownlie, *Public International Law*, p. 280.

12. Brierly, *Law of Nations*, pp. 7–16. See Bodin, *République* (n.p.: Scientia Aalen, 1961), Book One, chap. 8.

13. This is discussed in Brownlie, chap. 5, pp. 89–108.

14. On the relation of international agreements with the duty of nonintervention, particularly in the case of human rights, see Louis Henkin, "Human Rights and 'Domestic Jurisdiction'," in Thomas Buergenthal, ed., *Human Rights, International Law and the Helsinki Accords* (New York: Universe Books, 1977), pp. 21–40, and Thomas Buergenthal, "Domestic Jurisdiction, Intervention, and Human Rights: The International Law Perspective," in Peter G. Brown and Douglas Maclean, eds., *Human Rights and U.S. Foreign Policy* (Lexington, MA: Lexington Books, 1979), pp. 111–20. Both agree that even when the right of domestic jurisdiction over human rights has been "signed away" by a state, military intervention against it is proscribed. This doctrine, a product of the United Nations era, has replaced the nineteenth-century doctrine that permitted humanitarian intervention on behalf of oppressed peoples. The legal issues are discussed in the readings collected in Richard B. Lillich and Frank C. Newman, eds., *International Human Rights: Problems of Law and Policy* (Boston: Little, Brown and Company, 1979), pp. 484–544. The case analyzed there is India's 1971 intervention into Bangladesh; on this see also Oriana Fallaci's interview with Zulfikar Ali Bhutto, in *Interview with History* (Boston: Houghton Mifflin, 1976), pp. 182–209.

15. I adopt this terminology from Hannah Arendt, "Civil Disobedience," in *Crises of the Republic* (New York: Harcourt, Brace, Jovanovich, 1972), pp. 85–87. See also her *On Revolution* (New York: Viking, 1965), pp. 169–71. It

appears also in Michael Walzer, "The Problem of Citizenship," *Obligations* (New York: Simon & Schuster, 1970), p. 207.

16. Walzer, *Just and Unjust Wars* (New York: Basic Books, 1977), p. 54.

17. Giovanni Gentile, *Genesis and Structure of Society*, trans. H. S. Harris (Urbana: University of Illinois Press, 1966), pp. 121–22.

18. Gerald Doppelt, "Walzer's Theory of Morality in International Relations," *Philosophy & Public Affairs* 8, no. 1 (fall 1978): 9.

19. Walzer would, it seems, agree; see *Just and Unjust Wars*, p. 98.

20. See *Amnesty International Report 1978* (London: Amnesty International Publications, 1979), pp. 89–92, and Amnesty's *Human Rights in Uganda* (London: Amnesty International Publications, 1978).

21. See *Amnesty International Report 1978*, pp. 167–70, for detailed instances.

22. "A profound moral and political issue is at stake. Which is the greater evil: the continuation of a tyrannical and murderous regime, or a flagrant violation of national sovereignty? ... the Carter Administration ... decided without hesitation ... that the violation of Cambodia's sovereignty was a greater enormity than the Cambodian regime's violations of human rights...." Henry Kamm, "The Cambodian Dilemma," *The New York Times Magazine*, February 4, 1979, pp. 54–55. Evidently, this view was shared by the United Nations, which voted recently to seat a delegation from the deposed Pol Pot government rather than the Vietnam-supported Heng Samrin regime, on the grounds that no matter how unappetizing the behavior of the former, it would be wrong to condone aggression by recognizing the latter.

In citing these examples I am not entering any large moral claims on behalf of Vietnam or Tanzania, both of which are accountable for their share of human rights violations. Here I am in agreement with Walzer (*Just and Unjust Wars*, p. 105) that pure motives and clean hands are not necessary to morally justify an intervention. The present essay was written in early 1979, before the current Cambodian famine, in which it appears that the policies of Vietnam may be just as horrifying as those of the Khmer Rouge.

23. Other analyses of the concept of "human right" are possible. Walzer, for example, makes the interesting suggestion that the beneficiary of human rights is not a person, but humanity itself (*Just and Unjust Wars*, p. 158). Such an analysis has much to recommend it, but it does not concern us here, for humanity will still enjoy its rights through particular men and women.

24. I take this concept from Henry Shue, "Foundations for a Balanced U.S. Policy on Human Rights: The Significance of Subsistence Rights" (College Park, MD: Center for Philosophy and Public Policy Working Paper HRFP-I, 1977), pp. 3–4. Shue discusses it in detail in *Basic Rights: Subsistence, Affluence, and U.S. Foreign Policy* (Princeton, NJ: Princeton University Press, 1980), chap. 1 [reprinted in *Global Justice: Seminal Essays*, 84–103].

25. Ibid., pp. 3, 6–12.

26. The new definition also allows us to make sense of an interesting and plausible suggestion by Melzer, namely that a just war (in the sense of *jus ad bellum*) conducted in an unjust way *(jus in bello)* becomes unjust *(jus ad bellum)*, in other words, that the *jus ad bellum* is "anchored" in the *jus in bello*. On the new definition this would follow from the fact that a war conducted in a sufficiently unjust way would violate proportionality. See Melzer, pp. 87–93.

27. Walzer, *Just and Unjust Wars*, p. 57. See also Charles R. Beitz, *Political Theory and International Relations* (Princeton: Princeton University Press, 1979), pp. 175–76. [Part III of Beitz's book, in which the referenced pages are, is based on his essay "Justice and International Relations," first published in *Philosophy and Public Affairs* 4: 4, (summer 1975): 360–89, reprinted in *Global Justice: Seminal Essays*, 21–48, at 44.]

28. Walzer, *Just and Unjust Wars*, pp. 87–91.

29. As Walzer expressly denies, p. 94.

30. I take Doppelt to be making a similar point when he suggests that a people can be "aggressed" against by its own state as well as by a foreign state, "Walzer's Theory," p. 8. My argument in this section is quite in sympathy with Doppelt's, pp. 10–13.

31. Walzer, p. 88.

32. Quoted by Hannah Arendt, *Men in Dark Times* (New York: Harcourt, Brace & World, 1968), p. 213.

33. Walzer, *Just and Unjust Wars*, p. 82 n.

34. Ibid., p. xvi.

Some of the ideas in Sections II and III were suggested to me by George Friedman. I received helpful criticism of an early draft of this paper from Boleslaw Boczek and my colleagues Douglas Maclean and Henry Shue. Any resemblance between my remaining mistakes and their beliefs is wholly accidental. Finally, I wish to thank the Editors of *Philosophy & Public Affairs*, who spared the reader some rococo diction and bad arguments.

4. MICHAEL WALZER

Walzer defends his theory of just war in "The Moral Standing of States: A Response to Four Critics" against criticisms that his doctrine of nonintervention is too statist. The critics argue that Walzer is too conservative in prohibiting most interventions against tyrannical and authoritarian states. His defense strongly asserts the value of national self-determination. States are (or at least ought to be treated as) the result of deep-rooted cultural and political processes that are crucially incomprehensible to foreigners. Moreover, though locals are not obligated to defend their oppressive governments against foreign intervention, they often legitimately do so. Military interventions, even when they would clearly result in a change of government from tyranny to liberal democracy, thus cannot be justified on the perceptions of foreigners. The critics, Walzer argues, wrongly deny the value of lengthy processes of self-determination, and thereby fail to distinguish between the legitimacy states have toward their own citizens and the legitimacy states have toward other states in the world. While a failure of internal legitimacy may give citizens a right to revolt, this right does not transfer to foreigners. Except in dire circumstances, foreigners must presume that governments have a certain fit with those they govern. Based on the interest in self-determination, governments have a claim on one another to a presumption of legitimacy that, so long as it is intact, forbids (especially military) intervention.

The Moral Standing of States: A Response to Four Critics

First published in Philosophy and Public Affairs *9: 3 (spring 1980): 209–29.*

I

The argument of *Just and Unjust Wars* has been criticized in a number of ways, most of them overtly political in character, as if in paraphrase of Clausewitz's famous maxim: writing about war is a continuation of writing about politics....[1] That is not an entirely false maxim; indeed, it contains, as will be apparent below, unavoidable truth. And yet it is the purpose of a *theory* of just war to produce principles that, however they apply in this or that case, cannot be conscripted permanently into the service of any particular political creed or of any state or party. They are critical principles, and they open all states and parties to moral criticism. The principles I have put forward are of this sort, and I am less concerned—at least in this journal—to defend the casuistic judgments through which they were worked out than the overall structure of the argument.

But there is one set of criticisms to which I want to respond here because it does raise deep questions about the overall structure. Four writers, in substantial reviews or articles, have adopted the same position, developed it in somewhat different ways, arrived at a common conclusion: that *Just and Unjust Wars*, despite its putative foundation in a theory of individual rights, is ultimately "statist" in character. "The rights of states, and not the rights of individuals," says Wasserstrom, "come in the end to enjoy an exalted, primary status within the moral critique of aggression."[2] The book, says Doppelt, "furnishes a rhetoric of morality in international relations which places the rights of de facto states above those of individuals."[3] Beitz and Luban, while trying to suggest what an alternative morality might look like, make similar arguments.[4] The criticism of these writers rests in places upon a misreading of my own position, but it rests more largely upon significant philosophical disagreements about the nature of political life. And so it is worth pursuing.

The immediate issue is the doctrine of nonintervention, a feature of *jus ad bellum,* the part of the theory that explains the criminality of aggressive war. Wasserstrom, Doppelt, Beitz, and Luban all argue that the theory as I have formulated it (1) protects states that should not be protected against foreign intervention and (2) does so on grounds that are either inadequate or incoherent. The theory has, on their view, conservative implications, and what it conserves is the authority or sovereignty of illegitimate, that is tyrannical, regimes. They, on the other hand, are more open, given certain qualifications about proportionality, to an activist and interventionist politics aimed at overthrowing such regimes and maximizing the enjoyment of individual rights. This is not a line of criticism that I anticipated with any clarity. My own worries had a different focus: I thought the theory might be too permissive with regard to secessionist movements and foreign support for such movements. Hence, in responding now, I shall have to enlarge upon the argument of the book, and at one or two points, indicated below, I shall have to amend or qualify the argument. But the basic position remains intact. The state is presumptively, though by no means always in practice, the arena within which self-determination is worked out and from which, therefore, foreign armies have to be excluded.

II

The real subject of my argument is not the state at all but the political community that (usually) underlies it. And I will compound my putative conservatism by saying at the outset that that community rests most deeply on a contract, Burkeian in character, among "the living, the dead, and those who are yet to be born." It is hard, therefore, to imagine the assembly at which it was ratified. Contract, as I wrote in the book, is a metaphor. The moral understanding on which the community is founded takes shape over a long period of time. But the idea of communal integrity derives its moral and political force from the rights of contemporary men and women to live as members of a historic community and to express their inherited culture through political forms worked out among themselves (the forms are never entirely worked out in a single generation). I shall describe later on, with several examples, how these individual rights are violated when communal integrity is denied, even if the denial is benevolent in intention.

The members of the community are bound to one another. That is Luban's "horizontal" contract, and it constitutes the only form of political obligation.[5] There is no "vertical" or governmental contract—at least, not one that is mutually binding. Though the community requires a government, it is not the case that the citizens are bound to the government to defend it against foreigners. Rather, the government is bound to the citizens to defend them against foreigners. That is what it is for, or one of the things it is for. The citizens defend one another and their common life; the government is merely their instrument. But sometimes this instrument is turned against the citizens: Perhaps it still defends them against foreigners, but it also constrains and represses their common life; it denies their civil liberties; it imposes religious uniformity; it blocks attempts at self-help against political or economic oppression. It is a tyrannical government. Now it is the claim of my four critics, if I understand them correctly, that such a government, because it has no standing with its own people (no moral claim upon their allegiance), has no standing in international society, either. It is an outlaw government, without rights, or it is simply an ugly government, with something less than the usual complement of rights, subject to attack by anyone capable of attacking it and altering (for the better) the conditions of its rule. That is a large claim, for countries with tyrannical governments make up the greater part of international society. But it is a false claim—false not only in the law, as the law currently stands, but false morally, too, for reasons I shall come to below. The international standing of governments derives only indirectly from their standing with their own citizens. The derivation is complex because it is mediated by foreigners and because foreigners are not confronted (as citizens are) by a naked government, but by a state.

The state is constituted by the union of people and government, and it is the state that claims against all other states the twin rights of territorial integrity and political sovereignty. Foreigners are in no position to deny the reality of that union, or rather, they are in no position to attempt anything more than speculative denials. They don't know enough about its history, and they have no direct experience, and can form no concrete judgments, of the conflicts and harmonies, the historical choices and cultural affinities, the loyalties and resentments, that underlie it. Hence their conduct, in the first instance at least, cannot be determined by either knowledge or judgment. It is, or it ought to be, determined instead by a morally necessary presumption: that there exists a certain "fit" between the community and its government and that the state is "legitimate." It is not a gang of rulers acting in its own interests, but a people governed in accordance with its own traditions. This presumption is simply the respect that foreigners owe to a historic community and to its internal life. Like other presumptions in morality and law, it can be rebutted and disregarded, and what I have called "the rules of disregard" are as important as the presumption itself. So long as it stands, however, the boundaries of international society stand with it. This first presumption entails a second: that if a particular state were attacked, its citizens would think themselves bound to resist, and would in fact resist, because they value their own community in the same way that we value ours or in the same way that we value communities in general. The general valuation is, of course, crucial to the argument, but I won't stop to defend it until I am in a position to consider alternatives. In any case, it is the expectation of resistance that establishes the ban on invasion.

The obligation of citizens to fight for the state is something very different from the expectation that they will in fact fight. The expectation arises, or ought to arise, from the mere existence of a state, any state—with important exceptions to which I will come later. The obligation arises from the existence of a state of a certain sort, shaped to the requirements of moral and political philosophy. Now, this particular state is of that sort, or not; the obligation is real, or it isn't. These are questions open to argument, and foreigners, even foreign officials, are free to argue that the citizens of a particular state have no such obligations, and then to make further arguments about consent, freedom, participation, and so on. But they are not free to act on such arguments and go to war against a state whose citizens are not (so the foreigners think) bound to fight. They cannot claim that such states are literally indefensible. For as long as substantial numbers of citizens believe themselves bound and are prepared, for whatever reasons, to fight, an attack upon their state would constitute aggression. And again, foreigners are required (with exceptions…) to assume the belief and the preparedness, whether the obligation is real or not.

In a footnote in *Just and Unjust Wars*, I wrote that "the question of when territory and sovereignty can rightly be defended is closely connected to the question of when individual citizens have an obligation to join the defense." Doppelt takes this sentence to say that the citizens of a *sovereign* state, whatever its character and whatever their convictions about its character, are bound to fight on its behalf.[6] I meant only to suggest, as I went on to say, that both questions "hang on issues in social contract theory" (and to point readers to the arguments that I put forward in *Obligations*). But the sentence is misleading. In fact, a state whose citizens are not bound to fight may still find citizens ready to fight against an invading army, and it can hardly be doubted that these citizens (with exceptions...) have a right to fight and that the invaders are guilty of aggressive war. If no citizens come forward, or if they immediately surrender, then the state simply isn't defended. And then the invasion is a lesser crime than the crime we commonly call aggression, or it isn't a crime at all.[7] Nothing in my book was meant to suggest that citizens are bound to one another to defend tyrannical states (and they certainly are not bound to their tyrants). They are as free not to fight as they are free to rebel. But that freedom does not easily transfer to foreign states or armies and become a right of invasion or intervention; above all, it does not transfer at the initiative of the foreigners.

Hence states can be presumptively legitimate in international society and actually illegitimate at home. The doctrine of legitimacy has a dual reference. It is this dualism to which I referred when I wrote in *Just and Unjust Wars* that intervention is not justified whenever revolution is.[8] The two justifications do not coincide because they are addressed to different audiences. First, then, a state is legitimate or not depending upon the "fit" of government and community, that is, the degree to which the government actually represents the political life of its people. When it doesn't do that, the people have a right to rebel. But if they are free to rebel, then they are also free not to rebel—because they (or the greater number of them) judge rebellion to be imprudent or uncertain of success or because they feel that "slowness and aversion . . . to quit their old Constitutions," which Locke noted in his *Second Treatise*. That is, they still believe the government to be tolerable, or they are accustomed to it, or they are personally loyal to its leaders. And so arguments about legitimacy in this first sense of the word must be addressed to the people who make up a particular community. Anyone can make such arguments, but only subjects or citizens can act on them.

The second set of arguments concerns the presumptive legitimacy of states in international society. These arguments too can be made by anyone, including subjects and citizens, but they are properly addressed to foreigners, for it is foreigners who must decide whether to intervene or not. They are not to intervene unless the absence of "fit" between the government and community is radically apparent. Intervention in any other case usurps the rights of subjects and citizens. Wasserstrom asks: If the established government already deprives subjects and citizens of their rights, how can an attack narrowly aimed at that government add to the deprivation?[9] But the tyranny of established governments gives rise to a right of revolution, held individually by each subject or citizen, rightly exercised by any group of them, of which they cannot be deprived. When invasions are launched by foreign armies, even armies with revolutionary intentions, and even when revolution is justified, it is entirely plausible to say that the rights of subjects and citizens have been violated. Their "slowness" has been artificially speeded up, their "aversion" has been repudiated, their loyalties have been ignored, their prudential calculations have been rejected—all in favor of someone else's conceptions of political justice and political prudence. But this argument, Wasserstrom and Doppelt claim, suggests a Hobbesian theory of legitimacy: Any Leviathan state that is stable, that manages successfully to control its own people, is therefore legitimate.[10] In a sense, that is right. In international society, Leviathan states, and many other sorts of states, too, enjoy the rights of territorial integrity and political sovereignty. It has to be said, however, that Hobbes's argument is directed to the subjects of Leviathan, and it is not my intention, not by any means, to recommend its acceptance by that audience.

The first kind of legitimacy is or is likely to be singular in character. The judgments we make reflect our democratic values and suggest that there is only one kind of legitimate state or only a narrow range of legitimacy. Given an illiberal or undemocratic government, citizens are always free to rebel, whether they act on that right or not, and whether they believe themselves to have it or not. Their opinions are not relevant, for whatever they think, we can argue that such a government does not and cannot represent the political community.[11] But the second kind of legitimacy is pluralist in character. Here the judgments we make reflect our recognition of diversity and our respect for communal integrity and for different patterns of cultural and political development. And now the opinions of the people, and also their habits, feelings, religious convictions, political culture, and so on, do matter, for all these are likely to be bound up with, and partly explanatory of, the form and character of their state. That's why states objectively illegitimate are able, again and again, to rally subjects and citizens against invaders. In all such cases, though the "fit" between government and community is not of a democratic sort, there is still a "fit" of some sort, which foreigners are bound to respect.

The confusion of these two kinds of legitimacy, or the denial of the distinction between them, is the fundamental error of these four writers. They insist that the theory of *Just and Unjust Wars* requires me to call tyrannical states legitimate. My actual claim is that foreign officials must act as if they were legitimate, that is, must not make war against them. My critics are uneasy with the politics of *as if*, more uneasy with the presumption that underlies it, and most uneasy, I think, with the pluralism that that presumption mandates. They are committed to the view that the first kind of legitimacy is the only kind, and they are prepared to press international society toward a kind of reiterated singularity—the same government or roughly the same sort of government for every political community. But I won't try to address their positive arguments until I have worked through the cases where I am prepared to allow intervention and until I have indicated the far greater extent of their own allowance.

III

Though the concept of state sovereignty is, as Luban says, "insensitive" to legitimacy in its first sense, it is not insensitive to "the entire dimension of legitimacy," for there is such a thing as an illegitimate state even in international society, and there are cases when sovereignty can be disregarded.[12] These are the rules of disregard as I describe them in *Just and Unjust Wars*.[13] First, when a particular state includes more than one political community, when it is an empire or a multinational state, and when one of its communities or nations is in active revolt, foreign powers can come to the assistance of the rebels. Struggles for secession or national liberation justify or may justify intervention because in such cases there is no fit at all between government and community, and the state cannot claim, once the rebellion has reached certain proportions, even a presumptive legitimacy. While some citizens will probably feel bound to resist an intervention, it can be assumed that the citizens of the rebellious nation won't resist, and hence military action on their behalf does not count as aggression.

Second, when a single community is disrupted by civil war, and when one foreign power intervenes in support of this or that party, other powers can rightfully intervene in support of the other party.

Counterinterventions of this sort can be defended without reference to the moral character of the parties. Hence it may be the case that a foreign state has a right to intervene even when, given certain political principles, that would not be the right thing to do (similarly, the right may exist where intervention isn't the wise or prudent thing to do). Some of my critics object to the neutrality of the rule, but that kind of neutrality is a feature of all the rules of war; without it there could be no rules at all but only permissions addressed to the Forces of Good entitling them to do whatever is necessary (though only what is *necessary*) to overcome their enemies.

Third, interventions can be justified whenever a government is engaged in the massacre or enslavement of its own citizens or subjects.[14] In such cases, the usual presumption is reversed, and we ought to assume either that there is no "fit" between the government and the community or that there is no community. I think that I would now add to massacre and enslavement the expulsion of very large numbers of people (not simply the retreat of political opponents after a revolution or the transfer of populations that sometimes follows upon national liberation struggles—though these can be brutal enough). The example of Bangladesh that I used in the book to suggest the meaning of massacre may also be used to suggest the meaning of expulsion. The Indian intervention might as easily have been justified by reference to the millions of refugees as by the reference to the tens of thousands of murdered men and women. The purpose of stressing these extreme forms of oppression is, of course, to rule out intervention in cases of "ordinary" oppression. By democratic standards, most states throughout human history have been oppressive (and illegitimate), but those are not necessarily or usually the standards by which they are judged among their own people. On the other hand, we can always assume that murder, slavery, and mass expulsion are condemned, at least by their victims.

I will consider now some examples suggested by my critics—and first, the example of South Africa, referred to briefly by Wasserstrom and more extensively by Doppelt.[15] It is important to both these writers to assimilate the treatment of blacks in South Africa to the category of ordinary oppression so that they can challenge the limits set by the three exceptions. But politically active blacks do not, in fact, talk about their own situation in this manner. Their arguments fall readily into the structure of the theory I have presented; they claim that South Africa is an exceptional case in two different ways.[16] (1) They describe black South Africans as near-slaves, virtual slaves, in-effect-slaves, and true (for the moment at least) to the logic of that description, they call for measures short of military intervention—economic boycott, for example. But it would not, I think, be an unreasonable extension of the argument to hold that, from a moral standpoint, in-effect-slaves (if that description is accurate) and legal slaves count in the same way and that foreign intervention on behalf of either is justifiable.[17] (2) They describe the struggle of black South Africans as a struggle for national liberation. This is especially plausible since it parallels the official position of the South African government: that blacks are a separate nation and that they are not entitled to full citizenship in the Republic of South Africa. The policy of apartheid turns internal revolution into national liberation, even though the actual separation of the races is not such as to make possible a black secession. And so it opens the possibility of external support for the subject people. I would guess that if such support ever takes military forms, it will be defended in one or another of these two ways.

But South Africa is a stalking horse for a larger argument that is better examined in a case where my critics would permit intervention and the theory of *Just and Unjust Wars* would prohibit it. Consider secondly, then, the recent revolution in Nicaragua, which Luban treats in some detail.[18] The Sandinista struggle in Nicaragua extended over many years and culminated in two periods of civil war, the first of which (in August and September of 1978) resulted in a defeat for the rebels. The fighting was resumed in the summer of 1979, and the Somoza government was overthrown. What happened in the months between the two military campaigns usefully illustrates the meaning of self-determination under conditions of political oppression. During that time, the rebels regrouped, rearmed (with some outside help), and, what is most important for us, negotiated a significant broadening of the revolutionary "front." In the course of those negotiations, they were required to commit themselves in fairly explicit ways as to the character of the regime they hoped to establish. Now, had there been a foreign intervention at the time of the first campaign, aimed at rescuing the rebels from defeat, as Luban believes there should have been, this internal process of bargaining and commitment would have been cut short. And then the character of the new regime would have been determined by the intervening state together with whatever faction of rebels it chose to support. It is my claim that such an intervention would have violated the right of Nicaraguans as a group to shape their own political institutions and the right of individual Nicaraguans to live under institutions so shaped. Wasserstrom is wrong, then, to say that this individual right comes to nothing more than the right to live in "a civil society of almost any sort."[19] It is, in this case, the right to live in a civil society of a Nicaraguan sort.

But what if the Sandinistas, facing defeat in September 1978, had asked for foreign military intervention? Can the right of revolution transfer at the initiative of the revolutionaries? It does exactly that in the case of a national liberation struggle, when the revolutionaries are themselves, in a sense, at war with foreigners and are assumed to have the support of their own people. But in the case of revolution and civil war, no such assumption is possible. In principle, revolutionaries who enjoy the active and visible support of a clear majority of their own people can invite foreign armies to intervene on their behalf. But I do not believe that revolutionaries are ever in that position until they are well beyond the point where they need foreign help. All that they need then is that there be no help for the government. The case that Mill envisioned in his essay on nonintervention is more realistic: A group of rebels fighting for the freedom of the people and claiming their passive support, hard-pressed militarily, asks for the help of some foreign state. The rebels, Mill argued, must mobilize their own (putative) supporters, not some alien army.[20] Only a popular mobilization will pave the way for the establishment of a free government. I would add that only such a mobilization, which makes foreign assistance superfluous, could also make it justifiable.

In practice, the request for foreign help is an admission of domestic weakness. It is probably for that reason that the Sandinistas never asked for help (except for equipment to match what the government was receiving or had received). They thought themselves to have, or they thought themselves capable of achieving, majority support. And they were "unrealistic" in the same way I am, according to Wasserstrom. "It is surprisingly unrealistic to suppose that a modern state cannot control its citizens effectively without their genuine consent."[21] The Sandinistas believed, at the least, that the Somoza government could not control its citizens against their active opposition. They wanted their own victory to build upon and reflect that opposition, that is, to be a popular victory. And that is what foreigners should want, too, if they are committed to Nicaraguan self-determination.

In most civil wars, it just isn't possible to determine whether the government or the rebels (or which faction among the rebels) has majority support. Most citizens hide if they can, or profess to support whatever forces control the territory in which they live, or try to guess who will win and join the winners as early as possible. And then, the right of revolution can't and doesn't transfer to foreigners, whatever invitations are offered. Foreign states can't join a civil war, when no other states have joined, simply because they admire the principles of the party that has invited them in or even because they believe that that party would, under ideal conditions, win a free election. If they intervene successfully, the party on whose behalf they have intervened will certainly win the elections, but the conditions will not be ideal. In any case, they have no right to make their own principles or their own beliefs definitive for other people.

But if the eventual outcome, writes Doppelt, "reflects nothing but the balance of internal military might, I see no more reason for calling this process one of 'self-determination' … than I do for denying that it is self-determination on the mere basis that foreign troops have played some role in it."[22] In fact, however, there is no such thing as a bare "balance of internal military might." Armies and police forces are social institutions; soldiers and policemen come from families, villages, neighborhoods, classes. They will not fight cohesively, with discipline, or at length unless the regime for which they are fighting has some degree of social support. A civil war is the sign of a divided society. As an extended insurrection indicates popular support for the rebels (that's why the Viet Cong, despite the claims of the United States Government, could not have been sustained entirely from North Vietnam), so an extended resistance to insurrection indicates popular support for the government. That support may be ignorant, passive, bewildered; it may reflect nothing more than the people's "slowness and aversion" to change. Still, no foreigner can rightly override it. Of course, the actual outcome of a particular struggle will also reflect factors "irrelevant from a moral point of view." There is no way to guarantee the "right" result. But foreign troops are more irrelevant than any local factor, for their strength depends upon the character of their own government and community, their historical traditions, loyalties, and so on, and bears no relation at all to the history and culture of the people whose fate they are determining.

I am inclined to doubt that the issues raised in the last few paragraphs are, in any simple sense, empirical issues. At any rate, they are not susceptible to empirical resolution. We have no reliable indices of popular sentiment in time of civil war. For more or less similar reasons, it is virtually impossible to judge the strength or likely endurance of some established tyranny. There is no point at which foreigners can point to a tyrannical regime and say, "Self-determination has clearly failed; there is nothing to do but intervene." For revolution often comes unexpectedly, as it came to the Iran of the Shah, a sudden upsurge of previously invisible political currents. Intervention denies the political significance of such currents or it denies their moral significance. These are not denials that can be empirically justified. They are instead principled denials of self-determination itself—because it is too slow or too costly, or because its outcome is not foreknown, or because the likely outcome is thought to be unattractive. Underlying all such reasons, however, there must be some alternative principle. The alternative figures only implicitly in Doppelt's article; it is called "reform intervention" by Beitz;[23] Luban provides its formulas; and Wasserstrom gives it an appropriate theoretical label: "the utilitarianism of rights."[24] This principle poses a radical challenge to communal integrity, and I want now to consider it in some detail.

IV

It is easiest to begin with Luban's formulas, the most important of which is simply this: "A just war is (i) a war in defense of socially basic human rights (subject to proportionality)...."[25] Socially basic rights include security rights, against tyrannical governments as well as against foreign invaders, and subsistence rights. Luban would not justify a war fought for the sake of democracy or social justice, though Doppelt and Beitz apparently would.[26] Still, this is a far-reaching license. Or something more than a license: Since socially basic rights "are the demands of all of humanity on all of humanity," it might be Luban's view that we are bound to fight all the just wars we are able to fight—up to the point of exhaustion and incapacity. Then "the utilitarianism of rights" would have the same consequence as ordinary utilitarianism, leaving us no time to ourselves. But I won't pursue this line of argument.

If rights don't require us to intervene, however, then it is difficult to see why they should be called rights (in Luban's sense) or why Luban should object to my own argument, which would also permit interventions against governments that murdered or starved their own people. I suspect that he is reaching for a wider permissiveness—as the others certainly are—not only against governments that violate his list of rights, narrowly conceived, but against all repressive governments and against all governments that are or seem to be indifferent to the poverty of their people. Hence, the phrase "in defense of rights," though technically correct, is politically misleading. Since these are rights that people don't, in the relevant cases, enjoy and may not know themselves to have, the actual purpose of just wars might be better described: to establish or enforce rights, or to maximize their effectiveness, or to enlarge the population for which they are effective. Maximizing rights is very much like maximizing well-being—hence "the utilitarianism of rights"—though with the important proviso that the maximization can be pursued only up to a certain point by military force. But any extra enjoyment of rights, like any extra well-being, probably wouldn't balance the costs of the fighting anyway.

To whom is this far-reaching license granted? Who is to make the crucial calculations? In principle, I suppose, the license is extended to any and all foreigners; in practice, today, to the officials of foreign states; tomorrow, perhaps, to some set of global bureaucrats acting by themselves or as advisers to and agents of a Universal Assembly. Now, why them? And here a more serious sort of rights argument properly begins. Rights are in an important sense distributive principles. They distribute decision-making authority. When we describe individual rights, we are assigning to individuals a certain authority to shape their own lives, and we are denying that officials, even well-meaning officials, are authorized to interfere. The description of communal rights makes a similar assertion and a similar denial. In the individual case, we fix a certain area for personal choice; in the communal case, we fix a certain area for political choice. Unless these areas are clearly marked out and protected, both sorts of choices are likely to become problematic.

But unless they are democratically made, my critics might argue, political choices are already problematic and can't plausibly count as the free choices of the community. The area within which tyrants, oligarchs, ruling classes, priestly castes, and military cliques make their choices isn't worth protecting. Only liberal or democratic states have rights against external intervention. This claim plays on a (pretended) domestic equivalent: that only the uncoerced choices of minimally rational individuals are protected against intervention. But it is not the sign of some collective derangement or radical incapacity for a political community to produce an authoritarian regime. Indeed, the history, culture, and religion of the community may be such that authoritarian regimes come, as it were, naturally, reflecting a widely shared worldview or way of life. Such views and ways may be wrong or badly conceived; they are not necessarily insane. The authoritarian regime is not, to be sure, freely chosen, but then no set of political institutions is ever freely chosen from the full range of alternatives by a single set of people at a single moment in time. Institutions have histories; they are the products of protracted struggles. And it can't be the case that communities are protected against intervention only if those struggles have a single philosophically correct or universally approved outcome (or one of a small number of correct or approved outcomes). That would not be the same thing as protecting only free individuals; it would be more like protecting only individuals who had arrived at certain opinions, lifestyles, and so on.

The difference between my own views and those of my critics may be sharpened if we consider a hypothetical case designed to neutralize the proportionality qualification and all the other issues raised by the use of force and to focus exclusively on the question of communal integrity. Imagine, then, a country called Algeria in which a group of revolutionaries comes to power pledged to create a democratic and secular state, with equal rights for all citizens. The regime they actually create, or that is created as a result of their struggles with one another, is very different: a military dictatorship and a religious "republic," without civil and political liberties, and brutally repressive, not only because a new political elite has established itself and resists all challenges but also because women have been returned to their traditional religious subordination to patriarchal authority. It is clear, however, that this regime (in contrast to the one the revolutionaries originally had in mind) has deep roots in Algerian history and draws importantly upon Algerian political and religious culture. It is not a democratic regime; its popularity has never been tested in a democratic way; but there can be no doubt that it is an Algerian regime. Now, imagine further that the Swedish government had in its possession a wondrous chemical that, if introduced into the water supply of Algeria, would turn all Algerians, elites and masses, into Swedish-style social democrats. It would wipe out of their minds their own political and religious culture (though it would leave them with no sense of loss). And it would provide them instead with the knowledge, capacity, and will to create a new regime in which basic security rights, political and civil liberties, too, would be respected, women would be treated as equals, and so on. Should they use the chemical? Do they have a right to use it? The force of the argument depends upon the reader's readiness to value Swedish social democracy far above Algerian "socialism." I assume that valuation, and yet I am certain that the Swedes should not use the chemical. They should not use it because the historical religion and politics of the Algerian people are values for the Algerian people (even though individual Algerians have not chosen their religion and politics from among a range of alternatives), which our valuation cannot override. It may seem paradoxical to hold that the Algerian people have a right to a state within which their rights are violated. But that is, given the case as I have described it, the only kind of state that they are likely to call their own.

Nor would the case be different if there were a democratic political movement or a feminist movement within Algeria. For foreigners cannot judge the relative strength of such movements or allow them to substitute themselves for the people as a whole, not until they have won sufficient support to transform Algerian politics on their own. That may be a long process; it will certainly involve compromises of different sorts; and the movements if and when they win will be different from what they were when they began. All that is Algerian self-determination, a political process that also has value, even if it isn't always pretty, and even if its outcome doesn't conform to philosophical standards of political and social justice.

Individual rights may well derive, as I am inclined to think, from our ideas about personality and moral agency, without reference to political processes and social circumstances. But the enforcement of rights is another matter. It is not the case that one can simply proclaim a list of rights and then look around for armed men to enforce it. Rights are only enforceable within political communities where they have been collectively recognized, and the process by which they come to be recognized is a political process that requires a political arena. The globe is not, or not yet, such an arena. Or rather, the only global community is pluralist in character, a community of nations, not of humanity, and the rights recognized within it have been minimal and largely negative, designed to protect the integrity of nations and to regulate their commercial and military transactions.

Beitz seems to believe that this pluralist world order has already been transcended and that communal integrity is a thing of the past. In a world of increasing interdependence, he argues, it is an "evident falsity" to claim "that states are relatively self-enclosed arenas of political development."[27] Just as no man is an island, so no state is an island—not even Britain, Japan, or Singapore. We are all involved in one another's politics, responsible for one another, and open (it seems) to one another's interventions. I don't know what evidence might be presented for this view, what sorts of comparisons might be drawn with what previous historical periods. Perfect self-enclosure has probably never existed. Relative self-enclosure seems to me an evident truth. Anyone doubting it would have to account on psychological grounds for the enormous importance colonial peoples attach to their recently won independence and the enormous importance revolutionary groups attach to the seizure of power in their own political communities. In fact, psychological explanations are quite unnecessary. Political power within a particular community remains the critical factor in shaping the fate of the members. Of course, that fate (like all fates) is shaped within political and economic limits, and these can be more or less narrow; there are some states with relatively little room for maneuver. And yet, even economically dependent states, locked into international markets they can't control, can dramatically alter the conditions of their dependence and the character of their domestic life. Surely the histories of Yugoslavia since World War II, of Cuba since 1960, and of Iran over the last two years suggest strongly that what actually happens within a country is a function, above all, of local political processes. An internal decision (or an internal revolution) can turn a country around in a way no decision by another country, short of a decision to invade, can possibly do.

So the political community with its government, that is, the state, is still the critical arena of political life. It has not been transcended, and there are two important reasons, I think, for hesitating a long time before attempting the transcendence. The first reason is prudential. If the outcome of political processes in particular communal arenas is often brutal, then it ought to be assumed that outcomes in the global arena will often be brutal, too. And this will be a far more effective and therefore a far more dangerous brutality, for there will be no place left for political refuge and no examples left of political alternatives.

The second reason has to do with the very nature of political life. Politics (as distinct from mere coercion and bureaucratic manipulation) depends upon shared history, communal sentiment, accepted conventions—upon some extended version of Aristotle's "friendship." All this is problematic enough in the modern state; it is hardly conceivable on a global scale. Communal life and liberty requires the existence of "relatively self-enclosed arenas of political development." Break into the enclosures and you destroy the communities. And that destruction is a loss to the individual members (unless it rescues them from massacre, enslavement, or expulsion), a loss of something valuable, which they clearly value, and to which they have a right, namely their participation in the "development" that goes on and can only go on within the enclosure. Hence the distinction of state rights and individual rights is simplistic and wrongheaded. Against foreigners, individuals have a right to a state of their own. Against state officials, they have a right to political and civil liberty. Without the first of these rights, the second is meaningless: As individuals need a home, so rights require a location.

V

My own argument is perhaps best understood as a defense of politics, while that of my critics reiterates what I take to be the traditional philosophical dislike for politics. This dislike is most readily recognized in utilitarian argument, commonly addressed to real or imaginary bureaucrats. But it is also apparent among rights theorists, whenever the enforcement of rights is assigned to authorities who stand outside the political arena or who are allowed (or required) to act even in the absence of prior consent. Some such assignment, I don't doubt, is necessary even to my own argument, as the three exceptions suggest, and so it might be said that the question is only where to draw the line between external (bureaucratic or military) enforcement, on the one hand, and political decision making on the other. But I suspect that the disagreement goes deeper than that formulation allows. It has to do with the respect we are prepared to accord and the room we are prepared to yield to the political process itself, with all its messiness and uncertainty, its inevitable compromises, and its frequent brutality. It has to do with the range of outcomes we are prepared to tolerate, to accept as presumptively legitimate, though not necessarily to endorse. "For Walzer," writes Doppelt, states that possess the collective right of sovereignty "may violate the individual rights of all or some group of [their] citizens."[28] No, I do not give out permissions of that sort; obviously, I oppose all such violations. But I don't believe that the opposition of philosophers is a sufficient ground for military invasion. Perhaps, indeed, like Prince Hamlet, we are born to set things right, but we do that, or try to do it, by making arguments, not by summoning up armies.

NOTES

1. Michael Walzer, *Just and Unjust Wars* (New York, 1977).

2. Richard Wasserstrom, *Harvard Law Review* 92 (December 1978): 544.

3. Gerald Doppelt, "Walzer's Theory of Morality in International Relations," *Philosophy & Public Affairs* 8, no. 1: 26.

4. Charles R. Beitz, "Bounded Morality: Justice and the State in World Politics," *International Organization* 33: 405–24; David Luban, "Just War and Human Rights," *Philosophy & Public Affairs* 9, no. 2: 161–81 [reprinted herein 29–50].

5. Luban, p. 167 [herein 36].

6. Doppelt, p. 14.

7. This claim parallels the argument in *Just and Unjust Wars* (p. 330) about nonviolence. If citizens choose civil rather than military resistance, then the criminality of the aggressor is diminished, for he has evidently not forced them to fight, risk their lives, and die for their rights. If the invaders are welcomed by a clear majority of the people, then it would be odd to accuse them of any crime at all. But it is almost certain that such a welcome would be extended only in circumstances that make for the three exceptions that I take up below. And then the invasion will be blameless even before it is welcomed.

8. *Just and Unjust Wars*, p. 89.

9. Wasserstrom, p. 540.

10. Ibid., p. 542; Doppelt, p. 16.

11. Hence the Italian nationalist Mazzini was wrong to say (in his opening address to Young Europe in 1847) that "There is no international question as to forms of government, but only a national question." Instead, a simple distinction holds. The philosophical question is indeed international (or transnational or universal), but the political question can only rightly be answered by some national process of decision making.

12. Luban, p. 166 [herein 34].

13. The following paragraphs summarize the argument of *Just and Unjust Wars*, pp. 89–108.

14. For reasons I cannot understand, Doppelt takes me to mean by "enslavement" the "forced resettlement of masses of people" (p. 7), referring to a discussion of Spanish policy in Cuba in 1898. But all that I say about Spanish policy is that it was carried out "with so little regard for the health of the people involved that thousands of them suffered and died" (*Just and Unjust Wars*, p. 102). No, by "enslavement" I mean enslavement: The dictionary definition will do well enough. I offer no examples because, so far as I know, enslavement has never been made the occasion for (even the pretext for) a military intervention. Hence Doppelt's reference to the American South (p. 20) is otiose. Slaves are not to be conceived of as participants in any social or political process of self-determination.

15. Wasserstrom, p. 544; Doppelt, pp. 20, 23–25.

16. I can't refer authoritatively here to any body of South African literature; my reference is to arguments made in leaflets and at political meetings in the United States.

17. It is a problem, of course, that even ordinary oppression can be and commonly is described in the language of enslavement—as in the Marxist phrase "wage slavery." But that only suggests the importance of drawing a line that protests internal political and social processes (not against philosophical criticism or domestic resistance and revolution but only) against military intervention.

18. Luban, pp. 170–71 [herein 38–39].

19. Wasserstrom, p. 542.

20. See the discussion of Mill's argument, *Just and Unjust Wars*, pp. 87–91.

21. Wasserstrom, p. 542.

22. Doppelt, p. 13.

23. Beitz, p. 413.

24. The notion of a "utilitarianism of rights" was first formulated by Robert Nozick in *Anarchy, State, and Utopia* (New York, 1974), p. 28. Nozick goes on to argue, on Kantian grounds, that rights must be understood as constraints on action rather than as goals of a maximizing politics. Though I don't share his views as to the substance of a rights theory, the same conception of its structure underlies my own position in *Just and Unjust Wars*.

25. Luban, p. 175 [herein 42].

26. I am not sure, however, that Beitz means to defend *military* intervention. Reviewing a book on war, he certainly seems to do so. But in his own book, he introduces a similar argument by saying that he wishes "to bracket the case of military intervention" and talk only of "policies of interference that ... fall short of the actual use of violence" (*Political Theory and International Relations*, Princeton, 1979, p. 72). For myself, I was concerned in *Just and Unjust Wars* only with military intervention, but the arguments I constructed do rule out any external determination of domestic constitutional arrangements (as an example below will suggest). I don't, however, mean to rule out every effort by one state to influence another or every use of diplomatic and economic pressure. Drawing the line is sure to be difficult, but the precise location of the line is not at issue here, for all my critics, with only the possible exception of Beitz, are ready for "the actual use of violence" in other people's countries, in order to do them good.

27. Beitz, pp. 422–23.

28. Doppelt, p. 25.

5. MICHAEL W. DOYLE

Doyle examines the impact of liberal principles and institutions on liberal states' conduct of foreign affairs—an impact that, he claims, has not been clearly apprehended by either the bulk of citizens of such states, or by diplomats and academics. On the one hand, there is a tendency to cast liberalism in a patriotic or peace-loving light, and on the other, to perceive it as being at odds with the hard realities of balance-of-power international relations. Doyle maintains that each of these perceptions of the effect of liberalism on foreign affairs is mistaken, though each contains elements of truth. Liberalism, though not inherently peace-loving, has increased the chances of achieving world peace by strengthening the effect of the establishment of a group of mutually peaceful liberal states and through the manifestation of peaceful intent and restraint in at least some of the foreign policy conducted by liberal states. Doyle's diagnosis is that, while liberal practice toward other liberal societies has been very successful, liberal practice toward nonliberal societies has been clouded with confusion. He turns to the liberal writings of Kant to help dispel this confusion.

Kant, Liberal Legacies, and Foreign Affairs, Part 1

First published in Philosophy and Public Affairs *12: 3 (summer 1983): 205–35.*

I

What difference do liberal principles and institutions make to the conduct of the foreign affairs of liberal states? A thicket of conflicting judgments suggests that the legacies of liberalism have not been clearly appreciated. For many citizens of liberal states, liberal principles and institutions have so fully absorbed domestic politics that their influence on foreign affairs tends to be either overlooked altogether or, when perceived, exaggerated. Liberalism becomes either unselfconsciously patriotic or inherently "peace-loving." For many scholars and diplomats, the relations among independent states appear to differ so significantly from domestic politics that influences of liberal principles and domestic liberal institutions are denied or denigrated. They judge that international relations are governed by perceptions of national security and the balance of power; liberal principles and institutions, when they do intrude, confuse and disrupt the pursuit of balance-of-power politics.[1]

Although liberalism is misinterpreted from both these points of view, a crucial aspect of the liberal legacy is captured by each. Liberalism is a distinct ideology and set of institutions that has shaped the perceptions of and capacities for foreign relations of political societies that range from social welfare or social democratic to laissez-faire. It defines much of the content of the liberal patriot's nationalism. Liberalism does appear to disrupt the pursuit of balance-of-power politics. Thus its foreign relations cannot be adequately explained (or prescribed) by a sole reliance on the balance of power. But liberalism is not inherently "peace-loving"; nor is it consistently restrained or peaceful in intent. Furthermore, liberal practice may reduce the probability that states will successfully exercise the consistent restraint and peaceful intentions that a world peace may well require in the nuclear age. Yet the peaceful intent and restraint that liberalism does manifest in limited aspects of its foreign affairs announces the possibility of a world peace this side of the grave or of world conquest. It has strengthened the prospects for a world peace established by the steady expansion of a separate peace among liberal societies.

Putting together these apparently contradictory (but, in fact, compatible) pieces of the liberal legacy begins with a discussion of the range of liberal principle and practice. This article highlights the differences between liberal practice toward other liberal societies and liberal practice toward nonliberal societies. It argues that liberalism has achieved extraordinary success in the first and has contributed to exceptional confusion in the second. Appreciating these liberal legacies calls for another look at one of the greatest of liberal philosophers, Immanuel Kant, for he is a source of insight, policy, and hope.

II

Liberalism has been identified with an essential principle—the importance of the freedom of the individual. Above all, this is a belief in the importance of moral freedom, of the right to be treated and a duty to treat others as ethical subjects, and not as objects or means only. This principle has generated rights and institutions.

A commitment to a threefold set of rights forms the foundation of liberalism. Liberalism calls for freedom from arbitrary authority, often called "negative freedom," which includes freedom of conscience, a free press and free speech, equality under the law, and the right to hold, and therefore to exchange, property without fear of arbitrary seizure. Liberalism also calls for those rights necessary to protect and promote the capacity and opportunity for freedom, the "positive freedoms." Such social and economic rights as equality of opportunity in education and rights to health care and employment, necessary for effective self-expression and participation, are thus among liberal rights. A third liberal right, democratic participation or representation, is necessary to guarantee the other two. To ensure that morally autonomous individuals remain free in those areas of social action where public authority is needed, public legislation has to express the will of the citizens making laws for their own community.

These three sets of rights, taken together, seem to meet the challenge that Kant identified:

> To organize a group of rational beings who demand general laws for their survival, but of whom each inclines toward exempting himself, and to establish their constitution in such a way that, in spite of the fact their private attitudes are opposed, these private attitudes mutually impede each other in such a manner that [their] public behavior is the same as if they did not have such evil attitudes.[2]

But the dilemma within liberalism is how to reconcile the three sets of liberal rights. The right to private property, for example, can conflict with equality of opportunity and both rights can be violated by democratic legislation. During the 180 years since Kant wrote, the liberal tradition has evolved two high roads to individual freedom and social order; one is laissez-faire or "conservative" liberalism and the other is social welfare, or social democratic, or "liberal" liberalism. Both reconcile these conflicting rights (though in differing ways) by success-fully organizing free individuals into a political order.

The political order of laissez-faire and social welfare liberals is marked by a shared commitment to four essential institutions. First, citizens possess juridical equality and other fundamental civic rights such as freedom of religion and the press. Second, the effective sovereigns of the state are representative legislatures deriving their authority from the consent of the electorate and exercising their authority free from all restraint apart from the requirement that basic civic rights be preserved.[3] Most pertinently for the impact of liberalism on foreign affairs, the state is subject to neither the external authority of other states nor to the internal authority of special prerogatives held, for example, by monarchs or military castes over foreign policy. Third, the economy rests on a recognition of the rights of private property, including the ownership of means of production. Property is justified by individual acquisition (for example, by labor) or by social agreement or social utility. This excludes state socialism or state capitalism, but it need not exclude market socialism or various forms of the mixed economy. Fourth, economic decisions are predominantly shaped by the forces of supply and demand, domestically and internationally, and are free from strict control by bureaucracies.

In order to protect the opportunity of the citizen to exercise freedom, laissez-faire liberalism has leaned toward a highly constrained role for the

TABLE 1

Period	Liberal Regimes and the Pacific Union (By date "liberal")[a]	Total Number
18th century	Swiss Cantons[b] French Republic 1790–1795 the United States[b] 1776–	3
1800–1850	Swiss Confederation, the United States France 1830–1849 Belgium 1830– Great Britain 1832– Netherlands 1848– Piedmont 1848– Denmark 1849–	8

TABLE 1 (cont.)

Period	Liberal Regimes and the Pacific Union (By date "liberal")[a]	Total Number
1850–1900	Switzerland, the United States, Belgium, Great Britain, Netherlands Piedmont –1861, Italy 1861– Denmark –1866 Sweden 1864– Greece 1864– Canada 1867– France 1871– Argentina 1880– Chile 1891–	13
1900–1945	Switzerland, the United States, Great Britain, Sweden, Canada Greece –1911, 1928–1936 Italy –1922 Belgium –1940 Netherlands –1940 Argentina –1943 France –1940 Chile –1924, 1932 Australia 1901– Norway 1905–1940 New Zealand 1907– Colombia 1910–1949 Denmark 1914–1940 Poland 1917–1935 Latvia 1922–1934 Germany 1918–1932 Austria 1918–1934 Estonia 1919–1934 Finland 1919– Uruguay 1919– Costa Rica 1919– Czechoslovakia 1920–1939 Ireland 1920– Mexico 1928– Lebanon 1944–	29

TABLE 1 (cont.)

Period	Liberal Regimes and the Pacific Union (By date "liberal")[a]	Total Number
1945[c]–	Switzerland, the United States, Great Britain, Sweden, Canada, Australia, New Zealand, Finland, Ireland, Mexico	49
	Uruguay –1973;	
	Chile –1973;	
	Lebanon –1975	
	Costa Rica –1948, 1953–	
	Iceland 1944–	
	France 1945–	
	Denmark 1945–	
	Norway 1945–	
	Austria 1945–	
	Brazil 1945–1954, 1955–1964	
	Belgium 1946–	
	Luxemburg 1946–	
	Netherlands 1946–	
	Italy 1946–	
	Philippines 1946–1972	
	India 1947–1975, 1977–	
	Sri Lanka 1948–1961, 1963–1977, 1978–	
	Ecuador 1948–1963, 1979–	
	Israel 1949–	
	West Germany 1949–	
	Peru 1950–1962, 1963–1968, 1980–	
	El Salvador 1950–1961	
	Turkey 1950–1960, 1966–1971	
	Japan 1951–	
	Bolivia 1956–1969	
	Colombia 1958–	
	Venezuela 1959–	
	Nigeria 1961–1964, 1979–	
	Jamaica 1962–	
	Trinidad 1962–	
	Senegal 1963–	
	Malaysia 1963–	
	South Korea 1963–1972	
	Botswana 1966–	
	Singapore 1965–	
	Greece 1975–	
	Portugal 1976–	
	Spain 1978–	
	Dominican Republic 1978–	

TABLE 1 (cont.)

Notes

a. I have drawn up this approximate list of "Liberal Regimes" according to the four institutions described as essential: market and private property economies; polities that are externally sovereign; citizens who possess juridical rights; and "republican" (whether republican or monarchical), representative, government. This latter includes the requirement that the legislative branch have an effective role in public policy and be formally and competitively, either potentially or actually, elected. Furthermore, I have taken into account whether male suffrage is wide (that is, 30 percent) or open to "achievement" by inhabitants (for example, to poll-tax payers or householders) of the national or metropolitan territory. Female suffrage is granted within a generation of its being demanded; and representative government is internally sovereign (for example, including and especially over military and foreign affairs) as well as stable (in existence for at least three years).

Sources: Arthur Banks and W. Overstreet, eds., *The Political Handbook of the World, 1980* (New York: McGraw-Hill, 1980); Foreign and Commonwealth Office, *A Year Book of the Commonwealth 1980* (London: HMSO, 1980); *Europa Yearbook, 1981* (London: Europa, 1981); W. L. Langer, *An Encyclopedia of World History* (Boston: Houghton-Mifflin, 1968); Department of State, *Country Reports on Human Rights Practices* (Washington, DC: Government Printing Office, 1981); and *Freedom at Issue*, no. 54 (January–February 1980).

b. There are domestic variations within these liberal regimes. For example, Switzerland was liberal only in certain cantons; the United States was liberal only north of the Mason-Dixon Line until 1865, when it became liberal throughout. These lists also exclude ancient "republics," since none appear to fit Kant's criteria. See Stephen Holmes, "Aristippus in and out of Athens," *American Political Science Review* 73, no. 1 (March 1979).

c. Selected list, excludes liberal regimes with populations less than 1 million.

state and a much wider role for private property and the market. In order to promote the opportunity of the citizen to exercise freedom, welfare liberalism has expanded the role of the state and constricted the role of the market.[4] Both, nevertheless, accept these four institutional requirements and contrast markedly with the colonies, monarchical regimes, military dictatorships, and communist party dictatorships with which they have shared the political governance of the modern world.

The domestic successes of liberalism have never been more apparent. Never have so many people been included in, and accepted the domestic hegemony of, the liberal order; never have so many of the world's leading states been liberal, whether as republics or as constitutional monarchies. Indeed, the success of liberalism as an answer to the problem of masterless men in modern society is reflected in the growth in the number of liberal regimes from the three that existed when Kant wrote to the more than forty that exist today. But we should not be complacent about the domestic affairs of liberal states. Significant practical problems endure: among them are enhancing citizen participation in large democracies, distributing "positional goods" (for example, prestigious jobs), controlling bureaucracy, reducing unemployment, paying for a growing demand for social services, reducing inflation, and achieving large-scale restructuring of industries in response to growing foreign competition.[5] Nonetheless, these domestic problems have been widely explored though they are by no means solved. Liberalism's foreign record is more obscure and warrants more consideration.

III

In foreign affairs liberalism has shown, as it has in the domestic realm, serious weaknesses. But unlike liberalism's domestic realm, its foreign affairs have experienced startling but less than fully appreciated successes. Together they shape an unrecognized dilemma, for both these successes and weaknesses in large part spring from the same cause: the international implications of liberal principles and institutions.

The basic postulate of liberal international theory holds that states have the right to be free from foreign intervention. Since morally autonomous citizens hold rights to liberty, the states that democratically represent them have the right to exercise political independence. Mutual respect for these rights then becomes the touchstone of international liberal theory.[6] When states respect each other's rights, individuals are free to establish private international ties without state interference. Profitable exchanges between merchants and educational exchanges among scholars then create a web of mutual advantages and commitments that bolsters sentiments of public respect.

These conventions of mutual respect have formed a cooperative foundation for relations among liberal democracies of a remarkably effective kind. *Even though liberal states have become involved in numer-ous wars with nonliberal states, constitutionally secure liberal states have yet to engage in war with one another.*[7] No one should argue that such wars are impossible; but preliminary evidence does appear to indicate that there exists a significant predisposition against warfare between liberal states. Indeed, threats of war also have been regarded as illegiti-mate. A liberal zone of peace, a pacific union, has been maintained and has expanded despite numerous particular conflicts of economic and strategic interest.

During the nineteenth century the United States and Britain negotiated the northern frontier of the United States. During the American Civil War the commercial linkages between the Lancashire cotton economy and the American South and the sentimental links between the British aristocracy and the Southern plantocracy (together with numerous disputes over the rights of British shipping against the Northern blockade) brought Great Britain and the Northern states to the brink of war, but they never passed over that brink. Despite an intense Anglo-French colonial rivalry, crises such as Fashoda in 1898 were resolved without going to war. Despite their colonial rivalries, liberal France and Britain formed an entente before World War I against illiberal Germany (whose foreign relations were controlled by the Kaiser and the Army). During 1914–15, Italy, the liberal member of the Triple Alliance with illiberal Germany and Austria, chose not to fulfill its obligations under the Triple Alliance to either support its allies or remain neutral. Instead, Italy, a liberal regime, joined the alliance with France and Britain that would prevent it from having to fight other liberal states, and declared war on Austria and Germany, its former allies. And despite generations of Anglo-American tension and British restrictions on American trade, the United States leaned toward Britain and France from 1914 to 1917. Nowhere was this special peace among liberal states more clearly proclaimed than in President Woodrow Wilson's "War Message" of April 2, 1917: "Our object now, as then, is to vindicate the principles of peace and justice in the life of the world as against selfish and autocratic power and to set up amongst the really free and self-governed peoples of the world such a concert of purpose and of action as will henceforth ensure the observance of those principles."[8]

TABLE 2

*International Wars Listed Chronologically**

British–Maharattan (1817–1818)
Greek (1821–1828)
Franco Spanish (1823)
First Anglo–Burmese (1823–1826)
Javanese (1825–1830)
Russo–Persian (1826–1828)
Russo–Turkish (1828–1829)
First Polish (1831)
First Syrian (1831–1832)
Texan (1835–1836)
First British–Afghan (1838–1842)
Second Syrian (1839–1840)
Franco–Algerian (1839–1847)
Peruvian–Bolivian (1841)
First British–Sikh (1845–1846)
Mexican–American (1846–1848)
Austro–Sardinian (1848–1849)
First Schleswig–Holstein (1848–1849)
Hungarian (1848–1849)
Second British–Sikh (1848–1849)
Roman Republic (1849)
La Plata (1851–1852)
First Turco–Montenegran (1852–1853)
Crimean (1853–1856)
Anglo–Persian (1856–1857)
Sepoy (1857–1859)
Second Turco–Montenegran (1858–1859)
Italian Unification (1859)
Spanish–Moroccan (1859–1860)
Italo–Roman (1860)
Italo–Sicilian (1860–1861)
Franco–Mexican (1862–1867)
Ecuadorian–Colombian (1863)
Second Polish (1863–1864)
Spanish–Santo Dominican (1863–1865)
Second Schleswig–Holstein (1864)
Lopez (1864–1870)
Spanish–Chilean (1865–1866)
Seven Weeks (1866)
Ten Years (1868–1878)
Franco–Prussian (1870–1871)
Dutch–Achinese (1873–1878)
Balkan (1875–1877)
Russo–Turkish (1877–1878)
Bosnian (1878)

Second British–Afghan (1878–1880)
Pacific (1879–1880)
British–Zulu (1879)
Franco–Indochinese (1882–1884)
Mandist (1882–1885)
Sino–French (1884–1885)
Central American (1885)
Serbo–Bulgarian (1885)
Sino–Japanese (1894–1895)
Franco–Madagascan (1894–1895)
Cuban (1895–1898)
Italo–Ethiopian (1895–1896)
First Philippine (1896–1898)
Greco–Turkish (1897)
Spanish–American (1898)
Second Philippine (1899–1902)
Boer (1899–1902)
Boxer Rebellion (1900)
Ilinden (1903)
Russo–Japanese (1904–1905)
Central American (1906)
Central American (1907)
Spanish–Moroccan (1909–1910)
Italo–Turkish (1911–1912)
First Balkan (1912–1913)
Second Balkan (1913)
World War I (1914–1918)
Russian Nationalities (1917–1921)
Russo–Polish (1919–1920)
Hungarian–Allies (1919)
Greco–Turkish (1919–1922)
Riffian (1921–1926)
Druze (1925–1927)
Sino–Soviet (1929)
Manchurian (1931–1933)
Chaco (1932–1935)
Italo–Ethiopian (1935–1936)
Sino–Japanese (1937–1941)
Changkufeng (1938)
Nomohan (1939)
World War II (1939–1945)
Russo–Finnish (1939–1940)
Franco–Thai (1940–1941)
Indonesian (1945–1946)
Indochinese (1945–1954)

TABLE 2 (cont.)
*International Wars Listed Chronologically**

Madagascan (1947–1948)	Bangladesh (1971)
First Kashmir (1947–1949)	Philippine–MNLF (1972–)
Palestine (1948–1949)	Yom Kippur (1973)
Hyderabad (1948)	Turco–Cypriot (1974)
Korean (1950–1953)	Ethiopian–Eritrean (1974–)
Algerian (1954–1962)	Vietnamese–Cambodian (1975–)
Russo–Hungarian (1956)	Timor (1975–)
Sinai (1956)	Saharan (1975–)
Tibetan (1956–1959)	Ogaden (1976–)
Sino–Indian (1962)	Ugandan–Tanzanian (1978–1979)
Vietnamese (1965–1975)	Sino–Vietnamese (1979)
Second Kashmir (1965)	Russo–Afghan (1979–)
Six–Day (1967)	Irani–Iraqi (1980–)
Israeli–Egyptian (1969–1970)	
Football (1969)	

* The table is reprinted by permission from Melvin Small and J. David Singer from *Resort to Arms* (Beverly Hills, CA: Sage Publications, 1982), pp. 79–80. This is a partial list of international wars fought between 1816 and 1980. In Appendices A and B of *Resort to Arms*, Small and Singer identify a total of 575 wars in this period; but approximately 159 of them appear to be largely domestic, or civil wars.

This definition of war excludes covert interventions, some of which have been directed by liberal regimes against other liberal regimes. One example is the United States' effort to destabilize the Chilean election and Allende's government. Nonetheless, it is significant (as will be apparent below) that such interventions are not pursued publicly as acknowledged policy. The covert destabilization campaign against Chile is recounted in US Congress, Senate, Select Committee to Study Government Operations with Respect to Intelligence Activities, *Covert Action in Chile, 1963–73*, 94th Congress, 1st Session (Washington, DC: U.S. Government Printing Office, 1975).

The argument of this article (and this list) also excludes civil wars. Civil wars differ from international wars not in the ferocity of combat but in the issues that engender them. Two nations that could abide one another as independent neighbors separated by a border might well be the fiercest of enemies if forced to live together in one state, jointly deciding how to raise and spend taxes, choose leaders, and legislate fundamental questions of value. Notwithstanding these differences, no civil wars that I recall upset the argument of liberal pacification.

Statistically, war between any two states (in any single year or other short period of time) is a low-probability event. War between any two adjacent states, considered over a long period of time, may be somewhat more probable. The apparent absence of war among the more clearly liberal states, whether adjacent or not, for almost two hundred years thus has some significance. Politically more significant, perhaps, is that, when states are forced to decide, by the pressure of an impinging world war, on which side of a world contest they will fight, liberal states wind up all on the same side, despite the real complexity of the historical, economic, and political factors that affect their foreign policies. And historically, we should recall that medieval and early modern Europe were the warring cockpits of states, wherein France and England and the Low Countries engaged in near-constant strife. Then in the late eighteenth century there began to emerge liberal regimes. At first hesitant and confused, and later clear and confident as liberal regimes gained deeper domestic foundations and longer international experience, a pacific union of these liberal states became established.

The Realist model of international relations, which provides a plausible explanation of the general insecurity of states, offers little guidance in explaining the pacification of the liberal world. Realism, in its classical formulation, holds that the state is and should be formally sovereign, effectively unbounded by individual rights nationally and thus capable of determining its own scope of authority. (This determination can be made democratically, oligarchically, or autocratically.) Internationally, the sovereign state exists in an anarchical society in which it is radically independent; neither bounded nor protected by international "law" or treaties or duties, and hence, insecure. Hobbes, one of the seventeenth-century founders of the Realist approach, drew the international implications of Realism when he argued that the existence of international anarchy, the very independence of states, best accounts for the competition, the fear, and the temptation toward preventive war that characterize international relations. Politics among nations is not a continuous combat, but it is in this view a "state of war ... a tract of time, wherein the will to contend by battle is sufficiently known."[9]

In international relations theory, three "games" explain the fear that Hobbes saw as a root of conflict in the state of war. First, even when states share an interest in a common good that could be attained by cooperation, the absence of a source of global law and order means that no one state can count upon the cooperative behavior of the others. Each state therefore has a rational incentive to defect from the cooperative enterprise even if only to pursue a good whose value is less than the share that would have been obtained from the successful accomplishment of the cooperative enterprise (this is Rousseau's "stag dilemma"). Second, even though each state knows that security is relative to the armaments level of potential adversaries and even though each state seeks to minimize its arms expenditure, it also knows that, having no global guarantee of security, being caught unarmed by a surprise attack is worse than bearing the costs of armament. Each therefore arms; all are worse off (this is the "security dilemma," a variant of the "prisoner's dilemma"). Third, heavily armed states rely upon their prestige, their credibility, to deter states from testing the true quality of their arms in battle, and credibility is measured by a record of successes. Once a posture of confrontation is assumed, backing down, although rational for both together, is not rational (first best) for either individually if there is some chance that the other will back down first (the game of "chicken").[10]

Specific wars therefore arise from fear as a state seeking to avoid a surprise attack decides to attack first; from competitive emulation as states lacking an imposed international hierarchy of prestige struggle to establish their place; and from straightforward conflicts of interest that escalate into war because there is no global sovereign to prevent states from adopting that ultimate form of conflict resolution. Herein lie Thucydides' trinity of "security, honor, and self-interest" and Hobbes's "diffidence," "glory," and "competition" that drive states to conflict in the international state of war.[11]

Finding that all states, including liberal states, do engage in war, the Realist concludes that the effects of differing domestic regimes (whether liberal or not) are overridden by the international anarchy under which all states live.[12] Thus Hobbes does not bother to distinguish between "some council or one man" when he discusses the sovereign. Differing domestic regimes do affect the quantity of resources available to the state as Rousseau (an eighteenth-century Realist) shows in his discussion of Poland, and Morgenthau (a twentieth-century Realist) demonstrates in his discussion of morale.[13] But the ends that shape the international state of war are decreed for the Realist by the anarchy of the international order and the fundamental quest for power that directs the policy of all States, irrespective of differences in their domestic regimes. As Rousseau argued, international peace therefore depends on the abolition of international relations either by the achievement of a world state or by a radical isolationism (Corsica). Realists judge neither to be possible.

First, at the level of the strategic decision maker, Realists argue that a liberal peace could be merely the outcome of prudent diplomacy. Some, including Hobbes, have argued that sovereigns have a natural duty not to act against "the reasons of peace."[14] Individuals established (that is, should establish) a sovereign to escape from the brutalities of the state of nature, the war of all against all, that follows from competition for scarce goods, scrambles for prestige, and fear of another's attack when there is no sovereign to provide for lawful acquisition or regularized social conduct or personal security. "Dominions were constituted for peace's sake, and peace was sought for safety's sake"; the natural duty of the sovereign is therefore the safety of the people. Yet prudent policy cannot be an enforceable right of citizens because Hobbesian sovereigns, who remain in the state of nature with respect to their subjects and other sovereigns, cannot themselves be subjects.

Nevertheless, the interstate condition is not necessarily the original brutality only now transposed to the frontiers. The sovereign is personally more secure than any individual in the original state of nature and soldiers too are by nature timorous. Unlike individuals, states are not equal; some live more expansively by predominance, others must live only by sufferance. Yet a policy of safety is not a guarantee of peace. The international condition for Hobbes remains a state of war. Safety enjoins a prudent policy of forewarning (spying) and of forearming oneself to increase security against other sovereigns who, lacking any assurance that you are not taking these measures, also take them. Safety also requires (morally) taking actions "whatsoever shall seem to conduce to the lessening of the power of foreigners whom they [the sovereign] suspect, whether by slight or force."[15] If preventive wars are prudent, the Realists' prudence obviously cannot account for more than a century and a half of peace among independent liberal states, many of which have crowded one another in the center of Europe.

Recent additions to game theory specify some of the circumstances under which prudence could lead to peace. Experience; geography; expectations of cooperation and belief patterns; and the differing payoffs to cooperation (peace) or conflict associated with various types of military technology all appear to influence the calculus.[16] But when it comes to acquiring the techniques of peaceable interaction, nations appear to be slow, or at least erratic, learners. The balance of power (more below) is regarded as a primary lesson in the Realist primer, but centuries of experience did not prevent either France (Louis XIV, Napoleon I) or Germany (Wilhelm II, Hitler) from attempting to conquer Europe, twice each. Yet some, very new, black African states appear to have achieved a twenty-year-old system of impressively effective standards of mutual toleration. These standards are not completely effective (as in Tanzania's invasion of Uganda); but they have confounded expectations of a scramble to redivide Africa.[17] Geography—"insular security" and "continental insecurity"—may affect foreign policy attitudes; but it does not appear to determine behavior, as the bellicose records of England and Japan suggest. Beliefs, expectations, and attitudes of leaders and masses should influence strategic behavior. A survey of attitudinal predispositions of the American public indicate that a peaceable inclination would be enhanced by having at the strategic helm a forty-five-year-old, black, female, pediatrician of Protestant or Jewish faith, resident in Bethesda, Maryland.[18] Nevertheless, it would be difficult to determine if liberal leaders have had more peaceable attitudes than leaders who lead nonliberal states. But even if one did make that discovery, he also would have to account for why these peaceable attitudes only appear to be effective in relations with other liberals (since wars with nonliberals have not been uniformly defensive).

More substantial contributions have been made in the logic of game theory decision under differing military technologies. These technologies can alter the payoffs of the "security dilemma": making the costs of noncooperation high, reducing the costs of being unprepared or surprised, reducing the benefits of surprise attack, or increasing the gains from cooperation. In particular, Jervis recently has examined the differing effects of situations in which the offense or the defense has the advantage and in which offensive weapons are or are not distinguishable from defensive weapons. When the offense has the advantage and weapons are indistinguishable, the level of insecurity is high, incentives for preemptive attack correspondingly are strong. When offensive weapons do not have an advantage and offensive weapons are distinguishable, the incentives for preemptive attack are low, as are the incentives for arms races. Capable of signaling with clarity a nonaggressive intent and of guaranteeing that other states pose no immediate strategic threat, statesmen should be able to adopt peaceable policies and negotiate disputes. But, this cannot be the explanation for the liberal peace. Military technologies changed from offensive to defensive and from distinguishable to nondistinguishable, yet the pacific union persisted and persisted only among liberal states. Moreover, even the "clearest" technical messages appear subject to garbling. The pre-1914 period, which objectively represented a triumph of the distinguishable defense (machine guns, barbed wire, trench warfare) over the offensive, subjectively, as Jervis notes, was a period that appeared to military leaders to place exceptional premiums on the offensive and thus on preemptive war.[19]

Second, at the level of social determinants, some might argue that relations among any group of states with similar social structures or with compatible values would be peaceful.[20] But again, the evidence for feudal societies, communist societies, fascist societies, or socialist societies does not support this conclusion. Feudal warfare was frequent and very much a sport of the monarchs and nobility. There have not been enough truly totalitarian, fascist powers (nor have they lasted long enough) to test fairly their pacific compatibility; but fascist powers in the wider sense of nationalist, capitalist, military dictatorships fought each other in the 1930s. Communist powers have engaged in wars more recently in East Asia. And we have not had enough socialist societies to consider the relevance of socialist pacification. The more abstract category of pluralism does not suffice. Certainly Germany was pluralist when it engaged in war with liberal states in 1914; Japan as well in 1941. But they were not liberal.

And third, at the level of interstate relations, neither specific regional attributes nor historic alliances or friendships can account for the wide reach of the liberal peace. The peace extends as far as, and no farther than, the relations among liberal states, not including nonliberal states in an otherwise liberal region (such as the North Atlantic in the 1930s) nor excluding liberal states in a nonliberal region (such as Central America or Africa).

At this level, Raymond Aron has identified three types of inter-state peace: empire, hegemony, and equilibrium.[21] An empire generally succeeds in creating an internal peace, but this is not an explanation of peace among independent liberal states. Hegemony can create peace by overawing potential rivals. Although far from perfect and certainly precarious, United States hegemony, as Aron notes, might account for the interstate peace in South America in the postwar period during the height of the Cold War conflict. However, the liberal peace cannot be attributed merely to effective international policing by a predominant hegemon—Britain in the nineteenth century, the United States in the postwar period. Even though a hegemon might well have an interest in enforcing a peace for the sake of commerce or investments or as a means of enhancing its prestige or security; hegemons such as seventeenth-century France were not peace-enforcing police, and the liberal peace persisted in the interwar period when international society lacked a pre-dominant hegemonic power. Moreover, this explanation overestimates hegemonic control in both periods. Neither England nor the United States was able to prevent direct challenges to its interests (colonial competition in the nineteenth century, Middle East diplomacy and conflicts over trading with the enemy in the postwar period). Where then was the capacity to prevent all armed conflicts between liberal regimes, many of which were remote and others strategically or economically insignificant? Liberal hegemony and leadership are important (see Section V below), but they are not sufficient to explain a liberal peace.

Peace through equilibrium (the multipolar classical balance of power or the bipolar "cold war") also draws upon prudential sources of peace. An awareness of the likelihood that aggressive attempts at hegemony will generate international opposition should, it is argued, deter these aggressive wars. But bipolar stability discourages polar or superpower wars, not proxy or small-power wars. And multipolar balancing of power also encourages warfare to seize, for example, territory for strategic depth against a rival expanding its power from internal growth.[22] Neither readily accounts for general peace or for the liberal peace.

Finally, some Realists might suggest that the liberal peace simply reflects the absence of deep conflicts of interest among liberal states. Wars occur outside the liberal zone because conflicts of interest are deeper there. But this argument does nothing more than raise the question of why liberal states have fewer or less fundamental conflicts of interest with other liberal states than liberal states have with nonliberal, or nonliberal states have with other nonliberals. We must therefore examine the workings of liberalism among its own kind—a special pacification of the "state of war" resting on liberalism and nothing either more specific or more general.

IV

Most liberal theorists have offered inadequate guidance in understanding the exceptional nature of liberal pacification. Some have argued that democratic states would be inherently peaceful simply and solely because in these states citizens rule the polity and bear the costs of wars. Unlike monarchs, citizens are not able to indulge their aggressive passions and have the consequences suffered by someone else. Other liberals have argued that laissez-faire capitalism contains an inherent tendency toward rationalism, and that, since war is irrational, liberal capitalisms will be pacifistic. Others still, such as Montesquieu, claim that "commerce is the cure for the most destructive prejudices," and "Peace is the natural effect of trade."[23] While these developments can help account for the liberal peace, they do not explain the fact that liberal states are peaceful only in relations with other liberal states. France and England fought expansionist, colonial wars throughout the nineteenth century (in the 1830s and 1840s against Algeria and China); the United States fought a similar war with Mexico in 1848 and intervened again in 1914 under President Wilson. Liberal states are as aggressive and war prone as any other form of government or society in their relations with nonliberal states.

Immanuel Kant offers the best guidance. "Perpetual Peace," written in 1795, predicts the ever-widening pacification of the liberal pacific union, explains that pacification, and at the same time suggests why liberal states are not pacific in their relations with nonliberal states. Kant argues that Perpetual Peace will be guaranteed by the ever-widening acceptance of three "definitive articles" of peace. When all nations have accepted the definitive articles in a metaphorical "treaty" of perpetual peace he asks them to sign, perpetual peace will have been established.

The First Definitive Article holds that the civil constitution of the state must be republican. By republican Kant means a political society that has solved the problem of combining moral autonomy, individualism, and social order. A basically private property and market-oriented economy partially addressed that dilemma in the private sphere. The public, or political, sphere was more troubling. His answer was a republic that preserved juridical freedom—the legal equality of citizens as subjects—on the basis of a representative government with a separation of powers. Juridical freedom is preserved because the morally autonomous individual is by means of representation a self-legislator making laws that apply to all citizens equally including himself. And tyranny is avoided because the individual is subject to laws he does not also administer.[24]

Liberal republics will progressively establish peace among themselves by means of the "pacific union" described in the Second Definitive Article of the Eternal Peace. The pacific union is limited to "a treaty of the nations among themselves" which "maintains itself, prevents wars, and steadily expands." The world will not have achieved the "perpetual peace" that provides the ultimate guarantor of republican freedom until "very late and after many unsuccessful attempts." Then right conceptions of the appropriate constitution, great and sad experience, and goodwill will have taught all the nations the lessons of peace. Not until then will individuals enjoy perfect republican rights or the full guarantee of a global and just peace. But in the meantime, the "pacific union" of liberal republics *steadily expands* [my emphasis]" bringing within it more and more republics (despite republican collapses, backsliding, and war disasters) and creating an ever-expanding separate peace.[25] The pacific union is neither a single peace treaty ending one war nor a world state or state of nations. The first is insufficient; the second and third are impossible or potentially tyrannical. Kant develops no organizational embodiment of this treaty, and presumably he does not find institutionalization necessary. He appears to have in mind a mutual nonaggression pact, perhaps a collective security agreement, and the cosmopolitan law set forth in the Third Definitive Article.[26]

The Third Definitive Article of the Eternal Peace establishes a cosmopolitan law to operate in conjunction with the pacific union. The cosmopolitan law "shall be limited to conditions of universal hospitality." In this he calls for the recognition of the "right of a foreigner not to be treated with hostility when he arrives upon the soil of another [country]," which "does not extend further than to the conditions which enable them [the foreigners] to attempt the developing of intercourse [commerce] with the old inhabitants." Hospitality does not require extending either the right to citizenship to foreigners or the right to settlement, unless the foreign visitors would perish if they were expelled. Foreign conquest and plunder also find no justification under this right. Hospitality does appear to include the right of access and the obligation of maintaining the opportunity for citizens to exchange goods and ideas, without imposing the obligation to trade (a voluntary act in all cases under liberal constitutions).[27]

Kant then explains each of the three definitive articles for a liberal peace. In doing so he develops both an account of why liberal states do maintain peace among themselves and of how it will (by implication, has) come about that the pacific union will expand. His central claim is that a natural evolution will produce "a harmony from the very disharmony of men against their will."[28]

The first source derives from a political evolution, from a *constitutional law*. Nature (providence) has seen to it that human beings can live in all the regions where they have been driven to settle by wars. (Kant, who once taught geography, reports on the Lapps, the Samoyeds, the Pescheras.) "Asocial sociability" draws men together to fulfill needs for security and material welfare as it drives them into conflicts over the distribution and control of social products. This violent natural evolution tends toward the liberal peace because "asocial sociability" inevitably leads toward republican governments and republican governments are a source of the liberal peace.

Republican representation and separation of powers are produced because they are the means by which the state is "organized well" to prepare for and meet foreign threats (by unity) and to tame the ambitions of selfish and aggressive individuals (by authority derived from representation, by general laws, and by nondespotic administration). States that are not organized in this fashion fail. Monarchs thus cede rights of representation to their subjects in order to strengthen their political support or to obtain tax revenue. This argument provides a plausible, logical connection between conflict, internal and external, and republicanism; and it highlights interesting associations between the rising incidence of international war and the increasing number of republics.

Nevertheless, constant preparation for war can enhance the role of military institutions in a society to the point that they become the society's rulers. Civil conflict can lead to praetorian coups. Conversely, an environment of security can provide a political climate for weakening the state by constitutional restraints.[29] Significantly, the most war-affected states have not been liberal republics.[30] More important, the argument is so indistinct as to serve only as a very general hypothesis that mobilizing self-interested individuals into the political life of states in an insecure world will eventually engender pressures for republican participation. Kant needs no more than this to suggest that republicanism and a liberal peace are possible (and thus a moral obligation). If it is possible, then sometime over the course of history it may be inevitable. But attempting to make its date of achievement predictable—projecting a steady trend—he suggests, may be asking too much. He anticipates backsliding and destructive wars, though these will serve to educate the nations to the importance of peace.[31]

Kant shows how republics, once established, lead to peaceful relations. He argues that once the aggressive interests of absolutist monarchies are tamed and once the habit of respect for individual rights is ingrained by republican government, wars would appear as the disaster to the people's welfare that he and the other liberals thought them to be. The fundamental reason is this:

> If the consent of the citizens is required in order to decide that war should be declared (and in this constitution it cannot but be the case), nothing is more natural than that they would be very cautious in commencing such a poor game, decreeing for themselves all the calamities of war. Among the latter would be: having to fight, having to pay the costs of war from their own resources, having painfully to repair the devastation war leaves behind, and, to fill up the measure of evils, load themselves with a heavy national debt that would embitter peace itself and that can never be liquidated on account of constant wars in the future. But, on the other hand, in a constitution which is not republican, and under which the subjects are not citizens, a declaration of war is the easiest thing

in the world to decide upon, because war does not require of the ruler, who is the proprietor and not a member of the state, the least sacrifice of the pleasure of his table, the chase, his country houses, his court functions, and the like. He may, therefore, resolve on war as on a pleasure party for the most trivial reasons, and with perfect indifference leave the justification which decency requires to the diplomatic corps who are ever ready to provide it.[32]

One could add to Kant's list another source of pacification specific to liberal constitutions. The regular rotation of office in liberal democratic polities is a nontrivial device that helps ensure that personal animosities among heads of government provide no lasting, escalating source of tension.

These domestic republican restraints do not end war. If they did, liberal states would not be warlike, which is far from the case. They do introduce Kant's "caution" in place of monarchical caprice. Liberal wars are only fought for popular, liberal purposes. To see how this removes the occasion of wars among liberal states and not wars between liberal and nonliberal states, we need to shift our attention from constitutional law to international law, Kant's second source.

Complementing the constitutional guarantee of caution, *international law* adds a second source—a guarantee of respect. The separation of nations that asocial sociability encourages is reinforced by the development of separate languages and religions. These further guarantee a world of separate states—an essential condition needed to avoid a "global, soul-less despotism." Yet, at the same time, they also morally integrate liberal states "as culture progresses and men gradually come closer together toward a greater agreement on principles for peace and understanding."[33] As republics emerge (the first source) and as culture progresses, an understanding of the legitimate rights of all citizens and of all republics comes into play; and this, now that caution characterizes policy, sets up the moral foundations for the liberal peace. Correspondingly, international law highlights the importance of Kantian publicity. Domestically, publicity helps ensure that the officials of republics act according to the principles they profess to hold just and according to the interests of the electors they claim to represent. Internationally, free speech and the effective communication of accurate conceptions of the political life of foreign peoples is essential to establish and preserve the understanding on which the guarantee of respect depends. In short, domestically just republics, which rest on consent, presume foreign republics to be also consensual, just, and therefore deserving of accommodation. The experience of cooperation helps engender further cooperative behavior when the consequences of state policy are unclear but (potentially) mutually beneficial.[34]

Lastly, *cosmopolitan law* adds material incentives to moral commitments. The cosmopolitan right to hospitality permits the "spirit of commerce" sooner or later to take hold of every nation, thus impelling states to promote peace and to try to avert war.

Liberal economic theory holds that these cosmopolitan ties derive from a cooperative international division of labor and free trade according to comparative advantage. Each economy is said to be better off than it would have been under autarky; each thus acquires an incentive to avoid policies that would lead the other to break these economic ties. Since keeping open markets rests upon the assumption that the next set of transactions will also be determined by prices rather than coercion, a sense of mutual security is vital to avoid security-motivated searches for economic autarky. Thus avoiding a challenge to another liberal state's security or even enhancing each other's security by means of alliance naturally follows economic interdependence.

A further cosmopolitan source of liberal peace is that the international market removes difficult decisions of production and distribution from the direct sphere of state policy. A foreign state thus does not appear directly responsible for these outcomes; states can stand aside from, and to some degree above, these contentious market rivalries and be ready to step in to resolve crises. Furthermore, the interdependence of commerce and the connections of state officials help create crosscutting transnational ties that serve as lobbies for mutual accommodation. According to modern liberal scholars, international financiers and transnational, bureaucratic, and domestic organizations create interests in favor of accommodation and have ensured by their variety that no single conflict sours an entire relationship.[35]

No one of those constitutional, international or cosmopolitan sources is alone sufficient, but together (and only where together) they plausibly connect the characteristics of liberal polities and economies with sustained liberal peace. Liberal states have not escaped from the Realists' "security dilemma," the insecurity caused by anarchy in the world political system considered as a whole. But the effects of international anarchy have been tamed in the relations among states of a similarly liberal character. Alliances of purely mutual strategic interest among liberal and nonliberal states have been broken, economic ties between liberal and nonliberal states have proven fragile, but the political bond of liberal rights and interests have proven a remarkably firm foundation for mutual nonaggression. A separate peace exists among liberal states.

V

Where liberal internationalism among liberal states has been deficient is in preserving its basic preconditions under changing international circumstances, and particularly in supporting the liberal character of its constituent states. It has failed on occasion, as it did in regard to Germany in the 1920s, to provide international economic support for liberal regimes whose market foundations were in crisis. It failed in the 1930s to provide military aid or political mediation to Spain, which was challenged by an armed minority, or to Czechoslovakia, which was caught in a dilemma of preserving national security or acknowledging the claims (fostered by Hitler's Germany) of the Sudeten minority to self-determination. Farsighted and constitutive measures have only been provided by the liberal international order when one liberal state stood preeminent among the rest, prepared and able to take measures, as did the United States following World War II, to sustain economically and politically the foundations of liberal society beyond its borders. Then measures such as the British Loan, the Marshall Plan, NATO, GATT, the IMF, and the liberalization of Germany and Japan helped construct buttresses for the international liberal order.[36]

Thus, the decline of US hegemonic leadership may pose dangers for the liberal world. This danger is not that today's liberal states will permit their economic competition to spiral into war, but that the societies of the liberal world will no longer be able to provide the mutual assistance they might require to sustain liberal domestic orders in the face of mounting economic crises.

These dangers come from two directions: military and economic. Their combination is particularly threatening. One is the continuing asymmetry of defense, with the United States (in relation to its GNP) bearing an undue portion of the common burden. Yet independent and more substantial European and Japanese defense establishments pose problems for liberal cooperation. Military dependence on the United States has been one of the additional bonds helpful in transforming a liberal peace into a liberal alliance. Removing it, without creating a multilaterally directed and funded organization among the liberal industrial democracies, threatens to loosen an important bond. Economic instabilities could make this absence of a multilateral security bond particularly dangerous by escalating differences into hostility. If domestic economic collapses on the pattern of the global propagation of depressions in the 1930s were to reoccur, the domestic political foundations of liberalism could fall. Or, if international economic rivalry were to continue to increase, then consequent attempts to weaken economic interdependence (establishing closed trade and currency blocs) would break an important source of liberal accommodation.[37] These dangers would become more significant if independent and substantial military forces were established. If liberal assumptions of the need to cooperate and to accommodate disappear, countries might fall prey to a corrosive rivalry that destroys the pacific union.

Yet liberals may have escaped from the single, greatest, traditional danger of international change—the transition between hegemonic leaders. When one great power begins to lose its preeminence and to slip into mere equality, a warlike resolution of the international pecking order becomes exceptionally likely. New power challenges old prestige, excessive commitments face new demands; so Sparta felt compelled to attack Athens, France warred Spain, England and Holland fought with France (and with each other), and Germany and England struggled for the mastery of Europe in World War I. But here liberals may again be an exception, for despite the fact that the United States constituted Britain's greatest challenger along all the dimensions most central to the British maritime hegemony, Britain and the United States accommodated their differences.[38] After the defeat of Germany, Britain eventually, though not without regret, accepted its replacement by the United States as the commercial and maritime hegemon of the liberal world.

The promise of a peaceable transition thus may be one of the factors helping to moderate economic and political rivalries among Europe, Japan, and the United States.

Consequently, the quarrels with liberal allies that bedeviled the Carter and Reagan Administrations should not be attributed solely to the personal weaknesses of the two presidents or their secretaries of state. Neither should they be attributed to simple failures of administrative coordination or to the idiosyncrasies of American allies. These are the normal workings of a liberal alliance of independent republics. There is no indication that they involve a dissolution of the pacific union; but there is every indication that, following the decline in American preponderance, liberal states will be able to do little to reestablish the union should the international economic interdependence that binds them dissolve and should the domestic, liberal foundations of its central members collapse. But should these republican foundations and commercial sources of interdependence remain firm, then the promise of liberal legacies among liberal regimes is a continuing peace, even when the leadership of the liberal world changes hands.

When in *The Snows of Kilimanjaro*, Julian (F. Scott Fitzgerald) tells his friend (Hemingway), "The very rich are different from you and me," his friend replies, "Yes, they have more money." But the liberals are fundamentally different. It is not just, as the Realists might argue, that they have more or less resources, better or worse morale. Their constitutional structure makes them—realistically—different. They have established peace among themselves. But the very features that make their relations to fellow liberals differ from the state of war that all other states inhabit also make their relations with nonliberals differ from the prudent, strategic calculation that Realists hope will inform the foreign policies of states in an insecure world. These failings are the subject of the second part of this article.

NOTES

This is the first half of a two-part article. The article has benefited from the extensive criticisms of William Ascher, Richard Betts, William Bundy, Joseph Carens, Felix Gilbert, Amy Gutmann, Don Herzog, Stanley Hoffman, Marion Levy, Judith Shklar, Mark Uhlig, and the Editors of *Philosophy & Public Affairs*. I have also tried to take into account suggestions from Fouad Ajami, Steven David, Tom Farer, Robert Gilpin, Ernest van den Haag, Germaine Hoston, Robert Jervis, Donald Kagan, Robert Keohane, John Rawls, Nicholas Rizopoulos, Robert W. Tucker, Richard Ullman, and the members of a Special Seminar at the Lehrman Institute, February 22, 1983. The essay cannot be interpreted as a consensus of their views.

[Note added by author in 2007:] Because there is space to reprint only the first part of my two-part essay, I am concerned to preempt the impression that I think of liberal states as inherently peaceful. In fact, in the second part of the 1983 essay I develop the opposite view: that liberal states are not inherently peaceful, that indeed many are tempted to aggress partly inspired by commerce, democratic decision making, and (often perverted) drives to implement human rights.

1. The liberal-patriotic view was reiterated by President Reagan in a speech before the British Parliament on June 8, 1982. There he proclaimed "a global campaign for democratic development." This "crusade for freedom" will be the latest campaign in a tradition that, he claimed, began with the Magna Carta and stretched in this century through two world wars and a cold war. He added that liberal foreign policies have shown "restraint" and "peaceful intentions" and that this crusade will strengthen the prospects for a world at peace (*New York Times*, June 9, 1982). The skeptical scholars and diplomats represent the predominant Realist interpretation of international relations. See ns. 4 and 12 for references.

2. Immanuel Kant, "Perpetual Peace" (1795) in *The Philosophy of Kant*, ed. Carl J. Friedrich (New York: Modern Library, 1949), p. 453.

3. The actual rights of citizenship have often been limited by slavery or male suffrage, but liberal regimes harbored no principle of opposition to the extension of juridical equality; in fact, as pressure was brought to bear they progressively extended the suffrage to the entire population. By this distinction, the nineteenth-century United States was liberal; twentieth-century South Africa is not. See Samuel Huntington, *American Politics: The Promise of Disharmony* (Cambridge, MA: Harvard University Press, 1981).

4. The sources of classic, laissez-faire liberalism can be found in Locke, the *Federalist Papers*, Kant, and Robert Nozick, *Anarchy, State and Utopia* (New York: Basic Books, 1974). Expositions of welfare liberalism are in the work of the Fabians and John Rawls, *A Theory of Justice* (Cambridge, MA: Harvard University Press, 1971). Amy Gutmann, *Liberal Equality* (Cambridge: Cambridge University Press, 1980), discusses variants of liberal thought.

Uncomfortably paralleling each of the high roads are "low roads" that, while achieving certain liberal values, fail to reconcile freedom and order. An overwhelming terror of anarchy and a speculation on preserving property can drive laissez-faire liberals to support a law-and-order authoritarian rule that sacrifices democracy. Authoritarianism to preserve order is the argument of Hobbes's *Leviathan*. It also shapes the argument of right-wing liberals who seek to draw a distinction between "authoritarian" and "totalitarian" dictatorships. The justification sometimes advanced by liberals for the former is that they can be temporary and educate the population into an acceptance of property, individual rights, and, eventually, representative government. See Jeane Kirkpatrick, "Dictatorships and Double Standards," *Commentary* 68 (November 1979): 34–45. Complementarily, when social inequalities are judged to be extreme, the welfare liberal can argue that establishing (or reestablishing) the foundations of liberal society requires a nonliberal method of reform, a second low road of redistributing authoritarianism. Aristide Zolberg reports a "liberal left" sensibility among US scholars of African politics that justified reforming dictatorship. (See *One Party Government in the Ivory Coast* [Princeton: Princeton University Press, 1969], p. viii.) And the argument of "reforming autocracy" can be found in J. S. Mill's defense of colonialism in India.

5. Fred Hirsch, *The Social Limits to Growth* (Cambridge, MA: Harvard University Press, 1977).

6. Charles Beitz, *Political Theory and International Relations* (Princeton: Princeton University Press, 1979), offers a clear and insightful discussion of liberal ideas on intervention and nonintervention.

7. There appear to be some exceptions to the tendency for liberal states not to engage in a war with each other. Peru and Ecuador, for example, entered into conflict. But for each, the war came within one to three years after the establishment of a liberal regime, that is, before the pacifying effects of liberalism could become deeply ingrained. The Palestinians and the Israelis clashed frequently along the Lebanese border, which Lebanon could not hold secure from either belligerent. But at the beginning of the 1967 War, Lebanon seems to have sent a flight of its own jets into Israel. The jets were repulsed. Alone among Israel's Arab neighbors, Lebanon engaged in no further hostilities with Israel. Israel's recent attack on the territory of Lebanon was an attack on a country that had already been occupied by Syria (and the PLO). Whether Israel actually will withdraw (if Syria withdraws) and restore an independent Lebanon is yet to be determined.

8. Imperial Germany is a difficult case. The Reichstag was not only elected by universal male suffrage but, by and large, the state ruled under the law, respecting the civic equality and rights of its citizens. Moreover, Chancellor Bismarck began the creation of a social welfare society that served as an inspiration for similar reforms in liberal regimes. However, the constitutional relations between the imperial executive and the representative legislature were

sufficiently complex that various practices, rather than constitutional theory, determined the actual relation between the government and the citizenry. The emperor appointed and could dismiss the chancellor. Although the chancellor was responsible to the Reichstag, a defeat in the Reichstag did not remove him nor did the government absolutely depend on the Reichstag for budgetary authority. In practice, Germany was a liberal state under republican law for domestic issues. But the emperor's direct authority over the army, the army's effective independence from the minimal authority of the War Ministry, and the emperor's active role in foreign affairs (including the influential separate channel to the emperor through the military attachés) together with the tenuous constitutional relationship between the chancellor and the Reichstag made imperial Germany a state divorced from the control of its citizenry in foreign affairs.

This authoritarian element not only influenced German foreign policy-making, but also shaped the international political environment (a lack of trust) the Reich faced and the domestic political environment that defined the government's options and capabilities (the weakness of liberal opinion as against the exceptional influence of Junker militaristic nationalism). Thus direct influence on policy was but one result of the authoritarian element. Nonetheless, significant and strife-generating episodes can be directly attributed to this element. They include Tirpitz's approach to Wilhelm II to obtain the latter's sanction for a veto of Chancellor Bethmann-Hollweg's proposals for a naval agreement with Britain (1909). Added to this was Wilhelm's personal assurances of full support to the Austrians early in the Sarajevo Crisis and his, together with Moltke's, erratic pressure on the Chancellor throughout July and August of 1914, which helped destroy whatever coherence German diplomacy might otherwise have had, and which led one Austrian official to ask, "Who rules in Berlin? Moltke or Bethmann?" (Gordon Craig, *The Politics of the Prussian Army* [New York: Oxford University Press, 1964], pp. xxviii and chap. 6). For an excellent account of Bethmann's aims and the constraints he encountered, see Konrad H. Jarausch, "The Illusion of Limited War: Chancellor Bethmann-Hollweg's Calculated Risk, July 1914," *Central European History* 2 (1969).

The liberal sources of Italy's decision are pointed out in R. Vivarelli's review of Hugo Butler's *Gaetano Salvemini und die Italienische Politik vor dem Ersten Weltkrieg* in the *Journal of Modern History* 52, no. 3 (September 1980): 541.

The quotation from President Wilson is from Woodrow Wilson, *The Messages and Papers of Woodrow Wilson*, ed. Albert Shaw (New York: The Review of Reviews, 1924), p. 378.

9. Thomas Hobbes, *Leviathan* (New York: Penguin, 1980), I, chap. 13, 62; p. 186.

10. Robert Jervis, "Cooperation Under the Security Dilemma," *World Politics* 30, no. 1 (January 1978).

11. Thucydides, *The Peloponnesian Wars*, trans. Rex Warner (Baltimore, MD: Penguin Books, 1954) I: 76; and Hobbes, *Leviathan*, I, chap. 13, 61, p. 185. The coincidence of views is not accidental; Hobbes translated Thucydides. And Hobbes's portrait of the state of nature appears to be drawn from Thucydides' account of the revolution in Corcyra.

12. Kenneth N. Waltz, *Man, the State, and War* (New York: Columbia University Press, 1954, 1959), pp. 120–23; and see his *Theory of International Politics* (Reading, MA: Addison-Wesley, 1979). The classic sources of this form of Realism are Hobbes and, more particularly, Rousseau's "Essay on St. Pierre's Peace Project" and his "State of War" in *A Lasting Peace* (London: Constable, 1917), E. H. Carr's *The Twenty Year's Crisis: 1919–1939* (London: Macmillan & Co., 1951), and the works of Hans Morgenthau.

13. Jean-Jacques Rousseau, *The Government of Poland*, trans. Willmoore Kendall (New York: Bobbs-Merrill, 1972); and Hans Morgenthan, *Politics Among Nations* (New York: Alfred A. Knopf, 1967), pp. 132–35.

14. Hobbes, "De Cive," *The English Works of Thomas Hobbes* (London: J. Bohn, 1841), 2: 166-67.

15. Ibid., p. 171.

16. Jervis, "Cooperation Under the Security Dilemma," pp. 172–86.

17. Robert H. Jackson and Carl G. Rosberg, "Why West Africa's Weak States Persist," *World Politics* 35, no. 1 (October 1982).

18. Interpreted from Michael Haas, *International Conflict* (New York: Bobbs-Merrill, 1974), pp. 80–81, 457–58.

19. Jervis, "Cooperation Under the Security Dilemma," pp. 186–210, 212. Jervis examines incentives for cooperation, not the existence or sources of peace.

20. There is a rich contemporary literature devoted to explaining international cooperation and integration. Karl Deutsch's *Political Community and the North Atlantic Area* (Princeton: Princeton University Press, 1957) develops the idea of a "pluralistic security community" that bears a resemblance to the "pacific union," but Deutsch limits it geographically and finds compatibility of values, mutual responsiveness, and predictability of behavior among decision makers as its essential foundations. These are important, but their particular content, liberalism, appears to be more telling. Joseph Nye in *Peace in Parts* (Boston: Little, Brown & Co., 1971) steps away from the geographic limits Deutsch sets and focuses on levels of development; but his analysis is directed toward explaining integration—a more intensive form of cooperation than the pacific union.

21. Raymond Aron, *Peace and War* (New York: Praeger, 1968), pp. 151–54. Progress and peace through the rise and decline of empires and hegemonies has been a classic theme. Lucretius suggested that they may be part of a more general law of nature: "Augescunt aliae gentes, aliae miniuntur/Inque brevis spatio mutantur saecula animantum,/Et quasi cursores vitai lampada tradunt." [Some peoples wax and others wane/And in a short space the order of living

things is changed/And like runners hand on the torch of life.] *De Rer. Nat.* ii, 77–79.

22. Kenneth Waltz, *Theory of International Politics*, chap. 8; and Edward Gulick, *Europe's Classical Balance of Power* (New York: Norton, 1967), chap. 3.

One of the most thorough collective investigations of the personal, societal, and international systemic sources of war has been the Correlates of War Project. See especially Melvin Small and J. David Singer, *Resort to Arms* (Beverly Hills, CA: Sage, 1982) for a more comprehensive list and statistical analysis of wars. J. David Singer ("Accounting for International War: The State of the Discipline," *Journal of Peace Research* 18. no. 1 [1981]) drew the following conclusions: "The exigencies of survival in an international system of such inadequate organization and with so pervasively dysfunctional a culture require relatively uniform response (p. 11).... domestic factors are negligible;" war "cannot be explained on the basis of relatively invariant phenomena" (p. 1).

Michael Haas, *International Conflict*, discovers that, at the systemic level, "collective security, stratification, and hegemonization systems are likely to avoid a high frequency in violent outputs" (p. 453); but "no single [causal] model was entirely or even largely satisfactory" (p. 452). At the social level, war correlates with variables such as: "bloc prominence, military mobilizations, public perceptions of hostility toward peoples of other countries, a high proportion of gross national product devoted to military expenditures..." (p. 461). These variables appear to describe rather than explain war. A cluster analysis he performs associates democracy, development, and sustained modernization with the existence of peaceful countries (pp. 464–65). But these factors do not correlate with pacification during the period 1816–1965 according to M. Small and J. D. Singer, "The War Proneness of Democratic Regimes," *Jerusalem Journal of International Relations* 50, no. 4 (summer 1976).

Their conclusions follow, I think, from their homogenization of war and from their attempt to explain all wars, in which a myriad of states have engaged. I attempt to explain an interstate peace, which only liberal regimes, a particular type of state and society, have succeeded in establishing.

23. The incompatibility of democracy and war is forcefully asserted by Paine in *The Rights of Man*. The connection between liberal capitalism, democracy, and peace is argued by, among others, Joseph Schumpeter in *Imperialism and Social Classes* (New York: Meridian, 1955); and Montesquieu, *Spirit of the Laws* I, bk. 20, chap. 1. This literature is surveyed and analyzed by Albert Hirschman, "Rival Interpretations of Marker Society: Civilizing, Destructive, or Feeble?" *Journal of Economic Literature* 20 (December 1982).

24. Two classic sources that examine Kant's international theory from a Realist perspective are Stanley Hoffmann, "Rousseau on War and Peace" in the *State of War* (New York: Praeger, 1965) and Kenneth Waltz, "Kant, Liberalism, and War," *American Political Science Review* 56, no. 2 (June 1962). I have benefited from their analysis and from those of Karl Friedrich, *Inevitable Peace* (Cambridge, MA: Harvard University Press, 1948); F. H. Hinsley, *Power and*

the Pursuit of Peace (Cambridge: Cambridge University Press, 1967), chap. 4; W. B. Gallie, *Philosophers of Peace and War* (Cambridge: Cambridge University Press, 1978), chap. 1; and particularly Patrick Riley, *Kant's Political Philosophy* (Totowa, NJ: Rowman & Littlefield, 1983). But some of the conclusions of this article differ markedly from theirs.

Kant's republican constitution is described in Kant, "Perpetual Peace," *The Philosophy of Kant*, p. 437 and analyzed by Riley, *Kant's Political Philosophy*, chap. 5.

25. Kant, "Universal History," *The Philosophy of Kant*, p. 123. The pacific union follows a process of "federalization" such that it "can be realized by a gradual extension to all states, leading to eternal peace." This interpretation contrasts with those cited in n. 24. I think Kant meant that the peace would be established among liberal regimes and would expand as new liberal regimes appeared. By a process of gradual extension the peace would become global and then perpetual; the occasion for wars with nonliberals would disappear as nonliberal regimes disappeared.

26. Kant's "pacific union," the *foedus pacificum*, is thus neither a *pactum pacis* (a single peace treaty) nor a *civitas gentium* (a world state). He appears to have anticipated something like a less formally institutionalized League of Nations or United Nations. One could argue that these two institutions in practice worked for liberal states and only for liberal states. But no specifically liberal "pacific union" was institutionalized. Instead liberal states have behaved for the past 180 years as if such a Kantian pacific union and treaty of Perpetual Peace had been signed. This follows Riley's views of the legal, not the organizational, character of the *foedus pacificum*.

27. Kant, "Perpetual Peace," pp. 444–47.

28. Kant, the fourth principle of "The Idea for a Universal History" in *The Philosophy of Kant*, p. 120. Interestingly, Kant's three sources of peace (republicanism, respect, and commerce) parallel quite closely Aristotle's three sources of friendship (goodness, pleasure or appreciation, and utility). See *Nicomachean Ethics*, bk. 8, chap. 3, trans. J.A.K. Thomson (Baltimore: Penguin, 1955).

29. The "Prussian Model" suggests the connection between insecurity, war, and authoritarianism. See *The Anglo-American Tradition in Foreign Affairs*, ed. Arnold Wolfers and Laurence Martin (New Haven: Yale University Press, 1956), "Introduction," for an argument linking security and liberalism.

30. Small and Singer, *Resort to Arms*, pp. 176–79.

31. Kant, "The Idea for a Universal History," p. 124.

32. Immanuel Kant, "Perpetual Peace" in *The Enlightenment*, ed. Peter Gay (New York: Simon & Schuster, 1974), pp. 790–92.

Gallie in *Philosophers of Peace and War* criticizes Kant for neglecting economic, religious, nationalistic drives toward war and for failing to appreciate that "regimes" make war in order to enhance their domestic political support. But Kant holds that these drives should be subordinated to justice in a liberal society (he specifically criticizes colonial wars stimulated by rapaciousness). He also argues that *republics* derive their legitimacy from their accordance with law and representation, thereby freeing them from crises of domestic political support. Kant thus acknowledges both Gallie's sets of motives for war but argues that they would not apply within the pacific union.

33. Kant, *The Philosophy of Kant*, p. 454. These factors also have a bearing on Karl Deutsch's "compatibility of values" and "predictability of behavior" (see n. 20).

34. A highly stylized version of this effect can be found in the Realist's "Prisoner's Dilemma" game. There a failure of mutual trust and the incentives to enhance one's own position produce a noncooperative solution that makes both parties worse off. Contrarily, cooperation, a commitment to avoid exploiting the other party, produces joint gains. The significance of the game in this context is the character of its participants. The "prisoners" are presumed to be felonious, unrelated apart from their partnership in crime, and lacking in mutual trust—competitive nation-states in an anarchic world. A similar game between fraternal or sororal twins—Kant's republics—would be likely to lead to different results. See Robert Jervis, "Hypotheses on Misperception," *World Politics* 20, no. 3 (April 1968), for an exposition of the role of presumptions; and "Cooperation Under the Security Dilemma," *World Politics* 30, no. 2 (January 1978), for the factors Realists see as mitigating the security dilemma caused by anarchy.

Also, expectations (including theory and history) can influence behavior, making liberal states expect (and fulfill) pacific policies toward each other. These effects are explored at a theoretical level in R. Dacey, "Some Implications of 'Theory Absorption' for Economic Theory and the Economics of Information," in *Philosophical Dimensions of Economics*, ed. J. Pitt (Dordrecht, Holland: D. Reidel, 1980).

35. Karl Polanyi, *The Great Transformation* (Boston: Beacon Press, 1944), chaps. 1–2, and Samuel Huntington and Z. Brzezinski, *Political Power: USA/USSR* (New York: Viking Press, 1963, 1964), chap. 9. And see Richard Neustadt, *Alliance Politics* (New York: Columbia University Press, 1970) for a detailed case study of interliberal politics.

36. Charles Kindleberger, *The World in Depression* (Berkeley: University of California Press, 1973); Robert Gilpin, *U.S. Power and the Multinational Corporation* (New York: Basic Books, 1975); and Fred Hirsch and Michael Doyle, "Politicization in the World Economy" in Hirsch, Doyle, and Edward Morse, *Alternatives to Monetary Disorder* (New York: Council on Foreign Relations/McGraw-Hill, 1977).

37. Robert Gilpin, "Three Models of the Future," *International Organization* 29, no. 1 (winter 1975).

38. George Liska identifies this peaceful, hegemonic transition as exceptional in *Quest for Equilibrium: America and the Balance of Power on Land and Sea* (Baltimore, MD: The Johns Hopkins University Press, 1977), chap. 4,

p. 75. Wilson's speeches, including his "War Message," suggest the importance of ideological factors in explaining this transition: "Neutrality is no longer feasible or desirable where the peace of the world is involved and the freedom of its peoples, and the menace to that peace and freedom lies in the *existence* [emphasis supplied] of autocratic governments backed by organized force which is controlled wholly by their will, not by the will of their people." This quotation is from Woodrow Wilson, *The Messages and Papers of Woodrow Wilson*, ed. Albert Shaw (New York: The Review of Reviews, 1924), p. 378. Ross Gregory in *The Origins of American Intervention in the First World War* (New York: Norton, 1971) offers an interpretation along these lines, combining commercial, financial, strategic, and ideological factors in his account of the policy that brought the United States onto a collision course with Germany.

6. CHARLES R. BEITZ

Beitz seeks to explain the continuing influence of what, following Sidgwick, he calls the "national ideal"—that is, the view that foreign policy
should strive to promote the interests of the members of the nation, rather
than the interests of everyone. The national ideal, Beitz suggests, rests
on the thesis that compatriots take priority over noncompatriots. What,
though, might justify this thesis? Beitz considers a number of putative
justifications, arguing that, though some are not without force, none supports the standard view on such priority. He suggests in conclusion that
the national ideal might also be supported by certain kinds of reasons
that are neither moral nor self-interested.

Cosmopolitan Ideals and National Sentiment

First published in The Journal of Philosophy *80: 10, Part 1: Eightieth Annual
Meeting of the American Philosophical Association, Eastern Division (October
1983): 591–600.*

Henry Sidgwick's exploration of the immigration question led him to
notice a "general conflict between the cosmopolitan and the national
ideals of political organization." According to the national ideal, foreign
policy should "promote the interests of a determinate group of human
beings, bound together by the tie of a common nationality"; according
to the cosmopolitan ideal, it should strive impartially to promote the
interests of everyone. While conceding that the cosmopolitan ideal was
"perhaps the ideal of the future," Sidgwick defended the national ideal,
which he identified with the standpoint of commonsense morality.[1]

The national ideal is still dominant in commonsense moral thought.
For example, I doubt that many would disagree with Sidgwick that a

government may legitimately restrict immigration in order to protect the stability and cohesion of domestic political life. Similarly, it seems to be widely accepted that a government may give greater weight in redistributing income to improving the welfare of its domestic poor than to improving that of the poor elsewhere—even if the domestic poor are already better off than the foreign poor.

For reasons I shall sketch, I do not believe these sentiments can be defended as plausibly as Sidgwick maintained. However, my main purpose here is not to argue for a more cosmopolitan view. These arguments are clear enough.[2] The more difficult problem is to explain the continuing influence of the national ideal on our thinking, even after the force of cosmopolitan considerations has been appreciated. I would like to take up this problem here in a preliminary way. I begin with brief comments on the meaning of the national ideal and the reason why it needs justification, despite its prominence in commonsense moral thought. Then, I consider several arguments that are often advanced in its support. It will emerge that although these arguments are not without force, none supports the national ideal in its familiar form. Finally, I speculate about how the residual influence of this ideal might be explained, and indicate the kind of dilemma it poses for practical reasoning. My space is limited; so my remarks throughout will be regrettably schematic, but I hope to say enough to show why the "general conflict" that Sidgwick noticed is more complex and intractable than it might appear.

THE MEANING OF THE NATIONAL IDEAL

The national ideal is not the same as what has sometimes been called "national egoism" or *raison d'état*. Sidgwick emphasized (and I think commonsense morality would agree) that a state's pursuit of its citizens' interests should be limited by "the rules restraining it from attacking or encroaching on other States" (309). Presumably, states are also subject to the rules of ordinary morality, such as the principles of charity, beneficence, and fidelity. The distinguishing feature of the national ideal is not that it takes no account of the interests of foreigners, but rather that it takes account of (at least some of) their interests in a different way from that in which it takes account of the interests of compatriots. Adopting Henry Shue's phrase, we might say that the national ideal rests on the thesis that "compatriots take priority."[3]

As with any principle that sanctions unequal treatment, we are bound to wonder whether the priority thesis has a moral warrant. This question will seem especially pressing where, as here, the basis on which the principle discriminates is a characteristic that is possessed nonvoluntarily and where the effect of following the principle would be to reinforce existing inequalities. For it might be that discrimination on the basis of citizenship is like discrimination on the basis of race or sex: Priority for compatriots, like priority for whites and priority for males, could be nothing more than a reflection of relations of social power that have nothing, morally speaking, to be said for them. If this is not the case, we should be able to say why.

THE MORAL CONTENT OF THE PRIORITY THESIS

The priority thesis might arise at either an intermediate or a foundational level of moral thought. At the intermediate level, the thesis derives from reasoning at a deeper level where everyone's interests are treated equally. At the foundational level, the thesis asserts that the interests of compatriots should be given priority even when, all things considered, this cannot be justified by any principle of equal treatment.

Most efforts to justify priority for compatriots occur at the intermediate level. I cannot discuss these here in any detail, but I will comment briefly on two views, which are based, respectively, on consequentialist and contractarian interpretations of equal treatment. The consequentialist justification seems least likely to be persuasive: As with analogous efforts to justify priority for the interests of the self, any consequentialist argument for priority for compatriots will probably involve either implausible empirical premises or an eccentric standard of value. At a minimum, it would presuppose a more-or-less equal background distribution of natural resources and talents; without this, given standard assumptions about the diminishing marginal value of increasing income, there is no reason to think that overall value could not be increased by the redistribution that would result from wealthy states acting on a more impartial principle than priority for compatriots.

This familiar difficulty infects one of Sidgwick's arguments against open immigration. He claimed that open immigration "would not be really in the interest of humanity at large" because it would defeat the state's efforts to maintain its society's internal cohesion, promote the growth of culture, and preserve the order and integrity of its domestic political process (309). Initially, this argument may seem appealing because it recognizes that these features of communal life have great value, and because it reflects a realistic awareness that they could be endangered if governments adhered to the cosmopolitan ideal. Nevertheless, if the basis of the argument in "the interest of humanity at large" is taken seriously, the argument will not be persuasive: Under contemporary conditions, it is most unlikely that the value derived by their citizens from the cohesion and order of relatively well-endowed societies is greater than the value that could be gained by others from the redistribution of labor (or wealth) that would be brought about by adherence to cosmopolitan policies. Thus, I believe that Michael Walzer[4] is correct to suggest that the intuitive appeal of Sidgwick's argument flows from a different source than consequentialist balancing; on the other hand, it is not as clear to me as it is to Walzer that the argument's appeal has some other distinctively "moral basis"—a point I return to at the end.

It might seem that a better foundation for the priority thesis could be found in a contractarian moral theory like that set forth by John Rawls. On the assumption that national societies are self-sufficient schemes of social cooperation, Rawls restricts membership in the original position to compatriots until after the principles of distributive justice have been chosen; when others are finally admitted, it is only for the purpose of choosing regulative principles for diplomacy and war. The result is a strong form of the priority thesis: Since the scope of the difference principle is limited to national societies, the responsibilities of governments to outsiders derive only from the laws of nations (such as the nonintervention principle) and the natural duties (such as that of mutual aid).[5]

I have argued elsewhere (PTIR 129–36, 143–53 [cf. GJSE 23–26, 32–40]) that the membership of the original position should be global rather than national because national societies are not, in fact, self-sufficient: The system of global trade and investment, organized within a structure of international institutions and conventions, constitutes a scheme of social cooperation in Rawls's sense. Therefore, the principles of justice should apply in the first instance to the world at large. I now think that this argument misses the point (although I still accept its conclusion). If the original position is to represent individuals as equal moral persons for the purpose of choosing principles of institutional or background justice, then the criterion of membership is possession of the two essential powers of moral personality—a capacity for an effective sense of justice and a capacity to form, revise, and pursue a conception of the good.[6] Since human beings possess these essential powers regardless of whether, at present, they belong to a common cooperative scheme, the argument for construing the original position globally need not depend on any claim about the existence or intensity of international social cooperation. Of course, the construction would be pointless if there were no feasible scheme of institutions to which principles of justice could apply. But a *feasibility* condition is different from an *existence* condition, which I had earlier thought was necessary. Unless international cooperation according to the principles of justice can be shown to be infeasible, limiting the scope of the principles to national societies on the grounds that international cooperation does not exist today (or, as Brian Barry[7] argues, because present-day international cooperation lacks the requisite mutuality) would arbitrarily favor the status quo.[8]

One might wonder how these points would be affected if Rawls's theory were regarded as a "constructivist moral conception"—that is, as an effort "to articulate and make explicit those shared notions and principles thought to be already latent in common sense; or . . . if common sense is uncertain . . . to propose to it certain conceptions and principles congenial to its most essential convictions and historical traditions."[9] On such an interpretation, embedded in the original position are distinctive conceptions of the person and of the social role of morality. Though these are supposed to be widely accepted or presupposed in our culture, they are not seen as independently given or necessarily acceptable to all human beings as such. As a result, it may seem that the principles chosen would be applicable only to societies that share the conceptions embedded in the original position. If one assumes that the conceptions on which the theory relies are parochial to modern democratic societies, it would follow that the principles of justice are appropriate only to these societies, and do not apply globally (or to domestic societies of other kinds).[10]

These matters are complex and require more detailed attention than is possible here. Offhand, however, there are two reasons for doubting that the view as outlined is correct, at least as regards the international application of the principles. First, the parochialism assumption is questionable on empirical grounds: It is hardly clear that there is greater agreement in modern democratic societies than elsewhere on those elements of the conception of the person that animate the original position.[11] More fundamentally, even if the assumption is true, it would not justify limiting the original position to representatives of any particular democratic society. Although the basis of the conception of the person may be parochial, the conception itself, as Rawls describes it, is not. Once the conception of the person is specified by defining the moral powers, the argument for conceiving the original position in global terms is straightforward. One might say that we are compelled to take a global view in matters of social justice by features internal to our conception of moral personality, however parochial it may be.

None of this rules out the possibility that the parties to a *global* original position would accept the priority thesis. They might think, for example, that owing to various unalterable features of human social life, people would fare better in a world of states, each of which gave priority to its own citizens, than in a fully cosmopolitan world. By analogy with the parallel consequentialist defense of the thesis, however, this version of a contractarian defense would be plausible only as part of an ideal theory of global justice that also provided for background institutions at the international level that would compensate for the uneven distribution of natural and cultural resources among states.[12] Since the commonsense notion of priority for compatriots does not presuppose any such background, it will not find much support in a global original position.[13]

So far, I have been considering the priority thesis at the intermediate level—that is, as a principle based on considerations at a deeper level of moral reasoning at which everyone's interests are treated equally. However, if my doubts about the thesis were to be borne out by further examination of the arguments I have briefly sketched, this would not establish that it lacks significant moral content; for it might be that priority for compatriots can be explained at the foundational level instead.

The most plausible explanation of this type is suggested by the following remark of Thomas Nagel:

> There is some public analogue to the individual's right to lead his own life free of the constant demand to promote the best overall results, but it appears in the relations of states to one another rather than in their relations to their citizens: states can remain neutral in external disputes, and can legitimately favor their own populations—though not at any cost whatever to the rest of the world.[14]

Of course, the fact that there is a public analogue to a true principle of private morality does not imply that the public analogue is also true. We must ask whether there is a reason for accepting the principle of priority for compatriots that is comparable in its persuasiveness to our reason for accepting the element of private morality to which Nagel alludes. Two strategies for answering this question present themselves. Priority for compatriots might be supported by reasons pertaining to states that are themselves *analogues* of the reasons pertaining to persons which support the corresponding element of private morality. Or, priority for compatriots might be based on the *same* reasons that support the corresponding element of private morality.

The first of these strategies is not very promising. The element of private morality in question is a limited permission to aim at results that are less good, according to some impersonal standard, than other results that one is in a position to produce.[15] We recognize such a permission, within private morality, because of the importance we attach to being sufficiently free of impersonal moral constraints to be able to pursue the projects and commitments that express our separate identities as autonomous persons. This importance might be accounted for on consequentialist grounds, but it seems more likely to be a direct reflection in moral thought of what Samuel Scheffler calls "the independence of the personal point of view."[16]

There is room for dispute about whether this permission is properly conceived as internal to private morality or as an external motivational constraint. But even if the permission is understood as a part of personal morality, it does not have a plausible analogue pertaining to states. It is unrealistically romantic to characterize states qua states as expressing their separate identities by forming and pursuing projects and commitments; we have no conception of national agency, analogous to our conception of personal agency, that could give sense to something like "the independence of the national point of view"; and, in any case, it is a mystery why we should regard the national point of view as having the kind of significance for morality that attaches naturally to the personal point of view.

I turn therefore to the second strategy for explaining a foundational commitment to priority for compatriots: This is the strategy of deriving the commitment from the same considerations that motivate our acceptance of the principle of priority for the interests of the self. If individuals have a right to resist some of the sacrifices that impersonal morality demands in order to pursue their own commitments, then their governments may not require such sacrifices of them. Accordingly, there is an upper bound to the cost that a state can be morally required to bear in connection with pursuit of cosmopolitan goals (or any other goals). This upper bound defines the degree of priority that a government may accord to the interests of compatriots.

I believe that some such reasoning yields the most plausible account available of the moral content of priority for compatriots. But it must be emphasized that the priority thesis, so construed, will have significant limits. These limits derive from two sources. One is the underlying permission for individuals to favor themselves when necessary to protect their pursuit of important personal projects and commitments. This permission is itself limited; one may not forgo the chance to do great good for others in order to avoid a trifling sacrifice for oneself. This limit on the personal permission (however it is defined) will be reflected in the national permission as well. The other source involves the difference between individual and group sacrifice. One of the ways in which our individual sacrifices may be excessively burdensome is in setting us at a disadvantage relative to others who have sacrificed less. Where sacrifices are imposed on an entire population, however, this problem may not arise (supposing that the sacrifices are fairly allocated). Hence, it might be that a state may demand more of its people than its people, as individuals, must demand of themselves when cosmopolitan goals require sacrifices of them.

PATRIOTISM AND LOYALTY

It seems likely that the influence of the priority thesis in commonsense moral thought extends beyond what can be justified by the kinds of considerations discussed so far. The moral content of the national ideal is only part of the content of the national ideal. What is the rest?

A tempting answer is that the residual influence of the priority thesis is nothing more than a psychological or sociological artifact, whose significance for practical reasoning is merely that of an obstacle to be accommodated until it can be eliminated altogether.

In the end, this may prove to be correct. However, I do not think it is *obviously* correct, since it takes no account of at least two kinds of nonmoral but also non-self-interested reasons that back up some (though certainly not all) instances of patriotic sentiment. Some such reasons flow from a sense of shared loyalty: the feeling that I have obligations to compatriots simply because this is *our* country. I believe that such feelings are real and that they are primitive in the sense of being irreducible to feelings with a basis either in impersonal morality or in self-interest.[17] To some extent, the influence of loyalty in practical reasoning might be explained with reference to its role in our projects and commitments, but I doubt that such an explanation would be fully satisfactory. (I do not know what a better explanation would be like, however.) Another kind of reason that sometimes backs up patriotic sentiment is perfectionist. Just as we can see ourselves as striving to realize in our own lives various forms of individual perfection, so we can see our countries as striving for various forms of social or communal perfection. Again, it does not appear in either case that the influence of perfectionist reasons can be fully explained on moral grounds; yet, in both cases, this influence is persistent and clearly distinguishable from that of self-interest.

To return to where we began, the influence of both types of reasons can be detected in our thinking about immigration policy. For example, some combination of them surely provides the best explanation of the appeal of Sidgwick's argument that open borders would lead to the corruption of domestic culture and politics—an appeal that persists even if we think, contrary to Sidgwick, that open borders would better serve "the interest of humanity at large." If this is right, his "general conflict" reproduces on the large scale a pervasive dilemma of practical reasoning: how to combine different kinds of reasons for action when these reasons conflict and lack a common basis in virtue of which they can be reconciled. To make progress in international ethics, we need to recognize this dilemma and to understand more fully its nonmoral (as well as its moral) sources.

NOTES

This paper was presented at an APA symposium on International Justice, December 30, 1983; Henry Shue was co-symposiast, and Kai Nielsen was commentator; see *The Journal of Philosophy* 80: 10 (October 1983): 600–608 and 608–10, respectively, for their contributions.

1. Henry Sidgwick, *The Elements of Politics* (London: Macmillan, 4th ed., 1919), p. 309; parenthetical page references to Sidgwick are to this book.

2. I have argued against the national ideal, and in favor of one form of cosmopolitanism, in *Political Theory and International Relations* (Princeton, NJ: University Press, 1979), parts II and III (henceforth, PTIR). [Part III is based on the essay "Justice and International Relations," first published in *Philosophy and Public Affairs* 4(4), (summer 1975): 360–89, reprinted in *Global Justice: Seminal Essays*, 21–48.] See also Henry Shue, *Basic Rights: Subsistence, Affluence, and American Foreign Policy* (Princeton, NJ: University Press, 1980), pp. 131–52.

3. Op. cit., p. 132. As Shue points out, there is more to be said about how the thesis should be formulated in detail. But I do not believe it is necessary to explore the possible variations here.

4. "The Distribution of Membership," in Peter G. Brown and Henry Shue, eds., *Boundaries: National Autonomy and Its Limits* (Totowa, NJ: Rowman and Littlefield, 1981): 1–35, pp. 8–9 [reprinted in *Global Justice: Seminal Essays*, 145–77, 151–52].

5. *A Theory of Justice* (Cambridge, MA: Harvard University Press, 1971), pp. 4, 378–9.

6. Rawls, "Kantian Constructivism in Moral Theory," *The Journal of Philosophy*, LXXVII, 9 (September 1980): 515–72, pp. 521, 525.

7. "Humanity and Justice in Global Perspective," in J. Roland Pennock and John W. Chapman, eds., *Nomos XXIV: Ethics, Economics, and the Law* (New York: NYU Press, 1982): 219–52, pp. 232–34 [reprinted in *Global Justice: Seminal Essays*, 179–209, 190–92].

8. Here I am accepting a criticism of my earlier view advanced by David A. J. Richards, "International Distributive Justice," in Pennock and Chapman, op. cit.: 275–99, pp. 287–93.

9. Rawls, "Kantian Constructivism," p. 518.

10. Rawls himself apparently assumes that the conceptions are parochial in this way. Ibid.

11. For helpful comments, see Thomas W. M. Pogge, "Kant, Rawls, and Global Justice," unpublished Ph.D. dissertation, Harvard University, 1983, pp. 107–13.

12. Compare Rawls's discussion of the role of background institutions in maintaining the justice of market arrangements at the domestic level. *A Theory of Justice*, pp. 265–84.

13. For a discussion of the obligations of rich countries in the nonideal world under global principles of justice, see PTIR, pp. 169–76 [cf. *GJSE* 40–45].

14. "Ruthlessness in Public Life," in *Mortal Questions* (New York: Cambridge, 1979), p. 84.

15. By "some impersonal standard," I mean any agent-neutral standard for ranking outcomes according to the amount of overall goodness that they contain. It does not matter, for present purposes, how such a standard is defined.

16. *The Rejection of Consequentialism* (New York: Oxford, 1982), pp. 61–62.

17. See Andrew Oldenquist, "Loyalties," *The Journal of Philosophy*, LXXIX, 4 (April 1982): 173–93.

7. ALASDAIR MACINTYRE

MacIntyre begins by making certain clarificatory remarks on the nature of patriotism. He then contrasts two accounts of morality, a liberal conception in which it is difficult to find any place for patriotism at all, and an alternative account in which patriotism is a central virtue. Given that these two accounts of morality are incompatible, he argues, one cannot combine them, but must choose between them. MacIntyre then considers various considerations bearing on this choice, arguing that it is especially difficult for the liberal account to provide the motivational structure necessary to maintain a commitment to its standards.

Is Patriotism a Virtue?

First published as Is Patriotism a Virtue? *(The Lindley Lecture at the University of Kansas) Lawrence, KS: University Press of Kansas, 1984.*

I

One of the central tasks of the moral philosopher is to articulate the convictions of the society in which he or she lives so that these convictions may become available for rational scrutiny. This task is all the more urgent when a variety of conflicting and incompatible beliefs are held within one and the same community, either by rival groups who differ on key moral questions or by one and the same set of individuals who find within themselves competing moral allegiances. In either of these types of case the first task of the moral philosopher is to render explicit what is at issue in the various disagreements, and it is a task of this kind that I have set myself in this lecture.

For it is quite clear that there are large disagreements about patriotism in our society. And although it would be a mistake to suppose that there are only two clear, simple, and mutually opposed sets of beliefs about patriotism, it is at least plausible to suggest that the range of conflicting views can be placed on a spectrum with two poles. At one end is the view, taken for granted by almost everyone in the nineteenth century, a commonplace in the literary culture of the McGuffey readers, that "patriotism" names a virtue. At the other end is the contrasting view, expressed with sometimes shocking clarity in the 1960s, that "patriotism" names a vice. It would be misleading for me to suggest that I am going to be able to offer good reasons for taking one of these views rather than the other. What I do hope to achieve is a clarification of the issues that divide them.

A necessary first step in the direction of any such clarification is to distinguish patriotism properly so-called from two other sets of attitudes that are all too easily assimilated to it. The first is that exhibited by those who are protagonists of their own nation's causes because and only because, so they assert, it is their nation which is *the* champion of some great moral ideal. In the Great War of 1914–18, Max Weber claimed that Imperial Germany should be supported because its was the cause of *Kultur*, while Emile Durkheim claimed with equal vehemence that France should be supported because its was the cause of *civilisation*. And here and now there are those American politicians who claim that the United States deserves our allegiance because it champions the goods of freedom against the evils of communism. What distinguishes their attitude from patriotism is twofold: First, it is the ideal and not the nation that is the primary object of their regard; and second, insofar as their regard for the ideal provides good reasons for allegiance to their country, it provides good reasons for anyone at all to uphold their country's cause, irrespective of their nationality or citizenship.

Patriotism by contrast is defined in terms of a kind of loyalty to a particular nation that only those possessing that particular nationality can exhibit. Only Frenchmen can be patriotic about France, while anyone can make the cause of *civilisation* their own. But it would be all too easy in noticing this to fail to make a second equally important distinction. Patriotism is not to be confused with a mindless loyalty to one's own particular nation that has no regard at all for the characteristics of that particular nation. Patriotism does generally and characteristically involve a peculiar regard not just for one's own nation, but for the particular characteristics and merits and achievements of one's own nation. These latter are indeed valued *as* merits and achievements and their character as merits and achievements provides reasons supportive of the patriot's attitudes. But the patriot does not value in the same way precisely similar merits and achievements when they are the merits and achievements of some nation other than his or hers. For he or she—at least in the role of patriot—values them not just as merits and achievements, but as the merits and achievements of this particular nation.

To say this is to draw attention to the fact that patriotism is one of a class of loyalty-exhibiting virtues (that is, if it *is* a virtue at all), other members of which are marital fidelity, the love of one's own family and kin, friendship, and loyalty to such institutions as schools and cricket or baseball clubs. All these attitudes exhibit a peculiar action-generating regard for particular persons, institutions, or groups, a regard founded upon a particular historical relationship of association between the person exhibiting the regard and the relevant person, institution, or group. It is often, although not always, the case that associated with this regard will be a felt gratitude for the benefits that the individual takes him or herself to have received from the person, institution, or group. But it would be one more mistake to suppose patriotism or other such attitudes of loyalty to be at their core or primarily responses of gratitude. For there are many persons, institutions, and groups to which each of us have good reason to feel grateful without this kind of loyalty being involved. What patriotism and other such attitudes involve is not just gratitude, but a particular kind of gratitude; and what those who treat patriotism and other such loyalties as virtues are committed to believing is not that what they owe their nation or whomever or whatever it is is simply a requital for benefits received, based on some relationship of reciprocity of benefits.

So although one may as a patriot love one's country, or as a husband or wife exhibit marital fidelity, and cite as partially supporting reasons one's country's or one's spouse's merits and one's own gratitude to them for benefits received, these can be no more than *partially* supporting reasons, just because what is valued is valued precisely as the merits of *my* country or spouse or as the benefits received by *me* from *my* country or spouse. The particularity of the relationship is essential and ineliminable, and in identifying it as such we have already specified one central problem. What *is* the relationship between patriotism as such, the regard for this particular nation, and the regard that the patriot has for the merits and achievements of his or her nation and for the benefits he or she has received? The answer to this question must be delayed, for it will turn out to depend upon the answer to an apparently even more fundamental question, one that can best be framed in terms of the thesis that, if patriotism is understood as I have understood it, then "patriotism" is not merely not the name of a virtue, but must be the name of a vice, since patriotism thus understood and morality are incompatible.

II

The presupposition of this thesis is an account of morality that has enjoyed high prestige in our culture. According to that account, to judge from a moral standpoint is to judge impersonally. It is to judge as any rational person would judge, independently of his or her interests, affections, and social position. And to act morally is to act in accordance with such impersonal judgments. Thus to think and to act morally involve the moral agent in abstracting him or herself from all social particularity and partiality. The potential conflict between morality so understood and patriotism is at once clear. For patriotism requires me to exhibit peculiar devotion to my nation and you to yours. It requires me to regard such contingent social facts as where I was born and what government ruled over that place at that time, who my parents were, who my great-great-grandparents were, and so on, as deciding for me the question of what virtuous action is—at least insofar as it is the virtue of patriotism, which is in question. Hence the moral standpoint and the patriotic standpoint are systematically incompatible.

Yet although this is so, it might be argued that the two standpoints need not be in conflict. For patriotism and all other such particular loyalties can be restricted in their scope so that their exercise is always within the confines imposed by morality. Patriotism need be regarded as nothing more than a perfectly proper devotion to one's own nation, which must never be allowed to violate the constraints set by the impersonal moral standpoint. This is indeed the kind of patriotism professed by certain liberal moralists, who are often indignant when it is suggested by their critics that they are not patriotic. To those critics, however, patriotism thus limited in its scope appears to be emasculated, and it does so because in some of the most important situations of actual social life either the patriotic standpoint comes into serious conflict with the standpoint of a genuinely impersonal morality or it amounts to no more than a set of practically empty slogans. What kinds of circumstances are these? They are at least twofold.

The first kind arises from scarcity of essential resources, often historically from the scarcity of land suitable for cultivation and pasture, and perhaps in our own time from that of fossil fuels. What your community requires as the material prerequisites for your survival as a distinctive community and your growth into a distinctive nation may be exclusive use of the same or some of the same natural resources as my community requires for its survival and growth into a distinctive nation. When such a conflict arises, the standpoint of impersonal morality requires an allocation of goods such that each individual person counts for one and no more than one, while the patriotic standpoint requires that I strive to further the interests of my community and you strive to further those of yours, and certainly where the survival of one community is at stake, and sometimes perhaps even when only large interests of one community are at stake, patriotism entails a willingness to go to war on one's community's behalf.

The second type of conflict-engendering circumstance arises from differences between communities about the right way for each to live. Not only competition for scarce natural resources, but incompatibilities arising from such conflict-engendering beliefs may lead to situations in which once again the liberal moral standpoint and the patriotic standpoint are radically at odds. The administration of the *pax Romana* from time to time required the Roman *imperium* to set its frontiers at the point at which they could be most easily secured, so that the burden of supporting the legions would be reconcilable with the administration of Roman law. And the British Empire was no different in its time. But this required infringing upon the territory and the independence of barbarian border peoples. A variety of such peoples—Scottish Gaels, Iroquois Indians, Bedouin—have regarded raiding the territory of their traditional enemies living within the confines of such large empires as an essential constituent of the good life; whereas the settled urban or agricultural communities that provided the target for their depredations have regarded the subjugation of such peoples and their reeducation into peaceful pursuits as one of their central responsibilities. And on such issues once again the impersonal moral standpoint and that of patriotism cannot be reconciled.

For the impersonal moral standpoint, understood as the philosophical protagonists of modern liberalism have understood it, requires neutrality not only between rival and competing interests, but also between rival and competing sets of beliefs about the best way for human beings to live. Each individual is to be left free to pursue in his or her own way that way of life he or she judges to be best; while morality by contrast consists of rules which, just because they are such that any rational person, independently of his or her interests or point of view on the best way for human beings to live, would assent to them, are equally binding on all persons. Hence in conflicts between nations or other communities over ways of life, the standpoint of morality will once again be that of an impersonal arbiter, adjudicating in ways that give equal weight to each individual person's needs, desires, beliefs about the good and the like, while the patriot is once again required to be partisan.

Notice that in speaking of the standpoint of liberal impersonal morality in the way in which I have done, I have been describing a standpoint whose truth is both presupposed by the political actions and utterances of a great many people in our society and explicitly articulated and defended by most modern moral philosophers; and that it has at the level of moral philosophy a number of distinct versions—some with a Kantian flavor, some utilitarian, some contractarian. I do not mean to suggest that the disagreements between these positions are unimportant. Nonetheless, the five central positions that I have ascribed to that standpoint appear in all these various philosophical guises: first, that morality is constituted by rules to which any rational person would under certain ideal conditions give assent; second, that those rules impose constraints upon and are neutral between rival and competing interests—morality itself is not the expression of any particular interest; third, that those rules are also neutral between rival and competing sets of beliefs about what the best way for human beings to live is; fourth, that the units that provide the subject matter of morality as well as its agents are individual human beings and that in moral evaluations each individual is to count for one and nobody for more than one; and fifth, that the standpoint of the moral agent constituted by allegiance to these rules is one and the same for all moral agents and as such is independent of all social particularity. What morality provides are standards by which all actual social structures may be brought to judgment from a standpoint independent of all of them. It is morality so understood allegiance to which is not only incompatible with treating patriotism as a virtue, but which requires that patriotism—at least in any substantial version—be treated as a vice.

But is this the only possible way to understand morality? As a matter of history, the answer is clearly "No." This understanding of morality invaded post-Renascence Western culture at a particular point in time as the moral counterpart to political liberalism and social individualism, and its polemical stances reflect its history of emergence from the conflicts that those movements engendered and themselves presuppose alternatives against which those polemical stances were and are directed. Let me therefore turn to considering one of those alternative accounts of morality, whose peculiar interest lies in the place that it has to assign to patriotism.

III

According to the liberal account of morality, *where* and *from whom* I learn the principles and precepts of morality are and must be irrelevant both to the question of what the content of morality is and to that of the nature of my commitment to it, as irrelevant as *where* and *from whom* I learn the principles and precepts of mathematics are to the content of mathematics and the nature of my commitment to mathematical truths. By contrast, on the alternative account of morality which I am going to sketch, the questions of *where* and *from whom* I learn my morality turn out to be crucial for both the content and the nature of moral commitment.

On this view it is an essential characteristic of the morality each of us acquires that it is learned from, in, and through the way of life of some particular community. Of course, the moral rules elaborated in one particular historical community will often resemble and sometimes be identical with the rules to which allegiance is given in other particular communities, especially in communities that have a shared history or that appeal to the same canonical texts. But there will characteristically be *some* distinctive features of the set of rules considered as a whole, and those distinctive features will often arise from the way in which members of that particular community responded to some earlier situation or series of situations in which particular features of difficult cases led to one or more rules being put in question and reformulated or understood in some new way. Moreover, the form of the rules of morality as taught and apprehended will be intimately connected with specific institutional arrangements. The moralities of different societies may agree in having a precept enjoining that a child should honor his or her parents, but what it is so to honor and indeed what a father is and what a mother is will vary greatly between different social orders. So that what I learn as a guide to my actions and as a standard for evaluating them is never morality as such, but always the highly specific morality of some highly specific social order.

To this the reply by the protagonists of modern liberal morality might well be: Doubtless this is how a comprehension of the rules of morality is first acquired. But what allows such specific rules, framed in terms of particular social institutions, to be accounted moral rules at all is the fact they are nothing other than applications of universal and general moral rules, and individuals acquire genuine morality only because and insofar as they progress from particularized socially specific applications of universal and general moral rules to comprehending them as universal and general. To learn to understand oneself as a moral agent just is to learn to free oneself from social particularity and to adopt a standpoint independent of any particular set of social institutions, and the fact that everyone or almost everyone has to learn to do this by starting out from a standpoint deeply infected by social particularity and partiality goes no way toward providing an alternative account of morality. But to this reply a threefold rejoinder can be made.

First, it is not just that I first apprehend the rules of morality in some socially specific and particularized form. It is also and correlatively that the goods by reference to which and for the sake of which any set of rules must be justified are also going to be goods that are socially specific and particular. For central to those goods is the enjoyment of one particular kind of social life, lived out through a particular set of social relationships, and thus what I enjoy is the good of *this* particular social life inhabited by me and I enjoy *it* as what *it* is. It may well be that it follows that I would enjoy and benefit equally from similar forms of social life in other communities; but this hypothetical truth in no way diminishes the importance of the contention that my goods are as a matter of fact found *here*, among *these* particular people, in *these* particular relationships. Goods are never encountered except as thus particularized. Hence the abstract general claim, that rules of a certain kind are justified by being productive of and constitutive of goods of a certain kind, is true only if these and these and these particular sets of rules incarnated in the practices of these and these and these particular communities are productive of or constitutive of these and these and these particular goods enjoyed at certain particular times and places by certain specifiable individuals.

It follows that *I* find *my* justification for allegiance to these rules of morality in *my* particular community; deprived of the life of that community, *I* would have no reason to be moral. But this is not all. To obey the rules of morality is characteristically and generally a hard task for human beings. Indeed, were it not so, our need for morality would not be what it is. It is because we are continually liable to be blinded by immediate desire, to be distracted from our responsibilities, to lapse into backsliding, and because even the best of us may at times encounter quite unusual temptations that it is important to morality that *I* can only be a moral agent because *we* are moral agents, that I need those around me to reinforce my moral strengths and assist in remedying my moral weaknesses. It is in general only within a community that individuals become capable of morality, are sustained in their morality, and are constituted as moral agents by the way in which other people regard them and what is owed to and by them as well as by the way in which they regard themselves. In requiring much from me morally, the other members of my community express a kind of respect for me that has nothing to do with expectations of benefit; and those of whom nothing or little is required in respect of morality are treated with a lack of respect that is, if repeated often enough, damaging to the moral capacities of those individuals. Of course, lonely moral heroism is sometimes required and sometimes achieved. But we must not treat this exceptional type of case as though it were typical. And once we recognize that typically moral agency and continuing moral capacity are engendered and sustained in essential ways by particular institutionalized social ties in particular social groups, it will be difficult to counterpose allegiance to a particular society and allegiance to morality in the way in which the protagonists of liberal morality do.

Indeed, the case for treating patriotism as a virtue is now clear. *If* first of all it is the case that I can only apprehend the rules of morality in the version in which they are incarnated in some specific community; and *if* secondly it is the case that the justification of morality must be in terms of particular goods enjoyed within the life of particular communities; and *if* thirdly it is the case that I am characteristically brought into being and maintained as a moral agent only through the particular kinds of moral sustenance afforded by my community, *then* it is clear that deprived of this community, I am unlikely to flourish as a moral agent. Hence my allegiance to the community and what it requires of me—even to the point of requiring me to die to sustain its life—could not meaningfully be contrasted with or counterposed to what morality required of me. Detached from my community, I will be apt to lose my hold upon all genuine standards of judgment. Loyalty to that community, to the hierarchy of particular kinship, particular local community, and particular natural community, is on this view a prerequisite for morality. So patriotism and those loyalties cognate to it are not just virtues, but central virtues. Everything however turns on the truth or falsity of the claims advanced in the three preceding if-clauses. And the argument so far affords us no resources for delivering a verdict upon that truth or falsity. Nonetheless, some progress has been achieved, and not only because the terms of the debate have become clearer. For it has also become clear that this dispute is not adequately characterized if it is understood simply as a disagreement between two rival accounts of morality, as if there were some independently identifiable phenomenon situated somehow or other in the social world waiting to be described more or less accurately by the contending parties. What we have here are two rival and incompatible moralities, each of which is viewed from within by its adherents as morality-as-such, each of which makes its exclusive claim to our allegiance. How are we to evaluate such claims?

One way to begin is to be learned from Aristotle. Since we possess no stock of clear and distinct first principles or any other such epistemological resource that would provide us with a neutral and independent standard for judging between them, we shall do well to proceed dialectically. And one useful dialectical strategy is to focus attention on those accusations that the adherents of each bring against the rival position which the adherents of that rival position treat as of central importance to rebut. For this will afford at least one indication of the issues about the importance of which both sides agree and about the characterization of which their very recognition of disagreement suggests that there must also be some shared beliefs. In what areas do such issues arise?

IV

One such area is defined by a charge that it seems reasonable at least prima facie for the protagonists of patriotism to bring against morality. The morality for which patriotism is a virtue offers a form of rational justification for moral rules and precepts whose structure is clear and rationally defensible. The rules of morality are justifiable if and only if they are productive of and partially constitutive of a form of shared social life whose goods are directly enjoyed by those inhabiting the particular communities whose social life is of that kind. Hence *qua* member of this or that particular community I can appreciate the justification for what morality requires of me from within the social roles that I live out in my community. By contrast, it may be argued, liberal morality requires of me to assume an abstract and artificial—perhaps even an impossible—stance, that of a rational being as such, responding to the requirements of morality not *qua* parent or farmer or quarterback, but *qua* rational agent who has abstracted him or herself from all social particularity, who has become not merely Adam Smith's impartial spectator, but a correspondingly impartial actor, and one who in his impartiality is doomed to rootlessness, to be a citizen of nowhere. How can I justify to myself performing this act of abstraction and detachment?

The liberal answer is clear: Such abstraction and detachment is defensible, because it is a necessary condition of moral freedom, of emancipation from the bondage of the social, political, and economic status quo. For unless I can stand back from every and any feature of that status quo, including the roles within it which I myself presently inhabit, I will be unable to view it critically and to decide for myself what stance it is rational and right for me to adopt toward it. This does not preclude that the outcome of such a critical evaluation may not be an endorsement of all or some of the existing social order; but even such an endorsement will only be free and rational if I have made it for myself in this way. (Making just such an endorsement of much of the economic status quo is the distinguishing mark of the contemporary conservative liberal, such as Milton Friedman, who is as much a liberal as the liberal liberal who finds much of the status quo wanting—such as J. K. Galbraith or Edward Kennedy—or the radical liberal.) Thus liberal morality does after all appeal to an overriding good, the good of this particular kind of emancipating freedom. And in the name of this good it is able not only to respond to the question about how the rules of morality are to be justified, but also to frame a plausible and potentially damaging objection to the morality of patriotism.

It is of the essence of the morality of liberalism that no limitations are or can be set upon the criticism of the social status quo. No institution, no practice, no loyalty can be immune from being put in question and perhaps rejected. Conversely, the morality of patriotism is one that, precisely because it is framed in terms of the membership of some particular social community with some particular social, political, and economic structure, must exempt at least some fundamental structures of that community's life from criticism. Because patriotism has to be a loyalty that is in some respects unconditional, so in just those respects rational criticism is ruled out. But if so, the adherents of the morality of patriotism have condemned themselves to a fundamentally irrational attitude—since to refuse to examine some of one's fundamental beliefs and attitudes is to insist on accepting them, whether they are rationally justifiable or not, which is irrational—and have imprisoned themselves within that irrationality. What answer can the adherents of the morality of patriotism make to this kind of accusation? The reply must be threefold.

When the liberal moralist claims that the patriot is bound to treat his or her nation's projects and practices in some measure uncritically, the claim is not only that at any one time certain of these projects and practices will be being treated uncritically; it is that some at least must be permanently exempted from criticism. The patriot is in no position to deny this; but what is crucial to the patriot's case is to identify clearly precisely what it is that is thus exempted. And at this point it becomes extremely important that in outlining the case for the morality of patriotism—as indeed in outlining the case for liberal morality—we should not be dealing with straw men. Liberalism and patriotism are not positions invented by me or by other external commentators; they have their own distinctive spokesmen and their own distinctive voices. And although I hope that it has been clear throughout that I have only been trying to articulate what those voices would say, it is peculiarly important to the case for patriotic morality at this point that its actual historical protagonists be identified. So what I say next is an attempt to identify the common attitudes on this point of Charles Péguy and Charles de Gaulle, of Bismarck and of Adam von Trott. You will notice that in these pairs one member is someone who was at least for a time a member of his nation's political establishment, the other someone who was always in a radical way outside that establishment and hostile to it, but that even those who were for a time identified with the status quo of power, were also at times alienated from it. And this makes it clear that whatever is exempted from the patriot's criticism the status quo of power and government and the policies pursued by those exercising power and government never need be so exempted. What then is exempted? The answer is: the nation conceived *as a project*, a project somehow or other brought to birth in the past and carried on so that a morally distinctive community was brought into being that embodied a claim to political autonomy in its various organized and institutionalized expressions. Thus one can be patriotic toward a nation whose political independence is yet to come—as Garibaldi was; or toward a nation that once was and perhaps might be again—like the Polish patriots of the 1860s. What the patriot is committed to is a particular way of linking a past that has conferred a distinctive moral and political identity upon him or her with a future for the project that is his or her nation, which it is his or her responsibility to bring into being. Only this allegiance is unconditional, and allegiance to particular governments or forms of government or particular leaders will be entirely conditional upon their being devoted to furthering that project rather than frustrating or destroying it. Hence there is nothing inconsistent in a patriot's being deeply opposed to his country's contemporary rulers, as Péguy was, or plotting their overthrow as Adam von Trott did.

Yet although this may go part of the way toward answering the charge of the liberal moralist that the patriot must in certain areas be completely uncritical and therefore irrationalist, it certainly does not go all the way. For everything that I have said on behalf of the morality of patriotism is compatible with it being the case that on occasion patriotism might require me to support and work for the success of some enterprise of my nation as crucial to its overall project, crucial perhaps to its survival, when the success of that enterprise would not be in the best interests of mankind, evaluated from an impartial and an impersonal standpoint. The case of Adam von Trott is very much to the point.

Adam von Trott was a German patriot who was executed after the unsuccessful assassination attempt against Hitler's life in 1944. Trott deliberately chose to work inside Germany with the minuscule, but highly placed, conservative opposition to the Nazis with the aim of replacing Hitler from within, rather than to work for an overthrow of Nazi Germany, which would result in the destruction of the Germany brought to birth in 1871. But to do this he had to appear to be identified with the cause of Nazi Germany and so strengthened not only his country's cause, as was his intention, but also as an unavoidable consequence the cause of the Nazis. This kind of example is a particularly telling one, because the claim that such and such a course of action is "to the best interests of mankind" is usually at best disputable, at worst cloudy rhetoric. But there are a very few causes in which so much was at stake—and that this is generally much clearer in retrospect than it was at the time does not alter that fact—that the phrase has clear application: The overthrow of Nazi Germany was one of them.

How ought the patriot then to respond? Perhaps in two ways. The first begins by reemphasizing that from the fact that the particularist morality of the patriot is rooted in a particular community and inextricably bound up with the social life of that community, it does not follow that it cannot provide rational grounds for repudiating many features of that country's present organized social life. The conception of justice engendered by the notion of citizenship within a particular community may provide standards by which particular political institutions are found wanting: When Nazi anti-Semitism encountered the phenomena of German Jewish ex-soldiers who had won the Iron Cross, it had to repudiate German particularist standards of excellence (for the award of the Iron Cross symbolized a recognition of devotion to Germany). Moreover, the conception of one's own nation having a special mission does not necessitate that this mission may not involve the extension of a justice originally at home only in the particular institutions of the homeland. And clearly particular governments or agencies of government may defect and may be understood to have defected from this mission so radically that the patriot may find that a point comes when he or she has to choose between the claims of the project that constitutes his or her nation and the claims of the morality that he or she has learned as a member of the community whose life is informed by that project. Yes, the liberal critic of patriotism will respond, this indeed *may* happen; but it may not and it often will not. Patriotism turns out to be a permanent source of moral danger. And this claim, I take it, cannot in fact be successfully rebutted.

A second possible, but very different type of answer on behalf of the patriot would run as follows. I argued earlier that the kind of regard for one's own country that would be compatible with a liberal morality of impersonality and impartiality would be too insubstantial, would be under too many constraints, to be regarded as a version of patriotism in the traditional sense. But it does not follow that some version of traditional patriotism may not be compatible with some other morality of universal moral law, which sets limits to and provides both sanction for and correction of the particularist morality of the patriot. Whether this is so or not is too large and too distinct a question to pursue in this present paper. But we ought to note that even if it is so—and all those who have been both patriots and Christians *or* patriots and believers in Thomistic natural law *or* patriots and believers in the Rights of Man have been committed to claiming that it is so—this would not diminish in any way the force of the liberal claim that patriotism is a morally dangerous phenomenon.

That the rational protagonist of the morality of patriotism is compelled, if my argument is correct, to concede this does not mean that there is not more to be said in the debate. And what needs to be said is that the liberal morality of impartiality and impersonality turns out also to be a morally dangerous phenomenon in an interestingly corresponding way. For suppose the bonds of patriotism to be dissolved: Would liberal morality be able to provide anything adequately substantial in its place? What the morality of patriotism at its best provides is a clear account of and justification for the particular bonds and loyalties that form so much of the substance of the moral life. It does so by underlining the moral importance of the different members of a group acknowledging a shared history. Each one of us to some degree or other understands his or her life as an enacted narrative; and because of our relationships with others, we have to understand ourselves as characters in the enacted narratives of other people's lives. Moreover, the story of each of our lives is characteristically embedded in the story of one or more larger units. I understand the story of my life in such a way that it is part of the history of my family or of this farm or of this university or of this countryside; and I understand the story of the lives of other individuals around me as embedded in the same larger stories, so that I and they share a common stake in the outcome of that story and in what sort of story it both is and is to be: tragic, heroic, comic.

A central contention of the morality of patriotism is that I will obliterate and lose a central dimension of the moral life if I do not understand the enacted narrative of my own individual life as embedded in the history of my country. For if I do not so understand it I will not understand what I owe to others or what others owe to me, for what crimes of my nation I am bound to make reparation, for what benefits to my nation I am bound to feel gratitude. Understanding what is owed to and by me and understanding the history of the communities of which I am a part is on this view one and the same thing.

It is worth stressing that one consequence of this is that patriotism, in the sense in which I am understanding it in this paper, is only possible in certain types of national community under certain conditions. A national community, for example, that systematically disowned its own true history or substituted a largely fictitious history for it, or a national community in which the bonds deriving from history were in no way the real bonds of the community (having been replaced for example by the bonds of reciprocal self-interest) would be one toward which patriotism would be—from any point of view—an irrational attitude.

For precisely the same reasons that a family whose members all came to regard membership in that family as governed only by reciprocal self-interest would no longer be a family in the traditional sense, so a nation whose members took up a similar attitude would no longer be a nation, and this would provide adequate grounds for holding that the project which constituted that nation had simply collapsed. Since all modern bureaucratic states tend toward reducing national communities to this condition, all such states tend toward a condition in which any genuine morality of patriotism would have no place and what paraded itself as patriotism would be an unjustifiable simulacrum.

Why would this matter? In modern communities in which membership is understood only or primarily in terms of reciprocal self-interest, only two resources are generally available when destructive conflicts of interest threaten such reciprocity. One is the arbitrary imposition of some solution by force; the other is appeal to the neutral, impartial, and impersonal standards of liberal morality. The importance of this resource is scarcely to be underrated; but how much of a resource is it? The problem is that some motivation has to be provided for allegiance to the standards of impartiality and impersonality which both has rational justification and can outweigh the considerations provided by interest. Since any large need for such allegiance arises precisely and only when and insofar as the possibility of appeals to reciprocity in interests has broken down, such reciprocity can no longer provide the relevant kind of motivation. And it is difficult to identify anything that can take its place. The appeal to moral agents *qua* rational beings to place their allegiance to impersonal rationality above that to their interests has, just because it is an appeal to rationality, to furnish an adequate reason for so doing. And this is a point at which liberal accounts of morality are notoriously vulnerable. This vulnerability becomes a manifest practical liability at one key point in the social order.

Every political community except in the most exceptional conditions requires standing armed forces for its minimal security. Of the members of these armed forces it must require both that they be prepared to sacrifice their own lives for the sake of the community's security and that their willingness to do so be not contingent upon their own individual evaluation of the rightness or wrongness of their country's cause on some specific issue, measured by some standard that is neutral and impartial relative to the interests of their own community and the interests of other communities. And, that is to say, good soldiers may not be liberals and must indeed embody in their actions a good deal at least of the morality of patriotism. So the political survival of any polity in which liberal morality had secured large-scale allegiance would depend upon there still being enough young men and women who rejected that liberal morality. And in this sense liberal morality tends toward the dissolution of social bonds.

Hence the charge that the morality of patriotism can successfully bring against liberal morality is the mirror image of that which liberal morality can successfully urge against the morality of patriotism. For while the liberal moralist was able to conclude that patriotism is a permanent source of moral danger because of the way it places our ties to our nation beyond rational criticism, the moralist who defends patriotism is able to conclude that liberal morality is a permanent source of moral danger because of the way it renders our social and moral ties too open to dissolution by rational criticism. And each party is in fact in the right against the other.

V

The fundamental task that confronts any moral philosopher who finds this conclusion compelling is clear. It is to inquire whether, although the central claims made on behalf of these two rival modern moralities cannot both be true, we ought perhaps not to move toward the conclusion that both sets of claims are in fact false. And this is an inquiry in which substantial progress has already been made. But history in its impatience does not wait for moral philosophers to complete their tasks, let alone to convince their fellow citizens. The *polis* ceased to be the key institution in Greek politics even while Aristotle was still restating its rationale, and any contemporary philosopher who discusses the key conceptions that have informed modern political life since the eighteenth century is in danger of reliving Aristotle's fate, even if in a rather less impressive way. The owl of Minerva really does seem to fly at dusk.

Does this mean that my argument is therefore devoid of any immediate practical significance? That would be true only if the conclusion that a morality of liberal impersonality and a morality of patriotism must be deeply incompatible itself had no practical significance for our understanding of our everyday politics. But perhaps a systematic recognition of this incompatibility will enable us to diagnose one central flaw in the political life characteristic of modern Western states, or at least of all those modern Western states that look back for their legitimation to the American and the French revolutions. For polities so established have tended to contrast themselves with the older regimes that they displaced by asserting that, while all previous polities had expressed in their lives the partiality and one-sidedness of local customs, institutions, and traditions, they have for the first time given expression in their constitutional and institutional forms to the impersonal and impartial rules of morality as such, common to all rational beings. So Robespierre proclaimed that it was an effect of the French Revolution that the cause of France and the cause of the Rights of Man were one and the same cause. And in the nineteenth century the United States produced its own version of this claim, one that at the level of rhetoric provided the content for many Fourth of July orations and at the level of education set the standards for the Americanization of the late-nineteenth-century and early-twentieth-century immigrants, especially those from Europe.

Hegel employs a useful distinction, which he masks by his use of words *Sittlichkeit* and *Moralität*. *Sittlichkeit* is the customary morality of each particular society, pretending to be no more than this. *Moralität* reigns in the realm of rational universal, impersonal morality, of liberal morality, as I have defined it. What those immigrants were taught in effect was that they had left behind countries and cultures where *Sittlichkeit* and *Moralität* were certainly distinct and often opposed and arrived in a country and a culture whose *Sittlichkeit* just is *Moralität*. And thus for many Americans the cause of America, understood as the object of patriotic regard, and the cause of morality, understood as the liberal moralist understands it, came to be identified. The history of this identification could not be other than a history of confusion and incoherence, if the argument I have constructed in this lecture is correct. For a morality of particularist ties and solidarities has been conflated with a morality of universal, impersonal, and impartial principles in a way that can never be carried through without incoherence.

One test therefore of whether the argument that I have constructed has or has not empirical application and practical significance would be to discover whether it is or is not genuinely illuminating to write the political and social history of modern America as in key part the living out of a central conceptual confusion, a confusion perhaps required for the survival of a large-scale modern polity that has to exhibit itself as liberal in many institutional settings, but that also has to be able to engage the patriotic regard of enough of its citizens, if it is to continue functioning effectively. To determine whether that is or is not true would be to risk discovering that we inhabit a kind of polity whose moral order requires systematic incoherence in the form of public allegiance to mutually inconsistent sets of principles. But that is a task that—happily—lies beyond the scope of this lecture.

8. ONORA O'NEILL

O'Neill considers what three different kinds of moral theory say ought to be done about hunger and famine. She criticizes utilitarianism for requiring calculations that we are unable to make and for failing to prioritize human needs. Against theories that take human rights as basic, O'Neill points out that they are divided on the issue of whether some "welfare" rights—such as a right to subsistence—are human rights. Those who deny that such rights are human rights neglect human needs, she argues, while those who endorse such rights have yet to show convincingly who bears the correlative obligations. Many human rights theorists also fall short by denying that there are obligations of humanity or beneficence. O'Neill herself advocates a third kind of theorizing that takes human obligations as basic and, in particular, the Kantian obligation never to act in ways in which others cannot in principle also act. Such a theory, she argues, provides a better normative response to hunger and famine than utilitarianism and human rights approaches.

Rights, Obligations and World Hunger

First published in Poverty and Social Justice: Critical Perspectives: A Pilgrimage Toward Our Own Humanity, *ed. Francisco Jiménez (Tempe, AZ: Bilingual Press, 1987), 86–100.*

HUNGER AND FAMINE

Some of the facts of world hunger and poverty are now widely known. Among them are the following six:

1. World population is now over 5 billion and rising rapidly. It will exceed 6 billion by end of this century.

2.   In many Third World countries, investment and growth have so far concentrated in an urbanized modern sector, whose benefits reach a minority.

3.   In many poor countries, the number of destitute and landless increases even when there is economic growth.

4.   In many African countries, harvests have been falling for two decades and dependence on imported grain is growing.

5.   The rich countries of the North (for these purposes "the North" means the countries of North America, the EEC, and Australasia!) grow vast surpluses of grain. The grain that goes to poor countries is mostly sold.

6.   The rural poor of the Third World are sometimes harmed by grain imports, which are distributed in towns, so depriving peasants of customers for their crops. These peasants then migrate to shantytowns.

And then there is Ethiopia. We can understand the famine in Ethiopia better in the wider context of world hunger. Famines are not unexpected natural catastrophes, but simply the harshest extreme of hunger. We know well enough where in the world poverty and hunger are constantly bad enough for minor difficulties to escalate into famine. Ethiopia had its last famine only ten years ago. We know which other regions in Africa, Asia, and Latin America are now vulnerable to famines. Famine is the tip of the iceberg of hunger. It is the bit that is publicized and to which we react; but the greater part of the suffering is less lurid and better hidden.

Most hungry people are not migrating listlessly or waiting for the arrival of relief supplies. They are leading their normal lives with their normal economic, social, and familial situations, earning and growing what they normally earn or grow, yet are always poor and often hungry. These normal conditions are less spectacular than famine, but affect far more people.

We are tempted to set famine aside from other, endemic hunger and poverty. We blame natural catastrophes such as floods, drought, blight, or cold for destroying crops and producing famines. But harsh circumstances cause famines only when social and economic structures are too fragile to absorb such natural shocks. Californians know that desert climates need not lead to famines. Minnesotans know that a ferocious winter need not be reflected in countless annual deaths from cold. Yet both regions would have catastrophic annual mortality if they lacked appropriate social and economic structures. Many natural catastrophes produce human catastrophes only when social structures are inadequate.

FOCUS ON ACTION

We could list the facts of world hunger, poverty, and famine endlessly. But facts alone do not tell us what to do. What surely matters is action. But here we meet a problem. Which action we advocate depends partly on our perception of the facts, and this perception itself depends partly on the particular ethical outlook we adopt. Both our perception of problems and our prescriptions for action reflect our ethical theory. Ethical theories are not elegant trimmings that decorate our reasoning about practical problems. They determine our entire focus. They lead us to see certain facts and principles as salient and others as insubstantial. They focus our action—or our inertia.

I shall here consider three theories of what ought to be done about hunger and famine. Two are widely known and discussed in present debates in the English-speaking world, while the third, though in many ways older and more familiar, now receives rather less public attention. I shall offer certain criticisms of the two prevailing approaches and recommend the third to your attention.

The first approach is one that makes human happiness and well-being the standard for assessing action. Its most common modern version is *utilitarianism*. For utilitarians, all ethical requirements are basically a matter of beneficence to others. The second approach takes respect for human rights as basic and interprets the central issues of world hunger as matters of justice, which can be secured if all rights are respected. The third approach takes fulfillment of human obligations as basic and insists that these obligations include both obligations of justice and obligations of help or beneficence to others, and above all to others in need. Since no famine policy or development strategy would be adequate if it guided only individual action, all three of these positions will be considered as ways in which public and institutional policies as well as individual action might be guided.

MEASURING AND MAXIMIZING HAPPINESS

The central idea of all ethical reasoning that focuses on consequences or results is that action is right if it produces good results. The specifically utilitarian version of such thinking insists that the goodness of results be assessed by their contribution to total human happiness, and specifically that the best results are those that maximize human happiness. This position is very familiar to many of us because restricted versions of it are incorporated in economic theory and in business practice, and often used in daily decision making. It leads naturally to the question: What will maximize human happiness?

This seems such a simple question, but it has been given many unclear answers. Even discussions of hunger and famine, where the means to greater happiness may seem obvious, jangle with incompatible claims. The debates of the last decade show radical disagreements between utilitarian writers on world hunger.

The Australian philosopher Peter Singer has used simple economic considerations to argue that any serious utilitarian should undertake radical redistribution of his or her possessions and income to the poor. Standard marginalist considerations suggest that we can increase happiness by transferring resources from the rich to the poor. Any unhappiness caused by the loss of a luxury—such as a car—will be more than outweighed by the happiness produced by using the same funds to buy essential food for the hungry.

But the United States writer on famine, population, and ecological problems, Garrett Hardin, argues on the contrary that help to the poorest is forbidden on utilitarian grounds because it will in the end lead to the greatest misery. Drawing on the thought of the early-nineteenth-century economist and population theorist Thomas Malthus, he argues that food given to the poor will lead to population increases and ultimately to more people than can be fed and so ultimately to devastating famine and maximal misery.

It is an urgent practical question whether utilitarians can resolve these disagreements. The founder of utilitarianism, the late-eighteenth-century radical philosopher and polemicist Jeremy Bentham, thought we could do so with scientific rigor: It was only a matter of measuring and aggregating seven dimensions of human happiness. To help us he provided a pithy mnemonic verse in his *Introduction to the Principles of Morals and of Legislation*:

> *Intense, long, certain, speedy, fruitful, pure,*—Such marks in *pleasures* and in *pains* endure. Such pleasures seek if *private* be thy end: If it be *public* wide let them *extend*.[1]

But this is simply not enough. Despite the recurrent optimism of some economists and decision theorists about measuring happiness in limited contexts, we know we cannot generally predict or measure or aggregate happiness with any precision.

ACCURACY, PRECISION, AND NEEDS

Yet we can, it seems, often make approximate judgments of human happiness. And perhaps that is enough. After all, we do not need great precision, but only reasonable (even if vague) accuracy. We know that hunger and destitution mean misery and that enough to eat ends that sort of misery. Do we need to know more?

If we are to be utilitarians, we do need to know more. We need not only to know what general result to aim at, but to work out what means to take. Since very small changes in actions and policies may vastly alter results, precise comparisons of many results are indispensable. Examples of some unsuspected results of intended beneficence make the point vivid. Some food aid policies have actually harmed those whom they were intended to benefit or to benefit those who were not in the first place the poorest. (This is not to say that food aid is dispensable—especially in cases of famine—but it is never enough to end misery, and it can be damaging if misdirected.) Some aid policies aimed at raising standards of life, for example by encouraging farmers to grow cash crops, have damaged the livelihood of subsistence farmers, and harmed the poorest. The benefits of aid are often diverted to those who are not in the greatest need. The ubiquity of corruption also shows how essential it is for utilitarians to make precise and not vague judgments about how to increase human happiness. Benevolent intentions are quite easy to identify; but beneficent policies cannot be identified if we cannot predict and compare results precisely.

To do their calculations, utilitarians need not only precise measurements of happiness, but precise prediction of which policies lead to which results. They need the sort of comprehensive and predictive social science to which many researchers have aspired, but not attained. At present we cannot resolve even very basic disagreements between rival utilitarians. We cannot show whether happiness is maximized by attending to nearby desires where we can intervene personally (even if these are desires that reflect no needs), or by concentrating all our help on the neediest. Indeed, we often know too little even to predict which public policies will benefit the poor most.

If utilitarians somehow developed the precise methods of prediction and calculation that they lack, the results might not endorse help for the poor. Utilitarian thinking assigns no special importance to human need. Happiness produced by meeting the desires of those around us—even their desires for unneeded goods—may count as much as, or more than, happiness produced by ending real misery. All that matters is which desire is more intense. Since the neediest may be so weakened and apathetic that they no longer have strong desires, their need may count less and not more in a utilitarian calculus. But we know that charity that begins at home, where others' desires are evident to us, can find so much to do there that it often ends at home, too. So we can see that unless needs are given a certain priority in ethical thinking, they may be greatly neglected.

Meanwhile, utilitarian thinking unavoidably leaves vital dilemmas unclarified and unresolved. Was it beneficent, and so right, to negotiate massive development loans, although soaring interest rates have meant that much of poor countries' export earnings are now swallowed by interest payments? The present rich countries developed during a period of low and stable interest rates: They now control the ground rules of a world economy that does not provide that context of opportunity for remaining poor countries. Has it been happiness maximizing to provide development loans for poor countries in these conditions? Might happiness not be greater if poor countries had relied on lesser but indigenous sources of investment? Or would the cost of slower growth have been a larger total of human misery that could have been avoided by higher interest rates?

These are bitter questions, and I do not know the answer in general or for particular countries. I raise them as an example of the difficulty of relying on predictions and calculations about maximal happiness in determining what ought to be done, and what it would be wrong to do.

THE HUMAN RIGHTS MOVEMENT

The difficulties of utilitarian thinking may seem to arise from its ambitious scope. Utilitarianism tries to encompass the whole of morality under a single principle, and to select acts and policies that are not only right, but best or optimal. One alternative might be to aim for rather less. This might be done by looking at principles for evaluating acts and rejecting those that are wrong, rather than at grand proposals to find just those acts and policies that provide optimal results.

The most common contemporary embodiment of this approach is that of the human rights movement, which I shall consider next. The rhetoric of human rights is all around us—perhaps never more so than at present in the English-speaking world, and particularly in the United States. The sources of the rhetoric are well known. The earlier ones are the grand eighteenth-century documents, such as Tom Paine's *The Rights of Man*, and the declaration of rights of the United States and the French revolutions. The more recent growth of concern for human rights reflects a considerable revival of such thinking in the post-World War II search for foundations for a new international order, which gave rise to various United Nations documents, such as the Universal Declaration of Human Rights of 1948. The modern human rights movement gained impetus from the commitment of the Carter administration to a foreign policy that hoped to secure respect for human rights in other countries. While the Reagan administration and the Thatcher government have not taken a comprehensive commitment to human rights to heart, both have based their political outlook on a certain restricted picture of human rights, in which rights to property and one range of economic freedoms are given special emphasis. All these approaches take the central ethical requirement in human affairs to be respect for justice and construe justice as a matter of respect for rights.

LIBERTY RIGHTS AND WELFARE RIGHTS

Within the tradition of discussion of human rights there is considerable disagreement about the list of rights that justice comprises. In
general terms, the more right-wing proponents of the tradition assert
that there are only rights to liberty, hence that we have only the corresponding obligations of noninterference with others' liberty. Other
more left-wing proponents of human rights assert that there are also
certain "welfare" rights, hence certain positive obligations to help and
assist others. Those who think that all rights are liberty rights point to
supposed rights to life, liberty, and the pursuit of happiness, including
the right to unregulated economic activity. On this view it is unjust to
interfere with others' exercise of democratic political rights or capitalist
economic rights. Those who think that there are also "welfare" rights
point to supposed rights to food or basic health care or welfare payments. Since rights to unregulated economic activity are incompatible
with these, they reject unrestricted economic "rights."

These disagreements cannot be settled by appeal to documents. The
United Nations documents were a political compromise and resolutely
confer *all* sorts of rights. Proponents of liberty rights therefore think
that these documents advocate some spurious "rights," which are neither
part of nor compatible with justice. However, it is worth remember-
ing that this political compromise has in fact been accepted by nearly
all governments, who therefore have a prima facie institutionalized
treaty obligation to enact both liberty and "welfare" rights. This can be
an awkward point given that many people in the West tend to fault
the Eastern bloc countries for their violation of liberty rights but to
overlook the systematic denial in the West of certain economic and
welfare rights (such as a right to employment), which the international
documents endorse.

HUMAN RIGHTS AND HUMAN NEEDS

It matters hugely for the destitute which interpretation of rights is
acceptable and is used to guide policies and decisions. If human rights
are all liberty rights, then justice to the poor and hungry is achieved
by laissez-faire—provided we do not curtail their liberties, all is just.
For example, if a transnational suddenly closes its operations in a poor

country, so devastating the local economy, no injustice has been done. Or if the IMF requires severe economic retrenchment so that interest payments can be made, this is just, whatever hardships are inflicted. Or if commodity price shifts leave those who depend on a single cash crop—such as coffee, rubber, or palm oil—greatly impoverished, this is just, since no liberties will have been violated. If all human rights are liberty rights, then the needs of the poor are of no concern in working out what may be done without injustice.

But if some human rights are welfare or economic rights, justice will require that some of these needs be met. For example, if there are rights to food or to subsistence, then it is unjust not to meet these needs, and unjust not to regulate any economic activities that will prevent their being met. However, any claim that there are "welfare" rights is mere rhetoric unless the corresponding obligations are justified and allocated. And here the advocates of human rights are often evasive. It is a significant and not a trivial matter that there is no human obligations movement.

RIGHTS, LIBERTY, AND AUTONOMY

These disputes cannot be settled unless we can show which rights there are. The eighteenth-century pioneers often claimed that certain rights were self-evident. This claim now seems brazen, and in any case cannot settle disputes between the advocates of different sets of rights. The most impressive line of argument aimed at settling these disputes takes it that human rights constitute collectively the largest possible realization of human *liberty* or of human *autonomy*. However, even if we could justify assuming that either liberty or autonomy is the most fundamental of moral concerns, these two approaches lead to quite divergent claims about what rights there are. In addition, the advocates of each approach often disagree among themselves about exactly which rights there are.

Those who think that what is fundamental is *liberty*, understood as mere, "negative" noninterference by others, allow only for liberty rights. The idea of a consistent partitioning of human liberty would collapse as soon as we try to add rights to receive help or services, for the obligations that make these "welfare" rights a reality will be incompatible with various rights of action that basic liberty rights include. If we are obligated to provide food for all who need it, we cannot have unrestricted rights to do what we want with any food we have. At best certain societies may use their liberty rights to set up institutionalized rights to certain benefits—e.g., to education, welfare, health care—as has been done in most of the economically advanced nations. But an institutionalized right is not a natural or human right. The rights institutionalized in the developed countries have no bearing on the hunger and poverty in the Third World, where such rights have not been set up.

Those who think that it is autonomy rather than mere noninterference that is fundamental insist that there are some "welfare" rights to goods and services, such as a right to subsistence. For without adequate nutrition and shelter, human autonomy is destroyed, and liberty rights themselves would be pointless. But the advocates of subsistence rights have so far produced no convincing arguments to show who should bear obligations to feed others. Yet this is the question that matters most if "rights to subsistence" are to meet human needs.

RIGHTS AND CHARITY

Many advocates of human rights point out that we should not worry too much if rights theory neglects human needs. We should remember that justice is not the whole of morality, which can also require voluntarily given help. The needs of the poor can be met by charity. This thought appeals to many people. But it is an unconvincing one in the context of a theory of human rights. The rights perspective itself undercuts the status of charity, regarding it not as any sort of obligation, but as something that we are free to do or to omit, a matter of supererogation rather than of obligation. Such a view of help for the needy may be comfortable for the "haves" of this world, since it suggests that they go beyond duty and do something especially good if they help others at all. But it is depressing for the "have-nots" who cannot claim help of anybody, since it is not a matter of right. They can just hope help will happen; and usually what happens will be witheringly inadequate.

HUMAN AGENCY, RIGHTS, AND OBLIGATIONS

Justice need not be understood in the terms either of the human rights movement or of the utilitarian view of justice as just one contribution among others to human happiness. One way in which a different approach can be taken is by looking first at obligations rather than at rights. This has been a standard approach to ethical questions, both before and throughout the Christian tradition. Rights are eighteenth-century upstarts in moral discourse, as is the elevation of individual happiness to be the arbiter of moral judgment. Both these approaches see human beings in a somewhat passive way. This is plain enough in the utilitarian picture of human beings as loci of pains and pleasures. But it is less obvious that men and women are seen as passive in the theory of human rights. On the contrary, the turn to rights is sometimes defended on the grounds that it assigns a more active role to the powerless, who are to see themselves as wronged claimants rather than as the humble petitioners of more traditional, feudal pictures.

It is true that the human rights movement sees human beings *more* as agents than did feudal and utilitarian theories. But it still does not see them as fully autonomous: Claimants basically agitate for others to act. When we claim liberty rights or rights of authority, our first demand is that others act, so yielding us a space or opportunity in which we may or may not act. When we claim "welfare" rights, we need not picture ourselves as acting at all, but must see whoever bears the corresponding obligations as acting. By contrast, when we talk about obligations, we are speaking directly to those agents and agencies with the power to produce or refuse changes—the very audience that the rights perspective addresses only indirectly.

The French philosopher Simone Weil, writing during the Second World War, put the point this way in *The Need for Roots:*

> The notion of obligations comes before that of rights, which is subordinate and relative to the former. A right is not effectual by itself, but only in relation to the obligation to which it corresponds, the effective exercise of a right springing not from the individual who possesses it, but from other men who consider themselves as being under a certain obligation towards him.[2]

We do not know what a right amounts to until we know who has what obligation to do what for whom under which circumstances. When we try to be definite about rights, we always have to talk about obligations.

A fundamental difficulty with the rhetoric of rights is that it addresses only part—and the less powerful part—of the relevant audience. This rhetoric may have results if the poor are not wholly powerless; but where they are, claiming rights provides meager pickings. When the poor are powerless, it is the powerful who must be convinced that they have certain obligations—whether or not the beneficiaries claim the performance of these obligations as their right. The first concern of an ethical theory that focuses on action should be obligations, rather than rights.

WHAT OBLIGATIONS OF JUSTICE ARE THERE?

A theory of obligations can help deliberation about world hunger only if it is possible to show what obligations human beings have. The effort to show this without reliance on theological assumptions was made in the eighteenth century by the German philosopher Immanuel Kant. Recently Kant's work has often been seen as one more theory of human rights. This may be because he based his argument for human obligations on a construction analogous to that used in thinking of human rights as a partitioning of maximal human liberty or autonomy. For he asks what principles of action could consistently be shared by all agents. The root idea behind such a system of principles is that human obligations are obligations never to act in ways in which others cannot in principle also act. The fundamental principles of action must be shareable, rather than principles available only to a privileged few. Kant's method of determining the principles of obligation cannot be applied to the superficial detail of action: We evidently cannot eat the very grain another eats or have every one share the same roof. But we can try to see that the deep principles of our lives and of our institutions are shareable by all, and then work out the implications of these deep principles for particular situations.

If we use the Kantian construction, we can reach some interesting conclusions about human obligations. One obligation of justice that emerges from the construction is that of noncoercion. For a fundamental principle of coercion in some matter cannot be shared by all, since those who are coerced are prevented from acting, and so cannot share the principle of action. Coercion, we might say with Kant, is not *universalizable*.

This argument alone does not tell us what noncoercion requires in particular situations. Clearly it rules out many things that respect for liberty rights rules out. For example, a principle of noncoercion rules out killing, maiming, assaulting, and threatening others. This range of obligations not to coerce are as important for the well fed as for the hungry. But other aspects of noncoercion are peculiarly important for the hungry. Those who aim to act on a principle of noncoercion must take account of the fact that it is always rather easy to coerce those who are weak or vulnerable by activities that would not coerce richer or more powerful people.

Avoiding coercion is not just a matter of avoiding a short list of interferences in others' action, as rights approaches would have us imagine. Avoiding coercion means making sure that in our dealings with others we leave them room either to accept or to refuse the offers and suggestions made. This shows why an emphasis on obligations not to coerce is particularly telling in evaluating our dealings with the poor: They are so easily coerced. We can make them "offers they cannot refuse" with the greatest of ease. What might be genuine offers among equals, which others can accept or reject, can be threatening and unrefusable for the needy and vulnerable. They can be harmed in ways that threaten life by standard commercial or legal procedures, such as business deals that locate dangerous industrial processes in urban areas, or exact stiff political concessions for investment, or for what passes as aid, or that set harsh commercial conditions on "aid," such as mandating unneeded imports from a "donor" nation.

Arrangements of these sorts can coerce even when they use the outward forms of commercial bargaining and legality. These forms of bargaining are designed for use between agents of roughly equal power. They may not be enough to protect the powerless. Hence both individuals and agencies such as corporations and national governments (both of the North and of the South) and aid agencies must meet exacting standards if they are not to coerce the vulnerable in ordinary legal, diplomatic, and commercial dealings. Economic or material justice cannot be achieved without avoiding institutionalized as well as individual forms of coercion.

A second fundamental obligation of justice is that of avoiding deception. A principle of deception, too, is not universalizable, because victims of deception, like victims of coercion, are in principle precluded from sharing the perpetrator's principle of action, which is kept hidden from them. However, since the obligation of nondeception is relevant to all public and political life, and not solely for dealings that affect the poor, the hungry, and the vulnerable (although they are more easily deceived), I shall not explore its implications here.

OBLIGATIONS TO HELP: EMERGENCY RELIEF, DEVELOPMENT, AND RESPECT

In a rights framework, the whole of our moral obligations are brought under the heading of justice. But an obligations approach of the Kantian type also justifies obligations that are not obligations of justice and whose performance cannot be claimed as rights. Some types of action cannot be done for all others, so they cannot be a universal obligation or have corresponding rights. Yet they also are not contingent on any special relationship, so they cannot be a matter of special, institutionalized obligation. Yet they can be a matter of obligation. A theory of obligation, unlike a theory of rights, can allow for "imperfect" obligations, which are not allocated to specified recipients and so cannot be claimed.

This provides a further way in which an appreciation of need can enter into a theory of human obligations. We know that others in need are vulnerable and not self-sufficient. It follows that, even if they are not coerced, they may be unable to act, and so unable to become or remain autonomous agents who could act on principles that can be universally shared. Hence, if our fundamental commitment is to treat others as agents who could share the same principles that we act on, then we must be committed equally to strategies and policies that enable them to become and to remain agents. If we do anything less, we do not view others as doers like ourselves. However, nobody and no agent can do everything to sustain the autonomy of all others. Hence obligations to help are not and cannot be obligations to meet all needs; but they can be obligations not to base our lives on principles that are indifferent to or neglectful of others' need and what it actually takes to sustain their agency. In particular situations such "imperfect" obligations may require specific and arduous action. The fact that we cannot help everyone only shows that we have no obligation to help everyone, and not that we have no obligation to help anyone.

If we are not indifferent or neglectful of the requirements for sustaining others' autonomy we will, I suggest, find ourselves committed not only to justice but to various further principles in our action toward the poor and vulnerable. First we will be committed to material help that sustains agency, by helping people over the threshold of poverty below which possibilities for autonomous action are absent or meager. Since sustained and systematic help is needed if vulnerability and dependence are not to recur endlessly, this implies a commitment to development policies as well as to emergency food aid.

Unreliable aid does not secure autonomy. But nor, of course, can withholding food aid in emergencies secure autonomy. Since human needs are recurrent, food aid is not enough. Food is eaten and is gone; help can secure others' agency only if it constructs social and economic institutions that can meet human needs on a sustained basis. This means that help to the poorest and most vulnerable must seek sustainable production to make sure that when a given cycle of consumption is past, more is in the pipeline. Development of the relevant sort is evidently not only an economic matter, it also includes the development of human skills by appropriate education and institutional changes that help poor and vulnerable people to gain some control over their lives.

Since the basis of these obligations to help is the claim that principles of action must be shareable by all, the pursuit of development must not itself reduce or damage others' agency. It must not fail to respect those who are helped. Their desires and views must be sought, and their participation respected. Agency is not fostered if the poor experience "donor" agencies as new oppressors. Others' autonomy is not sustained if they are left feeling that they have been the victims of good works.

CONCLUSIONS AND AFTERTHOUGHTS

The theory of obligations just sketched is surprisingly familiar to most of us. It is not distant from pictures of human obligation that we find in the Christian tradition, and in the idiom of much of our social life. And it chimes closely with other traditions, too. Many of the voluntary aid agencies are fond of quoting a Chinese proverb that runs: Give a man a fish and you feed him for a day; teach him to fish and you feed him for life. President Reagan too has quoted this saying.

Although the position is traditional and familiar, the favored ethical theories of today do not endorse it. Utilitarian perspectives endorse the pursuit of happiness without specific concern to meet needs; human rights perspectives do not vindicate obligations to help those in need. It therefore seems appropriate to end with some polemical questions rather than a feeling of reassurance. How and why have we allowed uncertain images of maximal happiness and self-centered visions of claiming human rights to distort our understanding of central ethical notions such as justice, beneficence, and respect for human agents? Why have so many people been sure that our obligations to others are a matter of not interfering in their concern—of doing. . . nothing?

If human obligations are based on the requirements for respecting and securing one another's agency, then we may find another of Simone Weil's remarks to the point:

> The obligation is only performed if the respect is effectively expressed in a real, not a fictitious, way; and this can only be done through the medium of Man's earthly needs. . . . On this point, the human conscience has never varied. Thousands of years ago, the Egyptians believed that no soul could justify itself after death unless it could say, "I have never let anyone suffer from hunger." All Christians know they are liable to hear Christ say to them one day, "I was an hungered, and ye gave me no meat." Every one looks on progress as being, in the first place, a transition to a state of human society in which people will not suffer from hunger.[3]

To make that transition is indeed no longer a matter of feeding the beggar at the gate. Modern opportunities are broader and demand political as well as—perhaps more than—merely individual action. Of course, no individual can do everything. But this will daunt only those who are riveted by an exclusively individual conception of human endeavor and success. If we remember that many human activities and successes are not individual, we need not be daunted. We can then act in the knowledge that no individual and no institution is prevented from making those decisions within its power in ways that help fulfill rather than spurn obligations to the hungry.

NOTES

1. Jeremy Bentham, *Introduction to the Principles of Morals and of Legislation* (New York: Hafner Publishing Co., 1948), p. 29.

2. Simone Weil, *The Need for Roots* (New York: Harper & Row, 1952), p. 3.

3. Ibid., p. 6.

9. AMARTYA SEN

In "The Concept of Development," Amartya Sen lays out the fundamental features of development economics. The values at stake in development, while clearly intertwined with economics in general, have a unique domain. Simply measuring the expansion of national wealth tells one little about changes in the quality of life of individual citizens. As such, the concept of development comprises much more than the growth of a country's gross national product. Sen argues that in order to understand quality of life, and hence to measure and promote development, one needs to examine individuals' "functionings" and "capabilities." A person's functioning is her ability to do and to be certain important things, such as eating enough or being literate. But simply doing and being is not a sufficiently rich description of human life—freedom to choose is a critical component. Hence capabilities, alternative sets of functionings available to individuals, are necessary to explain human welfare.

The Concept of Development

First published in Handbook of Development Economics, *Volume I, ed. Hollis Chenery and T. N. Srinivasan (Amsterdam: Elsevier Science Publishers B. V., 1988), 9–26.*

1. THE BACKGROUND

"The French grow too fast," wrote Sir William Petty in 1676. Whether or not this was in fact the first recorded expression of what is clearly a traditional English obsession, it was certainly a part of one of the earliest discussions of development economics. Petty was concerned not merely with the growth of numbers and of incomes, but he also took a broad view of development problems, including concern with the exact content of the standard of living. Part of his statistical analysis was meant "to show" that "the King's subjects are not in so bad a condition as discontented Men would make them." While Petty had estimated national income by using both the "income method" and the "expenditure method," he had also gone on to judge the conditions of people in a broad enough way to include "the Common Safety" and "each Man's particular Happiness."[1]

Petty is regarded, with justice, as one of the founders of modern economics, and specifically a pioneer of quantitative economics.[2] He was certainly also a founder of development economics. Indeed, in the early contributions to economics, development economics can hardly be separated out from the rest of economics, since so much of economics was, in fact, concerned with problems of economic development. This applies not only to Petty's writings, but also to those of the other pioneers of modern economics, including Gregory King, Francois Quesnay, Antoine Lavoisier, Joseph Louis Lagrange, and even Adam Smith. *An Inquiry into the Nature and Causes of the Wealth of Nations* was, in fact, also an inquiry into the basic issues of development economics.

The fact that in the early writings in economics there was this noticeable congruence of development economics and economics in general is a matter of some interest, especially in the context of investigating the nature of "the concept of development." Interest in development problems has, traditionally, provided one of the deepest *motivations* for the pursuit of economics in general, and this broad basis of development economics has to be borne in mind when investigating the details of the concept of development. Having started off, rightly, with an ell, development economics can scarcely settle for an inch.

It is not hard to see why the concept of development is so essential to economics in general. Economic problems do, of course, involve logistic issues, and a lot of it is undoubtedly "engineering" of one kind or another. On the other hand, the success of all this has to be judged ultimately in terms of what it does to the lives of human beings. The enhancement of living conditions must clearly be an essential—if not *the* essential—object of the entire economic exercise, and that enhancement is an integral part of the concept of development. Even though the logistic and engineering problems involved in enhancing living conditions in the poor, developing countries might well be very different from those in the rich, developed ones, there is much in common in the respective exercises on the two sides of the divide [on this see Bauer (1971)].

Sometimes development economists have been rather protective of their own domain, insisting on separating development economics from the rest of economics. While the underlying motivation behind this effort is easy to understand, it is important not to make too much of the divide, nor to confuse separateness with independence. Tools of standard economics may have much fruitful use in development economics as well, even when the exact problems addressed happen to be quite specialized. It is, however, arguable that for one reason or another, a good deal of standard economics has tended to move away from broad issues of poverty, misery, and well-being, and from the fulfilment of basic needs and enhancing the quality of life. Development economists have felt it necessary to emphasize and justify their involvement with these—rather "old-fashioned"—problems, even though the relevance of these problems is by no means confined to development economics. There are also institutional differences that separate out the logistic issues in developing countries from those of developed ones, in the pursuit of economic development and the enhancement of living conditions.

Certainly, the systematic differences in institutional features is a matter of great moment in arriving at policies and deriving practical lessons regarding what is to be done. But the first issue—the emphasis on development objectives—is not a matter only for development economics as such, but of importance for economics in general [see Hirschman (1970)]. In this respect, too, insisting on a sharp division between development economics and other types of economics would be rather counterproductive. Development economics, it can be argued, has to be concerned not only with protecting its "own" territory, but also with keeping alive the foundational motivation of the subject of economics in general. The literature on the "concept of development"—whether explicitly put forward or discussed by implication—has to be examined in this broad perspective related to economics in general, rather than only in terms of "development economics" narrowly defined.

2. PRODUCTION, GROWTH, AND DEVELOPMENT

The close link between economic development and economic growth is simultaneously a matter of importance as well as a source of considerable confusion. There can scarcely be any doubt that, given other things, an expansion of opulence must make a contribution to the living conditions of the people in question. It was, therefore, entirely natural that the early writings in development economics, when it emerged as a subject on its own after the Second World War, concentrated to a great extent on ways of achieving economic growth, and in particular increasing the gross national product (GNP) and total employment [see Rosenstein-Rodan (1943), Mandelbaum (1945), Dobb (1951), Datta (1952), Singer (1952), Nurkse (1953), Dasgupta (1954), Lewis (1955), Baran (1957), Hirschman (1958)]. The process of economic development cannot abstract from expanding the supply of food, clothing, housing, medical services, educational facilities, etc., and from transforming the productive structure of the economy, and these important and crucial changes are undoubtedly matters of economic growth.

The importance of "growth" must depend on the nature of the variable the expansion of which is considered and seen as "growth." The crucial issue, therefore, is not the time-dimensional focus of growth, but the salience and reach of GNP and related variables on which usual measures of growth concentrate. The relation between GNP and living conditions is far from simple.[3] To illustrate the problem, figures for GNP per head and life expectancy at birth in 1984 are given in Table 1.1 for five different countries, namely, China, Sri Lanka, Brazil, Mexico, and South Africa. South Africa, with about seven times the GNP per head of China and Sri Lanka, has a substantially lower expectation of life than the latter countries. Similarly, Brazil and Mexico, also with many times the income of China and Sri Lanka, have achieved considerably less in longevity than these two much poorer countries. To point to this contrast is not, of course, the same thing as drawing an immediate policy conclusion as to exactly what should be done, but the nature of the contrast has to be borne in mind in refusing to identify economic development with mere economic growth. Even though an expansion of GNP, *given other things*, should enhance the living conditions of people, and will typically expand the life expectancy figures of that country, there are many other variables that also influence the living conditions, and the concept of development cannot ignore the role of these other variables.

TABLE 1.1
GNP and Life Expectancy

	GNP per head, 1984 (U.S. Dollars)	Life expectancy at birth, 1984 (years)
China	310	69
Sri Lanka	360	70
Brazil	1,720	64
Mexico	2,040	66
South Africa	2,340	54

Source: World Bank (1986).

Life expectancy is, of course, a very limited measure of what has been called "the quality of life." Indeed, in terms of what it directly measures, life expectancy is more an index of the "quantity" of life rather than of its quality. But the forces that lead to mortality, such as morbidity, ill health, hunger, etc., also tend to make the living conditions of the people more painful, precarious, and unfulfilling, so that life expectancy may, to some extent, serve as a proxy for other variables of importance as well. Furthermore, if we shift our attention from life expectancy to these other important variables, the relationship with GNP per head does not become any more immediate. Indeed, some of the variables related to living conditions, e.g., the prevalence of crime and violence, may sometimes have even a perverse relationship with average material prosperity.

This is a problem that applies not only to the poor, developing countries, but also to the richer ones. In fact, various studies of perception of welfare done in Western Europe have suggested a rather limited role of real income in self-assessment of personal welfare [see van Praag (1978), Allardt (1981), van Herwaarden and Kapteyn (1981), Erikson, Hansen, Ringen, and Uusitalo (1986)]. Reliance of self-assessment based on questionnaire information does, of course, have some problematic features also, but nevertheless there is enough evidence here to question the rather straightforward connection between material prosperity and welfare that is sometimes taken for granted in standard economic analysis.

In drawing a distinction between development and growth, a number of different sources of contrast have to be clearly distinguished from each other. First of all, insofar as economic growth is concerned only with GNP per head, it leaves out the question of the *distribution* of that GNP among the population. It is, of course, possible for a country to have an expansion of GNP per head while its distribution becomes more unequal, possibly even the poorest groups going down absolutely in terms of their own real incomes. Noting this type of possibility does not question the relevance of income considerations as such, but argues against taking only an aggregated view of incomes. Undoubtedly, some of the cases in which achievements in living conditions fall far behind what might be expected on the basis of average per capita GNP (e.g., in South Africa, and to a lesser extent in Brazil and Mexico, as reflected in Table 1.1) relate closely to the distributional question. Indeed, the contrast can be brought out even more sharply by looking also at the distribution of life expectancy (and of mortality and morbidity rates) over the population (e.g., between the racial and class groups in South Africa, and class and regional categories in Brazil and Mexico).

A second source of difference between growth and development relates to the question of *externality* and *nonmarketability*. The GNP captures only those means of well-being that happen to be transacted in the market, and this leaves out benefits and costs that do not have a price tag attached to them. Even when nonmarketed goods are included (e.g., peasant outputs consumed at home), the evaluation is usually restricted to those goods that have a market and for which market prices can be easily traced.[4] The importance of what is left out has become increasingly recognized, as awareness of the contribution of the environment and natural resources to our well-being has grown [see Dasgupta and Heal (1979), Dasgupta (1982)]. The argument can be applied to the social environment as well as to the physical one [see Hirschman (1958, 1970)].

Third, even when markets do exist, the valuation of commodities in the GNP will reflect the *biases* that the markets may have. There are important problems in dealing with different relative prices in different parts of the world. As has been shown by Usher (1968, 1976) and others, this can make quite a substantial quantitative difference. Even for a given economy, the relative importance that is attached to one commodity compared with another may be distorted vis-a-vis what might be achieved under perfectly competitive conditions if the market operations happen to be institutionally "imperfect," or if equilibrium outcomes do not prevail. There is an extensive welfare-economic literature on this, and the connection of that range of issues with the concept of development is obvious enough.

Fourth, the real income enjoyed by a person in a given year reflects at best the extent of well-being enjoyed by that person at that period of time. However, in assessing what kind of a life the person has succeeded in living, we have to take a more *integral* view of that person's life. The issues to be considered include interdependences over time [e.g., interperiod complementarities emphasized by Hicks (1965) among others], as well as the more elementary question of the *length* of that life. It is easy to construct two scenarios in which the time series of *per capita* GNP as well as *aggregate* GNP (and, of course, the population size) happen to be exactly the same in the two cases (period by period), but in one society people live twice as long as those in the other. There are difficult evaluative problems in judging what the "trade-off" should be between larger number, on the one hand, and longer life, on the other, but no matter in which direction one argues, there is an issue here of great importance to the assessment of development that is completely obscured by the GNP information. Even if GNP did everything it is expected to do (and there are very strong reasons for doubting this possibility), even then the information provided by GNP must remain fundamentally inadequate for the concept of development.

Finally, it must be noted that GNP is, in fact, a measure of the amount of the *means* of well-being that people have, and it does not tell us what the people involved are succeeding in getting out of these means, given their ends. To take a crude example, two persons with different metabolic rates and consuming the same amount of food will quite possibly achieve rather different levels of nourishment. Insofar as being well nourished is an important end, their actual achievements will be different, despite the congruence of their command over the *means* of achieving nourishment. As it happens, "poverty lines" have typically been defined in developing countries in the light of the "requirements" of some basic commodities, in particular food, and the interpersonal as well as the intrapersonal variability in the relationship between food and nourishment have been, in this context, a major problem to deal with.[5]

Ultimately, the assessment of development achieved cannot be a matter only of quantification of the *means* of that achievement. The concept of development has to take note of the actual achievements themselves. The assessment of development has to go well beyond GNP information, *even when* the other difficulties referred to earlier (such as distributional variation, presence of externalities and nonmarketabilities, imperfect price mechanisms, etc.) were somehow overcome.

3. CHARACTERISTICS, FUNCTIONINGS, AND LIVING

Insofar as development is concerned with the achievement of a better life, the focus of development analysis has to include the nature of the life that people succeed in living. This incorporates, of course, the *length* of the life itself, and thus life expectancy data have an immediate relevance to the living standard and through that to the concept of development. But the nature of the life that people succeed in living in each period is also a matter of importance. People value their ability to do certain things and to achieve certain types of beings (such as being well nourished, being free from avoidable morbidity, being able to move about as desired, and so on). These "doings" and "beings" may be generically called "functionings" of a person.

The well-being of a person can be seen as an evaluation of the functionings achieved by that person. This approach has been implicitly used by Adam Smith (1776) and Karl Marx (1844) in particular, and more recently in the literature on "the quality of life" [see, for example, Morris (1979), Streeten (1981)].[6] It can be more explicitly developed, conceptually defended, and empirically applied [on this see Sen (1980, 1985a)]. The functioning achievements are, of course, causally related to commodity possession and use, and thus the constituent elements of the GNP do enter the *determination* of functioning achievements. Indeed, these elements are the means of which the functionings are the ends—a point of view clearly presented by Aristotle in *Nicomachean Ethics* and *Politics*.

In recent departures in consumer theory, developed by Gorman (1956, 1976) and Lancaster (1966, 1971), commodities are viewed in terms of their characteristics. This is clearly a move in the right direction as far as well-being is concerned, since the functionings achieved by a person relate to the characteristics of the commodities used. On the other hand, no index of characteristics as such could possibly serve as an indicator of the achievements of a person, since the conversion of characteristics into functionings can and does vary from person to person. Characteristics of commodities are impersonal in a way that functionings cannot be, since the latter are features of *persons*, whereas the former are features of *commodities*. The relationships between commodities, characteristics, and functionings, and the sources of variations in their interconnections, have been discussed elsewhere [see Sen (1980, 1985a, 1985b)].

The achievement of functionings depends not only on the commodities owned by the person in question, but also on the availability of public goods, and the possibility of using private goods freely provided by the state. Such achievements as being healthy, being well nourished, being literate, etc., would depend naturally also on the public provisions of health services, medical facilities, educational arrangements, and so on. In recognizing this, there is no need yet to enter into the debate, which is important but need not be pursued here, as to whether provision by the state is a cost-effective way of enhancing the relevant functionings involved. That debate about development strategy will involve logistic and engineering issues, which require careful assessment. What is being pointed out here is the importance of judging development in terms of *functionings achieved*, and of seeing in that light the availability and use of the *means* to those functionings (in the form of possession of commodities, availability of public goods, and so on).

4. FREEDOM AND CAPABILITY

One of the functionings that may be thought to be particularly important in assessing the nature of development is the freedom to choose. Sometimes this concept is used in a rather narrow and limited way, so that the *actual* freedom to choose is not assessed, but instead the focus is on whether there are *restraints* imposed by others that hinder the actual freedom. That "negative" perspective, much pursued in the libertarian literature, does have, of course, philosophical standing of its own [see Hayek (1960), Berlin (1969), Nozick (1974)]. However, what is important to recognize in the present context is the fact that the "negative" emphasis on the absence of restraint is part of a moral approach that does not judge the goodness of a society in terms of the actual qualities of life *achieved* by the members of the society, and concentrates instead on the correctness of the *processes* through which these and other achievements come about. It is possible to debate whether the particular insistence on *processes* that do not involve such restraint is, in fact, as convincing as it clearly is to some exponents of this point of view. But in the present context, we need not enter into that large and important debate. It is sufficient here to note that as far as the living standards of the people are concerned, there is no escape from focusing on *achievements*, and processes come into all this mainly as means to and antecedents of those achievements, rather than being *independently* valuable in this context.

However, the *positive* freedom to be able to choose is, in fact, an important functioning on its own rights. Two persons who have identical achievements of *other* functionings may not still be seen as enjoying the same level of well-being if one of the two has no option to choose any other bundle of functionings, whereas the second person has significant options. Being able to freely choose to lead a particular life may be a point of a richer description of the life we lead, including the choices we are able to make [on this perspective, see Sen (1985a)].

A person's capability can be seen as the set of alternative functioning n-tuples any one of which the person can choose. One way of introducing the importance of freedom in the determination of well-being is to see well-being as a function not only of the actual functioning achievement, but also of the capability set from which that n-tuple of functionings is chosen. In this way of formally characterizing the problem, the list of functionings need not include "choosing" as such, but the value of choosing will be reflected in the evaluation by making that evaluation depend both on the chosen n-tuple of functionings, *and* on the nature and the range of the capability set itself.

There are difficult analytical problems involved in the evaluation of a set, in the light of the freedom it offers [on this see Koopmans (1964),

Kreps (1979), Sen (1985b)]. But insofar as the assessment of the quality of life and of development achievements involves these considerations, it is important not to lose sight of this perspective, even though it may not be immediately possible to make extensive use of this approach in actual empirical exercises.

A different way of looking at this problem involves incorporating the freedom to choose in the nature of the functionings themselves by defining them in a "refined" way [see Sen (1985a)]. Choosing to do x when one could have chosen any member of a set S, can be defined as a "refined functioning" x/S. The point can be brought out by considering the functioning of "fasting." When a person fasts he is clearly starving, but the nature of that functioning includes the choice *not* to so starve. A person who has no option but to starve (because, say, of his extreme poverty) cannot be said to be fasting. In assessing the achievements of the persons and of the society, the distinction between fasting and willy-nilly starving may well be very important. The route of "refined functionings," taking note of substantive exercise of choice, provides one particular way of incorporating the aspect of freedom in the assessment of functionings.

5. WEIGHTS AND RANKINGS

It should be clear that the perspective of functionings and capabilities specifies a *space* in which evaluation is to take place, rather than propos-ing one particular formula for evaluation. The exercise has to begin with an identification of valuable functionings. In the context of economic development, there might well be considerable agreement as to what functionings are valuable, even though there might be disagreement on the *relative* values to be attached to the different functionings. When an agreed list has been arrived at, the approach of "dominance" provides a *minimal* partial order on that space (in terms of greater achievement in *every* respect).

To go further than this will require more articulate evaluation functions. But these evaluations need not be based on a unique set of "indifference curves." The relative values may be specified as belonging to particular ranges, and corresponding to such specification of ranges, the overall ranking may be a partial order more extensive than the minimal dominance order but probably well short of a complete ordering. As the ranges of relative values are narrowed, the partial ordering will be extended. The mathematical technology involved in such evaluation (based on "intersection partial orderings") has been extensively used in other contexts [see, for example, Sen (1970), Blackorby (1975), Fine (1975), Basu (1979)]. The important thing to note here is that the problem of evaluation need not be seen in an all-or-nothing way. It is possible to extend the partial order by narrowing the ranges of weights, and how far one can go on the basis of agreement on evaluation will depend contingently on the nature of the exercise in question.

Even the specification of the space of functionings and capabilities does, however, have considerable cutting power. Achievements of real income and opulence may differ quite substantially from that of functionings and capabilities. To give just one example, in a comparison of the states in India, Kerala always figures as one of the poorest, in terms of GNP per head. On the other hand, in terms of many of the more important functionings, including living long, being educated, etc., Kerala does better than any other Indian state. Given this contrast, it is interesting to ask whether Kerala should be seen as having *more* achievement *or* rather *less* than the other Indian states. This relates to a question of considerable importance to the formulation of the concept of development. The argument for placing Kerala at the high end, rather than the low end, turns on the evaluation of functionings and capabilities as the right approach to development.

A crude assessment of functionings and capabilities in terms only of a few indicators like longevity, literacy, etc., will, of course, be inadequate and have to be revised and extended, but the exercise can be systematically done if and only if the concept of development is seen in terms of ends rather than means. As it happens, use of information regarding *morbidity* detracts somewhat from Kerala's high record, since the extent of illness seems to be rather large in Kerala, in comparison with some other Indian states, even after taking note of the greater "awareness" of health conditions in a population that is more educated and better served by public health services [on this see Panikar and Soman (1984), Kumar (1987)]. The adoption of the perspective of functionings and capabilities will call for a great deal of empirical as well as theoretical work being done within that general format.

As was argued earlier, that format is, of course, an old one in economics, even though the focus on opulence on the one hand and utility on the other has tended to deflect attention from that fundamental concern. Aside from discussions by Aristotle, Smith, and Marx, to which reference was made earlier, it should be mentioned that ad hoc uses of this perspective can be found extensively in the economic literature. In many planning exercises, the specification of objectives has included a clear recognition of the importance of certain functionings, e.g., in the specification of a "minimum level of living" [see Pant (1962)]. The literature on development indicators has also brought in some of these functionings, along with many other types of variables [see, for example, Adelman and Morris (1973), Adelman (1975), Kakwani (1981), Streeten (1981)].

The literature on "basic needs" also relates to this question, since the specification of basic needs of commodities has to be related to the recognition of their role in the achievement of functionings. Even though the *space* in which the basic needs have typically been specified has been that of commodities rather than of functionings and capabilities, the motivation clearly does relate to attaching importance to the latter [see, for example, Streeten (1981), and Streeten et al. (1981)].

The literature on basic needs has been growing rapidly in the recent years, but clear discussions of this question can be found even in Pigou's classic book *Economics of Welfare* (1952). Of course, Pigou related his focus on the command over a minimal basket of commodities to the utilitarian perspective, whereas in the modern literature quite often the foundational features have not been specified. It is arguable that these foundational questions are ultimately quite important for the concept of development, and it is precisely in that context that the capability approach provides a different strategy of assessment, more clearly geared to the evaluation of living as such rather than merely of the happiness generated by that living (as in the utilitarian approach). This is not the occasion to pursue the philosophical differences further [I have tried to do this elsewhere; Sen (1985a)], but there is no escape from recognizing the importance of this foundational question underlying the concept of development.

6. VALUES, INSTRUMENTS, AND OBJECTS

One of the difficulties in adequately characterizing the concept of development arises from the essential role of evaluation in that concept. What is or is not regarded as a case of "development" depends inescapably on the notion of what things are valuable to promote.[7] The dependence of the concept of development on evaluation becomes a problem to the extent that (1) the valuation functions accepted by different people differ from each other, and (2) the process of change involved in development alters the valuations of the people involved. These two problems may be called respectively "value-heterogeneity" and "value-endogeneity".

The problem of value-heterogeneity was already addressed earlier in the context of valuations of functionings and capabilities. It was pointed out that even when there are disagreements on the relative values to be attached to different functionings and capabilities, it is still possible to get uncontroversial partial orderings, based minimally on "dominance," but more extensively on "intersections" of the class of acceptable valuation functions. It is, of course, a matter of substantive normative analysis to argue in favor of some valuation functions against others, and insofar as the ranges of disagreement could be reduced through this means, the scope and reach of "intersection partial orderings" can be correspondingly enhanced.

Much of traditional development economics has proceeded on the basis of implicitly assuming a fairly large intersection of valuations related to objects of development. Even though the original discussions of economic development had tended to concentrate on the GNP and real income as such, the evaluation underlying that approach was implicitly based on assuming a widespread agreement on the *ends* to which real income and opulence are *means*. The shift in the focus of attention to basic needs, quality of life, and functionings and capabilities in general would not change the assumed agreement on the underlying basis of development analysis. The problem of value-heterogeneity is undoubtedly serious, but it is by no means absurd to think that the actual extent of agreement is indeed quite large. Most of the debates on development policy have tended to concentrate on the relationship between policy instruments and *agreed* ends (accepted in the analysis of policy).

It is, however, possible that a more explicit characterization of well-being and of people's freedom to achieve what they would value achieving will increase the demand for data and information in the conceptualization of development. For example, the scope for using more demographic and health-related information is certainly great in assessing the real achievements of development, and recent works dealing with the past as well as the present have outlined the necessity of seeking this type of information, neglected in traditional development analysis.[8]

It is possible that once these informational needs are recognized, there might again emerge a fair degree of consensus on what is to be valued and how. On the other hand, it is also possible that there might be much disagreement regarding the respective importance of different aspects of well-being. Some of these differences might involve scientific argumentation as to the precise role of different variables in human functioning. For example, whether an expansion of body size related to the process of economic development is an achievement of importance can be disputed in terms of the alleged presence or absence of relations between body size and performance. The conversion of nutrients into body characteristics *and* the role of body characteristics in achieving valuable functionings both call for close scrutiny.[9]

Other disputes may turn not on factual relations, but on what is to be regarded as an important part of a valuable life and how valuable it is. It would be idle to pretend that disputes on the relative importance of different types of functionings can be fully resolved on the basis of scientific argument alone. It is, therefore, particularly important to build into the concept of development the possibility of persistent incompleteness in ranking. Seeing the agreed ranking as the intersection of the partly divergent valuation functions must, of necessity, entail this.

The value-endogeneity problem raises issues of a somewhat different kind from those raised by value-heterogeneity. With value-heterogeneity the intersection partial ordering may have to be silent on some comparisons, but insofar as judgments are possible, they can be made on the basis of a *given* valuation function (whether or not complete). Value-endogeneity, on the other hand, raises what is, in some ways, a deeper problem, to wit, the *dependence* of the valuation function on the thing that is being valued. The process of development may bring about changes in what is regarded as valuable and what weights are attached to these objects. There are complex philosophical issues involved in judging changed conditions, when those changes bring about alterations in the values attached to these conditions.[10]

However, in this problem too there is a possibility of using an "intersection" technique. A change may be judged to be an improvement if it is superior *both* in terms of the antecedent values *and* subsequent values, i.e., prospectively better than the available alternatives and also retrospectively better than the rejected alternatives. In this case, there may be at least a pragmatic argument in favor of regarding this to be a genuine improvement, even though a purist might doubt whether such judgments can at all be taken as definitive when they are *generally* volatile (even though not, as it happens, in a way that affects the judgment of *this particular* change). Even this pragmatic justification will not obtain if the judgments based on antecedent values differ on the particular issue under discussion from those based on subsequent ones. It is possible for a change to be regarded as worse in terms of the earlier values, but better in terms of valuations made after the event.

In the more philosophical literature, the case for seeing valuations as having a certain measure of objectivity has increasingly gained ground compared with the situation that obtained some decades ago.[11] The "objectivist" position is, in fact, in line with very old traditions in ethics and political economy (going back at least to Aristotle), even though it was extremely unfashionable at the time development economics emerged as a subject, when the dominant schools of methodology were "positivism" of various types. The "objectivist" position would tend to support the possibility of resolving the conflicts involved in intertemporal changes in values by rational assessment.

These foundational issues will not be pursued further here. It is sufficient for the present purpose to note that no matter what view is taken of the nature of valuation, the practical problems of making judgment in the situation of value-heterogeneity and value-endogeneity must be enormous. Even if these differences could in principle be resolved through rational assessment, the possibility of actually resolving these differences in practice may be severely limited. Given that fact, the necessity of settling for partial orders in response to value-endogeneity as well as value-heterogeneity is, to some extent, inescapable.

Explicitly facing these problems of valuation has some advantages that should be emphasized. First, separating out relatively uncontroversial judgments from the controversial ones related to value-heterogeneity and value-endogeneity helps to clarify what can be asserted with some confidence, and what can be said only with much greater hesitation. A lot of the debates on policy-making in the context of economic development relates to valuation problems that are not unduly problematic. Whether state intervention or reliance on the market may be better means of enhancing living conditions is, of course, both important and controversial, but the controversy has typically centered, rightly, on the relationship between means and achievements rather than on differences in valuation. By explicitly facing the sources of the difficulties in valuation, it is possible to give those debates a deeper foundation without compromising the broad motivation underlying development economics.

Second, in some parts of the development literature, values have been treated as if they are simply *instrumental* to economic development, rather than the ultimate basis of judging the nature of development itself. For example, encouraging the valuation of profits and that of enterprise has often been seen as good *means* of development. Certainly, in terms of the dependence of economic growth on particular motivations, these propositions can be helpfully presented and assessed. On the other hand, it is also important to recognize that values are not *just* instruments, but also views about what should or should not be promoted. This dual role of values—both important and neither sacrificable—was recognized clearly enough by pioneers of modern economics, including Adam Smith (1776, 1790) and Karl Marx (1844, 1875). The foundational role of values can be neglected in favor of an instrumental view only by trivializing the basis of the concept of development.

7. CONCLUSION

The concept of development is by no means unproblematic. The different problems underlying the concept have become clearer over the years on the basis of conceptual discussions as well as from insights emerging from empirical work. Insofar as these problems have become clearer, something of substance has in fact been achieved, and the demise of the brashness that characterized the initiation of development economics need not be seen entirely as a loss. A clearer recognition of the difficulties and problems is certainly a step in the direction of enhancing our ability to tackle them.

Work on valuational problems will undoubtedly continue. Meanwhile, the agreed valuations in the form of emphasizing the importance of certain basic achievements in life make it possible for us to pursue practical debates on policy and action on the basis of an acceptable valuational foundation. Since many of these debates relate to matters of life and death, well-being and illness, happiness and misery, freedom and vulnerability, the underlying objectives are perspicuous enough and command broad agreement. Work on development economics need not await a complete "solution" of the concept of development.

NOTES

For helpful discussions and comments, I am most grateful to Hollis Chenery, T. N. Srinivasan, and Paul Streeten.

1. *Political Arithmetick*, in which these passages occur, was written by Petty around 1676, but it was published posthumously in 1691. The text could be found in Hull (1899, vol. I). The passages referred to can be found on pages 241–42, 311.

2. It may be remembered that it was Petty, the anatomist and musicologist, turned economist, who had insisted at the Royal Society that in discussions in the society, "no word might be used but what marks either number, weight, or measure" [Hull (1899, vol. I, p. lxiv)]. Those who complain about the "recent craze" for mathematical economics might have to put up with the fact that the recent times began a long time ago.

3. For discussions on this, see Adelman and Morris (1973), Sen (1973), Adelman (1975), Grant (1978), Morris (1979), Kakwani (1981), Streeten (1981), Streeten et al. (1981), Stewart (1985), Anand and Harris (1986).

4. Even when such market prices exist, reflecting the balance of actual demand and supply, the proper valuation of the nontraded units of tradeable variables may be far from easy. On the problem of including the value of leisure and leisure time expended at home, in the light of wage rates, see Nordhaus and Tobin (1972).

5. For arguments on different sides of this debate, see Bardhan (1974), Sukhatme (1977), Srinivasan (1982), Lipton (1983), Gopalan (1983), Dasgupta and Ray (1986), Kakwani (1986), Osmani (1987).

6. See also Sen (1973, 1985b), Adelman (1975), Scanlon (1975), Gwatkin,

Wilcox, and Wray (1980), Floud and Wachter (1982), Fogel, Engerman, and Trussell (1982), Gopalan (1983), Panikar and Soman (1984), UNICEF (1986), Chen (1986), Williams (1987).

7. On this general question, see Marglin and Marglin (1986).

8. See, in particular, Sen (1973, 1985b), Floud and Wachter (1982), Fogel, Engerman, and Trussell (1982), Gopalan (1983), Panikar and Soman (1984), UNICEF (1986), Williams (1987).

9. For different views on this subject, see, for example, Sukhatme (1977), Srinivasan (1982), Gopalan (1983), Fogel (1986), Dasgupta and Ray (1986), Kakwani (1986), Osmani (1987).

10. For an interesting discussion of this question, see Elster (1979, 1983). Some similar issues are raised in consumer theory when tastes are taken as endogenous [see, for example, von Weizsacker (1971), Pollak (1978)]. See also Hirschman (1970).

11. See in particular McDowell (1981), Nagel (1980, 1986), Hurley (1985), Wiggins (1985).

REFERENCES

Adelman, I. (1975) Development Economics—A Reassessment of Goals. *American Economic Review, Papers and Proceedings*, 65.

Adelman, I., and C. T. Morris (1973) *Economic Growth and Social Equity in Developing Countries*. Stanford: Stanford University Press.

Allardt, E. (1981) Experiences from the Comparative Scandinavian Welfare Study, with a Bibliography of the Project, *European Journal of Political Research*, 9.

Anand, S., and C. Harris (1986) Food and Living Standard: Implications for Food Strategies. WIDER, Helsinki, mimeo.

Baran, P. (1957) *Political Economy of Growth*. New York: Monthly Review Press.

Bardhan, P. K. (1974) On the Incidence of Poverty in Rural India in the Sixties, in T. N. Srinivasan and P. K. Bardhan, eds. *Poverty and Income Distribution in India*. Calcutta: Statistical Publishing Society.

Basu, K. (1979) *Revealed Preference of Government*. Cambridge: Cambridge University Press.

Bauer, P. T. (1971) *Dissent on Development*. London: Weidenfeld & Nicholson.

Berlin, I. (1969) *Four Essays on Liberty*. Oxford: Clarendon Press.

Blackorby, C. (1975) Degrees of Cardinality and Aggregate Partial Ordering. *Econometrica*, 43.

Chen, L. C. (1986) Primary Health Care in Developing Countries: Overcoming Operational, Technical, and Social Barriers. *Lancet*, 2.

Dasgupta, A. K. (1954) Keynesian Economics and Underdeveloped Countries. *Economic Weekly*, 6 (January 26). Reprinted in *Planning and Economic Growth*. London: Allen & Unwin (1965).

Dasgupta, P. (1982) *The Control of Resources*. Oxford: Blackwell.

Dasgupta, P., and G. Heal (1979) *Economic Theory and Exhaustible Resources*. London: James Nisbet; Cambridge: Cambridge University Press.

Dasgupta, P., and D. Ray (1986) Adapting to Undernourishment: The Biological Evidence and Its Implications. WIDER, Helsinki, in Drèze and Sen (1988).

Datta, B. (1952) *Economics of Industrialization*. Calcutta: World Press.

Dobb, M. H. (1951) *Some Aspects of Economic Development*. Delhi: Delhi School of Economics.

Drèze, J., and A. Sen (1988) *The Political Economy of Hunger: Volume I, Entitlement and Well-Being*. Oxford and New York: Clarendon Press, 1990.

Elster, J. (1979) *Ulysses and the Sirens*. Cambridge: Cambridge University Press.

Elster, J. (1983) *Sour Grapes*. Cambridge: Cambridge University Press.

Erikson, R., E. J. Hansen, S. Ringen, and H. Uusitalo (1987) *The Scandinavian Model: Welfare States and Welfare Research* (Comparative Public Policy Analysis Series). Armonk, NY: M.E. Sharpe.

Fine, B. (1975) A Note on "Interpersonal Comparisons and Partial Comparability." *Econometrica*, 43.

Floud, R., and K. W. Wachter (1982) Poverty and Physical Stature: Evidence on the Standard of Living of London Boys, 1770–1870. *Social Science History*, 6.

Fogel, R. W. (1986) Nutrition and the Decline in Mortality since 1700: Some Additional Preliminary Findings, National Bureau of Economic Research, Cambridge, MA, working paper 182.

Fogel, R. W., S. L. Engerman, and J. Trussell (1982) Exploring the Use of Data on Height: The Analysis of Long-Term Trends in Nutrition, Labour Productivity. *Social Science History*, 6.

Gopalan, C. (1983) Measurement of Undernutrition: Biological Considerations.

Economic and Political Weekly, 19 (April 9).

Gorman, W. M. (1956) The Demand for Related Goods. Iowa Experimental Station, Ames, IA, journal paper J3129.

Gorman, W. M. (1976) Tricks with Utility Function, in M. J. Artis and A. R. Nobay, eds., *Essays in Economic Analysis*. Cambridge: Cambridge University Press.

Grant, J. P. (1978) *Disparity Reduction Rates in Social Indicators*. Washington, DC: Overseas Development Council.

Gwatkin, D. R., J. R. Wilcox, and J. D. Wray (1980) The Policy Implications of Field Experience in Primary Health and Nutrition. *Social Science and Medicine*, 14C.

Hayek, F. A. (1960) *The Constitution of Liberty*. London: Routledge & Kegan Paul.

Hicks, J. R. (1965) *Capital and Growth*. Oxford: Clarendon Press.

Hirschman, A. O. (1958) *The Strategy of Economic Development*. New Haven: Yale University Press.

Hirschman, A. O. (1970) *Exit, Voice and Loyalty*. Cambridge, MA: Harvard University Press.

Honderich, T., ed. (1985) *Morality and Objectivity*. London: Routledge.

Hull, C. H., ed. (1899) *The Economic Writings of Sir William Petty*. Cambridge: Cambridge University Press.

Hurley, S. (1985) Objectivity and Disagreement, in T. Honderich (1985).

Kakwani, N. C. (1981) Welfare Measures: An International Comparison, *Journal of Development Economics*, 8.

Kakwani, N. C. (1986) On Measuring Undernutrition, in *Oxford Economic Papers*, New Series 41: 3 (July): 528–52.

Koopmans, T. C. (1964) On the Flexibility of Future Preferences, in M. W. Shelly and G. L. Bryan, eds. *Human Judgements and Optimality*. New York: Wiley.

Kreps, D. M. (1979) A Representation Theorem for "Preference for Flexibility," *Econometrica*, 47.

Kumar, B. G. (1987) Poverty and Public Policy: Government Intervention and Levels of Living in Kerala, India. D. Phil. dissertation, Oxford University.

Lancaster, K. J. (1966) A New Approach to Consumer Theory. *Journal of Political Economy*, 74.

Lancaster, K. J. (1971) *Consumer Demand: A New Approach*. New York: Columbia University Press.

Lewis, W. A. (1955) *The Theory of Economic Growth*. Homewood, IL: Irwin.

Lipton, M. (1983) *Poverty, Undernutrition and Hunger*. World Bank Staff Working Paper. Washington, DC: World Bank.

McDowell, J. (1981) Noncognitivism and Rule-Following, in S. H. Holtzman and C. M. Leich, eds. *Wittgenstein: To Follow a Rule*. London: Routledge & Kegan Paul.

McMurrin, S. (1980) *Tanner Lectures on Human Values*, vol. I. Cambridge: Cambridge University Press.

Mandelbaum (Martin), K. (1945) *The Industrialization of Backward Areas*. Oxford: Blackwell.

Marglin, F. and S. Marglin, eds. (1986) Development and Technological Transformation in Traditional Societies: Alternative Approaches. Papers presented at a WIDER conference. See *Dominating Knowledge: Development, Culture, and Resistance*. Oxford and New York: Clarendon Press, 1990.

Marx, K. (1844) *The Economic and Philosophic Manuscript of 1844*. English translation. London: Lawrence & Wishart.

Marx, K. (1875) *Critique of the Gotha Programme*. English translation. New York: International Publishers.

Morris, M. D. (1979) *Measuring the Conditions of the World's Poor: The Physical Quality of Life Index*. Oxford: Pergamon.

Nagel, T. (1980) The Limits of Objectivity, in S. McMurrin (1980).

Nagel, T. (1986). *The View from Nowhere*. Oxford: Clarendon Press.

Nordhaus, W., and J. Tobin (1972) Is Growth Obsolete? in National Bureau of Economic Research. *Economic Growth: Fiftieth Anniversary Colloquium*. New York: NBER.

Nozick, R. (1974) *Anarchy, State and Utopia*. Oxford: Blackwell.

Nurkse, R. (1953) *Problems of Capital Formation in Underdeveloped Countries*. Oxford: Blackwell.

Osmani, S. R. (1987) Nutrition and the Economics of Food: Implications of Some Recent Controversies. WIDER, Helsinki, in Drèze and Sen (1988).

Panikar, P. G. K. and C. R. Soman (1984) *Health Status of Kerala*. Trivandrum: Centre for Development Studies.

Pant, P. et al. (1962) *Perspective of Development 1961–1976: Implication of Planning for a Minimum Level of Living.* New Delhi: Planning Commission of India.

Parfit, D. (1984) *Reasons and Persons.* Oxford: Clarendon Press.

Petty, W. (1676) *Political Arithmetick.* Republished in C. H. Hull (1899).

Pigou, A. C. (1952) *The Economics of Welfare.* 4th ed., with eight new appendices. London: Macmillan.

Pollak, R. A. (1978) Endogenous Tastes in Demand and Welfare Analysis. *American Economic Review, Papers and Proceedings*, 68.

Rosenstein-Rodan, P. (1943) Problems of Industrialization in Eastern and Southeastern Europe. *Economic Journal*, 53.

Scanlon, T. M. (1975) Preference and Urgency. *Journal of Philosophy*, 73.

Sen, A. K. (1970) Interpersonal Aggregation and Partial Comparability. *Econometrica*, 38; A correction, *Econometrica*, 40.

Sen, A. K. (1973) On the Development of Basic Income Indicators to Supplement GNP measures. *Economic Bulletin for Asia and the Far East (United Nations)*, 24.

Sen, A. K. (1980) Equality of What? in S. McMurrin (1980) [reprinted in *Global Justice: Seminal Essays*, 61–81].

Sen, A. K. (1985a) Well-Being, Agency and Freedom: The Dewey Lectures, 1984. *Journal of Philosophy*, 82.

Sen, A. K. (1985b) *Commodities and Capabilities.* Amsterdam: North-Holland.

Singer, H. W. (1952) The Mechanics of Economic Development. *Indian Economic Review.* Reprinted in A. N. Agarwala and A. P. Singh, eds. *The Economics of Underdevelopment.* London: Oxford University Press.

Smith, A. (1776) *An Inquiry into the Nature and Causes of the Wealth of Nations.* Republished; edited by R. H. Campbell and A. S. Skinner. Oxford: Clarendon Press (1976).

Smith, A. (1790) *The Theory of Moral Sentiments.* Rev. ed. Republished; edited by D. D. Raphael and A. L. Macfie. Oxford: Clarendon Press (1975).

Srinivasan, T. N. (1982) Hunger: Defining It, Estimating Its Global Incidence and Alleviating It, in D. Gale Johnson and E. Schuh, eds. *Role of Markets in the World Food Economy.*

Stewart, F. (1985) *Planning to Meet Basic Needs.* London: Macmillan.

Streeten, P. (1981) *Development Perspectives.* London: Macmillan.

Streeten, P. et al. (1981) *First Things First: Meeting Basic Needs in Developing Countries*. New York: Oxford University Press.

Sukhatme, P. V. (1977) *Nutrition and Poverty*. New Delhi: Indian Agricultural Research Institute.

UNICEF (1986) *The State of the World's Children 1986*. New York: United Nations.

Usher, D. (1968) *The Price Mechanism and the Meaning of National Income Statistics*. Oxford: Clarendon Press.

Usher, D. (1976) The Measurement of Real Income. *Review of Income and Wealth*, 22.

Van Herwaarden, F. G. and A. Kapteyn (1981) Empirical Comparison of the Shape of Welfare Functions. *European Economic Review*, 15.

Van Praag, B. M. S. (1978) The Perception of Welfare Inequality. *European Economic Review*, 10.

von Weizsacker, C. C. (1971) Notes on Endogenous Changes in Tastes. *Journal of Economic Theory*, 3.

Wiggins, D. (1985) Claims of Need, in Honderich (1985).

Williams, A. (1987) What is Wealth and Who Creates It? York University, mimeo.

World Bank (1986) *World Development Report, 1986*. New York: Oxford University Press.

10. AVISHAI MARGALIT AND JOSEPH RAZ

Margalit and Raz examine the moral justification of the case for national self-determination—specifically, for the "right to determine whether a certain territory shall become, or remain, a separate state (and possibly also whether it should enjoy autonomy within a larger state)." They consider which groups might qualify as having a right to self-determination and suggest six characteristics of groups that, taken together, might be relevant in deciding this. The authors are specifically concerned to investigate these issues with respect to the real world, rather than an idealized one.

National Self-Determination

First published in The Journal of Philosophy *87: 9 (September 1990): 439–61.*

In the controversy-ridden fields of international law and international relations, the widespread recognition of the existence of national rights to self-determination provides a welcome point of agreement. Needless to say, the core consensus is but the eye of a raging storm concerning the precise definition of the right, its content, its bearers, and the proper means for its implementation. This paper will not address such questions, though indirectly it may help with their investigation. Its concern is with the moral justification of the case for national self-determination. Its purpose is critical and evaluative, its subject lies within the morality of international relations rather than within international law and international relations proper.

It is assumed throughout that states and international law should recognize such a right only if there is a sound moral case for it. This does not mean that international law should mirror morality. Its concern is with setting standards that enjoy the sort of clarity required to make them the foundations of international relations between states and fit for recognition and enforcement through international organs. These concerns give rise to special considerations that should be fully recognized in the subtle process of applying moral principles to the law. The derivation of legal principles from moral premises is never a matter of copying morality into law. Still, the justification of the law rests ultimately on moral considerations, and therefore those considerations should also help shape the contours of legal principles. That is why the conclusions of this paper bear on controversies concerning the proper way in which the law on this subject should develop, even though such issues are not here discussed directly.

Moral inquiry is sometimes understood in a utopian manner, i.e., as an inquiry into the principles that should prevail in an ideal world. It is doubtful whether this is a meaningful enterprise, but it is certainly not the one we are engaged in here. We assume that things are roughly as they are, especially that our world is a world of states and of a variety of ethnic, national, tribal, and other groups.[1] We do not question the justification for this state of affairs. Rather, we ask whether, given that this is how things are and for as long as they remain the same, a moral case can be made in support of national self-determination.

I. ISOLATING THE ISSUE

The core content of the claim to be examined is that there is a right to determine whether a certain territory shall become, or remain, a separate state (and possibly also whether it should enjoy autonomy within a larger state). The idea of national self-determination or (as we shall refer to it in order to avoid confusion) the idea of self-government encompasses much more. The value of national self-government is the value of entrusting the general political power over a group and its members to the group. If self-government is valuable, then it is valuable that whatever is a proper matter for political decision should be subject to the political decision of the group in all matters concerning the group and its members. The idea of national self-government, in other words, speaks of groups determining the character of their social and economic environment, their fortunes, the course of their development, and the fortunes of their members by their own actions, i.e., by the action of those groups, inasmuch as these are matters that are properly within the realm of political action.[2] Given the current international state system, in which political power rests, in the main, with sovereign states,[3] the right to determine whether a territory should be an independent state is quite naturally regarded as the main instrument for realizing the ideal of self-determination. Consideration of this right usually dominates all discussions of national self-determination. To examine the justification of the right is the ultimate purpose of this article. But we shall continuously draw attention to the fact that, as we shall try to show, the right of self-determination so understood is not ultimate, but is grounded in the wider value of national self-government, which is itself to be only instrumentally justified.

The next section deals with the nature of the groups that might be the subject of such a right. Section III considers what value, if any, is served by the enjoyment of political independence by such groups. Section IV examines the case for conceding that there is a moral right to self-determination. This examination may lead to revising our understanding of the content of the right. It may reveal that moral considerations justify only a narrower right, or that the argument that justifies the right warrants giving it a wider scope. But the core as identified here will provide the working base from which to launch the inquiry.

Before we start, a few words about this way of identifying the problem may be in place. In two ways the chosen focus of our examination is narrower than many discussions of self-determination in international relations. First, we disregard the claims made, typically by Third World countries, in the name of self-determination, against the economic domination of multinational companies, the World Bank, or against powerful regional or world powers. The considerations canvassed in this paper are relevant to such issues, but fall short of directly tackling them. To be complete, a discussion of a right must examine both its grounds and its consequences. This paper is concerned mostly with the grounds for the right of self-determination. It asks the question: Who has the right and under what conditions is it to be exercised? It does not go into the question of the consequences of the right beyond the assumption, already stated, that it is a right that a territory be a self-governing state. A good deal of the current turmoil in international law, and international relations, has to do with the exploration of that last notion. What is entailed by the fact that a state is a sovereign, self-governing, entity? The claims that economic domination violate the right to self-determination belong to that discussion. The conclusions of this paper provide part of the grounds by which such claims are to be settled. But we do not propose to pursue this question here.

Second, claims of self-determination are invariably raised whenever one state invades and occupies another, or a territory belonging to another. Yet it is important to distinguish between the wrongness of military invasion or occupation, and the rights available against it, and the right (whatever it may turn out to be) to self-determination. In a word, the latter is a source of title, whereas the former is a possessory right based largely on public-order considerations. Any legal system, international law not excluded, recognizes certain ways as legitimate ways of solving disputes and outlaws others. Subject to the exceptions of legitimate self-defense and self-help, the use of violence is forbidden. Violation of that prohibition gives rise to a right to have the status quo ante restored, before the deeper sources of the dispute between the parties are examined; that is, regardless of the soundness of one's title to a territory, one may not use force to occupy it. This is why the right to recover a territory lost by force is a possessory right. It does not depend on the ultimate soundness of one's title, and that is why it was said to be based on public-order considerations. A large part of its justification is in the need to establish that the proper means of dispute resolution be the only ones resorted to.

Not surprisingly, invocation of this possessory right is, however, accompanied by a claim of good title (the merits of which are not immediately relevant). The underlying title is often the right to self-determination. Hence the temptation to confuse the two. But notice that, apart from the different justificatory foundations, the two are far from identical in consequence. They merely overlap. The claims of a people who have been for many years ruled by another cannot be based on the possessory right that applies only against a recent occupier. On the other hand, the occupation of portions of Antarctica, or of some uninhabited island, do violate the possessory right, but not the right of self-determination. The latter is that of the inhabitants, and does not apply when there are no inhabitants.[4]

II. GROUPS

Assuming that self-determination is enjoyed by groups, what groups qualify? Given that the right is normally attributed to peoples or nations, it is tempting to give that as the answer and concentrate on characterizing "peoples" or "nations." The drawbacks of this approach are two: It assumes too much and it poses problems that may not require a solution.

It is far from clear that peoples or nations rather than tribes, ethnic groups, or linguistic, religious, or geographical groups are the relevant reference group. What is it that makes peoples particularly suited to self-determination? The right concerns determination whether a certain territory shall be self-governing or not. It appears to affect most directly the residents of a territory, and their neighbors. If anyone, then residents of geographical regions seem intuitively to be the proper bearers of the right. Saying this does not get us very far. It does not help in identifying the residents of which regions should qualify. To be sure, this is the crucial question. But even posing it in this way shows that the answer, "the largest regions inhabited by one people or nation," is far from being the obvious answer.

We have some understanding of the benefits self-government might bring. We need to rely on this in looking for the characteristics that make groups suitable recipients of those benefits. We want, in other words, to identify groups by those characteristics that are relevant to the justification of the right. If it turns out that those do not apply to peoples or nations, we shall have shown that the right to self-determination is misconceived and, as recognized in international law, unjustified. Alternatively, the groups identified may encompass peoples (or some peoples) as well as other groups. This will provide a powerful case for redrawing the boundaries of the right. Either way we shall be saved much argument concerning the characterization of nations which, interesting as it is in itself, is irrelevant to our purpose.

Having said that, it may be useful to take nations and peoples as the obvious candidates for the right. We need not worry about their defining characteristics. But we may gain insight by comparing them with groups, e.g., the fiction-reading public, or Tottenham Football Club supporters, which obviously do not enjoy such a right. Reflection on such examples suggests six characteristics that in combination are relevant to a case for self-determination.

1. The group has a common character and a common culture that encompass many, varied, and important aspects of life, a culture that defines or marks a variety of forms or styles of life, types of activities, occupations, pursuits, and relationships. With national groups we expect to find national cuisines, distinctive architectural styles, a common language, distinctive literary and artistic traditions, national music, customs, dress, ceremonies and holidays, etc. None of these is necessary. They are but typical examples of the features that characterize peoples and other groups that are serious candidates for the right to self-determination. They have pervasive cultures, and their identity is determined at least in part by their culture. They possess cultural traditions that penetrate beyond a single or a few areas of human life, and display themselves in a whole range of areas, including many that are of great importance for the well-being of individuals.

2. The correlative of the first feature is that people growing up among members of the group will acquire the group culture, will be marked by its character. Their tastes and their options will be affected by that culture to a significant degree. The types of careers open to one, the leisure activities one learned to appreciate and is therefore able to choose from, the customs and habits that define and color relations with strangers and with friends, patterns of expectations and attitudes between spouses and among other members of the family, features of lifestyles with which one is capable of empathizing and for which one may therefore develop a taste—all these will be marked by the group culture.

They need not be indelibly marked. People may migrate to other environments, shed their previous culture, and acquire a new one. It is a painful and slow process, success in which is rarely complete. But it is possible, just as it is possible that socialization will fail and one will fail to be marked by the culture of one's environment, except negatively, to reject it. The point made is merely the modest one that, given the pervasive nature of the culture of the groups we are seeking to identify, their influence on individuals who grow up in their midst is profound and far-reaching. The point needs to be made in order to connect concern with the prosperity of the group with concern for the well-being of individuals. This tie between the individual and the collective is at the heart of the case for self-determination.

As one would expect, the tie does not necessarily extend to all members of the group, and failure of socialization is not the only reason. The group culture affects those who grow up among its members, be they members or not. But to say this is no more than to point to various anomalies and dilemmas that may arise. Most people live in groups of these kinds, so that those who belong to none are denied full access to the opportunities that are shaped in part by the group's culture. They are made to feel estranged and their chances to have a rewarding life are seriously damaged. The same is true of people who grow up among members of a group so that they absorb its culture, but are then denied access to it because they are denied full membership of the group.

Nothing in the above presupposes that groups of the kind we are exploring are geographically concentrated, let alone that their members are the only inhabitants of any region. Rather, by drawing on the transmission of the group culture through the socialization of the young, these comments emphasize the historical nature of the groups with which we are concerned. Given that they are identified by a common culture, at least in part, they also share a history, for it is through a shared history that cultures develop and are transmitted.

3. Membership in the group is, in part, a matter of mutual recognition. Typically, one belongs to such groups if, among other conditions, one is recognized by other members of the group as belonging to it. The other conditions (which may be the accident of birth or the sharing of the group culture, etc.) are normally the grounds cited as reasons for such recognition. But those who meet those other conditions and are yet rejected by the group are at best marginal or problematic members of it. The groups concerned are not formal institutionalized groups, with formal procedures of admission. Membership in them is a matter of informal acknowledgment of belonging by others generally, and by other members specifically. The fiction-reading public fails our previous tests. It is not identified by its sharing a wide-ranging pervasive culture. It also fails the third test. To belong to the fiction-reading public all we have to do is to read fiction. It does not matter whether others recognize us as fiction-reading.[5]

4. The third feature prepares the way for, and usually goes hand in hand with, the importance of membership for one's self-identification. Consider the fiction-reading public again. It is a historically signifi-

cant group. Historians may study the evolution of the fiction-reading public, how it spread from women to men, from one class to others, from reading aloud in small groups to silent reading, from reliance on libraries to book buying, etc.; how it is regarded as important to one's qualification as a cultured person in one country, but not in another; how it furnishes a common topic of conversation in some classes but not in others; how belonging to the group is a mark of political awareness in some countries, while being a sign of escapist retreat from social concerns in another.

Such studies will show, however, that it is only in some societies that the existence of these features of the fiction-reading public is widely known. For the most part, one can belong to the group without being aware that one is a typical reader, that one's profile is that of most readers. Sometimes this is a result of a mistaken group image's being current in that society. Our concern is rather with those cases where the society lacks any very distinct image of that group. This indicates that, in such societies, membership of that group does not have a highly visible social profile. It is not one of the facts by which people pigeonhole each other. One need not be aware of who, among people one knows, friends, acquaintances, shopkeepers one patronizes, one's doctor, etc., shares the habit. In such societies, membership of the fiction-reading public is not highly visible, that is, it is not one of the things one will normally know about people one has contact with, one of the things that identify "who they are." But it happens in some countries that membership of the reading public becomes a highly visible mark of belonging to a social group, to the intelligentsia, etc. In such countries, talk of the recently published novel becomes a means of mutual recognition.

One of the most significant facts differentiating various football cultures is whether they are cultures of self-recognition: whether identification as a fan or supporter of this club or that is one of the features that are among the main markers of people in the society. The same is true of occupational groups. In some countries, membership is highly visible and is among the primary means of pigeonholing people, of establishing "who they are"; in others, it is not.

Our concern is with groups, membership of which has a high social profile, that is, groups, membership of which is one of the primary facts by which people are identified, and which form expectations as to what they are like, groups membership of which is one of the primary clues for people generally in interpreting the conduct of others. Since our perceptions of ourselves are in large measure determined by how we expect others to perceive us, it follows that membership of such groups is an important identifying feature for each about himself. These are groups, members of which are aware of their membership and typically regard it as an important clue in understanding who they are, in interpreting their actions and reactions, in understanding their tastes and their manner.

5. Membership is a matter of belonging, not of achievement. One does not have to prove oneself, or to excel in anything, in order to belong and to be accepted as a full member. To the extent that membership normally involves recognition by others as a member, that recognition is not conditional on meeting qualifications that indicate any accomplishment. To be a good Irishman, it is true, is an achievement. But to be an Irishman is not. Qualification for membership is usually determined by nonvoluntary criteria. One cannot choose to belong. One belongs because of who one is. One can come to belong to such groups, but only by changing, e.g., by adopting their culture, changing one's tastes and habits accordingly—a very slow process indeed. The fact that these are groups, membership of which is a matter of belonging and not of accomplishment, makes them suitable for their role as primary foci of identification. Identification is more secure, less liable to be threatened, if it does not depend on accomplishment. Although accomplishments play their role in people's sense of their own identity, it would seem that at the most fundamental level our sense of our own identity depends on criteria of belonging rather than on those of accomplishment. Secure identification at that level is particularly important to one's well-being.

6. The groups concerned are not small face-to-face groups, members of which are generally known to all other members. They are anonymous groups where mutual recognition is secured by the possession of general characteristics. The exclusion of small groups from consideration is not merely ad hoc. Small groups that are based on personal familiarity of all with all are markedly different in the character of their relationships and interactions from anonymous groups. For example, given the importance of mutual recognition to members of

these groups, they tend to develop conventional means of identification, such as the use of symbolic objects, participation in group ceremonies, special group manners, or special vocabulary, which help quickly to identify who is "one of us" and who is not.

The various features we listed do not entail each other but they tend to go together. It is not surprising that groups with pervasive cultures will be important in determining the main options and opportunities of their members, or that they will become focal points of identification, etc. The way things are in our world, just about everyone belongs to such a group, and not necessarily to one only. Membership is not exclusive and many people belong to several groups that answer to our description. Some of them are rather like national groups, e.g., tribes or ethnic groups. Others are very different. Some religious groups meet our conditions, as do social classes, and some racial groups. Not all religions or racial groups did develop rich and pervasive cultures. But some did and those qualify.

III. THE VALUE OF SELF-GOVERNMENT

(A) The Value of Encompassing Groups

The description of the relevant groups in the preceding section may well disappoint the reader. Some will be disappointed by the imprecise nature of the criteria provided. This would be unjustified. The criteria are not meant to provide operational legal definitions. As such they clearly would not do. Their purpose is to pick on the features of groups which may explain the value of self-determination. As already mentioned, the key to the explanation is in the importance of these groups to the well-being of their members. This thought guided the selection of the features. They are meant to assist in identifying that link. It is not really surprising that they are all vague matters of degree, admitting of many variants and many nuances. One is tempted to say "that's life." It does not come in neatly parceled parts. While striving to identify the features that matter, we have to recognize that they come in many shapes, in many shades, and in many degrees rife with impurities in their concrete mixing.

A more justified source of disappointment is the suspicion that we have cast the net too wide. Social classes clearly do not have a right to self-determination. If they meet the above conditions, then those conditions are at best incomplete. Here we can only crave the reader's patience. We tried to identify the features of groups that help explain the value of self-determination. These may apply not only beyond the sphere in which the right is commonly recognized. They may apply to groups that really should not possess it for other reasons yet to be explored.

The defining properties of the groups we identified are of two kinds. On the one hand, they pick out groups with pervasive cultures; on the other, they focus on groups, membership of which is important to one's self-identity. This combination makes such groups suitable candidates for self-rule. Let us call groups manifesting the six features *encompassing groups*. Individuals find in them a culture that shapes to a large degree their tastes and opportunities, and that provides an anchor for their self-identification and the safety of effortless, secure belonging.

Individual well-being depends on the successful pursuit of worthwhile goals and relationships. Goals and relationships are culturally determined. Being social animals means not merely that the means for the satisfaction of people's goals are more readily available within society. More crucially it means that those goals themselves are (when one reaches beyond what is strictly necessary for biological survival) the creatures of society, the products of culture. Family relations, all other social relations between people, careers, leisure activities, the arts, sciences, and other obvious products of "high culture" are the fruits of society. They all depend for their existence on the sharing of patterns of expectations, on traditions preserving implicit knowledge of how to do what, of tacit conventions regarding what is part of this or that enterprise and what is not, what is appropriate and what is not, what is valuable and what is not. Familiarity with a culture determines the boundaries of the imaginable. Sharing in a culture, being part of it, determines the limits of the feasible.

It may be no more than a brute fact that our world is organized in a large measure around groups with pervasive cultures. But it is a fact with far-reaching consequences. It means, in the first place, that membership of such groups is of great importance to individual well-being, for it greatly affects one's opportunities, one's ability to engage in the relationships and pursuits marked by the culture. Second, it means that the prosperity of the culture is important to the well-being of its members.

If the culture is decaying, or if it is persecuted or discriminated against, the options and opportunities open to its members will shrink, become less attractive, and their pursuit less likely to be successful.

It may be no more than a brute fact that people's sense of their own identity is bound up with their sense of belonging to encompassing groups and that their self-respect is affected by the esteem in which these groups are held. But these facts, too, have important consequences. They mean that individual dignity and self-respect require that the groups, membership of which contributes to one's sense of identity, be generally respected and not be made a subject of ridicule, hatred, discrimination, or persecution.

All this is mere common sense and is meant to be hedged and qualified in the way our common understanding of these matters is. Of course, strangers can participate in activities marked by a culture. They are handicapped, but not always very seriously. Of course, there are other determinants of one's opportunities, and of one's sense of self-respect. Membership of an encompassing group is but one factor. Finally, one should mention that groups and their culture may be pernicious, based on exploitation of people, be they their members or not, or on the denigration and persecution of other groups. If so, then the case for their protection and flourishing is weakened, and may disappear altogether.

Having regard for this reservation, the case for holding the prosperity of encompassing groups as vital for the prosperity of their members is a powerful one. Group interests cannot be reduced to individual interests. It makes sense to talk of a group's prospering or declining, of actions and policies as serving the group's interest or of harming it, without having to cash this in terms of individual interests. The group may flourish if its culture prospers, but this need not mean that the lot of its members or of anyone else has improved. It is in the interest of the group to be held in high regard by others, but it does not follow that, if an American moon landing increases the world's admiration for the United States, Americans necessarily benefit from this. Group interests are conceptually connected to the interests of their members but such connections are nonreductive and generally indirect. For example, it is possible that what enhances the interest of the group provides opportunities for improvement for its members, or that it increases the chance that they will benefit.

This relative independence of group interest is compatible with the view that informs this article: that the moral importance of the group's interest depends on its value to individuals. A large decline in the fortunes of the group may, e.g., be of little consequence to its members. There is no a priori way of correlating group interest with that of its members or of other individuals. It depends on the circumstances of different groups at different times. One clear consequence of the fact that the moral significance of a group's interest is in its service to individuals is the fact that it will depend, in part, on the size of the group. The fortunes of a larger group may be material to the well-being of a larger number of people. Other things being equal, numbers matter.

(B) The Instrumental Case

Does the interest of members in the prosperity of the group establish a right to self-determination? Certainly not, at least not yet, not without further argument. For one thing, we have yet to see any connection between the prosperity of encompassing groups and their political independence. The easiest connection to establish under certain conditions is an instrumental one. Sometimes the prosperity of the group and its self-respect are aided by, sometimes they may be impossible to secure without, the group's enjoying political sovereignty over its own affairs. Sovereignty enables the group to conduct its own affairs in a way conducive to its prosperity.[6] There is no need to elaborate the point. It depends on historical conditions. Hence the prominence of a history of persecution in most debates concerning self-determination. But a history of persecution is neither a necessary nor a sufficient condition for the instrumental case for self-government. It is not a necessary condition, because persecution is not the only reason why the groups may suffer without independence. Suffering can be the result of neglect or ignorance of or indifference to the prosperity of a minority group by the majority. Such attitudes may be so well entrenched that there is no realistic prospect of changing them.

Persecution is not a sufficient condition for there may be other ways to fight and overcome persecution, and because, whatever the advantages of independence, it may, in the circumstances, lead to economic decline, cultural decay, or social disorder, which only make their members worse off. Besides, as mentioned above, pernicious groups may not deserve protection, especially if it will help them to pursue repressive practices with impunity. Finally, there are the interests of nonmembers to be considered. In short, the instrumental argument (as well as others) for self-government is sensitive to counterarguments pointing to its drawbacks, its cost in terms of human well-being, possible violations of human rights, and so on.

We shall return to these issues below. First, let us consider the claim that the instrumental argument trivializes the case for self-government by overlooking its intrinsic value. Of the various arguments for the intrinsic value of self-government that have been and can be advanced, we examine one that seems the most promising.

(C) An Argument for the Intrinsic Value of Self-Government

The argument is based on an extension of individual autonomy or of self-expression (if that is regarded as independently valuable). The argument unravels in stages: (1) people's membership of encompassing groups is an important aspect of their personality, and their well-being depends on giving it full expression; (2) expression of membership essentially includes manifestation of membership in the open, public life of the community; (3) this requires expressing one's membership in political activities within the community. The political is an essential arena of community life, and consequently of individual well-being; (4) therefore, self-government is inherently valuable, it is required to provide the group with a political dimension.

The first premise is unexceptionable. So is the second, though an ambiguity might be detected in the way it is often understood. Two elements need separating. First, given the importance of membership to one's well-being, it is vital that the dignity of the group be preserved. This depends, in part, on public manifestations of respect for the group and its culture, and on the absence of ridicule of the group, etc., from the public life of the society of which one is a member. One should not have to identify with or feel loyalty to a group that denigrates an encompassing group to which one belongs. Indeed, one should not have to live in an environment in which such attitudes are part of the common culture. Second, an aspect of well-being is an ability to express publicly one's identification with the group and to participate openly in its public culture. An encompassing group is centered on mutual recognition and is inevitably a group with a public culture. One cannot enjoy the benefits of membership without participation in its public culture, without public participation in its culture.

Both elements are of great importance. Both indicate the vital role played by public manifestations of group culture and group membership among the conditions of individual well-being. To the extent that a person's well-being is bound up with his identity as a member of an encompassing group it has an important public dimension. But that dimension is not necessarily political in the conventional narrow sense of the term. Even where it is, its political expression does not require a political organization whose boundaries coincide with those of the group. One may be politically active in a multinational, multicultural polity.

Here supporters of the argument for the intrinsic value of self-government may protest. The expression of membership in the political life of the community, they will say, involves more than its public expression. It involves the possibility of members of an encompassing group participating in the political life of their state, and fighting in the name of group interests in the political arena. Such actions, they will insist, may be not only instrumentally valuable to the group, but intrinsically important to its politically active members. They are valuable avenues of self-fulfilment. These points, too, have to be readily admitted. There is no reason to think that everyone must take part in politics, or else his or her development is stunted and personality or life are deficient. In normal times, politics is but an option that people may choose to take or to leave alone. Although its availability is important, for its absence deprives people of valuable opportunities, its use is strictly optional. Even if it is possible to argue that one's personal well-being requires some involvement with larger groups, and the avoidance of exclusive preoccupation with one's own affairs and those of one's close relations or friends, that involvement can take nonpolitical forms, such as activity in a social club, interest in the fortunes of the arts in one's region, and the like.

Politics is no more than an option, though this is true in normal times only. In times of political crises that have moral dimensions, it may well be the duty of everyone to stand up and be counted. In Weimar, Germans had a moral duty to become politically involved to oppose Nazism. There are many other situations where an apolitical attitude is not morally acceptable. But all of them are marked by moral crises. In the absence of crisis there is nothing wrong in being nonpolitical.

Having said this, we must repeat that the option of politics must remain open, and with it the option of fighting politically for causes to do with the interests of one's encompassing groups. But there is nothing here to suggest that this should be done in a political framework exclusive to one's group or dominated by it. There is nothing wrong with multinational states, in which members of the different communities compete in the political arena for public resources for their communities. Admittedly, prejudice, national fanaticism, etc., sometimes make such peaceful and equitable sharing of the political arena impossible. They may lead to friction and persecution. This may constitute a good argument for the value of self-government, but it is an instrumental argument of the kind canvassed above. There is nothing in the need for a public or even a political expression of one's membership of an encompassing group that points to an intrinsic value of self-government.

(D) The Subjective Element

In an indirect way, the attempt to argue for the intrinsic value of self-government does point to the danger of misinterpreting the instrumental approach to the question. First, the argument does not deny the intrinsic value of the existence of the political option as a venue for activity and self-expression to all (adult) members of society. We are not advocating a purely instrumentalist view of politics generally. The intrinsic value to individuals of the political option does not require expression in polities whose boundaries coincide with those of encompassing groups. That is the only point argued for above.

Second, the pragmatic, instrumentalist character of the approach advocated here should not be identified with an aggregating impersonal consequentialism. Some people tend to associate any instrumentalist approach with images of a bureaucracy trading off the interest of one person against that of another on the basis of some cost-benefit analysis designed to maximize overall satisfaction; a bureaucracy, moreover, in charge of determining for people what is really good for them, regardless of their own views of the matter. Nothing of the kind should be countenanced. Of course, conflicts among people's interests do arise and call for rational resolution that is likely to involve sacrificing some interests of some people for the sake of others. Such conflicts, however, admit of a large degree of indeterminacy, and many alternative resolutions may be plausible or rational. In such contexts, talking of maximization, with its connotations of comparability of all options, is entirely out of place.

Furthermore, nothing in the instrumentalist and pragmatic nature of our approach should be allowed to disguise its sensitivity to subjective elements, its responsiveness to the perceptions and sensibilities of the people concerned. To a considerable extent, what matters is how well people feel in their environment: Do they feel at home in it or are they alienated from it? Do they feel respected or humiliated? etc. This leads to a delicate balance between "objective" factors and subjective perceptions. On the one hand, when prospects for the future are concerned, subjective perceptions of danger and likely persecution, etc., are not necessarily to be trusted. These are objective issues on which the opinion of independent spectators may be more reliable than that of those directly involved. On the other hand, the factual issue facing the independent spectators is how people will respond to their conditions, what will be their perceptions, their attitudes to their environment, to their neighbors, etc. Even a group that is not persecuted may suffer many of the ills of real persecution if it feels persecuted. That its perceptions are mistaken or exaggerated is important in pointing to the possibility of a different cure: removing the mistaken perception. But that is not always possible, and up to a point in matters of respect, identification, and dignity, subjective responses, justified or not, are the ultimate reality so far as the well-being of those who have them is concerned.

IV. A RIGHT TO SELF-DETERMINATION

It may seem that the case for self-government establishes a right to self-determination. That is, it establishes the reasons for the right sort of group, an encompassing group, to determine that a territory shall be self-governing. But things are not that simple. The case for self-government shows that sometimes, under certain conditions, it is best that the political unit be roughly an encompassing group. A group's right to self-determination is its right to determine that a territory be self-governing, regardless of whether the case for self-government, based on its benefits, is established or not. In other words, the right to self-determination answers the question "Who is to decide?"—not "What is the best decision?" In exercising the right, the group should act responsibly in light of all the considerations we mentioned so far. It should, in particular, consider not only the interests of its members but those of others who may be affected by its decision. But if it has the right to decide, its decision is binding even if it is wrong, even if the case for self-government is not made.[7]

The problem in conceding the existence of such a right is, of course, not the possibility that a group that would best be self-governing does not wish to be so. Given the strong subjectivist element in the instrumentalist argument, such reluctance to assume independence would suggest that the case for its being self-governing is much weakened. The problem is that the case for self-government is hedged by considerations of the interest of people other than members of the groups, and by the other interests of members of the groups, i.e., other than their interests as members of the groups. These include their fundamental individual interests which should be respected, e.g., by a group whose culture oppresses women or racial minorities. These considerations raise the question whether encompassing groups are the most suitable bodies to decide about the case for self-government. Can they be entrusted with the decision in a matter in which their group interests are in conflict with other interests of members of the group as well as with the interests of other people? At the very least this suggests that the right must be qualified and hedged to protect other interests.

More fundamental still is the question of how the right of self-determination fits within our general conception of democratic decision making. We are used to a two-level structure of argument concerning social issues, such as just taxation, the provision of public education, etc. First, we explore the principles that should govern the matter at issue. Second, we devise a form of democratic procedure for determining what shall be done. The first level answers the question "What should be done?" The second responds to the question, "Who should decide?"

On a simple majoritarian view, the issue of self-government seems to defy a democratic decision procedure. The question is "What is the relevant democratic unit?" and that question cannot be democratically decided, at least not entirely so. In fact, of course, we are not simple majoritarians. We adopt a whole range of democratic procedures such as constitution-making privileged majorities, ordinary legislative processes, plebiscites, administrative processes, and decisions by special agencies under conditions of public accountability and indirect democratic control. We match various democratic processes with various social and political problems. This means that there is no universal democratic formula serving as the universal answer to "Who decides?" questions. Rather, we operate a mixed principled-democratic system in which principles, whose credentials do not derive entirely from their democratic backing, determine what form of a democratic procedure is suited for what problem. Within this mixed principled-democratic framework, the right to self-determination fits as just another qualified democratic process suited to its object.

What are the principles involved? It is tempting to see here a principle giving the part veto over the issue of membership in a larger whole. To form a new political unit, or to remain part of an existing one, all component parts should agree. To break up a political unit, or to foil the creation of a new one, all that is required is the will of the group that wants to secede or to stay out. This principle derives its appeal from its voluntaristic aura. It seems to regard the justification of all political units as based on consent. But this is an undesirable illusion. It is undesirable since, as was explained above regarding encompassing groups, the more important human groupings need to be based on shared history, and on criteria of nonvoluntaristic (or at least not wholly contractarian) membership to have the value that they have. The principle presents no more than an illusion of a contractarian principle since it refers to groups, not to individuals. But the whole contractarian ethos derives its appeal from the claim that each individual's consent is a condition of the legitimacy of political units. Beyond all that, the principle simply begs the question that it is meant to answer, namely, what are the parts? Which groupings have the veto and which do not? Can the group of all the people whose surnames begin with a "g" and end with an "e" count for these purposes? Do they have the veto on membership in a larger political unit?

The right to self-determination derives from the value of membership in encompassing groups. It is a group right, deriving from the value of a collective good, and as such opposed in spirit to contractarian-individualistic[8] approaches to politics or to individual well-being. It rests on an appreciation of the great importance that membership in and identification with encompassing groups has in the life of individuals, and the importance of the prosperity and self-respect of such groups to the well-being of their members. That importance makes it reasonable to let the encompassing group that forms a substantial majority in a territory have the right to determine whether that territory shall form an independent state in order to protect the culture and self-respect of the group, provided that the new state is likely to respect the fundamental interests of its inhabitants, and provided that measures are adopted to prevent its creation from gravely damaging the just interests of other countries. This statement of the argument for the right requires elaboration.

(1) The argument is an instrumental one. It says, essentially, that members of a group are best placed to judge whether their group's prosperity will be jeopardized if it does not enjoy political independence. It is in keeping with the view that, even though participation in politics may have intrinsic value to individuals, the shape and boundaries of political units are to be determined by their service to individual well-being, i.e., by their instrumental value. In our world, encompassing groups that do not enjoy self-government are not infrequently persecuted, despised, or neglected. Given the importance of their prosperity and self-respect to the well-being of their members, it seems reasonable to entrust their members with the right to determine whether the groups should be self-governing. They may sacrifice their economic or other interests for the sake of group self-respect and prosperity. But such a sacrifice is, given the circumstances of this world, often not unreasonable.

One may ask why should such matters not be entrusted to international adjudication by an international court, or some other international agency. Instead of groups' having a right to self-determination, which makes them judges in their own cause, the case for a group's becoming self-governing should be entrusted to the judgment of an impartial tribunal. This would have been a far superior solution to the question "Who is to decide?" Unfortunately, there simply does not exist any international machinery of enforcement that can be relied upon in preference to a right of self-determination as the right of self-help, nor is there any prospect of one coming into existence in the near future. In the present structure of international relations, the most promising arrangement is one that recognizes group rights to self-determination and entrusts international bodies with the duty to help bring about its realization, and to see to it that the limits and preconditions of the right are observed (these are enumerated in the points two to five below).

(2) The right belongs to the group. But how should it be exercised? Not necessarily by a simple majority vote. Given the long-term and irreversible nature of the decision (remember that while independence is up to the group, merger or union is not), the wish for a state must be shared by an overwhelming majority, reflecting deep-seated beliefs and feelings of an enduring nature, and not mere temporary popularity. The precise institutional requirements for the exercise of the right are issues that transcend the topic of this paper. They are liable to vary with the circumstances of different national and ethnic groups. Whatever they are they should reflect the above principle.

(3) The right is over a territory. This simply reflects the territorial organization of our political world. The requirement that the group be a substantial majority of the territory stems from further considerations aimed at balancing the interest in self-government against the interests of nonmembers. First, it is designed to ensure that self-government for a territory does not generate a problem as great as it is meant to solve, by ensuring that the independence will not generate a large-scale new minority problem. That risk cannot be altogether avoided. As was remarked before, numbers count in the end.

A further factual assumption underlying this condition is that people are, even today, most directly affected by the goings-on in their region. It is true that one's economic conditions are affected by the economic activities in faraway places. This, however, is more and more true of the international system generally. The ideal of economic autarchy died a natural death. (Correspondingly, the condition of economic viability that used to figure in theories of the states in international relations has little role in the modern world.) What can be secured and protected, and what vitally matters to the quality of life, is its texture as determined by the local culture and custom, the nature of the physical environment, etc. Hence the right is given only to a group that is the majority in a territory. The case for self-government applies to groups that are not in the majority anywhere, but they do not have the right to self-determination anywhere. Their members, like other people, may have a right to immigration on an individual basis to a territory of their choice. But their case is governed by general principles of freedom of movement and the sovereign rights of existing states. This means that their communal interests remain an important consideration to be borne in mind by the decision makers, but they have no right, i.e., the decision is not up to them.

Do historical ties make a difference? Not to the right if voluntarily abandoned. Suppose that the group was unjustly removed from the country. In that case, the general principle of restitution applies, and the group has a right to self-determination and control over the territory it was expelled from, subject to the general principle of prescription. Prescription protects the interests of the current inhabitants. It is based on several deep-seated concerns. It is meant to prevent the revival of abandoned claims, and to protect those who are not personally to blame from having their life unsettled by claims of ancient wrongs, on the ground that their case now is as good as that of the wronged people or their descendants. Prescription, therefore, may lose the expelled group the right even though its members continue to suffer the effects of the past wrong. Their interest is a consideration to be borne in mind in decisions concerning immigration policies, and the like, but because of prescription they lost the right to self-determination. The outcome is not up to them to decide.

(4) The right is conditional on its being exercised for the right reasons, i.e., to secure conditions necessary for the prosperity and self-respect of the group. This is a major protection against abuse. Katanga cannot claim a right to self-determination as a way of securing its exclusive control over uranium mines within its territory. This condition does not negate the nature of a right. The group is still entrusted with the right to decide, and its decision is binding even if wrong, even if the case for self-government does not obtain, provided the reasons that motivate the group's decision are of the right kind.

(5) Finally, there are the two broad safeguards on which the exercise of the right is conditional. First, that the group is likely to respect the basic

rights of its inhabitants, so that its establishment will do good rather than add to the ills of this world. Second, since the establishment of the new state may fundamentally endanger the interests of inhabitants of other countries, its exercise is conditional on measures being taken to prevent or minimize the occurrence of substantial damage of this kind. Such measures, which will vary greatly from case to case, include free-trade agreements, port facilities, granting of air routes, demilitarization of certain regions, and so on.

Two kinds of interests do not call for special protection. One is the interest of a people to regard themselves as part of a larger rather than a smaller grouping or country. The English may have an interest in being part of Great Britain, rather than mere Englanders. But that interest can be justly satisfied only with the willing cooperation of, e.g., the Scots. If the other conditions for Scottish independence are met, this interest of the English should not stand in its way. Second, unjust economic gains, the product of colonial or other form of exploitation of one group by another, may be denied to the exploiting group without hesitation or compensation (barring arrangements for a transitory period). But where secession and independence will gravely affect other and legitimate interests of other countries, such interests should be protected by creating free-trade zones, demilitarized areas, and the like.

(6) A right in one person is sufficient ground to hold some other person(s) to be under a duty.[9] What duties arise out of the right to self-determination? How is this matter to be settled? As the previous discussion makes clear, the right of self-determination is instrumentally justified, as the method of implementing the case for self-government, which itself is based on the fact that in many circumstances self-government is necessary for the prosperity and dignity of encompassing groups. Hence, in fixing the limits of the right, one has to bear in mind the existing system of international politics, and show that, given other elements in that system, certain duties can be derived from the right to self-determination, whereas others cannot. The first and most important duty arising out of the right is the duty not to impede the exercise of the right, i.e., not to impede groups in their attempts to decide whether appropriate territories should be independent, so long as they do so within the limits of the right. This duty affects in practice first and foremost the state that governs the territory concerned and its inhabitants.

Other duties may follow from the right of self-determination. In particular, there may be a duty on the state governing the territory to provide aid in exercising the right, and a duty on other states to aid the relevant group in realizing its right, and thus to oppose the state governing the territory if it impedes its implementation. But the extent of these duties must be subject to the general principles of international morality, which indicate what methods may and may not be used in pursuit of worthwhile goals and in preventing the violation of rights. As indicated at the outset, the examination of the details of such implications of the right is beyond the scope of this article.

This brings to an end our consideration of the outlines of the case for a right to self-determination and its limits. It is an argument that proceeds in several stages from fundamental moral concerns to the ways in which they can be best implemented, given the way our world is organized. The argument is meant to present the normal justification for the right. It does not claim that there could not be alternative justifications. But it does claim to be the central case, which alternatives presuppose or of which they are variations.[10]

Two conclusions emerge from this discussion. On the one hand, the right to self-determination is neither absolute nor unconditional. It affects important and diverse interests of many people, from those who will be citizens of the new state, if it comes into being, to others far away from it. Those who may benefit from self-government cannot insist on it at all costs. Their interests have to be considered along those of others. On the other hand, the interests of members of an encompassing group in the self-respect and prosperity of the group are among the most vital human interests. Given their importance, their satisfaction is justified even at a considerable cost to other interests. Furthermore, given the absence of effective enforcement machinery in the international arena, the interest in group prosperity justifies entrusting the decision concerning self-government to the hands of an encompassing group that constitutes the vast majority of the population in the relevant territory, provided other vital interests are protected.

NOTES

We are grateful to Lea Brilmayer, Moshe Halbertal, David Heyd, and the editors of *The Journal of Philosophy* for helpful comments on an earlier draft.

1. This fact is doubly relevant. It is a natural fact about our world that it is a populated world with no unappropriated lands. It is a social and a moral fact that it is a world of nations, tribes, peoples, etc., that is, that people's perception of themselves and of others and their judgments of the opportunities and the responsibilities of life are shaped, to an extent, by the existence of such groups and their membership of them. It may be meaningful to claim that our views regarding national self-determination apply only to a populated world like ours. One may point to different principles that would prevail in a world with vast unoccupied fertile lands. Such speculation is utopian but it may serve to highlight some of the reasons for the principles that apply in our condition. To speculate concerning a reality different from ours in its basic social and moral constitution is pointless in a deeper way. Such social facts are constitutive of morality. Their absence undercuts morality's very foundations. We could say that under such changed conditions people will have normative beliefs and will be guided by some values. But they are not ones for which we can claim any validity.

2. This qualification is to take account of the fact that, according to doctrines of limited government, certain matters are outside the realm of politics, and no political action regarding them may be undertaken.

3. Among the exceptions to this rule are the slowly growing importance of supernational, especially regional, associations, such as the European Community, the growth of a doctrine of sovereignty limited by respect for fundamental human rights, and the continuing (usually thinly veiled) claims of some states that they are not bound by the international law regarding the sovereignty of states.

4. The substantive right protected indirectly by the possessory right in cases of this kind is one of the other rights providing a title in a territory. The right to self-determination is only one of the possible sources of title.

5. The fiction-reading public can take the character of a literary elite with mutual recognition as part of its identity. The importance of "acceptability" in such groups has often been noted and analyzed.

6. This is not meant to suggest that there are not often drawbacks to self-rule. They will be considered below.

7. It should be made clear that these observations relate to the right to self-determination as it is commonly understood in the discourse of international relations and international morality. In principle, there could be a different right of self-determination, i.e., a right that, when the case for self-government is established, self-government should be granted, i.e., that all the international agents have a duty to take what action is necessary to grant self-government

to the encompassing group regarding which the case for self-government has been established. That is, there could in principle have been a substantive right to have self-government when it is right that one should have it, rather than a "who is to decide" right, that an encompassing group should be entitled to decide whether it should be self-governing. Below we touch briefly on the reasons that explain why the right of self-determination as we know it today is not of this kind.

8. The reference is to moral individualism, or value individualism, not to methodological individualism. It is impossible here to deal with the matter adequately. Let us simply indicate our position briefly. There is no accepted characterization of the term. In *The Morality of Freedom* [(New York: Oxford, 1986), p. 198], Raz identified moral individualism with the view that only individual goods, and no collective goods, have intrinsic values. According to individualism so understood, membership of encompassing groups, and the prosperity of such groups, cannot be of intrinsic value. But we believe that it is intrinsically valuable. Hence, on this definition our approach is not individualistic. In "Three Grades of Social Involvement" [*Philosophy and Public Affairs*, 18: 2 (spring 1989), pp. 133–57], George Sher characterizes moral individualism as the belief that moral justification proceeds through premises relating to individuals and their preferences. His characterization is too vague to be conclusively disputed (e.g., all holistic justifications will include premises relating to preferences as well as to everything else—does that make them individualistic?). But if Sher has in mind the standard type of (actual or hypothetical) contractarian justifications, then our approach is not individualistic. Because actual individual preferences heavily depend on social practices, there is no reason to give them justificatory primacy. The content of hypothetical preferences is either too indefinite to yield any results or is made definite by assuming a certain social context to give them meaning. Either way it cannot be endowed with justificatory primacy, though of course people's capacity to respond to various conditions, and to form various goals and attachments, is central to any moral justification.

9. See Raz, *The Morality of Freedom*, chap. 7: "The Nature of Rights." On the relations of moral and legal rights, see also Raz, "Legal Rights," *Oxford Journal of Legal Studies*, IV (1984), p. 1. Raz has applied this analysis to the case of constitutional rights in general in chap. 10 of *The Morality of Freedom*.

10. On the notion of a "normal justification," and the reasons why it cannot be analyzed as either a necessary or a sufficient condition, see Raz, *The Morality of Freedom*, chap. 3.

11. HENRY SHUE

In order to decide whether a comprehensive treaty covering all greenhouse gases is the best next step after UNCED, one needs to distinguish among the four questions about the international justice of such international arrangements: (1) What is a fair allocation of the costs of preventing the global warming that is still avoidable? (2) What is a fair allocation of the costs of coping with the social consequences of the global warming that will not in fact be avoided? (3) What background allocation of wealth would allow international bargaining (about issues like 1 and 2) to be a fair process? and (4) What is a fair allocation of emissions of greenhouse gases (over the long term and during the transition to the long-term allocation)? In answering each question we must specify from whom any transfers should come and to whom any transfers should go. In justifying answers we usually face a choice between fault-based principles and no-fault principles.

Subsistence Emissions and Luxury Emissions

First published in Law and Policy *15: 1 (January 1993): 39–59.*

I. INTRODUCTION

The United Nations Framework Convention on Climate Change adopted in Rio de Janeiro at the United Nations Conference on Environment and Development (UNCED) in June 1992 establishes no dates and no dollars: No dates are specified by which emissions are to be reduced by the wealthy states and no dollars are specified with which the wealthy states will assist the poor states to avoid an environmentally dirty development like our own. The convention is toothless because throughout the negotiations in the Intergovernmental Negotiating Committee during 1991 to 1992 the US played the role of dentist: Whenever virtually all the other states in the world (with the notable exceptions of Saudi Arabia and Kuwait) agreed to convention language with teeth, the US insisted that the teeth be pulled out.

The Clinton administration now faces a strategic question: Should the next step aim at a comprehensive treaty covering all greenhouse gases (GHGs), or at a narrower protocol covering only one, or a few, gases, for example, only fossil-fuel carbon dioxide (CO_2)? Richard Stewart and Jonathan Wiener (1992) have argued for moving directly to a comprehensive treaty, while Thomas Drennen (1993) has argued for a more focused beginning. I will suggest that Drennen is essentially correct that we should not try to go straight to a comprehensive treaty, at least not of the kind advocated by Stewart and Wiener. First I would like to develop a framework into which to set issues of equity or justice of the kind introduced by Drennen.

II. A FRAMEWORK FOR INTERNATIONAL JUSTICE

A. Four Kinds of Questions

It would be easier if we faced only one question about justice, but several questions are not only unavoidable individually but are entangled with each other. In addition, each question can be given not simply alternative answers but answers of different kinds. In spite of this multiplicity of possible answers to the multiplicity of inevitable and interconnected questions, I think we can lay out the issues fairly clearly and establish that commonsense principles converge to a remarkable extent upon what ought to be done, at least for the next decade or so.

Leaving aside the many important questions about justice that do not have to be raised in order to decide how to tackle threats to the global environment, we will find four questions that are deeply involved in every choice of a plan for action. (1) What is a fair allocation of the costs of preventing the global warming that is still avoidable? (2) What is a fair allocation of the costs of coping with the social consequences of the global warming that will not in fact be avoided? (3) What background allocation of wealth would allow international bargaining [about issues like (1) and (2)] to be a fair process? (4) What is a fair allocation of emissions of greenhouse gases (over the long term and during the transition to the long-term allocation)? Our leaders can confront these four questions explicitly and thoughtfully, and thereby hope to deal with them more wisely, or they can leave them implicit and unexamined and simply blunder into positions on them while thinking only about the other economic and political considerations that always come up. What leaders cannot do is evade taking actions that will in fact be just or unjust. The subject of justice will not go away. Issues of justice are inherent in the kinds of choices that must immediately be made. Fortunately, these four issues that are intertwined in practice can be separated for analysis.

1. Allocating the Costs of Prevention

Whatever sums are spent in the attempt to prevent additional warming of the climate must somehow be divided up among those who are trying to deal with the problem. The one question of justice that most people readily see is this one: Who should pay for whatever is done to keep global warming from becoming any worse than necessary?

One is tempted to say: "to keep it from becoming any worse than it is already going to be as a result of gases that are already in the air." Tragically, we will in fact continue to make it worse for some time, no matter how urgently we act. Because of the Industrial Revolution, the earth's atmosphere now contains far more accumulated CO_2 than it was normal for it to contain during previous centuries of human history. This is not speculation: Bubbles of air from earlier centuries have been extracted from deep in the polar ice, and the CO_2 in these bubbles has been directly measured. Every day we continue to make large net additions to the total concentration of CO_2.

Several industrial nations have unilaterally committed themselves to reducing their emissions of CO_2 by the year 2000 to the level of their emissions in 1990. This may sound good, and it is obviously better than allowing emissions levels to grow in a totally uncontrolled manner, as the United States and many other industrial nations are doing. The 1990 level of emissions, however, was making a net addition to the total every day, because it was far in excess of the capacity of the planet to recycle CO_2 without raising the surface temperature of the planet. A reduction to the 1990 level of emissions means *reducing the rate* at which we are adding to the atmospheric total to a rate below the current rate of addition, but it also means *continuing to add to the total*.

Stabilizing emissions at a level as high as the 1990 level will not stabilize temperature—it will continue the pressure to drive it up. In order to stabilize temperature, emissions must be reduced to a level at which the accumulated *concentration* of CO_2 in the atmosphere is stabilized. CO_2 must not be added by human processes faster than natural processes can handle it by means that do not raise the surface temperature. Natural processes will, of course, have to "handle"whatever concentration of CO_2 we choose to produce, one way or another; some of those ways involve adjustments in parameters like surface temperature that *we* will have a hard time handling. There is, therefore, nothing magic about the 1990 level of emissions. On the contrary, at that historically unprecedented level of emissions, the atmospheric concentration would continue to expand rapidly—it merely would not expand as quickly as it will at present levels or at the higher business-as-usual future levels now to be expected.

Emissions must be stabilized at a much lower level than the 1990 level, which means that emissions must be sharply reduced. The most authoritative scientific consensus said that in order to stabilize the atmospheric concentration of CO_2, emissions would have to be reduced below 1990 levels by more than 60 percent! (Houghton, Jenkins & Ephraums, 1990: xviii, Table 2). Even if this international scientific consensus somehow were a wild exaggeration and the reduction needed to be, say, a reduction of only 20 percent from 1990 levels, we would still face a major challenge. Every day that we continue to add to the growing concentration, we increase the size of the reduction from current emissions necessary to stabilize the concentration at an acceptable total.

The need to reduce emissions, not merely to stabilize them at an already historically high level, is only part of the bad news for the industrial countries. The other part is that the CO_2 emissions of most countries that contain large percentages of the human population will be rising for some time. I believe that the emissions from these poor, economically less-developed countries also ought to rise insofar as this rise is necessary to provide a minimally decent standard of living for their now-impoverished people. This is, of course, already a (very weak) judgment about what is fair: namely, that those living in desperate poverty ought not to be required to restrain their emissions, thereby remaining in poverty, in order that those living in luxury should not have to restrain their emissions. Anyone who cannot see that it would be unfair to require sacrifices by the desperately poor in order to help the affluent avoid sacrifices will not find anything else said in this article convincing, because I rely throughout on a common sense of elementary fairness. Any strategy of maintaining affluence for some people by keeping other people at or below subsistence is, I take it, patently unfair because so extraordinarily unequal—intolerably unequal.

Be the fairness as it may, the poor countries of the globe are in fact not voluntarily going to refrain from taking the measures necessary to create a decent standard of living for themselves in order that the affluent can avoid discomfort. For instance, the Chinese government, presiding over more than 22 percent of humanity, is not about to adopt an economic policy of no-growth for the convenience of Europeans and North Americans already living much better than the vast majority of Chinese, whatever others think about fairness. Economic growth means growth in energy consumption, because economic activity uses energy. And growth in energy consumption, in the foreseeable future, means growth in CO_2 emissions.

In theory, economic growth could be fueled entirely by forms of energy that produce no greenhouse gases (solar, wind, geothermal, nuclear [fission or fusion], and hydroelectric). In practice, these forms of energy are not now economically viable (which is not to say that none of them would be if public subsidies, including government-funded research and development, were restructured). China specifically has vast domestic coal reserves, *the* dirtiest fuel of all in CO_2 emissions, and no economically viable way in the short run of switching to completely clean technologies or importing the cleaner fossil fuels, like natural gas, or even the cleaner technologies for burning its own coal, which do exist in wealthier countries. In May 1992, Chen Wang-xiang, general secretary of China's Electricity Council, said that coal-fired plants would account for 71 to 74.5 percent of the 240,000 megawatts of generating capacity planned for China by the year 2000 (1992). So, until other arrangements are made and financed, China will most likely be burning vast and rapidly increasing quantities of coal with, for the most part, neither the best available coal-burning technology, nor the best energy technology overall. The only alternative China actually has with its current resources is to choose to restrain its economic growth, which it will surely not do, rightly or wrongly. (I think rightly.)

Fundamentally, then, the challenge of preventing additional avoidable global warming takes this shape: How does one reduce emissions for the world as a whole while accommodating increased emissions by some parts of the world? The only possible answer is: by *reducing* the emissions by one part of the world by an amount *greater than* the increase by the other parts that are increasing their emissions.

The battle to reduce total emissions should be fought on two fronts. First, the increase in emissions by the poor nations should be held to the minimum necessary for the economic development that they are entitled to. From the point of view of the rich nations, this would serve to minimize the increase that their own reductions must exceed. Nevertheless, the rich nations must, second, also reduce their own emissions somewhat, however small the increase in emissions by the poor, if the global total of emissions is to come down while the contribution of the poor nations to that total is rising. The smaller the increase in emissions necessary for the poor nations to rise out of poverty, the smaller the reduction in emissions necessary for the rich nations—environmentally sound development by the poor is in the interest of all.

Consequently, two complementary challenges must be met—and paid for—which is where the less obvious issues of justice come in.[1] First, the economic development of the poor nations must be as "clean" as possible—maximally efficient in the specific sense of creating no unnecessary CO_2 emissions. Second, the CO_2 emissions of the wealthy nations must be reduced by more than the amount by which the emissions of the poor nations increase. The bills for both must be paid: Someone must pay to make the economic development of the poor as clean as possible, and someone must pay to reduce the emissions of the wealthy. These are the two components of the first issue of justice: allocating the costs of prevention.

2. Allocating the Costs of Coping

No matter what we do for the sake of prevention from this moment forward, it is highly unlikely that all global warming can be prevented, for two reasons. First, what the atmospheric scientists call a "commitment to warming" is already in place simply because of all the additional greenhouse gases that have been thrust into the atmosphere by human activities since around 1860. Today is already the morning after. We have done whatever we have done, and now its consequences, both those we understand and those we do not understand, will play themselves out, if not this month, some later month. Temperature at the surface level—at our level—may or may not already have begun to rise. But the best theoretical understanding of what would make it rise tells us that it will sooner or later rise because of what we have already done—and are unavoidably going to continue doing in the short and medium term. Unless the theory is terribly wrong, the rise will begin sooner rather than later. In the century and a quarter between the beginnings of the Industrial Revolution and 1993, and especially in the half century since World War II, the industrializing nations have pumped CO_2 into the atmosphere with galloping vigor. As of today the concentration has already ballooned.

Second, even if starting tomorrow morning everyone in the world made every exertion she could possibly be expected to make to avoid as much addition as possible to today's concentration, we would continue to add CO_2 much faster than it can be recycled without a rise in temperature for an indeterminate number of years to come. A sudden huge decline in the rate of addition to the total is not physically, not to mention economically, feasible. Further, needless to say, not everyone in the world is prepared to make every reasonable exertion. The "leadership" of the United States, the world's largest injector of CO_2 into the planet's atmosphere, will not even commit itself to cap CO_2 emissions by 2000 at 1990 levels, as easy as that would be (and as little good as it by itself would do). Consequently, even a good-faith transition to sustainable levels of CO_2 emissions would make the problem of warming worse for quite a few years before it could begin to allow it to become better. Years of fiddling while our commitment to the warming of future generations expands will make their problem considerably worse still than it already has to be.

The second issue of justice, then, is: How should the costs of coping with the unprevented human consequences of global warming be allocated? The two thoughts that immediately spring to mind are, I believe, profoundly misguided; they are, crudely put, to-each-his-own and wait-and-see. The first thought is: Let each nation that suffers negative consequences deal with "its own" problems, since this is how the world generally operates. The second is: Since we cannot be sure what negative consequences will occur, it is only reasonable to wait and see what they are before becoming embroiled in arguments about who should pay for dealing with which of them. However sensible these two strategic suggestions may seem, I believe that they are quite wrong and that this issue of paying for coping is both far more immediate and much more complex than it seems. This brief overview is not the place to pursue the arguments in any depth, but I would like to telegraph why I think these two obvious-seeming solutions need at the very least to be argued for.

(a) To-each-his-own

Instantly adopting this solution depends upon assuming without question a highly debatable description of the nature of the problem, namely, as it was put just above, "Let each nation that suffers negative consequences deal with 'its own' problems." The fateful and contentious assumption here is that whatever problems arise within one's nation's territory are *its own*, in some sense that entails that it can and ought to deal with them on its own, with (only) its own resources. This assumption depends in turn upon both of two implicit and dubious premises.

First, it is taken for granted that every nation now has all its own resources under its control. Stating the same point negatively, one can say that it is assumed that no significant proportion of any nation's own resources are physically, legally, or in any other way outside its own control. This assumes, in effect, that the international distribution of wealth is perfectly just, requiring no adjustments whatsoever across national boundaries! To put it mildly, that the world is perfectly just as it is, is not entirely clear without further discussion. Major portions of the natural resources of many of the poorer nations are under the control of multinational firms operated from elsewhere. Many Third

World states are crippled by burdens of international debt contracted for them, and then wasted, by illegitimate authoritarian governments. Thus, the assumption that the international distribution of wealth is entirely as it should be is hard to swallow.

Second is an entirely independent question that is also too quickly assumed to be closed: It is taken for granted that no responsibility for problems resulting within one nation's territory could fall upon another nation or upon other actors or institutions outside the territory. Tackling this question seriously means attempting to wrestle with slippery issues about the causation of global warming and about the connection, if any, between causal responsibility and moral responsibility, issues to be discussed more fully later. Once the issues are raised, however, it is certainly not a foregone conclusion, for instance, that coastal flooding in Bangladesh (or the total submersion of, for example, the Maldives and Vanuatu) would be entirely the responsibility of, in effect, its victims and not at least partly the responsibility of those who produced, or profited from, the greenhouse gases that led to the warming that made the ocean water expand and advance inland. On quite a few readings of the widely accepted principle of the "polluter pays," those who caused the change in natural processes that resulted in the human harm would be expected to bear the costs of making the victims whole. Once again, I am not trying to settle the question here, but merely to establish that it is indeed open until the various arguments are heard and considered.

(b) Wait-and-see

The other tactic that is supposed to be readily apparent and eminently sensible is: Stay out of messy arguments about the allocation of responsibility for potential problems until we see which problems actually arise—we can then restrict our arguments to real problems and avoid imagined ones. Unfortunately, this too is less commonsensical than it may sound. To see why, one must step back and look at the whole picture.

The potential costs of any initiative to deal comprehensively with global warming can be divided into two separate accounts, corresponding to two possible components of the initiative. The first component, introduced in the previous section of this article, is the attempted prevention of as much warming as possible, the costs of which can be thought of as falling into the prevention account. The second component, briefly sketched in this section, is the attempted correction of, or adjustment to—what I have generally called "coping with"—the damage done by the warming that for whatever reasons goes unprevented.

It may seem that if costs can be separated into prevention costs and coping costs, the two kinds of costs could then be allocated separately, and perhaps even according to unrelated principles. Indeed, the advice to wait-and-see about any coping problems assumes that precisely such independent handling is acceptable. It assumes in effect that prevention costs can be allocated—or that the principles according to which they will be allocated, once they are known, can be agreed upon—and prevention efforts put in motion, before the possibly unrelated principles for allocating coping costs need to be agreed upon. What is wrong with this picture of two basically independent operations is that what is either a reasonable or a fair allocation of the one set of costs may—I will argue, does—depend upon how the other set of costs is allocated. The respective principles for the two allocations must not merely not be unrelated but be complementary.

In particular, the allocation of the costs of prevention will directly affect the ability to cope later of those who abide by their agreed-upon allocation. To take an extreme case, suppose that what a nation was being asked to do for the sake of prevention could be expected to leave it much less able to cope with "its own" unprevented problems, on its own, than it would be if it refused to contribute to the prevention efforts—or refused to contribute on the specific terms proposed—and instead invested all or some of whatever it might have contributed to prevention in its own preparations for its own coping. For example, suppose that in the end more of Shanghai could be saved from the actual eventual rise in sea level due to global warming if China simply began work immediately on an elaborate and massive Dutch-style system of seawalls, dikes, canals, and sophisticated floodgates—a kind of Great Seawall of China—rather than spending its severely constrained resources on, say, purification technologies for its new coal-fueled electricity generating plants and other prevention measures. From a strictly Chinese point of view, the Great Seawall might be preferable even if China's refusal to contribute to the prevention efforts resulted in a higher sea level at

Shanghai than would result if the Chinese did cooperate with prevention (but then did not have time or resources to build the Seawall fast enough or high enough).

This fact that the same resources that might be contributed to a multilateral effort at prevention might alternatively be invested in a unilateral effort at coping raises two different questions, one primarily ethical and one primarily nonethical (although these two questions are not unrelated, either). First, would it be fair to expect cooperation with a multilateral initiative on prevention, given one particular allocation of those costs, if the costs of coping are to be allocated in a specific other way (which may or may not be cooperative)? Second, would it be reasonable for a nation to agree to the one set of terms, given the other set of terms—or, most relevantly, given that the other set of terms remained unspecified? Doing your part under one set now while the other set is up for grabs later leaves you vulnerable to the possibility of the second set's being stacked against you in spite of, or because of, your cooperation with the first set. It is because the fairness and the reasonableness of any way of allocating the costs of prevention depends partly upon the way of allocating the costs of coping that it is both unfair and unreasonable to propose that binding agreement should be reached now concerning prevention, while regarding coping we should wait-and-see.

3. The Background Allocation of Resources and Fair Bargaining

This last point about potential vulnerability in bargaining about the coping terms, for those who have already complied with the prevention terms, is a specific instance of a general problem so fundamental that it lies beneath the surface of the more obvious questions, even though it constitutes a third issue of justice requiring explicit discussion. The outcome of bargaining among two or more parties, such as various nations, can be binding upon those parties that would have preferred a different outcome only if the bargaining situation satisfies minimal standards of fairness. An unfair process does not yield an outcome that anyone ought to feel bound to abide by if she can in fact do better. A process of bargaining about coping in which the positions of some parties were too weak precisely because they had invested so much of their resources in prevention would be unfair in the precise sense that those parties that had already benefited from the invested resources of the consequently weakened parties were exploiting that very weakness for further advantage in the terms on which coping would be handled.

In general, of course, if several parties (individuals, groups, or institutions) are in contact with each other and have conflicting preferences, they obviously would do well to talk with each other and simply work out some mutually acceptable arrangement. They do not need to have and apply a complete theory of justice before they can arrive at a limited plan of action. If parties are more or less equally situated, the method by which they should explore the terms on which different parties could agree upon a division of resources or sacrifices (or a process for allocating the resources or sacrifices) is actual direct bargaining. Other things being equal, it may be best if parties can simply work out among themselves the terms of any dealings they will have with each other.

Even lawyers, however, have the concept of an unconscionable agreement; and ordinary nonlawyers have no difficulty seeing that voluntarily entered agreements can have objectionable terms if some parties were subject, through excessive weakness, to undue influence by other parties. Parties can be unacceptably vulnerable to other parties in more than one way, naturally, but perhaps the clearest case is extreme inequality in initial positions. This means that morally acceptable bargains depend upon initial holdings that are not morally unacceptable—not, for one thing, so outrageously unequal that some parties are at the mercy of others.

Obviously this entails in turn that the recognition of acceptable bargaining presupposes knowledge of standards for fair shares, which are one kind of standard of justice. If we do not know whether the actual shares that parties currently hold are fair, we do not know whether any actual agreement they might reach would be morally unconscionable. The simple fact that they all agreed is never enough. The judgment that an outcome ought to be binding presupposes a judgment that the process that produced it was minimally fair. While this may not mean that they must have "a complete theory of justice" before they can agree upon practical plans, it does mean that they need to know the relevant criteria for minimally fair shares of holdings before they can be confident that any plan they actually work out should in any way constrain those who might have preferred different plans.

If bargaining among nations about the terms on which they will cooperate to prevent global warming is to yield any outcome that can be morally binding on the nations who do not like it, the "initial" holdings at the time of the bargaining must be fair. Similarly, the "initial" holdings at the time of the bargaining about the terms on which they will cooperate to cope with the unprevented damage from global warming depends, once again, upon minimally fair shares at that point. Holdings at the point of bargaining over the arrangements for coping will have been influenced by the terms of the cooperation on prevention. Consequently, one requirement upon the terms for prevention is that they should not result in shares that would be unfair at the time that the terms of coping are to be negotiated. The best way to prevent unfair terms of coping would appear to be to negotiate both sets of terms at the same time and to design them to be complementary and fair taken together. This would deal with all the first three issues of justice at once. First, however, one needs to know the standard of fairness by which to judge. This is the third issue of justice.

4. Allocating Emissions: Transition and Goal

The third kind of standard of justice is general but minimal: general in that it concerns all the resources and wealth that contribute to the distribution of bargaining strength and weakness, and minimal in that it specifies, not thoroughly fair distributions, but distributions not so unfair as to undermine the bargaining process. The fourth kind of standard is neither so general nor so minimal. It is far less general because its subject is not the international distribution of all wealth and resources, but the international distribution only of greenhouse gas emissions in particular. And rather than identifying a minimal standard, it identifies an ultimate goal: What distribution of emissions should we be trying to end up with? How should shares of the limited global total of emissions of a greenhouse gas like CO_2 be allocated among nations and among individual humans? Once the efforts at prevention of avoidable warming are complete, and once the tasks of coping with unprevented harms are dealt with, how should the scarce capacity of the globe to recycle the net emissions be divided?

So far, of course, nations and firms have behaved as if each of them had an unlimited and unshakable entitlement to discharge any amount of greenhouse gases that it was convenient to release. Everyone has simply thrust greenhouse gases into the atmosphere at will. The danger of global warming requires that a ceiling—probably a progressively declining ceiling—be placed upon total net emissions. This total must somehow be shared among the nations and individuals of the world. By what process and according to what standards should the allocation be done?

I noted above the contrast between the minimal and general third kind of standard and this fourth challenge of specifying a particular (to greenhouse emissions) final goal. I should also indicate a contrast between this fourth issue and the first two. Both of the first two issues are about the allocation of costs: who pays for various undertakings (preventing warming and coping with unprevented warming)? The fourth issue is about the allocation of the emissions themselves: of the total emissions of CO_2 compatible with preventing global warming, what percentage may, say, China and India use—and, more fundamentally, by what standard do we decide? Crudely put, issues one and two are about money, and issue four is about CO_2. We need separate answers to, who pays? and to, who emits? because of the distinct possibility that one nation should, for any of a number of reasons, pay so that another nation can emit more. The right answer about emissions will not simply fall out of the right answer about costs, or vice versa.[2]

We will be trying to delineate a goal: a just pattern of allocation of something scarce and valuable, namely greenhouse-gas emissions capacities. However, a transition period during which the pattern of allocation does not satisfy the ultimate standard may well be necessary because of political or economic obstacles to an immediate switch away from the status quo. For instance, current emissions of CO_2 are very nearly as unequal as they could possibly be: A few rich countries with small populations are generating the vast bulk of the emissions, while the majority of humanity, living in poor countries with large populations, produces less altogether than the rich minority. It seems reasonable to assume that, whatever exactly will be the content of the standard of justice for allocating emissions, the emissions should be divided somewhat more equally than they currently are. Especially if the total cannot be allowed to keep rising, or must even be reduced, the per capita emissions of the rich few will have to decline so that the per capita emissions of the poor majority can rise.

Nevertheless, members of the rich minority who do not care about justice will almost certainly veto any change they consider too great an infringement upon their comfort and convenience, and they may well have the power and wealth to enforce their veto. The choice at that point for people who are committed to justice might be between vainly trying to resist an almost certainly irresistible veto and temporarily acquiescing in a far-from-ideal but significant improvement over the status quo. In short, the question would be: Which compromises, if any, are ethically tolerable? To answer this question responsibly, one needs guidelines for transitions as well as ultimate goals: not, however, guidelines for transitions instead of ultimate goals, but guidelines for transitions *in addition to* ultimate goals. For, one central consideration in judging what is presented as a transitional move in the direction of a certain goal is the distance traveled toward the goal. The goal must have been specified in order for this assessment to be made.[3]

B. Two More Kinds of Questions

A principle of justice may specify to whom an allocation should go, from whom the allocation should come, or, most usefully, both. The distinction between the questions, from whom and to whom, would seem too obvious to be worth comment except that "theories" of justice actually tend in this regard to be only half-theories. They tend, that is, to devote almost all their attention to the question "to whom," and to fail to tackle the challenges to the firm specification of the sources for the recommended transfers. This is one legitimate complaint practical people tend to have against such "theories": "You have shown me it would be nice if so-and-so received more, but you have not told me who is to keep less for that purpose—I cannot assess your proposal until I have heard the other half."

Unfortunately, the answer to "from whom?" does not flow automatically from all answers to "to whom?" Often a given specification of the recipients of transfers leaves open a wide variety of possible allocations of the responsibility for making the transfers. For instance, if the principle governing the allocation of certain transfers were, "to those who had been severely injured by the pollution from the process," the potential sources of the transfers would include: those who were operating the process, the owners of the firm that authorized the process, the insurance company for the firm, the agency that was supposed to be regulating the process, society in general, only the direct beneficiaries of the process and no one else, and so on. Quite often proposals about justice are not so much wrong as too incomplete to be judged either right or wrong.

I have phrased the first four kinds of issues about justice, which arise from different aspects of the challenge of global warming, as, in effect, from-whom questions, precisely because this is the neglected side of the discussion of justice. What we are now noticing is simply that there is, in addition, always the question "to whom?" It is more likely that "to whom?" will have an obvious answer than it is that "from whom?" will, but it is always necessary to check. If we are discussing the costs of coping, for example, it might seem obvious that from whomsoever the transfers should come, they should go to those having the most difficulty coping. However, if the specification of the sources of the transfers is "those who caused the problem being coped with," then country A, which did in fact cause the problem in country X, might be expected to assist country X, and not country Y, even though country Y was having much more difficulty coping (but with problems that were not A's responsibility). Not much, unfortunately, is obvious, although I will try to show that a great deal is actually fairly simple, given commonsense principles of fairness.

One vital point that this abstract example of A, X, and Y illustrates is: Answers to "from whom?" and answers to "to whom?" are interconnected. Once one has an answer to one question or the other, certain answers to the remaining question are inappropriate and, sometimes, another answer to the remaining question becomes the only one that really makes any sense. Often these logical connections are very helpful.

C. TWO KINDS OF ANSWERS

We saw, in section A, that if one thinks hard enough about how the international community should respond to global warming, questions about justice arise unavoidably at four points:

1. Allocating the costs of prevention

2. Allocating the costs of coping

3. The background allocation of resources and fair
    bargaining

4. Allocating emissions: transition and goal.

And in section B we have just now observed that besides these more difficult questions about identifying the bearers of responsibility who should be the sources of any necessary transfers, there is always in principle, and often in practice, a further question in each case about the appropriate recipients of any transfers.

Before attempting to sort out specific proposed answers to this array of questions, it is helpful, I think, to notice that individual principles of justice for the assignment of responsibility fall into one or the other of two general kinds, which I will call fault-based principles and no-fault principles. A well-known fault-based principle is: "The polluter pays"; and a widely accepted no-fault principle is "Payment according to ability to pay." The principle of payment according to ability to pay is no-fault in the sense that alleged fault, putative guilt, and past misbehavior in general are all completely irrelevant to the assignment of responsibility to pay. Those with the most should pay at the highest rate, but this is not because they have done wrong in acquiring what they own, even if they have in fact done wrong. The basis for the assignment of progressive rates of contribution, which are the kind of rates that follow from the principle of payment according to ability to pay, is not how wealth was acquired but simply how much is held.

In contrast, the polluter-pays principle is based precisely upon fault or causal responsibility. "Why should I pay for the cleanup?" "Because you created the problem that has to be cleaned up." The kind of fault invoked here need not be a moralized kind—the fault need not be construed as moral guilt so much as simply a useful barometer or symptom to be used to assign the burden of payment to the source of the need for the payment. That is, one need not, in order to rely upon this principle, believe that polluters are wicked or even unethical in some milder sense (although one can also believe they are). The rationale for relying upon polluter-pays could, in particular, be an entirely amoral argument about incentives: The polluter should pay because this assignment of cleanup burdens creates the strongest disincentive to pollute. Even so, this would be a fault-based principle in my sense of "fault-based," which simply means that the inquiry into who should pay depends upon a factual inquiry into the origins of the problem. The moral responsibility for contributing to the solution of the problem is proportional to the causal responsibility for creating the problem. The pursuit of this proportionality can itself in turn have a moral basis (guilty parties deserve to pay) or an amoral basis (the best incentive structure makes polluters pay). The label "fault-based" has the disadvantage that it may sound as if it must have a moral basis, which it may or may not have, as well as having a moral implication about who ought to pay, which it definitely does have.

An alternative label, which avoids this possible moralistic misunderstanding of "fault-based," would have been to call this category of principles, not "fault-based," but "causal" or "historical," since such principles make the assignment of responsibility for payment depend upon an accurate understanding of how the problem in question arose. This, however, has the greater disadvantage of suggesting as the natural label for what I call "no-fault" principles, "acausal," or "ahistorical" principles. That would, I think, be more misleading still because it would make the no-fault principles sound much more ethereal and oblivious to the facts than they are. "Payment according to ability to pay" does not call for an inquiry into the origins of the problem, but neither is it ahistorical or acausal. A historical analysis or a view about the dynamics of political economy might be a part of the rationale for an ability-to-pay principle, so it would be seriously misleading to label this principle "ahistorical" or "acausal" just because it does not depend upon a search for the villain in the not-necessarily-moralistic sense in which "fault-based" principles do depend upon identifying the villain, that is, in the sense of who produced the problem. So, I will stick with "fault-based" for principles according to which the answer to "from whom?" depends upon an inquiry into the question, "By whom was this problem caused?" and to "no-fault" for principles according to which "from whom?" can be answered on grounds other than an analysis of the production of the problem.

Principles for answering the second kind of question noted in section B, "to whom transfers should be made," also fall into the general categories of fault-based and no-fault. The principle, "make the victims whole," is ultimately fault-based in that the rightful recipients of required transfers are identified as specifically those who suffered from the faulty behavior on the basis of which it will be decided from whom the transfers should come: On this principle, the transfers should come from those who caused the injury or harm and go to those who suffered the injury or harm. Indeed, one of the great advantages of fault-based principles is precisely that their cause-and-effect structure provides complementary answers to both questions: Transfers go to those negatively affected, from those who negatively affected them. This specific principle, "make the victims whole," embodies a perfectly ordinary view—and an especially clear one, since it also partly answers the third question, how much should be transferred, by indicating that the transfer should be at least enough to restore the victims to their condition prior to the infliction of the harm. The victims (to whom?) are to be "made whole" (how much?—minimum amount, anyway) by those who left them less than whole (from whom?). This principle does not completely answer the question of "how much?" because it leaves open the option that the victims are entitled to more than enough merely to restore them to their condition ex ante, that is, it leaves open the possibility of additional compensation.

An ordinary example of a kind of no-fault principle for answering to whom an allocation should go is: "Maintain an adequate minimum." Naturally, the level of what was claimed to be the minimum would have to be specified and defended for this to be a usably concrete version of this kind of principle. It has the general advantage of all no-fault principles, however, in that no inquiry needs to be conducted into who was in fact injured, who injured them, how much they were injured and to what extent their problems had other sources, and so forth. Transfers go to those below the minimum until they reach the minimum; then something else happens (for example, they are retrained for available jobs). Quite a bit of information is still needed to use such a no-fault principle, both to justify the original specification of the minimum level and to select those who are in fact below it. Yet this information is of different types from the information needed to apply a fault-based principle: One does not need an understanding of possibly highly complex systems of causal interactions and positive and negative feedbacks and/or lengthy chains of historical connections among potentially vast numbers of agents and multiple levels of analysis. The information needed to apply no-fault principles tends to be contemporaneous information about current functioning, which is often easier to obtain than the convincing analysis of fault needed for the use of a fault-based principle.

The evident disadvantage of a no-fault principle for specifying to whom transfers go is that it lacks the kind of naturally complementary identification of from whom the transfers should come that flows from the cause-and-effect structure of fault-based principles. In particular, it does not imply that the transfers should come from whomever caused those who are below the minimum to be below the minimum; in fact, it does not even assume that there is any clear answer or, for that matter, any meaningful question of the form, "Who caused those below the minimum to be there?" The consequence of the absence of the convenient complementary answers implied by fault-based principles is that with no-fault principles the answers to the "to whom" question and the "from whom" question must be argued for and established separately, not by a single argument like arguments about fault. It might be, for example, that if the answer to the question "to whom?" is "those below the minimum," the answer to the question "from whom?" may be "those with the greatest ability to pay." The point, however, is that the argument for using ability-to-pay to answer the one question and the argument for using maintenance-of-a-minimum to answer the other question have to be two separate arguments.

III. COMPREHENSIVENESS VERSUS JUSTICE

With this framework in mind, one can return to the choice between the recommendations of Stewart and Wiener on the one hand and Drennen on the other. Stewart and Wiener make a kind of mistake that is often made by lawyers who take economics too seriously and equity not seriously enough. One of their chief arguments in favor of moving directly to a comprehensive treaty is that under a comprehensive treaty each nation could engage in what I will call homogenizing calculations of cost-effectiveness (Stewart & Wiener, 1992: 93–95). A major advantage of the comprehensive treaty is supposed to be that each nation could look at all uses of all GHGs and select the least-cost options. That is, one could begin the reduction of GHG emissions by eliminating the specific sources of specific gases the elimination of which would produce the smallest subtraction of economic value. The crucial feature of this approach to cost-effectiveness—the feature that leads me to call the approach "homogenizing"—is that all gas-sources (every source of every gas) are thrown into the same pot. Not a single distinction is made among gas sources, not even the distinction between essential and nonessential.

Now it may initially seem strange not to embrace a thoroughgoing least-cost-first approach, but I would like to try to argue not only that hesitation is not unreasonable but, further, that equity demands qualifications on that approach. First, I would like to explain my earlier slur against some economics and expand a bit on the worry about "homogenization." For standard economic analysis everything is a preference: the epicure's wish for a little more seasoning and the starving child's wish for a little water, the collector's wish for one more painting and the homeless person's wish for privacy and warmth, all are preferences. Quantitatively, they are different because some are backed up by a greater "willingness to pay" than others, but qualitatively a preference is a preference. For a few purposes, perhaps, we might choose to treat preferences only quantitatively, in terms of willingness to pay. To choose, however, to discard all the qualitative distinctions built up during the evolution of human history is to deprive ourselves of a rich treasure of sophistication and subtlety. Some so-called preferences are vital, and some are frivolous. Some are needs, and some are mere wants (not needs). The satisfaction of some "preferences" is essential for survival, or for human decency, and the satisfaction of others is inessential for either survival or decency.

Distinctions like the one between needs and wants, or the one between the urgent and the trivial, are of course highly contested and messy, which is why we yearn for the simplicity provided by everything being a so-called preference, differing only in strength (willingness to pay). To ignore *these* distinctions, however, is to discard the most fundamental differences in kind that we understand. This is a general complaint against much mainstream economics. My specific complaint against Stewart and Wiener does not depend upon this stronger, more general one—I mention the general thesis because my specific thesis concerns a parallel form of clarity-abandoning homogenization.

To suggest simply that it is a good thing to calculate cost-effectiveness across all sources of all GHGs is to suggest that we ignore the fact that some sources are essential and even urgent for the fulfillment of vital needs and other sources are inessential or even frivolous. What if, as is surely in fact the case, some of the sources that it would cost least to eliminate are essential and reflect needs that are urgent to satisfy, while some of the sources that it would cost most to eliminate are inessential and reflect frivolous whims? What if, to be briefly concrete, the economic costs of abandoning rice paddies are less than the economic costs of reducing miles-per-gallon in luxury cars? Does it make no difference that some people need those rice paddies in order to feed their children, but no one needs a luxury car?!

It would be nuts not to follow the principle of least-cost-first as long as one was dealing with matters of comparable significance: To do otherwise would be to choose a more expensive means to an end that could be reached by a less expensive means—that *is* fundamentally irrational. While the elimination of *N* thousand hectares of rice paddy might well cost less in economic terms than the tightening of corporate average fuel efficiency (CAFE) standards enough to produce the same reduction in GHG emissions, however, the human consequences of reducing food production and of reducing inefficient combustion are far from comparable in their effects upon the quality of life—indeed, in the case of the food, upon the very possibility of life. These are not two different means to the very same end. The ends of the two different measures could be the same in the amount of GHG emissions they eliminate, but the ends are otherwise as different as reducing vital supplies of food and making luxury a tad more costly. Consequently, to apply a homogenizing form of cost-effectiveness calculation, as if the two measures differed only in how much they each cost to produce the same reduction in emissions, is seriously to distort reality. This kind of comprehensiveness obscures distinctions that are fundamental, most notably the distinction between necessities and luxuries.

The central point about equity is that it is not equitable to ask some people to surrender necessities so that other people can retain luxuries.

It would be unfair to the point of being outrageous to ask that some (poor) people spend more on better feed for their ruminants in order to reduce methane emissions so that other (affluent) people do not have to pay more for steak from less crowded feedlots in order to reduce their methane and nitrous oxide emissions, even if less-crowded feedlots for fattening luxury beef for the affluent world would cost considerably more than a better quality of feed grain for maintaining the subsistence herds of the poor.

It is of course a different story if *all* incremental costs for reducing emissions, wherever incurred, are to be allocated according to ability to pay. If the beef eaters will pay for the better feed grain for the subsistence herds of the poor with *additional* funds not already owed for some other purpose like development assistance, it might, as far as the equity of the arrangements for reducing emissions goes, not be unfair to start with the least-cost measures. The least-cost measure paid for by those *most* able to pay is not at all the same as the least-cost measure paid for by those *least* able to pay. In terms of the framework laid out above, this would combine a no-fault answer to the question "from whom?" (ability to pay) with a no-fault answer to the question "to whom? " (maintenance of an adequate minimum).

If these two answers were fully justified—naturally, they require fuller argument—one or the other of two routes ought to be followed.[4] The homogenizing form of calculation of cost-effectiveness could be neutralized if it were accompanied by a firm commitment that costs are to be paid according to ability to pay and the actual establishment of mechanisms for enforcing the necessary transfers. Otherwise the costs ought to be partitioned—perhaps more than once but surely at least once—into costs that impinge upon necessities for the poor and costs that only impinge upon luxuries for the wealthy.

Thomas Drennen has suggested one type of such a partitioning, and he has based it upon two kinds of considerations: centrally upon the consideration of equity, but also upon the difficulties in measuring agricultural and other biological emissions of methane and verifying any mandated reductions. (It is ironic that the US, which held up the control of nuclear weapons for years with exaggerated worries about verification, now wants to plunge ahead with the much messier matter of methane.) Drennen has arrived at his partitioning between what should be within the scope of the treaty, and what should not, by combining type of gas and type of use. The gases that Drennen would have under protocol control are CO_2 and methane, presumably because they are the largest contributors to global warming that are subject to human control. (Water vapor is larger but not controllable.) The uses that he would like to see reduced are the "industrial-related" ones, not the agricultural ones. Drennen's strategy is to control nonbiological anthropogenic emissions of CO_2 and methane. This is a much more sophisticated formulation than the much-discussed one that deals only with fossil-fuel CO_2. I would nevertheless suggest that a definition of the scope different from Drennen's, based even more directly on considerations of equity, would be preferable; although I also acknowledge that practical consider-ations may require that Drennen's pair, nonindustrial-related CO_2 and nonindustrial-related methane, still be used as proxies for, and as the nearest practical approximation of, the specifications that flow directly from attention to equity.

My main doubts—and they are relatively minor—are about the division into industrial-related and non-industrial-related. This division reflects quite well, as I understand them, the difficulties of measurement and verification of methane emissions. It is much easier to calculate (and change!) leaks from natural gas pipelines than to calculate (and change!) emissions from various varieties of rice and various species of ruminants. Precisely this division reflects less well, however, the concern about equity that Drennen and I share. Just as the methane emissions from beef feedlots are in service of the desires of the wealthy, many of the CO_2 emissions in China and India *could be*—I am not assum-ing that they all in fact are—in service of the needs of the poor. Some agricultural methane emissions are a luxury, and some industrial CO_2 emissions are a necessity. By the standard of equity we do not want to leave all the former uncontrolled, and control all the latter.

Now insofar as we really cannot measure, or even accurately estimate, biological emissions of methane, the lack of perfect fit with equity does not for now matter. Yet I am somewhat impressed by the contention by Stewart and Wiener that we should be able to arrive at accurate enough estimates for our purposes, especially if, as I contend, our purposes ought not to include the control of subsistence emissions. For the sake of scientific understanding we must eventually be able to measure all kinds of emissions, but the measurements of the kinds that we are not going to control can be rough in the beginning.

We should not have a homogenized—undifferentiated—market in emissions allowances in which the wealthy can buy up the allowances of the poor and leave the poor unable to satisfy even their basic needs for lack of emissions allowances. Drennen's partition between industrial-related and nonindustrial-related may be the best approximation we can in practice make: Most agricultural emissions are probably for subsistence and many industrial emissions are not. Better still, if it is practical, would be a finer partitioning that left the necessary industrial activities of the developing countries uncontrolled (not, of course, unmeasured) and brought the unnecessary agricultural services of the developed world, as well as their superfluous industrial activities, under the system of control.

If there is to be an international market in emissions allowances, the populations of poor regions could be allotted inalienable—unmarketable—allowances for whatever use they themselves consider best. Above the inalienable allowances, the market could work its magic, and the standard of cost-effectiveness could reign supreme. But the market for emissions allowances would not be fully comprehensive, as Stewart and Wiener recommend. The poor in the developing world would be guaranteed a certain quantity of protected emissions, which they could produce as they choose. This would allow them some measure of control over their lives rather than leaving their fates at the mercy of distant strangers.

NOTES

1. Less obvious, that is, than the issue whether the poor should have to sacrifice their own economic development so that the rich can maintain all their accustomed affluence. As already indicated, if someone honestly thought this demand could be fair, we would belong to such different worlds that I do not know what I could appeal to that we might have in common.

2. For imaginative and provocative suggestions about the final allocations of emissions themselves, see Agarwal and Narain (1991).

3. A serious attempt to deal with issues about a compromise transition is in Grubb and Sebenius's chapter, "Participation, Allocation and Adaptability in International Tradable Emission Permit Systems for Greenhouse Gas Control" in *Climate Change* (1992).

4. I have provided some relevant arguments in Shue (1992). Justice, or equity, is also discussed in several chapters in the UNCTAD publication, *Combating Global Warming: A Study on a Global System of Tradeable Carbon Emission Entitlements* (1992).

REFERENCES

Agarwal, Anil, and Sunita Narain (1991) *Global Warming in an Unequal World: A Case of Environmental Colonialism*. New Delhi: Centre for Science and Environment.

Drennen, Thomas E. (1993) "After Rio: Measuring the Effectiveness of the International Response," *Law & Policy* 15: 15–37.

Grubb, Michael, and James K. Sebenius (1992) "Participation, Allocation and Adaptability in International Tradeable Emission Permit Systems for Greenhouse Gas Control." In *Climate Change: Designing a Tradeable Permit System*, by Organisation for Economic Co-operation and Development (OECD). Paris: OECD.

Houghton, J. T., G. J. Jenkins, And J. J. Ephraums (1990) *Climate Change: The IPCC Scientific Assessment*. Report by Working Group I. New York: Cambridge University Press for the Intergovernmental Panel on Climate Change.

Shue, Henry (1992) "The Unavoidability of Justice." In *The International Politics of the Environment: Actors, Interests, and Institutions*, edited by Andrew Hurrell and Benedict Kingsbury. Oxford: Clarendon Press.

Stewart, Richard B., and Jonathan B. Wiener (1992) "The Comprehensive Approach to Global Climate Policy: Issues of Design and Practicality." *Arizona Journal of International and Comparative Law* 9: 83–113.

Bureau of National Affairs (BNA) (1992) "Top Environmental Official Welcomes Summit Aid Pledges from Developed Nations—China." *International Environment Reporter: Current Reports* 15 (July 1): 444.

United Nations Conference on Trade and Development (UNCTAD) (1992) *Combating Global Warming: A Study on a Global System of Tradeable Carbon Emission Entitlements*. UNCTAD/RDP/DFP/1. New York: United Nations.

12. SUSAN MOLLER OKIN

Are the theories devised by feminists in affluent states relevant to the problems faced by the poorest women in poor countries? Arguing against those who claim that it is mistakenly "essentialist" to talk in terms of the problems of women "as such," Okin argues that many of the problems faced by the poorest women in poor countries are similar, but worse than those faced by women in wealthier settings, and that the theories devised by Western feminists are therefore indeed highly relevant to the problems of poor women. She finishes by raising some doubts about whether it is feasible or desirable to formulate a theory of justice entirely by listening to the point of view of each individual or group.

Gender Inequality and Cultural Differences

First published in Political Theory *22: 1 (February 1994): 5–24.*

Theories of justice are undergoing something of an identity crisis. How can they be universal, principled, founded on good reasons that all can accept, and yet take account of the many differences there are among persons and social groups? Feminists have been among the first to point out that large numbers of persons have typically been excluded from consideration in purportedly universalist theories. And some feminists have gone on to point out that many feminist theories, while taking account of sexist bias or omission, have neglected racist, heterosexist, class, religious, and other biases. Yet, joining our voices with those of others, some of us discern problems with going in the direction of formulating a theory of justice entirely by listening to every concrete individual's or group's point of view and expression of its needs. Is it possible, by taking this route, to come up with any principles at all? Is it a reliable route, given the possibility of "false consciousness"? Doesn't stressing differences, especially cultural differences, lead to a slide toward relativism? The problem that is being grappled with is an important one. There can no longer be any doubt that many voices have not been heard when most theories of justice were being shaped. But how can all the different voices express themselves and be heard and still yield a coherent and workable theory of justice? This question is one I shall (eventually) return to in this essay.

FEMINISM, DIFFERENCE, AND ESSENTIALISM

Feminists have recently had much to say about difference. One aspect of the debate has been a continuation of an old argument—about how different women are from men, what such differences may be due to, and whether they require that laws and other aspects of public policy should treat women any differently from men.[1] Another, newer, aspect of the debate is about differences among women. It is "essentialist," some say, to talk about women, the problems of women, and especially the problems of women "as such."[2] White middle- and upper-class feminists, it is alleged, have excluded or been insensitive to not only the problems of women of other races, cultures, and religions, but even those of women of other classes than their own. "Gender" is therefore a problematic category, those opposed to such essentialism say, unless always qualified by and seen in the context of race, class, ethnicity, religion, and other such differences (Childers and hooks 1990; Harris 1990; hooks 1984; Lorde 1984; Minow and Spelman 1990; Spelman 1988).

The general allegation of feminist essentialism certainly has validity when applied to some work. Feminists with such pedigrees as Harriet Taylor, Charlotte Perkins Gilman, Virginia Woolf, Simone de Beauvoir, and Betty Friedan (in *The Feminine Mystique*) all seem to have assumed, for example, that the women they were liberating would have recourse to servants. With the partial exception of Woolf, who remarks briefly on the difficult lot of maids, they did not pay attention to the servants, the vast majority of whom were also, of course, women. The tendency of many white middle- and upper-class feminists in the mid-nineteenth century to think only of women of their own class and race (some were explicitly racist) is what makes so poignant and compelling Sojourner

Truth's words in her famous "Ain't I a woman?" speech.[3] However, I think, and will argue, that this problem is far less present in the works of most recent feminists. But the charges of "essentialism" seem to grow ever louder. They are summed up in Elizabeth Spelman's (1988) recent claim that "the focus on women 'as women' has addressed only one group of women—namely, white middle-class women of Western industrialized countries" (p. 4). This has come to be accepted in some circles as virtually a truism.

The claim that much recent feminist theory is essentialist comes primarily from three (to some extent, overlapping) sources—European-influenced postmodernist thought; the work of African-American and other minority feminist women in the United States and Britain; and, in particular, Spelman's recent book, *Inessential Woman* (hereafter *IW*). Postmodernism is skeptical of all universal or generalizable claims, including those of feminism. It finds concepts central to feminist thinking, such as "gender" and "woman," as illegitimate as any other category or generalization that does not stop to take account of every difference. As Julia Kristeva, for example, says,

> The belief that "one is a woman" is almost as absurd and obscurantist as the belief that "one is a man" [W]e must use "we are women" as an advertisement or slogan for our demands. On a deeper level, however, a woman cannot "be"; it is something which does not even belong in the order of *being*. (Quoted in Marks and de Courtivron 1981, 137)

In the same interview, she also says that, because of the very different history of Chinese women, "It is absurd to question their lack of 'sexual liberation'" (in Marks and de Courtivron 1981, 140). Clearly, she thinks we could have no cross-cultural explanations of or objections to gender inequality.

Spelman argues that "the phrase 'as a woman' is the Trojan horse of feminist ethnocentrism" (*IW*, 13). The great mistakes of white middle-class feminists have been to exclude women different from themselves from their critiques or, even when they are included, to assume that, whatever their differences, their experience of sexism is the same. At best, she says, what is presented is "[a]n additive analysis [which] treats the oppression of a black woman in a society that is racist as well as sexist as if it were a further burden when in fact it is a *different burden"* (*IW*, 123; emphasis added).

These antiessentialist arguments, however, are often long on theory and very short on empirical evidence. A large proportion of Spelman's examples of how women's experiences of oppression are different are taken from periods of slavery in ancient Greece and, especially, in the pre–Civil War South. It is not clear, though, how relevant is the obvious contrast between the experience of white slaveholders' wives and black female slaves to most issues involving the sameness or difference of forms of gender oppression today.

Apart from the paucity of relevant evidence (which I shall return to), there seem to me to be two other related problems with Spelman's general antiessentialist argument. One is the claim that unless a feminist theorist perceives gender identity as intrinsically bound up with class, race, or other aspects of identity, she ignores the effects of these other differences altogether. Spelman writes, "If gender were isolatable from other forms of identity, if sexism were isolatable from other forms of oppression, then what would be true about the relation between any man and any woman would be true about the relation between any other man and any other woman" (*IW*, 81). But this does not follow at all. One can argue that sexism is an identifiable form of oppression, many of whose effects are felt by women regardless of race or class, without at all subscribing to the view that race and class oppression are insignificant. One can still insist, for example, on the significant difference between the relation of a poor black woman to a wealthy white man and that of a wealthy white woman to a poor black man.

The second problem is that Spelman misplaces the burden of proof, which presumably affects her perception of the need for her to produce evidence for her claims. She says, "Precisely insofar as a discussion of gender and gender relations is really, even if obscurely, about a particular group of women and their relation to a particular group of men, it is unlikely to be applicable to any other group of women" (*IW*, 114). But why? Surely the burden of proof is on the critic. To be convincing, she needs to show that and how the theory accused of essentialism omits or distorts the experience of persons other than those few the theorist allegedly does take account of. This, after all, is the burden that many of the feminists Spelman considers "essentialist" have themselves taken on in critiquing "malestream" theories. One of the problems of antiessentialist feminism (shared, I think, with much of postmodernist critique) is that it tends to substitute the cry "We're all different" for both argument and evidence.

There are, however, exceptions, and they tend to come from feminists who belong to racial minorities. One of the best critiques of feminist essentialism that I know of is that by Angela Harris (1990), in which she shows how ignorance of the specifics of a culture mars even thoroughly well-intentioned feminist analyses of women's experiences of oppression within that culture. She argues, for example, that in some respects, black women in the United States have had a qualitatively rather than simply quantitatively different experience of rape than that of white women (see esp. 594, 598–601). Even here, though, I think the antiessentialist critique is only partly convincing. Although more concerned with evidence for the salience of differences than most antiessentialists seem to be, Harris raises far more empirical questions than she provides answers. She provides just one example to support her assertion that black women's experience of rape is, even now, radically different from that of white women—that it is "an experience as deeply rooted in color as in gender" (p. 598).[4] Yet she, like Spelman, is as much disturbed by white feminists' saying that black women are "just like us only more so" as she is by their marginalizing black women or ignoring them altogether. As I shall argue, this "insult[ing]" conclusion—that the problems of other women are "similar to ours but more so"—is exactly the one I reach when I apply some Western feminist ideas about justice to the situations of poor women in many poor countries.

In this essay, I put antiessentialist feminism to what I think is a reasonably tough test. In doing this, I am taking up the gauntlet that Spelman throws down. She says, referring to the body of new work about women that has appeared in many fields,

> Rather than assuming that women have something in common as women, these researchers should help us look to see whether they do. Rather than first finding out what is true of some women as women and then inferring that this is true of all women , we have to investigate different women's lives and see what they have in common. (*IW*, 137)

Trained as a philosopher, she does not seem to consider it appropriate to take up the challenge of actually looking at some of this empirical evidence. Having said the above, she turns back to discussing Plato. Trained as a political scientist, I shall attempt to look at some comparative evidence. I'll put some Western feminist ideas about justice and inequality to the test (drawing on my recent book and the many feminist sources I use to support some of its arguments) by seeing how well these theories—developed in the context of women in well-off Western industrialized countries—work when used to look at the very different situations of some of the poorest women in poor countries. How do our accounts and our explanations of gender inequality stand up in the face of considerable cultural and socioeconomic difference?

DIFFERENCES AND SIMILARITIES IN GENDER OPPRESSION: POOR WOMEN IN POOR COUNTRIES

Does the assumption "that there is a generalizable, identifiable and collectively shared experience of womanhood" (Benhabib and Cornell 1987, 13) *have* any validity, or is it indeed an essentialist myth, rightly challenged by Third World women and their spokesfeminists? Do the theories devised by First World feminists, particularly our critiques of nonfeminist theories of justice, have anything to say, in particular, to the poorest women in poor countries, or to those policy-makers with the potential to affect their lives for better or for worse?

In trying to answer these questions, I shall address, in turn, four sets of issues, which have been addressed both by recent feminist critics of Anglo-American social and political theory and by those development scholars who have in recent years concerned themselves with the neglect or distortion of the situation of women in the countries they study. First, why and how has the issue of the inequality between the sexes been ignored or obscured for so long and addressed only so recently? Second, why is it so important that it be addressed? Third, what do we find, when we subject households or families to standards of justice—when we look at the largely hidden inequalities between the sexes? And finally, what are the policy implications of these findings?

WHY ATTENTION TO GENDER IS COMPARATIVELY NEW

In both development studies and theories of justice, there has, until recently, been a marked lack of attention to gender—and in particular to systematic inequalities between the sexes. This point has been made about theories of justice throughout the 1980s (e.g., Kearns 1983; Okin 1989b; Crossthwaite 1989). In the development literature, it was first made earlier, in pioneering work by Ester Boserup, but has lately been heard loud and strong from a number of other prominent development theorists (Chen 1983; Dasgupta 1993; Sen 1990a, 1990b; Jelin 1990). In both contexts, the neglect of women and gender seems to be due primarily to two factors. The first is the assumption that the household (usually assumed to be male-headed) is the appropriate unit of analysis. The dichotomy between the public (political and economic) and the private (domestic and personal) is assumed valid, and only the former has been taken to be the appropriate sphere for development studies and theories of justice, respectively, to attend to. In ethical and political theories, the family is often regarded as an inappropriate context for justice, since love, altruism, or shared interests are assumed to hold sway within it. Alternatively, it is sometimes taken for granted that it is a realm of hierarchy and injustice. (Occasional theorists, like Rousseau, have said both!) In economics, development and other, households until recently have simply been taken for granted as the appropriate unit of analysis on such questions as income distribution. The public/private dichotomy and the assumption of the male-headed household have many serious implications for women as well as for children that are discussed below (Dasgupta 1993; Jaquette 1982, 283; Okin 1989b, 10–14, 124–33; Olsen 1983; Pateman 1983).

The second factor is the closely related failure to disaggregate data or arguments by sex. In the development literature, it seems to appear simply in this form (Chen, Huq, and D'Souza 1981, 68; Jaquette 1982, 283–84). In the justice literature, this used to be obscured by the use of male pronouns and other referents. Of late, the (rather more insidious) practice that I have called "false gender neutrality" has appeared. This consists in the use of gender-neutral terms ("he or she," "persons," and so on), when the point being made is simply invalid or otherwise false if one actually applies it to women (Okin 1989b, esp. 10–13, 45). But the effect is the same in both literatures; women are not taken into account, so the inequalities between the sexes are obscured.

The public/domestic dichotomy has serious implications for women. It not only obscures intrahousehold inequalities of resources and power, as I discuss below, but it also results in the failure to count a great deal of the work done by women as work, since all that is considered "work" is what is done for pay in the "public" sphere. All of the work that women do in bearing and rearing children, cleaning and maintaining households, caring for the old and sick, and contributing in various ways to men's work does not count as work. This is clearly one of those instances in which the situation of poor women in poor countries is not qualitatively *different* from that of most women in rich countries but, rather, "similar but worse," for even more, in some cases far more, of the work done by women (and children) in poor countries is rendered invisible, not counted, or "subsumed under men's work." The work of subsistence farming, tending to animals, domestic crafts (if not for the market), and the often arduous fetching of water and fuel are all added to the category of unrecognized work of women that already exists in richer countries.[5] Chen notes that women who do all these things "are listed [by policy-makers] as housewives," even though "their tasks are as critical to the well-being of their families and to national production as are the men's" (Chen 1983, 220; see also Dasgupta 1993; Drèze and Sen 1989, chap. 4; Jaquette 1982, citing Bourgue and Warren 1979; Waring 1989).

WHY DOES IT MATTER?

This may seem like a silly question. Indeed, I hope it will soon be unnecessary, but it isn't—yet. I therefore argue, at the outset of *Justice, Gender, and the Family*, that the omission from theories of justice of gender, and of much of women's lives, is significant for three major reasons. Each of these reasons applies at least as much to the neglect of gender in theories of development. The first is obvious: Women matter (at least they do to feminists), and their well-being matters at least as much as that of men. As scholars of development have recently been making clear, the inequalities between the sexes in a number of poor countries have not only highly detrimental but *fatal* consequences for millions of women. Sen (1990a) has recently argued that as many as 100 million fewer women exist than might normally be expected on the basis of male/female mortality rates in societies less devaluing of women—not only the Western industrialized world but much of sub-Saharan Africa, too (see also Dasgupta 1993; Drèze and Sen 1989, chap. 4; Drèze and Sen 1990, Introduction, 11–14; but cf. Harriss 1990; Wheeler and Abdullah 1988). So here too we can reasonably say that the issue of the neglect of women is "similar but *much* worse."

The second reason I have raised (in the US context) for the necessity for feminist critique of theories of social justice is that equality of opportunity—for women and girls—but also for increasing numbers of boys—is much affected by the failure of theories of justice to address gender inequality. This is in part due to the greater extent of economic distress in female-headed households. In the United States, nearly 25 percent of children are being raised in single female-headed households, and three-fifths of all chronically poor households with children are among those supported by single women. It has been recently estimated that throughout the world one-third of households are headed by single females, with the percentage much higher in regions with significant male out-migration (Chen 1983, 221; Jaquette 1982, 271). Many millions of children are affected by the higher rate of poverty among such families.[6] Theories of justice or of economic development that fail to pay attention to gender ignore this, too.

In addition, the gendered division of labor has a serious and direct impact on the opportunities of girls and women, which crosses the lines of economic class. The opportunities of females are significantly affected by the structures and practices of family life, particularly by the fact that women are almost invariably primary caretakers, which has much impact on their availability for full-time wage work. It also results in their frequently being *over*worked, and renders them less likely than men to be considered economically valuable. This factor, too, operates "similarly but more so" within poor families in many poor countries. There, too, adult women suffer—often more severely—many of the same effects of the division of labor as do women in richer countries. But, in addition, their daughters are likely to be put to work for the household at a very young age, are much less likely to be educated and to attain literacy than are sons of the same households, and, worst of all—less valued than their brothers—they have less chance of staying alive because they are more likely to be deprived of food or of health care (Dasgupta 1993; Drèze and Sen 1990, chap. 4; Sen 1990a; Papanek 1990).

Third, I have argued that the failure to address the issue of just distribution within households is significant because the family is the first, and arguably the most influential, school of moral development (Okin 1989b, esp. 17–23). It is the first environment in which we experience how persons treat each other, in which we have the potential to learn how to be just or unjust. If children see that sex difference is the occasion for obviously differential treatment, they are surely likely to be affected in their personal and moral development. They are likely to learn injustice by absorbing the messages, if male, that they have some kind of "natural" enhanced entitlement and, if female, that they are *not* equals and had better get used to being subordinated if not actually abused. So far as I know, this point was first made in the Western context by John Stuart Mill, who wrote of the "perverting influence" of the typical English family of his time—which he termed "a school of despotism" (Mill [1869] 1988, 88). I have argued that the still remaining unequal distribution of benefits and burdens between most parents in two-parent heterosexual families is likely to affect their children's developing sense of justice (Okin 1989b, e.g., 21–23, 97–101). In the context of poor countries, as Papanek (1990) notes, "Domestic groups in which age and gender difference confer power on some over others are poor environments in which to unlearn the norms of inequality" (pp. 163–65). She also notes that "given the persistence of gender-based inequalities in power, authority, and access to resources, one must conclude that socialization for gender inequality is by and large very successful" (p. 170). When such basic goods as food and health care are unequally distributed to young children according to sex, a very strong signal about the acceptability of injustice is surely conferred. The comparison of most families in rich countries with poor families in poor countries—where distinctions between the sexes often start earlier and are much more blatant and more harmful to girls—yields, here too, the conclusion that, in the latter case, things are not so much different as "similar but more so." Many Third World families, it seems, are even worse schools of justice and more successful inculcators of the inequality of the sexes as natural and appropriate than are their developed world equivalents. Thus there is even more need for attention to be paid to gender inequality in the former context than in the latter.

Justice in the Family

What do we find when we compare some of Anglo-American feminists' findings about justice within households in their societies with recent discoveries about distributions of benefits and burdens in poor households in poor countries? Again, in many respects, the injustices of gender are quite similar.

In both situations, women's access to paid work is constrained both by discrimination and sex segregation in the workplace and by the assumption that women are "naturally" responsible for all or most of the unpaid work of the household (Bergmann 1986; Fuchs 1988; Gerson 1985; Okin 1989b, 147–52, 155–56; Sanday 1974). In both situations, women typically work longer total hours than men:

> Time-use statistics considering all work (paid and unpaid economic activity and unpaid housework) reveal that women spend more of their time working than men in all developed and developing regions except northern America and Australia, where the hours are almost equal. (United Nations Report 1991, 81 and chap. 6 passim; see also Bergmann 1986; Hochschild 1989)

In both situations, developed and less developed, vastly more of women's work is not paid and is not considered "productive."[7] Thus there is a wide gap between men's and women's *recorded* economic participation. The perception that women's work is of less worth (despite the fact that in most places they do more, and it is crucial to the survival of household members) contributes to women's being devalued and having less power both within the family and outside the household (Blumstein and Schwartz 1983; Dasgupta 1993; Drèze and Sen 1990, chap. 4; Okin 1989b, chap. 7; Sanday 1974; Sen 1990a, 1990b). This in turn adversely affects their capacity to become economically less dependent on men. Thus they become involved in "a cycle of socially caused and distinctly asymmetric vulnerability" (Okin 1989b, 138; Drèze and Sen 1989, 56–59). The devaluation of women's work, as well as their lesser physical strength and economic dependence on men, allows them to be subject to physical, sexual, and/or psychological abuse by men they live with (Gordon 1988; United Nations Report 1991, 19–20). However, in many poor countries, as I have mentioned, this power differential extends beyond the abuse and overwork of women to deprivation in terms of the feeding, health care, and education of female children—and even to their being born or not: "of 8,000 abortions in Bombay after parents learned the sex of the foetus through amniocentesis, only one would have been a boy" (United Nations Report 1991, see also Dasgupta 1993; Drèze and Sen 1989, chap. 4; Sen 1990a).

In cross-regional analyses, both Sen and Dasgupta have found correlations between the life expectancies of females relative to males and the extent to which women's work is perceived as having economic value. Thus in both rich and poor countries, women's participation in work outside the household can improve their status within the family, but this is not necessarily assured. It is interesting to compare Barbara Bergmann's (1986) analysis of the situation of "drudge wives" in the United States, who work full-time for pay and who also perform virtually all of the household's unpaid labor, with Peggy Sanday's earlier finding that, in some Third World contexts, women who do little of the work that is considered "productive" have low status, whereas many who do a great deal of it become "virtual slaves" (Sanday 1974, p. 201; Bergmann 1986, pp. 260–73).[8]

This leads us to the issue of women's economic dependence (actual and perceived). Although most poor women in poor countries work long hours each day, throughout the world they are often economically dependent on men. This, too, is "similar to but worse than" the situation of many women in richer countries. It results from so much of their work being unpaid work, so much of their paid work being poorly paid work, and, in some cases, from men's laying claim to the wages their wives and daughters earn. Feminist critics since Ester Boserup (1970) have argued that women's economic dependency on men was in many cases exacerbated by changes that development theory and development policy-makers saw only as "progressive." All too ready to perceive women as dependents, mainstream theorists did not notice that technology, geographical mobility, and the conversion from subsistence to market economies were not, from the female point of view, "unalloyed benefits, but processes that cut women out from their traditional economic and social roles and thrust them into the modern sector where they are discriminated against and exploited, often receiving cash incomes below the subsistence level, in turn increas(ing) female dependency" (Jaquette 1982; see also Boserup 1970; Rogers, in Jaquette).[9]

In both rich and poor countries, women who are the sole economic support of families often face particular hardship. However, whereas some are, not all of the reasons for this are the same. Discrimination against women in access to jobs, pay, retention, and promotion are common to most countries, with obviously deleterious effects on female-supported families. In the United States, the average full-time working woman earns a little more than two-thirds of the pay of a full-time male worker, and three-fifths of the families with children who live in chronic poverty are single female-parent families. Many such women in both rich and poor countries also suffer from severe "time poverty."

But the situation of some poor women in poor countries is different from—as well as distinctly worse than—that of most Western women today. It is more like the situation of the latter in the nineteenth century: Even when they have no other means of support, they are actually *prohibited* (by religiously based laws or oppressive cultural norms) from engaging in paid labor. Martha Chen (Chen 1995) has studied closely the situation of such women in the Indian subcontinent. Deprived of the traditional economic support of a male, they are prevented from taking paid employment by rules of caste, or *purdah*. For such women, it can indeed be liberating to be helped (as they have been by outsiders like Chen) to resist the sanctions invoked against them by family elders, neighbors, or powerful social leaders. Although many forms of wage work, especially those available to women, are hardly "liberating," except in the most basic sense, women are surely distinctly less free if they are *not* allowed to engage in it, especially if they have no other means of support. Many employed women in Western industrialized countries still face quite serious disapproval if they are mothers of young children or if the family's need for their wages is not perceived as great. But at least, except in the most oppressive of families or subcultures, they are *allowed* to go out to work. By contrast, as Chen's work makes clear, the basic right to be allowed to make a much needed living for themselves and their children is still one that many women in the poorest of situations in other cultures are denied.

Here, then, is a real difference—an oppressive situation that most Western women no longer face. But to return to similarities: Another that I discovered, while comparing some of our Western feminist ideas about justice with work on poor women in poor countries, has to do with the dynamics of power within the family. The differential exit potential theory that I adopt from Albert Hirschman's work to explain power within the family has recently been applied to the situation of women in poor countries (cf. Okin 1989b, chap. 7, with Dasgupta 1993 and Sen 1990b). Partha Dasgupta (1993) also uses exit theory in explaining the "not uncommon" desertion by men of their families during famines. He writes, "The man deserts [his wife] because *his* outside option in these circumstances emerges higher in his ranking than any feasible allocation within the household" (p. 329). He regards the "hardware" he employs—John Nash's game-theoretic program—as "needed if we are to make any progress in what is a profoundly complex matter, the understanding of household decisions" (p. 329). But the conclusion he reaches is very similar to the one that I reach, drawing on Hirschman's theory of power and the effects of persons' differential exit potential: Any factor that improves the husband's exit option or detracts from the wife's exit option thereby gives him additional voice, or bargaining power, in the relationship. Likewise, anything that improves the wife's exit option—her acquisition of human or physical capital, for example—will increase her autonomy and place her in a better bargaining position in the relationship (Dasgupta 1993, 331–33; Okin 1989b, chap. 7).[10]

In the United States, recent research has shown that women's and children's economic status (taking need into account) typically deteriorates after separation or divorce, whereas the average divorcing man's economic status actually improves (McLindon 1987; Weitzman 1985; Wishik 1986). This, taken in conjunction with the exit/voice theory, implies less bargaining power for wives within marriage. In poor countries, where circumstances of severe poverty combine with a lack of paid employment opportunities for women, increasing women's dependency on men, men's power within the family—already in most cases legitimized by highly patriarchal cultural norms—seems very likely to be enhanced. Although, as Dasgupta (1993) points out, Nash's formula was not intended as a normative theory, employed in this context, the theory not only *explains* (much as does my employment of Hirschman's theory) the cyclical nature of women's lack of power within the family. It also points to the injustice of a situation in which the assumption of women's responsibility for children, their disadvantaged position in the paid workforce, and their physical vulnerability to male violence all contribute to giving them little bargaining room when their (or their children's) interests conflict with those of the men they live with, thereby in turn worsening their position relative to that of men. The whole theory, then, whether in its more or its less mathematical form, seems just as applicable to the situations of very poor women in poor countries as it is to women in quite well-off households in rich countries. Indeed, one must surely say, in this case, too, "similar but *much* worse," for the stakes are undeniably higher—no less than life or death for more than 100 million women, as has recently been shown (Drèze and Sen 1990, chap. 4; Sen 1990a).

POLICY IMPLICATIONS

Some of the *solutions* to all these problems, which have been suggested recently by scholars addressing the situation of poor women in poor countries, closely resemble solutions proposed by Western feminists primarily concentrating on their own societies. (By "solutions to problems" I mean to refer to both what theorists and social scientists need to do to rectify their analyses and what policy-makers need to do to solve the social problems themselves.) First, the dichotomization of public and domestic spheres must be strongly challenged. As Chen (1983) writes, in the context of poor rural regions, "So long as policy-makers make the artificial distinction between the farm and the household, between paid work and unpaid work, between productive and domestic work, women will continue to be overlooked" (p. 220). Challenging the dichotomy will also point attention to the inequities that occur within households—various forms of abuse, including the inequitable distribution of food and health care. As Papanek (1990) argues, "Given a focus on socialization for inequality, power relations within the household—as a central theme in examining the dynamics of households—deserve special attention" (p. 170).

Second, and following from the above, the unit of analysis both for studies and for much policy-making must be the individual, not the household.[11] Noting that, given the greater political voice of men, public decisions affecting the poor in poor countries are often "guided by male preferences, not [frequently conflicting] female needs," Dasgupta (1993) concludes that

> the maximization of well-being as a model for explaining household behaviour must be rejected. Even though it is often difficult to design and effect it, the target of public policy should be persons, not households. Governments need to be conscious of the household as a resource allocation mechanism. (pp. 335–36)

Especially as women are even more likely in poor countries than in richer ones to be providing the sole or principal support for their households, as Chen (1983) points out, they require as much access as men to credit, skills training, labor markets, and technologies (and, I would add, equal pay for their work) (p. 221). Policies prompting women's full economic participation and productivity are needed increasingly for the survival of their households, for women's overall socioeconomic status, and for their bargaining position within their families. As Drèze and Sen (1989) say, "important policy implications" follow from the "considerable evidence that greater involvement with outside work and paid employment does tend to go with less anti-female bias in intra-family distribution" (p. 58). Because of the quite pervasive unequal treatment of female children in some poor countries, the need for equal treatment of women by policy-makers is often far more urgent than the need of most women in richer countries—but again, the issue is not so much different as "similar but more so."

IMPLICATIONS FOR THINKING ABOUT JUSTICE

Finally, I shall speculate briefly about two different ways of thinking about justice between the sexes, in cultures very different from ours. I have tried to show that, for feminists thinking about justice, John Rawls's theory, if revised so as to include women and the family, has a great deal to be said for it, and the veil of ignorance is particularly important (Rawls 1971; Okin 1989a, 1989b). If everyone were to speak only from his or her own point of view, it is unclear that we would come up with any principles at all. But the very presence of the veil, which hides from those in the original position any particular knowledge of the personal characteristics or social position they will have in the society for which they are designing principles of justice, forces them to take into account as many voices as possible and especially to be concerned with those of the least well-off. It enables us to reconcile the requirement that a theory of justice be universalizable with the seemingly conflicting requirement that it take account of the multiple differences among human beings.

In a recent paper, Ruth Anna Putnam (Putnam 1995), arguing a strongly antiessentialist line, and accusing Rawls and myself of varying degrees of exclusionary essentialism, considers instead an "interactive" (some might call it "dialogic") feminism: "that we listen to the voices of women of color and women of a different class, and that we appropriate what we hear" (p. 21).[12] Listening and discussing have much to recommend them; they are fundamental to democracy in the best sense of the word. And *sometimes* when especially oppressed women are heard, their cry for justice is clear—as in the case of the women Martha Chen worked with, who became quite clear that being allowed to leave the domestic sphere in order to earn wages would help to liberate them. But we are not always enlightened about what is just by asking persons who seem to be suffering injustices what they want. Oppressed people have often internalized their oppression so well that they *have* no sense of what they are justly entitled to as human beings. This is certainly the case with gender inequalities. As Papanek (1990) writes, "The clear perception of disadvantages requires conscious rejection of the social norms and cultural ideal that perpetuate inequalities and the use of different criteria—perhaps from another actual or idealized society—in order to assess inequality as a prelude for action" (pp. 164–65). People in seriously deprived conditions are sometimes not only accepting of them but relatively cheerful— the "small mercies" situation. Deprivations sometimes become gagged and muffled for reasons of deeply rooted ideology, among others. But it would surely be ethically deeply mistaken to attach a correspondingly small value to the loss of well-being of such people because of their survival strategy.

Coming to terms with very little is no recipe for social justice. Thus it is, I believe, quite justifiable for those not thoroughly imbued with the inegalitarian norms of a culture to come forth as its constructive critics. Critical distance, after all, does not have to bring with it detachment:

Committed outsiders can often be better analysts and critics of social injustice than those who live within the relevant culture. This is why a concept such as the original position, which aims to approximate an Archimedean point, is so valuable, at least in addition to some form of dialogue. Let us think for a moment about some of the cruelest or most oppressive institutions and practices that are or have been used to "brand" women—foot binding, clitoridectomy, and *purdah*. As Papanek shows, "well socialized" women in cultures with such practices internalize them as necessary to successful female development. Even though, in the case of the former two practices, these women may retain vivid memories of their own intense pain, they perpetuate the cruelties, inflicting them or at least allowing them to be inflicted on their own daughters.

Now, clearly, a theory of human flourishing, such as Nussbaum and Sen have been developing, would have no trouble delegitimizing such practices (Nussbaum 1992). But given the choice between a revised Rawlsian outlook or an "interactive feminist" one, as defined by Putnam, I'd choose the former any day, for in the latter, well-socialized members of the oppressed group are all too likely to rationalize the cruelties, whereas the men who perceive themselves as benefiting from them are unlikely to object. But behind the veil of ignorance, is it not much more likely that both the oppressors and the oppressed would have second thoughts? What Moslem man is likely to take the chance of spending his life in seclusion and dependency, sweltering in head-to-toe solid black clothing? What prerevolutionary Chinese man would cast his vote for the breaking of toes and hobbling through life, if he well might be the one with the toes and the crippled life? What man would endorse gross genital mutilation, not knowing *whose* genitals? And the women in these cultures, required to think of such practices from a male as well as a female perspective, might thereby, with a little distance, gain more notion of just how, rather than perfecting femininity, they perpetuate the subordination of women to men.

Martha Nussbaum (1992) has recently written of what happens when outsiders, instead of trying to maintain some critical distance, turn to what amounts to the worship of difference. Citing some examples of sophisticated Western scholars who, in their reverence for the integrity of cultures, defend such practices as the isolation of menstruating women and criticize Western "intrusions" into other cultures, such as the provision of typhoid vaccine, Nussbaum finds a strange and disturbing phenomenon:

> Highly intelligent people, people deeply committed to the good of women and men in developing countries, people who think of themselves as progressive and feminist and antiracist, are taking up positions that converge with the positions of reaction, oppression, and sexism. Under the banner of their radically and politically correct "antiessentialism" march ancient religious taboos, the luxury of the pampered husband, ill health, ignorance, and death. (p. 204)

As Nussbaum later concludes, "Identification need not ignore concrete local differences: in fact, at its best, it demands a searching analysis of differences, in order that the general good be appropriately realized in the concrete case. But the learning about and from the other is motivated by the conviction that the other is one of us" (p. 241).

As the work of some feminist scholars of development shows, using the concept of gender and refusing to let differences gag us or fragment our analyses does not mean that we should overgeneralize or try to apply "standardized" solutions to the problems of women in different circumstances. Chen argues for the value of a situation-by-situation analysis of women's roles and constraints before plans can be made and programs designed. And Papanek, too, shows how helping to educate women to awareness of their oppression requires quite deep and specific knowledge of the relevant culture.

Thus I conclude that gender itself is an extremely important category of analysis and that we ought not be paralyzed by the fact that there are differences among women. So long as we are careful and develop our judgments in the light of empirical evidence, it is possible to generalize about many aspects of inequality between the sexes. Theories developed in Western contexts can clearly apply, at least in large part, to women in very different cultural contexts. From place to place, from class to class, from race to race, and from culture to culture, we find similarities in the specifics of these inequalities, in their causes and their effects, although often not in their extent or severity.

NOTES

I am grateful to Elisabeth Friedman, Elisabeth Hansot, Robert O. Keohane, Martha Nussbaum, and Louise Tilly for helpful comments on an earlier draft of this article.

1. This debate has been conducted mostly among feminist legal and political theorists. The legal literature is already so vast that it is difficult to summarize, and it is not relevant to this essay. For some references, see Okin (1991), ns. 1–3.

2. "Essentialism," employed in the context of feminist theory, seems to have two principal meanings. The other refers to the tendency to regard certain characteristics or capacities as "essentially" female, in the sense that they are unalterably associated with being female. Used in this second way, essentialism is very close to, if not always identical with, biological determinism. I am not concerned with this aspect of the term here.

3. In 1851, at an almost entirely white women's rights convention, Truth said,

> That man over there says women need to be helped into carriages, and lifted over ditches, and to have the best place everywhere. Nobody ever helps me into carriages, or over mud puddles, or gives me any best place! And ain't I a woman? Look at me! Look at my arm! I have ploughed, and planted, and gathered into barns, and no man could head me! And ain't I a woman? I could work as much and eat as much as a man—when I could get it—and bear the lash as well! And ain't I a woman? I have borne thirteen children, and seen most all sold off to slavery, and when I cried out with my mother's grief, none but Jesus heard me! And ain't I a woman?

4. The example is that of the many black women (and few white women) who answered Joann Little's appeal on behalf of Delbert Tibbs, a black man who had been falsely accused of raping a white woman and sentenced to death. I do not think the example clearly supports Harris's assertion that black women have "a unique ambivalence" about rape, any more than it supports the assertion she claims to refute—that their experience is similar, but different in magnitude. Black women's present experience of rape is surely similar to that of white women in several important respects: Many are raped (by acquaintances as well as by strangers), they fear being raped, they sometimes modify their behavior because of this fear, and they are victimized as witnesses at the trials of their rapists. But their experience is probably also worse because, in addition to all of this, they have to live with the knowledge and experience of black men's being victimized by false accusations, harsher sentences, and, at worst, lynchings. Only empirical research that involved asking them could show more

certainly whether the oppression of black men as alleged rapists (or the history of master/slave rape, which Harris also discusses) makes black women's entire contemporary experience of rape different from that of white women.

5. However, the detailed division of labor between the sexes varies considerably from culture to culture. As Jane Mansbridge (1993) has recently written, in a discussion of "gratuitous gendering":

> Among the Aleut of North America, for example, only women are allowed to butcher animals. But among the Ingalik of North America, only men are allowed to butcher animals. Among the Suku of Africa, only the women can plant crops and only the men can make baskets. But among the Kaffa of the Circum-Mediterranean, only the men can plant crops and only the women can make baskets. (p. 345)

Her analysis is derived from data in George P. Murdoch and Caterina Provost, "Factors in the Division of Labor by Sex: A Cross-Cultural Analysis," *Ethnology* 12 (1973): 203–25. However, the work done by women is less likely to be "outside" work and to be paid or valued.

6. Poverty is both a relative and an absolute term. The poorest households in poor countries are absolutely as well as relatively poor and can be easily pushed below subsistence by any number of natural, social, or personal catastrophes. Poverty in rich countries is more often relative poverty (although there is serious malnutrition currently in the United States for example, and drug abuse, with all its related ills, is highly correlated with poverty). Relative poverty, although not directly life-threatening, can however be very painful, especially for children living in societies that are not only highly consumer-oriented but in which many opportunities—for good health care, decent education, the development of talents, pursuit of interests, and so on—are seriously limited for those from poor families. Single parents also often experience severe "time poverty," which can have a serious impact on their children's well-being.

7. See Dasgupta (1993) on members' perceived "usefulness" affecting the allocation of goods within poor households in poor families. Western studies as well as non-Western ones show us that women's work is already likely to be regarded as less useful—even when it is just as necessary to family well-being. So when women are really made less useful (by convention or lack of employment opportunities), this problem is compounded. Dasgupta questions simple measures of usefulness, such as paid employment, in the case of girls (1993). Where young poor women are not entitled to parental assets and their outside employment opportunities are severely restricted, the only significant "employment" for them is as childbearers and housekeepers—so marriage becomes especially valued (even though its conditions may be highly oppressive).

8. There seems to be some conflicting evidence on this matter. See Papanek (1990, 166–68).

9. This seems similar to changes in the work and socioeconomic status of women in Western Europe in the sixteenth to eighteenth centuries.

10. I do not mean to imply here that most women, whether in developed or less developed societies, think about improving their exit options when making decisions about wage work and related issues. Indeed, in some cultures, women relinquish wage work as soon as their families' financial situation enable them to do so. But their exit option is nevertheless reduced, and their partner's enhanced, thereby in all likelihood altering the distribution of power within the family.

11. This point seems to have been first explicitly made in the context of policy by George Bernard Shaw, who argues in *The Intelligent Woman's Guide to Socialism and Capitalism* (New Brunswick, NJ: Transaction Books, 1984) that the state should require all adults to work and should allocate an equal portion of income to each—man, woman, and child.

12. As Joan Tronto has pointed out to me, the use of "appropriate" here is noteworthy, given Putnam's professed desire to treat these other women as her equals.

REFERENCES

Benhabib, Seyla and Drucilla Cornell (1987) "Introduction: Beyond the Politics of Gender." In *Feminism as Critique*. Minneapolis: University of Minnesota Press.

Bergmann, Barbara R. (1986) *The Economic Emergence of Women*. New York: Basic Books.

Blumstein, Philip, and Pepper Schwartz (1983) *American Couples*. New York: Morrow.

Boserup, Ester (1970) *Women's Role in Economic Development*. London: Allen & Unwin.

Chen, Lincoln C., Emdadul Huq, and Stan D'Souza (1981) "Sex Bias in the Family Allocation of Food and Health Care in Rural Bangladesh." *Population and Development Review* 7: 55–70.

Chen, Martha Alter (1983) *A Quiet Revolution: Women in Transition in Rural Bangladesh*. Cambridge, MA: Schenkman.

Chen, Martha Alter (1995) "A Matter of Survival: Women's Right to Employment in India and Bangladesh." In *Women, Culture and Development: A Study of Human Capabilities*, ed. Martha C. Nussbaum and Jonathan Glover Oxford: Oxford University Press, 1995, 37–57.

Childers, Mary, and bell hooks (1990) "A Conversation about Race and Class." In *Conflicts in Feminism*, ed. Marianne Hirsch and Evelyn Fox Keller. New

York: Routledge, Chapman & Hall.

Crossthwaite, Jan (1989) *Sex in the Original Position*. Unpublished manuscript. Department of Philosophy, University of Auckland.

Dasgupta, Partha (1993) *An Inquiry into Well-Being and Destitution*. Oxford: Clarendon.

Drèze, Jean, and Amartya Sen (1989) *Hunger and Public Action*. Oxford: Clarendon.

Drèze, Jean, and Amartya Sen, eds. (1990) *The Political Economy of Hunger: Vol. 1. Entitlement and Well-Being*. Oxford: Clarendon.

Fuchs, Victor (1988) *Women's Quest for Economic Equality*. Cambridge, MA: Harvard University Press.

Gerson, Kathleen (1985) *Hard Choices: How Women Decide about Work, Career, and Motherhood*. Berkeley: University of California Press.

Gordon, Linda (1988) *Heroes of Their Own Lives*. New York: Viking.

Harris, Angela P. (1990) "Race and Essentialism in Feminist Legal Theory." *Stanford Law Review* 42: 581–616.

Harriss, Barbara (1990) "The Intrafamilial Distribution of Hunger in South Asia." In *The Political Economy of Hunger: Vol 1. Entitlement and Well-Being*, ed. Jean Drèze and Amartya Sen. Oxford: Clarendon.

Hochschild, Arlie (1989) *The Second Shift: Working Parents and the Revolution at Home*. New York: Viking.

hooks, bell (1984) *Feminist Theory: From Margin to Center*. Boston: South End Press.

Jaquette, Jane S. (1982) "Women and Modernization Theory: A Decade of Feminist Criticism." *World Politics* 34: 267–84.

Jelin Elizabeth, ed. (1990) *Women and Social Change in Latin America*. London: Zed Books.

Kearns, Deborah (1983) "A Theory of Justice and Love: Rawls on the Family." *Politics (Journal of the Australasian Political Studies Association)* 18: 2, 36–42.

Lorde, Audre (1984) "An Open Letter to Mary Daly." In *Sister Outsider*, ed. Audre Lorde. Trumansburg, NY: Crossing Press.

Mansbridge, Jane (1993) "Feminism and Democratic Community." In *Democratic community*, ed. John Chapman and Ian Shapiro. New York: New York University Press.

Marks, Elaine, and Isabelle de Courtivron, eds. (1981) *New French Feminisms:*

An Anthology. New York: Schocken.

McLindon, James B. (1987) "Separate but Unequal: The Economic Disaster of Divorce for Women and Children." *Family Law Quarterly* 12: 3.

Mill John Stuart [1869] (1988) *The Subjection of Women*. Reprint. Indianapolis: Hackett.

Minow, Martha, and Elizabeth V. Spelman (1990) "In Context." *Southern California Law Review* 63: 6, 1597–652.

Nussbaum, Martha (1992) "Human Functioning and Social Justice: In Defense of Aristotelian Essentialism." *Political Theory* 20: 202–46. A version, "Human Capabilities, Female Human Beings" is in *Women, Culture and Development: A Study of Human Capabilities*, ed. Martha C. Nussbaum and Jonathan Glover. Oxford: Oxford University Press, 1995, 61-104 [reprinted in *Global Justice: Seminal Essays*, 495–551].

Okin, Susan Moller (1989a) "Reason and Feeling in Thinking about Justice." *Ethics* 99: 2, 229–49.

Okin, Susan Moller (1989b) *Justice, Gender, and the Family*. New York: Basic Books.

Okin, Susan Moller (1991) "Sexual Difference, Feminism, and the Law." *Law and Social Inquiry* 16: 3 553–573.

Olsen, Frances (1983) "The Family and the Market: A Study of Ideology and Legal Reform." *Harvard Law Review* 96: 7.

Papanek, Hanna (1990) "To Each Less than She Needs, from Each More Than She Can Do: Allocations, Entitlements, and Value." In Irene Tinker, ed., *Women and World Development*. New York and London: Oxford University Press.

Pateman, Carole (1983) "Feminist Critiques of the Public/Private Dichotomy." In *Public and Private in Social Life*, ed. Stanley Benn and Gerald Gaus. London: Croom Helm. Also in Pateman, *The Disorder of Women*. Stanford, CA: Stanford University Press, 1989.

Putnam, Ruth Anna (1995) "Why Not a Feminist Theory of Justice?" in *Women, Culture and Development: A Study of Human Capabilities*, ed. Martha C. Nussbaum and Jonathan Glover. Oxford: Oxford University Press, 1995, 298–331.

Rawls John (1971) *A Theory of Justice*. Cambridge, MA: Harvard University Press.

Sanday, Peggy R. (1974) "Female Status in the Public Domain." In Michelle Zimbalist Rosaldo and Louise Lamphere, eds. *Woman, Culture, and Society*. Stanford, CA: Stanford University Press.

Sen, Amartya (1990a) "More than 100 Million Women are Missing." *New York Review of Books* (December 20).

Sen, Amartya (1990b) "Gender and Co-Operative Conflicts." In Irene Tinker, ed. *Women and World Development*. New York and London: Oxford University Press.

Spelman, Elizabeth V. (1988) *Inessential Woman: Problems of Exclusion in Feminist Thought*. Boston: Beacon.

United Nations Report (1991) *The World's Women: Trends and Statistics, 1970–1990*. New York: United Nations Publication.

Waring, Marilyn (1989) *If Women Counted: A New Feminist Economics*. San Francisco: Harper & Row.

Weitzman, Lenore (1985) *The Divorce Revolution: The Unexpected Social and Economic Consequences for Women and Children*. New York: Free Press.

Wheeler, E. F., and M. Abdullah (1988) "Food Allocation within the Family: Response to Fluctuating Food Supply and Food Needs." In I. de Garine and G. A. Harrison, *Coping with Uncertainty in Food Supply*. Oxford: Clarendon.

Wishik, Heather Ruth (1986) "Economics of Divorce: An Exploratory Study." *Family Law Quarterly* 20: 1.

13. AMARTYA SEN

In "Population: Delusion and Reality," Amartya Sen debunks the notion that the growth of the world population poses an imminent threat and that coercive political controls are necessary to slow population growth. To start, the danger from population growth lies not in falling incomes or in potential famines, but in depletion and degradation of the environment and in poor quality of life for women who lack the freedom to choose. High birth and fertility rates are a result, not a cause, of low levels—particularly among women—of education and health care. Sen gives the example of the Indian state of Kerala, which despite its poverty affords advanced opportunities for education and work, especially to women. Tellingly, Kerala has lower birth and fertility rates than China, which also provides high levels of education and health care. The key difference between China and Kerala lies in their methods: China famously relies heavily on coercive political controls to limit population growth, whereas Kerala employs a voluntary approach focusing on education and family planning. Kerala, Sen argues, exemplifies a collaborative approach to population growth, emphasizing social development that will ease the real population problems.

Population: Delusion and Reality

First published in The New York Review of Books *41: 15 (September 22, 1994): 62–71. Reprinted with permission from* The New York Review of Books. *Copyright © 1994 NYREV, Inc.*

1

Few issues today are as divisive as what is called the "world population problem." With the approach this autumn of the International Conference on Population and Development in Cairo, organized by the United Nations, these divisions among experts are receiving enormous attention and generating considerable heat. There is a danger that in the confrontation between apocalyptic pessimism on the one hand and a dismissive smugness on the other, a genuine understanding of the nature of the population problem may be lost.[1]

Visions of impending doom have been increasingly aired in recent years, often presenting the population problem as a "bomb" that has been planted and is about to "go off." These catastrophic images have encouraged a tendency to search for emergency solutions that treat the people involved not as reasonable beings, allies facing a common problem, but as impulsive and uncontrolled sources of great social harm in need of strong discipline.

Such views have received serious attention in public discussions, not just in sensational headlines in the popular press, but also in seriously argued and widely read books. One of the most influential examples was Paul Ehrlich's *The Population Bomb*, the first three sections of which were headed "Too Many People," "Too Little Food," and "A Dying Planet."[2] A more recent example of a chilling diagnosis of imminent calamity is Garrett Hardin's *Living within Limits*.[3] The arguments on which these pessimistic visions are based deserve serious scrutiny.

If the propensity to foresee impending disaster from overpopulation is strong in some circles, so is the tendency in others to dismiss all worries about population size. Just as alarmism builds on the recognition of a real problem and then magnifies it, complacency may also start off from a reasonable belief about the history of population problems and fail to see how they may have changed by now. It is often pointed out, for example, that the world has coped well enough with fast increases in population in the past, even though alarmists had expected otherwise. Malthus anticipated terrible disasters resulting from population growth and consequent imbalance in "the proportion between the natural increase of population and food."[4] At a time when there were fewer than a billion people, he was quite convinced that "the period when the number of men surpass their means of subsistence has long since arrived." However, since Malthus first published his famous *Essay on Population* in 1798, the world population has grown nearly six times larger, while food output and consumption per person are considerably higher now, and there has been an unprecedented increase both in life expectancies and in general living standards.[5]

The fact that Malthus was mistaken in his diagnosis as well as his prognosis two hundred years ago does not, however, indicate that contemporary fears about population growth must be similarly erroneous. The increase in the world population has vastly accelerated over the last century. It took the world population millions of years to reach the first billion, then 123 years to get to the second, 33 years to the third, 14 years to the fourth, 13 years to the fifth billion, with a sixth billion to come, according to one UN projection, in another 11 years.[6] During the last decade, between 1980 and 1990, the number of people on earth grew by about 923 million, an increase nearly the size of the total world population in Malthus's time. Whatever may be the proper response to alarmism about the future, complacency based on past success is no response at all.

IMMIGRATION AND POPULATION

One current worry concerns the regional distribution of the increase in world population, about 90 percent of which is taking place in the developing countries. The percentage rate of population growth is fastest in Africa—3.1 percent per year over the last decade. But most of the large increases in population occur in regions other than Africa. The largest absolute increases in numbers are taking place in Asia, which is where most of the world's poorer people live, even though the rate of increase in population has been slowing significantly there. Of the worldwide increase of 923 million people in the 1980s, well over half occurred in Asia—517 million in fact (including 146 million in China and 166 million in India).

Beyond concerns about the well-being of these poor countries themselves, a more self-regarding worry causes panic in the richer countries of the world and has much to do with the current anxiety in the West about the "world population problem." This is founded on the belief that destitution caused by fast population growth in the Third World is responsible for the severe pressure to emigrate to the developed countries of Europe and North America. In this view, people impoverished by overpopulation in the "South" flee to the "North." Some have claimed to find empirical support for this thesis in the fact that pressure to emigrate from the South has accelerated in recent decades, along with a rapid increase in the population there.

There are two distinct questions here: First, how great a threat of intolerable immigration pressure does the North face from the South, and second, is that pressure closely related to population growth in the South rather than to other social and economic factors? There are reasons to doubt that population growth is the major force behind migratory pressures, and I shall concentrate here on that question. But I should note in passing that immigration is now severely controlled in Europe and North America, and insofar as Europe is concerned, most of the current immigrants from the Third World are not "primary" immigrants but dependent relatives—mainly spouses and young children—of those who had come and settled earlier. The United States remains relatively more open to fresh immigration, but the requirements of "labor certification" as a necessary part of the immigration procedure tend to guarantee that the new entrants are relatively better educated and more skilled. There are, however, sizable flows of illegal immigrants, especially to the United States and to a lesser extent to Southern Europe, though the numbers are hard to estimate.

What causes the current pressures to emigrate? The "job-worthy" people who get through the immigration process are hardly to be seen as impoverished and destitute migrants created by the sheer pressure of population. Even the illegal immigrants who manage to evade the rigors of border control are typically not starving wretches, but those who can make use of work prospects in the North.

The explanation for the increased migratory pressure over the decades owes more to the dynamism of international capitalism than to just the growing size of the population of the Third World countries. The immigrants have allies in potential employers, and this applies as much to illegal farm laborers in California as to the legally authorized "guest workers" in automobile factories in Germany. The economic incentive to emigrate to the North from the poorer Southern economies may well depend on differences in real income. But this gap is very large anyway, and even if it is presumed that population growth in the South is increasing the disparity with the North—a thesis I shall presently consider—it seems unlikely that this incentive would significantly change if the Northern income level were, say, twenty times that of the Southern as opposed to twenty-five times.

The growing demand for immigration to the North from the South is related to the "shrinking" of the world (through revolutions in communication and transport), reduction in economic obstacles to labor movements (despite the increase in political barriers), and the growing reach and absorptive power of international capitalism (even as domestic politics in the North has turned more inward-looking and nationalistic). To try to explain the increase in immigration pressure by the growth rate of total population in the Third World is to close one's eyes to the deep changes that have occurred—and are occurring—in the world in which we live, and the rapid internationalization of its cultures and economies that accompanies these changes.

FEARS OF BEING ENGULFED

A closely related issue concerns what is perceived as a growing "imbalance" in the division of the world population, with a rapidly rising share belonging to the Third World. That fear translates into worries of various kinds in the North, especially the sense of being overrun by the South. Many Northerners fear being engulfed by people from Asia and Africa, whose share of the world population increased from 63.7 percent in 1950 to 71.2 percent by 1990, and is expected, according to the estimates of the United Nations, to rise to 78.5 percent by 2050 A.D.

It is easy to understand the fears of relatively well-off people at the thought of being surrounded by a fast growing and increasingly impoverished Southern population. As I shall argue, the thesis of growing impoverishment does not stand up to much scrutiny; but it is important to address first the psychologically tense issue of racial balance in the world (even though racial composition as a consideration has only as much importance as we choose to give it). Here it is worth recollecting that the Third World is right now going through the same kind of demographic shift—a rapid expansion of population for a temporary but long stretch—that Europe and North America experienced during their Industrial Revolution. In 1650 the share of Asia and Africa in the world population is estimated to have been 78.4 percent, and it stayed around there even in 1750.[7] With the Industrial Revolution, the share of Asia and Africa diminished because of the rapid rise of population in Europe and North America; for example, during the nineteenth century, while the inhabitants of Asia and Africa grew by about 4 percent per decade or less, the population of "the area of European settlement" grew by around 10 percent every decade.

Even now the combined share of Asia and Africa (71.2 percent) is considerably *below* what its share was in 1650 or 1750. If the United Nations' prediction that this share will rise to 78.5 percent by 2050 comes true, then the Asians and the Africans would return to being proportionately almost exactly as numerous as they were before the European Industrial Revolution. There is, of course, nothing sacrosanct about the distributions of population in the past; but the sense of a growing "imbalance" in the world, based only on recent trends, ignores history and implicitly presumes that the expansion of Europeans earlier on was natural, whereas the same process happening now to other populations unnaturally disturbs the "balance."

COLLABORATION VERSUS OVERRIDE

Other worries involving the relation of population growth to food supplies, income levels, and the environment reflect more serious matters.[8] Before I take up those questions, a brief comment on the distinction between two rival approaches to dealing with the population problem may be useful. One involves voluntary choice and a collaborative solution, and the other overrides voluntarism through legal or economic coercion.

Alarmist views of impending crises tend to produce a willingness to consider forceful measures for coercing people to have fewer children in the Third World. Imposing birth control on unwilling people is no longer rejected as readily as it was until quite recently, and some activists have pointed to the ambiguities that exist in determining what is or is not "coercion."[9] Those who are willing to consider—or at least not fully reject—programs that would use some measure of force to reduce population growth often point to the success of China's "one child policy" in cutting down the national birth rate. Force can also take an indirect form, as when economic opportunities are changed so radically by government regulations that people are left with very little choice except to behave in ways the government would approve. In China's case, the government may refuse to offer housing to families with too many children—thus penalizing the children as well as the dissenting adults.

In India the policy of compulsory birth control that was initiated during the "emergency period" declared by Mrs. Gandhi in the 1970s was decisively rejected by the voters in the general election in which it—along with civil rights—was a major issue. Even so, some public health clinics in the northern states (such as Uttar Pradesh) insist, in practice, on sterilization before providing normal medical attention to women and men beyond a certain age. The pressures to move in that direction seem to be strong, and they are reinforced by the rhetoric of "the population bomb."

I shall call this general approach the "override" view, since the family's personal decisions are overridden by some agency outside the family—typically by the government of the country in question (whether or not it has been pressed to do so by "outside" agencies, such as international organizations and pressure groups). In fact, overriding is not limited to an explicit use of legal coercion or economic compulsion, since people's own choices can also be effectively overridden by simply not offering them the opportunities for jobs or welfare that they can expect to get from a responsible government. Override can take many different forms and can be of varying intensity (with the Chinese "one child policy" being something of an extreme case of a more general approach).

A central issue here is the increasingly vocal demand by some activists concerned with population growth that the highest "priority" should be given in Third World countries to family planning over other public commitments. This demand goes much beyond supporting family planning as a part of development. In fact, proposals for shifting international aid away from development in general to family planning in particular have lately been increasingly frequent. Such policies fit into the general approach of "override" as well, since they try to rely on manipulating people's choices through offering them only some opportunities (the means of family planning) while denying others, no matter what they would have themselves preferred. Insofar as they would have the effect of reducing health care and educational services, such shifts in public commitments will not only add to the misery of human lives, they may also have, I shall argue, exactly the opposite effect on family planning than the one intended, since education and health care have a significant part in the *voluntary* reduction of the birth rate.

The "override" approach contrasts with another, the "collaborative" approach, that relies not on legal or economic restrictions but on rational decisions of women and men, based on expanded choices and enhanced security, and encouraged by open dialogue and extensive public discussions. The difference between the two approaches does not lie in government's activism in the first case as opposed to passivity in the second. Even if solutions are sought through the decisions and actions of people themselves, the chance to take reasoned decisions with more knowledge and a greater sense of personal security can be increased by public policies, for example, through expanding educational facilities, health care, and economic well-being, along with providing better access to family planning. The central political and ethical issue concerning the "override" approach does not lie in its insistence on the need for public policy but in the ways it significantly reduces the choices open to parents.

THE MALTHUS-CONDORCET DEBATE

Thomas Robert Malthus forcefully argued for a version of the "override" view. In fact, it was precisely this preference that distinguished Malthus from Condorcet, the eighteenth-century French mathematician and social scientist from whom Malthus had actually derived the analysis of how population could outgrow the means of living. The debate between Condorcet and Malthus in some ways marks the origin of the distinction between the "collaborative" and the "override" approaches, which still compete for attention.[10]

In his *Essay on Population*, published in 1798, Malthus quoted—extensively and with approval—Condorcet's discussion, in 1795, of the possibility of overpopulation. However, true to the Enlightenment tradition, Condorcet was confident that this problem would be solved by reasoned human action: through increases in productivity, through better conservation and prevention of waste, and through education (especially female education), which would contribute to reducing the birth rate.[11] Voluntary family planning would be encouraged, in Condorcet's analysis, by increased understanding that if people "have a duty toward those who are not yet born, that duty is not to give them existence but to give them happiness." They would see the value of limiting family size "rather than foolishly... encumber the world with useless and wretched beings."[12]

Even though Malthus borrowed from Condorcet his diagnosis of the possibility of overpopulation, he refused to accept Condorcet's solution. Indeed, Malthus's essay on population was partly a criticism of Condorcet's enlightenment reasoning, and even the full title of Malthus's famous essay specifically mentioned Condorcet. Malthus argued that

> there is no reason whatever to suppose that anything beside the difficulty of procuring in adequate plenty the necessaries of life should either *indispose* this greater number of persons to marry early, or *disable* them from rearing in health the largest families.[13]

Malthus thus opposed public relief of poverty: He saw the "poor laws" in particular as contributing greatly to population growth.[14]

Malthus was not sure that any public policy would work, and whether "overriding" would in fact be possible: "The perpetual tendency in the race of man to increase beyond the means of subsistence is one of the great general laws of animated nature which we can have no reason to expect will change."[15] But insofar as any solution would be possible, it could not come from voluntary decisions of the people involved, or acting from a position of strength and economic security. It must come from overriding their preferences through the compulsions of economic necessity, since their poverty was the only thing that could "indispose the greater number of persons to marry early, or disable them from rearing in health the largest families."

DEVELOPMENT AND INCREASED CHOICE

The distinction between the "collaborative" approach and the "override" approach thus tends to correspond closely to the contrast between, on the one hand, treating economic and social development as the way to solve the population problem and, on the other, expecting little from development and using, instead, legal and economic pressures to reduce birth rates. Among recent writers, those such as Gerard Piel[16] who have persuasively emphasized our ability to solve problems through reasoned decisions and actions have tended—like Condorcet—to find the solution of the population problem in economic and social development. They advocate a broadly collaborative approach, in which governments and citizens would together produce economic and social conditions favoring slower population growth. In contrast, those who have been thoroughly skeptical of reasoned human action to limit population growth have tended to go in the direction of "override" in one form or another, rather than concentrate on development and voluntarism.

Has development, in fact, done much to reduce population growth? There can be little doubt that economic and social development, in general, has been associated with major reductions in birth rates and the emergence of smaller families as the norm. This is a pattern that was, of course, clearly observed in Europe and North America as they underwent industrialization, but that experience has been repeated in many other parts of the world.

In particular, conditions of economic security and affluence, wider availability of contraceptive methods, expansion of education (particularly female education), and lower mortality rates have had—and are currently having—quite substantial effects in reducing birth rates in different parts of the world.[17] The rate of world population growth is certainly declining, and even over the last two decades its percentage growth rate has fallen from 2.2 percent per year between 1970 and 1980 to 1.7 percent between 1980 and 1992. This rate is expected to go steadily down until the size of the world's population becomes nearly stationary.[18]

There are important regional differences in demographic behavior; for example, the population growth rate in India peaked at 2.2 percent a year (in the 1970s) and has since started to diminish, whereas most Latin American countries peaked at much higher rates before coming down sharply, while many countries in Africa currently have growth rates between 3 and 4 percent, with an average for sub-Saharan Africa of 3.1 percent. Similarly, the different factors have varied in their respective influence from region to region. But there can be little dispute that economic and social development tends to reduce fertility rates. The regions of the Third World that lag most in achieving economic and social development, such as many countries in Africa, are, in general, also the ones that have failed to reduce birth rates significantly. Malthus's fear that economic and social development could only encourage people to have more children has certainly proved to be radically wrong, and so have all the painful policy implications drawn from it.

This raises the following question: In view of the clear connection between development and lower fertility, why isn't the dispute over how to deal with population growth fully resolved already? Why don't we reinterpret the population problem simply as a problem of under-development and seek a solution by encouraging economic and social development (even if we reject the oversimple slogan "Development is the most reliable contraceptive")?

In the long run, this may indeed be exactly the right approach. The problem is more complex, however, because a "contraceptive" that is "reliable" in the long run may not act fast enough to meet the present threat. Even though development may dependably work to stabilize population if it is given enough time, there may not be, it is argued, time enough to give. The death rate often falls very fast with more widely available health care, better sanitation, and improved nutrition, while the birth rate may fall rather slowly. Much growth of population may meanwhile occur.

This is exactly the point at which apocalyptic prophecies add force to the "override" view. One claim, then, that needs examination is that the world is facing an imminent crisis, one so urgent that development is just too slow a process to deal with it. We must try right now, the argument goes, to cut down population growth by drastic and forceful means if necessary. The second claim that also needs scrutiny is the actual feasibility of adequately reducing population growth through these drastic means, without fostering social and economic development.

2

POPULATION AND INCOME

It is sometimes argued that signs of an imminent crisis can be found in the growing impoverishment of the South, with falling income per capita accompanying high population growth. In general, there is little evidence for this. As a matter of fact, the average population of "low-income" countries (as defined by the World Bank) has been not only enjoying a rising gross national product (GNP) per head, but a growth rate of GNP per capita (3.9 percent per year for 1980–92) that is much faster than those for the "high-income" countries (2.4 percent) and for the "middle-income" ones (0 percent).[19]

The growth of per capita GNP of the population of low-income countries would have been even higher had it not been for the negative growth rates of many countries in sub-Saharan Africa, one region in which a number of countries have been experiencing economic decline. But the main culprit causing this state of affairs is the terrible failure of economic production in sub-Saharan Africa (connected particularly with political disruption, including wars and military rule), rather than population growth, which is only a subsidiary factor. Sub-Saharan Africa does have high population growth, but its economic stagnation has contributed much more to the fall in its per-capita income.

With its average population growth rate of 3.1 percent per year, had sub-Saharan Africa suddenly matched China's low population growth of 1.4 percent (the lowest among the low-income countries), it would have gained roughly 1.7 percent in per-capita GNP growth. The real income per person would still have fallen, even with that minimal population growth, for many countries in the region. The growth of GNP per capita is *minus* 1.9 percent for Ethiopia, *minus* 1.8 percent for Togo, *minus* 3.6 percent for Mozambique, *minus* 4.3 percent for Niger, *minus* 4.7 percent for Ivory Coast, not to mention Somalia, Sudan, and Angola, where the political disruption has been so serious that no reliable GNP estimates even exist. A lower population growth rate could have reduced the magnitude of the fall in per capita GNP, but the main roots of Africa's economic decline lie elsewhere. The complex political factors underlying the troubles of Africa include, among other things, the subversion of democracy and the rise of combative military rulers, often encouraged by the Cold War (with Africa providing "client states"—from Somalia and Ethiopia to Angola and Zaire—for the superpowers, particularly from the 1960s onward). The explanation of sub-Saharan Africa's problems has to be sought in these political troubles, which affect economic stability, agricultural and industrial incentives, public health arrangements, and social services—even family planning and population policy.[20]

There is indeed a very powerful case for reducing the rate of growth of population in Africa, but this problem cannot be dissociated from the rest of the continent's woes. Sub-Saharan Africa lags behind other developing regions in economic security, in health care, in life expectancy, in basic education, and in political and economic stability. It should be no great surprise that it lags behind in family planning as well. To dissociate the task of population control from the politics and economics of Africa would be a great mistake and would seriously mislead public policy.

POPULATION AND FOOD

Malthus's exact thesis cannot, however, be disputed by quoting statistics of income per capita, for he was concerned specifically with food supply per capita, and he had concentrated on "the proportion between the natural increase of population and food." Many modern commentators, including Paul Ehrlich and Garrett Hardin, have said much about this, too. When Ehrlich says, in his *Population Bomb*, "too little food," he does not mean "too little income," but specifically a growing shortage of food.

Is population beginning to outrun food production? Even though such an impression is often given in public discussions, there is, in fact, no serious evidence that this is happening. While there are some year-to-year fluctuations in the growth of food output (typically inducing, whenever things slacken a bit, some excited remarks by those who anticipate an impending doom), the worldwide trend of food output per person has been firmly upward. Not only over the two centuries since Malthus's time, but also during recent decades, the rise in food output has been significantly and consistently outpacing the expansion of world population.[21]

But the total food supply in the world as a whole is not the only issue. What about the regional distribution of food? If it were to turn out that the rising ratio of food to population is mainly caused by increased production in richer countries (for example, if it appeared that US wheat output was feeding the Third World, in which much of the population expansion is taking place), then the neo-Malthusian fears about "too many people" and "too little food" may have some plausibility. Is this what is happening?

In fact, with one substantial exception, exactly the opposite is true. The largest increases in the production of food—not just in the aggregate but also per person—are actually taking place in the Third World, particularly in the region that is having the largest absolute increases in the world population, that is, in Asia. The many millions of people who are added to the populations of India and China may be constantly cited by the terrorized—and terrorizing—advocates of the apocalyptic view, but it is precisely in these countries that the most rapid rates of growth in food output per capita are to be observed. For example, between the three-year averages of 1979–81 and 1991–93, food production per head in the world moved up by 3 percent, while it went up by only 2 percent in Europe and went down by nearly 5 percent in North America. In contrast, per capita food production jumped up by 22 percent in Asia generally, including 23 percent in India and 39 percent in China.[22] (See Table 1.)

TABLE 1

Indices of Food Production Per Capita

	1979-1981 Base Period	1991-1993
World	100	103
Europe	100	102
North America	100	95
Africa	100	94
Asia	100	122
including		
India	100	123
China	100	139

Source: FAO Quarterly Bulletin of Statistics

During the same period, however, food production per capita went down by 6 percent in Africa, and even the absolute size of food output fell in some countries (such as Malawi and Somalia). Of course, many countries in the world—from Syria, Italy, and Sweden to Botswana in Africa—have had declining food production per head without experiencing hunger or starvation since their economies have prospered and grown; when the means are available, food can be easily bought in the international market if it is necessary to do so. For many countries in sub-Saharan Africa the problem arises from the fact that the decline in food production is an integral part of the story of overall economic decline, which I have discussed earlier.

Difficulties of food production in sub-Saharan Africa, like other problems of the national economy, are not only linked to wars, dictatorships, and political chaos. In addition, there is some evidence that climatic shifts have had unfavorable effects on parts of that continent. While some of the climatic problems may be caused partly by increases in human settlement and environmental neglect, that neglect is not unrelated to the political and economic chaos that has characterized sub-Saharan Africa during the last few decades. The food problem of Africa must be seen as one part of a wider political and economic problem of the region.[23]

THE PRICE OF FOOD

To return to "the balance between food and population," the rising food production per capita in the world as a whole, and in the Third World in general, contradicts some of the pessimism that characterized the gloomy predictions of the past. Prophecies of imminent disaster during the last few decades have not proved any more accurate than Malthus's prognostication nearly two hundred years ago. As for new prophecies of doom, they cannot, of course, be contradicted until the future arrives. There was no way of refuting the theses of W. Paddock and P. Paddock's popular book *Famine—1975!*, published in 1968, which predicted a terrible cataclysm for the world as a whole by 1975 (writing off India, in particular, as a basket case), until 1975 actually arrived. The new prophets have learned not to attach specific dates to the crises they foresee, and past failures do not seem to have reduced the popular appetite for this creative genre.

However, after noting the rather dismal forecasting record of doomsayers, we must also accept the general methodological point that present trends in output do not necessarily tell us much about the prospects of further expansion in the future. It could, for example, be argued that maintaining growth in food production may require proportionately increasing investments of capital, drawing them away from other kinds of production. This would tend to make food progressively more expensive if there are "diminishing returns" in shifting resources from other fields into food production. And, ultimately, further expansion of food production may become so expensive that it would be hard to maintain the trend of increasing food production without reducing other outputs drastically.

But is food production really getting more and more expensive? There is, in fact, no evidence for that conclusion, either. In fact, quite the contrary. Not only is food generally much cheaper to buy today, in constant dollars, than it was in Malthus's time, but it also has become cheaper during recent decades. As a matter of fact, there have been increasing complaints among food exporters, especially in the Third World, that food prices have fallen in relation to other commodities. For example, in 1992 a United Nations report recorded a 38 percent fall in the relative prices of "basic foods" over the last decade.[24] This is entirely in line with the trend, during the last three decades, toward declining relative prices of particular food items, in relation to the prices of manufactured goods. The World Bank's adjusted estimates of the prices of particular food crops, between 1953–55 and 1983–85, show similarly steep declines for such staples as rice (42 percent), wheat (57 percent), sorghum (39 percent), and maize (37 percent).[25]

Not only is food getting less expensive, but we also have to bear in mind that the current increase in food production (substantial and well ahead of population growth, as it is) is itself being kept in check by the difficulties in selling food profitably, as the relative prices of food have fallen. Those neo-Malthusians who concede that food production is now growing faster than population often point out that it is growing "only a little faster than population," and they are inclined to interpret this as evidence that we are reaching the limits of what we can produce to keep pace with population growth.

But that is surely the wrong conclusion to draw in view of the falling relative prices of food, and the current difficulties in selling food, since it ignores the effects of economic incentives that govern production. When we take into account the persistent cheapening of food prices, we have good grounds to suggest that food output is being held back by a lack of effective demand in the market. The imaginary crisis in food production, contradicted as it is by the upward trends of total and regional food output per head, is thus further debunked by an analysis of the economic incentives to produce more food.

DEPRIVED LIVES AND SLUMS

I have examined the alleged "food problem" associated with population growth in some detail because it has received so much attention both in the traditional Malthusian literature and in the recent writings of neo-Malthusians. In concentrating on his claim that growing populations would not have enough food, Malthus differed from Condorcet's broader presentation of the population question. Condorcet's own emphasis was on the possibility of "a continual diminution of happiness" as a result of population growth, a diminution that could occur in many different ways—not just through the deprivation of food, but through a decline in living conditions generally. That more extensive worry can remain even when Malthus's analysis of the food supply is rejected.

Indeed, average income and food production per head can go on increasing even as the wretchedly deprived living conditions of particular sections of the population get worse, as they have in many parts of the Third World. The living conditions of backward regions and deprived classes can decline even when a country's economic growth is very rapid on the average. Brazil during the 1960s and 1970s provided an extreme example of this. The sense that there are just "too many people" around often arises from seeing the desperate lives of people in the large and rapidly growing urban slums—*bidonvilles*—in poor countries, sobering reminders that we should not take too much comfort from aggregate statistics of economic progress.

But in an essay addressed mainly to the population problem, what we have to ask is not whether things are just fine in the Third World (they obviously are not), but whether population growth is the root cause of the deprivations that people suffer. The question is whether the particular instances of deep poverty we observe derive mainly from population growth rather than from other factors that lead to unshared prosperity and persistent and possibly growing inequality. The tendency to see in population growth an explanation for every calamity that afflicts poor people is now fairly well established in some circles, and the message that gets transmitted constantly is the opposite of the old picture postcard: "Wish you weren't here."

To see in population growth the main reason for the growth of overcrowded and very poor slums in large cities, for example, is not empirically convincing. It does not help to explain why the slums of Calcutta and Bombay have grown worse at a faster rate than those of Karachi and Islamabad (India's population growth rate is 2.1 percent per year, Pakistan's 3.1), or why Jakarta has deteriorated faster than Ankara or Istanbul (Indonesian population growth is 1.8 percent, Turkey's 2.3), or why the slums of Mexico City have become worse more rapidly than those of San José (Mexico's population growth rate is 2.0, Costa Rica's 2.8), or why Harlem can seem more and more deprived when compared with the poorer districts of Singapore (US population growth rate is 1.0, Singapore's is 1.8). Many causal factors affect the degree of deprivation in particular parts of a country—rural as well as urban—and to try to see them all as resulting from overpopulation is the negation of social analysis.

This is not to deny that population growth may well have an effect on deprivation, but only to insist that any investigation of the effects of population growth must be part of the analysis of economic and political processes, including the effects of other variables. It is the isolationist view of population growth that should be rejected.

THREATS TO THE ENVIRONMENT

In his concern about "a continual diminution of happiness" from population growth, Condorcet was a pioneer in considering the possibility that natural raw materials might be used up, thereby making living conditions worse. In his characteristically rationalist solution, which relied partly on voluntary and reasoned measures to reduce the birth rate, Condorcet also envisaged the development of less improvident technology: "The manufacture of articles will be achieved with less wastage in raw materials and will make better use of them."[26]

The effects of a growing population on the environment could be a good deal more serious than the food problems that have received so much attention in the literature inspired by Malthus. If the environment is damaged by population pressures, this obviously affects the kind of life we lead, and the possibilities of a "diminution in happiness" can be quite considerable. In dealing with this problem, we have to distinguish once again between the long and the short run. The short-run picture tends to be dominated by the fact that the per-capita consumption of food, fuel, and other goods by people in Third World countries is often relatively low; consequently the impact of population growth in these countries is not, in relative terms, so damaging to the global environment. But the problems of the local environment can, of course, be serious in many developing economies. They vary from the "neighborhood pollution" created by unregulated industries to the pressure of denser populations on rural resources such as fields and woods.[27] (The Indian authorities had to close down several factories in and around Agra, since the façade of the Taj Mahal was turning pale as a result of chemical pollution from local factories.) But it remains true that one additional American typically has a larger negative impact on the ozone layer, global warmth, and other elements of the earth's environment than dozens of Indians and Zimbabweans put together. Those who argue for the immediate need for forceful population control in the Third World to preserve the global environment must first recognize this elementary fact.

This does not imply, as is sometimes suggested, that as far as the global environment is concerned, population growth in the Third World is nothing to worry about. The long-run impact on the global environment of population growth in the developing countries can be expected to be large. As the Indians and the Zimbabweans develop economically, they too will consume a great deal more, and they will pose, in the future, a threat to the earth's environment similar to that of people in the rich countries today. The long-run threat of population to the environment is a real one.

3

WOMEN'S DEPRIVATION AND POWER

Since reducing the birth rate can be slow, this and other long-run problems should be addressed right now. Solutions will no doubt have to be found in the two directions to which, as it happens, Condorcet pointed: (1) developing new technology and new behavior patterns that would waste little and pollute less, and (2) fostering social and economic changes that would gradually bring down the growth rate of population.

On reducing birth rates, Condorcet's own solution not only included enhancing economic opportunity and security, but also stressed the importance of education, particularly female education. A better-educated population could have a more informed discussion of the kind of life we have reason to value; in particular it would reject the drudgery of a life of continuous child bearing and rearing that is routinely forced on many Third World women. That drudgery, in some ways, is the most immediately adverse consequence of high fertility rates.

Central to reducing birth rates, then, is a close connection between women's well-being and their power to make their own decisions and bring about changes in the fertility pattern. Women in many Third World countries are deprived by high birth frequency of the freedom to do other things in life, not to mention the medical dangers of repeated pregnancy and high maternal mortality, which are both characteristic of many developing countries. It is thus not surprising that reductions in birth rates have been typically associated with improvement of women's status and their ability to make their voices heard—often the result of expanded opportunities for schooling and political activity.[28]

There is nothing particularly exotic about declines in the birth rate occurring through a process of voluntary rational assessment, of which Condorcet spoke. It is what people do when they have some basic education, know about family planning methods and have access to them, do not readily accept a life of persistent drudgery, and are not deeply anxious about their economic security. It is also what they do when they are not forced by high infant and child mortality rates to be so worried that no child will survive to support them in their old age that they try to have many children. In country after country the birth rate has come down with more female education, the reduction of mortality rates, the expansion of economic means and security, and greater public discussion of ways of living.

DEVELOPMENT VERSUS COERCION

There is little doubt that this process of social and economic change will over time cut down the birth rate. Indeed, the growth rate of world population is already firmly declining—it came down from 2.2 percent in the 1970s to 1.7 percent between 1980 and 1992. Had imminent cataclysm been threatening, we might have had good reason to reject such gradual progress and consider more drastic means of population control, as some have advocated. But that apocalyptic view is empirically baseless. There is no imminent emergency that calls for a breathless response. What is called for is systematic support for people's own decisions to reduce family size through expanding education and health care, and through economic and social development.

It is often asked where the money needed for expanding education, health care, etc., would be found. Education, health services, and many other means of improving the quality of life are typically highly labor-intensive and are thus relatively inexpensive in poor countries (because of low wages).[29] While poor countries have less money to spend, they also need less money to provide these services. For this reason many poor countries have indeed been able to expand educational and health services widely without waiting to become prosperous through the process of economic growth. Sri Lanka, Costa Rica, Indonesia, and Thailand are good examples, and there are many others. While the impact of these social services on the quality and length of life have been much studied, they are also major means of reducing the birth rate.

By contrast with such open and voluntary developments, coercive methods, such as the "one child policy" in some regions, have been tried in China, particularly since the reforms of 1979. Many commentators have pointed out that by 1992 the Chinese birth rate has fallen to 19 per 1,000, compared with 29 per 1,000 in India, and 37 per 1,000 for the average of poor countries other than China and India. China's total fertility rate (reflecting the number of children born per woman) is now at "the replacement level" of 2.0, compared with India's 3.6 and the weighted average of 4.9 for low-income countries other than China and India.[30] Hasn't China shown the way to "solve" the population problem in other developing countries as well?

4

CHINA'S POPULATION POLICIES

The difficulties with this "solution" are of several kinds. First, if freedom is valued at all, the lack of freedom associated with this approach must be seen to be a social loss in itself. The importance of reproductive freedom has been persuasively emphasized by women's groups throughout the world.[31]

The loss of freedom is often dismissed on the grounds that because of cultural differences, authoritarian policies that would not be tolerated in the West are acceptable to Asians. While we often hear references to "despotic" Oriental traditions, such arguments are no more convincing than a claim that compulsion in the West is justified by the traditions of the Spanish Inquisition or of the Nazi concentration camps. Frequent references are also made to the emphasis on discipline in the "Confucian tradition"; but that is not the only tradition in the "East," nor is it easy to assess the implications of that tradition for modern Asia (even if we were able to show that discipline is more important for Confucius than it is for, say, Plato or Saint Augustine).

Only a democratic expression of opinion could reveal whether citizens would find a compulsory system acceptable. While such a test has not occurred in China, one did in fact take place in India during "the emergency period" in the 1970s, when Indira Gandhi's government imposed compulsory birth control and suspended various legal freedoms. In the general elections that followed, the politicians favoring the policy of coercion were overwhelmingly defeated. Furthermore, family planning experts in India have observed how the briefly applied programs of compulsory sterilization tended to discredit voluntary birth control programs generally, since people became deeply suspicious of the entire movement to control fertility.

Second, apart from the fundamental issue of whether people are willing to accept compulsory birth control, its specific consequences must also be considered. Insofar as coercion is effective, it works by making people do things they would not freely do. The social consequences of such compulsion, including the ways in which an unwilling population tends to react when it is coerced, can be appalling. For example, the demands of a "one-child family" can lead to the neglect—or worse—of a second child, thereby increasing the infant mortality rate. Moreover, in a country with a strong preference for male children—a preference shared by China and many other countries in Asia and North Africa—a policy of allowing only one child per family can easily lead to the fatal neglect of a female child. There is much evidence that this is fairly widespread in China, with very adverse effects on infant mortality rates. There are reports that female children have been severely neglected as well as suggestions that female infanticide occurs with considerable frequency. Such consequences are hard to tolerate morally, and perhaps politically also, in the long run.

Third, what is also not clear is exactly how much additional reduction in the birth rate has been achieved through these coercive methods. Many of China's long-standing social and economic programs have been valuable in reducing fertility, including those that have expanded education for women as well as men, made health care more generally available, provided more job opportunities for women, and stimulated rapid economic growth. These factors would themselves have reduced the birth rates, and it is not clear how much "extra lowering" of fertility rates has been achieved in China through compulsion.

For example, we can determine whether many of the countries that match (or outmatch) China in life expectancy, female literacy rates, and female participation in the labor force actually have a higher fertility rate than China. Of all the countries in the world for which data are given in the *World Development Report 1994*, there are only three such countries: Jamaica (2.7), Thailand (2.2), and Sweden (2.1)—and the fertility rates of two of these are close to China's (2.0). Thus the additional contribution of coercion to reducing fertility in China is by no means clear, since compulsion was superimposed on a society that was already reducing its birth rate and in which education and jobs outside the home were available to large numbers of women. In some regions of China the compulsory program needed little enforcement, whereas in other—more backward—regions, it had to be applied with much severity, with terrible consequences in infant mortality and discrimination against female children. While China may get too much credit for its authoritarian measures, it gets far too little credit for the other, more collaborative and participatory, policies it has followed, which have themselves helped to cut down the birth rate.

CHINA AND INDIA

A useful contrast can be drawn between China and India, the two most populous countries in the world. If we look only at the national averages, it is easy to see that China with its low fertility rate of 2.0 has achieved much more than India has with its average fertility rate of 3.6. To what extent this contrast can be attributed to the effectiveness of the coercive policies used in China is not clear, since we would expect the fertility rate to be much lower in China in view of its higher percentage of female literacy (almost twice as high), higher life expectancy (almost ten years more), larger female involvement (by three-quarters) in the labor force, and so on. But India is a country of great diversity, whose different states have very unequal achievements in literacy, health care, and economic and social development. Most states in India are far behind the Chinese provinces in educational achievement (with the exception of Tibet, which has the lowest literacy rate of any Chinese or Indian state), and the same applies to other factors that affect fertility. However, the state of Kerala in southern India provides an interesting comparison with China, since it too has high levels of basic education, health care, and so on. Kerala is a state within a country, but with its 29 million people, it is larger than most countries in the world (including Canada). Kerala's birth rate of 18 per 1,000 is actually lower than China's 19 per 1,000, and its fertility rate is 1.8 for 1991, compared with China's 2.0 for 1992. These low rates have been achieved without any state coercion.[32]

The roots of Kerala's success are to be found in the kinds of social progress Condorcet hoped for, including among others, a high female literacy rate (86 percent, which is substantially higher than China's 68 percent). The rural literacy rate is in fact higher in Kerala—for women as well as men—than in every single province in China. Male and female life expectancies at birth in China are respectively 67 and

71 years; the provisional 1991 figures for men and women in Kerala are 71 and 74 years. Women have been active in Kerala's economic and political life for a long time. A high proportion do skilled and semiskilled work and a large number have taken part in educational movements.[33] It is perhaps of symbolic importance that the first public pronouncement of the need for widespread elementary education in any part of India was made in 1817 by Rani Gouri Parvathi Bai, the young queen of the princely state of Travancore, which makes up a substantial part of modern Kerala. For a long time public discussions in Kerala have centered on women's rights and the undesirability of couples marrying when very young.

This political process has been voluntary and collaborative, rather than coercive, and the adverse reactions that have been observed in China, such as infant mortality, have not occurred in Kerala. Kerala's low fertility rate has been achieved along with an infant mortality rate of 16.5 per 1,000 live births (17 for boys and 16 for girls), compared with China's 31 (28 for boys and 33 for girls). And as a result of greater gender equality in Kerala, women have not suffered from higher mortality rates than men in Kerala, as they have in the rest of India and in China. Even the ratio of females to males in the total population in Kerala (above 1.03) is quite close to that of the current ratios in Europe and America (reflecting the usual pattern of lower female mortality whenever women and men receive similar care). By contrast, the average female to male ratio in China is 0.94 and in India as a whole 0.93.[34] Anyone drawn to the Chinese experience of compulsory birth control must take note of these facts.

The temptation to use the "override" approach arises at least partly from impatience with the allegedly slow process of fertility reduction through collaborative, rather than coercive, attempts. Yet Kerala's birth rate has fallen from 44 per 1,000 in the 1950s to 18 by 1991—not a sluggish decline. Nor is Kerala unique in this respect. Other societies, such as those of Sri Lanka, South Korea, and Thailand, which have relied on expanding education and reducing mortality rates—instead of on coercion—have also achieved sharp declines in fertility and birth rates.

TABLE 2
Fertility Rates in China, Kerala, and Tamil Nadu

	1979	1991
China	2.8	2.0
Kerala	3.0	1.8
Tamil Nadu	3.5	2.2

Source: For China, Xizhe Peng, *Demographic Transition in China* (Oxford University Press, 1991), Li Chengrui, *A Study of China's Population* (Beijing: Foreign Language Press, 1992), and *World Development Report* 1994. For India, *Sample Registration System* 1979–80 (New Delhi: Ministry of Home Affairs, 1982) and *Sample Registration System: Fertility and Mortality Indicators* 1991 (New Delhi: Ministry of Home Affairs, 1993).

It is also interesting to compare the time required for reducing fertility in China with that in the two states in India, Kerala and Tamil Nadu, which have done most to encourage voluntary and collaborative reduction in birth rates (even though Tamil Nadu is well behind Kerala in each respect).[35] Table 2 shows the fertility rates both in 1979, when the one-child policy and related programs were introduced in China, and in 1991. Despite China's one-child policy and other coercive measures, its fertility rate seems to have fallen much less sharply than those of Kerala and Tamil Nadu. The "override" view is very hard to defend on the basis of the Chinese experience, the only systematic and sustained attempt to impose such a policy that has so far been made.

FAMILY PLANNING

Even those who do not advocate legal or economic coercion sometimes suggest a variant of the "override" approach—the view, which has been getting increasing support, that the highest priority should be given simply to family planning, even if this means diverting resources from education and health care as well as other activities associated with development. We often hear claims that enormous declines in birth rates have been accomplished through making family planning services available, without waiting for improvements in education and health care.

The experience of Bangladesh is sometimes cited as an example of such success. Indeed, even though the female literacy rate in Bangladesh is only around 22 percent and life expectancy at birth no higher than 55 years, fertility rates have been substantially reduced there through the greater availability of family planning services, including counseling.[36] We have to examine carefully what lessons can, in fact, be drawn from this evidence.

First, it is certainly significant that Bangladesh has been able to cut its fertility rate from 7.0 to 4.5 during the short period between 1975 and 1990, an achievement that discredits the view that people will not voluntarily embrace family planning in the poorest countries. But we have to ask further whether family planning efforts may themselves be sufficient to make fertility come down to really low levels, without providing for female education and the other features of a fuller collaborative approach. The fertility rate of 4.5 in Bangladesh is still quite high—considerably higher than even India's average rate of 3.6. To begin stabilizing the population, the fertility rates would have to come down closer to the "replacement level" of 2.0, as has happened in Kerala and Tamil Nadu, and in many other places outside the Indian subcontinent. Female education and the other social developments connected with lowering the birth rate would still be much needed.

Contrasts between the records of Indian states offer some substantial lessons here. While Kerala, and to a smaller extent Tamil Nadu, have surged ahead in achieving radically reduced fertility rates, other states in India in the so-called "northern heartland" (such as Uttar Pradesh, Bihar, Madhya Pradesh, and Rajasthan), have very low levels of education, especially female education, and of general health care (often combined with pressure on the poor to accept birth control measures, including sterilization, as a qualifying condition for medical attention and other public services). These states all have high fertility rates—between 4.4 and 5.1. The regional contrasts within India strongly argue for the collaborative approach, including active and educated participation of women.

The threat of an impending population crisis tempts many international observers to suggest that priority be given to family planning arrangements in the Third World countries over other commitments such as education and health care, a redirection of public efforts that is often recommended by policy-makers and at international conferences. Not only will this shift have negative effects on people's well-being and reduce their freedoms, it can also be self-defeating if the goal is to stabilize population.

The appeal of such slogans as "family planning first" rests partly on misconceptions about what is needed to reduce fertility rates, but also on mistaken beliefs about the excessive costs of social development, including education and health care. As has been discussed, both these activities are highly labor intensive, and thus relatively inexpensive even in very poor economies. In fact, Kerala, India's star performer in expanding education and reducing both death rates and birth rates, is among the poorer Indian states. Its domestically produced income is quite low—lower indeed in per capita terms than even the Indian average—even if this is somewhat deceptive, for the greatest expansion of Kerala's earnings derives from citizens who work outside the state. Kerala's ability to finance adequately both educational expansion and health coverage depends on both activities being labor-intensive; they can be made available even in a low-income economy when there is the political will to use them. Despite its economic backwardness, an issue that Kerala will undoubtedly have to address before long (perhaps by reducing bureaucratic controls over agriculture and industry, which have stagnated), its level of social development has been remarkable, and that has turned out to be crucial in reducing fertility rates. Kerala's fertility rate of 1.8 not only compares well with China's 2.0, but also with the US's and Sweden's 2.1, Canada's 1.9, and Britain's and France's 1.8.

The population problem is serious, certainly, but neither because of "the proportion between the natural increase of population and food" nor because of some impending apocalypse. There are reasons for worry about the long-term effects of population growth on the environment; and there are strong reasons for concern about the adverse effects of high birth rates on the quality of life, especially of women. With greater opportunities for education (especially female education), reduction of mortality rates (especially of children), improvement in economic security (especially in old age), and greater participation of women in employment and in political action, fast reductions in birth rates can be expected to result through the decisions and actions of those whose lives depend on them.

This is happening right now in many parts of the world, and the result has been a considerable slowing down of world population growth. The best way of dealing with the population problem is to help to spread these processes elsewhere. In contrast, the emergency mentality based on false beliefs in imminent cataclysms leads to breathless responses that are deeply counterproductive, preventing the development of rational and sustainable family planning. Coercive policies of forced birth control involve terrible social sacrifices, and there is little evidence that they are more effective in reducing birth rates than serious programs of collaborative action.

NOTES

1. This paper draws on my lecture arranged by the Eminent Citizens Committee for Cairo '94 at the United Nations in New York on April 18, 1994, and also on research supported by the National Science Foundation.

2. Paul Ehrlich, *The Population Bomb* (Ballantine, 1968). More recently Paul Ehrlich and Anne H. Ehrlich have written *The Population Explosion* (Simon & Schuster, 1990).

3. Garrett Hardin, *Living within Limits* (Oxford University Press, 1993).

4. Thomas Robert Malthus, *Essay on the Principle of Population as It Affects the Future Improvement of Society with Remarks on the Speculation of Mr. Godwin, M. Condorcet, and Other Writers* (London: J. Johnson, 1798), chapter 8; in the Penguin classics edition, *An Essay on the Principle of Population* (1982), p. 123.

5. See Simon Kuznets, *Modern Economic Growth* (Yale University Press, 1966).

6. Note by the Secretary-General of the United Nations to the Preparatory Committee for the International Conference on Population and Development, Third Session, A/Conf.171/PC/5, February 18, 1994, p. 30.

7. Philip Morris Hauser's estimates are presented in the National Academy of Sciences publication *Rapid Population Growth: Consequences and Policy Implications*, vol. 1 (Johns Hopkins University Press, 1971). See also Simon Kuznets, *Modern Economic Growth*, chapter 2.

8. For an important collection of papers on these and related issues see Sir Francis Graham-Smith, F.R.S., editor, *Population—The Complex Reality: A Report of the Population Summit of the World's Scientific Academies*, issued by the Royal Society and published in the US by North American Press, Golden, Colorado. See also D. Gale Johnson and Ronald D. Lee, editors, *Population Growth and Economic Development, Issues and Evidence* (University of Wisconsin Press, 1987).

9. Garrett Hardin, *Living within Limits*, p. 274.

10. Paul Kennedy, who has discussed important problems in the distinctly "social" aspects of population growth, has pointed out that this debate "has, in one form or another, been with us since then," and "it is even more pertinent

today than when Malthus composed his *Essay*," in *Preparing for the Twenty-first Century* (Random House, 1993), pp. 5–6.

11. On the importance of "enlightenment" traditions in Condorcet's thinking, see Emma Rothschild, "Condorcet and the Conflict of Values," in *The Historical Journal*, 39: 3 (September 1996): 677–701.

12. Marie Jean Antoine Nicholas de Caritat Marquis de Condorcet's *Esquisse d'un Tableau Historique des Progrès de l'Esprit Humain*, Xe Epoque (1795). English translation by June Barraclough, *Sketch for a Historical Picture of the Progress of the Human Mind*, with an introduction by Stuart Hampshire (Weidenfeld & Nicolson, 1955), pp. 187–92.

13. T. R. Malthus, *A Summary View of the Principle of Population* (London: John Murray, 1830); Penguin classics edition (1982), p. 243; italics added.

14. On practical policies, including criticism of poverty relief and charitable hospitals, advocated for Britain by Malthus and his followers, see William St. Clair, *The Godwins and the Shelleys: A Biography of a Family* (Norton, 1989).

15. Malthus, *Essay on the Principle of Population*, chapter 17; in the Penguin classics edition, *An Essay on the Principle of Population*, pp. 198–99. Malthus showed some signs of weakening in this belief as he grew older.

16. Gerard Piel, *Only One World: Our Own to Make and to Keep* (Freeman, 1992).

17. For discussions of these empirical connections, see R. A. Easterlin, editor, *Population and Economic Change in Developing Countries* (University of Chicago Press, 1980); T. P. Schultz, *Economics of Population* (Addison-Wesley, 1981); J. C. Caldwell, *Theory of Fertility Decline* (Academic Press, 1982); E. King and M. A. Hill, eds., *Women's Education in Developing Countries* (Johns Hopkins University Press, 1992); Nancy Birdsall, "Economic Approaches to Population Growth" in *The Handbook of Development Economics*, edited by H. B. Chenery and T. N. Srinivasan (Amsterdam: North Holland, 1988); Robert Cassen, et al., *Population and Development: Old Debates, New Conclusions* (New Brunswick: Overseas Development Council/Transaction Publishers, 1994).

18. World Bank, *World Development Report, 1994* (Oxford University Press, 1994), Table 25, pp. 210–11.

19. Ibid., Table 2.

20. These issues are discussed in my joint book with Jean Drèze, *Hunger and Public Action* (Oxford University Press, 1989), and the three volumes edited by us, *The Political Economy of Hunger* (Oxford University Press, 1990), and also in my paper "Economic Regress: Concepts and Features," *Proceedings of the World Bank Annual Conference on Development Economics, 1993* (World Bank, 1994).

21. This is confirmed by, among other statistics, the food production figures regularly presented by the United Nations Food and Agricultural Organization (see the *FAO Quarterly Bulletin of Statistics*, and also the *FAO Monthly Bulletins*).

22. For a more detailed picture and references to data sources, see my "Population and Reasoned Agency: Food, Fertility and Economic Development," in *Population, Economic Development, and the Environment*, edited by Kerstin Lindahl-Kiessling and Hans Landberg (Oxford University Press, 1994); see also the other contributions in this volume. The data presented here have been slightly updated from later publications of the FAO.

23. On this see my *Poverty and Famines* (Oxford University Press, 1981).

24. See UNCTAD VIII, Analytical Report by the UNCTAD Secretariat to the Conference (United Nations, 1992), Table V-S, p. 235. The period covered is between 1979–81 to 1988–90. These figures and related ones are discussed in greater detail in my paper "Population and Reasoned Agency," cited earlier.

25. World Bank, *Price Prospects for Major Primary Commodities*, vol. II (World Bank, March 1993), Annex Tables 6, 12, and 18.

26. Condorcet, *Esquisse d'un Tableau Historique des Progrès de l'Esprit Humain*; in the 1968 reprint, p. 187.

27. The importance of "local" environmental issues is stressed and particularly explored by Partha Dasgupta in *An Inquiry into Well-Being and Destitution* (Oxford University Press, 1993).

28. In *India: Economic Development and Social Opportunity*, by Jean Drèze and myself (Oxford: Clarendon Press, 1995), we discuss the importance of women's political agency in rectifying some of the more serious lapses in Indian economic and social performance—not just pertaining to the deprivation of women themselves.

29. See Jean Drèze and Amartya Sen, *Hunger and Public Action* (Oxford University Press, 1989), which also investigates the remarkable success of some poor countries in providing widespread educational and health services.

30. World Bank, *World Development Report 1994*, p. 212; and *Sample Registration System: Fertility and Mortality Indicators 1991* (New Delhi: Ministry of Home Affairs, 1993).

31. See the discussions, and the literature cited, in Gita Sen, Adrienne German, and Lincoln Chen, editors, *Population Policies Reconsidered: Health, Empowerment, and Rights* (Harvard Center for Population and Development Studies/International Women's Health Coalition, 1994).

32. On the actual processes involved, see T. N. Krishnan, "Demographic Transition in Kerala: Facts and Factors," in *Economic and Political Weekly* 11 (1976), and P. N. Mari Bhat and S. I. Rajan, "Demographic Transition in Kerala Revisited," in *Economic and Political Weekly* 25 (1990).

33. See, for example, Robin Jeffrey, "Culture and Governments: How Women Made Kerala Literate," in *Pacific Affairs* 60 (1987).

34. On this see my "More Than 100 Million Women Are Missing," *New York Review of Books*, December 20, 1990; Ansley J. Coale, "Excess Female Mortality and the Balance of the Sexes: An Estimate of the Number of

'Missing Females'," *Population and Development Review* 17 (1991); Amartya Sen, "Missing Women," *British Medical Journal* 304 (March 1992); Stephan Klasen, "'Missing Women' Reconsidered," *World Development*, 22: 7 (July 1994): 1061–71.

35. Tamil Nadu has benefited from an active and efficient voluntary program of family planning, but these efforts have been helped by favorable social conditions as well, such as a high literacy rate (the second highest among the sixteen major states), a high rate of female participation in work outside the home (the third highest), a relatively low infant mortality rate (the third lowest), and a traditionally higher age of marriage. See also T. V. Antony, "The Family Planning Programme: Lessons from Tamil Nadu's Experience," *Indian Journal of Social Science* 5 (1992).

36. World Bank and Population Reference Bureau, *Success in a Challenging Environment: Fertility Decline in Bangladesh* (World Bank, 1993).

14. SAMUEL SCHEFFLER

The commonsense conception of normative responsibility attaches considerable significance to the distinction between doing something and failing to prevent it, and recognizes special obligations to family members and others. As such, it is a relatively restrictive conception, limiting the individual's normative responsibilities. Recent global developments have put great pressure on this conception of normative responsibility. This has led some to turn to a less restrictive conception of normative responsibility, such as a consequentialist conception. Scheffler, however, gives some reasons to doubt whether a consequentialist conception of normative responsibility could ever come to function as a guide to everyday thought and action. He tentatively concludes by suggesting that we might need to rethink the whole practice of treating the individual as the primary locus of normative responsibility.

Individual Responsibility in a Global Age

First published in Social Philosophy and Policy *12: 1 (winter 1995): 219–36.* © *Social Philosophy and Policy Foundation 1995. Reprinted with the permission of Cambridge University Press.*

INTRODUCTION

Europe has been undergoing a process of political transformation whose outcome cannot be predicted with confidence, in part because the process is being driven by two powerful but conflicting tendencies. The first is the movement toward greater economic and political union among the countries of Western Europe. The second is the pressure, in the aftermath of the collapse of the Soviet Union, for the countries of Eastern Europe to fragment along ethnic and communal lines.

However these conflicting tendencies may be resolved in practice, they pose a theoretical problem for contemporary liberalism, and for many other political philosophies as well. The problem arises because contemporary liberalism—like many other political philosophies—tends to treat the *individual society* as the appropriate unit of justification, while tacitly assuming a one-to-one correspondence between individual societies and sovereign states. Thus, the dominant focus of liberal thought is on the question of how the political institutions of an individual society are to be justified, and it is taken for granted that the society in question, although undoubtedly comprising a population that is highly diverse in various respects, will nevertheless be organized as a single nation-state.[1] In addition, it tends to be assumed that any adequate justification of such a society's institutions will be one that is addressed exclusively to the citizens of that society, and that the justice or injustice of the society will depend entirely on the way in which it adjudicates among the interests of its own citizens.[2] Questions of global justice are considered under the heading of "international" justice, if indeed they are considered at all; like international law, international justice is thought of as an area of specialized concern that is most naturally addressed once a body of principles for the more fundamental case of the individual nation-state is in hand. Thus, for example, John Rawls describes himself as working with "the notion of a self-contained national community."[3] His primary aim, he says, is to develop principles "for the basic structure of society conceived for the time being as a closed system isolated from other societies."[4] "The significance of this special case," he adds, "is obvious and needs no explanation."[5] In Rawls's view, investigation of "the principles of justice for the law of nations" may appropriately be postponed until after principles for a single society have been derived.[6]

As recent events in Europe demonstrate, this set of assumptions may be brought under pressure from two different directions at once. On the one hand, the growing economic and technological interdependence of the countries of the world, which has helped to produce the drive toward greater union in Western Europe, makes it natural to wonder whether one can in fact produce an adequate justification for the institutions of a single society by treating it as "a closed system isolated from other societies." Perhaps societies are so economically interdependent that the justice of the basic structure of any one of them essentially depends on the nature of its political and economic relations to the others. Or, more radically, some may wonder whether, in the conditions of the modern world, the political and economic institutions for which the strongest justification can be found will be those of the individual society or state at all, as opposed to some more inclusive form of organization.[7]

On the other hand, although a focus on the political institutions of a single society may seem, from some vantage points, excessively narrow, events in Eastern Europe—and, indeed, in many other places as well—serve forcefully to remind us that there are also perspectives from which such a focus may seem too broad, for it may seem to underestimate both the extent and the political significance of the cultural diversity that exists within most actual societies. Certainly the expectation that each society will be organized as a *nation-state*—as opposed, say, to a multination-state—is open to serious question, given the evident power of shared identifications based on factors like religion, ethnicity, language, and cultural history, and given the heterogeneity of the populations of most existing states. Such an expectation may seem to rest on an inflated estimate of the significance of shared citizenship in relation to communal bonds of other kinds.

Thus, although it continues to be widely assumed both that the individual society is the appropriate unit of political justification and that such societies will be organized as nation-states, these assumptions are under political and intellectual pressure from two different directions. Caught between powerful universalistic and equally powerful particularistic tendencies, they define a widely held intermediate position that seems increasingly to require defense. To the extent that a political philosophy simply takes this position for granted, it begs some important theoretical questions to which recent events have lent considerable urgency.

This problem is especially acute for contractarian versions of contemporary liberalism, because of their explicit focus on the individual society as the relevant unit of justification and their tacit reliance on the category of the nation-state; but the problem also arises for other versions of liberalism, and for various other political philosophies as well. There is, however, one theory for which it would appear to be less of a problem, and that is consequentialism.[8] In general, social and communal ties have no direct justificatory significance for consequentialism, and the bond of shared citizenship is no exception. Consequentialists hold that social and political institutions ought to be arranged in such a way as to produce the best overall outcomes, and they take the interests of *all* human beings to count equally in determining which outcomes are best. Thus, on the face of it, consequentialism would appear much better equipped than some other views to accommodate the universalistic tendencies in modern political life, and much less vulnerable to any charge that it takes the category of the nation-state for granted.

Indeed, consequentialists can manage to treat the individual society as a unit with special justificatory significance only by "arguing back" to this more conventional position from their own radically universalistic and apparently revisionary starting point: by arguing, in other words, that the interests of all human beings will best be served by a division of labor in which the human population is organized into different societies, each of which has its own political institutions that are specially concerned with the welfare of that society. In much the same way, consequentialism can attach justificatory significance to familial bonds only by arguing that the interests of all humanity will best be served if individuals devote special attention to the members of their own families. In principle, the method of "arguing back" provides consequentialism with a schematic strategy for attaching political significance not only to the individual society but to less-than-universal social groups of any size. However, it can hardly be said that this makes consequentialism directly responsive to particularist or communitarian concerns. On the contrary, what the method of arguing back provides is clearly a strategy for the indirect accommodation of particularist concerns, and one that the consequentialist is entitled to deploy only in circumstances where it is reasonable to assume that universalistic aims will, in fact, best be achieved through particularist structures. Even in these circumstances, moreover, the consequentialist remains committed to denying what the particularist is most concerned to affirm—namely, the unmediated moral significance of those special ties that bind members of a community to each other, but that, in so doing, also serve to set them apart from people outside the community.

In this essay, I will not be directly concerned with the question of whether the individual society is in fact the appropriate unit of justification in political philosophy, nor will I offer any argument about the proper status within political philosophy of the category of the nation-state.[9] Instead, I will be concerned with the universalistic and particularistic pressures that give these questions their present urgency, and, more specifically, with the way in which these conflicting pressures may be viewed in part as expressing conflicting conceptions of responsibility. My aim is to explore this conflict about responsibility and, in particular, to argue that its current political manifestations are in part the outgrowth of a variety of developments in the modern world that have combined to make some fundamental features of our thinking about responsibility look increasingly problematic.

TWO CONCEPTIONS OF NORMATIVE RESPONSIBILITY

Different normative ethical theories may be seen as articulating different conceptions of individual responsibility. That is, such theories offer different interpretations of what it is the responsibility of the individual agent to do and to avoid doing. We may say that they offer different conceptions of the individual's *normative responsibility*. Within commonsense moral thought, two doctrines about normative responsibility play a central role. One is the doctrine that individuals have a special responsibility for what they themselves do, as opposed to what they merely fail to prevent. This doctrine is sometimes expressed in the principle that negative duties are stricter than positive duties, where this means, roughly, that it is more important to avoid doing certain sorts of things *to* people than it is to prevent unwelcome occurrences from befalling them or to provide them with positive benefits. The principle that negative duties are stricter than positive duties itself has two sides. The first consists in the idea that the negative duties ordinarily take priority over the positive in cases of conflict. Thus, for example, I may not ordinarily harm one innocent person even in order to prevent harm from befalling two other innocent people, because my negative duty not to harm the one is stronger than my positive duty to aid the two. The second side of the principle that negative duties are stricter than positive duties consists in the idea that the former constitute a greater constraint on one's pursuit of one's own goals, projects, and commitments. For example, I may not be permitted to harm an innocent person in order to advance my career aims, for to do so would violate my duty not to harm. Yet I may be permitted to advance my career aims in other ways, even if by so doing I will miss out on an opportunity to prevent a comparably serious harm from befalling a comparably innocent person.

The other commonsense doctrine is that one has distinctive responsibilities—or "special obligations"—toward members of one's own family and others to whom one stands in certain significant sorts of relationships. It is true, as Sidgwick emphasized, that there is disagreement within commonsense morality about the specific types of relationships that give rise to special obligations.[10] Although close family relationships are undoubtedly the least controversial example, there is less consensus about relationships of other kinds. Nevertheless, the importance of special obligations in commonsense moral thought seems undeniable. By any measure, they serve to define a large portion of the territory of morality as it is ordinarily understood. The willingness to make sacrifices for one's family, one's community, one's friends, and one's comrades is seen as one of the marks of a good or virtuous person, and the demands of morality, as ordinarily interpreted, have less to do with abstractions like the overall good than with the specific web of roles and relationships that serve to situate a person in social space.

Because of the significance that it attaches to the distinction between doing and failing to prevent, and to the category of special obligations, the commonsense conception of responsibility may be described as a *restrictive* conception. For the commonsense doctrines that make use of these ideas serve not only to delineate but also to limit the individual's normative responsibilities. Admittedly, there is room within commonsense morality for significant disagreement about the precise content of people's positive and negative duties, and also about the precise degree by which the strength of the latter exceeds that of the former. On any plausible interpretation, however, the principle that negative duties are stricter than positive duties serves to limit normative responsibility in such a way that individuals may, provided they avoid certain types of proscribed behavior, exercise considerable discretion in the way they choose to lead their lives and to allocate their resources.

Similarly, the doctrine that one has special obligations toward certain classes of individuals has, as a corollary, the principle that one's responsibilities toward other people are more limited.

As has often been pointed out, part of the radicalism of consequentialism lies in the challenge it presents to ordinary notions of normative responsibility.[11] To appreciate the radical character of this challenge we have only to observe that consequentialism rejects both of the commonsense doctrines I have mentioned. Thus, in the case of the first doctrine, whereas commonsense morality regards individuals as having special responsibility for what they themselves do, consequentialism treats the outcomes that one fails to prevent as no less important in determining the rightness or wrongness of one's actions than those that one directly brings about. This greatly widens the scope of one's normative responsibility, in so far as it implies that one's positive duties are as strict as one's negative duties—so that, for example, one's duty to alleviate suffering that one has had no hand in causing is as great as one's duty to avoid inflicting pain oneself. This in turn has two further implications, corresponding to the two sides of the commonsense principle that negative duties are stricter than positive duties. The first implication is that one may be required to harm or even to kill an innocent person if that is the only way to prevent still greater harm or death. The second implication is that the permissibility of any activity or pursuit, however innocent it may appear, must always depend on the unavailability of any alternative that would produce greater net benefit overall. Thus, on this conception, those who spend money on relative luxuries like movies, restaurant meals, or consumer electronics, when the same money could instead be used to prevent suffering and death, are doing something that is the moral equivalent of killing innocent people. Indeed, in order for it to be legitimate, on this conception, to devote energy and attention to one's most fundamental projects and aspirations, it is not enough that those projects and aspirations should be innocent or benign in and of themselves. Rather, it must be the case that nothing else one could possibly do would produce greater net benefit for humanity as a whole. It scarcely seems necessary to point out how dramatically these tenets serve to widen the scope of individual responsibility, or how sharply they conflict with most people's commonsense moral understanding.

Consequentialism also rejects the second of the two commonsense doctrines I have mentioned. Whereas commonsense morality holds that one has distinctive responsibilities toward family members and others to whom one stands in certain special sorts of relationships, consequentialism maintains that the interests of all people, family members and strangers alike, count equally in determining what one ought to do. Thus, for example, if one can either provide a benefit for one's own child or a slightly greater benefit for a stranger's child, then, other things being equal, one ought to provide the benefit for the stranger's child. Here again, the effect of the consequentialist position is greatly to widen the scope of the individual's normative responsibility. And, in view of the prominence of special obligations in ordinary moral thought, consequentialism's refusal to recognize such obligations provides further testimony to the radicalism of its conception of responsibility.

Of course, although consequentialism neither assigns intrinsic moral significance to the distinction between doing and failing to prevent, nor recognizes special obligations as a fundamental moral category, some consequentialists may wish to "argue back" to restrictions on individual responsibility that mimic those embraced by the commonsense conception. However, commonsense morality takes the restrictions to operate at the level of fundamental principle, and it is this that consequentialism denies. At the foundational level, in other words, consequentialism remains resolutely *nonrestrictive*. Thus, the conflict between the consequentialist and commonsense conceptions may be viewed as a conflict about the legitimacy of restrictiveness in the assignment of normative responsibility.

GLOBAL TRENDS AND INDIVIDUAL RESPONSIBILITY

The restrictions imposed by the ordinary conception of responsibility serve, in effect, to limit the size of the agent's moral world. To the extent that such restrictions are part of moral common sense, these limits seem natural to us. However, this sense of naturalness does not exist in a vacuum. It is supported by a widespread though largely implicit conception of human social relations as consisting primarily in small-scale interactions, with clearly demarcated lines of causation, among independent individual agents. It is also supported by a complex phenomenology of agency: that is, by a characteristic way of experiencing ourselves as agents with causal powers. Within this phenomenology, acts have primacy over omissions, near effects have primacy over remote effects, and individual effects have primacy over group effects. Let me comment briefly on each of these three phenomenological features.

The primacy of acts over omissions means that whereas our acts are ordinarily experienced by us as acts, we experience our omissions as omissions only in special contexts. Among these are contexts in which we believe an omission to fly in the face of some specific obligation or norm: as, for example, when I remain silent as the blind person strolls toward the edge of the cliff, or when I neglect to feed my child or to return my suicidal patient's telephone calls, or when I fail to provide you with a promised loan at the appointed time. In each of these cases, my belief that I have an obligation to act in a certain way may lead me to experience my failure to do so *as* an omission or failure to act. With respect to my acts themselves, however, no comparable background conviction is required. I experience my acts as acts whether or not they violate any norms or expectations.

The primacy of near effects over remote effects means that we tend to experience our causal influence as inversely related to spatial and temporal distance. Of course, we know that we can do things that will have effects in distant lands and remote times, and sometimes these effects matter greatly to us. The phenomenology of agency, however, is such that our influence on our local surroundings in the present and the near future tends, as we say, to seem more real to us. This is both because the relevant causal connections are ordinarily easier to discern in these circumstances and because we are more likely to witness the effects of our acts firsthand.

The primacy of individual effects over group effects means that when an outcome is the joint result of the actions of a number of people, including ourselves, we tend to see our own agency as implicated to a much lesser extent than we do when we take an effect to have resulted solely from our own actions. Again, this does not mean that we never feel any causal responsibility for outcomes produced jointly by our actions in conjunction with the actions of other people. However, it does mean that outcomes we perceive as resulting solely from our own actions tend to loom much larger for us, and that it is often easier for us to overlook our causal contributions to those outcomes that are the joint result of the actions of many people.[12]

As I have said, the limits placed by commonsense morality on individual normative responsibility seem natural to us, but this sense of naturalness does not exist in a vacuum. I have been suggesting that it arises instead within a context that is defined in part by a certain conception of social relations, and by certain familiar features of the phenomenology of agency. At the same time, a variety of developments in the modem world have conspired to place that conception of social relations, as well as the image of ourselves that is implicit in the phenomenology of agency, under enormous pressure. These developments include, most notably, the remarkable advances in science and technology in recent decades; the continuing revolutions in travel, communications, and information processing; the increased economic and political interdependence among the countries of the world; and the enormous growth in world population.

These developments have made it more difficult than ever to sustain the conception of human social relations as consisting primarily in small-scale interactions among single individuals. The earth has become an increasingly crowded place. The lives of its inhabitants are structured to an unprecedented degree by large, impersonal institutions and bureaucracies. The interactions of these institutions across national borders have profound effects on the lives of people worldwide, and serve to link the fates of people in different parts of the world in multiple ways. Thus, the quality of life for people in any one part of the world is, to a large extent, a function of a network of institutional arrangements that supports a very different quality of life for people in other parts of the world. And important political and economic developments in one area of the globe often have rapid and dramatic effects on people in other areas, effects that are frequently intensified by the speed with which information about them is communicated. Moreover, in consequence of the growth of population and the development of new technologies, human behavior now has effects on the natural environment that are unprecedented in scale. These environmental effects distribute themselves in complicated ways within and across national boundaries—often with profound consequences, in turn, for the lives of widely dispersed individuals and communities. In addition, they raise urgent questions about the impact of contemporary behavior on the lives and circumstances of future generations of people. In this context, the image of human social life as defined primarily by small-scale personal relations among independent individual agents begins to seem like a significant distortion.

Similar remarks apply to the conception of human action that is suggested by the phenomenology of agency. Phenomenologically speaking, our actions loom larger than our omissions; near effects loom larger than remote ones; and outcomes produced individually loom larger than those produced jointly. Yet, in light of the developments I have mentioned, the phenomenology of agency seems like an increasingly poor guide to the dimensions of human action that are socially significant. For surely, any serious accounting of the most urgent problems now facing the human race, as well as any serious proposals for their solution, will need to refer both to what people have done and to what they have not done—as individuals, in groups, and through social institutions—with consequences both near and far. Whether we are seeking to identify the reasons for global warming, or for the threat to the survival of the Amazonian rain forests, or for the vast disparities in wealth and life expectancy among rich and poor nations, we will need to move beyond the phenomenology of agency if we are to understand the role of human beings in generating these problems.

Thus, although the restrictive conception of responsibility that is embodied in commonsense moral thought may indeed seem natural to us, reflection on the sources of this sense of naturalness should lead us to wonder whether it really counts in favor of the commonsense view. And these doubts will only be reinforced if we find ourselves tempted by the suggestion that "commonsense" morality is in fact a quite specific cultural product: a product, moreover, that has its deepest roots in those relatively affluent societies that have the most to gain from the widespread internalization of a doctrine that limits their responsibility to assist the members of less fortunate societies.

It is, of course, a premise of this essay that the commonsense conception of responsibility is controversial despite its seeming naturalness. The prominence of consequentialism is one obvious manifestation of this controversy at the theoretical level. More generally, however, I think it is fair to say that there has been, within the culture at large, a decline in confidence in the commonsense conception, even among many people who basically accept it. If indeed the culture's confidence in the commonsense conception has been shaken, this is surely due, at least in part, to the developments I have mentioned. The communications revolution that is itself one of those developments has meant that information about *all* of the developments has been disseminated widely and insistently. To the extent that those developments cast doubt on ways of understanding ourselves and our social world that are congenial to the commonsense conception, it is not surprising that the widespread awareness of them should serve to erode our confidence in that conception.

As I have suggested, the persistence of consequentialism is one symptom at the theoretical level of the decline in confidence in the commonsense conception. It is not the only such symptom, however. Another one, which I have discussed elsewhere,[13] is the reluctance of contemporary liberal philosophers, as well as some of their most prominent critics, to appeal to any preinstitutional notion of desert of the kind that is often associated with the commonsense conception of responsibility. This reluctance is related to a more general tendency, which is clearly illustrated by the modern revolution in tort law, to conceive of responsibility as something that it is the job of social and political institutions to assign or to allocate to individuals on grounds that make institutional sense. Although this broad tendency is one that is quite hospitable to consequentialism, it need not take a distinctively consequentialist form, since the grounds on which responsibility is to be allocated need not be understood in narrowly consequentialist terms.

Although confidence in the commonsense conception of responsibility may have declined, however, it would be rash to predict the imminent demise of that conception or its imminent replacement by a thoroughly nonrestrictive conception of individual responsibility. In order to have any hope of superseding the commonsense conception—any hope, that is, of taking over the place that it now occupies within commonsense moral thought—a nonrestrictive conception of responsibility would need, at a minimum, to be capable of being internalized and of coming to function as a guide to everyday thought and action. Yet, despite the decline in our culture's confidence in the commonsense conception, and despite the increasingly sophisticated articulation of alternative theoretical approaches to at least some questions of responsibility, it is by no means clear that any thoroughly nonrestrictive conception of responsibility could meet these conditions. This is not because moral common sense is immutable; as I have already indicated, what it seems plausible to us to refer to as commonsense morality is undoubtedly a highly specific cultural product in certain respects. It is one thing to acknowledge this, however, and quite another thing to produce a viable conception of individual responsibility that does not employ any category like the category of special obligations, or any distinction like the distinction between negative and positive duties.

There are two reasons for this. The first has to do with the depth of the hold that such ideas have on us. Thus, for example, the sheer human importance of interpersonal bonds and relationships of various kinds makes it difficult to imagine the widespread internalization of a conception of responsibility that does not leave substantial room for special responsibilities arising out of such relationships. The sheer phenomenological force of the distinction between acts and omissions makes it similarly difficult to imagine the widespread internalization of a conception of responsibility that treats them entirely symmetrically. This helps to explain why, despite the fact that consequentialism considered in the abstract offers a radically expansive conception of individual responsibility, defenders of the view so often find themselves "arguing back" to a more conventional position that does make room—albeit derivatively—for the analogues of special obligations and the distinction between negative and positive duties.

The second reason is more complicated. The developments that tend to erode our confidence in the commonsense conception, and to encourage us to look for a less restrictive alternative, have these effects because they make a global perspective on the lives and conduct of individual agents seem morally more salient than the narrower perspective that we are more accustomed to taking. But while these developments do indeed make the idea of a less restrictive conception of responsibility seem more plausible, they do not themselves present us with any clearly defined conception of this kind. An emphasis on the significance for human affairs of various large-scale global developments and dynamics—

economic, political, technological, and environmental—does not translate in any obvious way into a determinate picture of how ordinary individuals should conduct their lives. After all, the individual agent *qua* individual agent will typically have only the most limited opportunities to influence these global dynamics, and, indeed, cannot in general be assumed to have any but the sketchiest and most speculative notions about the specific global implications of his or her personal behavior. Here again, the example of consequentialism is instructive. Taken at face value, the consequentialist conception of responsibility is highly expansionist and thoroughly nonrestrictive. It requires individuals always to act in such a way as to produce the optimal state of the world from an impersonal standpoint. In so doing, however, it seems to many people to make wildly excessive demands on the capacity of agents to amass information about the global impact of the different courses of action available to them. Faced with this objection, the most common consequentialist response is to treat it as another reason for arguing back to a more conventional demarcation of individual responsibility, thus abandoning the attempt to provide a nonrestrictive conception of responsibility, except at the foundational level. This is, of course, just an instance of consequentialism's well-known normative schizophrenia: its tendency to alternate between presenting itself as a radically revisionist morality, on the one hand, and as a possibly surprising but basically conservative account of the foundations of ordinary moral thought, on the other. This very schizophrenia testifies to the difficulty of producing a credible alternative to a restrictive conception of individual responsibility.

Thus, to repeat, if we come to see the global perspective as morally salient, the immediate effect is not to present us with a developed alternative conception of individual normative responsibility. Instead, the global perspective highlights the importance of various large-scale causal processes and patterns of activity that the individual agent cannot in general control, but within which individual behavior is nevertheless subsumed in ways that the individual is, at any given time, unlikely to be in a position fully to appreciate. The claim that individual behavior is "subsumed" within such patterns and processes is not, of course, meant to deny that individual human beings are the fundamental units of agency. Instead, the claim comprises two theses. The first is simply that it is not uncommon for an important outcome to be the product of a large number of acts performed by many different people, few if any of whom actually intend to produce the outcome in question. The second thesis is that many of the options and choices with which people are presented throughout their lives, although experienced by them as entirely natural, are nevertheless structured to a considerable extent by institutional arrangements of enormous complexity. By structuring individual choices in the way that they do, these arrangements serve, in effect, to harness and channel human actions: to recruit them as contributions to larger processes that typically have little to do with people's reasons for performing those actions, but which often have profound and far-reaching effects. Frequently, moreover, the individual agents involved, far from intending to participate in the production of these effects, are scarcely even aware that they have done so. Their vision is obscured by the seeming naturalness of the choices presented to them, by the independent character of their own reasons for acting as they do, by the complexity of the larger processes to which their actions contribute, by the often minute contribution to those processes made by any single action considered individually, and by the phenomenological priority of individual over group effects. Thus it is that much of the daily behavior we take for granted is linked in complicated but often poorly appreciated ways to broader global dynamics of the greatest importance.[14]

In view of these considerations, the most immediate effect of coming to see the global perspective as morally salient may be, not to present us with a developed, nonrestrictive conception of normative responsibility, but rather to generate doubts about our practice of treating the individual agent as the primary locus of such responsibility. For although the larger processes within which individual behavior is subsumed frequently have effects of enormous moral significance, the individual agent's relation to these effects is clearly not what one finds in paradigm cases of individual responsibility. The effects to which principles of individual responsibility are paradigmatically responsive are those produced solely or primarily by the individual's own actions.[15] Among the salient features of the phenomenon of subsumption, however, are the limited contribution each agent makes to the larger processes in question; the limited control each agent has over those processes; the pervasiveness of the processes and the attendant difficulty of abstaining in any wholesale way from participation in them; the extraordinary difficulty of obtaining consistently reliable information about the processes and their effects; and the equally formidable difficulty of ascertaining the different contributions that would be made to such processes by each of the various options available to the agent at any given time. Thus, although these processes often have effects of such great moral significance that there is an evident need to bring them under the normative control of a viable system of responsibility, the structure of the individual's relations to the processes makes it doubtful whether we have available any principles of individual conduct that are capable of accomplishing this aim. What we appear to lack, in other words, is a set of clear, action-guiding, and psychologically feasible principles that would enable individuals to orient themselves in relation to the larger processes, and general conformity to which would serve to regulate those processes and their effects in a morally satisfactory way. In view of the moral importance both of the processes and of their effects, the absence of such principles raises an obvious question about the adequacy of a system of normative responsibility that treats the individual agent as the primary bearer of such responsibility.[16]

In brief, then, the second reason for doubting the imminent replacement of the commonsense conception of responsibility by a thoroughly nonrestrictive conception is this: The same global developments that make a more expansive conception of individual normative responsibility seem initially more plausible also raise doubts about the very practice of treating individuals as the primary bearers of such responsibility. Since it is by no means clear what the alternative to that practice might be, however, these developments also pose a more general threat to our deployment of the categories of normative responsibility.

If the argument I have been advancing is correct, our practices with respect to normative responsibility face a significant threat. The problem arises out of a perspective on human action that seems increasingly to be forced upon us by a variety of developments in modern life. Up to a point, these developments appear to undermine the commonsense conception of normative responsibility, for they make the limits on individual responsibility imposed by that conception seem anachronistic and difficult to defend. Rather than providing straightforward support for an alternative, nonrestrictive conception of responsibility, however, these same developments tend instead to raise a more fundamental question about the availability of a suitable locus of normative responsibility in an increasingly important range of cases. Thus, the net effect of these developments may be, not to encourage the substitution of a nonrestrictive conception of responsibility for more restrictive ideas, but rather to leave our thinking about responsibility in some disarray.

CONCLUSION

I began this essay by taking note of the pressure toward universalism, and the conflicting pressure toward particularism, in modern political life, and by suggesting that these conflicting pressures serve in part to express conflicting conceptions of normative responsibility. It is now possible to clarify and to elaborate on this suggestion. The universalistic pressure—the pressure toward greater social and political integration—is an outgrowth of the very same developments that have made a more expansive conception of responsibility seem more plausible. Moreover, in so far as the tendency of such pressure is to suggest a diminished justificatory role for national and communal ties, and a reduced reliance on the distinction between acts and omissions in favor of a more inclusive concern for the enhancement of human well-being, it may itself be viewed as a manifestation of support for a more expansive conception. At the same time, the pressure toward universalism has met with great resistance, and recent years have witnessed an often ferocious resurgence of particularist loyalties. These complex developments should not be oversimplified, but they serve in part to remind us of the powerful hold that more restrictive notions of responsibility have on people. Indeed, if the argument of this essay is correct, there is a serious question about the extent to which an entirely nonrestrictive conception of responsibility could ever fully dislodge such notions. The question arises not only because of the hold that restrictive ideas have on us, but also because the challenge to those ideas is fueled by the growing authority, or apparent authority, of a perspective whose strongest tendency may not be to support a nonrestrictive conception, but rather to pose a more general threat to our thinking about normative responsibility.

It should not be surprising that we are faced with such a threat at this time. Recent decades have brought what one historian has called some of "the most rapid and profound upheavals of human life in recorded history."[17] Few important areas of life have been untouched by those upheavals, and there is little reason to suppose that our thinking about responsibility, which developed in the context of a radically different social world, is one of them. On the contrary, there is abundant evidence that our ideas about responsibility are in flux. The conflicting tendencies toward global integration and ethnic fragmentation constitute one symptom of this phenomenon on the political level. As I have tried to suggest in this essay, however, the underlying problem is a broader one, and we are unlikely to find a solution to the political problem without attaining greater stability in our thinking about normative responsibility more generally. What remains to be seen, then, is whether we can emerge from this period of normative confusion with a defensible and psychologically feasible conception of responsibility that can help structure our social relations during the enormous additional upheavals that undoubtedly await us. In the meantime, we live in a world that seems increasingly divided, and dangerously so, between an ascendant high-tech global culture and a persistent web of fierce particularist loyalties.

NOTES

1. One liberal who does *not* take the nation-state for granted, but who recognizes that most liberals do, is Will Kymlicka in *Liberalism, Community, and Culture* (Oxford: Clarendon Press, 1989).

2. As Yael Tamir observes in *Liberal Nationalism* (Princeton, NJ: Princeton University Press, 1993), 10: "[M]any national elements, although unacknowledged, have been fused into liberal thought.... For example, the liberal conception of distributive justice is particularistic and applies only within well-defined, relatively closed social frameworks, which favor members over nonmembers." For a historical account of changes in the way the concept of a "nation" has been understood, see E. J. Hobsbawm, *Nations and Nationalism since 1780*, 2nd ed. (Cambridge: Cambridge University Press, 1992).

3. John Rawls, *A Theory of Justice* (Cambridge, MA: Harvard University Press, 1971), 457.

4. Ibid., 8.

5. Ibid.

6. Ibid., 457. In *Political Liberalism* (New York: Columbia University Press, 1993: 272n), Rawls writes: "[A]s a first approximation, the problem of social justice concerns the basic structure as a closed background system. To start with the society of nations would seem merely to push one step further back the task of finding a theory of background justice. At some level there must exist a closed background system, and it is this subject for which we want a theory. We are better prepared to take up this problem for a society (illustrated by nations) conceived as a more or less self-sufficient scheme of social cooperation and as possessing a more or less complete culture. If we are successful in the case of a society, we can try to extend and to adjust our initial theory as further inquiry requires."

In his essay on "The Law of Peoples," *Critical Inquiry* 20 (1993): 36–68 [the original version from which *Critical Inquiry* excerpted is reprinted in *Global Justice: Seminal Essays*, 421–60], and in his book of the same title (Harvard University Press, 1999) [§15 and §16 reprinted herein], Rawls makes good on his suggestion that the topic of international justice should be addressed once a theory of justice for a single society has been developed. In chapter 6 of his *Realizing Rawls* (Ithaca, NY: Cornell University Press, 1989), however, Thomas Pogge argues that we should "abandon Rawls's primary emphasis on domestic institutions in favor of globalizing his entire conception of justice" (240). For a similar suggestion, see Charles Beitz, *Political Theory and International Relations* (Princeton, NJ: Princeton University Press, 1979), Part 3 [based on his essay "Justice and International Relations," first published in *Philosophy and Public Affairs* 4: 4, (summer 1975): 360–89, reprinted in *Global Justice: Seminal Essays*, 21–48].

7. In "The Law of Peoples," Rawls writes: "I follow Kant's lead in *Perpetual Peace* in thinking that a world government—by which I mean a unified political regime with the legal powers normally exercised by central governments—would either be a global despotism or else a fragile empire torn by frequent civil strife as various regions and peoples try to gain their political autonomy" (46) [*GJSE* 431].

Thomas Nagel takes a similar position in *Equality and Partiality* (New York: Oxford University Press, 1991), chap. 15. For a defense of the Kantian idea of a "pacific union" of liberal states as the most plausible route to world peace, see the two-part article by Michael Doyle, "Kant, Liberal Legacies, and Foreign Affairs," *Philosophy & Public Affairs* 12 (1983): 205–35 [reprinted herein 73–106] and 323–53. See also Jeremy Waldron, "Special Ties and Natural

Duties," *Philosophy & Public Affairs* 22 (1993): 3–30 [reprinted in *Global Justice: Seminal Essays*, 391–419].

8. Consequentialism, as I understand it, is a view that first gives some principle for ranking overall states of affairs from best to worst from an impersonal standpoint, and then says that the right act or policy or institutional arrangement in any given situation is the one that will produce the highest-ranked state of affairs that is available.

9. For some interesting suggestions, see Tamir, *Liberal Nationalism*, ch. 7.

10. See Henry Sidgwick, *The Methods of Ethics*, 7th ed. (London: Macmillan and Company, Ltd., 1907), Book III, chaps. IV and XI. Sidgwick also emphasizes the absence of any consensus about the extent of many of these obligations. The point is not merely that the extent of the obligation depends on the type of special relationship involved, but that with respect to any single type of relationship, it is often difficult to say how far the obligations of the participants are thought to extend.

11. See, for example, Bernard Williams, "A Critique of Utilitarianism," in J. J. C. Smart and Bernard Williams, *Utilitarianism: For and Against* (Cambridge: Cambridge University Press, 1973), 77–150.

12. This is especially true in cases where the outcome in question results from the actions of an extremely large number of people, each of whom makes only a tiny contribution to the production of that outcome. For a discussion of the moral significance of such cases, see Part 1 of Derek Parfit's *Reasons and Persons* (Oxford: Clarendon Press, 1984), esp. ch. 3. For criticism of Parfit, see Michael Otsuka, "The Paradox of Group Beneficence," *Philosophy & Public Affairs*, 20 (1991): 132–49.

13. See my "Responsibility, Reactive Attitudes, and Liberalism in Philosophy and Politics," chapter 1 in *Boundaries and Allegiances: Problems of Justice and Responsibility in Liberal Thought* (Oxford: Oxford University Press, 2001), 12–31.

14. Consider, in this connection, Onora [Nell] O'Neill's claim that "[m]odern economic causal chains are so complex that only those who are economically isolated and self-sufficient could know" that they are "not part of any system of activities causing unjustifiable deaths" ("Lifeboat Earth," *Philosophy & Public Affairs* 4 (1975): 286 [reprinted in *Global Justice: Seminal Essays*, 1–20, 13]).

15. Consider, in this connection, the following remarks by H. L. A. Hart and Tony Honoré in *Causation in the Law*, 2nd ed. (Oxford: Clarendon Press,

1985), lxxx: "The idea that individuals are primarily responsible for the harm which their actions are sufficient to produce without the intervention of others or of extraordinary natural events is important, not merely to law and morality, but to the preservation of something else of great moment in human life. This is the individual's sense of himself as a separate person whose character is manifested in such actions. Individuals come to understand themselves as distinct persons, to whatever extent they do, and to acquire a sense of self-respect largely by reflection on those changes in the world about them which their actions are sufficient to bring about without the intervention of others and which are therefore attributable to them separately."

16. Compare Thomas Pogge in *Realizing Rawls*, 8–9: "The effects of my conduct reverberate throughout the world, intermingling with the effects of the conduct of billions of other human beings. . . . Thus, many morally salient features of the situations of human beings (persistent starvation in northeastern Brazil, civil war in El Salvador, famine in India) arise from the confluence of the often very remote effects of the conduct of vast numbers of human beings. We as individuals have no hope of coping with such complexity and interdependence if we take the existing ground rules for granted and merely ask 'How should I act?' . . . We can cope only by attending to the scheme of ground rules which shapes the way persons act and co-determines how their actions, together, affect the lives of others."

17. Hobsbawm, *Nations and Nationalism since 1780*, 174.

15. RICHARD RORTY

Rorty's concern is to analyze the current moral situation of well-off inhabitants of rich countries in terms of alternative answers to the question "Who are we?" He begins by contrasting this question, which he takes to be a political one, with the traditional metaphysical or scientific question "What are we?" (or Kant's "What is Man?"). In the thinking of Nietzsche and William James, religious, scientific, and other attempts to answer this metaphysical question should be seen, not as attempts at the reflection of reality, but as tools—and different purposes require different tools. Answers to the *who* question are, Rorty claims, "attempts to forge, or reforge, a moral identity." They are also answers about what purposes we choose to pursue. Hence, our answer to the *who* question will suggest an appropriate answer to the *what* question. The *who* question is in this sense prior. One purpose that inhabitants of rich countries can pursue is that of sharing their wealth with the world's poor. To do so might have been feasible in 1900, says Rorty, but is not feasible in today's world because the numbers of the poor have increased tremendously in the intervening period. The institutions of rich countries require a certain amount of wealth in order to be maintained, and this wealth would not be available if it were dispensed to the poor.

Who Are We?
Moral Universalism and
Economic Triage

First published in Diogenes *44: 173 (spring 1996): 5–15*

In what sort of situation might someone ask the question "Who are we?" It seems most appropriate in the mouth of someone trying to shape her audience into a more coherent community. It is the sort of rhetorical question a party leader might ask at a party rally. In such situations, it means something like "What unifying ideal can we find to make us less like a mob and more like an army, less like people thrown together by accident and more like people who have united to accomplish a task?"

"Who are we?" is quite different from the traditional philosophical question "What are we?" The latter is synonymous with Kant's question, "What is Man?" Both mean something like "How does the human species differ from the rest of the animal kingdom?" or "Among the differences between us and the other animals, which ones matter most?" This "what?" question is scientific or metaphysical.

By contrast, the "who?" question is political. It is asked by people who want to separate off the human beings who are better suited to some particular purpose than other human beings, and to gather the former into a self-conscious moral community: that is, a community united by reciprocal trust, and by willingness to come to fellow members' assistance when they need it. Answers to the "who?" question are attempts to forge, or reforge, a moral identity.

Traditional moral universalism blends an answer to the scientific or metaphysical "what?" question with an answer to the political "who?" question. Universalism presupposes that the discovery of traits shared by all human beings suffices to show why, and perhaps how, all human beings should organize themselves into a cosmopolis. It proposes a scientific or metaphysical foundation for global politics. Following the model of religious claims that human beings are made in the image of God, philosophical universalism claims that the presence of common traits testifies to a common purpose. It says that the form of the ideal human community can be determined by reference to a universal human nature.

The idea of human nature has, in recent Western philosophy, come to seem obsolete. Ever since Darwin, philosophers have become increasingly suspicious of the very idea of naturalness. Western philosophy has been trying to adapt itself to Darwin's claim that what we call biological species are the haphazard productions of chance—a claim that erases the Greek distinction between natural and artificial kinds. For if the paradigm cases of natural kinds—biological species—are accidental results of accidental encounters between mutated genes and environmental niches, then the very idea of naturalness begins to seem artificial. Darwin makes it hard to continue the practice, common to the Greeks and to the Enlightenment, of using the term "natural" as a term of praise.

When the idea of naturalness goes, so does the Greek picture of inquiry as substituting reality for appearance, the way things are in their own intrinsic nature for the various ways human beings find it useful to describe them. The beginnings of the attempt to abandon the reality-appearance distinction are found in Nietzsche's *Twilight of the Idols* and William James's *Pragmatism*. Both books argue that the idea of truth as correspondence to reality only makes sense if reality has an intrinsic nature, and that it is unclear how we could ever tell whether or not a given descriptive vocabulary "corresponds" to such a nature.

The idea that some such vocabularies are somehow closer to the intrinsic nature of reality than others makes sense to religious believers. For those who believe that a certain religion enshrines the Word, and thus the Will, of the Creator and Lord of the Universe, not only does the question "In what language does the universe demand to be described?" make sense, but the answer is already evident. For secularists, however, the only way to make sense of the idea that the universe demands description in a certain vocabulary is to turn to science. Enlightenment secularism suggested that the vocabulary of the natural sciences is nature's own—the divisions made by this vocabulary are the joints at which nature demands to be cut.

James and Nietzsche viewed this sort of scientism as an unfortunate persistence of religious ways of thinking. They urged that the vocabulary of physics is simply one useful vocabulary among others—useful for technological purposes but useless for any others. Both thought that the Enlightenment's attempt to put science in the place of theology was a mistake, as was the initial assumption that the universe somehow *demands* a certain description. Both saw the choice among descriptions as a choice among human purposes, not a choice between human purposes and those of something nonhuman. Their Darwinian view of the human situation persuaded them that descriptions were tools, not attempts to correspond to the nature of reality. Different purposes demand different tools.

Adopting this view means replacing the choice between theological, scientific, and metaphysical descriptions of the world with a choice between human purposes. But the choice of what purposes to have is almost always, in practice, a choice among groups of people rather than a choice among abstract formulae. A choice of purposes to which to devote one's life is typically a choice between actual or possible human communities: between the sort of people who have one overriding purpose and the sort of people who have another. So, on the pragmatist view common to both Nietzsche and James, metaphysical questions are concealed political questions, questions about the group or groups with which one hopes to affiliate oneself, or that one hopes to create.

For example, to adopt a physicalistic metaphysics is to opt for a human community devoted to mastering nature for the sake of what Bacon called "the improvement of man's estate." To reject that metaphysics, either in the terms in which religious fundamentalists would reject, or in those in which Gandhi or Heidegger would reject it, is to presuppose an alternative answer to the question "Who are we?" Such a rejection is part of an attempt to create a different sort of human community, organized around a different goal.

To sum up what I have been saying so far: I read Nietzsche and James as saying that the question "Who are we?" should replace "What are we?" as the primordial question of philosophy. For it is the one to which we shall always return—the one that has always already been answered when we answer other questions. Every account of what human beings are is, for pragmatists like Nietzsche and James, a disguised proposal for shaping a new human community. The question "Who are we?" replaces the Greek question "What is Being?" and also Kant's questions "What can I know?" and "What is Man?" It replaces all these with a new form of Kant's question, "What may I hope?"

In this new form Kant's question becomes "What may *we* hope?" For it is no longer, as it was for Kant, a question about the immortality of the individual soul, but about the future of the species. The question "Who are we?" is future oriented in a way in which the question "What are we?" is not. The "what?" question enshrines the pre-Darwinian notion of a human essence, which has its place in a Platonic heaven of other essences. The "who?" question sets aside the notion of essence, of intrinsic reality, and thus, as I have already said, of the distinction between reality and appearance. It thereby stops asking a timeless question, and asks a question about future time. But this question about the future is not a request for a prediction, but rather for a project. To ask who we are becomes a way of asking what future we should try, cooperatively, to build.

Nietzsche and James agree on the primordiality of this question, but disagree about the answer. The two have different projects in mind: Nietzsche's is an aristocratic project and James's democratic. Nietzsche's "we" consists of a happy few, Zarathustra's chosen companions. James's "we" are the inhabitants of a global cooperative commonwealth. James took for granted the universalistic assumption, common to Christianity and the Enlightenment, that our moral community should be identical with our biological species—defined not in any essentialistic way, but simply as consisting of any organism with which any of us can interbreed. This amounts to the project of distributing the planet's resources in such a way that no human child lacks the opportunities for individual development, the life-chances, available to any other human child.

Nietzsche, obviously, did not take this assumption, or this project, for granted. Were he to reappear among us, Nietzsche would presumably say that this project is even more absurd than it was a century before. For now, even if it were desirable, it is obviously unfeasible. In 1900, when there were only one and a half billion people in the world, and there were still forests on land and fish in the sea, such an egalitarian project might have made some sense. But in 2010 we shall have 7 billion people, almost no forest, and barely any fish. So, one can imagine Nietzsche saying, even if democratic egalitarianism had been a good idea in 1900, nobody can put it forward as a practical proposal now. Doing so is either hypocritical or self-deceptive.

Nietzsche's point can be restated and enlarged as follows: the part of the world that fostered Christianity and the Enlightenment was exceptionally lucky. The assumption that our moral community should be identical with our biological species could only have occurred to people who were lucky enough to have more material goods than they really needed. It is not an idea that could have occurred to those who had to struggle to survive. Moral universalism is an invention of the rich.

The rich parts of the world, the ones that have already realized some of the dreams of the Enlightenment, are also the places where technology took off. Technology began making Europe rich even before the Enlightenment began making it democratic. Only people who were already exceptionally rich, and therefore exceptionally secure, could have taken the idea of democracy, much less of global democracy, seriously. Moral idealism goes along with economic success. The latter is obviously not a sufficient condition for the former, but I think we should concede to Nietzsche that it is a necessary one.

I think that we also have to concede to Nietzsche that no foreseeable application of technology could make every human family rich enough to give their children anything remotely like the chances that a family in the lucky parts of the world now takes for granted for theirs. Nobody has written a scenario that ends with every child born in Peru, Angola, and Bangladesh going to school, rather than working, until the age of eighteen, and then, if talented, proceeding to a university for training that will enable it to realize its fullest potentialities. Nobody has even written a scenario showing how a family in these countries would acquire a reason to practice birth control, instead of trying to propagate as many sources of income as possible.

Furthermore, nobody has written a scenario that shows how the people in the lucky industrialized democracies might redistribute their wealth in ways that create bright prospects for the children of the undeveloped countries without destroying the prospects of their own children and of their own societies. The institutions of the rich democracies are now so intertwined with advanced methods of transportation and communication, and more generally with expensive technology, that it is hardly possible to imagine their survival if the rich countries had to reduce their share of the world's resources to a fraction of what they now consume. Democratic institutions in these countries depend on the existence of things like universal literacy, meritocratic social mobility, bureaucratic rationality, and the existence of many competing sources of information about public affairs. Free universities, a free press, incorruptible judges, and unbribable police officers do not come cheap.

To mention all these missing scenarios is to suggest that the rich parts of the world may be in the position of somebody proposing to share her one loaf of bread with a hundred starving people. Even if she does share, everybody, including herself, will starve anyway. So she may easily be guilty, as my hypothetical Nietzsche suggests, either of self-deception or hypocrisy.

I do not know—perhaps nobody knows—whether the project of constructing a global cooperative commonwealth is as hopeless as I have been suggesting it may be. Technology has surprised us before, and so has the success of moral idealists in bringing about the seemingly impossible. Both might surprise us again. Maybe somebody has written scenarios I have not read. But my present concern is not with predictions, either gloomy or optimistic, but rather with describing the present moral situation of the rich and lucky inhabitants of the world in terms of alternative answers to the question "Who are we?".

One way to get these alternatives in focus is to remark that a traditional expression of moral idealism is for a smaller group of people to identify themselves imaginatively with a larger group. Fifty-one years ago, a set of rich and lucky people imagined themselves to be "we, the people of the United Nations." One reason they chose those words was that 156 years earlier, some equally rich and lucky people had imagined themselves to be "We, the people of the United States."

It has often been suggested that the authors of the Constitution of the United States of America were not entitled to describe themselves as the people of the United States. They were, it is said, only entitled to call themselves something like "We, the representatives of the property-owning white males of the United States." Their black slaves, their white servants, and even their wives and daughters did not really come into the picture. Similarly, it has often been suggested that when the representatives of governments signed the Charter of the United Nations, the most that they were really entitled to say was something like "We, the representatives of the political classes of our respective countries."

The existence of a moral community that can plausibly and without qualification identify itself as "we, the people of the United States" is still a project rather than an actuality. In a few respects, my country is closer to accomplishing this project now than it has ever been, thanks to the Civil Rights Revolution of the 1960s and to the continuing pressure exerted by feminists. In most respects, however, it is losing ground. For the gap between rich and poor Americans is widening steadily, and the latter are increasingly bereft of hope for their children's future.

A recent article by Richard Posner, the only American jurist who is also a distinguished and widely known intellectual figure, contains a sentence that underlines this lack of hope. Judge Posner wrote that "the very high crime rate of young black [American] males is an aspect of the pathological situation of the black underclass, but there does not appear to be any remedies for this situation that are at once politically feasible and likely to work."[1] In the context in which Posner writes, "politically feasible" means "compatible with the fact that the American middle class will not let itself be taxed to save the children of the underclass." This unwillingness creates a situation in which those children cannot hope for a decent chance in life. To predict that this unwillingness will persist is to say that there will, in the future, no longer be any "we" that unites the political class of the US and those underclass children in a moral community. Those black children are no longer, if Posner's judgment of political feasibility is right, among "we, the people of the United States," any more than their slave ancestors were when the US Constitution was written.

I hope that Posner is wrong, and that the middle class of my own country will not prove to be as cruel and greedy as he predicts. But I have cited Posner on the United States only to pursue the analogy with the United Nations. I think it is important to ask whether it is any longer possible to use the phrase "We, the people of the United Nations" as the name of a moral community, a community that is identical with the human species. The crucial question here is whether it is merely the cruelty and greed of the rich nations that keeps this community from being formed, or whether the formation of such a community is simply impossible, even given all the goodwill in the world.

Suppose that it is impossible. That is, suppose that there is no imaginable way to make decent life-chances available to the poorer 5 billion citizens of the member states of the United Nations while still keeping intact the democratic sociopolitical institutions cherished by the richer 1 billion. Suppose that the hope of such availability is doomed to be either hypocritical or self-deceptive. Suppose that we have passed the point of no return in the balance between population and resources, and that it is now *sauve qui peut*. Suppose that the rich and lucky billion come to believe that this is the case—not out of selfishness and greed, but as a result of accurate economic calculation. Then they will begin to treat the poor and unlucky 5 billion as surplus to their moral requirements, unable to play a part in their moral life. The rich and unlucky people will quickly become unable to think of the poor and unlucky ones as their fellow humans, as part of the same "we."

This may seem overstated. For surely, it might be objected, one can have a sense of identification with people whose suffering one has no way of alleviating. The link between having a sense of community and being able to fulfill obligations to other members of that community—the link between ought and can, between morals and money—is not that tight.

This objection is plausible, but not, I think, convincing. Consider the analogy, suggested by Posner's phrase "pathological situation," between finding it politically unfeasible to give people hope and finding it medically unfeasible to do. When a hospital is deluged with an impossibly large flood of victims of a catastrophe, the doctors and nurses begin to perform triage: They decide which of the victims are "medically feasible"—which ones are appropriate recipients of the limited medical resources available. When the American underclass is told that it is politically unfeasible to remedy their situation, they are in the same situation as accident victims who are told that it is unfeasible to offer them medical treatment.

In both cases, those who make the decision about feasibility are answering the question "Who are we?" by excluding certain human beings from membership in "We, the ones who can hope to survive." When we realize that it is unfeasible to rescue a person or a group, it is as if they had already gone before us into death. Such people are, as we say, "dead to us." Life, we say, is for the living. For the sake of their own sanity, and for the sake of the less grievously wounded patients who *are* admitted to the hospital, the doctors and nurses must simply blank out on all those moaning victims who are left outside in the street. They must cease to think about them, pretend that they are already dead.

These doctors and nurses illustrate the point that if you cannot render assistance to people in need, your claim that they form part of your moral community is empty. This in turn is an illustration of a more general, philosophical point: that it only makes sense to attribute a belief to someone if such an attribution helps one to predict the person's future actions. Beliefs are, as Bain and Peirce said, habits of actions. If no actions can be predicted on the basis of a belief-attribution, then the purported belief turns out to be, at most, the mouthing of a formula, a meaningless incantation.

On this Peircean, pragmatic account of belief, to believe that someone is "one of us," a member of our moral community, is to exhibit readiness to come to their assistance when they are in need. To answer the question "Who are we?" in a way that is relevant to moral questions is to pick out whom one is willing to do something to help. Pressing Peirce's point, I would argue that one is answering the question "Who are we?" in a useful and informative way only if one thereby generates reliable predictions about what measures the group identified as "we" will take in specified circumstances.

It follows that it is neither useful nor informative to answer this question by reference to a class of people whom one has no idea how to help. Moral identification is empty when it is no longer tied to habits of action. That is why it is either hypocritical or self-deceptive for the doctors to think of those who are left outside the hospital as "us." It is why it is either hypocritical or self-deceptive for those who agree with Posner about the hopelessness of attempting to rescue the black American underclass from its pathological situation to continue to use a phrase like "We, the people of the United States." It would be equally self-deceptive or hypocritical for those who do not believe that the industrialized democracies can bring either hope or human rights to the billions who lack both to use the term "We, the people of the United Nations."

When the founders of the United States and of the United Nations originally used these terms, however, it was neither self-deceptive nor hypocritical. For the foundation of each of these institutions was part of a project—a project of forming a moral community out of a mass of people that was not yet such a community. Both were founded not only in a spirit of hope, but in the midst of a plethora of practical proposals—proposals that looked, at the time, as if they might be politically and economically feasible. At the time of the foundation of the United Nations, when the world's population was only half its present size and everybody assumed that the forests and the fish would last forever, many proposals seemed politically feasible that seem so no longer.

Perhaps there are feasible political proposals to be made, even today, that would entitle us to use the phrase "We, the people of the United Nations" in a way which is neither empty nor hypocritical. If I knew what they were, I would offer them. But I do not, and so I am making a merely philosophical point.

I can sum up this point as follows: an answer to the question "Who are we?" which is to have any moral significance has to be one that takes money into account. Marx may have overstated when he identified morality with the interests of an economic class, but he had a point. That point is that a politically feasible project of egalitarian redistribution of wealth requires there to be enough money around to insure that, after the redistribution, the rich will still be able to recognize themselves—will still think their lives worth living. The only way in which the rich can think of themselves as part of the same moral community with the poor is by reference to some scenario that gives hope to the children of the poor without depriving their own children of hope.

As I said earlier, I am not trying to make predictions. Nor am I offering recommendations for action. Rather, I have been putting forward a philosophical argument that depends upon three premises. The first is that the primordial philosophical question is not "What are we?" but "Who are we?" The second is that "Who are we?" means "What community of reciprocal trust do we belong to?" The third is that reciprocal trust depends on feasibility as well as on goodwill. The conclusion I draw from these premises is that thinking of other people as part of the same "we" depends not only on willingness to help those people but on belief that one is *able* to help them. In particular, answering the question "Who are we?" with "We are members of a moral community that encompasses the human species" depends on an ability to believe that we can avoid economic triage.

NOTES

1. Richard Posner, "The Most Punitive Nation," *Times Literary Supplement* (September 1, 1995), p. 3.

16. PETER UNGER

In these two excerpts from *Living High and Letting Die*, Unger aims to support Singer's claim that those of us who live in rich countries are morally obligated to give substantial sums of money to aid agencies (see chapter 1 of this volume). In certain cases, Unger points out, we tend to think that individuals in a position to help others in grave need are morally required to do so, while in other cases—including appeals for funds from aid agencies—we tend to think that they are not. According to some, such different reactions reflect important moral differences between the cases in question. Unger argues, however, that such reactions often reflect morally irrelevant factors that cloud our judgment, and lead us to underestimate the moral importance of the needs of those who are far away from us. He illustrates this claim by looking in some detail at two such cases.

Sections 1-3 of Chapter 1 and Chapter 2 of *Living High and Letting Die*

First published in his Living High and Letting Die: Our Illusion of Innocence *(New York: Oxford University Press, 1996), 3–13, 24–61*

CHAPTER 1: ILLUSIONS OF INNOCENCE: AN INTRODUCTION

Each year millions of children die from easy-to-beat diseases, from malnutrition, and from bad drinking water. Among these children, about 3 million die from dehydrating diarrhea. As UNICEF has made clear to millions of us well-off American adults at one time or another, with a packet of oral rehydration salts that costs about 15 cents, a child can be saved from dying soon.

By sending checks earmarked for Oral Rehydration Therapy, or ORT, to the US Committee for UNICEF, we Americans can help save many of these children. Here's the full mailing address:

United States Committee for UNICEF
United Nations Children's Fund
333 East 38th Street, New York, NY 10016

Now, you can write that address on an envelope well prepared for mailing. And, in it, you can place a $100 check made out to the *US Committee for UNICEF* along with a note that's easy to write:

WHERE IT WILL HELP THE MOST, USE THE ENCLOSED FUNDS FOR ORT.

So, as is reasonable to believe, you can easily mean a big difference for vulnerable children.

Toward realistically thinking about the matter, I'll use a figure far greater than just 15 cents per child saved: Not only does the US Committee have overhead costs, but so does UNICEF itself; and, there's the cost of transporting the packets, and so on. Further, to live even just one more year, many children may need several saving interventions and, so, several packets. And, quite a few of those saved will die shortly thereafter, anyway, from some sadly common Third World cause. So, to be more realistic about what counts most, let's multiply the cost of the packet by 10, or, better, by *20!*

For getting one more Third World youngster to escape death and live a reasonably long life, $3 is a more realistic figure than 15 cents and, for present purposes, it will serve as well as any. Truth to tell, in the light of searching empirical investigation, even this higher figure might prove too low. But, as nothing of moral import will turn on the matter, I'll postpone a hard look at the actual cost till quite late in the book.[1] As will become evident, for a study that's most revealing that's the best course to take.

With our $3 figure in mind, we do well to entertain this proposition: If you'd contributed $100 to one of UNICEF's most efficient lifesaving programs a couple of months ago, this month there'd be over thirty fewer children who, instead of painfully dying soon, would live reasonably long lives. Nothing here's special to the months just mentioned;

similar thoughts hold for most of what's been your adult life, and most of mine, too. And, more important, unless we change our behavior, similar thoughts will hold for our future. That nonmoral fact moved me to do the work in moral philosophy filling this volume [*Living High and Letting Die*]. Before presenting it, a few more thoughts about the current global life-and-death situation.

1.1 Some Widely Available Thoughts about Many Easily Preventable Childhood Deaths

As I write these words in 1995, it's true that, in each of the past thirty years, well over 10 million children died from readily preventable causes. And, except for a lack of money aimed at doing the job, most of the deaths could have been prevented by using any one of many means.

Before discussing a few main means, it's useful to say something about the regions where the easily preventable childhood deaths have been occurring. First, there's this well-known fact: Over 90 percent of these deaths occur in the countries of the so-called Third World. By contrast, here's something much less widely known: Though almost all these needless deaths occur in the materially poorest parts of the world, poverty itself is hardly the whole story. For a good case in point, take the poverty-ridden Indian state of Kerala. While per capita income in this state of about 30 million is notably lower than in India as a whole, life expectancy in Kerala is higher than in *any other* Indian state. And, the childhood mortality rate is *much* lower than in India as a whole.[2] Why? Without telling a long historical story, most of the answer may be put like this: In this vibrantly democratic and responsive state, Kerala's millions have food security, safe drinking water, and very basic health care. By contrast, many of the richer Indians *don't* have their basic needs met, and don't have their *children's* needs met. So, while often a factor, poverty itself hardly explains why millions of kids needlessly die each year.

In one direction, I'll amplify that remark.[3] As is well known, many millions of children don't get enough to eat. These related truths are less well known: First, for each child that dies in a famine, several die from *chronic malnutrition*. Second, even if she gets over 80 percent of the calories needed by a youngster of her age for excellent health, a child who regularly gets less than 90 percent is so malnourished that she'll have a dangerously inadequate immune system. Third, what happens to many such vulnerable children is that, because she's among the many millions who haven't been vaccinated against measles, when she gets measles she dies from it. So, fourth, each year mere measles still kills about a million Third World kids.[4]

Several means of reducing measles deaths are worth mentioning, including these: Semiannually, an underfed child can be given a powerful dose of vitamin A, with capsules costing less than 10 cents. For that year, this will improve the child's immune system. So, if she hasn't been vaccinated, during this year she'll be better able to survive measles. What's more, from her two capsules, she'll get a big bonus: With her immune system improved, this year she'll have a better chance of beating the two diseases that take far more young lives than measles claims, pneumonia and diarrhea.

Though usually all that's needed to save a child from it is the administration of antibiotics that cost about 25 cents, pneumonia now claims about 3.5 million young lives a year, making it the leading child-killing disease. And, in the text's first paragraph, I've related the score for diarrhea. But, let's again focus on measles.

Having already said plenty about vitamin A, I'll note that, for about $17 a head, UNICEF can vaccinate children against measles. On the positive side, the protection secured lasts a lifetime; with no need for semiannual renewal, there's no danger of failing to renew protection! What's more, at the same time each child can be vaccinated for lifetime protection against five other diseases that, taken together, each year kill about another million Third World kids: tuberculosis, whooping cough, diphtheria, tetanus, and polio. Perhaps best of all, these vaccinations will be part of a worldwide immunization campaign that, over the years, is making progress toward *eliminating* these vaccine-preventable diseases, much as smallpox was eliminated only a decade or two ago. Indeed, with no incidence in the whole Western Hemisphere since 1991, polio is quite close to being eliminated; with good logistical systems in place almost everywhere, the campaign's success depends mainly on funding.[5]

Finally, the vast majority of the world's very vulnerable children live in lands with UNICEF programs operating productively, including all 13 developing countries lately (1992) ranked among the world's 20 most populous nations: China, India, Indonesia, Brazil, Pakistan,

Bangladesh, Nigeria, Mexico, Vietnam, Philippines, Iran, Turkey and Thailand.[6] By now, we've seen the main point: Through the likes of UNICEF, it's well within your power, in the coming months and years, to lessen serious suffering.

For even modestly well-informed readers, what I've just related doesn't come as a big surprise. All they'll have learned are some particulars pertaining to what they've learned long ago: By directing donations toward the worthy end, well-off folks can be very effective in lessening serious suffering and loss. Indeed, so well accustomed are they to this thought that, when reading the presented particulars, the worldly individuals won't make any notable response. For far fewer readers, what I've related will be something completely new. From many of them, my remarks will evoke a very notable response, even if a fairly fleeting one, about how we ought to behave: The thought occurs that each of us ought to contribute (what's for her) quite a lot to lessen early deaths; indeed, it's *seriously* wrong not to do that.

But, soon after making such a strict response, the newly aware also become well accustomed to the thought about our power. And, then, they also make the much more lenient response that almost everyone almost always makes: While it's good for us to provide vital aid, it's *not even the least bit wrong* to do *nothing* to help save distant people from painfully dying soon. (The prevalence of the lenient response is apparent from so much passive behavior: Even when unusually good folks are vividly approached to help save distant young lives, it's very few who contribute anything.)[7]

Which of these two opposite responses gives the more accurate indication of what morality requires? Is it really seriously wrong not to do anything to lessen distant suffering; or, is it quite all right to do nothing? In this book [*Living High and Letting Die*], I'll argue that the first of these thoughts is correct and that, far from being just barely false, the second conflicts strongly with the truth about morality.

1.2 SINGER'S LEGACY: AN INCONCLUSIVE ARGUMENT FOR AN IMPORTANTLY CORRECT CONCLUSION

While directly concerned more with famine relief than with the children's health issues just highlighted, it was Peter Singer who first thought to argue, seriously and systematically, that it's the first response that's on target.[8] Both early on and recently, he offers an argument for the proposition that it's wrong for us not to lessen distant serious suffering. The argument's first premise is this general proposition:

> If we can prevent something bad without sacrificing anything of comparable significance, we ought to do it.[9]

So that it may help yield his wanted conclusion, Singer rightly has us understand this premise in a suitably strong sense, with its consequent, "we ought to do it," entailing "it's *wrong* for us *not* to do it," not just the likes of "it's better for us to do it than not." But, in such a strong sense, many think the premise to be unacceptable. Briefly, I'll explain why that's so.[10]

Wanting his first premise to find favor, Singer offers a compelling example that's an instance of the general proposition. Using his words, and some of my own, here's that justly famous case:[11]

> *The Shallow Pond.* The path from the library at your university to the humanities lecture hall passes a shallow ornamental pond. On your way to give a lecture, you notice that a small child has fallen in and is in danger of drowning. If you wade in and pull the child out, it will mean getting your clothes muddy and either cancelling your lecture or delaying it until you can find something clean and dry to wear. If you pass by the child, then, while you'll give your lecture on time, the child will die straightaway. You pass by and, as expected, the child dies.

Now, when responding to this example, almost everyone's intuitive moral judgment is that your conduct's abominable. Does this reflect a strong obligation to aid that's quite general? Needed for Singer's first premise, the thought that it does is a pretty plausible proposition. But, also pretty plausibly, many think our response to the Shallow Pond doesn't reflect anything very general at all.

What moves them most here is the fact that, to other cases with people in great need, our intuitive responses are markedly different. Indeed, from typical thoughts about UNICEF, there's suggested:

The Envelope. In your mailbox, there's something from (the US Committee for) UNICEF. After reading it through, you correctly believe that, unless you soon send in a check for $100, then, instead of each living many more years, over thirty more children will die soon. But, you throw the material in your trash basket, including the convenient return envelope provided, you send nothing, and, instead of living many years, over thirty more children soon die than would have had you sent in the requested $100.

To this example, almost everyone reacts that your conduct isn't even wrong at all. Just so, many hold that, well indicated by our disparate responses to the Shallow Pond and the Envelope, there's a big moral difference between the cases. As they pretty plausibly contend, rather than any general duty to aid folks in vital need, there are only more limited obligations, like, say, a duty to *rescue* certain people.

Since what I've just related has considerable appeal, there's no way that, by itself, any such general argument for Singer's importantly correct conclusion will convince those who'd give more weight to the response the Envelope elicits than they'd give his general reasoning's first premise, or any relevantly similar statement. So, for many years, there's been a stand-off here, with little progress on the issue.[12]

Deciding this philosophical issue amounts to the same thing as deciding between our two quite opposite responses to the thought that it's within a well-off person's power to lessen serious suffering significantly, the strict response made when first aware of that thought and the lenient response regularly made later. This disagreement between philosophers mirrors a difference, then, that many experience without the benefit of philosophy. It's important to provide the discrepancy with a rational resolution.

1.3 TWO APPROACHES TO OUR INTUITIONS ON PARTICULAR CASES: PRESERVATIONISM AND LIBERATIONISM

Toward that important end, we'll examine vigorously our moral reactions to many *particular cases*. And, we'll explore not only many cases where aiding's the salient issue, but also many other ethically interesting examples. Briefly, I'll explain why: As we've observed, a few philosophers think that, while some of our responses to aiding examples are good indications of morality's true nature, like our strict reaction to the Shallow Pond, others are nothing of the kind, like our lenient reaction to the Envelope. And, as we've also observed, many other philosophers think that (almost) all our responses to aiding examples are good indications of morality's true nature, including our response to the Envelope. Rather than being narrow or isolated positions, when intelligently maintained each flows from a broad view of the proper philosophical treatment for (almost) all of morality. Thus, the majority thinks that, or has their morally substantive writing actually guided by the proposition that, not just for aiding, but right across the board, our untutored intuitions on cases (almost) always are good indications of conduct's true moral status; by contrast, we in the minority think that, and have our morally substantive writing guided by the proposition that, right across the board, even as our responses to particular cases *often are* good indications of behavior's moral status, so, also, they *often aren't* any such thing at all.

Though few of them may hold a view that's so very pure, those in the majority hold a position that's a good deal like what's well called *Preservationism*: At least at first glance, our moral responses to particular cases appear to reflect accurately our deepest moral commitments, or our *Basic Moral Values*, from which the intuitive reactions primarily derive; with all these case-specific responses, or almost all, the Preservationist seeks to *preserve* these appearances. So, on this view, it's only by treating all these various responses as valuable data that we'll learn much of the true nature of these Values and, a bit less directly, the nature of morality itself. And, so, in our moral reasoning, any more general thoughts must (almost) always accommodate these reactions.

To be sure, our intuitive responses to particular cases are a very complicated motley. So, for Preservationism, any interesting principle that actually embodies our Values, and that may serve to reveal these Values, will be extremely complex. But, at the same time, the view has the psychology of moral response be about as simple as possible. For now, so much for Preservationism's methodological aspect.

Just as the view itself has it, the morally substantive aspect of Preservationism is whatever's found by employing the method at the heart of the position. So, unlike the minority view we're about to encounter, it hasn't any antecedent morally substantive aspect. For now, so much for Preservationism.[13]

By contrast with Preservationists, we in the minority hold that insight into our Values, and into morality itself, won't be achieved on an approach to cases that's anywhere near as direct, or as accommodating, as what's just been described. On our contrasting *Liberationist* view, folks' intuitive moral responses to many specific cases derive from sources far removed from our Values and, so, they fail to reflect the Values, often even pointing in the opposite direction. So, even as the Preservationist seeks (almost) always to *preserve* the appearances promoted by these responses, the Liberationist seeks often to *liberate* us from such appearances.

Not by itself, nor even when combined with our intuitive judgments for the Envelope and for the Shallow Pond, will much of moral substance follow from the methodological aspect of Liberationism, barely sketched just above. But, that's certainly no problem with the view. To the contrary, it's the position's substantive side that, in the first place, moves Liberationists to be so skeptical of many of our case-specific responses. Just so, on the Liberationist view, a sensible methodology for treating our responses to examples will be guided by some morally substantive propositions, even as it will guide us toward further statements with moral substance. While our formulations of it are all fair game for much revision, most of the substantial moral core will be taken correctly to defeat any opposing propositions.[14]

Very briefly, here's a fallible formulation of a fair bit of Liberationism's substantive side:[15] Insofar as they need her help to have a decent chance for decent lives, a person must do a great deal for those few people, like her highly dependent children, to whom she has the most serious sort of special moral obligation. Insofar as it's compatible with that, which is often very considerably indeed, and sometimes even when it's not so compatible, she must do a lot for other innocent folks in need, so that they may have a decent chance for decent lives. For now, so much for Liberationism's morally substantive side.

Just that much substance suffices to move the Liberationist to hold that, even as (in the morally most important respects) the Envelope's conduct is *at least as bad* as the Shallow Pond's behavior, so (in those most important respects) that conduct is seriously wrong.[16] Now, even if he merely judged the Envelope's conduct to be somewhat wrong, the Liberationist would want to provide a pretty ambitious account of why our response to the case is lenient. And, since he goes much further, the account he'll offer is so very ambitious as to run along these general lines: Not stemming from our Values, the Envelope's lenient response is generated by the work of *distortional* dispositions. But, concerning the very same moral matter, there are other cases, like the Shallow Pond, that don't encourage the working of those dispositions. Accurately reflecting our Values, and the true nature of morality, our responses to these other cases *liberate* us from the misleading appearances flowing from that distortional work.[17]

CHAPTER 2: LIVING HIGH AND LETTING DIE: A PUZZLE ABOUT BEHAVIOR TOWARD PEOPLE IN GREAT NEED

Let's explore a puzzle about our behavior toward people in great need. Centrally, it concerns our untutored reactions to two cases, the two *puzzle cases*. For the cases to pose a puzzle, they must be similar in many ways even while they differ in many others. For the puzzle to pack a punch, the cases should be pretty simple and realistic. And, there should be a strong contrast between our intuitive responses to the cases. Now, one of our two puzzle cases will be the Envelope. For a case to pair with it, there should be an example that, though similar to the Shallow Pond in many respects, goes well beyond it in a few. For instance, in the Shallow Pond there's *very little cost* to you, the case's agent; so, in a newly instructive contrast case, there'll be very *considerable* cost to you.

2.1 A PUZZLE ABOUT BEHAVIOR TOWARD PEOPLE IN GREAT NEED

With those thoughts in mind, this is the first of our cases:

> *The Vintage Sedan.* Not truly rich, your one luxury in life is a vintage Mercedes sedan that, with much time, attention and money, you've restored to mint condition. In particular, you're pleased by the auto's fine leather seating. One day, you stop at the intersection of two small country roads, both lightly travelled. Hearing a voice screaming for help, you get out and see a man who's wounded and covered with a lot of his blood. Assuring you that his wound's

confined to one of his legs, the man also informs you that he was a medical student for two full years. And, despite his expulsion for cheating on his second year final exams, which explains his indigent status since, he's knowledgeably tied his shirt near the wound so as to stop the flow. So, there's no urgent danger of losing his life, you're informed, but there's great danger of losing his limb. This can be prevented, however, if you drive him to a rural hospital fifty miles away. "How did the wound occur?" you ask. An avid bird-watcher, he admits that he trespassed on a nearby field and, in carelessly leaving, cut himself on rusty barbed wire. Now, if you'd aid this trespasser, you must lay him across your fine back seat. But, then, your fine upholstery will be soaked through with blood, and restoring the car will cost over five thousand dollars. So, you drive away. Picked up the next day by another driver, he survives but loses the wounded leg.

Except for your behavior, the example's as realistic as it's simple.

Even including the specification of your behavior, our other case is pretty realistic and extremely simple; for convenience, I'll again display it:

> *The Envelope.* In your mailbox, there's something from (the US Committee for) UNICEF. After reading it through, you correctly believe that, unless you soon send in a check for $100, then, instead of each living many more years, over thirty more children will die soon. But, you throw the material in your trash basket, including the convenient return envelope provided, you send nothing, and, instead of living many years, over thirty more children soon die than would have had you sent in the requested $100.

Taken together, these contrast cases will promote the chapter's primary puzzle.

Toward having the puzzle be instructive, I'll make two stipulations for understanding the examples. The first is this: Beyond what's explicitly stated in each case's presentation, or what's clearly implied by it, there aren't ever any bad consequences of your conduct for anyone and, what's more, there's nothing else that's morally objectionable about it.[1] In effect, this means we're to understand a proposed scenario so that it is as boring as possible. Easily applied by all, in short the stipulation is: *Be boring!*

Also easily effected, the other stipulation concerns an agent's motivation, and its relation to her behavior: As much as can make sense, the agent's motivation in one contrast case, and its relation to her conduct there, is like that in the other. Not chasing perfection, here it's easy to assume a motivational parallel that's strong enough to prove instructive: Far from being moved by any malice toward the needy, in both our puzzle cases, your main motivation is simply your concern to maintain your nice asset position. So, even as it's just this that, in the Envelope, mainly moves you to donate nothing, it's also just this that, in the Sedan, similarly moves you to offer no aid.

Better than ever, we can ask these two key questions: What's our intuitive moral assessment of your conduct in the Vintage Sedan? And, what's our untutored moral judgment of your behavior in the Envelope? As we react, in the Sedan your behavior was very seriously wrong. And, we respond, in the Envelope your conduct wasn't even mildly wrong. This wide divergence presents a puzzle: Between the cases, is there a difference that adequately grounds these divergent intuitive assessments?

Since at least five obvious factors favor the proposition that the Envelope's conduct was *worse* than the Sedan's, at the outset the prospects look bleak: First, even just financially, in the Vintage Sedan the cost to the agent is *over fifty times* that in the Envelope; and, with *non*financial cost also considered, the difference is greater still. Second, in the Sedan, the reasonably expected consequences of your conduct, and also the actual consequences, were that *only one* person suffered a serious loss; but, in the Envelope, they were that *over thirty* people suffered seriously. Third, in the Sedan the *greatest loss suffered* by anybody was the loss of a *leg*; but, in the Envelope the *least loss* suffered was *far greater* than that.[2] Fourth, because he was a mature and well-educated individual, the Sedan's serious loser was *largely responsible* for his own serious situation; but, being just little children, none of the Envelope's serious losers was *at all responsible* for her bad situation. And, fifth, the Sedan's man suffered his loss owing to his objectionable trespassing behavior; but, nothing like that's in the Envelope.

Now, I don't say these five are the only factors bearing on the morality of your conduct in the two cases. Still, with the differential flowing from them as tremendous as what we've just seen, it seems they're almost bound to prevail. So, for Preservationists seeking sense for both a lenient judgment of the Envelope's conduct and a harsh one of the Sedan's, there's a mighty long row to hoe.[3]

2.2 AN OVERVIEW OF THE CHAPTER: DISTINGUISHING THE PRIMARY FROM THE SECONDARY BASIC MORAL VALUES

In the next section, we'll start the hard work of investigating the "apparently promising" differences between the puzzle cases. Here, I'll provide an overview of how it will proceed and where it may lead.

There are enormously many differences, of course, between the two examples: Only one of them involves a Mercedes automobile. On the other side, only the Envelope involves the postal system. But, as is evident, very nearly all of these enormously many differences haven't any chance of helping to ground a stricter judgment for the Sedan's behavior than the Envelope's. So, the job at hand may well be manageable. First, we'll try to look at genuine differences one by one. But, sometimes we'll confront thoughts that, though they might first appear to locate differential factors, really don't find any. With some of these thoughts, the fault's that the idea doesn't really fasten on any factor at all. With others, the fault's that the factor's really present in both puzzle cases, not just the one where it's obvious.

Going beyond all such confusions, we'll note some factors that do differentiate between our puzzle cases. Each time that happens, we'll ask: Does *this* difference do much to favor a harsh judgment only for the Sedan's conduct, and not for the Envelope's? In trying to answer, each time we'll consult our two main guides. On the one hand, we'll note our *moral intuitions on particular cases.* On the other, we'll note the deliverance of what I'll call our *general moral common sense,* since this second sensibility is directed at matters at least somewhat more general than the first's proper objects. Pitched at a level somewhere between the extremely general considerations dominating the tenets of traditional moral theories, on one hand, and the quite fine-grained ones often dominating the particular cases philosophers present, on the other, it's at this moderately general level of discursive thought, I commonsensibly surmise, that we'll most often respond in ways reflecting our Values and, less directly, morality itself. Not yet having much confirmation, that's now just a sensible working hypothesis. At all events, after seeing what both these guides say about each of nine notable differences, we'll ask: Does any combination of the differences ground a harsh judgment just for the Sedan?

Increasingly, we'll see that, for the most part, the deliverance from our two guides will agree. Occasionally, however, we'll see disagreement. What will explain that discrepancy? Though we won't arrive at a fully complete answer, we'll see a partial explanation full enough to be instructive: Even while the imperiled folks peopling certain cases have absolutely vital needs to be met, since their dire needs *aren't conspicuous* to you, the examples' agent, our intuitive response has your conduct as quite all right. Rather than anything with much moral weight, it's this that largely promotes the lenient response to the Envelope's behavior. Correspondingly, our harsh response to the Sedan's conduct is largely promoted by a serious need that's so salient.[4]

To avoid many confusions, a few remarks should suffice: Generally, what's most conspicuous to you is what most fully attracts, and what most fully holds, your attention. Often, what's very conspicuous to you is distinct from what you perceive clearly and fully. Thus, while we may clearly and fully perceive them, the needs of a shabby person lying in one of New York City's gloomiest streets *aren't* very conspicuous to us. But, when someone's nicely groomed and dressed, and he's in a setting where no such troubles are expected, then, generally, his serious need is conspicuous.

As matters progress, these points about salience will become increasingly clear: When it's present in spades, as with the Vintage Sedan, then, generally, we'll judge harshly our agent's unhelpful behavior; when it's wholly absent, as with the Envelope, then, generally, we'll judge the agent's conduct leniently.

When the intuitive moral responses to cases are so largely determined by such sheer salience to the examples' agent(s), do they accurately reflect our Values? Straightforwardly, Preservationism's answer is that they do. By contrast, the best Liberationist answer isn't straightforward. Briefly, I'll explain.

At times, some people's great needs may be highly salient to you and, partly for that reason, it's then *obvious* to you that (without doing anything the least bit morally suspect) you can save the folks from suffering serious loss. Then, to you, it may be *obvious* that your letting them suffer *conflicts very sharply* with your Basic Moral Values (and, so, with the very heart of morality). To highlight this, let's say that, for you then, there's an Obvious Sharp Conflict. Now, since you're actually a quite decent person, when there's such an Obvious Sharp Conflict, generally it will be *hard* for you, psychologically, *not* to help meet people's great needs, even if you must incur a cost that's quite considerable. So, then, usually you won't behave in the way stipulated in the Vintage Sedan; rather, you'll behave helpfully.

In sharp contrast with that, there's this: When you let there be more folks who suffer serious loss by failing to contribute to the likes of UNICEF, then, even to you yourself, it's *far* from obvious that your conduct conflicts sharply with your Values, and with much of morality; indeed, as it usually appears, there *isn't* any such conflict. To highlight this contrasting situation, let's say that, for you *then*, there's No Apparent Conflict. Now, even though you're a decent person, when there's No Apparent Conflict, generally it will be *all too easy* for you, psychologically, not to help meet people's great needs. So, then, as with most decent folks, you'll behave in the unhelpful way stipulated for the Envelope.

With the difference between there being an Obvious Sharp Conflict and there being No Apparent Conflict, we've noted a contrast between the Envelope and the Sedan that *isn't* always morally irrelevant. Indeed, perhaps particularly when thinking whether to praise or to damn some conduct, *sometimes* it's appropriate to give this difference *great* weight. But, until the last chapter, in most of this book's [*Living High and Letting Die*] pages, even the mere mention of the difference would be misplaced. For, here the aim is to become clearer about what really are the Basic Moral Values and, perhaps less directly, what's really morally most significant. And, since that's our aim, it's useful to *abstract away from* questions of what psychological difficulty there may be for us, in one case or another, to behave in a morally acceptable manner. Thus, until the book's last chapter, I'll set contexts where, as is there perfectly proper, no weight at all will be given to such considerations.

For a good perspective on this methodological proposal, it's useful to compare the Liberationist's thoughts about the Envelope's behavior to a reasonably probing abolitionist's thoughts, addressed to an ordinary "good Southerner" some years before the Civil War. No Jefferson he, our Southerner thinks that, especially as it's practiced by so many nice enough folks all around him, slaveholding isn't so much as wrong. Now, without seeking to dole out blame, our abolitionist may compare a typical white slaveholder's conduct with respect to his black slaves and, say, the conduct of a white person who, without any good reason for assaulting anyone, punches another white hard on the jaw, rendering his hapless victim unconscious for a few minutes. (Perhaps, because he abstained from alcoholic beverages, and said as much, the victim refused to drink, say, to the puncher's favorite Virginian county.) As the abolitionist might painstakingly point out, first focusing on one contrast between the two behaviors, then another, and another, and another, in the morally most important respects, that bad assaulting behavior *wasn't as bad* as the much more common slaveholding behavior.

Paralleling the difference in psychological difficulty noted for the Envelope and the Sedan, there's a difference in the slaveholding conduct and the assaulting behavior. For the ordinary Old Southerners, there's No Apparent Conflict between common slaveholding conduct and the Basic Moral Values, whereas, even for them, there's an Obvious Sharp Conflict between the gratuitous punching conduct and the Values; and so on, and so forth. For both parties to the discussion, *that's* common knowledge right from the outset. Indeed, attempting to focus the discussion on any *such* difference is, really, just a move to opt out of any serious discussion of the moral status of the slaveholding. Now, what that abolitionist was doing with such controlling conduct as was then widespread, this Liberationist author is doing, or is going to try to do, with such unhelpful conduct as the Envelope's currently common behavior. So, as decently sensible readers will see, it's inappropriate to focus on the thought that there's an Obvious Sharp Conflict only with the Sedan, and not with the Envelope; for, that will be just a move to opt out of seriously discussing the moral status of such vitally unhelpful conduct that, with No Apparent Conflict, is now so commonly exemplified. Not perfect, the parallel between the abolitionist and the Liberationist is plenty strong enough for seeing the sense in my modest proposal.

By now, I've made all the section's main points. So, it's with hesitation that, in what remains, I try to say something of interest to readers who enjoy, as I do, making philosophical distinctions, and enjoy exploring what utility may derive therefrom. Hesitantly, I'll offer a distinction between our *Primary* and our *Secondary* Basic Moral Values, a contrast that may have only heuristic value.

I'll begin with some remarks about the Primary Values: Among them is, plainly, a value to the effect that (like any well-behaved person) you not contribute to the serious suffering of an innocent other, neither its initiation nor its continuation. In the Envelope, your conduct *didn't* conflict, apparently, with this obviously important Value; so vast is the sea of suffering in the world and so resolutely efficient are UNICEF's health-promoting programs that, even if you'd made as large a donation as you could possibly afford, there *still wouldn't* have been *anyone*, apparently, whose serious suffering *you'd* have averted, or even lessened much. Concerning an equally "ground level" moral matter, is there some *other* Primary Value the Envelope's conduct *did* contravene? Well, there's none that's obvious.

But, as Liberationists may suggest, perhaps the Envelope's conduct conflicts with an *unobvious* Value, near enough, a Primary Value to the effect that, about as much as you possibly can manage, you *lessen the number of (the world's) innocent others who suffer seriously.* Though it encompasses, apparently, your relations with many millions of needy people, this unobvious Value might be *just as central* to your Values as the obvious one so prominent in the previous paragraph.

As I'll trust, that's a useful start toward indicating the domain of the Primary Values. Perhaps a helpful indication of this domain can be given, briefly and roughly, along these more general lines: Knowing everything you ought about what's really the case morally, and knowing all that's relevant to your situation, it's in the domain of the Primary Values that you look when, being as morally well motivated as anyone could wish, you deliberate about what you morally ought to do. So, motivation needn't be a stranger to the Primary Values' domain: When someone has his conduct conflict with what morality *obviously* requires and, so, with what even a *modestly* cognizant moral agent *knows* it requires, then, (at least) for being motivated so poorly, the person's behavior does badly by his good Primary Values.

Well, then, what's in the domain of the Secondary Values? Here's a step toward an answer: As has long been recognized, part of morality concerns our *epistemic* responsibilities. Here, morality concerns what we *ought* to know about the *nonmoral facts* of our situation. A simple example: In an area frequented by little kids, when you park your car quickly, without taking care to know the space is free of kids, then, even if you cause no harm, there's *something morally wrong* with your behavior. Now, another step: Far less well recognized, another part of morality concerns what we ought to know about our *Values* and, perhaps less directly, about what's really *morally* the case. Again, suppose it's true that central to the Primary Values is a Value to the effect that, roughly, you have the number of innocents seriously suffering be as small as you can manage. Then, even though it may be hard to do, it may be that you ought to know that. And, should you fail to know it, you've failed your Secondary Values.

Further, our Secondary Values concern how our conduct *ought to be moved by* our knowing what's really the case morally. Generally, in an area of conduct, one must first do well by the epistemic aspect of these Values, just introduced, before one's in a position to do well by their motivational aspect, now introduced: In the area of slaveholding conduct, during their mature years Washington and Jefferson did well, apparently, by the epistemic aspect of the Secondary Values. This put them in at least some sort of position to do well, in this area, by the motivational aspect of these Values (and, so, to do well by the Primary Values). But, they did badly by this other aspect; and, so, they contravened the Primary Values.

In the area of the Envelope's conduct, the Liberationist suggests, we do badly even by the epistemic aspect of the Secondary Values. So, we're far from doing even modestly well by their motivational aspect (and, so, by the Primary Values). By abstracting away from questions of how well we may do by our Secondary Values, we can learn about our Primary Values. So, until the last chapter, I'll set contexts where weight's rightly given only to how well an agent does by the Primary Values. At that late stage, it will turn out, I'll do well to give the Secondary Values pride of place.

Both the Primary and the Secondary Values are concerned with motivational matters. What the Secondary Values alone concern is, I'll say, the *unobvious* things someone ought to know about her Values and *those* motivational matters most closely connected with *those* things. Now, this notion of the Secondary Values may harbor, irremediably, much arbitrariness: (1) Through causing doubts as to what's really the case in certain moral matters, a person's social setting may make it hard for her to know much about the matters and, so, she may know far less than what, at bottom, she ought to know. (2) Insofar as she knows what's what morally about the matter, the setting may make it hard for her to be moved much by what she does know and, so, she may be moved far less than what, at bottom, she ought to be moved. For both reasons, (1) and (2), someone may fail to behave decently. Of a particular failure, we may ask: Did it derive (mainly) from a failure of awareness; or did it derive (mainly) from a failure of will? Often, it may be arbitrary to *favor either* factor, (1) *or* (2), and *also* arbitrary to say they're *equally* responsible. So, with the offered contrast, I don't pretend to mark a deep difference.

Recall this leading question: When they reflect little more than the sheer conspicuousness, to this or that agent, of folks' great needs, how well do our case-specific responses reflect our Basic Moral Values? In terms of my heuristic distinction, the Liberationist answers: When that's what they do, then, properly placing aside Secondary matters, our intuitions on the cases promote a badly distorted conception of our *Primary* Values. In line with that useful answer, the chapter's inquiry will lead to this Liberationist solution of its central puzzle: According to the Primary Values, the Envelope's behavior is at least as badly wrong as the Sedan's. But, first, the Preservationist gets a good run for the money.

2.3 PHYSICAL PROXIMITY, SOCIAL PROXIMITY, INFORMATIVE DIRECTNESS, AND EXPERIENTIAL IMPACT

What might ground judging negatively only the Sedan's behavior, and not the Envelope's? Four of the most easily noted differences cut no moral mustard.

Easily noted is the difference in *physical distance*. In the Vintage Sedan, the wounded student was only a few feet away; in the Envelope, even the nearest child was many miles from you. But, unlike many physical forces, the strength of a moral force doesn't diminish with distance. Surely, our moral common sense tells us that much. What do our intuitions on cases urge?

As with other differential factors, with physical distance *two* sorts of example are most relevant: Being greatly like the Envelope in many respects, in one sort there'll be a *small* distance between those in need and whoever might aid them. Being greatly like the Sedan, in the other there'll be a far greater distance. To be terribly thorough, for each factor I'd have an apt example of *both* its most relevant sorts. Mercifully, with most factors, I won't have both, but just one. But, to show what could be done with each, with physical distance I'll go both ways. First, I'll present this "Envelopey" case:

> *The Bungalow Compound.* Not being truly rich, you own only a one-twelfth share in a small bungalow that's part of a beach resort compound in an exotic but poor country, say, Haiti. Long since there's been much strife in the land, right now it's your month to enjoy the bungalow, and you're there on your annual vacation. In your mailbox, there's an envelope from UNICEF asking for money to help save children's lives in the town nearest you, whichever one that is. In your very typical case, quite a few such needy kids are all within a few blocks and, just over the compound wall, some are only a few feet away. As the appeal makes clear, your $100 will mean the difference between long life and early death for nearby children. But, of course, each month such appeals are sent to many bungalows in many Haitian resort compounds. You contribute nothing and, so, more nearby children die soon than if you'd sent $100.

As most respond to this case, your behavior isn't so much as wrong at all.[5] Next, a "Sedanish" example:

> *The CB Radios.* Instead of coming upon the erstwhile student at a crossroads, you hear from him on the CB radio that's in your fine sedan. Along with the rest of his story, the trespasser informs you, by talking into his own much cheaper CB radio, that he's stranded there with an old jalopy, which can't even be started and which, to boot, is out of gas. Citing landmarks to each other, he truthfully says you're just ten miles from where he's stranded. He asks you to pick him up and take him to a hospital, where his leg can be saved. Thinking about an upholstery bill for over $5000, you drive in another direction. As a foreseen result of that, he loses his leg, though not his life.

As most react to this other case, your behavior was seriously wrong.

In the Bungalow Compound, you were only a short distance from the needy children; in the CB Radios, you were ten miles from the needy trespasser. Thus, our responses to relevant cases jibe with the deliverance from our more general moral common sense. So much for physical proximity.

Often, physical distance correlates with what we might call *social distance*. Following the instruction to be boring, we've thus supposed that the Sedan's trespasser was your compatriot and, so, he was socially somewhat close. As we've also supposed, the Envelope's children are all foreigners, all socially more distant. Can that difference matter much? Since all those children become dead little kids, our common sense says, "Certainly not." What do we get from examples?

As usual from now on, I'll hit the issue from just one side. Here, we'll confront a Sedanish example:

> *The Long Drive*. Rather than going for a short drive, you're spending the whole summer driving from your home, in the United States, to the far tip of South America and back. So, it's somewhere in Bolivia, say, that you stop where two country roads cross. There you confront an erstwhile Bolivian medical student who tells you of his situation, in Spanish, a language you know well. As you soon learn, he wants you to drive him to a hospital, where his leg can be saved. Thinking also of your upholstery, you drive elsewhere and, as a result, he loses a leg.

To the Long Drive, almost all respond that your behavior was abominable.

Perhaps it's only within certain limits that social proximity's morally irrelevant. But, insofar as they're plausible, such limits will leave so very much leeway as to be entirely irrelevant to our puzzle: Where those in need are socially *very* close to you, like your closest family members, there may be a very strong moral reason for you to meet *their* dire needs. But, in the Sedan, it wasn't your father, or your sister, or your son whose leg was at stake. Indeed, as we've been boringly supposing, the trespasser was a complete stranger to you. So much for social proximity.

A third difference concerns how the agent learns of the great need he can help meet. In the Sedan, much is learned by your direct perception of the wounded man. In the Envelope, the information is acquired far more indirectly, by your reading something that was produced by someone who herself collated reports, and so on. In this differential factor of *informative directness*, will there be much to favor a Preservationist solution? Well, when their information is only indirectly acquired, sometimes people aren't very sure of things, or they aren't very reasonable in being sure. But, nothing remotely like that's going on in the Envelope. So, our common sense now tells us this: Since you're quite certain of what will happen if you don't contribute to UNICEF, and since you're quite reasonable in being so certain, the fact that your information's indirectly acquired is morally insignificant. What's more, our responses to relevant cases often agree, as with our severe reaction to the CB Radios.

A fourth difference, *experiential impact*, often goes along with informative directness: In the Vintage Sedan, both the needy man himself and the condition of his great need entered into your own experience. But, that's not so in the Envelope. About this difference, common sense is clear: While the need may seem more compelling in the Sedan than with folks behind a wall, there's no moral weight here. And, our reactions to cases can agree with that good common sense: In the CB Radios, the man's awful plight doesn't enter your experience. Even the sounds you hear aren't the real deal: Electronics had as much to do with your audition as he. And, suppose the trespasser had signaled you in Morse code, with nonvocal "dots" and "dashes." It would still be seriously wrong to favor your leather over his leg.

Having considered four differences, we haven't moved one inch along the row to be hoed for a comfortably Preservationist solution. Might we fare better by looking in quite another direction?

2.4 THE THOUGHT OF THE DISASTROUS FURTHER FUTURE

When thinking about cases like the Envelope, many often have this *thought of the disastrous further future*: "If I help prevent some of these young children from dying soon, then, years from now, they'll produce yet more children, worsening the population explosion that, more than anywhere else, goes on precisely where there are so many imperiled children. If I donate to UNICEF, I'll just help create a situation, in the further future, when there'll be disastrously more little kids painfully dying. So, it's actually *better* to throw away the envelope. At the very least, it's not wrong."

As we'll soon see, this thought of the disastrous further future is a fallacious rationalization, at odds with the great bulk of available evidence.[6] More to the present point, even if the thought were true, it wouldn't help with our puzzle: Just as we wisely followed the instruction to be boring, so there's no clear implication, from the statement of our puzzle cases, to any disastrously large future population. And, when responding to cases, we directly comply with that instruction.

Recall the Long Drive. Now, you're right there at the crossroads with the Bolivian and, all of a sudden, you're thinking mainly of how your conduct can bear on the further future: "If I take this guy to the hospital, then, as he'll long continue to have both his legs, he'll long be a reasonably attractive guy and, even worse, a very mobile fellow. Whether in wedlock or not, he then may well father far too many little Bolivians. But, if he'll have only one leg, he probably won't contribute nearly as much, if anything at all, to a disastrous dying of Bolivians many years hence. Playing the odds well and thinking also of the *further* future, it's *better* to let him lose a leg. At the least, if I do that, I won't behave badly." Finally, we'll suppose that, moved mainly by those thoughts, you drive away and let him suffer the loss. Now, was *that* in the example to which we recently responded? Certainly not. And, if it *were* in our original specification, our response would still be severely negative.[7]

Since it doesn't bear on our puzzle, we needn't examine the data bearing on population in the further future. But, since the matter's of broad importance, it's important to know this: The available evidence strongly supports the thought that *decreasing* childhood mortality *stabilizes* population! To be sure, the increasingly widespread availability of modern contraceptives is partly responsible for the recent big decreases in how fast the world's population is growing, as many studies show. This is one reason, even if perhaps not the most important reason, to support the International Planned Parenthood Federation, or IPPF.[8] For us, that effective group's most relevant address is:

International Planned Parenthood Federation,
Western Hemisphere Region, Inc.
902 Broadway - 10th Floor
New York, NY 10010

[Mail Donation:
www.ippfwhr.org/donate/donate_mail_e.html
IPPF/WHR
120 Wall Street, 9th Floor
New York, NY 10005-3902

Online Donation:
https://secure.ga0.org/02/IPPFWHR]

Still, for population to stabilize, much more is needed than any fine group like that will provide.

What's also needed can be seen from many perspectives. For continuity, I'll again focus on the Indian state of Kerala: Since the Total Fertility Rate's already down to 1.9, or even lower, population won't just stabilize there; it will decline! Beyond widespread availability of contraceptive means, there are other reasons that fully 80 percent of Keralan couples actually use family planning measures: Because they know the *childhood mortality rate there is very low*, Keralans can be confident that, without having many kids, they'll have some surviving children. And, since they know the community will make sure their basic needs are met, Keralans know that, even without children to rely on, their *life expectancy is high*. And, since the *female literacy rate is very high*, marking much respect for women's interests, it's no surprise that in Kerala there's a population success story.[9] Not only does the thought of the disastrous further future bypass our puzzle, but it's also undermined by the evidence. So much for that unhappy thought.

2.5 Unique Potential Saviors and Multiple Potential Saviors

To many people, the most promising difference between our contrast cases is this: In the Vintage Sedan, you're the only one who can get the trespasser's leg saved; using jargon to highlight that, you're his *unique potential savior*. But, in the Envelope, there are more than enough well-off people to get the distant children saved; in kindred jargon, they're all the children's *multiple potential saviors*: "Because you're his unique potential savior, mightn't you have a great responsibility toward the trespasser? That may be why, in the Sedan, your behavior was wrong.

Because you're only one of their multiple potential saviors, you might not have much responsibility toward the Envelope's children. This may be why, in that case, your behavior wasn't wrong."

But, to our moral common sense, that's nonsense: You knew full well that, even though they *could* do so, almost all the other well-off folks *wouldn't* aid the needy children. You knew that, for all they'd do, there'd still be kids in dire need. So, while many others behaved very badly, you did, too.

Often, that much of our moral common sense is reflected in our intuitions on particular cases. Building on the preceding section, one case in point is:

> *The Wealthy Drivers.* In addition to you, there are three other drivers in the area with CB radios, all four of you hearing the pleas from the wounded trespasser. Even this much quickly develops on the air: Each of the others is less than five miles from the erstwhile student, while you're fully ten miles from him. And, each of the others is far wealthier than you. But, as each of the three complain, she doesn't want to get involved. So, none of you help the wounded man. Since those who can aid him don't, he loses his injured leg.

With multiple potential saviors, none is unique. But, as most react, even your conduct was badly wrong.

In closing the section, I'll note this: By pretty high epistemic standards, in the Wealthy Drivers you knew your help was needed. But, by *much higher* epistemic standards, in the Envelope you knew that (since the likes of UNICEF get far less than can be put to vital use), your money was needed.

2.6 THE THOUGHT OF THE GOVERNMENTS

When thinking of the likes of the Envelope, many entertain the *thought of the governments*: "Toward aiding the distant needy children, a person like me, who's hardly a billionaire, can do hardly anything. But, through taxation of both people like me and also billionaires, our government can do a great deal. Indeed, so wealthy is our country that the government can do just about everything that's most needed. What's more, if ours joined with the governments of other wealthy nations, like France and

Germany and Japan, then, for any one of the very many well-off people in all the wealthy nations, the financial burden would be very easily affordable. And, since making one's tax payments is a routine affair, the whole business would be nearly automatic. Just so, these governments really ought to stop so many children from dying young. And, since they really ought to do the job, it's all right for me not to volunteer." What are we to make of this common line of thought?

Well, whatever it precisely means, I suppose those governments ought to contribute, annually, the tens of billions of dollars that, annually, would ensure that only a tiny fraction of the world's poorest children suffer seriously. And, whatever it means, it's even true that their conduct is seriously wrong. But, what's the relevance of that to assessing your own behavior, and mine? There isn't any. For we know full well that, for all the governments will do, each year millions of Third World kids will die from easily preventable causes. And, knowing that, we can make use of the previous section.

In the morally important respects, in the Envelope your situation is the same as in the Wealthy Drivers: Since it was harder for you to help, and since the real cost to you would have been greater, it's credible that, in the Wealthy Drivers, your conduct wasn't *as bad* as the others' behavior. Even so, your conduct also was very bad. Similarly, in the Envelope it was harder for you to do much for distant needy children than it was for the wealthy governments, and perhaps the cost to you was greater. So, it's also credible that, in the Envelope, your behavior wasn't *as bad* as the wealthy governments' conduct. Yet further, it's also credible that the behavior of these wealthy governments wasn't *as bad* as the conduct of the German government, under Hitler, in the 1940s. So much for the thought of the governments.

2.7 The Multitude and the Single Individual

When thinking of the Envelope, we may feel overwhelmed by the enormous multitude of seriously needy people: "In the face of that vast multitude, I'm almost impotent." With this feeling of futility, is there something to distinguish between the Envelope and the Sedan? At first, it may seem so: "In the Sedan, there was just a *single individual* in need; in the Envelope, there were *so many altogether in a vast multitude.*

Though I had to help the single individual, mayn't I simply leave be such a vast multitude?"

But, just as were each of the world's most badly endangered children, the trespasser was also one of the very many greatly needy people in the world. And, while there are certain perspectives from which he'll seem an especially singular figure, that's also true of every last one of the needy children. So, in point of even mathematical fact, neither thoughts of the multitude nor thoughts of particular individuals can mark any distinction at all between our puzzle cases. So much for those confused thoughts.

2.8 THE CONTINUING MESS AND THE CLEANED SCENE

Related to thoughts of the multitude, there's the *thought of the continuing mess*: "Even if I do send the $100 to UNICEF, there'll still be many children very prematurely dying. Indeed, *no matter what I do*, there'll still be, for very many years, very many children dying from easily preventable causes." In this thought, is there something to distinguish between our puzzle cases? At first, it may seem so: "Unlike the Envelope's distant children, the Sedan's trespasser presented me with a particular distinct problem. If only I got him to the hospital, the problem would have been completely resolved. Starting with just such a problem, I'd finish with nothing less than a completely *cleaned scene*. How very different that is from the *continuing mess* involving all the distant children!"

But, this appearance also is illusory: Just as much as any distant child's diarrheal dehydration, the trespasser's infected leg was part of the "continuing mess in the world." As has long been true, and as will long be remain true, the world has many people with infected legs, many of whom will lose them. If distant children were part of a "continuing mess," *so was the trespasser*. No more than the Envelope does the Sedan offer the chance to have the world be a cleaned scene. So much for this confusion.

2.9 EMERGENCIES AND CHRONIC HORRORS

Rather than any genuine differences between our puzzle cases, in the previous few sections we've seen only some confusions. It's high time to observe a real difference between the Envelope and the Vintage

Sedan: In the Vintage Sedan, there's an *emergency*, while in the Envelope there's none. But, does that mean any moral ground for favoring the Envelope's conduct?

Our moral common sense speaks negatively. First, on the Vintage Sedan: Shared with many other emergencies, what are the main points to note about the bad bird-watching incident? Well, until recently, the erstwhile student was doing reasonably all right; at least, his main needs were regularly met. And, that was also true of the other people in his area. Then, all of a sudden, things got worse for him, and, for the first time in a long time, he had a big need on the verge of not being met. Next, the Envelope: The distant little children always were in at least pretty bad straits. And, in their part of the world, for a long time many people's great needs weren't met and, consequently, those many suffered seriously. But, then, even as there's no emergency in the Envelope, that situation's *far worse* than almost any emergency; to highlight this, we may say that, in the Envelope, there's a *chronic horror*.

Of course, their living in a chronic horror is no reason to think that, by contrast with the previously fortunate trespasser, it was all right to do nothing for long-suffering children. Indeed, such a thought's so preposterous that, indirectly, it points to a *sixth* factor favoring *stricter* judgment for the Envelope: During the very few years they've had before dying, those children were among the worst off people in the world, while the trespasser had quite a few years of a reasonably good life. (And, insofar as the exam-cheater's life was less than very happy, that was due mainly to his own bad behavior.) So, it's just for the Envelope's unhelpful conduct that *justice* wants an especially strict judgment. At all events, from our moral common sense, there's no good news for Preservationism.

Before remarking on our intuitive responses to particular emergency cases, I should say something about how, during the past thirty-five years, the world's chronic horrors have become less horrible, though there's still a long way to go. For the big picture, most of what's wanted comes when seeing the worldwide progress, from 1960 onward, in four basic categories:[10]

	1960	1970	1980	1990	1990–95
Life expectancy in years	46	53	58	62	64.4
Under-five deaths per 1000 births	216	168	138	107	86
Average births per woman (TFR)	6.0	5.7	4.4	3.8	3.1
Percentage of 6–11-year-olds in school	48	58	69	77	NA

(As population's been increasing most in the Third World, the more recent the numbers, the more they're determined by events there. So, there's been *more* progress *there* than these figures indicate.)

Especially as this section features emergencies, for a more fine-grained picture I turn to the cyclone-prone country of Bangladesh, where about 15 million people, out of about 115 million, live in the vulnerable coastal region. The victim of 7 of the century's 10 worst cyclones, in the past twenty-five years 3 big ones struck Bangladesh. When 1970's big cyclone struck the unprepared country, the windstorm killed about *3 million*, about 2.5 million succumbing, in the storm's devastating aftermath, to waterborne disease. Far beyond just helping to prompt the writing of Singer's "Famine, Affluence, and Morality" [reprinted herein 1–14], this disaster "sparked the founding of Oxfam America," about twenty-five years after the original Oxfam was founded in Oxford, England.[11] With help from such foreign non-governmental organizations (NGOs), and with hard work by Bangladeshi groups and individuals, by 1991 a lot was done to make the country's people less vulnerable to killing winds; when a big cyclone hit Bangladesh that year, only(!?) about *130 thousand* folks were killed, a dramatic improvement.[12] But, come to think of it, a great many poor folks still had to bury their children, or their parents, or their spouses, or their siblings, or their best friends. So, with continued support from far and near, Bangladeshis continued to work hard. So, by 1994 those Third Worlders had built nine hundred cleverly designed cyclone shelters, each able to protect thousands of people. Expressing a misleadingly *high* estimate, I'll end the paragraph with the first sentence of the piece in *Oxfam America News* so recently cited, with only the italics being my creation: On May 2, a 180 mph cyclone pummeled southeastern coastal Bangladesh, claiming just *under 200* lives.[13] Though it looks like there's a misprint, that's as well ordered as it's well warranted.

For ever so many years, really, but, especially in more recent years, most in the world's poorest countries, including Bangladesh, have lives that are actively effective, socially committed, and part of a palpable upward trend; their lives are clearly well worth living. When thinking whether to help these materially poor folks, so that more and more of them will bury fewer and fewer of their children, it's useful to have that in mind.

Just as UNICEF works effectively both to make chronic horrors less horrible and to address emergency situations, OXFAM, as Oxfam America is popularly known, is also effective across the board. Now, the 1994 cyclone left about 500,000 Bangladeshis homeless, many of whom still need help; so, in 1995 there's still something of an emergency even there. And, as every several months the group must address a brand-new emergency, I think you should know how to help the good group aid many folks newly in great need. All you need do is make out a sizable check to *Oxfam America* and mail it to this address:

Oxfam America
26 West Street
Boston, MA 02111

[www.oxfamamerica.org/contact_us
Oxfam America
226 Causeway St., 5th Floor
Boston, MA 02114]

With this added to the US Committee's address and IPPF's, you now know more than enough, I think, about how to be an effectively helpful person.

In closing the section mercifully, I'll help you escape from the Real World by taking you back to the Philosophy Room: Regarding *emergencies*, what's to be found in our responses to the cases? For good instruction in our Happy Room, I'll contrive a case where, first, there *is* an emergency, and, second, you *can* help folks in dire need, but, third, people's dire needs are *inconspicuous* to you:

The Emergency Envelope. UNICEF informs you of the terrible effects of a recent hurricane on, say, Haiti: Now, there are many additional Haitian kids who, without outside help, will soon die. By Haitian standards, these are upper-middle-class children. While they were doing quite well before the hurricane, now, they, too, are in mortal danger. So, if you don't soon send $100 to a special fund set up by UNICEF, within the next few weeks, not only will more poor Haitian kids die, but so will more of these others. Even so, you send nothing and, in consequence, that happens.

As most respond to this case, you didn't do anything so much as wrong. So much for emergency.

2.10 URGENCY

Often, it's especially important to act when matters are *urgent*. Along with that idea, there comes this line of thought: "When someone will lose life or limb *very soon* unless you help him, it's morally *required* that you aid. But, if there's lots of time before anything much happens, aiding isn't morally required. Mightn't this be ground for judging the Envelope's conduct more leniently than the Sedan's?"

It's plenty obvious that, in the Vintage Sedan, there's plenty of urgency: If you don't soon take him to the hospital, the trespasser will soon lose a leg. And, it appears that, in the Envelope, there's no urgency: Even if you put $100 in the mailbox just a minute from now, it will take at least a couple of weeks for that to translate into lifesaving aid for anyone. What's more, if you don't send anything right away, you can do it later, say, next month. Soon or not so soon, just as many will be vitally aided.

In these thoughts of a contrast, however, there's illusion and confusion. This isn't to deny that, in many cases, it's important both to act promptly and to have one's conduct determined by a clear sense of who's in the most imminent danger. Rather, it's to say that, even as the Sedan's a case with morally important urgency so is the Envelope.

Toward seeing that, I'll present two cases that really do differ in morally important urgency. For both, we'll make these suppositions: In room A, there's a man tied down with rope and, next to him, a time bomb's set to go off in just an hour. Unless he's untied and released from the room, its explosion will kill him. The same for room B, but the time is 24 hours. You can save either man, but not both.

For the first case, we'll go on to make the most natural further assumptions: After you save the man in A, not only will there still be time for someone to save the man in B, but, during the extra 23 hours, B's man enjoys *extra chances* for rescue that A's could never have.

For the second case, we'll make more unusual assumptions: As you know with absolute certainty, beyond what you'll do soon, there *aren't any* extra chances even for the man in B. So, simply and surely, you're to choose who'll live and who'll die.

In the first case, clearly you must save the man in A. But, what of the second case? Well, in some sense, perhaps it's still true that A's man's in a more urgent situation than B's. But, still, there's little reason to favor aiding him.

What have we learned? Well, at least for the most part, what moral weight attaches to urgency is due to the lesser chances of avoiding serious loss that, normally but not inevitably, are found in situations where there's little time to save the day. But, between the Sedan and the Envelope, there's never any such difference in the chances. Since that's not easy to see, I'll try to make enlightening remarks.

There's a continual flow of aid from some of the world's well-off folks to many of the most seriously needy. At it's far end, every day there are thousands of children on the very brink of death. Today, their vital need is *very* urgent. In the case of over 30,000 of these kids, this will be proven by the fact that, even as their need won't be met today, by tomorrow they'll be dead. Of course, just as urgent are the needs of thousands of others who, only through receiving today some *very* timely ORT, won't be dead tomorrow or, happily, anytime soon. To be sure, there are many more thousands of children whose vital needs today *aren't so very* urgent: For over 30,000 of these, in just two days, their needs *will be* that urgent. And, for over 30,000 *others*, in just three days they'll have such terribly urgent needs; and so on. Just so, for over 30,000 still other needy youngsters, their last day alive with danger will be in 30 days, or 31, that is, just a month from now.

Consider these "monthers." In some sense, it may be true that, over the next month, their needs will become more and more urgent. But, since we can be *certain* that, if you don't donate to UNICEF soon, more of these "monthers" will die, what moral relevance can *any such* increase in urgency have for your behavior? Clearly, none at all. By contrast, what matters is that, very soon, you begin to lessen the number of children who die a month from now and that, then, you help lessen the number who die shortly after that, and so on. So, facts like its taking a month for your mailed check to have a vital impact aren't morally significant. To think otherwise is like thinking that, in our second case with the two rooms, saving the man in A is morally much better than saving B's man.

In morally relevant respects, each greatly needy child is like a man in a room, tied down with a rope, with a time bomb set to explode. Some children's bombs are set to go off around noon tomorrow; others are set for five days hence; still others' are set for a month from now. But, since it's certain that, for all everyone else will do, even in a month's time, many of the children *still won't* have their ropes untied, in these different settings there's precious little moral weight. Because the ways of the world are slow to improve, for quite a while remarks like these will be quite true. And, *that's* more certain than that you yourself will be alive a day from now. So, our moral common sense delivers the message: As for morally weighty urgency, there's plenty in the Sedan *and* in the Envelope.

Hoping you won't forget that main thought, I'll present this less important idea: When not mixed with factors that help it promote the salience of vital needs, often urgency doesn't even influence our responses to particular cases. To see that, it's best to confront a case with *all sorts* of urgency, some as weighty as it's easily overlooked, and lots as slight as it's blatantly obvious:

> *The Super Express Fund.* The most bizarre thing in your mail today is an appeal from the SEF: By calling a certain number and using any major credit card, you can donate $500 to the SEF right away, night or day. The effect of such a prompt donation will be that one more child will receive ORT this very day and, in consequence, won't soon die. Of course, the SEF's appeal makes clear the reason that it will cost so much to provide ORT to just one child: Upon hearing from you, your credit card donation is attended to personally, directly, and completely. So, moments after your call, a certain ORT packet is rushed to the nearest international airport,

speeded to the next jet bound for Africa, and so on. Eventually, in a remote region, a paramedic rushes from a speeding vehicle. After examining several moribund children, he chooses one that, certainly, is today on the very brink of death. Then, he rapidly mixes the solution and administers it to just that most urgently needy little child. But, you don't ever make such a call and, in consequence, one more child soon dies than if you'd made the requested donation.

As everyone responds, you didn't do wrong. So, for now, we've learned enough about urgency.

2.11 Causally Focused Aid and Causally Amorphous Aid

From discussing thoughts bound to occur to many, I turn to some esoteric distinctions. Perhaps the most notable concerns *causally focused* aid and, by contrast, *causally amorphous* aid. First, a few words about causally focused aid: If you'd provided aid to the trespasser in the Vintage Sedan, your helpful behavior would've been causally focused on that particular needy person. In an enlarged but parallel case, you might helpfully take, in your large vintage Mercedes bus, fully thirty greatly needy trespassers to a hospital. In the *Vintage Bus*, the aid you'd provide would be causally focused on *each one* of those thirty people. Next, causally amorphous aid: In the Envelope, even if you'd behaved helpfully, there'd never be *anyone* for whom *you'd* have made the difference between suffering a serious loss and suffering none; there'd never be a child of whom it would be true that, had you sent in $100, she wouldn't have died prematurely. Rather, on one end of a causal chain, there are many donors contributing together and, on the other, there are all the people saved by the large effort they together support. The more support given, the more folks saved, and that's all she wrote.[14] Does this favor the Envelope's conduct?

As our moral common sense directs, there's no chance of that. Rather, since there's nothing morally objectionable about proceeding to aid greatly needy folks amorphously, no moral weight attaches to the precise character of the causal relations between the well-off and those whom, whether collectively or not, they might help save. Morally, the important thing is that the vulnerable don't suffer. And, with a well aimed case, our intuitive reactions confirm that decent deliverance:

The Special Relations Fund. You receive material from a group that assures you they'll find a moribund little child that your money, if you contribute, will prevent from dying prematurely. Since very many moribund little kids are out there, this won't be terribly difficult, or costly, but neither will it be very cheap and easy to have your vital aid be causally focused: So, if you donate $100 to the SRF, while only one less child will die soon, the group will ensure that your donation makes the big difference for the one child. But, you send nothing and, in consequence, one more child soon dies than if you'd made the requested donation.

Here, it's clear that any aid will be causally focused. But, as all respond, your conduct wasn't the least bit wrong. So, on our reactions to cases, this esoteric factor doesn't have any great effect.

2.12 SATISFYING NICE SEMANTIC CONDITIONS

Before noticing another esoteric distinction, I'd like to discuss a family of quite ordinary ideas that's closely related to, but that's not quite the same as, the one just considered. Just as the common concepts are well placed under the head *satisfying nice semantic conditions*, so the family's most salient notion prompts this suggestion: "When you can *save* folks from much suffering, it's wrong not to aid. But, perhaps, if you'll merely *help to prevent* folks from suffering seriously, you needn't help. Mightn't that ground a big difference between our puzzle cases?" Hardly. First, by contrast with the Shallow Pond, had you been helpful in the Vintage Sedan, a doctor's services would still be needed to save the leg; so, in strict truth, the very most we could have said for you would be that, then, *you and a doctor* would have saved the leg. Second, and much more important, there's this: Whatever their precise character, these semantic niceties don't matter morally; at any rate, abandoning the wounded man was wrong.

About other members of *saving*'s family, the same points hold true. For example, when you've the chance to be only a partial enabler of someone who might save a needy person, but you're needed, then, just as surely as the one who has the chance to star as the saver, you must play your supporting role. Certainly, our moral common sense tells us that.

Plenty well enough, we can also see the point by way of apt examples. As with many cases where a great need is conspicuous, this happens with:

> *The Indian Sewer.* While vacationing in India, you come upon a child who's on the verge of drowning in the waters of a sewer. When the child fell in, she knocked away the bar propping up the sewer's trapdoor grating, which is also now down in the sewer. So, the heavy door's now closed. For the child to be saved, three able adults are needed. One person, who's both strong and agile, must go down into the sewer and bring up the child. Being strong but not agile, you can't do that. Still, there's someone else there who can. For the agile man to play the central role in a rescue, two others must hold open the filthy, strangely-shaped grating, one holding it by one edge and the other by another. A third person is able and willing to hold one of these edges and, so, it's now all up to you. But, not wanting to soil your new suit, you walk away and, so, the child drowns.

As all strongly react, your behavior was monstrous. Now, recall the Shallow Pond, where you had a chance to *save* someone from suffering a serious loss. Was your behavior in the Indian Sewer any better? Very widespread is the comparative intuition on the cases: Your behavior in this new example is just as abominable as in that old one.

Of course, in the Envelope, you never had even the chance to fill any such fairly fulfilling supporting role as the one just noted; rather, you had, at most, only the chance to *contribute to enabling others* to save children. But, it's only a confusion to think that could give you even the slightest moral license.

Underlying the confusion, sometimes there may be the idea that, much as with writing poetry, for example, what we do for needy people constitutes personally fulfilling projects. To fulfill ourselves, each of us wants to write her own poems, or to grow her own garden, or whatever: If I'm just a pretty fair poet, not greatly talented, a poem written mainly by a great poet, with just marginal input from me, might well be much better than any I'd write by myself, or with only some help. But, quite rationally, my attitude is that it's not enough for there to be excellent poems in whose writing I had only a marginal role. By contrast with poetry, however, toward *people in serious trouble*, it's crazy to have an attitude that's even *remotely like that*, and for our conduct toward them to be determined by any such attitude.

2.13 EPISTEMIC FOCUS

Analogous to the distinction between aid that's causally focused and aid that's causally amorphous, there's a distinction between *epistemically focused* aid and *epistemically amorphous* aid: Even if you donated the $100 requested in the Envelope, and even if you thereby helped save some people, you *wouldn't know which* folks you helped save from an early death, or even aided at all. In the Vintage Sedan, by contrast, if you took the trespasser to the hospital and his leg was saved, you'd know whom you aided.[15] Can this favor the Envelope's behavior? Our common sense says that, morally, it doesn't matter whether you come to know whose dire needs you help meet. And, our reactions to cases can chime in nicely.

Though I resolved not to cover you with cases, here I'll bother to go both ways. First, here's an Envelopey case that's very like other recent examples:

> *The Very Special Relations Fund.* Not only does the VSRF make sure your $200 will go to save the life of a certain particular child, but it makes sure you'll get to know which kid that is. By providing you with her name and a picture of the child saved, you'll know precisely which child's life just your donation served to spare. Still, you don't send anything and, in consequence, one more child soon dies than if you'd made the requested donation.

To this epistemically focused case, we respond that your conduct was all right. Indeed, with lenient responses in mind, many *actually* refrained from donating to groups enormously like the VSRF. And, here's a suitable Sedanish example:

> *The Vintage Boat.* Your one real luxury in life is a vintage power boat. In particular, you're very happy with the fine wood trim of the handsome old boat. Now, there's been a big shipwreck in the waters off the coast where your boat's docked. From the pier, in plain

view several hundred are struggling. Though both Coast Guard boats and private boats are already on their way to the people, more boats are needed. Indeed, the more private boats out and back soon, the more people will be saved. But, it's also plain that, if you go out, still, owing to all the melee, nobody will ever know which people will have been benefited by *you*. Indeed, for each of the folks whom you might bring in, it will be true to say this: For all anyone will ever know, she'd have been brought in by *another* boat, in which case some *other* person, whom some other boat rescued, would've perished. On the other hand, this you do know: While there's no risk at all to you, if you go out, your boat's wood trim will get badly damaged, and you'll have to pay for expensive repairs. So, you leave your boat in dock and, in consequence, a few more plainly struggling folks soon die.

As almost all respond to this epistemically amorphous case, your conduct was seriously wrong.

It's worth noting, briefly, an extended form of this distinction: In the Vintage Sedan, even *beforehand* you know whom you'll aid, if only you bother to provide the aid there relevant; but, in the Envelope, you *certainly wouldn't* know *beforehand* whom you'll aid. Can *that* mean much for a comfortably Preservationist solution? Again, our moral common sense speaks negatively. As with the Vintage Boat, reactions to many cases can confirm that decent deliverance. So much for epistemic focus.

2.14 MONEY, GOODS, AND SERVICES

In the Sedan, to provide apt aid you must perform a *service* for a needy person. Moreover, one of your *goods* would be needed in the performance of the service, namely, your vintage car. By contrast, in the Envelope all you must contribute is *money*; and, beyond the trivial effort needed to mail the money, the monetary cost is all you'd incur. Can this difference favor the Envelope's behavior?

Often, the difference between mere money and, on the other side, actual goods and services, has a psychological impact on us: When there's a call for our money, generally we think of what's going on as just charity. And, when thinking this, it seems all right to decline. But, at least in blatantly urgent situations, when there's a call for services, or one of our especially apt goods, a fair number of us think we must rise to the occasion. Does this difference have much moral relevance?

On this point, our moral common sense is clear: It doesn't matter whether it's money, or goods, or services, or whatever, that's needed from you to lessen serious suffering. There isn't a stronger moral call on you when it's your goods or services that are needed aid than when it's just your money.

In everyday life, that's confirmed by our reactions to very many cases: When disasters strike, like earthquakes, hurricanes, or floods, organizations work to aid the imperiled victims. On many of us, these groups often call only for our money. But, on some, they call for goods or services: For example, one good group may suggest that, since you're well placed in the pharmaceutical industry, you might make calls to your associates, asking them to donate medicines needed by victims of last week's disaster. But, plenty often, in these ordinary cases, the needs *aren't salient* to the agent approached and, then, our uncritical reactions are lenient. So, plenty often, the fact that what's needed is an agent's services, or her goods, doesn't affect even our responses to cases.

2.15 COMBINATIONS OF THESE DIFFERENTIATING FACTORS

Though no single one of the most notable factors differentiating the puzzle cases can carry much moral weight, mightn't certain *combinations* of them carry great weight? If that's so, then our puzzle might have, after all, a comfortably Preservationist solution. But, it's not so.

To get a good grip on the matter, we'll list explicitly the notable differential factors. Besides sheer conspicuousness, we've noted nine. In the order of their first appearance, and "viewed from the side of the Vintage Sedan," they are: (1) physical proximity, (2) social proximity, (3) informational directness, (4) experiential impact, (5) unique potential savior, (6) emergency, (7) causal focus, (8) epistemic focus, and (9) goods and services.[16] What does our general moral common sense say about those nine factors? Just as it's already done, it keeps telling us, about every single one, that it's *morally irrelevant*. Quite as clearly, this common sense says the same thing about any more complex difference the simpler ones combine to form, namely, that *it's* morally irrelevant.[17]

Concerning this question of their combination, what do our untutored responses to examples tell us about the nine listed factors? For relevantly interesting data, we're to look only at cases, of course, where people's great needs are inconspicuous to the cases' agents. For, if there's one thing we're *not* concerned now to explore, it's the extent to which our nine factors can combine to promote sheer conspicuousness of people's terrible troubles.

Now, it might be very difficult to confront a case that, at once, both included all nine "Sedanish" features and had only such great needs to meet as were quite inconspicuous. But, however that may be, it doesn't much matter. For, even with decidedly fewer than all nine, we can get the right idea quite clearly enough and, from the examples we've already confronted, we've already done that. So, for the energetic reader, I'll leave the exercise of constructing a complex case of the sort lately indicated. For the less energetic, there's the note appended to this very sentence.[18]

2.16 HIGHLY SUBJECTIVE MORALITY AND OUR ACTUAL MORAL VALUES

In our Primary Values, how much weight's accorded to psychologically powerful salience? Of course, there may be great weight given to certain things *often associated* with it: Often, the people whose needs are most conspicuous to you are your closest relatives and friends. And, someone might have extra strong moral reason to meet the great needs of folks who, socially and personally, are extremely close to her. But, even as it remains when their needs become very obscure to you, as can occur when you travel, such extra reason won't derive, of course, from the salience of these folks' needs. So, we've yet to see any reason to think that moral weight's given to conspicuousness of need itself.

In at least two ways, we can see that the reverse is true. First, consider the choice between certainly saving 99 strangers whose dire needs are highly salient to you and, on the other side, certainly saving 100 whose equally dire needs are very *inconspicuous*. As our Primary Values direct, you ought to save the 100. Second, consider the choice between an attempt that has a 90 percent chance of success in saving a stranger whose dire need is highly salient to you and, on the other side, an attempt that has a 91 percent chance of success in saving one whose equal need is very inconspicuous. Here, our main Values direct you to make the attempt with the slightly greater chance of success.

According to the Values of certain possible people, and maybe even a few actual people, you'll be directed oppositely. Then, *just because* their dire needs are more conspicuous, you ought to favor saving *fewer* people over more folks; and, *just because* his dire need's more conspicuous, you ought to favor making the *less likely* attempt to meet someone's dire need. Those possible Values may be well called *Highly Subjective* Primary Values.

According to such Highly Subjective Values, conspicuousness to a particular agent is a factor that, in and of itself, has substantial moral weight. But, as we've just clearly seen, that's enormously different from our Primary Values. So, now, that fact will surprise few. What may remain surprising is an implication of the fact: In our Primary Values, nothing favors the Envelope's conduct over the Sedan's.

No doubt, our discussion's furthered our appreciation of the implication. Even so, there remains much resistance to thinking the Envelope's conduct is wrong. Accordingly, in the chapter's final sections, I'll make an attempt, to be further pursued in later chapters [of *Living High and Letting Die*], rationally to reduce this persistent resistance.

2.17 Resistance to the Puzzle's Liberationist Solution: The View That Ethics Is Highly Demanding

Here's one main line of persistent resistance: By contrast with judging the Sedan's conduct severely, if we do that with the Envelope's, then, since we can't reject certain boring truths we all know full well, we'll have to accept a certain general position that's very strict and demanding. Composed partly of purely moral propositions and partly of propositions relating moral ideas to our actual circumstances, it may be called the *View that Ethics Is Highly Demanding*, and it may be seen to have these implications: To behave in a way that's not seriously wrong, a well-off person, like you and me, must contribute to vitally effective groups, like OXFAM and UNICEF, most of the money and property she now has, and most of what comes her way for the foreseeable future.

Is there much substance in this line of resistance? To answer well, we'll proceed systematically. And, for that, we'll distinguish two statements that, if true, can each undermine the line. One is categorical:

(1)　The View that Ethics Is Highly Demanding is the correct view of our moral situation.

And, the other is a conditional proposition:

(2)　(Even) if this View isn't correct, a strict judgment for the Envelope (still) won't do any more toward committing us to the View than will a strict judgment for the Vintage Sedan.

Much later, in chapter 6 [of *Living High and Letting Die*], I'll argue for the View that Ethics Is Highly Demanding.[19] But, at this early stage, we'll learn most by focusing on the conditional. So, I'll argue that, if a strict judgment for the Sedan *doesn't* commit us to anything very costly, then neither does a strict judgment for the Envelope.

Now, even before looking for any such argument, we know that its conditional conclusion must be correct. How so? Well, we've *stipulated* that, to the cases' agent, the helpful conduct requested in the Sedan is *over fifty times* as costly as in the Envelope. Still, observing details can be instructive.

Often, it's good to treat morality as an infinity of moral *principles*, or *precepts*, each entailing infinitely many others, more and more specific. On that approach, I'll first present this relatively general principle:

> *Lessening (the Number of People Suffering) Serious Loss.* Other things being even nearly equal, if your behaving in a certain way will result in the number of people who suffer serious loss being less than the number who'll suffer that seriously if you don't so behave (and if you won't thereby treat another being at all badly or ever cause another any loss at all), then it's seriously wrong for you not to so behave.[20]

To indicate the scope I mean the maxim to have, I'll make some remarks about the intended range of "serious loss." First, some positive paradigms: Even if it happens painlessly, when someone loses her life very prematurely, she suffers a serious loss. And, if someone loses even just a foot, much less a leg, she also suffers seriously. And, it also happens when, without losing any of his parts, someone loses his eyesight. Next, some losses less than serious: There's your losing just a tooth. And, there are financial losses from which you can recover. Anyway, this precept clearly applies to both puzzle cases.

Clearly, this maxim makes no provision for financial costs to the agent. And, so, many will resist the idea that it's a genuine moral principle. By the book's [*Living High and Letting Die*] end, we'll see that such cares for costs conflict with any truly decent moral thinking. But, now, it's good to see how they can be accommodated.

How might it be ensured that, even when followed fully, a precept won't ever mean a terribly burdensome cost? Of course, we must see to it that, *in the principle itself,* there's a logical guarantee to that effect. So, I'll do that straightaway and, to save space, I'll make other obvious changes when going from Lessening Serious Loss to this more specific precept:

> *Pretty Cheaply Lessening Early Death.* Other things being even nearly equal, if your behaving in a certain way will result in the number of people who *very prematurely lose their lives* being less than the number who'll do so if you don't so behave and *if even so you'll still be at least reasonably well off,* then it's seriously wrong for you not to so behave.[21]

Before moving to a yet more appealingly lenient specific maxim, we'll notice two points about this one: First, complying with it can't have you be less than reasonably well off! And, second, while the Envelope's conduct gets a severe judgment from the precept, *not* so the Sedan!

Few truly rich folks, if any at all, will fully comply with Pretty Cheaply Lessening Early Death. So, for any particular billionaire, the cost of compliance will be very great: If the toll's not taken all at once, then a decently progressive sequence will soon turn any into someone who's just reasonably well off.[22] So, for a maxim that's appealing even to the very rich, we must have a precept that's a lot like:

> *Very Cheaply Lessening Early Death.* Other things being even nearly equal, if your behaving in a certain way will result in the

number of people who very prematurely lose their lives being less than the number who'll do so if you don't so behave and if even so you'll still be both (a) at least reasonably well off *and (b) very nearly as well off as you ever were*, then it's seriously wrong for you not to so behave.

Even for rich folks, this precept's full observance can't ever be very costly. And, since you're not very poor, you'll see clearly that, while it yields a strict judgment for the Envelope's conduct, it doesn't yield any for the Sedan's![23] So, it's very clearly indeed that we see the soundness of the section's main point: If a strict judgment for the Sedan doesn't commit us to anything onerous, then a strict judgment for the Envelope is *fully compatible* with a View that Ethics is Highly *Undemanding!*[24]

2.18 FURTHER RESISTANCE: DIFFERENT SORTS OF SITUATION AND THE ACCUMULATION OF BEHAVIOR

A good closing for the chapter can come from considering this other line of resistance: "In the Vintage Sedan, *the sort* of situation I encountered was a very *unusual* sort, and a quite *rare* sort. And, so, if I'd behaved well in the Sedan, then, pretty surely, I'd be off a certain moral hook for a good long while. By contrast, *the sort* of situation I faced in the Envelope was a very *common* sort of situation, a sort that's all too *frequent*; so, all too surely, I'll face a situation of *this other* sort again pretty soon. So, even if I'd behaved well in the Envelope, I wouldn't be off this other moral hook for long at all. Though hard to detail, that's a weighty moral difference between the cases." What's more, it seems this line may be furthered by a thought that, as was made clear by this text's very first page, we should all endorse: The fact that, in the Envelope, you failed to respond to an *appeal* has only minuscule moral weight. So, the line then continues like this: "With the sort of situation where I'll help save lives by contributing to UNICEF, there's hardly ever any stopping. But, nothing remotely like that holds for the sort in the Sedan. So, between the two cases, there's a huge moral difference."

Though it has a certain appeal, in this line there's really nothing more than in, say, the thought that people in a vast multitude are quite different from single individuals, that is, there's nothing whatsoever. But, since it's not obvious, I'll take pains to explain: Right at the line's start, we find the assumption that, in the Vintage Sedan, there actually is something that's *the one and only sort* of situation you encountered. But, that's as far from the truth as can be; for, in truth, you there encountered a situation of, or belonging to, *enormously many sorts*. For example, you confronted a situation of the sort *situations involving vintage automobiles* and, for another, *situations where there's the chance for someone to take another to a hospital*, and, for a third, *situations where someone's dire need is conspicuous to you*. Compounding errors, moments later there was made the equally defective assumption that, in the Envelope, there's something that's *the one and only sort* of situation you there encountered.

An appreciation of those twin troubles has us ask a properly pointed question: Perhaps rather rarely instanced, (and perhaps *not* rarely instanced) is there a *sort of situation* that (even as it *is* instanced by the Sedan and *not* by the Envelope) *can* ground strict judgment for the Sedan, but *can't* for the Envelope? At first glance, this question may seem to introduce new issues. But, for a simple reason, it really doesn't: If some such *sort* can effect this grounding, then certain *factors* must be similarly potent, namely, those serving to distinguish such a potent sort from less potent sorts. So, the question fails to locate anything we haven't already worked to investigate.

So far, the section's discussion has been very general and abstract. For a fuller sense of its main point, I'll illustrate with material more specific and concrete: Suppose that, though far from rich, you've already donated fully a fourth of your income this year to support effective programs conducted by OXFAM, UNICEF, and IPPF. Largely, you did this by responding quite positively to the many appeals that, during the year, you've received from the organizations. (As I'll bother to observe, unless you're "one in a million," this supposition is *wildly* false. Yet, because we've made it, we're set to hear a helpfully concrete little story.)[25] Near the year's end, it's now late December. Before the year's over, there appears in your mail, complete with material about ORT and a return envelope, yet another appeal from UNICEF. Throwing up your hands, you think this: "Even forgetting about the thousands I've given to OXFAM and IPPF this year, I've already sent UNICEF itself thousands of dollars. Now, I don't want to be a Scrooge, you understand; but, holy moly, enough is enough!" With that exasperating thought in mind, you throw away the most recent material.

Of course, there's another half to this little story: Later the same day, you go for a drive in your vintage Mercedes sedan. At a rural crossroads, you come upon a trespasser, evidently a harmless bird-watcher, with a badly wounded leg. After hearing his elaborate appeal, you throw up your hands and have the same thoughts as a few hours before. Finishing with another token of "Now, I don't want to be a Scrooge, you understand; but, holy moly, enough is enough!"—you drive away and he loses a leg.

For your conduct in this two-scene story, what are our intuitive moral assessments? For the scene where you tossed UNICEF's envelope in the trash, our response is lenient. But, for your conduct in the second scene, our response is strict. Of course, in a slightly different form, that's just our old puzzle.

As I've suggested, some may try to ground the divergent responses along a certain "sortal" line: "In the story's first part, I confronted a situation of *the same sort* I already often encountered this year. So, taking together all the situations of *that* sort, I'll have behaved quite well during the whole year. But, in the story's second part, I confronted a situation of a *new* sort. Now, taking together all the situations of this second sort, we find that, since there's only one of them, for my letting the trespasser lose his leg, I'll have acted very badly, during the whole year, in *all those* situations."

At this point, the absurdity of these sortal thoughts becomes clear quickly: In both the story's first part and its second, there was a situation belonging to enormously many sorts. Now, with the "Envelopey" situation faced first, it's only certain of its *morally irrelevant* sorts that do much to promote your quickly grouping it with other situations, for example, the sort *situations where you receive appeals from organizations that aid the vitally needy*. But, for accurate moral assessment, it's only certain *other* of its sorts that are relevant, for example, the sort *situations where behaving helpfully has no morally bad aspects and results in fewer folks suffering serious loss*. Of course, the Sedanish situation second in the story *doesn't* belong to the morally *irrelevant* sort just noted for its Envelopey predecessor, nor to ever so many *other* such irrelevant sorts. But, so what? It *does* belong to the ethically *relevant* sort lately noted. Indeed, (with our Secondary Values' domain rightly remaining to the side), as this chapter's work has helped show, *all* its morally relevant sorts are *also* instanced by its Envelopey predecessor.

Like the points surviving scrutiny in previous sections, the few here surviving support only a Liberationist solution to the chapter's puzzle, not a Preservationist answer. But, even now, many will think the Envelope's conduct isn't wrong at all, much less seriously so. With that in mind, in the next chapter [chap. 3 of *Living High and Letting Die*] I seek a deeper understanding of such commonly, but perhaps terribly, unhelpful behavior.

NOTES

1. Illusions of Innocence: An Introduction

1. In the summer of 1995, I fervently sought to learn how much it really costs, where the most efficient measures get their highest yield, to get vulnerable children to become adults. Beyond reading, I phoned experts at UNICEF, the Rockefeller Foundation, the Johns Hopkins School of Hygiene and Public Health and, finally, the World Bank. As I say in the text, nothing of moral import turns on my search's findings. For those to whom that isn't already clear, it will be made evident, I think, by the arguments of chapter 6 [of *Living High and Letting Die*]. Partly for that reason, it's there that I'll present the best empirical estimates I found.

2. Most of what I say about Kerala was first inspired by reading Frances Moore Lappé and Rachel Schurman, *Taking Population Seriously*, the Institute for Food and Development Policy, 1988. Almost all is well documented in a more recent book from the Institute, entirely devoted to the Indian state: Richard W. Franke and Barbara H. Chasin, *Kerala: Radical Reform as Development in an Indian State*, 1989. Still more recently, these statements are confirmed by material on pages 18–19 of the United Nations Development Programme's *Human Development Report 1993*, Oxford University Press, 1993.

3. Much of what I'll say about causes of childhood death, and about the interventions that can nullify these causes, is systematically presented in James P. Grant's *The State of the World's Children 1993*, published for UNICEF by the Oxford University Press in 1993. To a fair extent, not more, I've cross-checked this against the (somewhat independent) material I've skimmed in the more massive *World Development Report 1993*, published for the World Bank by the OUP in 1993.

4. But, happily, UNICEF's worldwide immunization campaign has been making great strides against measles for years. So, while just a few years ago measles claimed over 1.5 million young lives, in the past year, 1994, it claimed about 1 million.

5. In "Polio Isn't Dead Yet," The *New York Times*, June 10, 1995, Hugh Downs, the chairman of the U.S. Committee, usefully writes, "The United States spends $270 million on domestic [polio] immunization each year. For about half that amount polio could be eliminated worldwide in just five years, according to experts from Unicef and the World Health Organization. If the disease is wiped off the earth, we would no longer need to immunize American children and millions of dollars could be diverted to other pressing needs."

6. The widely available table I use is presented on page 135 of *The 1993 Information Please Almanac*, Houghton Mifflin, 1993. The statement that each of these countries has a well-established UNICEF program in place, and that it's currently (1995) easy for the program to work well in large parts of the nation, was told me by a US Committee staffer.

7. In a typical recent year, 1993, the US Committee for UNICEF mailed out, almost every month, informative appeals to over 450,000 potential donors. As a Committee staffer informed me, the prospects were folks whose recorded behavior selected them as *well above* the national average in responding to humanitarian appeals. With only a small overlap between the folks in each mailing, during the year over 4 million "charitable" Americans were vividly informed about what just a few of their dollars would mean. With each mailing, a bit less than 1 percent donated anything, a pattern persisting year after year.

8. See his landmark essay, "Famine, Affluence and Morality," *Philosophy and Public Affairs*, 1972 [reprinted herein 1–14].

9. See page 169 of the original edition of his *Practical Ethics*, Cambridge University Press, 1979. Without any change, this first premise appears on page 230 in the book's Second Edition, published by the CUP in 1993.

10. Now, without departing from it's original spirit, the premise may be reformulated so that, at least at first sight, there are more appealing arguments for its importantly correct conclusion, that it's wrong for us not to lessen serious suffering, and even for the wanted stronger conclusion that it's *seriously* wrong. For example, one more appealing formulation has us replace Singer's original first premise with this proposition that, briefly, will be discussed in chapter 2, section 17 [of *Living High and Letting Die*, herein 365–68]:

> *Pretty Cheaply Lessening Early Death.* Other things being even nearly equal, if your behaving in a certain way will result in the number of people who *very prematurely lose their lives* being less than the number who'll do so if you don't so behave and *if even so you'll still be at least reasonably well off*, then it's seriously wrong for you not to so behave.

But, in any event, at least one of the argument's premises will be a general proposition many will think unacceptable.

11. The case first appears in "Famine, Affluence and Morality" [reprinted herein 3–5]. The words I use come from the Second Edition of *Practical Ethics*.

12. For a complementary explanation of the impasse, see the subsection "The Methodological Objection," on pages 104–5 in Garrett Cullity's recent paper, "International Aid and the Scope of Kindness," *Ethics* 105: 1 (October 1994): 99–127. Taking the paper's text together with its footnotes, there's a useful overview of the discussion that, in the past couple of decades, pertains to Singer's contribution.

13. Many contemporary ethicists are *pretty close* to being (pure) Preservationists, prominently including Frances M. Kamm, in papers and, more recently, in *Morality/Mortality*, Oxford University Press, Volume 1, 1993 and Volume 2, 1996; Warren S. Quinn, in papers collected in *Morality and Action*, Cambridge University Press, 1993; and, Judith J. Thomson, in papers collected in *Rights, Restitution and Risk*, Harvard University Press, 1986 and, more recently, in *The Realm of Rights*, Harvard, 1990.

Whatever the *avowed* methodological stance, it's a radically rare ethicist who'll actually advocate, and continue to maintain, a morally substantive proposition that's strongly at odds with his reactions to more than a few cases he considers.

Of course, many gesture at the propositions presented in John Rawls's Outline of a Decision Procedure for Ethics," *Philosophical Review* (1951), fashionably uttering the words "reflective equilibrium". With the Liberationism this book [*Living High and Letting Die*] develops, perhaps there's a step toward putting some meat on some such schematic bones; in any case, there's more than just a gesture.

14. As I'll suppose, my fellow Liberationists, including Peter Singer, are reasonably flexible here.

15. The Liberationism whose moral substance is now to be spelled out, very incompletely, is the sort I myself favor. Others, like Peter Singer, will profess somewhat different guiding substantive moral beliefs, or Values. While those differences are important in certain contexts, in the context of this inquiry they aren't.

16. The expressions just bracketed in the text are to allow for certain nice ways these matters can be complicated by considerations of our *Secondary* Basic Moral Values, which Values aren't introduced in the text till the book's second chapter [herein 334–71]. For now, don't bother with that, but just note this: Even the staunchest Liberationist can establish semantic contexts in which it's *correct to say* that only the Shallow Pond's conduct is badly wrong, and even that the Envelope's isn't wrong at all. (It's not until the book's [*Living High and Letting Die*] last chapter that I'll provide the sort of semantic account that supports this note's qualification.)

17. On a third view, our responses to *both* cases fail to reflect anything morally significant: Just as it's all right not to aid in the Envelope, so, it's also perfectly all right in the Shallow Pond. Aptly named *Negativism*, this repellently implausible position has such very great difficulties that, in these pages,

I'll scarcely ever consider it. To keep the text itself free from mentions of such a hopeless view, on the few occasions when Negativism's addressed at all, the brief notices will be confined to footnotes.

2. Living High and Letting Die: A Puzzle about Behavior toward People in Great Need

1. To understand our cases according to this usefully simplifying stipulation, we should have a good idea of what's to count as clearly implied by the statement of an example. Toward that end, perhaps even just a few words may prove very helpful. First, some fairly general words: To be clearly implied by such a statement, a proposition needn't be logically entailed by the statement. Nor need it be entailed even by a conjunction of the statement and a group of logical, mathematical, analytical or purely conceptual truths. Rather, it's enough that the proposition be entailed by a conjunction of the statement with others that are each commonly known to be true. Second, some more specific words: With both our puzzle cases, it's only in a *very boringly balanced* way that we're to think of the case's relevantly vulnerable people. Thus, even as we're not to think of anyone who might be saved as someone who'll go on to discover an effective cure for AIDS, we're also not to think of anyone as a future despot who'll go on to produce much serious suffering.

2. Among other reasons, this accommodates the friends of John Taurek's wildly incorrect paper, but highly stimulating essay "Should the Numbers Count?" in *Philosophy and Public Affairs*, 1977. But, as even some of the earliest replies to it show, no accommodation is really necessary; flawed only by some minor errors, a reasonably successful reply is Derek Parfit's "Innumerate Ethics," *Philosophy and Public Affairs*, 1978. So, my making this accommodation is an act of philosophical supererogation.

3. For the moment, suppose that, as the five factors indicate, your conduct in the Envelope was at least as bad as in the Sedan. From a purely logical point of view, there's naught to choose between the two salient ways of adjusting our moral thinking: (1) *The Negativist Response*. While continuing to hold that your conduct in the Envelope *wasn't* wrong, we may hold that, despite initial appearances, your conduct in the Sedan *also wasn't* wrong. (2) *The Liberationist Response*. While continuing to hold that your conduct in the Sedan *was wrong*, we may hold that, despite initial appearances, your conduct in the Envelope *also was wrong*. But, since we've more than just logic to go on, we can see the Liberationist Response is far superior. So, unless there's a sound way to hoe that mighty long row, we should conclude, with Liberationism, that the Envelope's conduct was very seriously wrong.

4. As I'll use the term "salience" in this book [*Living High and Letting Die*], it will mean the same as the more colloquial but more laborious term, "conspicuousness." So, on my use of it, "salience" *won't* mean the same as "*deserved* conspicuousness."

5. Throughout this work [*Living High and Letting Die*], my statements about how "most respond" are to be understood like this: Informally and intermittently, I've asked many students, colleagues and friends for their intuitive moral assessments of the agent's behavior in a case I've had them just encounter. Even as this has been unsystematic, so, at any given point, I'll use reports about how "most respond" to a certain case mainly as a guide for proceeding in what then appears a fruitful direction. Without ever placing great weight on any one of the reports, it may be surprisingly impressive to feel the weight of them all taken together.

Trying to be more systematic, I asked a research psychologist at my home university to read an early draft of the book [*Living High and Letting Die*], with an eye to designing some telling experiments. Good enough to start with that, he asked graduate students to take on the project, and its onerous chores, as a doctoral dissertation; but, he found no takers. Having limited energy, I've left the matter there.

6. For an excellent analysis of population issues that's accessible even to laymen like me, I'm grateful for Amartya Sen's lucid essay, "Population: Delusion and Reality," *The New York Review of Books*, September 22, 1994 [reprinted herein 259–90]. As Sen there does much to make clear, our thought of the disastrous further future is little better than an hysterical fantasy.

7. More directly, a variant case chimes in with the same results: Suppose that, because he has a very large wound, our Bolivian's very life is greatly in danger. For him to live, you must take him to a hospital. Thinking about population problems and the further future, you drive away and let him die. As we intuitively react, your conduct's morally outrageous.

8. What's just been mentioned is only one of the good reasons to support IPPF. Here are others: First, with maternal mortality still standing at about 500,000 women a year, IPPF is cutting down the number and, so, lessening the number of children, still in the millions, who each year become motherless. Second, in IPPF clinics, many Third Worlders receive the basic health care they need. Right now I'll stop with this third point: Perhaps the greatest of all IPPF affiliates, Colombia's PROFAMILIA supports some clinics for men only. Owing to that, the terribly macho attitudes of many Colombian men have become much less macho, a big benefit to many Colombian women. At all events, in Colombia there's occurring a population success story.

9. Presented in literally graphic form, this paragraph's facts, and other fascinating data, cover page 49 of *The State of the World's Children 1995*, just off the press from the OUP at the time of this writing. For other fascinating facts, see Sen's essay, "Population: Delusion and Reality" [reprinted herein 259–90]. As careful readers will note, presenting data from India's Ministry of Home Affairs, on page 70 of his paper [herein 284], Sen's Table 2 shows Kerala to have even a slightly lower TFR, 1.8 rather than 1.9. But, of course, anything under 2.0 is happily remarkable.

Much more than living in a region with a high per capita income, and very much more than living in one where a liberal religion prevails, it's the factors I've just stressed that are important in determining the numbers of children that the region's women will bear. Just so, and very well worth noting, of all the world's pretty populous places, it's Italy, where even the Pope himself resides, that has the lowest Total Fertility Rate. With a TFR of just 1.3, Italy's set for a *big* decline in population!

10. For 1960, 1970, 1980, and 1990, I use the figures graphically presented on page 55 of *The State of the World's Children 1995*. For the estimated average year in the range 1990–95, the latest reliable estimate, I use the three figures found in *World Population Prospects: The 1994 Revision*, Population Division of the United Nations Secretariat, United Nations, New York, 1995. As a reliable estimate for more recent school enrollment is not available to me now, there's the "NA."

11. The quoted phrase, and much of the information about Bangladesh and cyclones here related, is from Fauzia Ahmed, "Cyclone Shelters Saving Lives," *Oxford America News*, summer 1994, page 5.

12. For those skeptical of what's to be found in such obscure places as *Oxfam America News*, I'll cite a piece in "the paper of record." From Sanjoy Hazarika, "New Storm Warning System Saved Many in Bangladesh," *New York Times*, May 5, 1994, I offer this sentence, "A major cyclone in 1991 killed an estimated 131,000 persons, wiping out entire villages and islands and leaving human corpses littering the countryside." As Oxfam's main source in Bangladesh, the Bangladesh Rural Advancement Committee, is closer to the ground than the *Times*' main source, apparently just the Bangladesh Government, their *News*' estimate for the 1991 toll, 138,000, is probably closer to the actual number of people killed then.

13. This is well in line with what's in the Hazarika piece, loc. cit., a Special to The *New York Times*. Here's its first sentence: "The comparatively low death toll in the huge storm that whipped across parts of southeastern Bangladesh on Monday night with winds of up to 180 miles an hour was attributed today to a combination of modern technology and simple steps that led to the evacuation of hundreds of thousands of villagers to high ground and storm shelters." Next, here's a scrap from later in the piece: ". . . according to Bangladesh Government officials, took the lives of 167. . . ." Finally, the piece's real kicker comes with its final sentence: "Most of the victims in the storm Monday were not Bangladeshis but Muslim refugees from Myanmar, formerly Burma, who had fled an army crackdown against followers of Islam in that country." So, without those unlikely and unlucky foreigners, the toll would have been *under 100*.

To my mind, far better than anything the *Times* offers on Bangladesh and its cyclones, there's a marvelous, and marvelously short, video on this amazing true story, called "Shelter," available from Oxfam America. Americans willing to make a contribution to OXFAM can get Shelter by calling this toll-free number: 1 - 800 - OXFAM-US, easily dialed as 1 - 800 - 693 - 2687.

14. On one logico-metaphysical view, there can't be casually amorphous relations. Though it appears false, it just might be true. If so, then this distinction marks no real difference. But, of course, it might well be false. And, since I should see if Liberationism prevails even on a "worst case scenario," I'll suppose that, in the Envelope, any aid would be causally amorphous.

15. Even here, some possible philosophers deny there's any real difference between the cases; skeptics about knowledge hold that, since we don't ever know anything, you'll never know anything about the fate of the trespasser. But, this can be passed over. And, from now on, I won't bother with philosophical views that deny an apparent difference between our two cases is a real one.

16. We've also discussed, of course, some candidates for being additional differential factors that proved unsuccessful. In the order discussed, and this time "viewed from the Envelope's side," they are: (a) worsening the further future—both factually false and contrary to our main stipulation, (b) leaving matters to the wealthy governments—at best just a modestly interesting instance of multiple potential saviors, (c) aiding only a very small part of an enormous multitude, as opposed to aiding a particular needy individual—a mere ethical illusion, (d) making only a decrease in the continuing mess rather than cleaning the scene—an even crazier illusion, (e) lacking important urgency—another illusion, and (f) failing to satisfy a nice semantic condition—not a genuinely differential factor, since, with a doctor's work needed, in the Sedan you couldn't really save someone's leg.

17. Perhaps, I may note a purely logical point: Those favoring stricter judgment for the Sedan aren't the only ones who can talk about combinations. Just as well, it can be done by those favoring a stricter judgment for the Envelope. But, since our common sense so clearly says that there's nothing substantial in any of this, it's silly to make a big deal about this logical symmetry.

18. In section 6 of the next chapter [chap. 3 of *Living High and Letting Die*], "Combination of Factors and Limited Conspicuousness," I work up a complex case with all the Sedan's listed factors, and with salience of need kept low. The example, the African Earthquake, has an obvious *variant* that's directly relevant to the present question. And, to this variant, we'll respond that unhelpful conduct isn't wrong.

19. Even while the View that Ethics Is Highly Demanding allows few exceptions to the sort of transfer of wealth just indicated, none will give you any substantial license to pursue your own happiness, or your own (nonmoral) fulfillment: Insofar as it gets you to be more helpful to those in direst need, as with earning more money to be given toward saving children's lives, not only may you spend money on yourself, but you positively must do that. And, insofar as it's needed to meet your strictest special moral obligations, as with getting your child a costly lifesaving operation, you must do that. In some detail, we'll discuss this in chapter 6 [of *Living High and Letting Die*] when, based on material from chapters that precede it, I'll argue that morality's far more demanding than we commonly suppose.

20. It's with thoughts about the causally amorphous aid you might have provided in the Envelope that I bother to formulate precepts, like this one, with rather lengthy locutions.

21. For economy, I haven't again inscribed the long bracketed clause, "(and if you won't thereby treat another being at all badly or ever cause another any loss at all)." But, as context makes clear, its thought's in all the section's precepts.

22. Though many may find this to be excessively demanding on rich folks, I think the maxim really doesn't make any excessive demand. But, biding my time till chapter 6 [of *Living High and Letting Die*], I won't argue that now.

23. While not poor, it may be that you're not rich, either. Then, there'll be at least two reasons why this precept doesn't yield a strict judgment for your conduct in the Sedan. Of course, one has been in play for a fair while: Unlike in the Envelope, in the Sedan there was never any question of any life being lost. Independent of that, another reason's this: Unlike when you're out only $100, when you're out over $5,000, it's probably fair to say you *aren't* very nearly as well off as you ever were.

24. As I hope you're coming to agree, at least for us in a world like this, any decent morality must be, at the very least, a *Pretty Highly* Demanding Ethics. And, while in chapter 6 [of *Living High and Letting Die*], I'll advance a View that's even much more ambitious than that, in the section now closing, all I needed to do, and all I aimed to do, was something extremely unambitious.

25. While quite a few give a lot to elite institutions, and while many give much to local religious groups, hardly anyone gives even a fortieth of her annual income toward anything even remotely as important, ethically, as those programs. Just so, each year well-off Americans give far more to Harvard University than to all three mentioned groups combined, UNICEF and OXFAM and IPPF; and far more to Yale than all three combined; and they also give more even to my less elite home institution, NYU, than to all combined. Owing to facts like these, what's in the text is a gross understatement.

17. THOMAS HURKA

Hurka considers whether nationalism, understood as partiality to one's own nation, is morally justified. After criticizing certain other attempts to provide such a justification, including that of Alasdair MacIntyre (chapter 7 in this volume), he argues that nationalism typically involves two different forms of partiality: a partiality to one's individual conationals as individuals, and a partiality to one's nation's impersonal good (for example, its survival as a nation). He then focuses on the first kind of partiality, arguing that it is indeed morally justified when it is based on a shared history of working together to produce significant benefits.

The Justification of National Partiality

First published in The Morality of Nationalism, *ed. Robert McKim and Jeff McMahan (Oxford University Press, 1997), 139–57.*

The moral issues about nationalism arise from the character of nationalism as a form of partiality. Nationalists care more about their own nation and its members than about other nations and their members; in that way nationalists are partial to their own national group. The question, then, is whether this national partiality is morally justified or, on the contrary, whether everyone ought to care impartially about all members of all nations. As Jeff McMahan emphasizes in "The Limits of National Partiality," a philosophical examination of this question must consider the specific features of nationalism as one form of partiality among others. Some partiality—for example, toward one's spouse and children—seems morally acceptable and even a duty. According to commonsense moral thinking, one not only may but also should care more about one's family members than about strangers. But other instances of partiality, most notably racial partiality, are in most circumstances widely condemned. Is national partiality more like familial partiality or more like racial partiality? To answer this question, we must know what in general justifies attitudes of partiality. Caring more about certain people is appropriate when one stands in certain special relations to those people. But what are these relations, and to what degree do they hold among members of the same nation? Assuming they are present within families and not within races, to what degree are they present within nations?

In addressing these questions, I will consider only "universalist" nationalism, the view that *all* people ought to be partial to their own nation and conationals. This is a more interesting and plausible position than the "particularist"—one could equally well say "chauvinist"—view that only one's own nation, say, only Canada, deserves special loyalty. And I will consider only intrinsic justifications of nationalism. There are various instrumental arguments for national partiality, ones claiming that, starting from impartial moral principles, we can show how people's being partial to their conationals will have good effects impartially considered. I do not find these instrumental arguments very persuasive. In any case, the more interesting philosophical question is whether national partiality can be justified noninstrumentally, or at the foundational level of morality. Many people believe that familial partiality is justified not just as a means to benefits for all but intrinsically or in itself. My question will be whether national partiality can be justified in the same foundational way.

My discussion will cover three separate topics. First, I will challenge one widely accepted view about the moral foundations of nationalism. Second, I will suggest that a full discussion of nationalism must recognize that it has two components, which raise distinct moral issues. Finally, I will sketch a moral defense of one of these aspects of nationalism. This defense will concede that along one important dimension the relations among conationals have less of the character that justifies partiality than do the relations among family members, but it will argue that along another dimension they have roughly as much. The result is not that we should be as partial to our conationals as we are to our children—that would be absurd—but that we may properly be partial to some degree.

NATIONALISM AND "EMBEDDED SELVES"

I have said that the moral issues about nationalism turn on whether certain relations hold within national groups. But many writers connect these issues to more abstract debates about the nature of morality and of moral agents. They say the impartialist view that we ought to care equally about all humans goes with the "Enlightenment" conception of morality as universal and impartial, whereas the defense of nationalism goes with a different "particularist" or "communitarian" conception of morality. According to this latter conception, moralities necessarily arise within the life of particular communities and therefore inevitably distinguish centrally between members and outsiders, requiring a certain priority to the interests of the former. David Miller expresses this kind of view. He says that moral impartialism sees the subject "as an abstract individual, possessed of the general powers and capacities of human beings—especially the power of reason," whereas a nationalist ethic sees the subject as "partly defined by its relationships, and the various rights, obligations, and so forth that go along with these, so these commitments themselves form a basic element of personality."[1] But although nationalism is often said to rest on these communitarian ideas about morality—let me summarize them in the slogan that "moral selves are embedded"—I do not see any connection between the two. Despite their prominence in the recent literature on nationalism, claims about the "embedded self" are not relevant to the intrinsic justification of national partiality. I can detect two arguments in defense of nationalism that may be suggested by the talk of embedded selves, which I will call the *cultural perfectionist* argument and the *metaethical particularist* argument. The cultural perfectionist argument does not go far enough to justify a universalist ethic of nationalism; the metaethical particularist argument goes too far. Let me start with the cultural perfectionist argument.

Perfectionism as a general normative view holds that the good for human beings consists in developing their "nature" or "identity."[2] More specifically, it holds that certain properties make an individual what he or she is and thereby constitute that person's nature or identity, and that his or her good consists in developing these properties to a high degree. In many classical versions of perfectionism—for example, those of Aristotle, Marx, and Nietzsche—the relevant nature is generic human nature, one shared by all human beings. But those who talk of "embedded selves" sometimes suggest a different perfectionist view. According to this view, human beings have natures or identities based on their membership in particular cultures, and their good consists at least partly in developing these narrower cultural identities. According to this "cultural" perfectionism, I as a Canadian have a specifically Canadian identity, a German has a German identity, and in each case our good consists at least partly in developing this cultural identity. One argument suggested by the talk of "embedded selves" is that this cultural perfectionism provides the justification for national partiality. If human beings had just an abstract or common human nature, this argument runs, a purely impartialist or cosmopolitan morality would be reasonable. But if, instead, their identities depend on their belonging to particular cultures, morality demands that they be specially loyal to those cultures.[3]

Though this is a less central point, I do not believe that cultural perfectionism is a very plausible version of perfectionism. In the most attractive versions of this general normative view, the properties that it is good for a human to develop constitute his or her identity in a strict or metaphysical sense. They are essential to the person in the strong sense that he or she could not exist as numerically the same individual without having these properties. This condition is satisfied by the classical perfectionisms of Aristotle, Marx, and Nietzsche; since I am essentially a human, no being that did not have the properties that make humans human could be identical to me. But the condition is not satisfied by cultural perfectionism. I was born in Canada and raised in Canadian culture. But we can easily imagine a different course of events, one in which, a few months after my birth, my parents return to their native Czechoslovakia and raise me there. And what we imagine in this course of events is that *I*, the very same individual, am raised in Czech culture. My being a Canadian, therefore, is not metaphysically essential to me and constitutes my identity in only a weaker, nonmetaphysical sense. And nonmetaphysical identities, it seems to me, cannot generate a plausible version of perfectionism.

As I said, however, this is a less central point. What is more important is that even if we accept cultural perfectionism, it does nothing to justify national partiality. Let us grant that humans have different goods based on their membership in different cultures. How does it follow that I should care more about the achievement by my conationals of their specific cultural good than about the achievement by people in other cultures of their specific good? What rules out the view that I should care impartially about all people's realizing their different cultural identities—that is, what rules out an impartialist cultural perfectionism? Such a perfectionism would recognize that the good of Canadians is different from the good of Germans but direct both Canadians and Germans to care equally about both. How does accepting cultural perfectionism as a general position rule this specific view out?[4] I am not suggesting that the writers who embrace cultural perfectionism do so in an impartialist way. Most, it seems to me, endorse national partiality. But the partiality they affirm does not follow from their cultural perfectionism, which is equally consistent with an impartialist approach. Their position therefore combines cultural perfectionism with claims about partiality that are independent of any ideas about cultural identities and cannot be justified by them.

Cultural perfectionists may object that I have ignored a crucial feature of their argument. This argument does not claim only that people in different cultures have different identities; it claims, beyond that, that those identities involve, as one component, a demand for partiality toward the culture's members. Thus my identity as a Canadian demands partiality toward Canadians, a German's identity demands partiality toward Germans, and neither of us can fully achieve his or her good by following an impartial morality.

If it takes this form, the cultural perfectionist argument requires a strong additional assumption. To show that national partiality is justified in *every* culture, it must assume that *every* culture involves as one component a demand for partiality, so there could never be a culture of pure impartialists. I find this assumption dubious, but let us grant it and ask what follows. If my identity involves as one component a demand for national partiality, I cannot fully achieve my good if I do what is right by impartialist standards. But this is no embarrassment or difficulty for an impartialist cultural perfectionism. It is merely one instance of the familiar fact that to do what is right, or has the best consequences impartially considered, agents must sometimes sacrifice some of their own good. Doing what is right often involves omitting what is best for oneself; here it involves omitting that part of one's good that consists in being partial. This familiar fact does not tell against impartial cultural perfectionism, and there is still no justification for national partiality.[5]

The difficulty with the cultural perfectionist argument is that it operates at the wrong level to justify national partiality. The affirmation of partiality concerns the *form* of an ethically appropriate concern. It says that whatever people's good consists in, we should care more about our conationals' good than about other people's. But cultural perfectionism makes claims about the *content* of our ethical concern, or about what people's good consists in. And no claims about what people's good consists in can justify the idea that we ought to care more about some people's good than about others'.

The second argument suggested by the talk of "embedded selves," which I called the metaethical particularist argument, does address issues about form. It claims that an impartialist morality, one requiring all humans to care equally about all others, is inconsistent with the true nature of moral codes and principles. These codes and principles, the argument says, always arise within particular cultures; they are addressed to the members of a culture as having the particular cultural identities they have and as occupying particular roles within that culture. Morality is always *our* morality, in these circumstances here. This means that the standpoint presupposed by impartial morality—outside all cultures and making judgments about them all—is not available. Morality must be partial because the impartialist alternative is conceptually incoherent.

The problem here is that the particularist argument excludes not only impartialist morality but also a universalist ethic of nationalism. For universalists, too, make claims about what is right in all cultures, namely, partiality toward them; their judgments, too, do not arise from their particular culture but apply equally to all cultures. Consider Alasdair MacIntyre's lecture, "Is Patriotism a Virtue?" [reprinted herein 119–38.] As its title indicates, this lecture asks a question about the value of patriotism in all cultures everywhere. And MacIntyre ties an affirmative answer to this question to what looks like a particularist metaethical view. On the view that underwrites patriotism, he writes, we never learn "morality as such, but always the highly specific morality of some highly specific social order." Later he claims that impartialist morality requires something that cannot be justified, namely, that we "assume an abstract and artificial—perhaps even an impossible—stance, that of a rational being as such, responding to the requirements of morality not *qua* peasant or farmer or quarterback, but *qua* rational agent who has abstracted him or herself from all social particularity."[6] But someone who really accepted this metaethical particularism could not ask the universalized question of MacIntyre's title. Such a person could only write a lecture titled "Is Canadian Patriotism a Virtue in Canada?" (if he or she was Canadian) or "Is German Patriotism a Virtue in Germany?" (if he or she was German). This person would not make any claims but would deny the intelligibility of claims about the value of patriotism in cultures other than his or her own. Any such universalist claims, no less than those of impartialist morality, issue from a standpoint that the particularist says is not available—namely, one abstracted from any particular social identity and addressed to all humans or all members of cultures as such. As I have said, the interesting affirmation of national partiality is the universalist one; it is also the one that all writers on this subject discuss. But this universalist affirmation cannot be supported by metaethical particularism; on the contrary, it is excluded by it.

Let me summarize my discussion of the "embedded self" by introducing some technical terminology. The interesting nationalist doctrine is both universalist and agent-relative. It is universalist because it claims that partiality toward one's nation and conationals is appropriate for all humans in all cultures. It is agent-relative because it says that what different humans should be partial to is different—namely, their *own* conationals. The cultural perfectionist argument does not go far enough to justify this doctrine, because it does not rule out an impartialist view according to which we ought to care equally about the realization of their different cultural identities by people in all the cultures in the world. The metaethical particularist argument goes too far to justify the doctrine, because it rules out not only impartialist but also all universal moral claims. Neither of the two arguments that I can see suggested by the talk of "embedded selves" does anything to justify national partiality. The real issues about the ethics of nationalism do not concern the nature of morality or of the self but are those I introduced at the start of this chapter. Assuming that special relations sometimes justify partiality, are the relations among conationals of the kind that do justify partiality, like those among family members, or of the kind that do not, like those among members of a race?

NATIONALISM AND IMPERSONAL GOODS

My second topic is the content of national partiality, or exactly what nationalists are partial to. Many writers speak simply of being partial to one's nation without explaining further what that means. Some speak, more specifically, of being partial toward one's conationals—that is, of giving more weight to the interests of individuals in one's nation than to those of other individuals. This is certainly one aspect of nationalism, but I believe there is often another aspect.

In a number of writings Charles Taylor has emphasized the importance of cultural survival as a good and value for minority groups. In *Multiculturalism and "The Politics of Recognition,"* for example, he writes: "It is axiomatic for Quebec governments that the survival and flourishing of French culture in Quebec is a good."[7] Noting the importance of this insight, McMahan says it shows how for participants in a culture its survival has "impersonal value."[8] I agree that in one important sense the survival of a culture is an "impersonal" value or good, but in another sense, which seems to be the one McMahan has in mind, it is not, or is not most importantly, impersonal.

The survival of a culture is an impersonal good in the sense that is not reducible to the goods of individual persons, or to goods located in individual persons' lives. Consider francophone Quebeckers who care deeply that there be a French culture in Quebec three generations from now. Do they believe that the survival of French culture is a good because better human lives will be lived if French culture survives than if it does not? Do they believe, more specifically, that their great-grandchildren will lead better lives if they are born and raised in a French culture than if, that culture having disappeared, those great-grandchildren are born and raised as full members of an English culture? I do not believe these Quebeckers need or even should, if they wish to avoid chauvinism, believe this. They should grant that after enough time the disappearance of French culture would not be worse for persons in the sense of making the lives lived by persons worse. If, despite this, they continue to view the survival of their culture as a good, they must view it as an impersonal good in the following sense: It would be better if French culture survived even if this would not make the lives persons live more valuable.[9]

Valuing cultural survival in this way does not require the metaphysical view that cultures or nations exist separately from, or over and above, their individual members. It is fully compatible with the reductionist view that facts about nations consist entirely in facts about individuals and the relations between them. According to this reductionist view, for French culture to survive in Quebec is only and entirely for individuals in Quebec to live and interact in certain ways. But while holding that the *existence* of a culture is reducible to facts about individuals, a nationalist can deny that the *good* of the culture's existing is reducible to the *goods* of individuals. The fact that people interact in certain ways can have a value that is separate from the values present in their individual lives.[10]

Cultural survival, then, is an impersonal good in the sense that it does not consist in the goods of individual persons. But the word "impersonal" is often used in another sense, one equivalent to "impartial." In this sense, an impersonal good is one it is appropriate for all agents to desire and pursue and to weigh impartially against other similar goods. This seems to be the sense McMahan has in mind when he calls cultural survival an "impersonal value." He introduces the topic of survival while discussing the instrumental arguments that can be given, from an impartialist standpoint, for endorsing some degree of national partiality, and he considers it alongside a value that cannot but be impersonal in this second sense—namely, that of the overall cultural diversity of the world. But it seems to me that cultural survival is valued by nationalists, and is thought by them appropriately valued, in a highly partial way. Who is it who cares about the survival of French culture in Quebec? It is surely, above all, francophone Quebeckers. And they do not care about their culture's survival only in an impartial way, or merely as contributing to a universal good such as overall cultural diversity. If they did, they would gladly accept the disappearance of French culture in Quebec if that somehow allowed the survival of two other cultures elsewhere in the world. This is not their attitude; they care specially about the survival of *their own* culture. In the same way, it seems to me, people outside a culture do not have nearly as much reason to care about its survival as a good. McMahan writes that people outside a culture "are capable of appreciating its intrinsic value" and of "perceiving in a particular alien culture a variety of merits that may not be replicated in any other culture." But these remarks, though true, do not suffice to establish the appropriateness of impartial concern for another culture. I can appreciate that the well-being of someone else's children is a good while believing that I ought to care much more about my own children's well-being. And in my view commonsense nationalism does not give people outside a culture much moral duty to care directly about the culture's survival. This is obscured in many actual situations by the fact that the members of the culture do desire its survival. Thus if francophone Quebeckers care deeply about their culture's survival, this gives other people, and especially anglophone Canadians, a reason of a more familiar kind to support measures that will ensure the culture's survival—namely, that Quebeckers desire it. But what if a majority of Quebeckers ceased to care about their culture's survival and instead preferred assimilating into English culture? In this situation I believe Quebeckers in the minority would still feel a strong duty to fight for their culture and to try to persuade the majority to change their minds. But non-Quebeckers would surely not feel any such strong duty, nor would they be failing in not feeling it. They might appropriately feel some mild regret about the loss of a distinctive culture and the loss of some overall diversity in the world, but they would not feel strongly bound to prevent the assimilation, for example, by offering subsidies to Quebeckers who retain their French culture. When it is considered in itself and apart from the desires it gives rise to in members, the survival of a culture does not seem to be something that, according to commonsense nationalism, nonmembers have a strong reason to care about or pursue.

I have suggested that cultural survival, though an impersonal good in the sense that it is not reducible to the goods of individuals, is the object of highly partial attitudes. The same can be true of other impersonal goals associated with a culture. For example, nationalists can care that their cultures not only survive but also achieve the full flowering or self-expression that comes through sovereignty and independent statehood. In this case the importance of the impersonal good may be harder to see because there can also be personal goods at stake in sovereignty. Thus nationalists may believe that the individuals in their culture will engage in more valuable political activity or live under more culturally sensitive institutions if their government is entirely their own. But if it is possible to value the survival of one's culture apart from any benefits to individuals, it is surely possible to value sovereignty and statehood in the same way, and I think those active in independence movements do commonly have this impersonal desire. They value their nation's sovereignty, as they value their culture's survival, as something good partly in itself. Thus a central force in the Quebec sovereignty movement has been the desire that francophone Quebeckers affirm their status as *un peuple* by establishing their own nation-state. In fact, nationalists can have many impersonal goals that they value in a partial way: that their culture flourish in the arts and sciences, that it be economically vigorous, that it produce athletes who win medals at the Olympics. Beyond this, nationalists can have impersonal political goals that they value partially: that their nation occupy a large territory, that it be militarily powerful, that it dominate its neighbors and even dictate to the world.

In this list of impersonal goals, there is a large moral difference between the innocuous first goal, cultural survival, and the politically threatening ones that come later, such as military power and world domination. But this is nothing new in the study of nationalism, which is often described as Janus-faced, attractive in some forms and terrifying in others. And our responses to the list may be guided by the view, which many writers on this subject endorse, that any acceptable form of national partiality must be constrained by respect for the basic rights of all individuals, no less in other countries than in one's own. One may pursue one's own nation's good and do so in preference to other nations' good but only in ways that respect fundamental rights.[11] As it happens, the more acceptable impersonal goals, such as cultural survival, can usually be pursued successfully without violating anyone's rights, whereas it is hard to see territorial expansion or world domination achieved without violating rights. The different impersonal goals may differ morally not so much in themselves, therefore, as in the means likely to be necessary for their achievement.

I do not claim that every form of nationalism involves concern for impersonal goods; some nationalists may favor only the interests of their individual conationals. But it seems to me that the two forms of partiality often go together, and I will therefore define *full-blooded nationalism* as combining a greater concern for the impersonal goods of one's own culture, such as its survival and flourishing, with a greater concern for the interests of one's conationals. In a phrase I have used above, full-blooded nationalism involves partiality both toward one's nation, seen as having certain impersonal goods, and toward one's conationals. If this characterization is correct, it has an important implication for the morality of nationalism.

If full-blooded nationalism involves two components, a successful moral justification of it must address both. It must show the appropriateness of partiality toward one's conationals and also toward one's nation's impersonal good. Here the difficulties facing the two justifications seem interestingly different.

Consider, first, partiality toward one's conationals. There is no doubt that one ought morally to care about one's conationals; they are people, and one ought in general to care about people. The difficulty is to show why one should care more about these people than about others who are not members of one's nation, or why partiality toward this particular group is appropriate. In the situation where partiality seems most clearly justified, that of the family, it rests on a special relationship between people that is both rich and intense. The members of a family care deeply about each other, have lived together for many years, and have to a significant degree shaped each other's characters. Their interactions have been as close as people's typically ever are. But the relations among conationals are nothing like this. I have never met the vast majority of my fellow Canadians and do not know who they are; the causal links between our lives are tenuous at best. Especially worrisome is the fact that these links do not seem closer than my links with many non-Canadians—for example, with Americans living just across the Alberta-Montana border. In fact, with respect to closeness, the relations among conationals seem comparable to those among members of a race, who likewise mostly have not met. If the relations between conationals hold only to a limited degree, and not much more than between non-nationals, how can they justify any substantial degree of partiality?

The justification of the second form of partiality, toward one's nation's impersonal good, faces the opposite difficulty. Here there does not seem to be a large problem about justifying the attitude's partiality. Only one culture or nation in the world is mine; all the others are not mine. This is not just a small difference in degree but a large difference, perhaps a difference in kind. So if the justification of strong partiality requires a large difference in linkage or connectedness, we have that here. The problem, rather, is to show that impersonal goods are morally appropriate objects of any concern in the first place. What can be called "individualist" theories of the good deny this. Individualist theories hold that the only goods there are, and thus the only objects of rational concern, are personal goods, or the goods of individuals.[12] According to individualism, nationalists who value the survival or flourishing of their culture apart from any effects on individuals are being irrational and fetishistic. Their attitude is objectionable not because of its partiality but because of its object, which is not a genuine good because it is not a feature of individuals' lives. Nor is it only individualism in the strict sense that counts against the second form of partiality. A more moderate view allows that there can be impersonal goods and rational concern for them but insists that these goods are always relatively minor and the concern they call for always of less weight than the concern required for individuals. According to this moderate view, a partial attitude toward one's nation's impersonal good is allowed but not in a strength that often allows promoting that good at the expense of benefits to individuals.

To summarize: If there are two forms of national partiality, they need two justifications, and the difficulties facing these justifications are different. That one should care somehow about one's conationals is not in doubt; the question is whether it is right to care more about them than about non-nationals. As for a nation's impersonal good, if some concern for it is appropriate, it seems plausible that this is a highly partial concern. The difficult question here is whether that initial concern is appropriate: whether impersonal goods are worth caring about or whether the only, or only important, goods are those of individuals.

PARTIALITY AND HISTORY

Having suggested the importance to nationalism of impersonal goods, I will now set them aside and consider the more commonly recognized aspect of nationalism: partiality toward one's conationals. This partiality has many more specific manifestations. Nationalists typically care much more about relieving economic hardship within the nation than outside it; compare what nations spend on domestic welfare programs with what they spend on foreign aid. Nationalists also want immigration policy decided primarily by considering the effects on people already within the nation rather than on those who want to join. These various positions may receive some support from concern for impersonal goals like the nation's flourishing as a collective, but they are primarily directed at individuals. Setting aside the impersonal component of nationalism, therefore, I will consider the moral justification of partiality toward one's individual conationals. When partiality toward certain individuals is justified, it is because certain special relations hold between oneself and them. To what degree do these relations hold between members of a nation?

Because the arena in which partiality seems most clearly justified is the family, defenders of nationalism often try to assimilate the relations among conationals to those among family members. As we have seen, however, this assimilation is problematic; especially in the degree of interaction they involve, nations are not like large families. To many writers, therefore, it has seemed that the degree of national partiality that is justified is even in the most favorable circumstances much less than most nationalists desire.

In this section I will sketch a reply to this widespread skepticism about national partiality. This reply concedes that along one important dimension the relations between conationals have much less of the character that justifies partiality than do familial relations, but it claims that along another dimension, which most writers ignore, they have roughly as much.

First, however, I must state a presupposition of my argument: that the basis of partiality among conationals must be an objective rather than a subjective relation and, in particular, cannot be just the fact that conationals care more about each other than about non-nationals. It may be, as is sometimes argued, that certain subjective facts—that is, certain attitudes on the part of individuals—are necessary for a nation to exist. For example, it may be that individuals must view membership in a group as an important part of their identity before the group constitutes a nation. But questions about when a nation exists are different from questions about when its members should be partial toward each other, and the latter questions cannot turn on mere facts about caring. There are two decisive arguments for this conclusion.[13] One is that a purely subjective basis could not rule out the racial partiality that most of us find morally offensive. The fact that racists care more about people with their own skin color would by itself make it right for them to do so. The second argument is that a subjective basis cannot justify what nationalists typically affirm—namely, a duty to favor one's conationals that is binding even on those who do not now care about their conationals. I will assume, then, that the basis of national partiality must be some objective relation—that is, some relation that holds independently of people's attitudes. To determine which relation this is, we must look more closely at the objective side of personal or familial relations.

Consider my relation to my wife. If I love her specially, it is partly for certain qualities that she has. Some of these qualities I am attracted to without judging them to be intrinsically good, such as her appearance and the sound of her voice. Others I do judge to be good, such as her trustworthiness, her intelligence, and her concern for other people. Especially with these latter qualities it is important that my beliefs about them be true, that she, in fact, have the qualities, and that they truly be good. But even if all my relevant beliefs are true, my wife's having these qualities does not explain all my emotional attachment to her. If it did, I would abandon my wife the moment someone else came along with the same properties to a higher degree. Or if, just before dying, my wife had a clone of herself made to stay with me, I would think myself no worse off for the exchange. But of course I would not trade in my wife in this way. Though I love her partly for her qualities, I do not do so in a way that would accept substitution. I also love her, in the common phrase, "as an individual," or for herself.

What does it mean to love a person "as an individual"? In my view, it does not mean loving a person apart from any qualities at all but rather loving the person for qualities that no one else can share. More specifically, it involves loving the person for certain historical qualities, ones deriving from his or her participation with one in a shared history. Thus I love my wife not only as trustworthy, intelligent, and so on, but also as the person who nursed me through that illness, with whom I spent that wonderful first summer, and with whom I discovered that hotel on Kootenay Lake. These historical qualities focus my love on my wife as an individual, since no substitute, not even a clone, can be the very person who did those things with me.

A highly romantic view of love and friendship holds that once these historical qualities are established they entirely determine the relationship, which should therefore never end and always imposes duties of partiality. This is the view expressed in Shakespeare's line: "Love is not love / Which alters when it alteration finds." But I think most of us believe that historical qualities, though part of the basis for love and friendship, are, again, not the entire basis. If my wife changes radically, losing the general or shareable qualities I admire and taking on ones I find despicable, I will no longer feel attached to her or bound by duties of partial concern. My love, in other words, has a dual basis. My wife's role in a shared history with me explains why I love her more than other people with similar general qualities, but her general qualities matter, too. If those qualities changed enough, our history would not be a sufficient basis to maintain my love or to continue to demand partiality toward her.

We can see the same dual basis in nationalists' attachment to their nation and conationals. Nationalists are, first, attracted to their culture and the activities that define it, thinking them to a considerable degree good. They need not believe that their culture is superior in the sense of being the single best in the world. That chauvinist belief would not be credible and, in any case, would justify not universalist nationalism but the belief that everyone in the world should promote the one best culture. Instead, nationalists need only believe that their culture is one of perhaps many in the world that are good. What attaches them specially to this culture and its members are historical facts: that this is the culture *they* grew up in, that their conationals share *with them* a history of being shaped by, participating in, and sustaining this culture. The favorable evaluation of their conationals' cultural activities is a necessary basis for this nationalist attachment, but it is not sufficient. There is also, and distinguishing their conationals from other people whose culture is equally good, the crucial fact of a shared cultural history.

This dual basis can lead to conflicts about national attachment. As Yael Tamir writes, "Citizens of a state involved in an unjust war may be torn between the feeling that they have an associative obligation to serve in the army together with their enlisted fellows, and their commitment to a moral code dictating they should refuse."[14] In the situation Tamir describes, the citizens' state is not now good; it has at least some general qualities that are evil. But the citizens are still historically connected to this state as the one they grew up under. How they resolve this conflict depends on which of the two bases of national attachment they find more important, which in many particular cases will depend on how evil their state currently is. If it is not irredeemably evil, the citizens may continue to feel special duties toward it and work harder to reform it than to reform other equally evil states elsewhere. But if their state degenerates too far, their historical connection to it may be outweighed and their feelings of national attachment, like love for an individual whose character has changed utterly, may end.

If national attachment rests partly on the belief that one's culture is good, it is important that that belief be true, which requires the culture to be, in fact, good. This is one point where evaluative considerations bear on the justification of national partiality, but there is another point as well. Considerations about good and evil also help determine when a shared history is of the right kind to justify partial concern and, when it is, what degree of partiality is justified.

Consider again a personal relationship like that between spouses. Here the shared history is predominantly one of mutual benefit or beneficence; two people have helped each other through difficult times and also shared good times, giving and taking pleasure in each other's company. And I think a history of reciprocal benefit or, alternatively, one where people have jointly benefited others, such as the students in a school where these people taught, can be a legitimate basis of partiality. The same is true of a history of shared suffering; people who lived in the same barracks in a Nazi labor camp and suffered the same evils there can appropriately feel on the basis of their shared history some greater concern for each other's well-being. But I do not think a shared history justifies partiality when it is a history of doing evil, as for former members of an SS unit that ran and terrorized a labor camp. Many of us find something obscene in the idea of nostalgic reunions, even at this late date, of former SS colleagues, and there is a similar obscenity in the idea of partiality toward former SS colleagues. If an SS veteran receives a letter from one of his former colleagues claiming financial hardship and requesting a loan of $1,000, should he feel a special duty to honor the request or to help his former colleague before helping others who are equally in need? It seems to me that he should not, even if his former colleague is now morally reformed. If anything, given the evil of the history they share, he should feel a duty not to associate with his former colleague and should contribute first to others who did not participate in that aspect of his past. Whereas a shared history of doing good or suffering evil can justify duties of partiality, a shared history of doing evil cannot.

These points suggest a general account of the basis of duties of partiality. Some activities and states of people, most notably their doing good or suffering evil, call for a positive, caring, or associative response. Others, such as their doing evil, call for a negative or dissociative response. Partiality between people is appropriate when they have shared in the past in the first kind of activity or state. For example, if two people have a shared history of doing good, either reciprocally or to others, partiality between them in the present is a way of honoring that good fact about their past. (This is why partiality among former SS colleagues is troubling; it seems to honor a past that properly calls for dishonor.) One should, in general, care more about people who have shared with one in activities and states that call for a caring response. This account does not claim to justify partiality of concern as a general moral phenomenon; on the contrary, it assumes it. It assumes that one has a special duty to honor past doings of good or sufferings of evil *that involved oneself.* But it does give particular duties of partiality a more abstract basis. In the many realms where partiality is appropriate—the family, private clubs, perhaps the nation—it is an appropriate response to a history that joins oneself and other people in activities or states that are good or that call for association.

This general account can explain our attitudes to racial partiality. As McMahan notes,[15] while we condemn racial discrimination by members of a dominant racial group, we often think it appropriate for minority races to celebrate their distinctness and even to implement discriminatory policies that benefit their members at the expense of others. In current conditions, black and aboriginal solidarity movements have a different moral status than white supremacy movements. The explanation, I would argue, is that minority racial groups have a shared history of the kind that makes partiality morally appropriate—namely, a shared history of suffering evil because of one's racial membership. But the history of dominant racial groups, which is largely one of oppressing the minority, is not of the kind that justifies partiality. Among members of the minority, there is a shared history that morally warrants partiality toward other members; among members of the majority, there is one that positively precludes it.

More important, the account suggests a defense of national partiality against the skeptical argument mentioned above. If certain people have a shared history of doing good, what determines the degree of partiality that is justified between them? Two factors suggest themselves: the degree to which the people's history is shared or involves interaction between them, and the amount of good their interaction produced. Other things being equal, people whose history involves closer relations or more intimate contact have stronger duties of partiality. Also, other things being equal, people whose interactions produced more good, for themselves or for others, have stronger duties of partiality.

The history of family members scores extremely high on the first of these dimensions—namely, closeness of contact. Family members interact intimately on a daily basis, with large effects on each other's lives. Family history also scores high on the dimension of good done, given the large benefits given by parents to their children, spouses to each other, and even children to their parents. Surely family members benefit each other as much as they do any individuals.

A nation's history, by contrast, scores very low on the first dimension. As I have said, I have not met the majority of my fellow Canadians and do not know who they are. But a nation's history does much better on the second dimension. Consider another example from my history. In the 1960s, Canadians created a national health care system that continues to provide high-quality medical care to all citizens regardless of their ability to pay. The benefit this medicare system provides any one citizen is probably less than that provided by his or her family, but it is still substantial, and it is one Canadians have provided together. Canadians derive equally substantial benefits from many other aspects of their political activity. When these benefits are added together, they constitute a significant counterweight to the weakness of national relations on the first dimension, that of closeness of contact. The critique of national partiality considers only this first dimension, of closeness. But if we believe that a necessary basis for justified partiality is a shared history, that this history must be good rather than evil, and that the degree of partiality a history justifies depends partly on the quantity of goodness it produces or embodies, we have some response to the critique. On the one dimension, a national history does indeed have much less of the character that justifies partiality than a family history. But on another dimension, the national history has roughly as much.

This account of the basis of national partiality fits most obviously those many nationalisms that point to glorious deeds in the nation's past, such as saving Europe for Christendom or inventing representative democracy. But the account should not be too closely tied to these nationalisms, for two reasons. First, if the basis of national partiality is objective rather than subjective, it must depend on the nation's actual history rather than on beliefs about that history that are all too often false. A national mythology with no basis in fact cannot justify nationalist policies today.[16] Second, the benefits produced in a nation's history need not be specially grand; on the contrary, they can be perfectly ordinary. Consider again familial partiality. The benefits my wife and I have given each other, such as companionship and love, are also given to each other by countless other couples. What ties my wife and me specially together is not that we have produced unique goods but that we have produced familiar goods jointly, in interactions with each other. The goods in a nation's history can likewise be familiar. Before enacting medicare, Canadians together maintained political institutions and through them the rule of law in Canada, which ensured liberty and security for all Canadian citizens. The same liberty and security were produced in other nations, but only my fellow Canadians produced them with me, and it is that historical fact that is decisive. According to the account I am proposing, it is important that a nation's history have produced significant benefits, but these benefits need not be the grand ones of national mythologies or even at all different from those produced in other nations' histories.

Nations as defined by political institutions[17] are not the only large groups that can have this kind of history. Consider a linguistic and cultural group. Its members have together sustained a language and through it the possibility of beneficial communication for all its speakers. Other groups have also sustained languages, but this group has done it here. They have also, as writers and readers, sustained a literature and an artistic tradition that provide further benefits. When political and cultural groups coincide, these two grounds of partiality reinforce each other. The nation's members have two separate reasons for being partial to the same individuals. But when political and cultural boundaries do not coincide, there can be conflicts about partiality. Consider franco-phone Quebeckers. They share a political history with all Canadians and a cultural history with a smaller number of francophone Canadians. Which group they feel more partial to will depend on how good they think the groups' present qualities are and how beneficial they think the groups' histories have been. Those who think of Canada as a successful country with an admirable political history will be strongly attached to the larger group; those who see present failure and a past of suppressing minorities will not.

Whether a nation is defined politically or culturally, its history differs from a family's in involving many more people, both as recipients of its benefits and as participants in producing them. If only the first of these differences, in the number of beneficiaries, mattered morally, the nation's history would score much higher on the dimension of good done than the family's, since its benefits are much more widely dispersed. The total good resulting from Canadian medicare, for example, is vastly greater than any produced in a family. But it is more plausible to count both differences about numbers, so that what matters for this dimension is not the total benefit produced in a history but something closer to the average benefit per participant, which in the national case roughly equals the average benefit per recipient.[18] Even when we take this view, however, the good produced in a national history is comparable to that in a family history. If we consider the benefits each Canadian receives from living under the rule of law and with social programs such as medicare, they are surely of similar size to those that person receives from his or her family. If this is so, a national history scores roughly as well on the dimension of good done as a family history. Since the national history scores less well on the dimension of interaction, the result on balance is that less partiality is justified toward one's conationals than toward one's family members. This is an intuitively plausible result. Not even the most ardent nationalist claims that one should care as much about one's conationals, as conationals, as about one's spouse or child. And the degree of concern that is justified toward conationals is considerably greater than toward non-nationals, since one's history with the latter scores very poorly on both dimensions. One not only has had no close interactions with non-nationals but also has produced no significant goods with them. The political and cultural institutions of a nation enable its members to cooperate, however indirectly, in producing significant benefits. But there are no comparable institutions joining non-nationals, even ones living just across a national border, and therefore no comparable goods they can be said jointly to have produced.

I wish I could say more precisely what degree of national partiality this historical account justifies. Unfortunately, that would require weighing against each other more precisely the two dimensions of closeness of contact and good done in a history, which I cannot now do. Nor do I see that more precise weightings of these dimensions follow from the general ideas I have advanced. So I will content myself with two more modest conclusions. The first is that, whatever degree of national partiality is intrinsically justified, it is more than the limited degree that the comparison with families initially suggested. Though a national history scores less well on one dimension than a family history, it scores comparably well on another and therefore justifies at least a moderate degree of partiality. It may be that any morally acceptable national partiality must be constrained by respect for the basic rights of all persons, both within one's nation and outside it. But familial partiality is likewise constrained by respect for rights, and it still has considerable room to express itself. The second conclusion is that it is no surprise that nations and cultures are prime objects of partial attitudes. According to the historical account, partiality is justified when the members of a group have worked together in the past to produce significant benefits. But nations and cultures embody just the institutions that make such beneficial interactions possible. My nation is an appropriate object of partial attitudes because it more than other similarly sized groups has allowed me to act with others to produce significant human goods.

NOTES

An earlier version of this essay was presented as a commentary on Jeff McMahan's "The Limits of National Partiality" at the Conference on the Ethics of Nationalism, University of Illinois at Urbana-Champaign, April 1994. Many of its ideas were stimulated by McMahan's fine essay; I am also grateful to him and to Robert McKim for helpful comments. [Jeff McMahan, "The Limits of National Partiality" in *The Morality of Nationalism*, ed. Robert McKim and Jeff McMahan (Oxford University Press 1997), 107–38.]

1. David Miller, "The Ethical Significance of Nationality," *Ethics* 98 (1988): 649–50 [reprinted in *Global Justice: Seminal Essays*, 235–53, 237–38]. The same view is defended in his *On Nationality* (Oxford: Clarendon Press, 1995).

2. See my *Perfectionism* (New York: Oxford University Press, 1993).

3. This argument is suggested in Michael Sandel, "The Procedural Republic and the Unencumbered Self," *Political Theory* 12 (1984): 81–96; and Yael Tamir, *Liberal Nationalism* (Princeton: Princeton University Press, 1993), chap. 1.

4. As an analogy, consider a different version of perfectionism defended by Rousseau, Humboldt, and Mill. They hold that the nature whose realization constitutes a person's good is not one shared with all other humans or even one shared with all members of one's culture but rather a nature distinctive of that person as an individual. Each person has a unique individual identity, by realizing which the person achieves "individuality." But do these writers say that each person ought to care only or even more about his or her own achievement of individuality than about other people's? They do not. They say that each person ought to care impartially about the achievement of individuality by all and to support those institutions, especially liberal institutions, that will permit individuality for all. But if this individualist perfectionism is compatible with full impartiality, surely cultural perfectionism is as well.

5. Could the cultural perfectionist claim that the demand for partiality is not just one component of every cultural identity but an essential component, so that if I do not care more about my conationals I do not realize my cultural identity to any degree at all? This claim surely is, as a claim about identities, utterly implausible. And even if it is accepted, it still does not show why, at a foundational level, I should care more about the realization to some rather than no degree of my nation's identity than of others'.

6. Alasdair MacIntyre, *Is Patriotism a Virtue?*, Lindley Lecture (Lawrence: University of Kansas, 1984), pp. 9, 12 [reprinted herein 119–38, 126, 129]. A weaker version of metaethical particularism is defended by Michael Walzer in *Spheres of Justice* (New York: Basic Books, 1983), chaps. 1–2 [chap. 2 of Walzer's book is based on his essay "The Distribution of Membership," first published in *Boundaries: National Autonomy and Its Limits*, ed. Peter G. Brown and Henry Shue (Totowa: Rowman & Littlefield, 1981), 1–35, reprinted in *Global Justice: Seminal Essays* 145–77], and *Interpretation and Social Criticism* (Cambridge, MA: Harvard University Press, 1987).

7. Charles Taylor, *Multiculturalism and "The Politics of Recognition,"* ed. Amy Gutmann (Princeton: Princeton University Press, 1992), p. 58.

8. See McMahan, "The Limits of National Partiality."

9. The importance of goods that are impersonal in this sense for the morality of war is brought out in Jeff McMahan and Robert McKim, "The Just War and the Gulf War," *Canadian Journal of Philosophy* 23 (1993): 522. Note that what Derek Parfit calls an "impersonal," as against a "person-affecting," principle of beneficence does not involve reference to impersonal goods in my sense (see

his *Reasons and Persons* [Oxford: Clarendon, 1984], pp. 386–87). Parfit's "impersonal" view holds that the best outcome is the one in which the best lives are lived, even though the people living those lives may be numerically different from the people in alternative outcomes. (Numerical nonidentity is especially likely when the outcomes involve large-scale and long-lasting changes, as the survival and disappearance of a culture do.) But Parfit's "impersonal" view still holds, with other versions of beneficence, that the relevant goods in the different outcomes are all states of individual persons. It is this latter claim that the affirmation of what I call impersonal goods denies. This affirmation rejects not only person-affecting beneficence but also the individualism about value still present in Parfit's "impersonal" view.

10. If the impersonal view accepts metaphysical reductionism, it embodies G. E. Moore's principle of "organic unities," according to which the value of a whole need not equal the sum of the values its parts would have if they existed alone. See Moore, *Principia Ethica* (Cambridge: Cambridge University Press, 1903), chap. 6.

11. See, for example, McMahan, "The Limits of National Partiality."

12. Individualism is affirmed in Avishai Margalit and Joseph Raz, "National Self-Determination," *Journal of Philosophy* 87 (1990): 439–61 [reprinted herein 181–206]; and Tamir, *Liberal Nationalism*, pp. 83–84. Interestingly, Margalit and Raz allow that the interest of a group is not reducible to the interests of its members (p. 450 [herein 192f]) but insist that only individual interests are relevant to the justification of national rights.

13. See McMahan, "The Limits of National Partiality."

14. Tamir, *Liberal Nationalism*, p. 102.

15. See McMahan, "The Limits of National Partiality."

16. It is also relevant that these beliefs usually concern the distant past, which in my view counts less in justifying partiality than does the recent past. Immediately after World War II, national partiality on the part of Germans would have been morally unthinkable because of the evil their nation had just done. It is much less so today, after fifty years of the Federal Republic.

17. Those of us who live in multicultural states, especially ones like Canada where two cultures are geographically separated, are much more likely than others to define "nation" in political rather than in ethnic or cultural terms. If we did not, we would be barred by language from any pan-Canadian "nationalism." The Canadian understanding of "nation" is nicely illustrated by an incident from the 1968 federal election campaign. The Progressive Conservatives, seeking to reverse decades of electoral failure in Quebec, announced a *deux nations* policy, according to which Canada was composed of French-speaking and English-speaking *nations*. Pierre Trudeau, recently elected leader of the Liberal Party, said he rejected this "two nations" policy. He did not favor the separation of Quebec but wanted Canada to remain one nation. Though Trudeau's reply benefited him electorally in English Canada, it was widely

regarded as linguistically mischievous. The English word "nation," it was said, is not equivalent to the French *nation*. While the French word has a primarily cultural significance, the English word is political. The correct translation of *deux nations* is therefore "two [founding] peoples," which does not carry, as "two nations" does, any implication of separate political institutions.

18. I owe this point to Jeff McMahan. Note that treating both differences as significant plausibly implies that members of small nations have just as strong duties of partiality as members of large nations. If only the number of recipients were significant, citizens of the United States would have a duty of partiality ten times as strong as that of Canadians because their history has benefited ten times as many people.

18. CHARLES TAYLOR

Taylor suggests that a genuine, unforced worldwide consensus on human rights would have to be something like what John Rawls calls an "overlapping consensus": an agreement on certain norms that persists despite disagreement about what justifies those norms. He argues that such norms should also be distinguished from the legal forms that give them force, which could also vary from society to society. He then looks at four cases in which there appear to be serious conflicts between current human rights language and major contemporary cultures, and seeks ways of resolving these conflicts in each case.

Conditions of an Unforced Consensus on Human Rights

First published in The East Asian Challenge for Human Rights, *ed. Joanne R. Bauer and Daniel A. Bell (Cambridge: Cambridge University Press, 1999), 124–44. © Carnegie Council on Ethics and International Affairs 1999. Reprinted with the permission of Cambridge University Press.*

INTRODUCTION

What would it mean to come to a genuine, unforced international consensus on human rights? I suppose it would be something like what Rawls describes in his *Political Liberalism* as an "overlapping consensus."[1] That is, different groups, countries, religious communities, and civilizations, although holding incompatible fundamental views on theology, metaphysics, human nature, and so on, would come to an agreement on certain norms that ought to govern human behavior. Each would have its own way of justifying this from out of its profound background conception. We would agree on the norms while disagreeing on why they were the right norms, and we would be content to live in this consensus, undisturbed by the differences of profound underlying belief.

The idea was already expressed in 1949 by Jacques Maritain: "I am quite certain that my way of justifying belief in the rights of man and the ideal of liberty, equality, fraternity is the only way with a firm foundation in truth. This does not prevent me from being in agreement on these practical convictions with people who are certain that their way of justifying them, entirely different from mine or opposed to mine,... is equally the only way founded upon truth."[2]

Is this kind of consensus possible? Perhaps because of my optimistic nature, I believe that it is. But we have to confess at the outset that it is not entirely clear around what the consensus would form, and we are only beginning to discern the obstacles we would have to overcome on the way there. I want to talk a little about both these issues here.

First, what would the consensus be on? One might have thought this was obvious: on human rights. That's what our original question was about, but there is an immediate obstacle that has often been pointed out. Rights talk is something that has roots in Western culture. Certain features of this talk have roots in Western history, and there only. This is not to say that something very like the underlying norms expressed in schedules of rights don't turn up elsewhere, but they are not expressed in this language. We can't assume without further examination that a future unforced world consensus could be formulated to the satisfaction of everyone in the language of rights. Maybe yes, maybe no. Or maybe partially yes, partially no, as we come to distinguish among the things that have been associated in the Western package.

This is not to say that we already have some adequate term for whatever universals we think we may discern between different cultures. Jack Donnelly speaks of "human dignity" as a universal value.[3] Onuma Yasuaki criticizes this term, pointing out that "dignity" has itself been a favorite term in the Western philosophical stream that has elaborated human rights. He prefers to speak of the "pursuit of spiritual and material well-being" as the universal.[4] Where "dignity" might be too precise and culture-bound a term, "well-being" might be too vague and general. Perhaps we are incapable at this stage of formulating the universal values in play here. Perhaps we shall always be incapable of this. This wouldn't matter, because what we need to formulate for an overlapping consensus are certain norms of conduct. There does seem to be some basis for hoping that we can achieve at least some agreement on these norms. One can presumably find in all cultures condemnations of genocide, murder, torture, and slavery, as well as of, say, "disappearances" and the shooting of innocent demonstrators.[5] The deep underlying values supporting these common conclusions will, in the nature of the case, belong to the alternative, mutually incompatible justifications.

I have been distinguishing between norms of conduct and their underlying justification. The Western rights tradition in fact exists at both of these levels. On one plane, it is a legal tradition, legitimating certain kinds of legal actions and empowering certain kinds of people to make them. We could, and people sometimes do, consider this legal culture as the proper candidate for universalization, arguing that its adoption can be justified in more than one way. Then a legal culture entrenching rights would define the norms around which world consensus would supposedly crystallize.

Some people already have trouble with this, such as Lee Kwan Yew and those in East Asia who sympathize with him. They see something dangerously individualistic, fragmenting, dissolvent of community in this Western legal culture. (Of course, they have particularly in mind—or in their sights—the United States.)[6] In their criticism of Western procedures, they also seem to be attacking the underlying philosophy, which allegedly gives primacy to the individual, whereas supposedly a "Confucian" outlook would have a larger place for the community and the complex web of human relations in which each person stands.

The Western rights tradition also contains certain views on human nature, society, and the human good and carries some elements of an underlying justification. It might help the discussion to distinguish these two levels, at least analytically, so that we can develop a more fine-grained picture of what our options are. Perhaps in fact, the legal culture could "travel" better if it could be separated from some of its underlying justifications. Or perhaps the reverse is true, that the underlying picture of human life might look less frightening if it could find expression in a different legal culture. Or maybe neither of these simple solutions will work (this is my hunch), but modifications need to be made to both; however, distinguishing the levels still helps, because the modifications are different on each level.

In any case, a good place to start the discussion would be to give a rapid portrait of the language of rights that has developed in the West and of the surrounding notions of human agency and the good. We could then proceed to identify certain centers of disagreement across cultures, and we might then see what if anything could be done to bridge these differences.

THE LANGUAGE OF RIGHTS

Many societies have held that it is good to ensure certain immunities or liberties to their members—or sometimes even to outsiders (think of the stringent laws of hospitality that hold in many traditional cultures). Everywhere it is wrong to take human life, at least under certain circumstances and for certain categories of persons. Wrong is the opposite of right, so this is relevant to our discussion.

A quite different sense of the word is invoked when we start to use the definite or indefinite articles, or to put it in the plural, and speak of "a right" or "rights," or when we start to attribute these to persons, and speak of "your rights" or "my rights." This is to introduce what has been called "subjective rights." Instead of saying that it is wrong to kill me, we begin to say that I have a right to life. The two formulations are not equivalent in all respects, because in the latter case the immunity or liberty is considered as it were the property of someone. It is no longer just an element of the law that stands over and between all of us equally. That I have a right to life says more than that you shouldn't kill me. It gives me some control over this immunity. A right is something that in principle I can waive.[7] It is also something I have a role in enforcing.

Some element of subjective right exists in all legal systems. The peculiarity of the West is that, first, the concept played a bigger role in European medieval societies than elsewhere in history, and, second, it was the basis of the rewriting of Natural Law theory that marked the seventeenth century. The older notion that human society stands under a Law of Nature, whose origin is the Creator, and that is thus beyond human will, became transposed. The fundamental law was reconceived as consisting of natural rights, attributed to individuals prior to society. At the origin of society stands a Contract, which takes people out of a State of Nature and puts them under political authority, as a result of an act of consent on their part.

Subjective rights are not only crucial to the Western tradition; even more significant is the fact that they were projected onto Nature and formed the basis of a philosophical view of humans and their society, one that greatly privileges individuals' freedom and their right to consent to the arrangements under which they live. This view has become an important strand in Western democratic theory of the last three centuries.

The notion of (subjective) rights both serves to define certain legal powers and also provides the master image for a philosophy of human nature, of individuals and their societies. It operates both as legal norm and as underlying justification. Moreover, these two levels are not unconnected. The force of the underlying philosophy has brought about a steady promotion of the legal norm in our politicolegal systems so that it now occupies pride of place in a number of contemporary polities. Charters of rights are now entrenched in the constitutions of a number of countries, and also of the European Union. These are the bases of judicial review, whereby the ordinary legislation of different levels of government can be invalidated on the grounds of conflict with these fundamental rights.

The modern Western discourse of rights involves, on one hand, a set of legal forms by which immunities and liberties are inscribed as rights, with certain consequences for the possibility of waiver and for the ways in which they can be secured—whether these immunities and liberties are among those from time to time granted by duly constituted authority or among those that are entrenched in fundamental law. On the other hand, it involves a philosophy of the person and of society, attributing great importance to the individual and making significant matters turn on his or her power of consent. In both these regards, it contrasts with many other cultures, including the premodern West, not because some of the same protections and immunities were not present, but because they had a quite different basis.[8]

When people protest against the Western rights model, they seem to have this whole package in their sights. We can therefore see how resistance to the Western discourse of rights might occur on more than one level. Some governments might resist the enforcement of even widely accepted norms because they have an agenda that involves their violation (for example, the contemporary Peoples Republic of China). Others, however, are certainly ready, even eager to espouse some universal norms, but they are made uneasy by the underlying philosophy of the human person in society. This seems to give pride of place to autonomous individuals, determined to demand their rights, even (indeed especially) in the face of widespread social consensus. How does this fit with the Confucian emphasis on close personal relationships, not only as highly valued in themselves, but as a model for the wider society? (See Joseph Chan, "A Confucian Perspective on Human Rights for Contemporary China" in *The East Asian Challenge for Human Rights*, ed. Joanne R. Bauer and Daniel A. Bell (Cambridge: Cambridge University Press 1999), 212–37.) Can people who imbibe the full Western human rights ethos, which reaches its highest expression in the lone courageous individual fighting against all the forces of social conformity for her rights, ever be good members of a "Confucian" society? How does this ethic of demanding what is due to us fit with the Theravada Buddhist search for selflessness, for self-giving and *dana* (generosity)?[9]

Taking the rights package as a whole is not necessarily wrong, because the philosophy is plainly part of what has motivated the great promotion enjoyed by this legal form. But the kinds of misgivings expressed in the previous paragraph, which cannot be easily dismissed, show the potential advantages of distinguishing the elements and loosening the connection between a legal culture of rights enforcement and the philosophical conceptions of human life that originally nourished it.

It might help to structure our thinking if we made a tripartite distinction. What we are looking for, in the end, is a world consensus on certain norms of conduct enforceable on governments. To be accepted in any given society, these would in each case have to repose on some widely acknowledged philosophical justification, and to be enforced, they would have to find expression in legal mechanisms. One way of putting our central question might be this: What variations can we imagine in philosophical justifications or in legal forms that would still be compatible with a meaningful universal consensus on what really matters to us, the enforceable norms?

Following this line of thinking, it might help to understand better just what exactly we might want to converge on in the world society of the future, as well as to measure our chances of getting there, if we imagine variations separately on the two levels. What I propose to do is look at a number of instances in which there seem to be obvious conflicts between the present language of human rights and one or more major contemporary cultures. The goal will be to try to imagine ways in which the conflict might be resolved and the essential norms involved in the human rights claim preserved, and this through some modification either of legal forms or of philosophy.

ALTERNATIVE LEGAL FORMS

I would like to look at four kinds of conflict. The first could be resolved by legal innovation, and I will briefly discuss this possibility, but it can best be tackled on the philosophical level. The other three involve the basic justification of human rights claims. In developing these, I will have to spell out much further the justificatory basis for Western thinking and practice about rights than I have in my rather sparse remarks about Natural Rights theory. I shall return to this later.

Let us take the kind of objection that I mentioned at the outset, that someone like Lee Kwan Yew might raise about Western rights practice and its alleged unsuitability for other societies, in particular East Asian ones. The basic notion is that this practice, obviously nourished by the underlying philosophy I described in the previous section, supposes that individuals are the possessors of rights and encourages them to act, to go out and aggressively seek to make good their rights. But this has a number of bad consequences. First of all, it focuses people on their rights, on what they can claim from society and others, rather than on their responsibilities, what they owe to the whole community or to its members. It encourages people to be self-regarding and leads to an atrophied sense of belonging. This in turn leads to a higher degree of social conflict, more and more many-sided, tending ultimately to a war of all against all. Social solidarity weakens, and the threat of violence increases.

This scenario seems rather overdrawn to some. However, it seems to have elements of truth to others, including to people within Western societies, which perhaps might make us doubt that we are on to a difference *between* civilizations here. In fact, there is a long tradition in the West warning against pure rights talk outside a context in which the political community has a strong positive value. This "communitarian" theorizing has taken on a new urgency today because of the experience of conflict and alienation and the fraying of solidarity in many Western democracies, notably but not only the United States. Does this mean that Lee Kwan Yew's formula might offer a solution to present-day America?

The absurdity of this suggestion brings us back to the genuine differences of culture that exist today. But if we follow through on the logic of the "communitarian" critique in the West, we can perhaps find a framework in which to consider these differences.

One of the key points in the critique of a too exclusive focus on rights is that this neglects the crucial importance of political trust. Dictatorships, as Tocqueville pointed out, try to destroy trust between citizens,[10] but free societies vitally depend on it. The price of freedom is a strong common commitment to the political formula that binds us, because without the commitment the formula would have to be aggressively enforced and this threatens freedom. What will very quickly dissolve the commitment for each and every one of us is the sense that others no longer share it or are willing to act on it. The common allegiance is nourished on trust.

This goes for a political regime centered on the retrieval of rights as much as for any other. The condition of our being able to go out and seek to enforce our own rights is that the system within which this is carried out retains the respect and allegiance of everybody. Once rights retrieval begins to eat into this, once it begins to create a sense of embattled grievance pitting group against group, undermining the sense of common allegiance and solidarity, the whole system of freewheeling rights enforcement is in danger.

The issue is not "individualism" as such. There are many forms of this, and some have grown up together with modern, democratic forms of political society. The danger is in any form of either individualism or group identity that undercuts or undermines the trust that we share a common allegiance as citizens of this polity.

I don't want to pursue here the conditions of political trust in Western democracies, at least not for its own sake,[11] but I want to use this requirement as a heuristic tool, in search of a point of consensus on human rights. One way of considering a claim, similar to that of Lee Kwan Yew's, that the Western rights focus does not fit a certain cultural tradition would be to ask how certain fundamental liberties and immunities could be guaranteed in the society in question, consistent with the maintenance of political trust. This means, of course, that one will not consider satisfactory any solution that does not preserve these liberties and immunities while accepting whatever modifications in legal form one needs to generate a sense of common acceptance of the guaranteeing process in the society concerned.

In the concrete case of Lee Kwan Yew's Singapore, this would mean that his claim in its present form is hardly receivable. There is too much evidence of the stifling of dissent and of the cramping (to say the least) of the democratic political process in Singapore. However, this kind of claim should lead us to reflect further on how immunities of the kinds we seek in human rights declarations can best be preserved in "Confucian" societies.

Turning back to Western societies, we note that judges and the judicial process enjoy in general a great deal of prestige and respect.[12] In some countries, this respect is based on a long tradition in which some notion of fundamental law played an important part, and hence in which its guardians had a special place. Is there a way of connecting rights retrieval in other societies to offices and institutions that enjoy the highest moral prestige there?

Adverting to another tradition, we note that in Thailand at certain crucial junctures the immense moral prestige of the monarchy has been used to confer legitimacy on moves to end military violence and repression and return to constitutional rule. This was the case following the student demonstrations in October 1973, and again in the wake of the popular reactions against the seizure of power by General Suchinda Kraprayoon in May 1992. In both cases, a military junta responded with violence, only to find its position unsustainable and to be forced to give way to a civilian regime and renewed elections. In both these cases, King Bhumibhol played a critical role.[13] The king was able to play this role because of elements in the traditions that have contributed to the Thai conception of monarchy, some of which go way back. For example, the conception of the king as *dharmaraja*, in the tradition of Ashoka,[14] sees the ruler as charged with establishing dharma in the world.

It was perhaps crucial to the upheavals of 1973 and 1992 that a king with this kind of status played the part he did. The trouble is that the power of the royal office can also be used in the other direction, as happened in 1976 when right-wing groups used the slogan "Nation, King and Religion" as a rallying cry in order to attack democratic and radical leaders. The movement of reaction culminated in the October 1976 coup, which relegated the democratic constitution once again to the wastebasket.[15]

The issue arising from all this is the following: Can the immense power to create trust and consensus that resides in the Thai monarchy be in some way stabilized, regularized, and channeled in support of constitutional rule and the defense of certain human rights, such as those concerned with the security of the person? In Weberian terms, could the charisma here be "routinized" enough to impart a stable direction to it without being lost altogether? If a way could be found to draw on this royal charisma, together with the legitimacy enjoyed by certain individuals of proven "merit" who are invested with moral authority as in the Thai tradition, to enhance support for a democratic order respectful of those immunities and liberties we generally describe as human rights, the fact that it might deviate from the standard Western model of judicial review initiated by individuals should be accorded less importance than the fact that it protects human beings from violence and oppression. We would have in fact achieved convergence on the substance of human rights, in spite of differences in form.

ALTERNATIVE FOUNDATIONS

Suppose we take the "communitarian" arguments against Western rights discourse emanating from other societies at another level, not questioning so much the legal forms but expressing disagreement with the underlying philosophical justification. My example is again drawn from Thailand. This society has seen in the last century a number of attempts to formulate reformed interpretations of the majority religion, Theravada Buddhism. Some of these have sought a basis in this form of Buddhism for democracy and human rights. This raises a somewhat broader issue than the one I'm focusing on because it concerns an alternative foundation for both democracy and human rights. The job of attaining a consensus on human rights in today's world will probably be simplified, however, if we don't try—at least at first—to come to agreement about forms of government, but concentrate solely on human rights standards. I believe that the developments in Thai thinking described here illustrate what is involved in coming to an "overlapping consensus" on the narrower basis as well.

One main stream of reform consists of movements that (as they see it) attempt to purify Buddhism, to turn it away from a focus on ritual, on gaining merit and even worldly success through blessings and acts of piety, and to focus more on (what they see as) the original goal of Enlightenment. The late Phutthathat (Buddhadasa) has been a major figure in this regard. This stream tries to return to what (it sees as) the original core of Buddhist teaching, about the unavoidability of suffering, the illusion of the self, and the goal of Nibbana. It attacks the "superstition" of those who seek potent amulets, the blessings of monks, and the like; it wants to separate the search for enlightenment from the seeking of merit through ritual; and it is very critical of the whole metaphysical structure of belief that has developed in mainstream Buddhism about heavens, hell, gods, and demons, which plays a large part in popular belief. It has been described by the Sri Lankan anthropologist Gananath Obeyesekere as a "protestant Buddhism."[16]

This stream seems to be producing new reflections on Buddhism as a basis for democratic society and human rights. Sulak Sivaraksa and Saneh Chamarik are among the leading figures whose writings reflect this. They and others in their milieu are highly active in social justice advocacy. They are concerned with alternative models of development, which would be more ecologically sound, concerned to put limits to growth, critical of "consumerism," and conducive to social equality. The Buddhist commitment lies behind all these goals. As Sulak explains it, the Buddhist commitment to nonviolence entails a nonpredatory stance toward the environment and calls also for the limitation of greed, one of the sources of anger and conflict.[17]

We can see here an agenda of universal well-being, but what specifically pushes to democracy, to ensuring that people take charge of their own lives rather than simply being the beneficiaries of benevolent rule? Two things seem to come together in this outlook to underpin a strong democratic commitment. The first is the notion, central to Buddhism, that ultimately each individual must take responsibility for his or her own Enlightenment. The second is a new application of the doctrine of nonviolence, which is now seen to call for a respect for the autonomy of each person, demanding in effect a minimal use of coercion in human affairs. This carries us far from the politics of imposed order, decreed by the wise minority, which has long been the traditional background to various forms and phases of nondemocratic rule. It is also evident that this underpinning for democracy offers a strong support for human rights legislation, and that, indeed, is how it is understood by thinkers like Sulak.[18]

There is an outlook here that converges on a policy of defense of human rights and democratic development but that is rather different from the standard Western justifications of these. It isn't grounded on a doctrine of the dignity of human beings as something commanding respect. The injunction to respect comes rather as a consequence of the fundamental value of nonviolence, which also generates a whole host of other consequences (including the requirement for an ecologically responsible development and the need to set limits to growth). Human rights don't stand out, as they often do in the West, as a claim on their own, independent from the rest of our moral commitments, even sometimes in potential conflict with them.

This Buddhist conception provides an alternative way of linking together the agenda of human rights and that of democratic development. Whereas in the Western framework, these go together because they are both seen as corequirements of human dignity, and indeed, as two facets of liberty, a connection of a somewhat different kind is visible among Thai Buddhists of this reform persuasion. Their commitment to people-centered and ecologically sensitive development makes them strong allies of those communities of villagers who are resisting encroachment by the state and big business, fighting to defend their lands and forests. This means that they are heavily into what has been recognized as a crucial part of the agenda of democratization in Thailand—decentralization, and in particular the recovery of local community control over natural resources.[19] They form a significant part of the NGO community committed to this agenda. A rather different route has been traveled to a similar goal.

Other differences stand out. Because of its roots in a certain justice agenda, the politics of establishing rights in the West has often been surrounded with anger, indignation, the imperative to punish historic wrongdoing. From this Buddhist perspective comes a caution against the politics of anger, itself the potential source of new forms of violence. My aim here is not to judge between these approaches but to point to these differences as the source of a potentially fruitful exchange within a (hopefully) emerging world consensus on the practice of human rights and democracy.

We can in fact see a convergence here on certain norms of action, however they may be entrenched in law. What is unfamiliar to the Western observer is the entire philosophical basis and its appropriate reference points, as well as the rhetorical source of its appeal. In the West, both democracy and human rights have been furthered by the steady advance of a kind of humanism that stressed that humans stood out from the rest of the cosmos, had a higher status and dignity than anything else. This has its origins in Christianity and certain strands of ancient thought, but the distance is greatly exacerbated by what Weber describes as the disenchantment of the world, the rejection of a view of the cosmos as a meaningful order. The human agent stands out even more starkly from a mechanistic universe. For Pascal, the human being is a mere reed, but of incomparably greater significance than what threatens to crush it, because it is a thinking reed. Kant echoes some of the same reflections in his discussion of the sublime in the third critique[20] and also defines human dignity in terms of the incomparably greater worth of human beings compared to the rest of the contents of the universe.[21]

The human rights doctrine based on this humanism stresses the incomparable importance of the human agent. It centers everything on him or her, makes his or her freedom and self-control a major value, something to be maximized. Consequently, in the Western mind, the defense of human rights seems indissolubly linked with this exaltation of human agency. It is because humans justifiably command all this respect and attention, at least in comparison to anything else, that their rights must be defended.

The Buddhist philosophy that I have been describing starts from a quite different place, the demand of *ahimsa* (nonviolence), and yet seems to ground many of the same norms. (Of course, there will also be differences in the norms grounded, which raises its own problems, but for the moment I just want to note the substantial overlap.) The gamut of Western philosophical emotions, the exaltation at human dignity, the emphasis on freedom as the highest value, the drama of age-old wrongs righted in valor, all the things that move us in seeing *Fidelio* well performed, seem out of place in this alternative setting. So do the models of heroism. The heroes of *ahimsa* are not forceful revolutionaries, not Cola di Rienzi or Garibaldi, and with the philosophy and the models, a whole rhetoric loses its basis.

This perhaps gives us an idea of what an unforced world consensus on human rights might look like. Agreement on norms, yes, but a profound sense of difference, of unfamiliarity, in the ideals, the notions of human excellence, the rhetorical tropes and reference points by which these norms become objects of deep commitment for us. To the extent that we can only acknowledge agreement with people who share the whole package and are moved by the same heroes, the consensus will either never come or must be forced.

This is the situation at the outset, in any case, when consensus on some aspect of human rights has just been attained. Later a process can follow of mutual learning, moving toward a "fusion of horizons" in Gadamer's term, in which the moral universe of the other becomes less strange. Out of this will come further borrowings and the creation of new hybrid forms.

After all, something of this has already occurred with another stream of the philosophy of *ahimsa*, that of Gandhi. Gandhi's practices of nonviolent resistance have been borrowed and adapted in the West, for example, in the American Civil Rights Movement under Martin Luther King. Beyond that, they have become part of a world repertory of political practices, invoked in Manila in 1988 and in Prague in 1989, to name just two examples.

Also worthy of remark is one other facet of this case that may be generalizable as well. An important part of the Western consciousness of human rights lies in the awareness of an historic achievement. Human rights define norms of respect for human beings, more radical and more exigent than have ever existed in the past. They offer in principle greater freedom, greater security from violence, from arbitrary treatment, from discrimination and oppression than humans have enjoyed at least in most major civilizations in history. In a sense they involve taking the exceptional treatment accorded to privileged people in the past, and extending it to everyone. That is why so many of the landmarks of the historical development of rights were in their day instruments of elite privilege, starting with Magna Carta.

There is a curious convergence in this respect with the strand of Reform Buddhism I have been describing. Here too there is the awareness that very exigent demands are being made that go way beyond what the majority of ordinary believers recognize as required practice. Reform Buddhism is practiced by an elite, as has been the case with most of its analogues in history. But here too, in developing a doctrine of democracy and human rights, Reform Buddhists are proposing to extend what has hitherto been a minority practice and entrench it in society as a whole. Here again there is a consciousness of the universalization of the highest of traditional minority practice.

It is as though in spite of the difference in philosophy this universalization of an exigent standard, which human rights practice at its best involves, was recognized as a valid move and re-created within a different cultural, philosophical, and religious world. The hope for a world consensus is that this kind of move will be made repeatedly.

HIERARCHY AND IDENTITY

This example drawn from Thailand provides one model for what the path to world consensus might look like—a convergence on certain norms from out of very different philosophical and spiritual backgrounds. The consensus at first doesn't need to be based on any deep mutual understanding of these respective backgrounds. Each may seem strange to the other, even though both recognize and value the practical agreement attained. Of course, this is not to say that there is no borrowing involved at all. Plainly, democracy and human rights practices originated somewhere and are now being creatively recaptured (perhaps in a significantly different variant) elsewhere, but a mutual understanding and appreciation of each other's spiritual basis for signing on to the common norms may be close to nonexistent.

This, however, is not a satisfactory end point. Some attempt at deeper understanding must follow or the gains in agreement will remain fragile, for at least two closely connected reasons. The first is that the agreement is never complete. We already saw that what we can call the *ahimsa* basis for rights connects to ecological concerns differently from the Western humanist basis, in that the place of anger, indignation, righteous condemnation, and punishment is different in the two outlooks. All this must lead to differences of practice, of the detailed schedule of rights, or at least of the priority ordering among them. In practice, these differences may not emerge in variant schedules of rights. They may be reflected in the way a given schedule is interpreted and applied in different societies. After all, entrenched charters have to be applied by courts, and the courts make their interpretations within the framework of the moral views prevalent in their society. Some, like the Canadian charter, specifically provide for this adaptive interpretation by calling on the courts to interpret the charter in the light of social requirements, including those of a democratic society.[22] The demands of a world consensus will often include our squaring these differences in practical contexts, our accommodating or coming to some compromise version that both sides can live with. These negotiations will be inordinately difficult unless each side can come to some more fine-grained understanding of what moves the other.

The second reason follows on from the first and is in a sense just another facet of it. The continued coexistence in a broad consensus that continually generates particular disagreements, which have in turn to be negotiated to renewed consensus, is impossible without mutual respect. If the sense is strong on each side that the spiritual basis of the other is ridiculous, false, inferior, unworthy, these attitudes cannot but sap the will to agree of those who hold these views while engendering anger and resentment among those who are thus depreciated. The only cure for contempt here is understanding. This alone can replace the too-facile depreciatory stories about others with which groups often tend to shore up their own sense of rightness and superiority. Consequently, the bare consensus must strive to go on toward a fusion of horizons.

In this discussion I have analytically distinguished consensus from mutual understanding and have imagined that they occur sequentially as successive phases. This is certainly a schematic oversimplification, but perhaps not totally wrong in the Thai case I was examining. However, in other situations some degree of mutual understanding is an essential condition of getting to consensus. The two cannot simply occur successively, because the path to agreement lies through some degree of sympathetic mutual comprehension.

I want to look now at another difference that seems to be of this latter type. To lay it out here, I will have to describe more fully another facet of the Western philosophical background of rights, which can hit a wall of incomprehension once one crosses the boundary to other cultures. This is the Western concern for equality, in the form of nondiscrimination. Existing charters of rights in the Western world are no longer concerned only with ensuring certain liberties and immunities to individuals. To an important degree, they also serve to counter various forms of discrimination. This represents a shift in the center of gravity of rights talk over the last centuries. One could argue that the central importance of nondiscrimination enters American judicial review with the Fourteenth Amendment, in the aftermath of the Civil War. Since then nondiscrimination provisions have been an important and growing part of schedules of rights both in the United States and elsewhere.

This connection is perhaps not surprising, although it took a long time to come to fruition. In a sense, the notion of equality was closely linked from the beginning to that of Natural Right, in contradistinction to the place of subjective rights in medieval systems of law, which were also those of certain estates or privileged individuals. Once right inheres in nature, then it is hard in the long run to deny it to anyone. The connection to equality is the stronger because of the thrust of modern humanism mentioned earlier, which defines itself against the view that we are embedded in a meaningful cosmic order. This latter has been a background against which various forms of human differentiation could appear natural, unchallengeable—be they social, racial, or sexual. The differences in human society, or gender roles, could be understood to reflect differentiations in the order of things and to correspond to differences in the cosmos, as with Plato's myth of the metals. This has been a very common form of thinking in almost all human societies.[23]

The destruction of this order has allowed for a process of unmasking existing social and gender differences as merely socially constructed, as without basis in the nature of things, as revocable and hence ultimately without justification. The process of working this out has been long, and we are not yet at the end, but it has been hard to resist in Western civilization in the last two centuries.

This aspect of Western rights talk is often very hard to export because it encounters societies in which certain social differences are still considered very meaningful, and they are seen in turn as intrinsically linked to certain practices that in Western societies are now regarded as discriminatory. However hard these sticking points may be for a Westerner to grasp in detail, it is not difficult to understand the general shape of the conflict, particularly because we in the West are far from having worked out how to combine gender equality with our conflicted ideas of gender difference.

To take this issue of gender equality as our example, we can readily understand that a certain way of framing the difference, however oppressive it may be in practice, also serves as the reference point for deeply felt human identities. The rejection of the framework can be felt as the utter denial of the basis of identity, and this not just for the favored gender, but also for the oppressed one. The gender definitions of a culture are interwoven with, among other things, its love stories, both those people tell and those they live.[24] Throwing off a traditional identity can be an act of liberation, but more than just liberation is involved here; without an alternative sense of identity, the loss of the traditional one is disorienting and potentially unbearable.

The whole shape of the change that could allow for an unforced consensus on human rights here includes a redefinition of identity, perhaps building on transformed traditional reference points in such a way as to allow for a recognition of an operative equality between the sexes. This can be a tall order, something we should have no trouble appreciating in the West because we have yet to complete our own redefinitions in this regard. This identity redefinition will be the easier to effect the more it can be presented as being in continuity with the most important traditions and reference points, properly understood. Correspondingly, it gets maximally difficult when it comes across as a brutal break with the past involving a condemnation and rejection of it.

To some extent, which of these two scenarios gets enacted depends on developments internal to the society, but the relation with the outside world, and particularly the West, can also be determining.

The more the outside portrayal, or attempt at influence, comes across as a blanket condemnation of or contempt for the tradition, the more the dynamic of a "fundamentalist" resistance to all redefinition tends to get in train, and the harder it will be to find unforced consensus. This is a self-reinforcing dynamic, in which perceived external condemnation helps to feed extreme reaction, which calls down further condemnation, and hence further reaction, in a vicious spiral. The world is already drearily familiar with this dynamic in the unhealthy relation between the West and great parts of the Islamic world in our time.

In a sense, therefore, the road to consensus in relation to this difference is the opposite from the one mentioned earlier. There, the convergence on norms between Western humanism and reform Buddhism might be seen as preceding a phase in which they come better to understand and appreciate and learn from each other. In the field of gender discrimination, it may well be that the order would be better reversed, that is, that the path to consensus passes through greater sympathetic understanding of the situation of each party by the other. In this respect, the West with its own hugely unresolved issues about equality and difference is often more of a menace than a help.

THE POLYVALENCE OF TRADITION

Before concluding, I want to look at another difference, which resembles in different respects both of the preceding. That is, it is certainly one in which the dynamic of mutual miscomprehension and condemnation is driving us away from consensus, but it also has potentialities like the Thai case, in that we can see how a quite different spiritual or theological basis might be found for a convergence on norms. I am thinking of the difference between international human rights standards and certain facets of the *Shari'a*, recently discussed in so illuminating a fashion by Abdullahi Ahmed An-Na'im.[25] Certain punishments prescribed by the *Shari'a*, such as amputation of the hand for theft or stoning for adultery, appear excessive and cruel in the light of standards prevalent in other countries.

It is worthwhile developing here, as I have in the other cases, the facet of Western philosophical thought and sensibility that has given particular force to this condemnation. This can best be shown through an example. When we read the opening pages of Michel Foucault's *Surveiller et Punir* we are struck by its riveting description of the torture, execution, and dismemberment of Damien, the attempted assassin of Louis XV in the mid-eighteenth century.[26] We cannot but be aware of the cultural change that we have gone through since the Enlightenment.[27] We are much more concerned about pain and suffering than our forebears; we shrink more from the infliction of gratuitous suffering. It would be hard to imagine people today taking their children to such a spectacle, at least openly and without some sense of unease and shame.

What has changed? We can distinguish two factors, one positive and one negative. On the positive side, we see pain and suffering and gratuitously inflicted death in a new light because of the immense cultural revolution that has been taking place in modernity, which I called elsewhere "the affirmation of ordinary life."[28] What I was trying to gesture at with this term is the momentous cultural and spiritual change of the early modern period, which dethroned the supposedly higher activities of contemplation and the citizen life, and put the center of gravity of goodness in ordinary living, production, and the family. It belongs to this spiritual outlook that our first concern ought to be to increase life, relieve suffering, foster prosperity. Concern above all for the "good life" smacked of pride, of self-absorption. Beyond that, it was inherently inegalitarian, because the alleged "higher" activities could only be carried out by an elite minority, whereas leading rightly one's ordinary life was open to everyone. This is a moral temper to which it seems obvious that our major concern must be our dealings with others, in justice and benevolence, and these dealings must be on a level of equality. This affirmation, which constitutes a major component of our modern ethical outlook, was originally inspired by a mode of Christian piety. It exalted practical agape, and was polemically directed against the pride, elitism, and one might say self-absorption of those who believed in "higher" activities or spiritualities.

We can easily see how much this development is interwoven with the rise of the humanism that stands behind the Western discourse of human rights. They converge on the concern for equality, and also for the security of the person against burdens, dangers, and suffering imposed from outside.

But this is not the whole story. There is also a negative change; something has been cast off. It is not as though our ancestors would have simply thought the level of pain irrelevant, providing no reason at all to desist from some course of action involving torture and wounds. For us, the relief of suffering has become a supreme value, but it was always an important consideration. It is rather that, in cases like that of Damien, the negative significance of pain was subordinated to other, weightier considerations. If it is necessary that punishment in a sense undo the evil of the crime, restore the balance—what is implicit in the whole notion of the criminal making *amende honorable*—then the very horror of regicide calls for a kind of theater of the horrible as the medium in which this undoing can take place. In this context, pain takes on a different significance; there has to be lots of it to do the trick. A principle of minimizing pain is trumped.

Thus, we relate doubly to our forebears of two centuries ago. We have new reasons to minimize suffering, but we also lack a reason to override the minimizing of suffering. We no longer have the whole outlook—linked as it was to the cosmos as meaningful order—that made sense of the necessity of undoing the crime, restoring the breached order of things, in and through the punishment of the criminal.

In general, contemporaries in the West are so little aware of the positive change they have gone through—they tend anachronistically to think that people must always have felt this way—that they generally believe that the negative change is the crucial one that explains our difference from our predecessors. With this in mind, they look at the *Shari'a* punishments as the simple result of premodern illusions, in the same category in which they now place the ancien régime execution scenarios. With this dismissive condemnation, the stage is set for the dynamic I described earlier, in which contemptuous denunciation leads to "fundamentalist" reaffirmations, which in turn provoke even more strident denunciations, and so on.

What gets lost in this struggle is what An-Na'im shows so clearly, the possibilities of reinterpretation and reappropriation that the tradition itself contains. What also becomes invisible is what could be the motor of this change, analogous to the role played by the cultural revolution affirming ordinary life in the West. What this or these could be is not easy for an outsider to determine, but the striking Islamic theme of the mercy and compassion of God, reinvoked at the beginning of almost every sura of the *Qur'an*, might be the locus of a creative theological development. This might help toward a convergence in this domain, in which case we might see a consensus among those of very different spiritual backgrounds, analogous to the Thai Buddhist views I discussed earlier.

CONCLUSION

I started this chapter with the basic notion that an unforced world consensus on human rights would be something like a Rawlsian "overlapping consensus," in which convergent norms would be justified in very different underlying spiritual and philosophical outlooks. I then argued that these norms have to be distinguished and analytically separated not just from the background justifications, but also from the legal forms that give them force. These two could vary with good reason from society to society, even though the norms we crucially want to preserve remain constant. We need, in other words, a threefold distinction: norms, legal forms, and background justifications, which each have to be distinguished from the others.

I then looked at four examples of differences. These by no means exhaust the field, though each is important in the present international exchange on human rights. One of these dealt with the issue of variations in legal forms. In the other three, I tried to discuss issues around the convergence on norms out of different philosophical and spiritual backgrounds.

Two important facets of these convergences emerged. In one way, they involve the meeting of very different minds, worlds apart in their premises, uniting only in the immediate practical conclusions. From another side, it is clear that consensus requires that this extreme distance be closed, that we come better to understand each other in our differences, that we learn to recognize what is great and admirable in our different spiritual traditions. In some cases, this kind of mutual understanding can come after convergence, but in others it seems almost to be a condition of it.

An obstacle in the path to this mutual understanding comes from the inability of many Westerners to see their culture as one among many. An example of this difficulty was visible in the last difference discussed. To an extent, Westerners see their human rights doctrine as arising simply out of the falling away of previous countervailing ideas—such as the punishment scenarios of the ancien régime—that have now been discredited to leave the field free for the preoccupations with human life, freedom, the avoidance of suffering. To this extent they will tend to think that the path to convergence requires that others too cast off their traditional ideas, that they even reject their religious heritage, and become "unmarked" moderns like us. Only if we in the West can recapture a more adequate view of our own history, can we learn to understand better the spiritual ideas that have been interwoven in our development and hence be prepared to understand sympathetically the spiritual paths of others toward the converging goal.[29] Contrary to what many people think, world convergence will not come through a loss or denial of traditions all around, but rather by creative reimmersions of different groups, each in their own spiritual heritage, traveling different routes to the same goal.

NOTES

1. John Rawls, *Political Liberalism* (New York: Columbia University Press, 1993), lecture IV.

2. From the Introduction to UNESCO, *Human Rights: Comments and Interpretations* (London: Allan Wingate, 1949), pp. 10–11; cited in Abdullahi An-Na'im, "Towards a Cross-Cultural Approach to Defining International Standards of Human Rights: The Meaning of Cruel, Inhuman, or Degrading Treatment or Punishment," in Abdullahi Ahmed An-Na'im, ed., *Human Rights in Cross-Cultural Perspectives* (Philadelphia: University of Pennsylvania Press, 1992), pp. 28–29.

3. Jack Donnelly, *Universal Human Rights in Theory and Practice* (Ithaca: Cornell University Press, 1989), pp. 28–37.

4. See Onuma Yasuaki, "Toward an Intercivilizational Approach to Human Rights" in *The East Asian Challenge for Human Rights*, ed. Joanne R. Bauer and Daniel A. Bell (Cambridge: Cambridge University Press 1999), 103–23.

5. See Sidney Jones, "The Impact of Asian Economic Growth on Human Rights," *Asia Project Working Paper Series* (New York: Council on Foreign Relations, January 1995), p. 9.

6. "I find parts of [the American system] totally unacceptable: guns, drugs, violent crime, vagrancy, unbecoming behaviour in public—in sum, the breakdown of civil society. The expansion of the right of the individual to behave or misbehave as he pleases has come at the expense of orderly society. In the East the main object is to have a well-ordered society so that everybody can have maximum enjoyment of his freedoms. This freedom can only exist in an ordered state and not in a natural state of contention." Fareed Zakaria, "Culture Is Destiny: A Conversation with Lee Kuan Yew," *Foreign Affairs* 73 (March/April 1994), p. 111.

7. Which is why Locke had to introduce a restrictive adjective to block this option of waiver, when he spoke of "inalienable rights." The notion of inalienability had no place in earlier natural right discourse, because this had no option of waiver.

8. According to Louis Henkin, "The Human Rights Idea in Contemporary China: A Comparative Perspective" in R. Randle Edwards, Louis Henkin, and Andrew J. Nathan, *Human Rights in Contemporary China* (New York: Columbia University Press, 1986), p. 21:

> In the Chinese tradition the individual was not central, and no conception of individual rights existed in the sense known to the United States. The individual's participation in society was not voluntary, and the legitimacy of government did not depend on his consent or the consent of the whole people of individuals. . . .

> In traditional China, the idea was not individual liberty or equality but order and harmony, not individual independence but selfless-ness and cooperation, not freedom of individual conscience but conformity to orthodox truth. . . . The purpose of society was not to preserve and promote individual liberty but to maintain the harmony of the hierarchical order and to see to it that truth prevailed.

9. See Sulak Sivaraksa, "Buddhism and Human Rights in Siam" (unpub-lished paper presented at Bangkok Workshop of the Human Rights Initiative, Carnegie Council on Ethics and International Affairs, March 1996), pp. 4–5. Sulak wonders whether the Western concept of freedom, closely allied with that of right, "has reached an end point in environmental degradation."

10. "L'égalité place les hommes à côté les uns des autres, sans lien commun qui les retienne. Le despotisme élève des barrières entre eux et les sépare. Elle les dispose à ne point songer à leurs semblables et il leur fait une sorte de vertu publique de l'indifférance." [Equality places people next to each other, without a common link that really keeps them together. Despotism elevates

barriers between people and keeps them apart. It predisposes individuals not to think of their compatriots and makes a kind of public virtue out of their indifference.] Alexis de Tocqueville: *De la Démocratie en Amérique*, vol. 2, part II, chapter IV (Paris: Edition Garnier-Flammarion, 1981), p. 131.

11. I have talked about substantially similar issues in somewhat different terms in the last chapter of *The Malaise of Modernity* (Toronto: Anansi Press, 1991), and in "Liberalism and the Public Sphere," *Philosophical Arguments* (Cambridge, MA: Harvard University Press, 1995), chapter 13.

12. That is what is so dangerous to public order in cases like the 1995 O. J. Simpson trial, which both show up and further entrench a deep lack of respect for and trust in the judicial process.

13. There is a Western analogue in the positive part played by Juan Carlos during the coup in Madrid in 1974.

14. See Stanley Tambiah, *World Conqueror and World Renouncer* (New York: Cambridge University Press, 1976).

15. See the discussion in John Girling, *Thailand: Society and Politics* (Ithaca: Cornell University Press, 1981), pp. 154–57. Frank Reynolds in his "Legitimation and Rebellion: Thailand's Civic Religion and the Student Uprising of October, 1973," in Bardweil L. Smith, ed., *Religion and Legitimation of Power in Thailand, Laos, and Burma* (Chambersburg, PA: Anima Books, 1978), discusses the use by the student demonstrators of the symbols of "Nation, Religion, Monarchy."

16. Richard Gombrich and Gananath Obeyesekere, *Buddhism Transformed: Religious Change in Sri Lanka* (Princeton, NJ: Princeton University Press, 1988), chapters 6 and 7.

17. See Sulak Sivaraksa, *Seeds of Peace: A Buddhist Vision for Renewing Society* (Berkeley and Bangkok: Parallax Press, 1992), chapter 9.

18. See ibid., especially part 2.

19. See the discussion in Vitit Muntarbhorn and Charles Taylor, *Roads to Democracy: Human Rights and Democratic Development in Thailand*, Bangkok and Montreal (International Centre for Human Rights and Democratic Development, July 1994), part 3.

20. *Kants Werke*, vol. 6: *Kritik der Urteilskraft* (Berlin: Walter de Gruyter, 1964), first part, second book, sections 28–29.

21. *Grundlegung zur Metaphysik der Sitten*, Berlin Academy edition (Berlin: Walter de Gruyter, 1968), vol. 4, p. 434.

22. See the discussion in Joseph Chan, "The Asian Challenge to Universal Human Rights: A Philosophical Appraisal," in James T. H. Tang, ed., *Human Rights and International Relations in the Asia-Pacific Region* (London: Pinter, 1995).

23. A good example is Pierre Bourdieu's description of the "correspondences" between the male–female difference and different colors, cardinal points, and oppositions like wet–dry, up–down, etc. See his *Outline of a Theory of Practice* (Cambridge: Cambridge University Press, 1977), chapter 3.

24. See, for example, Sudhir Kakar, *The Inner World* (Delhi: Oxford University Press, 1978), who claims that Hindu culture foregrounds a love story of the young married couple, already with children, as against the prevalent Western tale of the love intrigue that leads to marriage.

25. See his "Towards a Cross-Cultural Approach to Defining International Standards of Human Rights," chapter 1; also see Abdullahi A. An-Na'im, "The Cultural Mediation of Human Rights: The Al-Arqam Case in Malaysia" in *The East Asian Challenge for Human Rights*, ed. Joanne R. Bauer and Daniel A. Bell (Cambridge: Cambridge University Press 1999), 147–68.

26. Foucault, *Surveiller et Punir* (Paris: Gallimard, 1976).

27. Tocqueville was already aware of the change when he commented on a passage from Mme. de Sévigny in *De la Démocratie en Amérique*.

28. See Charles Taylor, *Sources of the Self* (Cambridge, MA: Harvard University Press, 1989), chapter 13.

29. I have discussed at greater length the two opposed understandings of the rise of modernity that are invoked here in "Modernity and the Rise of the Public Sphere," Grethe B. Peterson, ed., *The Tanner Lectures on Human Values* (Salt Lake City: University of Utah Press, 1993).

19. JOHN RAWLS

In this excerpt from *The Law of Peoples*, Rawls argues that "well-ordered" peoples have a duty to assist peoples burdened by unfavorable conditions. The aim of this duty is to help burdened societies attain liberal or "decent" institutions, secure human rights, and meet basic needs. When that aim is achieved, the duty in question has been fulfilled. Rawls then considers whether a more ambitious principle of global distributive justice may be appropriate, one aimed at institutionally limiting inequalities among peoples. He argues against such a principle, emphasizing two related factors: the role that the political culture of a society plays in its development, and the fact that such principles often lack a clear target and a cutoff point.

§15 and §16 of *The Law of Peoples*

First published in his The Law of Peoples *(Cambridge: Harvard University Press, 1999), 105–20. Copyright © 1999 by the President and Fellows of Harvard College. All rights reserved. Reprinted with the permission of Harvard University Press.*

§15. BURDENED SOCIETIES

15.1 UNFAVORABLE CONDITIONS

In noncompliance theory we have seen that the long-term goal of (relatively) well-ordered societies is somehow to bring the outlaw states into the Society of well-ordered Peoples. The outlaw states[1] of modern Europe in the early modern period—Spain, France, and the Hapsburgs—or, more recently, Germany, all tried at one time to subject much of Europe to their will. They hoped to spread their religion and culture and sought dominion and glory, not to mention wealth and territory. These states were among the more effectively organized and economically advanced societies of their day. Their fault lay in their political traditions and institutions of law, property, and class structure, with their sustaining religious and moral beliefs and underlying culture. It is these things that shape a society's political will; and they are the elements that must change before a society can support a reasonable Law of Peoples.

In what follows I take up the second kind of nonideal theory, namely, societies burdened by unfavorable conditions (henceforth, *burdened societies*). Burdened societies, while they are not expansive or aggressive, lack the political and cultural traditions, the human capital and know-how, and, often, the material and technological resources needed to be well-ordered. The long-term goal of (relatively) well-ordered societies should be to bring burdened societies, like outlaw states, into the Society of well-ordered Peoples. Well-ordered peoples have a *duty* to assist burdened societies. It does not follow, however, that the only way, or the best way, to carry out this duty of assistance is by following a principle of distributive justice to regulate economic and social inequalities among societies. Most such principles do not have a defined goal, aim, or cutoff point, beyond which aid may cease.

The levels of wealth and welfare among societies may vary, and presumably do so; but adjusting those levels is not the object of the duty of assistance. Only burdened societies need help. Furthermore, not all such societies are poor, any more than all well-ordered societies are wealthy. A society with few natural resources and little wealth can be well-ordered if its political traditions, law, and property and class structure with their underlying religious and moral beliefs and culture are such as to sustain a liberal or decent society.

15.2. FIRST GUIDELINE FOR DUTY OF ASSISTANCE

The first guideline to consider is that a well-ordered society need not be a wealthy society. I recall here three basic points about the principle of "just savings" (within a domestic society) as I elaborated it in *A Theory of Justice*, §44.

(a) The purpose of a just (real) savings principle is to establish (reasonably) just basic institutions for a free constitutional democratic society (or any well-ordered society) and to secure a social world that makes possible a worthwhile life for all its citizens.

(b) Accordingly, savings may stop once just (or decent) basic institutions have been established. At this point real saving (that is, net additions to real capital of all kinds) may fall to zero; and existing stock only needs to be maintained, or replaced, and nonrenewable resources carefully husbanded for future use as appropriate. Thus, the savings rate as a constraint on current consumption is to be expressed in terms of aggregate capital accumulated, resource use forgone, and technology developed to conserve and regenerate the capacity of the natural world to sustain its human population. With these and other essential elements tallied in, a society may, of course, continue to save after this point, but it is no longer a duty of justice to do so.

(c) Great wealth is not necessary to establish just (or decent) institutions. How much is needed will depend on a society's particular history as well as on its conception of justice. Thus the levels of wealth among well-ordered peoples will not, in general, be the same.

These three features of the savings process discussed in *A Theory of Justice* bring out the similarity between the duty of assistance in the Law of Peoples and the duty of just savings in the domestic case. In each instance, the aim is to realize and preserve just (or decent) institutions, and not simply to increase, much less to maximize indefinitely, the average level of wealth, or the wealth of any society or any particular class in society. In these respects the duty of assistance and the duty of just savings express the same underlying idea.[2]

15.3. Second Guideline

A second guideline for thinking about how to carry out the duty of assistance is to realize that the political culture of a burdened society is all-important; and that, at the same time, there is no recipe, certainly no easy recipe, for well-ordered peoples to help a burdened society to change its political and social culture. I believe that the causes of the wealth of a people and the forms it takes lie in their political culture and in the religious, philosophical, and moral traditions that support the basic structure of their political and social institutions, as well as in the industriousness and cooperative talents of its members, all supported by their political virtues. I would further conjecture that there is no society anywhere in the world—except for marginal cases[3]—with resources so scarce that it could not, were it reasonably and rationally organized and governed, become well-ordered. Historical examples seem to indicate that resource-poor countries may do very well (e.g., Japan), while resource-rich countries may have serious difficulties (e.g., Argentina). The crucial elements that make the difference are the political culture, the political virtues and civic society of the country, its members' probity and industriousness, their capacity for innovation, and much else. Crucial also is the country's population policy: it must take care that it does not overburden its lands and economy with a larger population than it can sustain. But one way or the other, the duty of assistance is in no way diminished. What must be realized is that merely dispensing funds will not suffice to rectify basic political and social injustices (though money is often essential). But an emphasis on human rights may work to change ineffective regimes and the conduct of the rulers who have been callous about the well-being of their own people.

This insistence on human rights is supported by Amartya Sen's work on famines.⁴ In his empirical study of four well-known historical cases (Bengal, 1943; Ethiopia, 1972–74; Sahel, 1972–73; and Bangladesh, 1974), he found that food decline need not be the main cause of famine, or even a minor cause. In the cases he studied, the drop in food production was not great enough to lead to famine given a decent government that cared for the well-being of all its people and had in place a reasonable scheme of backup entitlements provided through public institutions. The main problem was the failure of the respective governments to distribute (and supplement) what food there was. Sen concluded: "Famines are economic disasters, not just food crises."⁵ In other words, they are attributable to faults within the political and social structure, and its failure to institute policies to remedy the effects of shortfalls in food production. A government's allowing people to starve when it is preventable reflects a lack of concern for human rights, and well-ordered regimes as I have described them will not allow this to happen. Insisting on human rights will, it is to be hoped, help to prevent famines from developing, and will exert pressure in the direction of effective governments in a well-ordered Society of Peoples. (I note, by the way, that there would be massive starvation in every Western democracy were there no schemes in place to help the unemployed.)

Respecting human rights could also relieve population pressure within a burdened society, relative to what the economy of the society can decently sustain.[6] A decisive factor here appears to be the status of women. Some societies—China is a familiar example—have imposed harsh restrictions on the size of families and have adopted other draconian measures. But there is no need to be so harsh. The simplest, most effective, most acceptable policy is to establish the elements of equal justice for women. Instructive here is the Indian state of Kerala, which in the late 1970s empowered women to vote and to participate in politics, to receive and use education, and to own and manage wealth and property. As a result, within several years Kerala's birth rate fell below China's, without invoking the coercive powers of the state.[7] Like policies have been instituted elsewhere—for example, in Bangladesh, Colombia, and Brazil—with similar results. The elements of basic justice have proven themselves essential for sound social policy. Injustice is supported by deep-seated interests and will not easily disappear; but it cannot excuse itself by pleading lack of natural resources.

To repeat, there is no easy recipe for helping a burdened society to change its political culture. Throwing funds at it is usually undesirable, and the use of force is ruled out by the Law of Peoples. But certain kinds of advice may be helpful, and burdened societies would do well to pay particular attention to the fundamental interests of women. The fact that women's status is often founded on religion, or bears a close relation to religious views,[8] is not in itself the cause of their subjection, since other causes are usually present. One may explain that all kinds of well-ordered societies affirm human rights and have at least the features of a decent consultation hierarchy or its analogue. These features require that any group representing women's fundamental interests must include a majority of women (§8.3 [of *The Law of Peoples*]). The idea is that any conditions of the consultation procedure that are necessary to prevent violations of the human rights of women are to be adopted. This is not a peculiarly liberal idea but one that is also common to all decent peoples.

We can, then, bring this idea to bear as a condition on offered assistance without being subject to the charge of improperly undermining a society's religion and culture. The principle here is similar to one that is always followed in regard to the claims of religion. Thus, a religion cannot claim as a justification that its intolerance of other religions is necessary for it to maintain itself. In the same way a religion cannot claim as a justification for its subjection of women that it is necessary for its survival. Basic human rights are involved, and these belong to the common institutions and practices of all liberal and decent societies.[9]

15.4. THIRD GUIDELINE

The third guideline for carrying out the duty of assistance is that its aim is to help burdened societies to be able to manage their own affairs reasonably and rationally and eventually to become members of the Society of well-ordered Peoples. This defines the "target" of assistance. After it is achieved, further assistance is not required, even though the now well-ordered society may still be relatively poor. Thus the well-ordered societies giving assistance must not act paternalistically, but in measured ways that do not conflict with the final aim of assistance: freedom and equality for the formerly burdened societies.

Leaving aside the deep question of whether some forms of culture and ways of life are good in themselves, as I believe they are, it is surely a good for individuals and associations to be attached to their particular culture and to take part in its common public and civic life. In this way belonging to a particular political society, and being at home in its civic and social world, gains expression and fulfillment.[10] This is no small thing. It argues for preserving significant room for the idea of a people's self-determination and for some kind of loose or confederative form of a Society of Peoples, provided the divisive hostilities of different cultures can be tamed, as it seems they can be, by a society of well-ordered regimes. We seek a world in which ethnic hatreds leading to nationalistic wars will have ceased. A proper patriotism (§5.2 [of *The Law of Peoples*]) is an attachment to one's people and country, and a willingness to defend its legitimate claims while fully respecting the legitimate claims of other peoples.[11] Well-ordered peoples should try to encourage such regimes.

15.5. DUTY OF ASSISTANCE AND AFFINITY

A legitimate concern about the duty of assistance is whether the motivational support for following it presupposes a degree of affinity among peoples, that is, a sense of social cohesion and closeness, that cannot be expected even in a society of liberal peoples—not to mention in a society of all well-ordered peoples—with their separate languages, religions, and cultures. The members of a single domestic society share a common central government and political culture, and the moral learning of political concepts and principles works most effectively in the context of society-wide political and social institutions that are part of their shared daily life.[12] Taking part in shared institutions every day, members of the same society should be able to resolve political conflicts and problems within the society on a common basis in terms of public reason.

It is the task of the statesman to struggle against the potential lack of affinity among different peoples and try to heal its causes insofar as they derive from past domestic institutional injustices, and from the hostility among social classes inherited through their common history and antagonisms. Since the affinity among peoples is naturally weaker (as a matter of human psychology) as society-wide institutions include a larger area and cultural distances increase, the statesman must continually combat these shortsighted tendencies.[13]

What encourages the statesman's work is that relations of affinity are not a fixed thing, but may continually grow stronger over time as peoples come to work together in cooperative institutions they have developed. It is characteristic of liberal and decent peoples that they seek a world in which all peoples have a well-ordered regime. At first we may suppose this aim is moved by each people's *self-interest*, for such regimes are not dangerous but peaceful and cooperative. Yet as cooperation between peoples proceeds apace they may come to care about each other, and affinity between them becomes stronger. Hence, they are no longer moved simply by self-interest but by mutual concern for each other's way of life and culture, and they become willing to make sacrifices for each other. This mutual caring is the outcome of their fruitful cooperative efforts and common experiences over a considerable period of time.

The relatively narrow circle of mutually caring peoples in the world today may expand over time and must never be viewed as fixed. Gradually, peoples are no longer moved by self-interest alone or by their mutual caring alone, but come to affirm their liberal and decent civilization and culture, until eventually they become ready to act on the *ideals and principles* their civilization specifies. Religious toleration has historically first appeared as a *modus vivendi* between hostile faiths, later becoming a moral principle shared by civilized peoples and recognized by their leading religions. The same is true of the abolition of slavery and serfdom, the rule of law, the right to war only in self-defense, and the guarantee of human rights. These become ideals and principles of liberal and decent civilizations, and principles of the Law of all civilized Peoples.

§16. ON DISTRIBUTIVE JUSTICE AMONG PEOPLES

16.1 EQUALITY AMONG PEOPLES

There are two views about this. One holds that equality is just, or a good in itself. The Law of Peoples, on the other hand, holds that inequalities are not always unjust, and that when they are, it is because of their unjust effects on the basic structure of the Society of Peoples, and on relations among peoples and among their members.[14] We saw the great importance of this basic structure when discussing the need for toleration of decent nonliberal peoples (§§7.2–7.3 [of *The Law of Peoples*]).

I note three reasons for being concerned with inequality in domestic society and consider how each applies to the Society of Peoples. One reason for reducing inequalities within a domestic society is to relieve the suffering and hardships of the poor. Yet this does not require that all persons be equal in wealth. In itself, it doesn't matter how great the gap between rich and poor may be. What matters are the consequences. In a liberal domestic society that gap cannot be wider than the criterion of reciprocity allows, so that the least advantaged (as the third liberal principle requires) have sufficient all-purpose means to make intelligent and effective use of their freedoms and to lead reasonable and worthwhile lives. When that situation exists, there is no further need to narrow the gap. Similarly, in the basic structure of the Society of Peoples, once the duty of assistance is satisfied and all peoples have a working liberal or decent government, there is again no reason to narrow the gap between the average wealth of different peoples.

A second reason for narrowing the gap between rich and poor within a domestic society is that such a gap often leads to some citizens being stigmatized and treated as inferiors, and that is unjust. Thus, in a liberal or decent society, conventions that establish ranks to be recognized socially by expressions of deference must be guarded against. They may unjustly wound the self-respect of those not so recognized. The same would be true of the basic structure of the Society of Peoples should citizens in one country feel inferior to the citizens of another because of its greater riches, *provided* that those feelings are justified. Yet when the duty of assistance is fulfilled, and each people has its own liberal or decent government, these feelings are unjustified. For then each people adjusts the significance and importance of the wealth of its own society for itself. If it is not satisfied, it can continue to increase savings, or, if that is not feasible, borrow from other members of the Society of Peoples.

A third reason for considering the inequalities among peoples concerns the important role of fairness in the political processes of the basic structure of the Society of Peoples. In the domestic case this concern is evident in securing the fairness of elections and of political opportunities to run for public office. Public financing of political parties and campaigns tries to address these matters. Also, when we speak of fair equality of opportunity, more than formal legal equality is meant. We mean roughly that background social conditions are such that each citizen, regardless of class or origin, should have the same chance of attaining a favored social position, given the same talents and willingness to try. Policies for achieving this fair equality of opportunity include, for example, securing fair education for all and eliminating unjust discrimination. Fairness also plays an important role in the political processes of the basic structure of the Society of Peoples, analogous to, though not the same as, its role in the domestic case.

Basic fairness among peoples is given by their being represented equally in the second original position with its veil of ignorance. Thus the representatives of peoples will want to preserve the independence of their own society and its equality in relation to others. In the working of organizations and loose confederations of peoples, inequalities are designed to serve the many ends that peoples share (§4.5 [of *The Law of Peoples*]). In this case the larger and smaller peoples will be ready to make larger and smaller contributions and to accept proportionately larger and smaller returns. In addition, the parties will formulate guidelines for setting up cooperative organizations, and will agree to standards of fairness for trade as well as to certain provisions for mutual assistance. Should these cooperative organizations have unjustified distributive effects, these would have to be corrected in the basic structure of the Society of Peoples.

16.2. DISTRIBUTIVE JUSTICE AMONG PEOPLES

Several principles have been proposed to regulate inequalities among peoples and prevent their becoming excessive. Two of these are discussed by Charles Beitz.[15] Another is Thomas Pogge's Egalitarian Principle,[16] which is similar in many respects to Beitz's second principle of redistributive justice.

These are suggestive and much-discussed principles, and I need to say why I don't accept them. But, of course, I do accept Beitz's and Pogge's goals of attaining liberal or decent institutions, securing human rights, and meeting basic needs. These I believe are covered by the duty of assistance discussed in the preceding section.

First let me state Beitz's two principles. He distinguishes between what he calls "the resource redistribution principle" and a "global distribution principle." The distinction between them is as follows: Suppose first, that the production of goods and services in all countries is *autarkic*, that is, each country relies entirely on its own labor and resources without trade of any kind. Beitz holds that some areas have ample resources, and societies in such areas can be expected to make the best use of their natural riches and prosper. Other societies are not so fortunate, and despite their best efforts, may attain only a meager level of well-being because of resource scarcities.[17] Beitz views the resource redistribution principle as giving each society a fair chance to establish just political institutions and an economy that can fulfill its members' basic needs. Affirming this principle "provides assurance to persons in resource-poor societies that their adverse fate will not prevent them from realizing economic conditions sufficient to support just social institutions and to protect human rights."[18] He doesn't explain how the countries with sufficient resources are to redistribute them to resource-poor countries; but no matter.

The global distribution principle that Beitz discusses concerns a situation where production is no longer autarkic and there are flows of trade and services between countries. He believes that in this case a global system of cooperation already exists. In this instance Beitz proposes that a global difference applies (analogous to the principle used in the domestic case in *A Theory of Justice*), giving a principle of distributive justice between societies.[19] Since he believes that the wealthier countries are so because of the greater resources available to them, presumably the global principle (with its scheme of taxation, say) redistributes the benefits of greater resources to resource-poor peoples.

However, because, as I have said, the crucial element in how a country fares is its political culture—its members' political and civic virtues—and not the level of its resources,[20] the arbitrariness of the distribution of natural resources causes no difficulty. I therefore feel we need not discuss Beitz's resource redistribution principle. On the other hand, if a global principle of distributive justice for the Law of Peoples is meant to apply to our world as it is with its extreme injustices, crippling poverty, and inequalities, its appeal is understandable. But if it is meant to apply continuously without end—without a target, as one might say—in the hypothetical world arrived at after the duty of assistance is fully satisfied, its appeal is questionable. In the latter hypothetical world a global principle gives what we would, I think, regard as unacceptable results. Consider two illustrative cases:

Case (i): two liberal or decent countries are at the same level of wealth (estimated, say, in primary goods) and have the same size population. The first decides to industrialize and to increase its rate of (real) saving, while the second does not. Being content with things as they are, and preferring a more pastoral and leisurely society, the second reaffirms its social values. Some decades later the first country is twice as wealthy as the second. Assuming, as we do, that both societies are liberal or decent, and their peoples free and responsible, and able to make their own decisions, should the industrializing country be taxed to give funds to the second? According to the duty of assistance there would be no tax, and that seems right; whereas with a global egalitarian principle without target, there would always be a flow of taxes as long as the wealth of one people was less than that of the other. This seems unacceptable.

Case (ii) is parallel to (i) except that at the start the rate of population growth in both liberal or decent societies is rather high. Both countries provide the elements of equal justice for women, as required by a well-ordered society; but the first happens to stress these elements, and its women flourish in the political and economic world. As a consequence, they gradually reach zero population growth that allows for an increasing level of wealth over time. The second society, although it also has these elements of equal justice, because of its prevailing religious and social values, freely held by its women, does not reduce the rate of population growth and it remains rather high.[21] As before, some decades later, the first society is twice as wealthy as the second. Given that both societies are liberal or decent, and their peoples free and responsible, and able to make their own decisions, the duty of assistance does not require taxes from the first, now wealthier society, while the global egalitarian principle without target would. Again, this latter position seems unacceptable.

The crucial point is that the role of the duty of assistance is to assist burdened societies to become full members of the Society of Peoples and to be able to determine the path of their own future for themselves. It is a principle of *transition*, in much the same way that the principle of real saving over time in domestic society is a principle of transition. As explained in §15.2 [of *The Law of Peoples*, herein 432–33], real saving is meant to lay the foundation for a just basic structure of society, at which point it may cease. In the society of the Law of Peoples the duty of assistance holds until all societies have achieved just liberal or decent basic institutions. Both the duty of real saving and the duty of assistance are defined by a *target* beyond which they no longer hold. They assure the essentials of *political autonomy*: the political autonomy of free and equal citizens in the domestic case, the political autonomy of free and equal liberal and decent peoples in the Society of Peoples.

This raises the question of the difference between a global egalitarian principle and the duty of assistance.[22] That principle is designed to help the poor all over the world, and it proposes a General Resource Dividend (GRD) on each society to pay into an international fund to be administered for this purpose. The question to ask about it is whether the principle has a target and a cutoff point. The duty of assistance has both: It seeks to raise the world's poor until they are either free and equal citizens of a reasonably liberal society or members of a decent hierarchical society. That is its target. It also has by design a cutoff point, since for each burdened society the principle ceases to apply once the target is reached. A global egalitarian principle could work in a similar way. Call it an egalitarian principle with target. How great is the difference between the duty of assistance and this egalitarian principle? Surely there is a point at which a people's basic needs (estimated in primary goods) are fulfilled and a people can stand on its own. There may be disagreement about when this point comes, but that there is such a point is crucial to the Law of Peoples and its duty of assistance. Depending on how the respective targets and cutoff points are defined, the principles could be much the same, with largely practical matters of taxation and administration to distinguish between them.

16.3. CONTRAST WITH COSMOPOLITAN VIEW

The Law of Peoples assumes that every society has in its population a sufficient array of human capabilities, each in sufficient number so that the society has enough potential human resources to realize just institutions. The final political end of society is to become fully just and stable for the right reasons. Once that end is reached, the Law of Peoples prescribes no further target such as, for example, to raise the standard of living beyond what is necessary to sustain those institutions. Nor is there any justifiable reason for any society's asking for more than is necessary to sustain just institutions, or for further reduction of material inequalities among societies.

These remarks illustrate the contrast between the Law of Peoples and a cosmopolitan view (§11 [of *The Law of Peoples*]). The ultimate concern of a cosmopolitan view is the well-being of individuals and not the justice of societies. According to that view there is still a question concerning the need for further global distribution, even after each domestic society has achieved internally just institutions. The simplest illustrative case is to suppose that each of two societies satisfies internally the two principles of justice found in *A Theory of Justice*. In these two societies, the worst-off representative person in one is worse off than the worst-off representative person in the other. Suppose it were possible, through some global redistribution that would allow both societies to continue to satisfy the two principles of justice internally, to improve the lot of the worst-off representative person in the first society. Should we prefer the redistribution to the original distribution?

The Law of Peoples is indifferent between the two distributions. The cosmopolitan view, on the other hand, is not indifferent. It is concerned with the well-being of individuals, and hence with whether the well-being of the globally worst-off person can be improved. What is important to the Law of Peoples is the justice and stability for the right reasons of liberal and decent societies, living as members of a Society of well-ordered Peoples.

NOTES

1. Some may object to this term, yet these states were indeed outlaw societies. Their wars were essentially dynastic wars to which the lives and fundamental interests of most members of the societies were sacrificed.

2. The main idea I express here draws on J. S. Mill's *The Principles of Political Economy*, 1st ed. (London, 1848), book IV, chap. 6, "The Stationary State." I follow Mill's view that the purpose of saving is to make possible a just basic structure of society; once that is safely secured, real saving (net increase in real capital) may no longer be necessary. "The art of living" is more important than "the art of getting on," to use his words. The thought that real saving and economic growth are to go on indefinitely, upward and onward, with no specified goal in sight, is the idea of the business class of a capitalist society. But what counts for Mill are just basic institutions and the well-being of what Mill would call "the labouring class." Mill says: "...the decision [between a just system of private property and socialism] will depend mainly on one consideration, viz., which of the two systems is consistent with the greatest amount of human liberty and spontaneity. After the means of subsistence are assured, the next in strength of personal wants of human beings is liberty, and (unlike physical wants which as civilization advances become more moderate and more amenable to control) it increases instead of diminishing in intensity as intelligence and the moral faculties are more developed." From the 7th and last edition of the *Principles* published in Mill's lifetime, paragraph 9 of §3 of chap. 1 of book II. What Mill says here is perfectly consistent with the Law of Peoples and its structure of political values, though I could not accept it as it stands. References to Mill's *Principles* are from the paperback edition, edited by Jonathan Riley, in Oxford World Classics (Oxford: Oxford University Press, 1994). The complete text of the *Principles* is now in *The Complete Works of John Stuart Mill*, vols. 2 and 3, Introduction by V. W. Bladen, ed. J. M. Robson (London: University of Toronto Press, Routledge & Kegan Paul, 1965).

3. Arctic Eskimos, for example, are rare enough, and need not affect our general approach. I assume their problems could be handled in an *ad hoc* way.

4. See Amartya Sen, *Poverty and Famines* (Oxford: Clarendon Press, 1981). Sen's book with Jean Drèze, *Hunger and Public Action* (Oxford: Clarendon Press, 1989), confirms these points and stresses the success of democratic regimes in coping with poverty and hunger. See their summary statement in chap. 13, p. 25. See also the important work of Partha Dasgupta, *An Inquiry into Well-Being and Destitution* (Oxford: Clarendon Press, 1993), chaps. 1, 2, and 5.

5. Sen, *Poverty and Famines*, p. 162.

6. I do not use the term "overpopulation" here since it seems to imply the idea of optimal population; but what is that? When seen as relative to what the economy can sustain, whether there is population pressure is a clear enough question. I am indebted to Amartya Sen on this point.

7. See Amartya Sen, "Population: Delusion and Reality," *The New York Review of Books*, September 22, 1994, pp. 62–71 [reprinted herein 259–90]. On Kerala, see pp. 70ff [herein 282ff]. China's birth rate in 1979 was 2.8; Kerala's 3.0. In 1991 these rates were 2.0 and 1.8 respectively.

8. I say this because many Muslim writers deny that Islam sanctions the inequality of women in many Muslim societies, and attribute it to various historical causes. See Leila Ahmed, *Women and Gender in Islam* (New Haven: Yale University Press, 1992).

9. See *Political Liberalism*, V: §6.

10. Ibid., V: §7.

11. These are specified by the Law of Peoples.

12. Joshua Cohen, "A More Democratic Liberalism," *Michigan Law Review*, 92: 6 (May 1994), pp. 1532–33.

13. Here I draw on a psychological principle that social learning of moral attitudes supporting political institutions works most effectively through society-wide shared institutions and practices. The learning weakens under the conditions mentioned in the text. In a realistic utopia this psychological principle sets limits to what can sensibly be proposed as the content of the Law of Peoples.

14. My discussion of inequality is greatly indebted, as so often, to T. M. Scanlon.

15. Charles Beitz, *Political Theory and International Relations* (Princeton: Princeton Univerity Press, 1979). [The here relevant Part III of Beitz's book is based on his essay "Justice and International Relations," first published in *Philosophy and Public Affairs* 4: 4, (summer 1975): 360–89, reprinted in *Global Justice: Seminal Essays*, 21–48]

16. Pogge's global egalitarian principle as set out in "An Egalitarian Law of Peoples," PAPA 23: 3 (summer 1994) [reprinted in *Global Justice: Seminal Essays*, 461–93] is not a statement of his own preferred view, but one that he

sees as internal to *A Theory of Justice*. It states how he thinks the international system should be treated if it were treated as the domestic one is treated in *A Theory of Justice*.

17. Beitz, *Political Theory and International Relations*, p. 137 [cf. *GJSE* 27].

18. Ibid., p. 141 [cf. *GJSE* 31].

19. Ibid., pp. 153–63 [cf. *GJSE* 32–40].

20. This is powerfully (if sometimes a little too strongly) argued by David Landes in his book *The Wealth and Poverty of Nations* (New York: W. W. Norton, 1998). See his discussion of the OPEC countries, pp. 411–14. Landes thinks that the discovery of oil reserves has been a "monumental misfortune" for the Arab world (p. 414).

21. Because these basic elements of equal justice for women (including liberty of conscience and freedom of religion) are in place, I assume that the rate of population growth is voluntary, meaning that women are not coerced by their religion or their place in the social structure. This obviously calls for more discussion than I can give here.

22. For a statement of Pogge's own view see his "Human Flourishing and Universal Justice," in *Social Philosophy & Policy* 16: 1 (Winter 1999), 333–61. Pogge tells me that here his view does have a target and a cutoff point. I mention in the text that this raises the question of how great the difference may be between the duty of assistance and Pogge's global egalitarian view in "Universal Justice." Without the details of his discussion before us, I cannot discuss it further here.

20. STEPHEN M. GARDINER

Gardiner begins by criticizing the arguments of Garrett Hardin (chapter 2 in this volume). Hardin argues that the world population problem has a tragic structure, presenting us with a terrible choice between coercion and immense suffering. Gardiner argues that Hardin's arguments fail, in part because he ignores the fact that birth rates tend to fall as development takes place. Unfortunately, however, this response to concerns about population growth has a sting on its tail. For development, at least as currently practiced, tends to increase energy consumption and hence environmental impact. Consequently, the level of development needed to halt population growth, using current technologies, would lead to huge environmental problems. And certain of these environmental problems, Gardiner argues, really do have tragic structures.

The Real Tragedy of the Commons

First published in Philosophy and Public Affairs *30: 4 (autumn 2001): 387–416.*

In two celebrated and widely anthologized articles as well as several books, the biologist Garrett Hardin claims (a) that the world population problem has a certain structure: It is a tragedy of the commons; and, (b) that, given this structure, the only tenable solutions involve either coercion or immense human suffering.[1] In this article, I shall argue for two claims. First, Hardin's arguments are deeply flawed.[2] The population problem as he conceives it does not have the structure of a commons; and even if it did, this would not necessitate the extreme responses he canvasses. Second, nevertheless, much of Hardin's pessimism is justified. Some environmental problems associated with population size do have tragic structures, although these are of a different form than Hardin envisions. For example, the problem of global climate change has an intergenerational aspect that makes it significantly worse than Hardin's commons, and for this reason (as opposed to Hardin's) extreme responses may be needed to avert environmental catastrophe.[3]

I. HARDIN'S ANALYSIS

In 1804, after a wait of approximately 2 million years, human population reached 1 billion. One hundred twenty-three years later, in 1927, it topped 2 billion; thirty-three years later, in 1960, 3 billion. By 1974, fourteen years later, there were 4 billion people; thirteen years on, in 1987, 5 billion; and twelve years after that, in 1999, 6 billion.[4] This is an amazing rate of progression. Bill McKibben reports that if the world's population had increased by the same number each year throughout its history as it did in 1994, then thinking backward from its current total, the proverbial Adam and Eve would have to have started out in 1932.[5]

There are some positive signs. For example, the rate of increase in the number of humans appears to be slowing down.[6] Nevertheless, since this rate is being applied to an expanding base of people, the absolute number of births will only come down to what it is today by the second quarter of this century. Furthermore, because people are living longer, the total population will still be rising at the midcentury mark, and will then likely be around 9 billion; that is, by around 2054, global population will be 50 percent larger than it is today. Hence, the problem of population growth is very much with us.

Population is a problem because the increased absolute number of people, and the rate of increase itself, are both likely to have a severe impact on the planet. Extra people place extra demands on food, water, and energy supply, and their activities cause environmental damage. So, it is important to understand what or who[7] is causing the problem, and perhaps thereby determine what if anything can be done about it.

Hardin offers some dramatic answers to these questions. First, he claims that the population problem has a special structure—it is a commons problem—and that this structure "*remorselessly generates* tragedy."[8] The tragedy is that, left to their own devices, people have large families, causing misery to themselves and their communities and untold damage to the environment. Second, Hardin sees the problem as one primarily caused by, and affecting, those in the developing nations. Third, he argues that the only available solutions are severe. In one article, he argues that we should abandon the United Nation's declaration that freedom to reproduce is a fundamental human right.[9] Instead, Hardin thinks, we should use coercive instruments to prevent people from reproducing, or reproducing more than is wanted. In another article, Hardin argues that the affluent nations should refuse to assist their poorer neighbors in times of humanitarian crisis. Instead, he endorses Tertullian's claim that we would be wise to think of "pestilence, famine, wars, and earthquakes" as "prun[ing] away [their] luxuriant growth."[10]

Hardin's idea is that the earth provides a corrective to the problem of population through natural catastrophe. But, he thinks, human interference has disrupted the natural mechanism. Misguided altruism, in the form of the welfare state and food aid to overpopulated countries, has meant that the costs of overpopulation no longer fall on those who have the children. These institutions have created what Hardin calls "a tragedy of the commons."

The tragedy is illustrated with an example. Hardin asks us to imagine a group of farmers grazing cattle on common land. He says:

> As a rational being, each herdsman seeks to maximize his gain. Explicitly or implicitly, more or less consciously, he asks, "What is the utility to me of adding one more animal to my herd?" This utility has one negative and one positive component.
>
> (1) The positive component is a function of the increment of one animal. Since the herdsman receives all the proceeds from the sale of the additional animal, the positive utility is nearly +1.
>
> (2) The negative component is a function of the additional overgrazing created by one more animal. Since, however, the effects of overgrazing are shared by all the herdsmen, the negative utility for any particular decision-making herdsman is only a fraction of -1.
>
> Adding together the component partial utilities, the rational herdsman concludes that the only sensible course for him to pursue is to add another animal to his herd. And another.... But this is the conclusion reached by each and every rational herdsman sharing a commons. Therein is the tragedy. Each man is locked into a system that compels him to increase his herd without limit—in

a world that is limited. Ruin is the destination toward which all men rush, each pursuing his own best interest in a society that believes in the freedom of the commons. Freedom in a commons brings ruin to all.[11]

The commons, as Hardin understands it, seems to have two features. First, it is a multiperson prisoner's dilemma.[12] Second, it governs a single common resource. In this article, I shall focus on the first feature.[13]

II. THE PRISONER'S DILEMMA

A prisoner's dilemma is a situation with a certain structure. In the standard example, two prisoners are about to stand trial for a crime they are accused of committing together.[14] Each faces the following proposition. He can either confess or not confess. If both confess, then each gets five years. If neither confesses, then each gets one year on a lesser charge. But if one confesses and the other does not, then the confessor goes free, and the nonconfessor gets ten years. Neither knows for sure what the other will do; but each knows that the other faces the same choice situation.

Given this scenario, each person has the following preference ranking:

(1) I confess, the other prisoner doesn't. (Go free)
(2) Neither of us confess. (1 year)
(3) Both of us confess. (5 years)
(4) I don't confess, but the other prisoner does. (10 years)

This situation is usually expressed with a diagram:

| | | Person B | |
		don't confess	confess
Person A	don't confess	1, 1 (2nd, 2nd)	10, 0 (4th, 1st)
	confess	0, 10 (1st, 4th)	5, 5 (3rd, 3rd)

The reason why the situation is called a dilemma is as follows. Suppose I am one of the prisoners. I cannot guarantee what the other prisoner will do, and have no effective means to make it that I can do so. So I need to consider each possibility. Suppose he confesses. Then it is better for me to confess also (since five years in jail is better than ten). Suppose he does not confess. Then it is better for me to confess (since going free is better than one year in jail). So, whatever he does, I should confess. But the situation is exactly the same for him. So, reasoning in the same way I do, he will confess also. Hence, the outcome will be that both of us confess (getting five years each). But this yields a suboptimal outcome. Each of us prefers the outcome that comes from us both not confessing (one year each) over the outcome that comes from us both confessing (five years each).[15]

For our purposes, the problem can be (roughly) characterized as follows:

PD1: It is *collectively rational* to cooperate: each agent prefers the outcome produced by everyone cooperating over the outcome produced by no one cooperating.

PD2: It is *individually rational* not to cooperate: when each individual has the power to decide whether or not she will cooperate, each person (rationally) prefers not to cooperate, whatever the others do.

PD1 and PD2 generate the paradox as follows. In prisoner's dilemma situations, each individual has the power to decide whether or not she will cooperate. Hence, given PD2, if each person is individually rational, no one cooperates. But this means that each person ends up with an outcome that she prefers less than another outcome that is available. For, according to PD1, each prefers the cooperative over the noncooperative outcome.[16]

Hardin's description of this kind of situation as a tragedy is apt. For what happens is more than simply a bad thing. The situation as it stands drives people by an inexorable process toward a situation that is worse by their own lights, and away from a situation that is better. Indeed, it is the very same values that make cooperation preferable that drive each agent away from it. In the classic example, prisoners want less jail time, that is why they collectively prefer cooperation; but their desire for less jail time also makes it individually rational for them not to cooperate.

III. COERCION AND POPULATION

Now, suppose the population problem were a prisoner's dilemma. What would follow? Hardin suggests two things. In "Tragedy of the Commons," he says that we should mutually agree on the use of coercive instruments to prevent people from reproducing, or reproducing more than is wanted. In "Lifeboat Ethics" [herein 15–27] he argues that the affluent nations should refuse to assist their poorer neighbors in times of humanitarian crisis.

These recommendations are difficult to accept.[17] Indeed, there is a strong moral presumption against Hardin's solutions. For they imply that the rich countries should deliberately allow hundreds of millions of people to die, when the rich could help the poor at relatively small cost to themselves. This conflicts with even a very weak principle of beneficence.[18] It may also be resisted on other moral grounds.[19]

Given the presumptions against Hardin's solutions, surely we should think on moral grounds that if almost anything else will work, then that is what we should do. This makes it relevant to consider alternative ways in which prisoner's dilemma situations might be resolved, ways that do not involve coercion. At least three are pertinent here. The first is to change people's motives, and so alter the preference structure that generates the problem. Hence, one might try to make people value some aspect of the situation in a new way. For example, fairly recently, many people have been made to disparage Styrofoam cups to the extent that they have such a strong preference to drink from a reusable cup, that they are willing to carry one around with them. Or one might try to make people value cooperation itself.

The second solution is to appeal to broad considerations of self-interest. For example, it is well known that the dynamics of a prisoner's dilemma can be changed if the parties will meet again in other bargaining situations in the future. If we know that we must make a bargain again, we are much more likely to give up some gains from noncooperation now in exchange for the expectation of gains to be made from an overall strategy of cooperation.

The third solution is to appeal to a sense of fair play, and in particular to the notion of reciprocity. This is present in almost all societies, and supports a social attitude of rebuke to those who do not cooperate: They are socially shunned. This too can work to solve some problems without the need for coercive state interference.[20]

Now the problem for Hardin is that, even if the population problem were a prisoner's dilemma, it seems plausible to think that any one of these solutions (or some combination) might help to resolve it. The appeal to broad self-interest looks especially promising. The economic costs of having children are huge; and the noneconomic costs are also frequently high. Though, arguably, the noneconomic benefits of parenthood are similarly large, it seems more than possible to persuade people either to forgo these altogether (by having no children of their own, and making do with being biological or nonbiological aunts or uncles, for example), or to have fewer of these benefits (by having fewer children), in exchange for the savings incurred by not having children.[21] Indeed, arguably, this is at least part of what has already happened in the developed countries, and has reduced the number of children there.

However, Hardin seems to treat the possibility of such solutions with outright disdain. In particular, he seems to think that an appeal to broad self-interest will not work because self-interest is far too deeply tied to the production of children for any change in reproductive behavior to occur.[22] And he regards an appeal to fairness as not only ineffective, but also self-eliminating.

These attitudes of Hardin's suggest that he regards the population problem not just as a prisoner's dilemma, but a prisoner's dilemma that depends on circumstances of a particularly deep and intractable kind. So, in order to understand Hardin's attitudes, we must look at his arguments for the claim that population is a prisoner's dilemma.

IV. POPULATION AS A PRISONER'S DILEMMA

If population is a prisoner's dilemma, then it must have the following features:

Population-PD1: It is *collectively rational* to have smaller families: Each agent prefers the outcome produced by everyone having smaller families over the outcome produced by everyone having large families.

Population-PD2: It is *individually rational* to have a large family: when each individual has the power to decide whether or not she will have a large or small family, each person (rationally) prefers to have a large family, no matter what everyone else does.[23]

The first problem for Hardin, which is widely noted, is that, on the assumption that most actual people are individually rational to this extent, *Population-PD2* seems to be empirically false. This is true both of its content and its form.

With regard to content, the raw data is remarkably consistent. First, as is often pointed out, there has been a significant transition in Western Europe over the past one hundred years or so. All agree that Western Europe is *below* replacement level, and that this is almost true now in North America.[24] There was a spurt of population growth with industrialization, but now this is over. Furthermore, this happened without coercion. So, *Population-PD2* is not true of the behavior of people in these nations.[25] Second, the UN reports that *global* fertility rates have fallen significantly in the recent past (to 2.7 children per family in 1998, from 5 in the early 1950s); and, furthermore, this reflects a decline in fertility in *all* regions of the world (in the last twenty-five years, 6.6 to 5.1 in Africa, 5.1 to 2.6 in Asia, 5.0 to 2.7 in Latin America and the Caribbean).[26] So, *Population-PD2* seems unlikely to be true of the behavior of the world as a whole, either: All seem to be following the downward trend toward smaller family size.[27]

As well as being in stark conflict with the raw data, *Population-PD2* also takes an overly simplistic form. It reduces the question of reproduction to the issue of family size. But even in the developing nations, matters are much more complex than this. For example, the recent Indian census has suggested that ultrasound technology is enabling Indians to follow the Chinese in aborting female fetuses at abnormally high rates. In India, then, it seems clear that sex plays a significant role in reproductive choice, and one that affects family size. And this fact is clearly relevant for population policy.[28]

The second problem for Hardin is that *Population-PD2* seems independently implausible. Although *Population-PD1* seems plausible enough (it is undoubtably true that everyone is worse off if all have large families), what makes it in my interests to have a large family *whatever anyone else does?* Consider the following: For a prisoner's dilemma, we need this incentive structure:

		Couple B	
		merely replaces	has a large family
Couple A	merely replaces	2nd, 2nd *maintain current population*	4th, 1st
	has a large family	1st, 4th	3rd, 3rd *population explosion*

But why would we think that couples have these preferences, so that the preferred outcome for all is to have a large family, and what is feared most of all is for others to have large families while we do not? Under moderately favorable conditions, it seems more plausible that some people will prefer replacement, or close to replacement, no matter what everyone else does; that very few people will prefer having lots of children just for the sake of it; and that some will prefer no children (or one). Indeed, the empirical evidence from the developed countries suggests that overall, taking everyone's preferences into account, uncoerced decisions produce a level of reproduction that is *below* the replacement level for a whole society.

To resist this argument, Hardin has to claim that it is always to the advantage of the individual to have a large family.[29] But why should we believe this? It is not clear. But Hardin seems tempted by the view that it is because it is *biologically advantageous* to have a large family. For example, he says: ·

> *If* each human family were dependent only on its own resources;
> *if* the children of improvident parents starved to death; *if,* thus,
> overbreeding brought its own "punishment" to the germ line—*then*

there would be no public interest in controlling the breeding of families. But our society is deeply committed to the welfare state, and hence is confronted with another aspect of the tragedy of the commons. In a welfare state, how shall we deal with the family, the religion, the race, or the class (or indeed any distinguishable and cohesive group) that adopts overbreeding as a policy to secure its own aggrandizement? To couple the concept of freedom to breed with the belief that everyone born has an equal right to the commons is to lock the world into a tragic course of action.[30]

Now, this argument faces two problems. First, it is concerned with groups and germ lines. It says nothing about the interests of the *individuals* involved. Therefore, it does nothing to justify the claim that it is always to the advantage of the individual to have a large family. Second, this claim would be plausible only if one posited a strong correlation between the biological interests of a germ line and the self-interest of individuals carrying that germ line. But, on any plausible theory of the interests or well-being of an individual, an individual's self-interest does not consist in, nor is it dominated by, even his or her own biological interests, let alone the biological interests of the group.[31]

But perhaps Hardin has a second argument that does not depend on people's interests. When arguing against the idea that an appeal to conscience might solve the population problem (my "fair play suggestion"), he says:

> People vary. Confronted with appeals to limited breeding, some people will undoubtedly respond to the plea more than others. Those who have more children will produce a larger fraction of the next generation than those with more susceptible consciences. The difference will be accentuated, generation by generation.... The argument assumes that conscience or the desire to have children (no matter which) is hereditary—but hereditary only in the most general formal sense. The result will be the same whether the attitude is transmitted through germ cells, or exosomatically.... The argument has been stated in the context of the population problem, but it applies equally well to any instance in which society appeals to an individual exploiting a commons to restrain himself for the general good—by means of his conscience. To make such an appeal is to set up a selective system that works toward the elimination of conscience from the race.[32]

Hence, Hardin argues that reproductive restraint will be eliminated by natural selection: Those who practice restraint will have fewer descendants than those who do not, and since the attitude of restraint is transmitted between generations, this attitude will become progressively less common.

This argument faces serious practical, empirical, and theoretical problems. The practical problem is that natural selection works over very long time-scales. Hence, it is unlikely to happen fast enough to prevent the appeal to conscience working for a while. And perhaps a while is all we need worry about, if the benign demographic thesis is correct. The empirical problem is that if Hardin were right, we would expect people already to have the desire for as many children as possible, since we would expect the selection procedure to have been at work for generations.[33] But the empirical evidence suggests the opposite: Global fertility rates are falling. The theoretical problem is the assumption that the attitude of restraint is transmitted between generations. There is simply no reason to believe that peoples' consciences will be the same as their parents', nor in particular that they will have the same attitude toward reproduction. Indeed, the empirical evidence stands squarely against it.

So, I conclude that Hardin's analysis of the population problem as a prisoner's dilemma is untenable. It relies on flawed assumptions about human motivation that rest on extremely dubious appeals to evolutionary biology.

V. TOTAL ENVIRONMENTAL IMPACT

The discussion so far has shown that Hardin's analysis of the population problem as a tragedy of the commons is fatally flawed, and even if it were not, Hardin's solutions would not be justified. But there is one respect in which Hardin's account is close to the truth. At least one aspect of the population problem does have a tragic structure; and extreme solutions may be required to overcome it.

To begin, it is worth observing that the important issue about population is not how many people there are. In itself, this tells us nothing and threatens little. The real issue is the environmental impact that people have, in particular on the so-called carrying capacity of the earth.[34] Thus, if there is an issue of population, it is the issue of how the number of people in the world interacts with the environmental impact per person, to produce the total environmental impact of humanity.

On this issue, however, there is reason to believe that the most important variable is the environmental impact per person, not the total human population.[35] If this is right, the benign demographic thesis turns out not to be so encouraging after all. For that thesis suggests that the price of a decrease in the absolute number of people is development. But development as we presently understand it requires additional energy consumption, and this in turn tends to involve an increase in the environmental impact per person.[36] (For the major sources of energy currently supporting the developed countries, especially oil and coal, come with significant environmental impacts.) Indeed, the development necessary for the less developed nations to reach a stable or even declining population would, on present technologies, involve a catastrophic increase in energy consumption, and so in the environmental impact per person.[37]

This news is bad enough, but there is worse to come. For the problem of an escalating environmental impact per person seems to have a structure similar to the one that so worries Hardin in his misdiagnosis of the problem of world population. Indeed, the structure of this problem is in some respects worse than the one Hardin envisions, and so more of a tragedy.

VI. THE INTERGENERATIONAL ISSUE

There are both inter- and intragenerational problems involving environmental impact. Consider first the intergenerational problem. Much of the damage inflicted by energy consumption is by current generations on future generations.[38] For example, global climate change is caused mainly by emissions of carbon dioxide, but the effects of these emissions on the global temperature suffer from an important time-lag. The lifetime of carbon dioxide in the upper atmosphere is over one hundred years, so that the full (cumulative) effects of current emissions will not be felt until the beginning of the twenty-second century. By contrast, the benefit of burning fossil fuels, the energy thereby produced, is consumed by the present generation. Hence, whereas the present generation both causes the environmental damage and reaps the rewards, most of the costs fall on future generations.[39] This suggests that the current generation has a powerful self-interested reason to carry on polluting, and the future generations a powerful self-interested reason for wanting that pollution to stop.[40]

Now, it is true that this problem has a tragic structure, and is a commons. But it is not a tragedy of the commons in Hardin's sense. It is worse. Present and future generations both have an interest in the earth's relative climatic stability, and therefore in its capacity to absorb the by-products of fossil fuel emissions. But, of course, the future generations have no control over what the present generation does with that capacity; whether it stays within, uses up, or exceeds it. Indeed, they could not *in principle* have any such control. They are not around to present a claim, nor to represent their interests. Worse, even if they were around, or even if someone could represent them, they would have no bargaining power. There is nothing that they can offer the present generation in exchange for cooperation (or nothing that the present generation could not take anyway). So, what happens is completely up to the present generation. And it has powerful self-interested incentives to exceed the capacity and thereby alter the climate.

Given this analysis, other things being equal, it is reasonable to expect that the commons will be deeply harmed by the present generation. Furthermore, the same reasoning will apply to each future generation as it comes into being. However much it may deplore the effects of the previous generations decisions on it, each generation will face the same decision situation with respect to generations later than it. Hence, each generation will pollute, and the pollution will continue as long as the earth can bear it.

This analysis shares with Hardin's tragedy of the commons the claim that a suboptimal outcome might eventuate even if collectively all generations would agree that it would be better if the atmosphere were not so exploited. For this agreement would be based on what is better for the human race as a whole, or better for each generation bar the first if all others do the same. But this qualification about the first generation is extremely important. It makes the current problem worse than a prisoner's dilemma, for restricting pollution is not better for the first generation. And then, provided each generation takes its starting position as a given, it is not better for subsequent generations either. So, we get a sequential motive toward noncooperation and overpollution.

In short, the intergeneration problem has the following general features:

Intergenerational-1:   It is *collectively rational* for most generations to cooperate: (almost) every generation prefers the outcome produced by everyone restricting pollution over the outcome produced by everyone overpolluting.

Intergenerational-2:   It is *individually rational* for all generations not to cooperate: when each generation has the power to decide whether or not it will overpollute, each generation (rationally) prefers to overpollute, whatever the others do.

This structure is worse than the prisoner's dilemma structure in the following ways. First, *Intergenerational-1* is worse than *PD1* because it is not true that everyone prefers cooperation (hence, the "almost"). The first generation capable of overexploiting the atmosphere will prefer to do so, since it experiences no gains from cooperation. Second, *Intergenerational-2*: is worse than *PD2* because the reason for it is deeper. In the prisoner's dilemma, *PD2* arises because there is *in fact* no way for each prisoner or herdsman to ensure that the behavior of others is beneficial so long as his is beneficial. But here, *Intergenerational-2* arises because the situation is such that it is *in principle* impossible for one generation to ensure that the behavior of the others is beneficial so long as theirs is beneficial.

The intergenerational problem not only has a more tragic structure than Hardin's tragedy of the commons, it is also more resistant to solution. Earlier I argued, contrary to Hardin, that his problem could be resolved by standard noncoercive means, e.g., by appeal to broad self-interest or to a sense of fairness. But here such solutions are problematic. First, the usual appeals to broad self-interest rely on there being repeated interactions between the parties where mutually beneficial behavior is possible. But between present and future generations there is neither repeated interaction (by definition, there is no interaction at all), nor mutual benefit (there is little future generations can do to benefit present generations).[41] Second, similar difficulties arise for standard appeals to reciprocity: Future people cannot reciprocate. Still, perhaps one could argue that if the first generation capable of serious long-term pollution unilaterally restricts its activities, then subsequent generations can owe the obligation to their forefathers to restrict their pollution for the sake of future generations. (Subsequent generations get a benefit from not inheriting an overpolluted planet, but then must, out of fairness, pass this on, so that there is a kind of indirect reciprocity.) Unfortunately, this solution faces both theoretical and practical problems. The theoretical problem is that we need to assume that the initial generation makes a pure sacrifice of self-interest, with no compensation. So, their action cannot be justified by an appeal to (even indirect) *reciprocity*. The practical problem is that the antecedent is not satisfied: Significant long-term pollution has already occurred.[42]

These problems reflect the difference in structure of the cases already mentioned. For, in the prisoner's dilemma case, most of the proposed solutions rely on rearranging the situation so as to provide some kind of guarantee of the behavior of others when one cooperates. But in the intergenerational problem, there is no way to rearrange the situation in this way.[43] It is essential to the problem that the parties cannot interact, and so that the future generations are in no position to benefit nor to engage in reciprocal acts with their forebears.

VII. TWO INTERPRETATIONS OF THE INTRAGENERATIONAL PROBLEM

Suppose for the moment that the intergenerational problem can be overcome, and people in the present generation agree that they have a reason not to overpollute. Still there is a problem. For there remains a collective action problem at the intragenerational level. Again, let us take climate change as our example.

Now, there is some controversy about how to characterize the intragenerational aspect of the global warming problem. In particular, there seems to be some case for describing it as a Prisoner's Dilemma, and some for describing it as a Battle of the Sexes.[44] A full account of these matters would be beyond the scope of this article.[45] However, for current purposes we can make do with something more limited. I shall argue that, even without decisively resolving the theoretical dispute, in practice the intragenerational problem is best treated *as if* it were a prisoner's dilemma, and so as adding a further tragic structure to the general problem of global warming.[46]

To make this argument, I shall present a brief case for three claims: first, that, seen from a long-term perspective, there is a strong case for characterizing the intragenerational global warming problem as a prisoner's dilemma; second, that if there is uncertainty about whether it is a battle of the sexes or prisoner's dilemma, it should be treated as if it were a prisoner's dilemma; and, third, that in any case the importance of classifying it as a battle of the sexes instead of a prisoner's dilemma is undercut by the background presence of the intergenerational problem.

Let us begin with a preliminary case for a prisoner's dilemma interpretation. Consider the circumstances facing *individual members* of the present generation (or individual firms).[47] On the surface, these appear to generate a prisoner's dilemma. To begin with, even if the members of the present generation care about future generations, the marginal effects of any individual's pollution are small. Furthermore, there are powerful incentives to cheat. First, not polluting involves an absolute sacrifice of energy consumption, and so of self-interest. Second, it is cheaper to pollute than not to pollute; and the cheaper energy is a comparative advantage when one is producing things in the marketplace.[48] Third, cheating might be difficult to identify. Carbon dioxide emissions, for example, are very difficult to monitor and detect.[49] Fourth, policing will be difficult in another way: So long as everyone cheats, cheating does not harm anyone around at the moment; so there is no one presently around with a powerful interest in stopping it. Indeed, as we have already seen, all the present people have a powerful interest in polluting, no matter what others do, and so have an incentive to turn a blind eye to the pollution of others so long as others turn a blind eye to them.

If this is right, even without considering the intergenerational problem, members of the present generation seem to have the following preference structure:

1st preference: I pollute, you don't.

2nd preference: No one pollutes.

3rd preference: Everyone pollutes.

4th preference: You pollute, I don't.

But this, of course, is a prisoner's dilemma preference structure. Hence, other things being equal, left to their own devices each individual will choose a strategy of polluting, since it gets better outcomes than not polluting. But then everyone will pollute, which gives everyone only their third preference, and not their second.

Now, it is tempting to suppose that the prisoner's dilemma analysis applies not only to individuals and individual firms, but also to countries. But this extension may be questioned.[50] For it may be said that it neglects the fact that perhaps the collective good at stake can be achieved without *everyone* cooperating, and therefore that it may be rational for a subgroup to produce the good alone.[51] In this case, there will be a situation where, for N players:

Partial Cooperation: There is a number M (such that M < N) that is the minimum number of players whose cooperation is necessary if some situation, which is bad for all, is to be avoided.

Marginal Cooperation: If the number of others who are willing to cooperate is just short of M, then a given party prefers to cooperate, since he is better off enjoying the benefits of cooperation and paying his share of the cost than he is in the situation where not enough people cooperate.[52]

This situation is not a prisoner's dilemma. It is distinctive of a prisoner's dilemma that each party does at least as well by not cooperating as he does by cooperating, no matter what the others do. But in this situation, if the number of other cooperators is just short of M, then a given player does better by cooperating than not cooperating. This kind of situation is usually termed a many-person battle of the sexes.[53]

Interpreting the intragenerational global warming problem as a battle of the sexes has some initial appeal.[54] Principally, it reflects the undoubted theoretical fact that it is *total* global emissions that need to be cut, so that in principle there is no physical reason why the costs of any given percentage reduction need to be borne by all.[55] Furthermore, if the intragenerational problem were a battle of the sexes, this would be welcome news, practically speaking. For, unlike a prisoner's dilemma, a battle of the sexes may have internal solutions: that is, solutions that do not require a change in the payoffs available to the players, or to the basic psychology of self-interest.[56] So, solving the intragenerational problem would be easier than if it were a prisoner's dilemma.[57]

VIII. THE INTRAGENERATIONAL PROBLEM IN PRACTICE

Nevertheless, there are some reasons for concern about the battle of the sexes analysis. First, the idea of a fixed global percentage reduction does not adequately capture the dynamic nature of the problem and the exponential nature of growth.[58] To begin with, any actual talk of stabilization or a percentage reduction is relative to a fixed point (under Kyoto, 1990) where not all countries are making maximum use of fossil fuels (or, more broadly, of CO_2 emissions themselves), and it is quite likely that none are.[59] So what really needs to be looked at is the percentage reduction needed over the global total for maximum usage. This is unknown, as we don't know what possible uses of CO_2 emissions technological developments might make open to us. However, if, as a rough (and probably extremely conservative) estimate, we take current US emissions as the maximum per capita, based on current technology, we would get an astronomical total from which to cut back to, say, 1990.[60] Furthermore, this means that the costs must be borne by anyone with the potential ability to bring the global total above the optimal level of emissions. But (depending on the figures above, and especially if the gains in terms of self-interest from fossil fuel use have not yet been fully realized) this means everyone, or almost everyone.[61] Without full cooperation one is at best delaying global warming, not arresting it.[62]

If all this is right, it casts doubt on the partial compliance assumption. For it suggests one of two possibilities. If the size of the smallest player is large enough that it alone could ensure that the ceiling is broken regardless of what the others do, then the Partial Compliance Assumption is false. Alternatively, if M is large, and close to N, then the Partial Compliance Assumption is misleading in the context. For the nations excluded must have small populations and/or current emissions. Therefore, they will not be major players in the climate change problem, nor indeed in the wider international arena.[63] The focus on partial compliance is thus at best misleading.

Second, the Marginal Cooperation claim is also dubious. Consider it first in relation to Hardin's commons. In Hardin's commons, it is not true that only a subgroup of cooperators is required to secure the collective good. Instead, any attempt by a subgroup to secure the optimal productivity of the commons will be undermined by the remaining noncooperators. For it is true both (a) that it is possible for any noncooperating herdsman to increase his herd without limit, and (b) that each has an incentive to do so, since the benefits accrue only to him whereas the costs are shared by all. Indeed, this is just the fundamental dynamic that creates the commons problem in the first place.[64]

The lesson here is that one has a prisoner's dilemma, not a battle of the sexes, if it is possible for noncooperators to undermine the collective good produced by a subgroup, and if they have a strong enough incentive to do so. But just these features seem to be present in the global warming case. For, given what we have already said, it is empirically likely both that noncooperators can disrupt the ceiling of emissions, and that they have the incentive to do so.[65] Hence, the subgroup cannot enforce a ceiling, and would incur large costs if it tried. It seems, then, that the intragenerational global warming problem will be a prisoner's dilemma.

Now, the above constitutes a strong case for a prisoner's dilemma interpretation. Nevertheless, in the end, it is an empirical matter whether this interpretation is correct, or whether global warming turns out to be some other kind of collective action problem; and the empirical issues are complex and shrouded in uncertainty. So, it is helpful to have a secondary practical argument at hand. This goes as follows. If it is an empirical matter whether global warming is, say, a battle of the sexes or a prisoner's dilemma, then it is at least *possible* that the problem is a prisoner's dilemma (or worse). But then there are grounds to treat it *as if* it were a prisoner's dilemma. There are three reasons.

First, if it is possible that global warming is a prisoner's dilemma, this undermines the practical advantage of classifying the problem as a battle of the sexes, which was that such problems may have internal solutions.[66] For if the problem may turn out to be a prisoner's dilemma, we should not rely on internal solutions because they are unavailable for prisoner's dilemma. Instead, we should seek external solutions, such as payoff changes and motivation changes, because these can resolve *both* prisoner's dilemma and battle of the sexes. In general, if there is doubt about whether a situation is prisoner's dilemma or battle of the sexes, and if the noncooperative outcomes are potentially catastrophic, it seems to make sense to employ those solutions that apply to both; if one tries only battle of the sexes methods, then one might fail.

Second, even if the intragenerational problem were a battle of the sexes, the relevance of this fact would be undermined by the background presence of the intergenerational problem. So far, we have simply assumed that problem away in this section, but in practice it will likely corrupt the presence in the current generation of concerns for the distant future.

Third, a similar undermining occurs due to the presence within the present generation of localized variants of the intergenerational problem. For example, governments and businesses are typically headed by elites whose time horizons are extremely limited. They have a strong incentive to ignore altogether, or at least defer action on, problems whose solutions demand high costs to be instituted on the present set of voters and other politically influential groups for the sake of benefits to those who do not currently have any political power.

If these arguments are correct, then there are strong reasons for treating the intragenerational global warming problem as if it were a prisoner's dilemma. This news is bad enough. But matters are made worse by the fact that the usual solutions to prisoner's dilemma situations also tend to be undermined by the background presence of the intergenerational problem. First, the appeal to broad self-interest is problematic. Although the current generations do interact repeatedly, so that there are many gains to be made through cooperation, the accessibility of these gains does not depend on cooperation about pollution. In fact, restricting pollution actually lessens the potential gains of cooperation, perhaps even to the point where from a self-interested point of view it is better to pollute and not cooperate than to cooperate and not pollute. So, the potential gains to be made from cooperation do not have the same status as in normal prisoner's dilemma cases.[67] Second, the problem of monitoring compliance suggests that the appeal to fairness also may not work.[68] Hardin may be wrong that natural selection eliminates conscience, but it does seem plausible to say that, without an effective method of ensuring compliance, the market eliminates a sense of fairness, or at least a competitively disadvantageous sense of fairness. If some producers cheat on energy consumption, they will have a competitive advantage, through exploiting the externality costs. Hence, over time, they will eliminate more restrained competitors.[69]

IX. IMPLICATIONS

If my analysis of the inter- and intragenerational problems surrounding global warming are correct, two of Hardin's main claims are right after all. First, strong coercive regulatory regimes may be needed in order to stop overpollution, and so to address the pressing problem suggested by population growth.[70] Second, the benign demographic transition hypothesis should be treated with suspicion.

Nevertheless, Hardin and I differ in our reasons for making these claims, and this has practical consequences. In the first case, Hardin is not correct about who the primary subjects of coercion should be. For it is people in the rich countries who presently cause most of the pollution I have been concerned with, not those in the poor countries. Hence, while it is true that it would be disastrous for the poor countries to adopt the more energy- and pollution-intensive lifestyles of the West (and, as a result there is reason to prevent this happening), it is also true, and more important, that even without their contribution, the existing patterns of behavior in the West will have serious consequences, and must be stopped. This should be the political priority.[71]

In the second case, Hardin is skeptical about the benign demographic transition hypothesis because he doubts the scientific evidence, and is inclined toward a strong evolutionary account of human reproductive behavior. But I am skeptical because, although the empirical evidence for a decline in population seems compelling, I doubt that the expected transition will be benign. For it comes at the price of increased development, and so increased energy consumption and pollution. This locates the problem not in the deep nature of human beings and their germ lines, but rather in ways of life that all of us could, and should, give up.

NOTES

Parts of this article were presented to the International Society for Environmental Ethics at the American Philosophical Association (Eastern Division) meeting in Atlanta in 2001, and to the Australasian Association for Professional and Applied Ethics conference in Brisbane in 2000. I'd like to thank my audience on those occasions and, in particular, Dale Jamieson, Andrew Brennan, and my APA commentator, Margaret Holmgren. I have also benefited from discussions with Tim Bayne, Simon Blackburn, Roger Crisp, Philip Pettit, David Schmidtz, and Henry Shue; and from the written comments of an anonymous reviewer for *Philosophy & Public Affairs*. Some of the work on this article was completed while I was a visitor at Hertford College, Oxford University, and Cornell University, as the recipient of an Erskine Fellowship. I would like to thank all three institutions for their support. I owe most to Nicholas Sturgeon, who not only set me on this path, but also provided a fine example of how to do analytic philosophy well.

1. "Tragedy of the Commons," *Science* 162 (1968): 1243–48; "Living in a Lifeboat," *Bioscience* 24 (1974): 561–68. See also *Living Within Limits* (Cambridge: Cambridge University Press, 1993); *The Ostrich Factor: Our Population Myopia* (Oxford: Oxford University Press, 1999). Some estimation of the influence of Hardin's work and the esteem with which it is held in the scientific community can be found in Joanna Burger and Michael Gochfield, "The Tragedy of the Commons 30 Years Later," *Environment* (December 1998): 4–27; the responses in "The Tragedy of the Commons Revisited," *Environment* (March 1999): 4–5, 45; and Hardin's "Extensions of 'The Tragedy of the Commons'," *Science* 280 (1998): 682–83. Burger and Gochfield include a graph of the citation index from 1968 to 1997 showing persistent levels of over 100 citations per year among natural and social scientists.

2. Hardin's work has, of course, been criticized before, but I have not found the criticism I will make in the literature. First, most of the criticism is empirical, especially that offered by proponents of a benign demographic transition hypothesis, who maintain that population will be curbed by development. Unfortunately, valuable though it is, this work does not directly address Hardin's main argument, which is not empirical but theoretical. Second, much of the theoretical criticism of Hardin revolves around his metaphors in "Lifeboat Ethics," [herein 15–27] not those in "Tragedy of the Commons." For a good discussion of the major views and their weaknesses, see Jesper Ryberg, "Population and Third World Assistance," *Journal of Applied Philosophy* 14 (1997): 207–19.

3. The climate change problem is a useful illustration for two reasons: because it seems to be the most serious environmental problem we face at present; and because something like the same incentive structure appears to some degree in other environmental problems.

4. United Nations, Department of Economic and Social Affairs, Population Division, *1998 Update* (http://www.census.gov//ipc//www/worldpop.html).

5. Bill McKibben, "Reaching the Limit," *New York Review of Books* (May 29, 1997).

6. The U.S. Bureau of Census estimates the peak to have been in 1962 and 1963 at 2.19 percent per year.

7. This is not to say that the issue is one of whom to blame, in the moral sense. Hardin thinks blaming misses the point. In "Lifeboat," he says, "the concepts of blame and punishment are irrelevant. The question is, what are the operational consequences of establishing a world food bank?" (p. 563). In *Living Within Limits*, this is on his assumption that "each human being, like every other animal, is genetically programmed to seek its own good," so that "[t]he tragedy is brought on not by individual sin ('greed'), but by the system itself" (p. 218).

8. "Tragedy," p. 1244; emphasis added.

9. Ibid., p. 1246; *Ostrich*, p. 145.

10. "Lifeboat," p. 564.

11. "Tragedy," p. 1244. Repeated in *Living Within Limits*, pp. 217–18.

12. See Nick Griffin, "Lifeboat USA, Part 1," *International Journal of Moral and Social Studies* 3 (1988): 230–31.

13. The second feature also poses difficulties for Hardin. Environmental problems associated with population growth can impact resources at various levels (local, national, regional, and global). Presumably, then, the best candidate for a single common resource is the biosphere as a whole. But Hardin does not take this approach. Instead, in "Lifeboat," he rejects a "spaceship earth" metaphor in favor of speaking of the rich countries as individual lifeboats that should defend themselves against the lifeboats of the poor countries. But it is not clear what the ecological grounds could be for taking individual countries as single common resources. For further criticisms, see William W. Murdoch and Allen Oaten, "Population and Food: Metaphors and the Reality," *Bioscience* 25 (1975); reprinted in Louis Pojman, *Environmental Ethics*, 2d ed. (Belmont, CA: Wadsworth, 1998), 357–61.

14. The title and illustration are attributed to Albert Tucker, who used them to popularize ideas developed by Merrill Flood and Melvin Dresher in investigating global nuclear strategy. For more information, see Stephen Kuhn, "The Prisoner's Dilemma," *Stanford Encyclopedia of Philosophy*, http://setis.library.usyd.edu.au/stanford/entries/prisoner-dilemma/#Bib'.

15. But neither of us can get there as things stand. Suppose one of us thinks, It's a prisoner's dilemma, so we should not confess. Then, the other person knows that we know this. But if he thinks we are not going to confess, the rational thing for him to do is to confess, since this gives him a better outcome. Remember that the previous reasoning showed that a prisoner should confess, no matter what the other prisoner does.

16. The prisoner's dilemma structure is interesting for both theoretical and practical reasons. The theoretical reason is that it involves a paradox of rationality. It shows that in some situations, individuals reasoning purely on the basis of self-interest can be led to make decisions that are suboptimal in terms of self-interest. (Strictly-speaking, the problem does not depend on self-interested motivation per se, but might arise for any value system with a similar structure, including some moral views. See Derek Parfit, *Reasons and Persons* [Oxford: Oxford University Press, 1984], pp. 55–56, 95–110.) The practical reason is that there are real-world situations that have this structure.

17. Ryberg also argues that even if Hardin is right about the severity of the problem, it may not necessitate his solutions. Ryberg's argument relies on the idea that aid to the "overpopulated" countries coupled with regulation of population via famine and environmental disaster may still be best on Hardin's consequentialist grounds. See Ryberg, pp. 212–15. Hence, he disputes Hardin's empirical claims about the overall results of the prisoner's dilemma. By contrast, I take issue with Hardin's assumptions about what follows from the dilemma situation itself.

18. A principle of beneficence may be conceived of as either a principle of moral goodness (or virtue), or as a moral requirement. Here I directly intend the former, as beneficence is less controversial as a moral ideal (say, of charity), than as a moral requirement. But I also believe that the weak principle I have in mind is plausible as a requirement.

19. For example, some might argue that, in withholding aid, the rich countries seem to treat the people who starve as a result disrespectfully. For the starving seem to be treated in ways to which they could not in principle consent, and so can be conceived of as being coerced. (One might also say that they are thereby used by the rich as a means to solving a wider problem.) Hence, their actions conflict with major tenets of Kantian (and arguably commonsense) morality, which claim we should not treat others in ways to which we could not in principle consent, and that we should never treat them merely as a means. These claims are, of course, controversial, even amongst Kantians. But an approach to aid problems that makes moves of this sort has been defended by Onora O'Neill, "Ending World Hunger" in Tom Regan, ed., *Matters of Life and Death*, 3d ed. (Belmont, CA: Wadsworth, 1993), and *Faces of Hunger: An Essay on Poverty, Justice, and Development* (London: Allen & Unwin, 1985).

20. In the original standard "tit for tat" solutions to the prisoner's dilemma, the second and third strategies fit together. Robert Axelrod reported that "the two requisites for cooperation to thrive are that the cooperation be based on reciprocity, and that the shadow of the future is important enough to make this reciprocity stable." (Axelrod, *The Evolution of Cooperation* [New York: Basic Books, 1984]; selection reprinted in *Ethics*, Peter Singer, ed. [Oxford: Oxford University Press, 1994], pp. 88–92 at p. 90.) For egoists, these conditions hold

when there is prolonged interaction over time and where this interaction holds the promise of great benefits to both sides.

21. For an overview, see Andrew Hacker, "The Case Against Kids," *New York Review of Books*, vol. 47, no. 19 (November 30, 2000): 12–18.

22. Hardin says, "Ruin is the destination toward which all men rush, each pursuing his own best interest in a society that believes in the freedom of the commons" ("Tragedy," p. 1244, emphasis added); about the population problem in particular he says, "the individual benefits as an individual from his ability to deny the truth [about the population tragedy] even though society as a whole, of which he is a part, suffers" ("Tragedy," p. 1244).

23. Hardin tends to speak in terms of "overbreeding," and seems to mean by this "having as many healthy, surviving children as possible." But his general argument requires only the more modest "have a size of family above replacement level," and this is what I intend here. (I have avoided the use of "breeding" as this term may seem offensive, and in any case encourages the animalistic connotations Hardin tries to give human behavior, connotations I resist below.)

24. The North American population figures are complicated by large immigration to both the United States and Canada. Without immigration, North America is likely to be slightly below replacement.

25. It is not true even in those nations officially in favor of more rather than fewer children. For example: Italy is officially Catholic; but nineteenth-century Italy had a fertility rate of five children per woman; but now it is down to significantly below that necessary for replacement. Indeed, the United Nations predicts very substantial immigration will be necessary to maintain its current population.

26. United Nations, *1998 Update*. This data is used by optimists about population in support of their view that there will be a benign demographic transition to lower total population. The pessimists may argue that these declines are coming too late (and they may be right). But this does not help Hardin's argument, for this is an empirical question, to be answered by the data. But Hardin doesn't provide any data. He provides a conceptual argument to show that the population problem is a prisoner's dilemma, and that coercion is required.

27. For a good discussion of the data, see Elizabeth Willot, "Population Trends," in David Schmidtz and Elizabeth Willot, eds., *Environmental Ethics: What Really Matters, What Really Works* (Oxford: Oxford University Press, 2001).

28. A major cause of the problem seems to be (a) that these societies have no universal social security systems, and (b) that women are effectively relieved of all responsibilities for their own family when they marry. This tends to make the rationality of having a child depend on its sex, and perhaps the rationality of having an additional child depend on the sex of the preceding

children. See Celia W. Dugger, "Modern Asia's Anomaly: The Girls Who Don't Get Born," *The New York Times, Week in Review*, Sec. 4 (May 6, 2001): 4. The issue is discussed in depth by Amartya Sen, "Missing Women," *British Medical Journal* 304 (March 7, 1992): 587; and *Development as Freedom* (New York: Anchor, 1999), chap. 8.

29. Hardin seems to realize this. He says that the independent herdsman "dare not refrain" from overloading the commons, because if he did so he would "suffer more" than a "selfish" one who does overgraze ("Lifeboat," p. 562); furthermore, if he did refrain from overgrazing, the herdsman would be (correctly) condemned as a "simpleton" ("Tragedy," p. 1246).

30. "Tragedy," p. 1246; emphasis in original. As is often noted, this seems to be an inaccurate description of the motivation of those in above-replacement countries. People in some societies have reason to have lots of children because there is no one else to look after them when they become old and there is high infant mortality. This makes it risky not to have lots of children, from the point of view of self-interest. This is actually worse than a prisoner's dilemma situation. For here the parents are likely not to prefer the constrained outcome, because they fear abandonment in old age more than general population problems.

31. There is also a question about whether one can make sense of biological interests in evolutionary terms (and also, perhaps, whether one can make sense of the notion of biological interests). Such an approach is tried by Gary Varner, *In Nature's Interests? Interests, Animal Rights, and Environmental Ethics* (Oxford: Oxford University Press, 1998). But note that even Varner believes that individuals have psychological interests in addition to their biological interests, and that the psychological interests trump the biological.

32. "Tragedy," p. 1246.

33. That is, we would expect people already to have the desire for as many children as would maximize the chance of the genes being passed on. Against this, Hardin would presumably argue that the historical natural pruning had an effect on reproductive motivation, but one that is being undermined by the more recent welfare state and foreign aid programs. But here it is worth pointing out (a) that those countries without the welfare state have sustained high birth rates rather than held them back, and (b) that the decline in birth rates has occurred in rich countries even given the introduction of welfare. (Against [b], Hardin might argue that it is too early to tell what will happen in these countries, given that welfare is fairly recent; but still the empirical evidence does not look promising for him.)

34. Determining the carrying capacity is a difficult and extremely value-laden business, which raises philosophical issues of its own. For a helpful discussion, see Joel E. Cohen, *How Many People Can the Earth Support?* (New York: Norton, 1995), chap. 12, and app. 3 and 4.

35. See Griffin, "Lifeboat," pp. 223–24.

36. Global energy consumption rose from 21 to 318 exajoules between 1900 and 1988 (See William C. Clark, in *Managing Planet Earth* (New York: Freeman, 1990), p. 87. Bill McKibben reports that per capita consumption had risen from less than 1 megawatt-hour per person in 1800 to 19 megawatt hours per person in 1989 (McKibben, *The End of Nature* [New York: Anchor, 1989], p. 2).

37. For example, in 1997, India and China had commercial energy use per capita of 479 and 907 kg of oil equivalent respectively, compared to 3,863 and 8,079 for the United Kingdom and United States respectively. (See World Bank, *World Development Indicators 2000.*)

Hardin recognizes that energy consumption per capita is a useful partial measure of quality of life. He also points out the sharp difference between figures for developed and less developed countries. But he refused to see this as a global problem. Instead, he argues for a localizing principle: that parochial distribution of resources should be matched by parochial consumption; and so sees the problem as a local one. (For example, he all but suggests that Bangladesh should reduce its population from 104 million to 2.7 million, rather than bemoan its lack of resources.) But there are two problems for Hardin here. First, his defense of the principle ("there must be some sort of fragmentation of administrative tasks") is too weak either to justify the principle itself, or the conclusions he is prepared to draw from it. Second, Hardin admits that the principle does not apply to air and water, where a global approach is needed. But, as I shall stress below, the most serious environmental problems caused by current energy consumption involve atmospheric pollution, and so are global. (See Hardin "Cultural Carrying Capacity: A Biological Approach to Human Problems," *Bioscience* 36 (1986): 599–606, esp. 602–5.)

38. Future generations are often defined as those future people whom those presently alive will not live to meet (see, for example, Avner de-Shalit, *Why Posterity Matters: Environmental Policies and Future Generations* [London: Routledge, 1995], p. 138). For the sake both of simplicity, and of making clear the fundamental dynamics, I follow that usage here. However, "future generations" is also often used to refer to those not presently alive, and it is important to emphasize that many of the points I will make apply in a more nuanced way to this less restricted notion. This is because the crucial issue is not when those who will live when we have gone appear, but the extent of our present concern for their well-being. (This is what gives a point even to the more restrictive use of the term "future generations.") Indeed, it is worth noting that much of what is said about future people in the restricted sense applies not only to future people in the less restricted sense, but also (in a graduated way) to people already presently alive. For even when there is overlap, and we care about the well-being of at least some of the people who remain after we are dead, that concern tends to be less than our concern for people around now (even when the same people are at issue) and to decline over temporal

distance. (Such issues are important to a full account of the dynamics of the global warming problem, since there one would want to say more about the medium-range effects of climate change. But here I am offering only a basic outline, for illustrative purposes.)

39. Two qualifications are worth making here. First, not all of the rewards accrue to the present generation. Some are passed on in the form of technological advances and increases in the capital stock. This raises the prospect that future generations might be compensated for the damage they inherit through having better resources with which to deal with them. Such arguments are no doubt warranted in some cases: For example, some developing countries are probably right to think that they do best to improve their economic infrastructure rather than abate emissions at the moment, especially since the planet is already committed to some warming. However, in general, the point is limited by such factors as (a) that much of the benefit of emissions is not passed on but simply consumed; (b) that technology and capital are far from perfect substitutes for environmental quality; and (c) that the precise physical effects of global warming are likely to be unpredictable, severe, and possibly catastrophic (so that effective deployment of the inherited benefits to mitigate them may be extremely difficult).

Second, if the immediate effects of pollution are bad enough, the costs placed on the present generation may, of course, be high enough to give them a self-interested reason not to pollute. But this presently seems unlikely in the case of CO_2 emissions. (This is especially so because, even if the short-term future impact of climate change is significant, this will be caused by past emissions, and so is warming to which the present generation is already committed through the action of past generations.)

40. I leave aside the philosophical problem identified by Derek Parfit as the Non-Identity Problem. See Parfit, *Reasons and Persons*, chap. 16. But note than even Parfit thinks that we can carry on talking in terms of harms to future generations (Ibid., p. 367).

41. They might continue certain traditions and projects. See John O'Neill, "Future Generations: Present Harms," *Philosophy* 68 (1993): 35–51.

42. Perhaps it could be weaker. Perhaps all that is required is that some generation capable of making a difference make the sacrifice. Still, the theoretical problem remains. Presumably it is to be resolved at least in part by appeal to purely altruistic moral reasons.

43. Perhaps the point can be made clearer by looking at the preference structures that underlie the tragic situation. The intergenerational problem begins with a prisoner's dilemma structure:

> 1st preference: I pollute, previous generation does not.
> 2nd preference: Neither I nor previous generation pollutes.
> 3rd preference: I pollute, previous generation pollutes.
> 4th preference: I don't pollute, previous generation pollutes.

But for the first generation capable of serious overpollution, this becomes simply:

1st preference: I pollute.
2nd preference: I don't pollute.

So, this fixes the third option for the next generation, and so on for subsequent generations.

44. Climate change is explicitly described as a prisoner's dilemma by Marvin S. Sooros, *The Endangered Atmosphere: Preserving a Global Commons* (Columbia, SC: University of South Carolina Press, 1997); pp. 260–61. It seems to be implicit in many other analyses. By contrast, Jeremy Waldron makes the case for a Battle of the Sexes in an unpublished research paper kindly supplied to me by an anonymous referee for this journal. (Waldron, "Who Is to Stop Polluting? Different Kinds of Free-Rider Problem," June–July 1990. A Contribution to a project, Ethical Guidelines for Global Bargains, undertaken by the Program on Ethics and Public Life, Cornell University, with support from the Rockefeller Foundation. Waldron is applying a general approach to collective action problems put forth by Jean Hampton, "Free-Rider Problems in the Production of Collective Goods," *Economics and Philosophy* 3 [1987]: 245–73; and *Hobbes and the Social Contract Tradition* [Cambridge: Cambridge University Press, 1986].) The Battle of the Sexes analysis is also briefly suggested by some remarks of Nick Mabey, Stephen Hall, Claire Smith, and Sujata Gupta, *Argument in the Greenhouse: The International Economics of Controlling Global Warming* (London: Routledge, 1997), pp. 356–59; 409–10; and, for the specific issue of ratification of the Kyoto Protocol, Scott Barrett, "Political Economy of the Kyoto Protocol," *Oxford Review of Economic Policy* 14 (1998): 20–39; 36–37.

45. I hope to pursue the issues in more detail, and as applied to the Kyoto Protocol in particular, in a future paper tentatively entitled "The Global Warming Tragedy and the Dangerous Illusion of the Kyoto Protocol," *Ethics & International Affairs* 18 (1) (Winter 2004): 23-39. Some discussion of the Kyoto context is to be found in Barrett, "Political Economy."

46. There are two basic reasons why the structure of the intragenerational problem is unclear. First, solving the problem requires resolving a number of other collective action problems that are subordinate, or otherwise closely related, to it. Second, because of the uncertainty surrounding the magnitude and distribution of the various costs and benefits of climate change, the dynamics of the intragenerational and related problems are all subject to considerable uncertainty.

47. The writers noted above are all concerned with countries. But I begin with individuals for the sake of simplicity, since I believe that a prisoner's dilemma analysis would be widely accepted at that level. I make a case for extending the analysis to countries below.

48. This is in part because externality effects imply that compliance costs are likely to be high, and in part because there is an entrenched competitive advantage based on current patterns of energy use.

49. Things might be more promising if one considers the sources of carbon dioxide, namely the fossil fuels themselves. For most individuals have to buy their fuel from others; and most countries have to import much of their fuel from elsewhere. (But note that: [a] some countries do have significant fossil fuels of their own, e.g., China's coal reserves; [b] monitoring and enforcing limits on oil production, although one of the easier fuels to monitor, has proved difficult in the past, e.g., for OPEC, and for those imposing sanctions on Iraq; and [c] the emissions produced by any given unit of, say, oil vary considerably depending on use, in ways which make calculations of overall emissions levels difficult, even when the agents involved are compliant.)

50. Note that it would be possible to hold that countries confront a battle of the sexes, even if individuals confront a prisoner's dilemma. There are two reasons. First, the number of actors is very different, making it more plausible in the individual case that decisions made by one party do not directly affect decisions made by the others. Second, on the one hand, a many-person collective action problem often has the character of a prisoner's dilemma as far as a chooser is concerned if: (a) it involves an incremental good with indiscernible contributions; or (b) a step good, *and* either the threshold is indiscernible or it is not particularly proximate in terms of my choice (i.e., if I do not perceive the crossing of the threshold as a close thing, then what happens is that the effect of my contribution becomes less and less discernible). But, on the other hand, it has the character of a battle of the sexes for the individual if: (c) the good is incremental and contributions are discernible; or (d) there is a discernibly close threshold. Arguably, the intragenerational problem facing individuals seems best characterized by either (a) or (b): (b) with remoteness seems to be the way most people see it; or else (a) with fatalistic attitude. Hence, they are more likely to face a prisoner's dilemma. But one might argue that (c) or (d) is more likely for countries, since they are in a better position to gather information, make agreements, and guarantee certain levels of reduction. Hence, countries might face a battle of the sexes. (For this method of classification, I rely on Waldron, who relies on Hampton.)

51. Hampton says that many actual problems are mislabeled as prisoner's dilemmas when they really have this structure. See Hampton, "Free-Riding."

52. Waldron characterizes the global warming problem as follows in "Who Is to Stop Polluting," pp. 34–35:

(a) There are more than two players. Call the number of players N.

(b) There is a number M (such that M < N), which is the minimum number of players whose cooperation is necessary if some situation, which is bad for all, is to be avoided.

(c) If M players cooperate, all N players benefit.

(d) Each player prefers the situation in which M players cooperate but he is not one of them to the situation in which he is one of the M cooperators. In other words, cooperation is costly.

(e) The greater the number of cooperators, the smaller the cost to each of cooperating. Thus each, if he is a cooperator, prefers that the number of cooperators be as large as possible.

(f) If any cooperate, and the number of cooperators is less than M, then the cooperators suffer the cost and enjoy none of the benefits of cooperation. Each would prefer not to cooperate than to be in this situation.

(g) If the number of others who are willing to cooperate is just short of M, then a given party prefers to cooperate, since he is better off enjoying the benefits of cooperation and paying his share of the cost than he is in the situation where not enough people cooperate.

So, I have picked out Waldron's (b) and (g).

53. See Hampton, 1987. The basic structure of the Battle of the Sexes can be gleaned from the (unfortunately sexist) story from which it gets its name. A couple are deciding whether to go out on a date. The man would most prefer to go to see a game of baseball; the woman would most prefer a trip to the theater. But both prefer to go on the date rather than to go to their own favorite event (or stay at home) alone. This yields the following preference structure:

Battle of the Sexes

		Woman	
		Baseball	Theater
Man	Baseball	1st, 2nd	3rd, 3rd
	Theater	4th, 4th	2nd, 1st

In this situation, there is no natural equilibrium position, but the two cooperative solutions are better than either noncooperative solution. Hence, both players are motivated to compromise because both want to avoid the noncooperative outcome. (Note: The phrase "many-person battle of the sexes" is unfortunately ambiguous between a situation in which all prefer to cooperate, and one where all prefer that some cooperate. Hampton intends the latter.)

54. For example, it preserves the insight that climate change involves some form of collective action problem involving a strong incentive to try to free ride

(in this case, by getting others to form the subgroup). Furthermore, it appears to be supported by some aspects of recent real-world events. Even in the face of the decision by the United States—the world's single largest emitter—to refuse to support the Kyoto agreement, the other countries of the world have made an agreement that involves significant reductions in projected emissions for the other large emitters (prominently, the European Union and Japan). This suggests both the Partial and Minimal Cooperation claims.

55. This is mentioned by both Mabey et al. and Waldron, and seems to support the Partial Cooperation claim.

56. In particular, a battle of the sexes can be resolved if (a) a particular outcome is salient to both parties as the likely cooperative resolution (and so can act as a rallying point), and (b) for the party who must give up his most favored outcome to secure the salient one, the expected utility of conceding to the salient outcome is greater than that of holding out and so risking a noncooperative outcome.

57. Again, this initially appears to be supported by recent events.

58. The basic battle of the sexes analysis ignores some (further) important strategic factors that emerge once only some countries comply, namely the competitive advantages internal to not making cuts. (For example, one's energy costs are cheaper than one's competitors' not only because they are spending money cutting emissions that will be passed on to consumers in higher prices, but also because these efforts will lower the price of fossil fuels on the world markets by reducing demand for them and encourage emissions-intensive industries to migrate to countries with no restrictions.) And it is possible that they make at least some of the attempt to reduce total emissions self-defeating. (Interestingly, Mabey et al. consider the current scenario unstable, for they believe that defection the United States will make energy-intensive industries leave the cooperating countries in such numbers that the benefits of cooperation for those countries would be outweighed by their costs. See Mabey et al., *Arguing*, pp. 266, 299, 410.)

59. Of course, CO_2 is not the only greenhouse gas whose emissions are useful to humans; it is merely the one presently most important. (Methane is also very important; bringing the slightly comical problem of bovine flatulence to global prominence.) So, in the end, an even more comprehensive agreement is needed, as Kyoto envisages.

60. Very roughly, for a world population of 6 billion people, this would amount to 123 billion tons of carbon dioxide annually (based on 20.5 tons per capita emissions for the United States, the figure for 1995). This rises to 184.5 billion tons for a world population of 9 billion, which is projected by the US Census Bureau for mid-century.

Total projected emissions from energy consumption for 1991 was a mere 26.4 billion tons. (Hence, continuation at 1991 levels would allow a per capita average for emissions of 4.4 tons, which is only 20 percent of the US figure.) Hence, China alone (with a population of 1.2 billion in 1995, rising to 1.5

billion in 2025) could break the 1991 total, even if (as would never happen) other countries emitted nothing. (Slightly) more realistically, and simplifying considerably, even if all other countries cut back 20 percent from their levels in the early nineties—a huge reduction over projected "business-as-usual" growth—(to a total of 21.1 billion tons), a bloc of countries with very low current emissions and a combined population of over 250 million (i.e., 4 percent of the world's population) could conceivably break the 1991 total if they emitted at current US levels. As, of course, would the United States alone if it were the defector. (Figures from the World Resources Institute, as cited by the UNEP Climate Change Kit, http://www.unfccc.int/resource/iuckit/index.html.)

61. This is especially so if the marginal costs of reduction get higher and higher, which they do, so that the costs to a cooperating group goes up the more other countries pollute. This effect would be exacerbated by a reduction in the price of fossil fuels brought about by the withdrawal of demand by the core group.

62. And one might not be delaying it very much. Some say that the current agreement between Europe and Japan will only slow the growth in atmospheric carbon dioxide by six years. (This, of course, ignores the fact that the current agreement only covers emissions from 2008 to 2012, and envisions new targets for future years.)

63. There are still problems in leaving such nations out of an agreement over the long term. If they could increase population by reproduction or by immigration over time, then they might become a threat to the agreement; and there would be an incentive for individuals to emigrate there so long as an advantage existed for doing so: i.e., for CO2-rich ways of life. This would imply that partial cooperation is false after all.

Waldron's (e) also suggests that N-M will be small; (e) states that the greater the number of cooperators, the smaller the cost to each of cooperating. Thus each prefers that, if he is a cooperator, the number of cooperators be as large as possible. Hence, each cooperator has an incentive to use any other means at his disposal to put pressure on other countries outside the subgroup to join. Since the cooperation of the large and potentially economically powerful nations is required for success (given the dynamic problem), it will be small and economically not-so-powerful nations who fall into N-M, but these are the most susceptible to external pressure from these nations. Hence, it is to be expected that M will be equal, or very close, to N.

64. It is also worth noting that the more successful the subgroup is to begin with, the greater incentives to the noncooperators to do this, as the better the quality of the commons they can exploit. Furthermore, to maintain the commons, the M are under progressive pressure to do more and more, so that the costs on them in a dynamic context increase dramatically.

65. The theoretical difficulty here may be in treating total abatement as a step, rather than incremental, good. If abatement at some percentage of global 1990 levels really represented a threshold that benefited all, then one

might argue that even noncooperators would have an incentive not to disrupt it. But this argument would be a mistake, for two reasons. First, the influence of emissions is, as far as anyone knows, or at least as far as it is treated in the models of the problem, incremental, not a matter of threshold. Hence, there is a threat at the margin. Second, and even more important, since "disruption" here simply involves continuing to pollute on a business-as-usual basis (i.e., to the extent that it is a benefit irrespective of concerns about climate), this "solution" would actually turn noncooperators into cooperators. For bearing some of the costs of abatement here simply means not polluting on a business-as-usual basis.

66. Notice the "may" here. Internal solutions require the identification of a salient solution. But in the case of global warming, this is undermined by the complex nature of the problem. In particular, the identification of a relevant subgroup is undermined by uncertainty about the distribution of costs and by the range of potential contributors.

67. Note that if the intergenerational problem is to be solved, the first generation is already making an absolute sacrifice in terms of self-interest. This makes things difficult in dealing with noncooperators. Suppose they seem quite happy to pollute and not cooperate. Am I supposed to offer them further incentives to come back into the fold? But then I am giving up both my potential gains from polluting (to the future generations), and some of the further gains from cooperation (to the reluctant cooperators). This is a lot to ask. Just overpolluting myself will look very tempting.

68. The problem is that noncompliance, even global noncompliance, is actually a benefit to the present generation, so the incentives to enforce are not high.

69. The competitive pressures argument does not work in all contexts, but it does seem operative here. For some doubts about its general application, see Daniel Hausman and Michael McPherson, *Economic Analysis and Moral Philosophy* (Cambridge: Cambridge University Press, 1996), chap. 4.

70. In addition, note that the problem of overpollution would remain even in the absence of population growth, since energy consumption per capita is on an upward spiral.

71. Furthermore, it is probably a politically necessary prerequisite to preventing the developing countries from following a Western path.

21. DAVID MILLER

Miller's paper focuses on what he calls the "problem of remedial responsibility." This is the problem of determining what principles should be used in assigning special obligations to various parties to end avoidable suffering and deprivation. He considers four such principles, based respectively on causal responsibility, moral responsibility, capacity, and ties of community. He argues that though each principle has some plausibility, none is adequate by itself. He concludes that we must be pluralists about remedial responsibilities, and thus find some way of combining these four principles. He finishes by sketching one way of doing so, which he calls the "connection theory."

Distributing Responsibilities

First published in Journal of Political Philosophy *9: 4 (December 2001): 453–71.*

In this article I examine a question that arises frequently in moral and political debate, but has not to my knowledge been examined in much depth by philosophers. Our world contains all too many instances of deprived or suffering people—people whose basic rights to security, or subsistence, or health care are not being protected, and who as a result are in no position to live minimally decent lives. Nearly all of us believe that this is a situation that demands a remedy: Someone should provide the resources to end the suffering and deprivation.[1] The problem does not lie here, but in deciding which particular agent or agents should put the bad situation right. Very often there are many agents who could act in this way. The issue is how to identify one particular agent, or group of agents, as having a particular responsibility to remedy the situation. For unless we can do this, there is a danger that the suffering or deprivation will continue unabated, even though everyone agrees that it is morally intolerable, because no one is willing to accept the responsibility to step in and relieve it.

For an example of the problem I have in mind, consider the current plight of Iraqi children who are malnourished and lack access to proper medical care. No one doubts that their condition is a very bad one, nor is it difficult to grasp what would be needed to remedy it. But who has the responsibility for putting it right? Is it the United Nations, and more especially the Western powers, who on the one hand have contributed to the situation, or so it is alleged, by imposing economic sanctions on Iraq, and on the other are well placed to supply the necessary food and medical aid? Or is it Saddam Hussein and his henchmen, who have diverted a large percentage of Iraq's GNP to military expenditure, and who have deliberately (it is alleged) prevented aid from reaching poor families in an attempt to have the sanctions lifted? Or does responsibility lie with the Iraqi people as a whole, on the grounds that each nation has a duty to look after its own, which in this case might involve taking direct action to overthrow the current brutal regime?

I shall call this the problem of remedial responsibility. To be remedially responsible for a bad situation means to have a special obligation to put the bad situation right, in other words to be picked out, either individually or along with others, as having a responsibility toward the deprived or suffering party that is not shared equally among all agents. The problem is to find a principle, or set of principles, for assigning such responsibilities that carries moral weight, so that we can say that agents who fail to discharge their remedial responsibilities act wrongly and may properly be sanctioned. (What form the sanctioning may take will vary from case to case, and it is not part of my brief here to pursue this question. I mention sanctions simply to underline the point that when we are arguing about where the responsibility for remedying a bad situation should fall, we mean our answer to have some teeth.) In other words, the problem is: What connects a particular agent A to a particular patient P in such a way that A is singled out as having a remedial responsibility toward P that others, in general, do not have? Note that the agents in question may be individual people, but, as the example I gave above illustrates, they may also be collectives of various kinds—governments, states, corporations, even those amorphous entities called nations. Assigning responsibility to these collective bodies raises additional questions that I cannot address here.[2] Instead I shall assume that such assignments of collective responsibility are both meaningful and justifiable, and focus on the issue of how they should be distributed. In exploring this issue, I shall often refer to individual agents and patients, because we are likely to have better-formed judgments in these cases, but eventually our analysis should be applicable to collective cases, too.

Because the problem of distributing responsibilities is so urgent, human societies have evolved mechanisms whereby they are formally assigned to individual people or to institutions. If we ask who is responsible for safeguarding this particular battered child, the answer is likely to be the social worker who has been assigned to the case. I am not concerned here with such formally assigned responsibilities, but with the underlying principles that should guide us when we are in a position to make formal assignments, and that we should appeal to directly when no formal assignments have been made. Very often, in fact, the problem arises precisely because of the lack of any institutional mechanism that can assign responsibilities formally—the international arena is replete with examples. We may believe that we should move toward a situation where for any group of deprived or suffering people there is some agency that has formally been assigned the responsibility to remedy their condition. But clearly that day is a very long way off, and meanwhile the best we can do is to lay out some principles for distributing responsibilities that we hope will command widespread agreement. That is the task of the present article.

I. PRINCIPLES OF REMEDIAL RESPONSIBILITY

Perhaps the most obvious solution to our problem is to say that agents should be held remedially responsible for situations when, and to the extent that, they were responsible for bringing those situations about. In other words we look to the past to see how the deprivation and suffering that concerns us arose, and having established that, we are then able to assign remedial responsibility. In the case of the Iraqi children, for instance, we need to know why they are malnourished and sick: Who is responsible for bringing about this state of affairs?

Clearly this answer invokes a different sense of "responsibility" from the one that directly concerns us. But which sense? Unfortunately, few concepts in moral and political philosophy are more slippery than that of responsibility, and it is a fair bet that real debates on issues such as the plight of Iraqi children become muddied as the protagonists slip from one meaning of responsibility to the next.[3] So we need to draw some distinctions, and in particular a distinction between *causal* and *moral* responsibility.

To say that an agent is causally responsible for some state of affairs is simply to highlight the causal role played by the agent in the genesis of that state of affairs. Here I rely on what Hart and Honoré have called the commonsense understanding of causation according to which when we say that C caused E we are singling out C as one among a potentially large number of antecedent conditions for E's occurrence, distinguished from the other conditions by virtue of its abnormality (and also, in many cases, by virtue of its being a deliberate human action).[4] For an example of "bare" causal responsibility—causal responsibility that is not accompanied by moral responsibility—consider the case where I am walking along the pavement, taking ordinary care, but trip over a raised paving stone, knock down the person in front of me, and injure him. Then I am causally responsible for the injury, but not morally responsible, because I have done nothing that attracts moral praise or blame. My tripping is simply the unusual feature in the case that accounts for the unfortunate injury to the pedestrian.

Moral responsibility, on the other hand, involves an appraisal of the agent's conduct. In the cases that particularly concern us, the agent's role in bringing about the outcome must be such that it leaves the agent liable to moral blame. That in turn requires us to ask questions such as whether the agent intended the outcome, whether he foresaw it, whether his behavior violated some standard of reasonable care, and so forth. As the example above shows, moral responsibility is in one respect a narrower notion than causal responsibility, since there will be many cases in which someone's conduct is perfectly innocent but it just so happens that something he does is the main causal factor in injuring another. But in another respect it may be wider, for instance if I negligently fail to take steps to prevent something from occurring. Suppose I take my son Jamie and his friend Nick to the park to play, and in the course of some rather boisterous game Jamie manages to break Nick's arm. Meanwhile I am sitting on the bench with my head buried in a newspaper and fail to notice what is going on. Then I may be morally responsible for Nick's arm getting broken, even though it is clearly Jamie who is causally responsible according to the criteria suggested above (whether Jamie is also morally responsible will depend on the details of the case—essentially whether it is reasonable to expect a boy of that age to foresee the likely outcome of the rough-and-tumble that is taking place). I am morally responsible because I have failed in my duty to take care of the boys, something that I assumed when I offered to take them down to the park. I can properly be blamed for not preventing the broken arm.

Having clarified the distinction between causal and moral responsibility, we can now ask whether either of these yields an adequate principle for assigning remedial responsibility. The appeal of causal responsibility is straightforward. If A is the cause of P's deprived condition—and this appears to be something that can be established empirically—then what is more obvious than to hold A responsible for remedying it? If he was the sole cause, then remedial responsibility is his alone; if several agents together caused P's condition, then remedial responsibility should be distributed in proportion to causal responsibility. But on closer inspection the causal principle faces a number of damaging objections.

The first is simply that there are many cases in which no identifiable A has caused P's condition, and yet we would be reluctant to say that no one has any remedial responsibility toward P. Prominent here are instances in which P's condition results from natural causes—P starves because of crop failure or is stricken with cancer. Of course it is always possible in such instances to specify forms of action which, had certain agents taken them, would have prevented the condition from emerging. The crop failure would not have occurred if company A had installed an irrigation system; the cancer would not have occurred if health authority B had decided to invest an extra £X million in preventive medicine. But there are an infinite number of such counterfactuals, and so they will not, in general, identify any particular agents as causally responsible for P's condition. When a particular counterfactual seems relevant, that is because the agent it describes has already been identified as bearing responsibility for P's condition. Thus if company A had contracted to install an irrigation system in P's neighborhood, it *then* becomes appropriate to single out A's inaction as the cause of the crop failure. But in the absence of any such agreement, or other special link between A and P, there is no reason to distinguish A's failure to install an irrigation system from B's failure to supply fertilizer, from C's failure to make available genetically modified seeds, and so on—the list containing all those actions the performance of any one of which would have prevented the crop failure.[5]

A second, related, difficulty arises when there are several agents whose actions can be plausibly linked to P's condition. Here there seems to be no merely empirical way of dividing up causal responsibility as a basis for assigning remedial responsibility.[6] Return to the case of the deprived Iraqi children. Suppose it is true, as seems plausible, that if the UN had not decided to impose economic sanctions, more money would have been available to fund health and social security in Iraq. Suppose it is also true that if Saddam had decided to cut military expenditure, enough would have been left, even with the sanctions, to prevent the destitution. Both the UN and Saddam can then be described as causally responsible for the sufferings of the children. But how should we apportion responsibility between them? In answering this question, we cannot apparently avoid making moral appraisals of the relevant agents' conduct, especially examining how far their behavior was justified. If we think that Saddam's regime posed a serious threat to neighboring countries, and therefore that UN sanctions were justified, then we will single out Saddam's policy decisions as the cause of the children's suffering. If, by contrast, we see Iraq as a vulnerable regime surrounded by enemies, and therefore as justified in arming itself in self-defense, we shall lay causal responsibility at the door of the UN. Causal attributions are being determined by normative assumptions about justified behavior. But in that case we no longer have a causal principle in our original sense—the ethical question about who bears remedial responsibility for P's condition is no longer being answered just by looking empirically at who brought that condition about.

Finally, questions about justification appear to arise even in cases where there is only one agent who can plausibly be described as the cause of P's condition. For sometimes A may act in a way that is harmful to P, and yet bear no remedial responsibility for the harm he has caused, because we judge A's behavior to be legitimate. Suppose for instance that in a market setting A drives P out of business by offering a better service to customers, then provided he deals fairly we do not think that he bears any remedial responsibilities toward P. Or A may cast P into depression by marrying the love of his life. So it seems that the causal principle taken by itself cannot explain our remedial responsibilities. It falls down where no particular A can be identified as the cause of P's condition, and it also falls down where A is certainly causally responsible, in whole or in part, for the harm done to P, but A's behavior appears justifiable, and therefore does not bring remedial responsibilities in its train.

Yet it is interesting to notice that even innocent causation may place *some* special responsibility upon the agent. Return to the case where by simple mischance I stumble and knock down a pedestrian. Everyone in the vicinity is under some obligation to help him to his feet and make sure that he is not badly hurt; yet we believe that the responsibility is in the first place mine, so I have the primary obligation to act.[7] I did nothing wrong—indeed I could not help doing what I did—yet having done it, having been the cause of P falling to the ground, I seem to be linked to him more strongly than B who just happened to be passing by. (In the same way, it seems appropriate that I should apologize, or at least express regret for what has happened, even though I am not at all to blame for the event.)[8] This may seem mysterious; indeed some may find it disturbing that we can apparently incur responsibilities just by doing something as unintentional and innocent as walking along the street. I do not want to suggest that bare causation of this kind plays more than a minor part in distributing responsibilities. But the fact that it plays any part at all may help us in searching for the correct theory.

So let us now consider the alternative principle that A should be held remedially responsible for P's condition insofar as he is *morally responsible* for its occurrence, in the sense that carries with it ascriptions of fault and blame. This principle seems to capture nicely what is at stake in our original example: When we ask who is responsible for the plight of Iraqi children, we appear to be asking who is morally responsible for bringing about their condition of malnutrition and ill health, whether by acting wrongly (the UN and Saddam) or by failing to act as duty requires (the Iraqi people as a whole). We have seen already that moral responsibility is narrower than causal responsibility in some ways and wider in others, and it looks as though in both respects this enables it to fit better with our considered judgments about remedial responsibility. There are cases in which people are causally but not morally responsible for the outcome of their actions—for instance, those in which the chain of events connecting action and outcome is long and tortuous, so that the agent could not have reasonably foreseen the final result of her action—and here we are unlikely to hold them remedially responsible for the harm that may ensue. Equally, in cases where we judge people to be morally responsible for the occurrence of a harm, even though their causal role in bringing it about was merely a negative one—cases like the delinquent parent who is reading a newspaper when he should have been watching out for children—we *do* hold them remedially responsible. So at first glance it seems that the moral responsibility principle is going to perform better than the causal principle in explaining our remedial responsibilities.

But that is not to say that it explains everything. To begin with, it cannot explain why causation alone sometimes seems sufficient to generate remedial responsibilities—as in the example of the innocent pedestrian. Nor can it deal happily with cases of justified, but harmful, behavior. For instance, suppose that A must quickly find a certain drug to save Q's life, and the only way he can do this is to steal some from P, who needs the drug, too, but less urgently. We think that he should steal the drug from P, but that he then has a remedial responsibility to P to replace what he has taken.[9] But he is not morally responsible for harm suffered by P in the intervening period in the sense that leaves him liable to attributions of blame; provided he goes on to discharge his remedial responsibilities, his conduct is not faulty.

There is, however, an ambiguity in the meaning of moral responsibility that needs to be addressed at this point. As defined above, it is linked conceptually to liability to blame: To say of A that he is morally responsible for state S is to say that he has contributed to the bringing about of S in such a way as to incur blame. But one may sever this link and use a broader concept of moral responsibility according to which people are to be held morally responsible for the results of their actions, so long as these actions themselves satisfy certain conditions of intentionality, voluntariness, etc., without implying that they are blameable for what they did.[10] On this second view, A is morally responsible for the effects on P of stealing the drug, because he took the drug deliberately and freely, even though he was fully justified in acting as he did. The broader view, then, preserves the connection between moral responsibility and remedial responsibility in the drug case. But it runs into difficulties in cases where justified, but harmful, conduct appears not to bring remedial responsibilities with it—cases like that in which A engages in fair competition with P in a market setting. Suppose that A sets up a shop close to P's and by legitimate means attracts most of P's customers, then A is morally responsible for P's loss of earnings, on the broader view. Even if A did not intend the precise outcome that occurred, he went into business deliberately, and could reasonably have foreseen as one result of his competitive behavior that P would be damaged. Yet we do not feel that he owes P anything by way of remedy so long as he has acted fairly.

So neither of the two concepts of moral responsibility we have considered—neither the narrow concept linked to blame, nor the wide, morally neutral, concept—gives us the link we are looking for between moral and remedial responsibilities. The narrow concept fails to explain why there are remedial responsibilities in the drug case; but the wider concept, which holds people responsible for the results of all their voluntary actions, whether blameworthy or not, implies that there are remedial responsibilities in the shopkeeper case, too.[11] Neither concept appears to hit the target precisely.

The biggest problem with the moral responsibility principle, however—one that it shares with the causal principle—is that it looks too exclusively to the past in assigning remedial responsibilities. The question it asks is always "Who is responsible for bringing this bad situation about?" and never, for instance, "Who is best placed to put it right?" One obvious defect of the principle, therefore, is that it has nothing to say when the morally responsible agent proves to be incapable of discharging her remedial responsibilities—for instance when she is dead or incapacitated. Unless we want to say that remedial responsibilities disappear when we cannot find an agent who is both morally responsible for the situation in question and capable of remedying it, the principle remains incomplete.

Taking our cue from the last paragraph, consider next the principle of *capacity*, which holds that remedial responsibilities ought to be assigned according to the capacity of each agent to discharge them. The rationale for this is obvious enough. If we want bad situations put right, we should give the responsibility to those who are best placed to do the remedying. If there is a bather in trouble off the beach, and it makes most sense for one person to undertake the rescue, then we should choose the strongest swimmer. In other circumstances we may want to share responsibility among A, B, C . . . in proportion to their respective capacities to rectify P's condition, as suggested by the slogan "From each according to his abilities, to each according to his needs."

On closer inspection, however, the capacity principle seems to blend together two different factors that may not always point in the same direction. One has to do with the *effectiveness* of different agents in remedying the situation; the other has to do with the *costs* they must bear in the course of doing so. The strongest swimmer may also be fearful (so that although he is an effective rescuer, the rescue causes him considerable distress)—or perhaps he simply dislikes the kind of attention that goes along with a successful rescue. If A is slightly stronger than B, but A's costs are also much higher, is it obviously the right solution to hold A responsible for rescuing P? On the moral responsibility view, costs do not present ethical problems: If A has harmed P through some action of his, then he should remedy the harm regardless of the cost to himself; requiring that he should pay the cost here is justifiable in the light of what he has done.[12] But to apply the capacity principle, it seems, we have to begin by weighing effectiveness against cost to determine whose capacity is the greatest in the morally relevant sense.[13]

Another problem with the capacity principle is that, by focusing attention entirely on agents' present capacity to remedy some harm, it neglects to ask how variations in capacity have arisen. And so it is vulnerable to the grasshopper and ant objection: Assuming that the grasshoppers *could* have spent the summer gathering food for the winter rather than singing, we may wonder whether the ants, who now have the capacity to help the famished grasshoppers by virtue of their earlier diligence, have a remedial responsibility to do so. Perhaps the destitution of the grasshoppers imposes some residual responsibility on the ants, but not as much as if, say, the grasshoppers' store of food had been washed away by unexpected rain. The capacity view cannot explain why remedial responsibility is stronger in one case than in the other. This is the weakness that accompanies its strength: Its exclusive focus on the present necessarily blinds it to historical considerations.

Finally, we need to ask whether capacity alone—the simple physical ability to remedy P's bad condition—is sufficient to generate remedial responsibility in the absence of a stronger link between A and P. Return to the case of the drowning bather, and notice that we single out the strongest swimmer from among those already gathered on the beach. Perhaps, then, we appeal to capacity only after identifying a set of agents whose relationship to P is such that they already bear a special responsibility toward him; capacity is used to pick out one particular agent from the set.[14]

That thought suggests a fourth principle for distributing responsibilities which we might call the communitarian principle, using "community" here in a fairly loose sense to capture special ties of various kinds such as those that exist within families, collegial groups of various kinds, nations, and so forth. The claim is that when people are linked together by such ties, whether arising from shared activities and commitments, common identities, common histories, or other such sources, they also (justifiably) see themselves as having special responsibilities to one another, responsibilities that are greater than those they have toward humanity at large; and this in particular imposes special responsibilities toward any member of the relevant community who is harmed or in need.

The great merit of the communitarian principle is that it can make sense of much of our existing practice when responsibilities have to be distributed without resort to artificial devices. Consider, for example, a group of hikers out on a trip in the mountains together, where one of the party falls and injures herself. Here we simply take it for granted that the responsibility for bringing aid to the injured member falls in the first place collectively on the whole group, rather than on, say, other climbers who happen to be in the vicinity at the time. By forming ourselves into a group to make the expedition, we create the kind of relationship that generates special responsibilities as a matter of course, and there is no need to invoke a hypothetical contract among the members, or to suppose that somehow members of such a group are better placed to understand their fellow members' needs than nonmembers would be, in order to reach the conclusion that when one person gets injured, it is the group that bears the primary responsibility to remedy her condition.[15] But the communitarian principle does less well on two other counts.

First, and only too obviously, it cannot explain why remedial responsibilities sometimes exist in the absence of special relationships of the kind outlined above. But there are at least two cases in which their existence seems pretty clear-cut. One is the case in which A simply injures P without justification, particularly perhaps when the injury involves a violation of P's basic rights (to bodily integrity, say, or to subsistence). That A bears a remedial responsibility in such a case seems uncontroversial, and this is regardless of whether A and P are linked by some kind of communal bond. If I injure a complete stranger, someone not connected to me by nationality, religion, or any of the possible forms of communitarian tie, I still owe him a remedy for the injury I have caused.

Likewise, and only a little more controversially, A may be remedially responsible for P simply because he happens to be the only person currently in a position to do anything about P's condition. This assumes of course that P's condition is one of significant deprivation or injury. But if that is the case, then the general duty we all have to aid people who are seriously injured or deprived will devolve upon A simply because he is the only person able to discharge it, either because, for instance, he is the sole passerby when the skater on the pond falls through the ice, or because he alone has the know-how to sort out P's condition. Once again these responsibilities appear to transcend any communal bonds that might exist between A and P.[16]

The second limitation of the communitarian principle is that it has nothing directly to say about how responsibilities are to be distributed *within* the community. It can accommodate the fact that one community may nest inside another, so that A can bear special responsibilities to everyone in C, but also more extensive responsibilities still to everyone in C^1, a subset of C. But it cannot go beyond this in distributing responsibilities within C except by importing considerations that are not themselves of a communitarian character. Our belief that in some instances people with greater capacity to help P should bear more of the responsibility for doing so, as suggested by the capacity principle, cannot be generated from within the communitarian perspective alone. And since a full account of remedial responsibilities should aim to get beyond the group level and attribute responsibility to individuals, the communitarian principle taken by itself appears inadequate.[17]

II. TAKING STOCK

We seem to have reached an impasse. We have looked at four principles—causal responsibility, moral responsibility, capacity, and community—each of which seems prima facie plausible as a way of allocating remedial responsibilities, but none of which, on closer inspection, seems adequate by itself. So how should we proceed? There seem to be three main options. The first is to abandon the search for a general theory of remedial responsibilities. The grounds for doing this would be that my initial formulation of the problem—here is a group of deprived or suffering people; whose responsibility is it to put the situation right?—misleadingly amalgamates a range of quite different cases, in each of which a different principle applies. For example, that formulation glosses over the difference between the case in which P's deprivation or suffering is the result of human action, and the case where it has purely natural causes. So instead of looking for a general theory to explain our remedial responsibilities, we need to disaggregate the cases first, and then perhaps construct specific accounts of responsibility to fit each of them in turn.

The second option is to mount a defense of one of the principles canvassed above, and then argue that all of our considered judgments about remedial responsibility can in fact be captured by that principle. This may involve conceding that there are cases in which people are deprived or suffering but in which no one has a responsibility to help them. For instance, one might argue that agents have remedial responsibilities only when they are morally responsible for the deprivation and suffering in question. Someone who took that line would have to reject my original formulation in a different way: They would have to deny the premise that it is morally intolerable if (remediable) suffering and deprivation are allowed to continue, in other words that where they exist we are morally bound to hold *somebody* (some person or some collective agent) responsible for relieving them.

The third option is to construct a multiprinciple theory that combines the four principles I have identified in some fashion. There are various ways in which this might be done, but broadly speaking we can distinguish theories that rank the principles in a certain way—recommend that they should be applied sequentially, for instance—and theories that are more straightforwardly pluralist, in the sense that they ask us to balance or weigh the various principles against one another when responsibilities have to be assigned.

The first option is really a counsel of despair. If our aim in developing a theory of remedial responsibility is eventually to be able to pin these responsibilities on to particular agents and then exert pressure on them to discharge their obligations, a unified theory is a much better tool than a string of subtheories. But more important, few cases in real life will fall neatly into just one of the categories we might construct. The example with which I began illustrates this. When we think about who bears remedial responsibility for Iraqi children, we think about what certain agents have done, what other agents have failed to do, we think about who can claim to have acted with justification, and we also think about who is now best placed to help the children. It is not a simple case in which an identifiable A has unjustifiably injured an identifiable P, nor is it a simple case in which P's condition has purely natural causes. The same will hold in all but the most primitive cases of human deprivation and suffering. So it would be premature to abandon the search for a general theory of remedial responsibility.

The second option involves attempting to bring everything that we want to say about remedial responsibility under the auspices of one of the principles identified above. How might a theory of this kind be constructed? The most plausible candidates, I believe, are a backward-looking theory of moral responsibility and a forward-looking theory, some variant of the capacity view, which focuses on the effective relief of harm and deprivation. A theory of the first kind would hold that agents are only remedially responsible for situations when they are blameable for bringing them about, and a proponent of such a theory might be willing to accept that in cases where no such agent can be found, no remedial responsibilities exist (thus no-one should be held remedially responsible for the victims of natural disasters, though no doubt it would be a morally worthy act to help them). Such a theory looks entirely to the past; the only question it asks is "Who has done this thing?"

A wholly backward-looking theory of this kind finds itself trapped in the following dilemma: Either it leaves victims intolerably exposed, in the sense that many injuries will go unremedied, or inadequately remedied, or else it imposes an intolerable burden on agents—this could mean any one of us—by making us responsible for potentially enormous costs resulting from our actions. To see this, consider a case in which some slight act of carelessness on my part results in injuries to Smith that require millions of pounds to compensate. In this instance, we can either narrow the concept of moral responsibility so that I am no longer responsible for everything that results from my careless action—in which case Smith's condition will largely go unremedied—or else we broaden it so that I become remedially responsible for Smith's condition, in which case we would seriously limit our freedom as actors. Every time we acted, we would face a small but significant risk of landing ourselves with crippling remedial responsibilities.[18] A purely backward-looking theory cannot satisfy our underlying interest in protection against harm and deprivation without burdening us with liabilities that would make everyday life (driving to work, walking down the street) a potentially hazardous business.

Forward-looking theories tell us to assign responsibility in whatever way will best achieve our aim of relieving victims, and thus to ignore the past except insofar as it tells us things about agents that are now relevant in deciding who is most appropriately placed to remedy P's plight. Such theories look at the issue from the side of the victim, and their corresponding weakness is that they assign no intrinsic weight to the value we attach to moral responsibility. Suppose A injures P in a simple and straightforward way. A forward-looking theory asks "Who should now remedy P's condition?" and A will come into the frame only if we judge it most useful or beneficial to hold him responsible, either in the particular case, or because we think it a beneficial rule to assign remedial responsibility in such cases to the agent who brought about P's condition. But this does not take the past seriously enough: A has done this thing, he can now make amends, so why should we look any farther in assigning responsibility? The roundabout reasoning that a forward-looking theory requires seems to violate a basic belief that, at least in simple cases, people should be held responsible for the harm that they do.[19]

It seems, therefore, that an acceptable theory of remedial responsibility must make room in some fashion for each of the principles identified above. But how is this to be done? Again, there are different ways of constructing a multiprinciple theory. Let us consider some of the more plausible alternatives.

One possibility is that the relevant principles should be applied in sequence: We look to see whether there is any agent who can be held responsible for remedying P's condition under principle X, and if the answer is yes, that settles the matter; if the answer is no, we proceed to principle Y, and so forth. The plausibility of such a theory will depend on the sequence chosen, so rather than review all of the variations, let me focus on one likely candidate. This tells us to begin by applying the principle of moral responsibility. If we can find an agent who is responsible for P's plight, and also has the capacity to remedy it, then we should hold that agent remedially responsible for P. Failing that—if no morally responsible agent can be identified, or if the agent or agents who bear moral responsibility turn out to be incapable of supplying the remedy—we invoke another principle—causal responsibility, say, or community. Clearly there are different ways of completing the theory. But we need go no farther, because I do not think that the first move is defensible.

The problem is that moral responsibility is a matter of degree, and degrees of moral responsibility for P's condition do not necessarily correlate with other relevant features, especially with the capacity to relieve P's suffering or deprivation. We can lose sight of this fact by thinking in terms of very simple cases, namely those in which A is solely responsible for injuring P, does so by virtue of a deliberate act, and as a result has the resources that could now be used to compensate for the injury. But although such cases undoubtedly occur, we are more often confronted with ones in which A bears a lesser degree of moral responsibility, either by virtue of the character of his action—he acted negligently, for instance, rather than deliberately, or he acted with justification, harming P in pursuit of some greater good—or because responsibility has to be shared between a number of different agents. Moreover, the fact that A played some part in bringing about P's condition does not entail that he derived any tangible benefit from doing so. So if we think about a case such as the Iraqi children, we might well conclude that each of the agents identified in the case—the United Nations, Saddam's clique, and the Iraqi people—bore some share of moral responsibility for the suffering of those children, though the nature of the responsibility would differ in each case. The United Nations might be accused of pursuing a justifiable end by unacceptable means, the suffering of the children being a foreseeable side effect of the sanctions policy. Saddam might be accused, more harshly, of deliberately allowing the suffering to occur for propaganda purposes. About the Iraqi people, it could be said that their causal role in bringing about the suffering was almost entirely negative, but that in the circumstances they could reasonably have been expected to oppose Saddam's regime more effectively. If those judgments are accepted, we would have to conclude, first, that no agent can be singled out as uniquely morally responsible for the situation we want to have remedied; and, second, that the agent bearing the largest share of responsibility (Saddam's clique) is also worst placed to bring the children the help that they need. It is probably wrong to say that the Iraqi government is incapable of finding the resources in question. But clearly it would be very much easier for the Western powers to do so. In these circumstances, is it right to let our judgments of remedial responsibility be determined entirely by our prior beliefs about how far different agents are morally responsible for creating the situation that needs a remedy?

This suggests that, rather than applying principles of responsibility in strict sequence, our approach should be more openly pluralist: We should simply look to see which principle or principles apply in a particular case, and if we find that more than one applies, we should weigh their respective strengths. But before reaching this conclusion, we should consider a second way of ordering the principles. This approach sees them not as competing with one another, but as addressing different aspects of the allocation of responsibility. Again I shall focus on one particular version of this approach.

The position I have in mind holds that we need to distinguish *immediate* responsibility for relieving harm and suffering from *final* responsibility.[20] Where people are in distress or in danger of further injury, we need to identify the agents best placed to help them in the short term. But these may not be the agents who should bear the costs of such action in the long term. So A may be immediately responsible for relieving P, because A is the agent in a position to offer aid directly, but final responsibility may be B's, in which case B may have to compensate A for the resources she has provided to B or for incidental costs arising from the relief effort.

Adopting such a view, we might conclude that *capacity,* and to some extent *community,* are relevant principles when immediate responsibilities are being distributed, because these are criteria that tell us who is best able to relieve P's condition quickly and effectively. *Moral responsibility, causal responsibility,* and perhaps *community* again, are invoked when final responsibilities are the issue.[21] Now clearly there are cases where something like that picture seems to apply. If I negligently allow my child to fall into the river, but I cannot swim, then immediate responsibility for the rescue may fall on a passerby who can, while I remain ultimately responsible for my child's welfare once he is pulled out, and for any damage suffered by the rescuer. But what makes the picture appropriate is precisely the immediacy of the harm: If the child is not saved at once he will drown. It is that feature that makes capacity the overriding consideration in the short term. In many other cases, however, the deprivation or suffering that motivates our assigning of responsibility is relatively stable, in the sense that we have no reason to expect the situation to deteriorate suddenly, and here it seems that capacity becomes one relevant consideration to consider, alongside the others. And even where harm is immediate, capacity may not trump the other principles in a straightforward way: Where several swimmers could rescue the drowning child, we may not simply pick the strongest, but, for instance, the person who caused him to fall in, or the negligent parent who should have taken more care to keep him away from the water's edge.

III. THE CONNECTION THEORY

It appears that we must settle for a pluralist approach to distributing responsibilities. Attempts to eliminate all but one of the principles we have unearthed lead to unacceptable results. Attempts to impose a fixed order of application on those principles also lead us astray. But can a pluralist approach give us a satisfying theory of remedial responsibility? I shall sketch such a theory, which I propose to call the *connection* theory.[22]

This begins with the observation that all of us have a strong interest in the existence of mechanisms that protect us from harm and injury; more particularly, in the event that we find ourselves in a bad condition that it is difficult or impossible for us to remedy through our own devices, we want there to be some way of assigning responsibilities such that an identifiable A (or perhaps A, B, and C taken together) becomes responsible for rectifying our situation. We want A to feel that he is responsible, and to act accordingly, and we want everyone else to make the same judgment and therefore to put pressure of various kinds on A if he fails to act. Responsibility that is widely dispersed is no good, because then everyone will attempt to hang back in the hope that someone else will step in first, no one will be particularly liable to censure if the bad condition is not remedied, and so on.

The interest of potential P's in having clearly defined responsibilities is evident, reflecting the fact that all of us are vulnerable to outside events that may seriously harm our interests or threaten our lives. But equally, it may not matter so much, from P's point of view, which particular A is held responsible. There may be many agents who are able to remedy P's condition; it matters considerably to P that one such agent, or one group of agents, should be singled out, for the reasons given above, but apart from that P may be indifferent which agent this happens to be. In these circumstances we will fix responsibility on the agent who is already connected to P in some way; if several agents are so connected, we will choose the one whose link to P is strongest, or else, depending on the circumstances, divide up responsibility according to relative strength of connection. (Whether one agent is singled out, or responsibility shared between several, may depend on whether P's condition is better remedied by a single agent taking action or several agents acting in concert.)

What kind of connection is relevant here? My proposal is that we should return to the principles explored in the second section of the article, and now see them as specifying forms of connection between A and P that may, in particular cases, be sufficient to establish A's responsibility for remedying P's condition. That is, A may be remedially responsible for P either because he is causally responsible for P's condition, or morally responsible for it, or has the (special) capacity to rectify it, or already has a communal relationship with P. Any of these relations—causal responsibility, moral responsibility, capacity, or community— may establish the kind of special link between A and P that enables us to single out A as the one who bears the responsibility for supplying the resources that will remedy P's condition.

In many cases there will be independent moral reasons for using a particular connection as a basis for assigning remedial responsibility. This applies most obviously where the connection consists in A's moral responsibility for P's injury. There are two independent reasons for holding A remedially responsible in this case: First, where A has unjustly benefited from the injury he has inflicted on P—he has stolen something of P's, or exploited him, for example—then if A is made to compensate P by returning what he has taken or in some other way undoing the damage he has inflicted, then this will help to cancel out A's unjust gain, and so restore justice between them. Second, even if A has not benefited from his actions, he has wronged P, and should therefore make recompense to P as a way of acknowledging the wrong he has committed; remedying P's injury is an obvious way to do this. In the cases of capacity and community, too, we can provide a plausible rationale for basing remedial responsibilities on these forms of connection (these rationales will be quite different from the one just given in the case of moral responsibility). But causal responsibility, in the absence of the other forms of connection, seems not to have its own ethical rationale. If A is causally responsible for P's condition, but he is neither morally responsible for it (say he could not possibly have foreseen the results of his action) nor especially well placed to assist P, nor linked to P by special communal ties, there seems no independent reason to hold him remedially responsible for sorting P out. Yet we do seem to think that a bare causal connection is enough to generate special responsibilities, as the case of the innocent pedestrian who knocks down another shows. Perhaps it might be argued that in such cases holding the causal agent responsible will create incentives to take special care not to inflict accidental injury; thus the rationale is indirectly utilitarian.[23] But this interpretation seems forced: If the link between action and outcome is such that the agent could not be expected to anticipate the injury to P, then how is A supposed to alter his behavior? I suggest instead that causal responsibility as a source of remedial responsibility confirms the theory I am putting forward: We need some way of identifying an A to hold remedially responsible for P's condition, so in the absence of any other link between potential A's and P we fix upon the purely physical link of causality. This, admittedly, can be trumped fairly readily once other forms of connection come into play; but the fact that we are prepared to rely on bare causal connection in the first place underlines the necessity of finding some nonarbitrary way of assigning responsibility to a particular agent.

The connection theory successfully offers practical guidance in cases where only one of its four constituent principles is satisfied. There is nothing paradoxical, according to the theory, in assigning remedial responsibility on the basis of causation, say, in one case and on the basis of communitarian relations in the next case. Our overriding interest is to identify an agent who can remedy the deprivation or suffering that concerns us, and in pursuit of that aim we fix on whoever is linked to P according to one of the theory's four criteria, about which there is widespread agreement. Where two or more of the principles apply, the theory tells us to look at the strength of the various connections. Thus if A is weakly linked to P by virtue of moral responsibility, whereas B is strongly linked to P by virtue of capacity (B is in a far better position to remedy P's condition than any other agent), the theory instructs us to hold B remedially responsible. In some cases it may recommend dividing responsibility between two or more agents, where this makes practical sense, and the ties are of comparable strength. On the connection theory there is no algorithm that can tell us to apply principle 1 first and then move on to principle 2, and so forth—my reasons for rejecting such an algorithm have already been given. This means, of course, that when connections have to be weighed against each other, we can do no more than appeal to shared moral intuitions about which is the stronger.

The strength of the connection theory, as I see it, is that it treats the obligation to relieve deprivation and suffering as of overriding concern. By using multiple criteria, we ensure that there is always *some* agent who can be assigned responsibility for remedying P's condition. At the same time, it makes room for other moral considerations, such as the deeply held belief that where we can point the finger at a particular A as being morally responsible for the harm suffered by P, it is A himself who should remedy the harm wherever possible. Single-principle theories, I have suggested, will inevitably run up against such beliefs sooner or later. And although the connection theory is internally complex, this complexity may simply mirror the complexity of real-world cases in which remedial responsibility has to be assigned. If there were a simple answer to questions such as who is responsible for the current plight of Iraqi children, we would not argue about it politically in the way that we do. The connection theory does not offer a mechanical answer to questions of that kind, but it provides a way of thinking about them—highlighting their complexity—that may in the end prove to be more illuminating.

NOTES

Earlier versions of this article were presented to the Nuffield Political Theory Workshop and to the All Souls Seminar in Political Philosophy. I should like to thank both audiences for their helpful comments. I should particularly like to thank Jerry Cohen, Richard Dagger, Cécile Fabre, and Bob Goodin, plus three anonymous referees for *The Journal of Political Philosophy*, for their extensive written comments on earlier drafts of the article.

1. I say "nearly all" because there may be philosophers with libertarian instincts who hold that deprivation and suffering call for remedy only when they are the result of some agent violating the victims' rights. I examine this position briefly later in the article.

2. I have tackled some of them in a companion paper, "Holding Nations Responsible."

3. It is worth citing a story invented by Hart to illustrate the slipperiness of the concept: "As captain of the ship, X was responsible for the safety of his passengers and crew. But on his last voyage he got drunk every night and was responsible for the loss of the ship with all [others] aboard. It was rumored that he was insane, but the doctors considered that he was responsible for his actions. Throughout the voyage he behaved quite irresponsibly, and various incidents in his career showed that he was not a responsible person. He always maintained that the exceptional winter storms were responsible for the loss of the ship, but in the legal proceedings brought against him he was found criminally responsible for his negligent conduct, and in separate civil proceedings he was held legally responsible for the loss of life and property. He is still alive and he is morally responsible for the deaths of many women and children." H. L. A. Hart, *Punishment and Responsibility: Essays in the Philosophy of Law* (Oxford: Clarendon Press, 1968), p. 211.

4. See H. L. A. Hart and T. Honoré, *Causation in the Law*, 2nd ed. (Oxford, Clarendon Press, 1985), chap. 2 for this account. Their analysis raises many questions, not least the problem that the distinction between causes and (mere) conditions depends upon the perspective from which we are looking at any given event, which in turn determines what will be regarded as normal background conditions and what will be regarded as an abnormal intervening circumstance. This in turn raises the possibility that causal judgments are in part influenced by moral considerations that determine the perspective from which our causal inquiry is launched. I return briefly to this point later in the article. Here, I assume that we have a workable notion of causal responsibility that is distinct from moral responsibility, as illustrated by the example given in the text, even if there are ineliminable practical concerns that lie behind our judgments of causal responsibility.

5. Why not then treat *all* of these as in equal measure responsible for P's condition? If we do this then we lose the distinctive purpose of responsibility assignments as I understand them, which is to identify one or more agents who

are under some special obligation to relieve P's condition, and who therefore can properly be put under pressure to act. In other words, responsibility loses its practical force if it is diffused among all those agents of whom it is true that they *might* have acted in such a way that P's condition did not occur. I return later to the reasons we have for wanting specific assignments of responsibility, not diffuse ones.

6. This can apply even where A and P herself are the only agents involved, as pointed out in S. Perry, The Moral Foundations of Tort Law, *Iowa Law Review* 70 (1992), 449–514, at pp. 463–64.

7. Someone might argue here that we assign responsibility in this way because the person who knocked the pedestrian over is also likely to be the person best placed (by virtue of proximity) to take care of him afterward. However, if we think of the accident occurring in a crowded street, it seems that any advantage of this kind will be negligible, whereas our sense that it is the person who caused the fall who bears the primary responsibility is quite strong.

8. Cf. T. Honoré, Responsibility and Luck, *Law Quarterly Review,* 104 (1988), 530–53, at pp. 544–45.

9. A parallel case, involving a backpacker caught in a blizzard who breaks into an unoccupied hut and uses up what he finds there to keep himself alive, was introduced by Joel Feinberg in Voluntary Euthanasia and the Inalienable Right to Life, *Philosophy and Public Affairs* 7 (1978): 93–102, and has subsequently been widely discussed—see, for instance, J. J. Thomson, Rights and Compensation, in *Rights, Restitution and Risk* (Cambridge, MA: Harvard University Press, 1986), and L. Lomasky, Compensation and the Bounds of Rights, *Nomos XXXIII: Compensatory Justice,* ed. J. W. Chapman (New York: New York University Press, 1991).

10. It is not necessary here to spell this broader, nonappraisive concept of moral responsibility out in detail, except to say that it still remains distinct from causal responsibility: On the broader concept, A is morally responsible for the outcome of all the actions he deliberately performs, but not, for instance, for accidentally knocking down a pedestrian as a result of stumbling himself.

11. Can the moral responsibility principle be saved by adding in further conditions that differentiate the two cases? One difference between them is that P has a right to the drug that is stolen in the first case, but no right to his customers' patronage in the second case. This suggests the following: A is remedially responsible for P's condition if and only if he is morally responsible for a rights-violation that led to that condition. However, on closer inspection this turns out to be too restrictive. Suppose, for instance, that A publishes an unfair review of P's book, damaging his career. We may think that he has a responsibility to offset the damage (supposing there is some way he can do this) without believing that P has a right that has been infringed by the publication of the review. The wrongness of A's action together with the harm suffered by P seem sufficient in this case to generate a remedial responsibility without the invocation of a rights violation.

12. This claim requires some fine-tuning. Even if A is unquestionably at fault in acting as he did, he may be liable only for the effects of his action that a reasonable person would have foreseen, not for consequences that arise in peculiar ways or through the intervention of other actors. For discussion of this principle in the context of tort law, see Hart and Honoré, *Causation in the Law*, chap. 9, and A. Ripstein, *Equality, Responsibility and the Law* (Cambridge: Cambridge University Press, 1999), chap. 4.

13. We could of course simply define capacity as effectiveness, in which case we would have to allow in, as a separate and competing principle, the principle that remedial responsibilities should be assigned to the agents who would bear the least costs in discharging them.

14. Unfortunately, there is not sufficient space here to consider a close cousin of the capacity principle, the vulnerability principle defended in R. E. Goodin, *Protecting the Vulnerable: A Reanalysis of Our Social Responsibilities* (Chicago: University of Chicago Press, 1985). Goodin's central proposal is that protective responsibilities should be assigned in proportion to vulnerabilities: The more vulnerable P is to A, the greater A's responsibility to protect P from harm. I see this as a cousin of the capacity principle since, in general, the greater an agent's capacity to act, the greater her potential impact on others, and therefore the more vulnerable those others are to her decisions. However, P's vulnerability, considered simply by itself, seems to correlate with a responsibility on A's part to avoid causing harm to P, rather than a wider remedial responsibility to rectify P's suffering or deprivation. Suppose that P is the young author of a book on a topic on which I am recognized to be the leading authority, and I am asked to review the book. P is highly vulnerable to my actions: A damaging review will blight his career, a favorable one may launch it. I have a responsibility here not to harm P willfully or carelessly. If I think the book is a bad one I should say so, but I should take care, for instance, not to indulge my prejudices, precisely because the author is relatively junior, and therefore more vulnerable to my judgment than an established figure would be. So I have a limited responsibility to avoid causing P harm. But I seem to have no special responsibility to protect P from the harm that others may inflict—other reviewers less scrupulous than myself, for instance—and in the event that P is damaged, whether by my own (fair) review, or by other hands, I bear no remedial responsibilities. (If I review the book unfairly, and P's career suffers as a result, then I do have remedial responsibilities, but these are better explained by the moral responsibility principle discussed earlier than by the vulnerability principle; it is the faultiness of my conduct, not the simple fact of P's vulnerability, that creates such responsibilities.)

15. The best nonreductionist account of such special responsibilities known to me is to be found in S. Scheffler, Relationships and Responsibilities, *Philosophy and Public Affairs* 26 (1997): 189-209.

16. One may of course think that where communal bonds also exist this *strengthens* A's obligation, so that if A has to decide which of two endangered

skaters to rescue first, he should give precedence to the one who lives in his neighborhood or belongs to his church; similarly a medical specialist may give priority to treating critically ill patients in his own nation while also acknowledging some responsibility toward similar patients elsewhere.

17. In some cases, of course, responsibility does just rest with the group as a whole until it is assigned by some mechanism to individuals, as in the case of the mountaineering group who share responsibility equally for their injured comrade until, say, they draw straws to decide who should go back and call out the Mountain Rescue team. There is nothing to distinguish one member from another in the assigning of responsibility. But this will not be true in general.

18. Insurance provides a mechanism for offsetting this objection, and, as Honoré points out in relation to tort law, "some form of insurance is essential if a system of corrective justice is to operate fairly in modern conditions": T. Honoré, The Morality of Tort Law, *Philosophical Foundations of Tort Law*, ed. D. G. Owen (Oxford: Clarendon Press, 1995), p. 90. But it is of course only contingent that such a mechanism exists—so a ground-level theory of remedial responsibility cannot presuppose that it does (that is, we cannot argue that it is essentially fair to hold people remedially responsible for compensating all of the harm that may eventuate from their actions on the grounds that, if insurance mechanisms exist, they can choose to protect themselves from incurring excessive burdens).

19. Some considerations in support of this basic belief are advanced in Honoré, Responsibility and Luck.

20. I am grateful to an anonymous referee for *The Journal of Political Philosophy* for suggesting this position.

21. Community might appear in both places because, on the one hand, it can serve to identify agents who are physically proximate to P and therefore likely to be well placed to help him, and on the other hand, it picks out a group of agents who have a special concern for P's welfare.

22. In thinking about the general shape of this theory, I have drawn inspiration from Hume's theory of justice and property, as set out particularly in *A Treatise of Human Nature*, ed. L. A. Selby-Bigge, 2nd ed., revised P. H. Nidditch (Oxford: Clarendon Press, 1978), part III, sections 2–3, 6. Hume argued that we have a shared strong interest in the existence of rules that stably assign possessions to persons as their property. The specific rules employed, however, depended less on utilitarian considerations than on common mental dispositions that lead us to connect persons to material objects in particular ways. The connection theory of remedial responsibility proposed here has a similar general structure, though as readers have pointed out there are also significant disanalogies between the two theories.

23. Another suggestion might be that causal responsibility always carries traces of moral responsibility with it. How can we be sure that the pedestrian who was apparently taking good care to watch his step did not in fact have a momentary lapse of concentration and fail to notice the raised paving stone

which he ought to have noticed? Or alternatively perhaps we are all to some small degree morally responsible for *everything* that results from our action, no matter how remote the causal chain, or how careful we have been. In ways such as these, we can put a moral gloss on causal responsibility. But then again, might not this be a case of the tail wagging the dog? Might it not be that *because* we want to hold causal agents remedially responsible for the harm they bring about, in certain cases, we are driven to impute moral responsibility to them, in defiance of our more usual (and defensible) understanding of that idea?

22. RICHARD W. MILLER

Miller presents arguments in defense of two forms of priority that are deeply entrenched in ordinary thinking about aid to needy strangers: the priority in favor of compatriots, and the priority in favor of those who are literally nearby. In particular, he argues that both forms of priority are consistent with recognizing the equal worth of all. He goes on to argue, however, that a proper understanding of the justification of those forms of priority shows that, given certain features of the global order, those of us who live in rich countries do nevertheless have substantial duties to aid distant strangers abroad.

Moral Closeness and World Community

First published in The Ethics of Assistance: Morality and the Distant Needy, *ed. Deen K. Chatterjee (Cambridge: Cambridge University Press, 2004), 101–22. © Cambridge University Press 2004. Reprinted with the permission of Cambridge University Press.*

Ordinary moral thinking about aid to needy strangers discriminates in favor of the political closeness of compatriots and the literal closeness of people in peril who are close at hand. For example, in ordinary moral thinking, I have, as an American citizen, a much more demanding duty to support tax-financed aid to the poor of the United States than to support such aid to the foreign poor. I have a duty to save a drowning toddler I encounter at the cost of ruining my four-hundred-dollar suit, but not a duty to donate four hundred dollars to save children in a distant village from a yet more ghastly death from dysentery.

One of my goals is to defend these biases, showing that they express a deep commitment to moral equality. The other is to show that a proper understanding of their justification establishes substantial, if less demanding duties to help the foreign poor. In this way, a vindication of ordinary moral favoritism toward closeness grounds a case for extensive foreign aid that could be believable to the vast majority of nonphilosophers, who find it unbelievable that a strong duty of impartial concern for neediness, whether near or far, determines what should be done to help needy strangers.

A MORALITY OF EQUAL RESPECT

My framework for defending this favoritism is a cluster of interconnected moral judgments that provide a partial interpretation of the principle that a choice is wrong just in case it could not express appreciation of the equal worth of all. The elements of this cluster are individually plausible and mutually supportive, providing a coherent perspective of moral equality from which the biases toward political and physical closeness can be assessed.

If appreciation of the equal worth of all required equal *concern* for all, there would be little hope of reconciling it with the ordinary biases. But this equation of equal valuing of persons with equal concern is much too strict. I do not have the same concern for the girl who lives next door as for my daughter, but I certainly do not regard my daughter as having greater worth. Rather (to offer a first interpretive precept) my equal appreciation of their worth is a matter of equal respect, not equal concern.

Equal respect is not just a matter of noninterference. In refusing to rescue the drowning toddler at the cost of ruining my suit, I would show a failure to respect him, a failure to ascribe the same worth to him and to myself, even if I did not push him into the water. If I appreciate everyone's equal worth, I must take anyone's neediness to be a reason to help. But I may decline to help, while expressing equal respect, because of a legitimate excuse, i.e., a special consideration in virtue of which my not helping is not wrong.[1]

One important source of such an excuse is a response to sharing a part of one's life with a person that constitutes the proper valuing of one's relationship.[2] This form of valuing primarily consists of responding to a certain type of shared history (one's child's dependence, for example, or mutual liking, activities enjoyed in common and mutual emotional openness) with certain forms of special concern (parental nurturance, for example, or the loyalties of friendship.) If I properly value parenting, then I respond to my young child's dependence on me by embracing a special responsibility for her well-being. In recognizing that this is the right response for me to have, I recognize that similar responsiveness is right for others and that it is desirable to help others respond to a similar history by doing well in pursuing similar goals of caring. But my appreciation of the special goodness of this nurturant response to parenthood is primarily expressed in my own special engagement in it, engagement that precludes impartial concern to promote the relationship regardless of whose it is. Although I appreciate the goodness of anyone's parental nurturing, I would not express a proper valuing of it by abandoning my child because this enables me to help two other people to become nurturant parents of two other children.

With their usual zest for vivid examples, philosophers have filled the landscape of partiality based on special relationships with water accidents and fires, in which the very life of the dear one is at stake. If I probably will have just one chance to rescue and a person is drowning on each side of the lagoon, my attempting the less likely, more distant rescue first is normally wrong, but not if the more distant one is my daughter. But special responsibilities based on special relationships extend much farther than saving from death. The most extensive such responsibilities, toward one's dependent children, involve a special commitment to help a particular person gain access to a life in which she pursues worthwhile goals, with which she identifies, enjoyably and well, goals exercising a broad range of important capacities. Thus, my proper valuing of my relationship to my daughter provides an adequate reason to spend money to send her to a good college that could, instead, be donated to an Oxfam project that will probably save several children in a village in Mali from early death.

Not only can reasons for special concern deriving from special relationships make the expression of impartial concern nonobligatory, if they are sufficiently important they can make impartial conduct wrong. To abandon my child as part of a project of adding to the net frequency of nurturant parenting or to abandon my friend to free up time needed to introduce friendship into the lives of two friendless people would constitute a failure to respect the person to whom I am tied. By the same token, I can rightly refuse to treat my child or my friend as just one locus of needs among others on the grounds that this is incompatible with my self-respect.

Three further observations will also be useful in the moral assessment of aid to needy strangers. First, if a special responsibility for someone else's well-being can justify neglect of more urgent needs of others when this threatens to make her life worse by jeopardizing the pursuit of worthwhile, important personal goals, then what threatens to worsen one's own life can also provide one with such an excuse. For surely one appropriately takes responsibility for one's own life. The doctor who would do the most good as a workoholic emergency room physician in an understaffed inner-city hospital, nearly but not quite "burnt out" by his job's demands, does no wrong if he continues his suburban dermatology practice instead, in order to avoid worsening his own life.

A further consideration, which also tends to increase the scope of excuses for neglect of the neediest, is a certain primacy of rules. Full appreciation of everyone's equal worth is a feature of someone's character, the general dispositions she expresses as circumstances arise. So someone's excuse for neglect of another's urgent need on a particular occasion may depend on the costs of a standing commitment that would dictate this assistance, rather than the burden of aid on the occasion in question. World poverty and effective charities such as Oxfam produce many occasions on which a relatively affluent person in the per-capita best-off countries could donate enough to save a desperate stranger from dire peril at small cost to herself and those to whom she has valuable and demanding relationships. But someone who appreciates the equal worth of all need not take such an opportunity to give on a particular occasion, if a standing commitment to respond in this way would jeopardize her special responsibilities and her capacity to pursue her worthwhile goals enjoyably and well.

Finally, the rules for living determining the difference between right and wrong are not just private rules that someone can embrace as an expression of legitimate personal goals. They have a distinctive potential social function: The terms of self-governance in virtue of which someone conducts herself in a morally responsible way are terms that she could want all to share while respecting all. This potential social role is the basis for further alternative formulations of the nature of moral duty. An act is wrong just in case its performance in its circumstances violates all moral codes that anyone who respects all could want all willingly to embrace as part of a shared moral code. Equivalently, an act is wrong just in case it violates every code that all could self-respectfully share. (One respects all in seeking to live by a moral code that all could self-respectfully share, and one disrespects another if one wants her to regulate her life in a way that is incompatible with her self-respect even if the regulation is shared.) These connections between moral duty and universally acceptable shared commitment are a final general resource that I will use to assess duties of aid to needy strangers in a morality of equal respect.

TAX-FINANCED AID

Even assuming (as I do) that such centrally important intimate relationships as that of being someone's parent, child, or friend provide reasons for neglect of strangers' needs, it is by no means clear to what extent forms of closeness that bind one to some, but not all, needy strangers justify special concern for them. I will begin inquiry into the moral status of these colder types of closeness with the case that is central to public policy, the standard political bias toward compatriots.

In ordinary moral thinking, one has a duty to put needy compatriots first in political choices concerning tax-financed aid; even if one lives in a per-capita rich country, one knows that the most desperately poor mostly live abroad, in countries lacking adequate resources to relieve their dire burdens, and one thinks that it is typically cheaper to relieve a burden on a poor foreigner through foreign aid than a burden on a needy compatriot through domestic aid. How can this bias be reconciled with an appreciation of the equal worth of all?

When I make political choices, a morally central difference between my relationship to poor compatriots and my relationship to poor foreigners is that I take part, and willingly so, in the creation of laws and policies that my compatriots are forced to obey. Proper valuing of the compatriot relationship provides a reason for the patriotic bias, partly because of the special requirements for justifiable participation in a project of coercion.

Suppose that someone taking part in political choice realizes that she lives under a regime of inequality of the following kind. The current system of laws gives rise to situations in which some people lack the same opportunity as others to live a good life. This system is, let us say, a capitalist regime in which, inevitably, some lose while others win, and children of losers (or of successive generations of losers) have special difficulty leading a good life. There is an alternative (I assume it is capitalist, as well) in which those who suffer the most from inferior social opportunities under the present system would have better opportunities to lead a good life, through measures whose burdens on an advantaged compatriot would not be as great as the consequent improvement in life-prospects of the disadvantaged. This is a powerful moral reason for a citizen to support a shift to the more equal alternative. In general, one can respect others while refusing to worsen one's own life to relieve worse burdens of theirs. But one does show disrespect if one helps to force others to accept rules of self-advancement generating life-worsening disadvantages for them and opposes a change that worsens one's life by reducing benefits of social advantage, when the change is necessary to relieve more serious burdens due to the social disadvantages one helps to impose.

The duty of special concern for disadvantages imposed by shared political arrangements limits the pursuit of globally impartial beneficence, not just the pursuit of self-interest. A participant in the process of collective self-rule ought to treat the relief of an important burden suffered by a compatriot due to the system of laws that she helps to impose as a stronger reason to change the laws than an unmet need of a foreigner, even one that can be satisfied more efficiently than her compatriot's need. To fail to accept this special responsibility for reducing burdens that one would otherwise help to impose coercively is to fail properly to disvalue political subordination. It is as disrespectful as an overlord's telling his exploited serfs that his exactions are justified by his using them to improve the well-being of the more miserable serfs of a fellow-baron.

Still, this argument from coercively sustained social disadvantage would not support the duty of patriotic bias in its whole extent. Even if politically enforced rules of self-advancement gave rise to no burdensome inferiorities, some compatriots' access to a good life would be drastically restricted by calamitous natural, as opposed to social, processes, for example, specially long-lasting, severe illnesses. There is, in ordinary thinking, a duty to provide these sufferers with some tax-financed aid, if this would supplement their own, inadequate resources in an effective and dignified way. Moreover, ordinary moral thinking shows patriotic bias in this matter: It would be quite wrong to neglect these afflicted people, "our" afflicted people, because foreign aid is a more effective means of relieving affliction worldwide.

The moral basis for this further bias is the proper valuing of joint loyalty on which a life-determining collective project depends. Suppose that we are willing, self-respecting participants in a joint project, that is, we have willingly joined in it or, in any case, we would not willingly do without it. Its success has an important impact on the success in life of each of us, and its success depends on potentially demanding loyalty on the part of participants. Proper valuing of participation in such a project is expressed in special loyalty to the other loyal participants, that is, a commitment to use one's influence on the project to show special concern for them in times of special need. As in other cases of loyalty, for example, friendship, this special concern, while responsive to beneficial sharing, is not simply a consequence of gratitude and is not always required for fair play. (I am grateful for the pleasure of hearing Maurizio Pollini, but I have no duty of loyalty to him. A compatriot who is unable to do much to express her loyalty to the common political project or who has actually been called upon to do very little still merits substantial concern.)

This duty of mutual loyalty arises in many shared cooperative activities. Consider the duty of the healthy members of a philosophy department to give a colleague a break if her voice has begun to weaken from Parkinson's disease and she can no longer teach the sort of large service course, which no one wants to teach, that is part of everyone's expected mix of courses. It would be quite wrong for the healthy colleagues to say, "We are glad that you have been loyal to the department. But our sharing this loyalty is enough, without our being loyal to you." More specifically, loyal coparticipation should lead to loyalty to the coparticipant, which governs decision making in the joint project: Everyone in the department has a duty of loyalty to support a departmental decision in favor of special concern, but if the majority of one's colleagues were to vote for callous disloyalty in the crucial department meeting, one would have no duty to use one's own salary to reduce the harm. (Without a restriction to aid via the joint project, a requirement of loyal aid to coparticipants makes each, as a potential benefactor, too vulnerable to consequences of others' disloyalty.)

How much provision for needy participants a duty of mutual loyalty entails depends on the importance of the project to all concerned, on how potentially demanding the required institutional loyalties are, and on how effective the cooperative project is as a means of helping the needy. Such proportionality is needed to ration the demands of mutual loyalty in a cooperative project, which compete, in anyone's life, with the demands of mutual loyalty in other projects, with other special responsibilities, and with legitimate self-concern. These considerations of proportionality make the political project of collective self-rule the source of a specially extensive duty of concern. For the institutional loyalty it requires is potentially extremely demanding, its effects on members' lives are pervasive and fundamental, and it is a particularly effective means of attending to members' needs.

Extensive as its political demands have turned out to be, the proper valuing of civic loyalty might seem incapable of explaining one further component of the duty of special concern for afflicted compatriots, as most people see it. This duty extends to those so afflicted since birth that they have never been in a position to be loyal participants. Suppose that we live in a country, among the most affluent per capita, in which some children are orphans who suffer from a painful, severely debilitating congenital disease that permanently prevents their political participation—say, a form of spina bifida. Whatever the legitimate excuses for withholding tax-financed aid might be, the following seems quite inadequate: "We will let these children among us with spina bifida suffer because the money that might go to their care is more effectively spent preventing afflictions just as grave by improving sanitation in poor foreign countries." How can special concern for our most pitiable compatriots be a duty, when all who suffer as much worldwide are equally deserving of our pity?

Obviously, any active compatriot's duty of concern for one of the orphans with spina bifida will not respond to any duty of this severely afflicted compatriot actually to engage in activities helping to sustain their shared institutions. Still, both the able and the severely afflicted compatriot can fall within the scope of an obligation to do what one can loyally to sustain the shared political institutions. If you are born in the territory of a government worthy of loyalty, then you have a duty loyally to participate in the shared political process if you can, unless you emigrate. If people did not generally recognize this duty, governments could not be stable and effective vehicles of justice.

In light of this principle, someone born with a severe disability, such as the paralysis of spina bifida, has the same duty as any compatriot loyally to participate if she can—but she cannot. She is like an utterly impoverished parent who has any parent's duty to do the best he can to guard his child's health, but who can do nothing to discharge this duty, since he cannot afford the only medicine that could help his child. So, if the concern that *active* participants in a worthwhile political project have a right to expect from each other is concern for each as someone doing what she can to discharge a duty to participate, it would be arbitrary of them not to show the same concern for congenitally severely disabled compatriots, who are also doing the best they can, viz., nothing, to discharge the same duty. And in fact, doing what one can to discharge the conditional duty of loyalty *is* the basis on which active participants properly expect concern.

The mutual loyalty that responsible active participants seek involves using their common project to express special concern *for one another*. So their well-wishing must not be contingent on the good fortune of being able to meet the ability-condition. Imposing this condition for aid, in this context, would show that one was not concerned for the other, but only for the payoff of her participation. Even if I am never disabled until death suddenly strikes me down in vigorous old age, my compatriots have never been concerned for me if they would tell me, if I were disabled, "You are not useful to us and resources for insurance were equally distributed, so your distress is no concern of ours." Such well-wishing might constitute concern to avoid disproportion between what I contributed or would have if called on and what I receive, but not concern for me as a person.

It follows that if I withhold special concern from those who are bound to a common political project by the same duty of loyalty as me, withholding it because they are physically unable to follow through, I do not have an attitude of concern toward them that I ought to expect from others and show toward others, as part of a proper valuing of loyal joint citizenship. So, in withholding this special concern, I would be making an arbitrary distinction, discriminating in a way that violates moral integrity. But I make no arbitrary distinction in withholding the same concern from similarly needy foreigners who, similarly, do not and cannot participate in my political project. For the shared special concern that I ought to seek and offer among compatriots reflects the sharing of a duty of loyal participation that foreigners do not share.

FOREIGN AID

These ways of grounding bias toward compatriots in political choices on a morality of equal respect for all are very far from justifying utter nonprovision of humanitarian aid to poor foreigners by the governments of countries in which average material well-being is high on a world scale. On the contrary, each rationale implies a reason (albeit a less weighty reason) why aid should be provided—in response to current institutions, not just common humanity.

Political coercion that could be supported by someone who respects all does not solely affect people within the governed territory. It can be used, and is, in fact, used to keep needy foreigners out and to exclude them from exploitation of domestic natural resources. Those who suffer from closed borders or an inferior local share of the world's resources ought to receive what they would enjoy in an impartially justifiable scheme of access.

Similarly, the commitment to mutual loyalty has an international echo. One can imagine a world in which the governments of poor countries are disposed to expropriate the property of foreign investors, cancel foreign financial obligations, and invade richer countries whenever this would benefit their citizens on balance. Perhaps this is our world, and fear of the consequences *is* the only current constraint. Still, someone rationally committed to self-respectful unforced acceptability to all will not want to live in such a world. For the rationality of his willingness to forgo benefits that are not justifiable on the basis of self-respectful unforced acceptability involves a desire that the reliability of others not depend on their fear of retaliation. After all, the basing of reliability on self-respectful trust is what he would lose if he were Louis XIV, depending on the reliable oppression of peasants—and this luxurious situation repels him. So a morally responsible citizen of a rich country will want the reliability of international norms to depend on loyal self-respectful support in rich and poor countries. Extrapolating domestic reasoning, she will, then, want our norm-governed international system to become one in which concern for others throughout the world responds to such freely given loyalty. In part, foreign aid is a first step in the construction of such a system, a first step incumbent on the richest countries, since their citizens are less needy, their resources for aid are greater, and their economic dominance puts them in a position to abuse others' loyalty to international norms.

Despite their importance, these considerations dictate less aid than their domestic analogues. In all or virtually all countries, even those with average income that is high on a world scale, the duties deriving from the need to justify domestic coercion produce much larger claims on resources for aid than the corresponding international duties.[3] Suffering due to transnational political coercion that could be supported by someone who has equal respect for all is a relatively small part of world poverty. For example, sovereign control over natural resources is rarely a major determinant of national prosperity or poverty, which largely depends, instead, on commercial and technological capacities. Similarly, while immigration restrictions significantly affect the prospects of some, most of the world's poor would be in no position to take advantage of the removal of those obstacles; they might, indeed, be hurt by the flight of specially skilled and productive compatriots. In any case, in a country that is among the best off per-capita, aid needed to compensate for burdens imposed by immigration restrictions is apt to be far less than aid needed to compensate for imposed domestic disadvantages. Since all per-capita well-off countries with substantial immigration restrictions jointly contribute to suffering due to the blocked opportunities, they share in the duty to alleviate it. In contrast, people in a per-capita well-off country have a unique duty to attend to the social disadvantages of their own compatriots, and this can be extremely expensive: Consider how expensive it is to provide victims of the severest social disadvantages in such a country with access to secure, interesting, valued work.

As for the relevant duties of mutual loyalty: They are proportionate to the potential demands of the needed institutional loyalty and the impact of the shared institutions. Since international institutions are less important on both dimensions, duties of loyalty will dictate less concern for fellow participants in international institutions than for compatriots.

Still, the rationales for patriotic bias do entail substantial reasons for foreign aid, grounded on special relationships that now bind humans one to another worldwide, not just on the ancient fact of common humanity. The existence of global relationships sharing the moral authority of compatriotism to some significant degree is a grain of truth in the idea of world community.

PRIVATE AID

Taxation in the per-capita richest countries, especially the United States, often leaves intact large personal surpluses over and above what is needed to discharge special responsibilities to intimates. (Certainly, tax-financed nonmilitary aid to less developed countries is no threat to these surpluses in the United States. In 2000, its per-capita cost was $35.)[4] In this setting, discussions of the moral significance of closeness rightly give much prominence to the morality of voluntary giving: In what ways, if any, should relationships of closeness affect the allocation of voluntary aid to needy strangers? My case for patriotic bias in tax-financed aid concerned the avoidance of disrespectful political coercion and the use of shared political institutions to express a proper valuing of institutional loyalties. So no guidance concerning the question of voluntary giving results—and fortunately so. One wants to avoid the patriotic stupidity of condemning Americans who check the "Where the need is greatest" box, rather than the "United States only" box, when they tell the Save the Children Foundation whom they want to help through their private donations.

Questions about biases in aid are not, as such, questions about the total extent of duties to aid. However, a description of the extent of one's general duty to respond to neediness with aid will turn out to be a help in assessing both the importance of closeness and the claims of world community in nonpolitical choices. In the morality of equal respect that I sketched at the outset, this duty of beneficence is described in a precept that I will call "the Principle of Sympathy":

> One's underlying disposition to respond to neediness ought to be sufficiently demanding that giving which would express greater underlying concern would impose a significant risk, on balance, of worsening one's life, if one fulfilled all further responsibilities; and it need not be any more demanding than this.

By "one's underlying disposition to respond to neediness," I mean the responsiveness to neediness with aid that would express the general importance one ascribes to relieving others' burdens, apart from special relationships and circumstances. Such ultimate concerns are not precise and determinate. So a change to a different, more demanding sensitivity in response to the same background of worldwide need would be expressed in a substantial increase in giving.

If the Principle of Sympathy is valid, such a substantial increase in giving may, at present, be an obligation of most affluent people. For a reduction in funds to spend on nonphilanthropic pursuits need not worsen one's life just because the reduction makes it more difficult to satisfy desires expressing one's worthwhile goals. Given my goal of aesthetically interesting eating, I have desires that are more easily satisfied if I have more money to spend at nice restaurants. But being served a mediocre meal when I would have been in a position to have a better one if I had given less to charity does not, in itself, make my life worse. Even fairly frequent disappointment of this kind need not make for a worse life. On the other hand, one's life is worsened by the inability to pursue, enjoyably and well, the range of worthwhile goals with which one intelligently identifies, or could readily intelligently identify, as giving point and order to one's choices. If I could hardly ever afford to eat at a restaurant serving interesting and delicious meals (unless I sacrificed a worthwhile goal that is as important to me as my goal of gastronomic exploration), my life would be worse.[5]

Both the duty-generating aspect and the permissive aspect of the Principle of Sympathy can be derived from the morality of equal respect. If I could be more responsive to neediness without imposing a significant risk of worsening my own life or neglecting further responsibilities, then the costs to me of greater responsiveness are not an adequate excuse for my neglect of people's needs, not a basis for reconciling unequal concern with equal respect. Lesser underlying concern for serious deprivation in others motivated by fear of trivial expected costs to oneself expresses the attribution of lesser importance to others' lives. Yet such personal costs of greater responsiveness are the only excuse that is left if further responsibilities have been taken into account, as they are in the Principle of Sympathy. On the other hand, as I argued before, I have an adequate excuse not to ascribe greater importance than I do to others' neediness as such if the consequent increased disposition to give would impose a significant risk of making my life worse. The responsibility to a dependent that justifies a refusal to display concern for neediness as such that imposes a significant risk of worsening his life corresponds to a similar prerogative in the case of one's ultimate dependent, oneself.

Perhaps my life would have been better, happier, and healthier if I had never developed my gastronomic interest, or my sartorial interest in displaying my aesthetic sensibility and engaging in the fun of mutual aesthetic recognition, and had formed a deeper commitment than my own to serve the world's poor. But the activities with which one can intelligently readily identify as the basis for a life that is rewarding to oneself are not the same as those with which one once could have identified. After all, poverty worsens the lives of those who would not be worsened if a different upbringing had given them the outlook of monks and nuns in ascetic orders.

MERE CLOSENESS

Returning from the question of how concerned an individual must be to relieve neediness in general to the question of favoritism toward needy strangers who are in some sense close, one encounters a stark contrast in ordinary moral thinking between those with urgent needs who are literally close to a potential benefactor and those who are not: We ordinarily take ourselves to have a strong (i.e., potentially quite demanding) duty to rescue someone in peril close at hand, but no strong duty, in general, to rescue someone in peril, regardless of distance. In light of further reflection, this ordinary bias in aid has sometimes seemed perverse. In the essay at the origins of current discussions of closeness and aid, Singer notes this aspect of ordinary moral thinking and protests, "If we accept any principle of impartiality, universality, morality or whatever, we cannot discriminate against anyone merely because he is far away from us."[6] An adequate defense of the discrimination in duties must show that the ordinary special connection between closeness and the duty to rescue is justifiable in a perspective of equal respect for all.

Obviously, ordinary morality does acknowledge plenty of demanding duties to help imperiled distant strangers, based on special responsibilities (e.g., the forest ranger's, as she surveys the vast forest from the observation tower) and special histories (e.g., the negligent toxic-waste-disposer's obligation to help the now-dispersed victims of his negligence). So the live issue concerning literal closeness and aid to needy strangers is not whether strong duties to help strangers stop at the boundary of the near. Obviously, they do not. Also, ordinary insistence on a strong duty to rescue those in peril close at hand presupposes normal background circumstances of human interaction. In a ghastly circumstance of frequent encounter, every day, with innocents in imminent dire peril, it might even be morally permissible for someone to neglect a drowning toddler close at hand, because he must ration individually easy aid to nearby victims to take adequate care of his loved ones and his life. In a science fiction in which humans have become so adapted to contact via the internet that attention and control are much easier at a distance than closeby, there seems to be no strong duty of nearby rescue.

The live issue in the assessment of the ordinary connection between closeness and obligatory aid is the justification of the presence in an otherwise acceptable moral code of (something like) the following principle, asserting a special linkage between potentially demanding rescues and closeness, taken to govern rescues in the normal background circumstances of human interaction:

> (The Principle of Nearby Rescue.) One has a duty to rescue someone encountered closeby who is currently in danger of severe harm and whom one can help to rescue with means at hand, if the sacrifice of rescue does not itself involve a grave risk of harm of similar seriousness or of serious physical harm, and does not involve wrongdoing.

I will offer reasons why the morality of equal respect precludes a revision of ordinary morality giving rise to a moral code lacking the Principle of Nearby Rescue or any similar special connection between closeness and rescue. What reasons come into play in the course of this vindication depends on what alternatives are to be precluded.

If the question is whether the reference to closeness should be deleted in the Principle of Nearby Rescue, then the crucial consideration is one that helped to sustain the Principle of Sympathy, namely, the avoidance of excessive demands. In what are now the normal circumstances of human interaction, which include the prevalence of severe peril and inadequate local resources in some parts of the world and far-reaching means of aid elsewhere, many of the world's better-off can reject the distance-deleted alternative to Nearby Rescue, without showing unequal respect: Such a standing commitment to help those in peril near or far would involve their imposing on themselves a serious risk of a worse life, for lack of resources needed to pursue, enjoyably and well, worthwhile goals to which they are attached. In contrast, commitment to a moral code including the Principle of Nearby Rescue imposes no risks that someone who ascribes equal value to everyone's life can reject. Because of our shared human vulnerability, our shared need to monitor goings-on close at hand and our typically greater capacity to intervene nearby with means close at hand than to intervene in distant processes or with distant means, the expected net cost of a shared commitment to Nearby Rescue is trivial at most, in the course of a morally responsible person's life. One may gain, as beneficiary, from the shared commitment, on account of vulnerability. One may lose, as benefactor, but the ex ante probability of substantial net loss in the course of a life in normal circumstances is nil or minute. Because the expected loss from shared commitment to the rule of nearby rescue is trivial, at most, rejecting this commitment to save people in dire peril because it demands too much would show a failure to appreciate the equal worth of every person's life.

Of course, commitment to the Principle of Nearby Rescue could come due in costly ways in unusual circumstances. But this is true of quite uncontroversial moral principles, which clearly are requirements of equal respect, for example, principles requiring the keeping of a promise that has become surprisingly costly when the stakes to the promisee are substantial and the possibility of adequate compensation is uncertain.

However, considerations of demandingness will not justify the inclusion of the Principle of Nearby Rescue *in addition to* the Principle of Sympathy in a shared system of principles that must be acceptable to anyone who equally respects all. Here, the vindication of Nearby

Rescue must rebut the objection that the singling out of nearby victims is arbitrary, not the objection that it requires too little giving. Although commitment to rescue from nearby peril is one relevantly nonburdensome way for someone to respond to neediness, the same could be said of other rules enjoining specific kinds of aid that are not mandatory, for example, "Give at least a small amount to the prevention or treatment of cancer every year." In general, people have a broad prerogative to pick and choose among possible ingredients in the total personal practice of giving that expresses their ultimate concern for others' neediness. Singling out a worthy cause as mandatory almost always justifies a complaint of arbitrariness on the part of those who specially care about other causes, as potential beneficiaries or benefactors. Why isn't it arbitrary to insist that the Principle of Nearby Rescue be in everyone's package of beneficent rules?

The answer to this question must appeal to special values of closeness that provide everyone who respects all with a reason for including Nearby Rescue among her rules of aid. There are at least three such reasons.

(a) *The relationship of encounter.* Personal encounter is our minimal special relationship, the pervasive (if usually fleeting) basis for mutual recognition. Quite apart from the value of assurance of aid in case of disaster, life goes better if people encountering each other are in a position to assume that the other would benevolently attend to a peril that strikes in the course of the encounter. Even if I know that I will never collapse on a sidewalk, my encounters with passersby are better if I know that they would not simply step over me if I did collapse. So a proper valuing of special relationships is expressed in special attentiveness to the needs of those closeby.

(b) *Coordination.* A special inclination to help those in peril close at hand is pervasive among us humans. It functions reasonably well as a way of assigning responsibility to those able to help, avoiding buck-passing and inefficiency without making relevantly excessive demands. No rival, relevantly undemanding basis for coordination of personal efforts to aid is feasible. So this is a disposition that one would want to continue to be prevalent, if one values everyone's life. One would, then, be a parasite not to share the disposition.[7]

(c) *Trusteeship.* A self-respecting person expects others to be inclined to respect her space, giving her free passage and letting her continue to leave her imprint on her environment. Of course, the spatial prerogative that we rightly claim is hardly absolute. Still, others' obligation not to interfere with my movement and not to keep me from going about my business where I happen to be is more demanding than their general obligation to take my interests into account. Stopping someone in his tracks is, in general, much more serious than creating a reason for someone, now distant, to take a different path. On the other hand, it shows a failure of equal respect to insist that others be specially concerned to leave one in control of one's immediate environment without accepting a responsibility to pay special attention to events within this space that provide a serious reason for concern. A moral code that all could self-respectfully share will include both the spatial prerogative and the correlative responsibility of trusteeship.[8]

The appeal to specific values of closeness is essential in explaining why the special connection between closeness and the duty of aid is nonarbitrary. But this appeal does not provide a convincing explanation of why reference to closeness should not be deleted in the Principle of Nearby Rescue, a move to a morality that would require aid to nearby victims and much more, besides. So, when morally relevant values of closeness are described in a defense of the ordinary connection between closeness and obligatory aid, there is legitimate cause for concern that these considerations lack the power to justify neglect of dire need. On the other hand, when the ordinary connection between closeness and obligatory aid is defended on the ground that the restriction to those closeby avoids excessive demands, there is cause for concern that strong demands have been avoided at the cost of an arbitrary distinction. These worries are overcome by taking account of the distinctive role of each kind of consideration at a different stage in the vindication of the ordinary connection between literal closeness and obligatory aid.

FROM CLOSENESS TO DISTANCE

Like the case for special concern for compatriots in tax-financed aid, the case for Nearby Rescue rests on an appreciation of closeness that also suggests considerations supporting duties of concern for distant strangers. To some extent, the support is direct: Considerations that I have labeled "values of closeness" lend special value to caring interactions between a potential beneficiary and a distant imperiled stranger, sustaining a duty of special concern. For example, considerations of encounter and coordination create a special duty to help when emergencies arise in the course of communication, however remote. If the distant salesperson taking down my order over the telephone shows unmistakable signs of having a heart attack, I have a duty to help him in addition to any background duty to help victims of heart attacks in general. I believe that the values of closeness sustain other such duties of aid to particular distant people in circumstances that are sufficiently similar to closeness. But these duties would not connect many people in the richest countries with many people in poor countries, in the relatively moderate morality that I am exploring. In general, the monitoring and fulfillment of a far-flung network of obligations to particular people engendered in ways beyond the agent's control would constitute an excessive distraction from the pursuit of worthwhile personal goals.

The most important contribution of the case for Nearby Rescue to the case for aid to distant strangers is less direct. The justification of Nearby Rescue depended on the moral relevance of certain values, singling out nearby victims, to anyone's choices of whom to aid. Analogously, a different universal value, which also commands the attention of any morally responsible benefactor, could provide a reason to implement the general demands of sympathy in ways that benefit needy people in poor foreign countries. Specifically, in current world circumstances, the proper valuing of willing cooperation has a crucial moral role to play in channeling aid from affluent people in rich countries to the foreign poor. Those benefactors must be sensitive to the exploitive relationship between their affluence and desperate foreign needs; without this sensitivity, they would be free to regulate their beneficence by considerations that are apt to crowd out aid to the foreign poor.

Suppose that a citizen of one of the per-capita richest countries is at least fairly affluent, and has worthwhile personal goals, valuable relationships, and special responsibilities that are not unusually demanding. The Principle of Sympathy will require substantial aid to help others avoid deprivations. However, even if giving to the desperately needy in poor countries is the most efficient way of relieving the most desperate needs, one must not conclude, in the absence of further considerations, that such a person has a duty to send substantial aid abroad. People with serious needs that are not the most severe or with burdens that are hard to lift could rightly complain of a general requirement that private aid to needy strangers always be channeled in ways that do the most to relieve the most serious needs. So could benefactors who seek to give in ways that express special values and acknowledge special relationships that enrich their lives. Benefactors express their love of opera and ballet through giving that avoids cultural deprivations. Preferential attention to needy compatriots or needy people in one's city or neighborhood is justifiable, even if it is not dictated, by a variety of considerations. It can be an expression of civic friendship, that is, a way of expressing appreciation of goodwill and courage in the face of adversity on the part of the disadvantaged who take part in one's own social milieu, through which they contribute to mutual respect and trust. Often, such local aid involves a commitment to continue an inherently valuable tradition and expectation of sharing. If the suffering of the domestic disadvantaged reflects a shortfall in meeting the special demands of domestic justice, a special interest in helping them is one way, even if it is not an obligatory way, of affirming the importance of the underlying values of political respect and loyalty.

If good causes that would crowd out aid to the foreign poor are close to the benefactor's heart, what compelling moral reason could there be for such a person to allocate a substantial portion of his aid to needy people in poor countries? This question has great practical importance. In the actual charitable donations of typical affluent people in the per-capita best-off countries, the allocation to needy people in poor countries is not substantial. In the United States in 2001, only 2 percent of donations to tax-exempt nonprofit organizations went to those whose primary interest was international, including those concerned with international security, foreign affairs, and cultural exchange as well as those concerned with development assistance and humanitarian relief.[9] Only about 7 percent of households made any contribution to any of these international agencies.[10] Development assistance by private voluntary agencies based in the United States amounted to $16 per US resident.[11]

In implementing the demands of sympathy, someone who regards the lives of all as equally valuable must count efficiency in relieving the burdens of the neediest as a significant reason to donate to a cause. Still, it does not seem that this consideration—which I take to favor poor people in poor countries—must play an important role, in the final analysis, in the benefactions of affluent people in per-capita rich countries, given the pressure of competing good causes that are close to their hearts. What does require a substantial allocation of aid to desperately needy people in poor countries is a more specific obligatory concern, the proper valuing of willing cooperation, entailing a concomitant disvaluing of exploitation.

Someone who respects all, equally valuing their lives, must value cooperative relationships in which no party benefits from severe bargaining disadvantages of others that deprive them of access to a good life. One could hardly rationally commit oneself to observing a moral code whose terms of self-governance everyone could willingly, self-respectfully share if one did not care whether one benefited from the extraction of burdensome concessions from others that they are forced to yield on account of dire need. If I benefit from others' agreeing to work on terms incompatible with a good life because their bargaining position is weak, then a proper valuing of willing cooperation requires a special disposition on my part to use my gains to help relieve their disadvantages, at least if this does not impose a significant risk of worsening my life or interfering with my special responsibilities. My use of these gains from the severe disadvantages of some in charitable relief of the deprivations of others would be an expression of contempt, unless, perhaps, this use much more effectively relieves needs at least as serious or effectively relieves much more urgent needs. My using benefits from the weak bargaining power of people fleeing grinding rural poverty for the sweatshops of Southeast Asia to help the needy of my hometown would be wrongful channeling of beneficence, like rushing past a toddler sinking into quicksand in order to visit a lonely sick friend before the end of hospital visiting hours.

These days, affluent people in the per-capita richest countries are apt to derive considerable material benefits from such bargaining disadvantages of poor foreigners. They gain from the consequent cheapness of labor and raw materials while their own special skills or financial assets shield them from costs that globalization can impose on their less affluent compatriots. Moreover, this transnational benefit does not just derive from desperate neediness of foreigners actually engaged in the advantageous transactions. Well-positioned buyers are advantaged by actual sellers' fears of concessions that might be made by even more desperately needy potential sellers, elsewhere. So, in their charitable activities (which might have to be extensive, given the Principle of Sympathy), affluent people in per-capita rich countries ought to give substantial and distinctive consideration to the neediest foreigners, in general. These are people whose desperation contributes to their prosperity.

Once the duty to channel substantial aid to the foreign poor is established, it contributes to the political duty to support tax-financed aid as well. For everyone adequately responsive to foreign needs has reasons to favor significant reliance on taxation as a means of discharging such responsibilities, reasons that include the importance of scale and coordination in the development of infrastructure in a poor economy, the absence of adequate voluntary responsiveness to foreign needs, and the danger that those who voluntarily do as much as they should in their charitable endeavors will, by giving up financial resources, place themselves at a competitive disadvantage to those who give much less than they should. In principle, increases in tax-financed foreign aid could end the moral pressure on the affluent to show substantial concern for poor foreigners in their private contributions. But typical affluent people in per-capita well-off countries have not reached this point, and people in the United States are especially far from it.

CONCLUSION

The conflict between reasons expressing the moral importance of neediness as such and reasons expressing the independent importance of relationships of closeness is a recurrent, troubling feature of moral experience. At present, the outcome of this conflict among most people in the per-capita best-off countries (and, especially, in the United States) is a low level of effective concern for neediness in poor countries. If (as I believe) this level is too low, the underlying moral error might seem to be a failure to appreciate the ultimately greater authority of the perspective of impartial concern. But the arguments of this essay suggest that this is a false diagnosis, diverting attention from the arguments most apt to help the world's poor.

The authoritative moral perspective is one of equal respect, not equal concern. In seeking to specify the demands of equal respect, the friends of the world's poor have no need to debunk ordinary biases toward closeness. For a sympathetic understanding of these biases uncovers powerful rationales for concern for needy strangers who are not close. The avoidance of disrespectful coercion and valuing of loyalty that justify the political bias toward needy compatriots also provide important reasons for tax-financed aid to needy foreigners. An understanding of the rationales for a specific, potentially demanding duty to aid those in peril close at hand helps to explain why typical affluent people in rich countries have a duty to allocate substantial donations to aid needy people in poor countries.

The strength of these moral reasons to aid distant strangers reflects the nature of current transnational interactions, for example, the importance of global institutions that ought to be sustained by global loyalties, the significance of immigration restrictions as a barrier to opportunities, the existence of far-reaching transnational facilities for aid, public and private, and the extent of transnational benefits from neediness abroad. Because these interactions give rise to such important transnational duties, public and private, the world is now a moral community. The moral importance of this far-flung community is illuminated, rather than obscured, by a proper appreciation of the moral importance of closeness.

NOTES

1. There is another usage in which excuses reduce the blameworthiness of a person for doing what is wrong, typically on account of some diminished capacity. My topic, in using the term, will always be the wrongness of what is done.

2. To adopt a phrase of Scanlon's see T. M. Scanlon, *What We Owe to Each Other* (Cambridge: Harvard University Press, 1998), p. 89 and elsewhere. Samuel Scheffler, "Relationships and Responsibilities," *Philosophy & Public Affairs* 26 (1997): 189–209 is another recent examination of special relationships that is generally supportive of my view of their role in moral obligation.

3. The exceptions would be per-capita well-off countries within which it is easy to remove all serious burdens due to inferior social opportunities and to do what can be done to alleviate specially severe natural misfortunes. I am not sure such countries exist.

4. This includes concessionary loans less repayment of principal, as well as grants, and contributions to multilateral programs, as well as bilateral aid. See *World Development Indicators: 2002* (Washington: World Bank, 2002), pp. 358f. In 1995, 72.7 percent of this aid was subject to restrictions on procurement sources, presumably favorable to US manufacturing and agricultural interests (ibid., p. 357, where no more recent figure is provided for the United States)

5. Some might disagree with my assessment of the impact of the disappointing meal, claiming that it makes my life worse but only insignificantly so. I do not think that this disagreement matters for present purposes. At the cost of some awkwardness, those who have this alternative assessment can take "worse" to abbreviate "significantly worse," wherever the disagreement would otherwise lead them to resist my arguments about aid.

6. Peter Singer, "Famine, Affluence, and Morality," *Philosophy & Public Affairs* 1 (1972): 232 [reprinted herein 1–14, 4].

7. In "The Possibility of Special Duties," *Canadian Journal of Philosophy* 16 (1986): 651–76, Philip Pettit and Robert Goodin emphasize the benefits of widely shared norms allocating special responsibilities. They are not concerned, however, with the moral status of closeness and deploy a rule-consequentialist framework that has very different consequences, especially for foreign aid, from the morality of equal respect that I am exploring.

8. Here, I have benefited from Kamm's intriguing tentative suggestion that the duty "to take care of what is associated with oneself: for example, the area near one" is "the flip side" of the "prerogative to give greater weight to one's own interests rather than giving equal weight to oneself and to others." (See Frances Kamm, "Faminine Ethics," in Dale Jamieson, ed., *Singer and His Critics* [Oxford: Blackwell, 1999], p. 200.) However, an alleged duty to take care of what is associated with oneself seems much too broad in scope. After all, the former owner has no responsibility to continue to take care of his distinctive, monogrammed cast-off clothes. One needs to find a prerogative specifically concerned with what is closeby that directly generates a responsibility for what happens there without further appeal to mere "association."

9. Center on Philanthropy at Indiana University, *Giving USA 2002* (Indianapolis: AAFRC Trust for Philanthropy, 2002), pp. 19, 125. This amount included corporate and foundation as well as individual giving.

10. Ibid., p. 147.

11. See Table 13, OECD, *2002 Development Cooperation Report*, www.oecd.org/xls/M00037000/M00037866.xls.

23. THOMAS POGGE

Citizens of affluent countries tend to think about the global poor in terms of duties of assistance. The popular belief that such positive duties generate our only moral obligations with respect to the global poor rests on mistaken empirical beliefs about the roles of local factors in explaining poverty. Pogge offers the analogy of a classroom—variation in student performance is not exclusively determined by the abilities of students; the "global" factor of teacher quality clearly plays a role as well. Explaining global poverty without reference to the pervasive global economic order imposed upon the global poor is a similar fallacy. Insofar as we benefit from a system that foreseeably and avoidably causes widespread misery, citizens of affluent countries are violating negative duties not to harm the global poor. We have, in turn, obligations to reduce the harm we will cause and to compensate for any harm we do cause. These obligations are of a very different nature from a duty to assist.

"Assisting" the Global Poor

First published in The Ethics of Assistance: Morality and the Distant Needy, *ed. Deen K. Chatterjee (Cambridge: Cambridge University Press, 2004), 260–88.* © *Cambridge University Press 2004. Reprinted with the permission of Cambridge University Press.*

We citizens of the affluent countries tend to discuss our obligations toward the distant needy mainly in terms of donations and transfers, assistance and redistribution: How much of our wealth, if any, should we give away to the hungry abroad? Using one prominent theorist to exemplify this way of conceiving the problem, I show how it is a serious error—and a very costly one for the global poor.

1. THE THESIS OF THE PURELY DOMESTIC CAUSATION OF POVERTY (PDPT) IN RAWLS

In his book *The Law of Peoples*, John Rawls adds an eighth law to his previous account: "Peoples have a duty to assist other peoples living under unfavorable conditions that prevent their having a just or decent political and social regime."[1] The addition is meant to show that Rawls's proposal can give a plausible account of global economic justice, albeit a less egalitarian one than his cosmopolitan critics have been urging upon him.[2] This newly added duty is, however, more than Rawls's account can justify and less than what is needed to do justice to the problem of world poverty.

It is doubtful that the new amendment would be adopted in Rawls's international original position, which represents liberal and decent peoples only. Each such representative is rational[3] and seeking an international order that enables his or her own people to be stably organized according to its own conception of justice or decency.[4] Such representatives may well agree to assist one another in times of need. But why is it rational for them to commit to assisting poor peoples that never had a liberal or decent institutional order?

This challenge highlights how Rawls's international original position is too strongly focused on safeguarding the well-orderedness of liberal and decent societies and therefore triply implausible: First, peoples neither liberal nor decent are not represented in the international original position, and the interests of their members are thereby discounted completely.[5] Second, because (liberal and decent) *peoples* count equally, the interests of their individual members (in the viability and stability of their domestic order) are represented unequally to the detriment of those who belong to more populous peoples.[6] Third, other important interests of members of liberal or decent peoples are not represented—for example, their interest in their socioeconomic position relative to that of other societies.[7]

Though more demanding than what his international original position can justify, Rawls's duty of assistance is not demanding enough. This duty stipulates only an *absolute* target: No people should be prevented by poverty from organizing itself as a liberal or decent society. Rawls opposes any *relative* target: Above the absolute threshold, international inequalities are unconstrained and hence a matter of moral indifference.

Rawls suggests why he opposes any relative target: Once a people has attained the modest economic capacities necessary to sustain a liberal or decent institutional order, it is morally free to decide whether to make further net savings. If it does not, then its per capita income may fall further and further behind that of other peoples who save and invest more. It has a right to make this decision. But it also must then accept responsibility for the consequences. It cannot plausibly complain later about the evolved discrepancy in affluence—let alone demand a share of the much greater incomes other societies have become able to generate.[8]

One might adduce against this argument that the effects of crucial decisions made for a society are often borne by persons who had no role in this decision—by later generations, or by persons at the bottom of a "decent hierarchical society."[9] Both parts of Rawls's second principle of domestic justice forbid social institutions that impose the burdens (above some absolute threshold) of costly decisions made for a family upon members of this family alone. Decent societies, as Rawls describes them, may well be committed to similar domestic burden sharing. So it is unclear why liberal and decent societies should be categorically opposed to any analogous scheme of *international* burden sharing, even to a scheme that demands little from the wealthier societies and is adjusted according to the actual impact of perverse incentives and moral hazards.[10]

A further point is that the global institutional context in which national decisions are made codetermines their effects. Consider two ways in which the global order can be structured. It can be structured so that the rules of the world economy reflect the bargaining power of the various states, effectively preventing the smaller and poorer societies from achieving the solid rates of economic growth that are easily available to the bigger and richer ones. Or this order can be structured so that it, regardless of the distribution of power, maintains fair and open markets that actually make it easier for poorer than for richer countries to achieve high rates of economic growth. Without any burden sharing, the latter design would clearly engender much less hardship and inequality than the former would. The choice of global order then codetermines what the effects of poor national decisions are. Even rejecting any and all international burden sharing, Rawls could still have expressed a preference over these contrasting institutional designs. The contrast suggests that he should have complemented his duty of assistance after all, perhaps by a duty to help structure the global order so as to minimize personal poverty and international inequality.

Rawls does not see this point, I think, because he believes that the causes of severe poverty lie within the poor countries themselves. He stresses repeatedly that this is true of the world as it is: "the causes of the wealth of a people and the forms it takes lie in their political culture and in the religious, philosophical, and moral traditions that support the basic structure of their political and social institutions, as well as in the industriousness and cooperative talents of its members, all supported by their political virtues. ... the political culture of a burdened society is all-important.... Crucial also is the country's population policy."[11] When societies fail to thrive, "the problem is commonly the nature of the public political culture and the religious and philosophical traditions that underlie its institutions. The great social evils in poorer societies are likely to be oppressive government and corrupt elites."[12]

These passages suggest that poverty is due to domestic factors, not to foreign influences. This empirical view about poverty leads rather directly to the important moral error to be exposed: to the false idea that the problem of world poverty concerns us citizens of the rich countries mainly as potential helpers. I will therefore examine in detail the empirical view of the domestic causation of severe poverty, showing why it is false and also why it is so widely held in the developed world.

2. REASONS AGAINST THE PDPT

It is well to recall that existing peoples have arrived at their present levels of social, economic, and cultural development through a historical process that was pervaded by enslavement, colonialism, even genocide. Though these monumental crimes are now in the past, they have left a legacy of great inequalities that would be unacceptable even if peoples were now masters of their own development. Even if the peoples of Africa had had, in recent decades, a real opportunity to achieve similar rates of economic growth as the developed countries, achieving such growth could not have helped them overcome their initial 30:1 disadvantage in per capita income. Even if, starting in 1960, African annual growth in per capita income had been a full percentage point above ours each and every year, the ratio would still be 20:1 today and would not be fully erased until early in the twenty-fourth century.[13] It is unclear then whether we may simply take for granted the existing inequality as if it had come about through choices freely made within each people. By seeing the problem of poverty merely in terms of assistance, we overlook that our enormous economic advantage is deeply tainted by how it accumulated over the course of *one* historical process that has devastated the societies and cultures of four continents.

But let us leave aside the continuing legacies of historical injustice and focus on the empirical view that at least in the postcolonial era, which brought impressive growth in global per capita income, the causes of the *persistence* of severe poverty, and hence the key to its eradication, lie within the poor countries themselves. Many find this view compelling in light of the great variation in how the former colonies have evolved over the last forty years. Some of them have done quite well in economic growth and poverty reduction while others exhibit worsening poverty and declining per capita incomes. Isn't it obvious that such strongly divergent national trajectories must be due to differing *domestic* causal factors in the countries concerned? And isn't it clear, then, that the persistence of severe poverty has local causes?

This reasoning connects three thoughts: There are great international variations in the evolution of severe poverty. These variations must be caused by local (country-specific) factors. These factors, together, fully explain the overall evolution of severe poverty worldwide. To see the fallacy, consider this parallel: There are great variations in the performance of my students. These variations must be caused by local (student-specific) factors. These factors, together, fully explain the overall performance of my class.

Clearly, the parallel reasoning results in a falsehood: The overall performance of my class also crucially depends on the quality of my teaching and on various other "global" factors as well. This shows that the second step is invalid. To see this more precisely, one must appreciate that there are two distinct questions about the evolution of severe poverty. One question concerns observed *variations* in national trajectories. In the answer to this question, local factors must play a central role. Yet, however full and correct, this answer may not suffice to answer the second question, which concerns the *overall* evolution of poverty worldwide: Even if student-specific factors fully explain observed variations in the performance of my students, the quality of my teaching may still play a major role in explaining why they did not on the whole do much better or worse than they actually did. Likewise, even if country-specific factors fully explain the observed variations in the economic performance of the poor countries, global factors may still play a major role in explaining why they did not on the whole do much better or worse than they did in fact.

This is not merely a theoretical possibility. There is considerable international economic interaction regulated by an elaborate system of treaties and conventions about trade, investments, loans, patents, copyrights, trademarks, double taxation, labor standards, environmental protection, use of seabed resources, and much else. In many ways, such rules can be shaped to be more or less favorable to various affected parties such as, for instance, the poor or the rich societies. Had these rules been shaped to be more favorable to the poor societies, much of the great poverty in them today would have been avoided.

Let me support this point with a quote from the *Economist* which—being strongly supportive of WTO globalization and having vilified, on its cover and in its editorial pages, the protesters of Seattle, Washington, and Genoa as enemies of the poor[14]—is surely not biased in my favor:

> Rich countries cut their tariffs by less in the Uruguay Round than poor ones did. Since then, they have found new ways to close their markets, notably by imposing anti-dumping duties on imports they deem "unfairly cheap." Rich countries are particularly protectionist in many of the sectors where developing countries are best able to compete, such as agriculture, textiles, and clothing. As a result, according to a new study by Thomas Hertel, of Purdue University, and Will Martin, of the World Bank, rich countries' average tariffs on manufacturing imports from poor countries are four times higher than those on imports from other rich countries. This imposes a big burden on poor countries. The United Nations Conference on Trade and Development (UNCTAD) estimates that they could export $700 billion more a year by 2005 if rich countries did more to open their markets. Poor countries are also

hobbled by a lack of know-how. Many had little understanding of what they signed up to in the Uruguay Round. That ignorance is now costing them dear. Michael Finger of the World Bank and Philip Schuler of the University of Maryland estimate that implementing commitments to improve trade procedures and establish technical and intellectual-property standards can cost more than a year's development budget for the poorest countries. Moreover, in those areas where poor countries could benefit from world trade rules, they are often unable to do so. ... Of the WTO's 134 members, 29 do not even have missions at its headquarters in Geneva. Many more can barely afford to bring cases to the WTO.[15]

Such effects of the going WTO rules show that the causes of the persistence of severe poverty do not, *pace* Rawls, lie solely in the poor countries themselves. The global economic order also plays an important role. It is not surprising that this order is shaped to reflect the interests of the rich countries and their citizens and corporations. In the world as it is, the 15.6 percent of humankind living in the "high-income economies" have 81 percent of global income while the other 84.4 percent of humankind share the remaining 19 percent.[16] It is of great importance for these other countries to be allowed access to the markets of the high-income economies, where per capita incomes are 23 times higher on average. This fact gives our governments greatly superior bargaining power. If our officials serve us well in intergovernmental negotiations about the ground rules of the world economy, they use this superior bargaining power, and their advantages in information and expertise, to shape each facet of the global order to our benefit, allowing us to capture the lion's share of the gains from economic interaction. In this way, large inequalities, once accumulated, have a tendency to intensify[17]—and this is happening, quite dramatically, on the global plane: "The income gap between the fifth of the world's people living in the richest countries and the fifth in the poorest was 74 to 1 in 1997, up from 60 to 1 in 1990 and 30 to 1 in 1960."[18]

If the global economic order plays a major role in the persistence of severe poverty worldwide and if our governments, acting in our name, are prominently involved in shaping and upholding this order, then the deprivation of the distant needy may well engage not merely positive duties to assist but also more stringent negative duties not to harm. Yet, this obvious thought is strangely absent from the debates about our relation to the distant needy. Even those who have most forcefully presented the eradication of severe poverty as an important moral task for us are content to portray us as mere bystanders. Thus, Peter Singer argues that we should donate most of our income to save lives in the poor countries. He makes his case by telling the story of a healthy young professor who, walking by a shallow pond, sees a small child in it about to drown. Surely, Singer says, the professor has a duty to save the child, even at the cost of dirtying his clothes. And similarly, he argues, we have a duty to send money to poverty relief organizations that can, for each few dollars they receive, save one more child from a painful hunger death.[19] It is, in one way, a virtue of Singer's argument that it reaches even those who subscribe to the Purely Domestic Poverty Thesis (PDPT), the view that the persistence of severe poverty is due solely to domestic causes. But by catering to this empirical view, Singer also reinforces the common moral judgment that the citizens and governments of the affluent societies, whom he is addressing, are as innocent in regard to the persistence of severe poverty abroad as the professor is in regard to the child's predicament.[20]

3. AN EXPLANATION FOR WHY THE PDPT IS SO WIDELY ACCEPTED

Having argued that the PDPT, though widely held in the developed countries, is nonetheless quite far from the truth, I should be able to give some reasons for its popularity. I can see four main such reasons. The first is that belief in this thesis is rather comfortable for people in the developed world. Most of us know at least vaguely of the horrendous conditions among the global poor. We confront poverty statistics such as these: Out of a total of 6130 million human beings (2001), some 2735 million live below \$2/day, and 1089 million of them live below the \$1/day international poverty line.[21] 799 million are undernourished, more than 1 billion lack access to safe water, 2.4 billion lack access to basic sanitation, and 876 million adults are illiterate.[22] More than 880 million lack access to basic health services.[23] Approximately 1 billion have no adequate shelter and 2 billion no electricity.[24] "Two out of five children in the developing world are stunted, one in three is underweight and one in ten is wasted."[25] 250 million children between 5 and 14 do wage work outside their household—often under harsh or cruel conditions: as soldiers, prostitutes, or domestic servants, or in agriculture, construction, textile or carpet production.[26] Roughly one-third of all human deaths, some 50,000 daily, are due to poverty-related causes, easily preventable through better nutrition, safe drinking water, vaccines, cheap rehydration packs, and antibiotics.[27] Severe deprivations on such a scale would be considerably more disturbing to us were we to see them as due, in part, to a global institutional order that also sustains our comparatively lavish lifestyles by securing our resources and economic dominance. The PDPT shields us from such discomfort.

A second reason for the popularity of the PDPT in the developed world is awareness of the great differences among developing countries' economic performance. These differences draw our attention to domestic factors and international differences and thus away from global factors. Many ignore the causal role of global factors completely, often falling prey to the fallacy discussed above. Others fall for a different fallacy by concluding from the success of a few developing countries that the existing global economic order is quite hospitable to poverty eradication. This reasoning involves a some–all fallacy: The fact that *some* persons born into poverty in the US become millionaires does not show that *all* such persons can do likewise.[28] The reason is that the pathways to riches are sparse. They are not rigidly limited, to be sure, but the US clearly cannot achieve the kind of economic growth rates needed for everyone to become a millionaire (keeping fixed the value of the currency and the real income millionaires can now enjoy). The same holds true for developing countries. The Asian tigers (Hong Kong, Taiwan, Singapore, and South Korea), which together constitute well under 2 percent of the population of the developing world, achieved impressive rates of economic growth and poverty reduction. They did so through a state-sponsored buildup of industries that mass produce low-tech consumer products. These industries were globally successful by using their considerable labor-cost advantage to beat competitors in the developed countries and by drawing on greater state support and/or a better-educated workforce to beat competitors in other developing countries.[29] Building such industries was hugely profitable for the Asian tigers. But if many other poor countries had adopted this same developmental strategy, competition among them would have rendered it much less profitable. We cannot conclude then that the existing global economic order, though less favorable to the poor countries than it might be, is still favorable enough for all of them to do as well as the Asian tigers have done in fact.

A third reason for the popularity of the PDPT in the developed world is the prevailing research focus among social scientists who, like the rest of us, pay much more attention to the differences among national and regional developmental trajectories than to the overall evolution of poverty and inequality worldwide. Across several academic disciplines, there is a vast literature analyzing the causal roles of the local climate, natural environment, resources, food habits, diseases, history, culture, social institutions, economic policies, leadership personalities, and much else.[30] Advice dispensed by development economists and others is also overwhelmingly focused on the design of national economic institutions and policies. Thus, libertarian economists of the "freshwater" school (so dubbed because its leading lights have taught in Chicago) argue that a country's best way to expel human misery is economic growth and its best way to achieve economic growth is to foster free enterprise with a minimum in taxes, regulations, and red tape. A competing, more left-leaning school of thought, represented by Amartya Sen, contends that poverty persists because poor countries have *too little* government: public schools, hospitals and infrastructure. Sen's favorite poster child is the poor Indian state of Kerala, whose socialist government has given priority to fulfilling basic needs and thereby achieved more for that population's health, education, and life expectancy than the governments of other, more affluent Indian states.[31] These hot and worthwhile debates about appropriate economic policies and social institutions for the poor countries overshadow the far more important question of what causal role the rules of our globalized world economy play in the persistence of severe poverty.

This research focus among social scientists is surely partly due to the first two reasons: They, too, and their readers, are overly impressed by dramatic international differentials in economic performance and feel emotionally more comfortable, and careerwise more confident, with work that traces the persistence of severe poverty back to local causes rather than to global institutions we are involved in upholding. But there is also a good methodological reason for the research bias toward national and local causes: There being only this one world to observe, it is hard to obtain solid evidence about how the overall incidence of poverty would have evolved differently if this or that global factor had been different. By contrast, solid evidence about the effects of national and local factors can be gleaned from many poor countries that differ in their natural environment, history, culture, political and economic system, and government policies.

A fourth reason for the popularity of the PDPT is the prevalence of brutal and corrupt governments and elites in the poor countries. It seems far-fetched, even preposterous, to blame the global economic order for the persistence of severe poverty in countries that are ruled by obvious thugs and crooks. It also seems that whatever benefits global institutional reforms might bring to such countries would be captured by their corrupt elites, bringing little relief to the general population while reinforcing the power of their oppressors. Many among us believe then that we should postpone reforms that would make the global order fairer to the poor countries until they will have put their house in order by making their national political and economic order fairer to the domestic poor.

4. IMPORTANT DOMESTIC FACTORS ARE THEMSELVES SUSTAINED BY FOREIGN INFLUENCES

This last reason, too, is a bad one, because the existing world order is itself a crucial causal factor in the prevalence of corruption and oppression in the poor countries. It was only in 1999, for example, that the developed countries finally agreed to curb their firms' bribery of foreign officials by adopting the OECD *Convention on Combating Bribery of Foreign Public Officials in International Business Transactions*.[32] Until then, most developed states did not merely legally authorize their firms to bribe foreign officials, but even allowed them to deduct such bribes from their taxable revenues, thereby providing financial inducements and moral support to the practice of bribing politicians and officials in the poor countries.[33] This practice diverts the loyalties of officials in these countries and also makes a great difference to which persons are motivated to scramble for public office in the first place. Developing countries have suffered staggering losses as a result, most clearly in the awarding of public contracts. These losses arise in part from the fact that bribes are priced in: Bidders on contracts must raise their price in order to get paid enough to pay the bribes. Additional losses arise as bidders can afford to be noncompetitive, knowing that the success of their bid will depend on their bribes more than on the substance of their offer. Even greater losses arise from the fact that officials focused on bribes pay little attention to whether the goods and services they purchase in their country's behalf are of good quality or even needed at all. Much of what developing countries have imported over the decades has been of no use to them—or even harmful, by promoting environmental degradation or violence (bribery is especially pervasive in the arms trade). Preliminary evidence suggests that the new *Convention* is ineffective in curbing bribery by multinational corporations.[34] But even if it were effective, it would be very hard to purge the pervasive culture of corruption that is now deeply entrenched in many developing countries thanks to the extensive bribery they were subjected to during their formative years.

The issue of bribery is part of a larger problem. The political and economic elites of poor countries interact with their domestic inferiors, on the one hand, and with foreign governments and corporations, on the other. These two constituencies differ enormously in wealth and power. The former are by and large poorly educated and heavily preoccupied with the daily struggle to make ends meet. The latter, by contrast, have vastly greater rewards and penalties at their disposal. Politicians with a normal interest in their own political and economic success can thus be expected to cater to the interests of foreign governments and corporations rather than to competing interests of their much poorer compatriots. And this, of course, is what we find: There are plenty of poor-country governments that came to power or stay in power only thanks to foreign support. And there are plenty of poor-country politicians and bureaucrats who, induced or even bribed by foreigners, work against the interests of their people: *for* the development of a tourist-friendly sex industry (whose forced exploitation of children and women they tolerate and profit from), *for* the importation of unneeded, obsolete, or overpriced products at public expense, *for* the permission to import hazardous products, wastes, or factories, *against* laws protecting employees or the environment, and so on.

To be sure, there would not be such huge asymmetries in incentives if the poor countries were more democratic, allowing their populations a genuine political role. Why then are most of these countries so far from being genuinely democratic? This question brings further aspects of the current global institutional order into view.

It is a very central feature of this order that any group controlling a preponderance of the means of coercion within a country is internationally recognized as the legitimate government of this country's territory and people—regardless of how this group came to power, of how it exercises power, and of the extent to which it is supported or opposed by the population it rules. That such a group exercising effective power receives international recognition means not merely that we engage it in negotiations. It means also that we accept this group's right to act for the people it rules, that we, most significantly, confer upon it the privileges freely to dispose of the country's natural resources (international resource privilege) and freely to borrow in the country's name (international borrowing privilege).

The *resource privilege* we confer upon a group in power is much more than mere acquiescence in its effective control over the natural resources of the country in question. This privilege includes the power[35] to effect legally valid transfers of ownership rights in such resources. Thus a corporation that has purchased resources from the Saudis or Suharto, or from Mobuto or Sani Abacha, has thereby become entitled to be—and actually *is*—recognized anywhere in the world as the legitimate owner of these resources. This is a remarkable feature of our global order. A group that overpowers the guards and takes control of a warehouse may be able to give some of the merchandise to others, accepting money in exchange. But the fence who pays them becomes merely the possessor, not the owner, of the loot. Contrast this with a group that overpowers an elected government and takes control of a country. Such a group, too, can give away some of the country's natural resources, accepting money in exchange. In this case, however, the purchaser acquires not merely possession, but all the rights and liberties of ownership, which are supposed to be—and actually *are*—protected and enforced by all other states' courts and police forces. The international resource privilege, then, is the legal power to confer globally valid ownership rights in the country's resources.

This international resource privilege has disastrous effects in poor but resource-rich countries, where the resource sector constitutes a large segment of the national economy. Whoever can take power in such a country by whatever means can maintain his rule, even against widespread popular opposition, by buying the arms and soldiers he needs with revenues from the export of natural resources and with funds borrowed against future resource sales. The resource privilege thus gives insiders strong incentives toward the violent acquisition and exercise of political power, thereby causing coup attempts and civil wars. Moreover, it also gives outsiders strong incentives to corrupt the officials of such countries who, no matter how badly they rule, continue to have resources to sell and money to spend.

Nigeria is a case in point. It produces about 2 million barrels of oil per day which, depending on the oil price, fetch some $10-20 billion annually, one-quarter to one-half of GDP. Whoever controls this revenue stream can afford enough weapons and soldiers to keep himself in power regardless of what the population may think of him. And so long as he succeeds in doing so, his purse will be continuously replenished with new funds with which he can cement his rule and live in opulence. With such a powerful incentive, it cannot be surprising that, during 28 of the past 32 years, Nigeria has been ruled by military strongmen who took power and ruled by force.[36] Nor can it be surprising that even a polished elected president fails to stop gross corruption: Olusegun Obasanjo knows full well that, if he tried to spend the oil revenues solely for the benefit of the Nigerian people, military officers could—thanks to the international resource privilege—quickly restore their customary perks.[37] With such a huge price on his head, even the best-intentioned president could not end the theft of oil revenues and survive in power.

The incentives arising from the international resource privilege help explain what economists have long observed and found puzzling: the significant *negative* correlation between resource wealth (relative to GDP) and economic performance.[38] This explanation is confirmed by a recent regression analysis by two Yale economists, which shows that the causal link from resource wealth to poor economic performance is mediated through reduced chances for democracy.[39] Holding the global order fixed as a given background, the authors do not consider how the causal link they analyze itself depends on global rules that grant the resource privilege to any group in power, irrespective of its domestic illegitimacy.

The *borrowing privilege* we confer upon a group in power includes the power to impose internationally valid legal obligations upon the country at large. Any successor government that refuses to honor debts incurred by an ever so corrupt, brutal, undemocratic, unconstitutional, repressive, unpopular predecessor will be severely punished by the banks and governments of other countries. At minimum it will lose its own borrowing privilege by being excluded from the international financial markets. Such refusals are therefore quite rare, as governments, even when newly elected after a dramatic break with the past, are compelled to pay the debts of their ever so awful predecessors.

The international borrowing privilege makes three important contributions to the incidence of oppressive and corrupt elites in the developing world. First, this privilege facilitates borrowing by destructive rulers who can borrow more money and can do so more cheaply than they could do if they alone, rather than the whole country, were obliged to repay. In this way, the borrowing privilege helps such rulers maintain themselves in power even against near-universal popular discontent and opposition.[40] Second, the international borrowing privilege imposes upon democratic successor regimes the often huge debts of their corrupt predecessors. It thereby saps the capacity of such democratic governments to implement structural reforms and other political programs, thus rendering such governments less successful and less stable than they would otherwise be. (It is small consolation that putschists are sometimes weakened by being held liable for the debts of their democratic predecessors.) Third, the international borrowing privilege strengthens incentives toward coup attempts: Whoever succeeds in bringing a preponderance of the means of coercion under his control gets the borrowing privilege as an additional reward.

By discussing several global systemic factors in some detail, I hope to have undermined a view that, encouraged by libertarian and more leftist economists alike, most people in the developed world are all too ready to believe: The persistence of severe poverty is due to causes that are indigenous to the countries in which it occurs and thus unrelated to the affluent societies and their governments. This view is dramatically mistaken. Yes, domestic factors contribute to the persistence of severe poverty in many countries. But these contributions often depend on features of the global institutional order, which sustain some of those factors and exacerbate the impact of others. In these ways, the nonindigenous factors I have discussed play a major causal role in the evolution of severe poverty worldwide. They are crucial for explaining the inability and especially the unwillingness of the poor countries' leaders to pursue more effective strategies of poverty eradication. And they are crucial therefore for explaining why global inequality is increasing so rapidly that substantial global economic growth since the end of the Cold War has not reduced income poverty and malnutrition[41]—*despite* substantial technological progress, *despite* a huge poverty reduction in China,[42] *despite* the post–Cold-War "peace dividend,"[43] *despite* a 10 percent drop in real food prices since 1990,[44] *despite* official development assistance (ODA), and *despite* the efforts of international humanitarian and development organizations. If we are serious about eradicating severe poverty worldwide, we must understand the causal role of such nonindigenous factors and be willing to consider ways of modifying them or of reducing their impact.[45]

If the PDPT were true, the moral issues the distant needy raise for us might plausibly be considered under the assistance label alone.[46] But since the PDPT is seriously mistaken, this label may be misleading insofar as we may also be *contributing to*, or *profiting from*, social factors that exacerbate severe poverty abroad.

5. HOW CAN OUR DESIGN OF THE GLOBAL ORDER BE ASSESSED MORALLY?

We can still deny that we are so contributing or profiting, even if we acknowledge the PDPT's collapse and accept our shared responsibility for the existing global order. We can say for instance that our imposition of this order benefits the global poor, or at least does not harm them by exacerbating their poverty. While such claims are often made, for the current WTO rules for example, it remains quite unclear what their meaning is supposed to be. Benefit, after all, is a comparative notion which implicitly appeals to some baseline scenario under which the global poor would be even worse off than they are now in the world as it is. What baseline might we adduce to show the global poor that they are benefiting from the present global order?

There are three options. We might invoke a *diachronic* comparison, appealing to the *trend* in the depth or incidence of severe poverty worldwide. But this argument fails for three independent reasons. Its premise is false: Severe income poverty and malnutrition are not actually in decline globally (note 41). Moreover, its inference is invalid: Severe poverty might be declining, in China for instance, *despite* the fact that the global economic order tends to exacerbate such poverty. A diachronic comparison does not permit us to judge this possibility one way or the other and is therefore useless for judging the impact of any specific causal factor. Finally, we must not simply assume that the preceding situation was morally unproblematic. Otherwise we would have to conclude that a man is benefiting his children if he beats them up ever less frequently, or that the US economic order of the early nineteenth century benefited the slaves if their enslavement became less brutal during this period.

Our second option is to invoke a *subjunctive* comparison with a *historical* baseline. To judge whether the Israeli occupation reduced illiteracy in the West Bank, we should not ask diachronically whether illiteracy declined, but counterfactually whether illiteracy is lower than it would have been without the occupation. Adopting this idea, we might argue that the existing global order is benefiting the global poor insofar as they are better off than they would be if some preceding set of rules had remained in force. But this argument makes the—here inappropriate—assumption that those preceding rules were neutral, neither harming nor benefiting the global poor. By the same reasoning the military junta under Senior General Than Shwe could be said to be benefiting the Burmese people if merely they are better off than they would now be if the predecessor junta under General Ne Win were still in power.

Our third option is to invoke a *subjunctive* comparison with a *hypothetical* baseline—arguing perhaps that even more people would live and die even more miserably in some fictional state of nature than in this world as we have made it. But this option, too, is unpromising so long as we lack a precise and morally uniquely appropriate specification of that fictional world and a morally uniquely appropriate standard for comparing the two worlds in regard to severe poverty. You may think that these worries are merely academic, that our world is surely vastly better in this regard than any conceivable state of nature. And so it indeed appears from our vantage point. And yet: "Worldwide 34,000 children under age five die daily from hunger and preventable diseases."[47] Try to conceive a state of nature that can match this amazing feat of our globalized civilization, not just briefly, but every day for decades on end![48]

None of our three options is suitable for explicating our question—whether the existing world order harms or benefits the global poor—in a way that is both clear and appropriate to the assessment of this order. This failure suggests the inverse strategy: Instead of basing our justice assessment of this order on whether it does harm (independently defined), we can make our judgment of whether the imposition of this order does harm turn on an assessment of this order by some harm-independent criterion of justice.

To illustrate the idea, consider the institutional order of the US in its infancy, which greatly disadvantaged women vis-à-vis men. Our judgment of this order as unjust is not based on a historical comparison with how women had fared under British rule. It is not based on a comparison with how women would have fared had British rule continued. And it is not based on a comparison with how women would fare in some state of nature. (All these comparisons can be more plausibly invoked to just-ify than to criticize the institutional order under consideration.) Rather, it is because it assigned women a status inferior to men's that we judge this order to have been unjust to women and its imposition therefore a harm done to them.

Many harm-independent criteria might be proposed for assessing the justice of our global order. Such criteria differ in at least three respects. They differ in how they identify the relevant affected parties: as individual persons, households, social groups, nations, or states. They differ in their *absolute* demands—requiring, for instance, that affected parties must enjoy security of self and property or access to basic necessities. And they differ in their *relative* demands—requiring perhaps that basic rights or basic educational or medical opportunities must be equal or that economic inequalities must be constrained in certain ways.

Even if our global order fails to meet compelling absolute or relative requirements, it may still be defended on the grounds that this failure is unavoidable. An assessment of its justice must be sensitive then to information about what alternatives are feasible and about the conditions such feasible alternatives would engender. With regard to alternatives that diverge greatly from the existing global order, it may be impossible to establish such information in a rigorous way. It is quite possible, however, to estimate the impact of the existing global order relative to its nearby institutional alternatives. We saw such estimates in the *Economist* passage quoted above: The developing countries are missing out on some $700 billion annually in export revenues because the developed countries insisted on grandfathering heavy protections of their markets—through tariffs, quotas, antidumping duties, export credits, and subsidies to domestic producers.[49] It is quite possible, though unseemly among economists, to extend this estimate to the number of poverty deaths that would have been avoided by a more symmetrical opening of markets.[50] The number is large, as $700 billion annually is nearly 12 percent of the gross national incomes of all developing countries, representing 84.4 percent of humankind.[51]

Many features of the existing global order embody similar trade-offs between the interests of the high-income countries and their citizens on the one hand and the global poor on the other. An unconditional resource privilege gives us access to a larger, cheaper, and more reliable supply of foreign resources, because we can acquire ownership of them from anyone who happens to exercise effective power without regard to whether the country's population either approves the sale or benefits from the proceeds. Advantageous also to putschists and tyrants in the developing world, broad resource and borrowing privileges are much worse, however, for the global poor than would be narrower such privileges conditional on minimal domestic legitimacy. The existing TRIPs Agreement is better for us and worse for the global poor than an alternative that would have required the rich countries to supply funds for shielding the global poor from exorbitant markups on drugs and seeds.[52] The existing Law of the Sea Treaty is better for us and worse for them than an alternative that would have guaranteed the poor countries some share of the value of harvested seabed resources.[53] It is better for us and worse for the global poor that we do not have to pay for the negative externalities we impose on them: for the pollution we have produced over many decades and the resulting effects on their environment and climate, for the rapid depletion of natural resources, for the contribution of our tourists to the AIDS epidemic, and for the violence caused by our demand for drugs and our war on drugs.

The cumulative impact of all these trade-offs upon the global poor is likely to be staggering. In the fourteen years since the end of the Cold War, some 250 million human beings have died prematurely from poverty-related causes, with 18 million more added each year (note 27). Had the developed countries shaping the global rules given more weight to the interests of the global poor, the toll in early deaths and deprivations would certainly and foreseeably have been vastly lower at negligible cost to our affluence. It is then very hard to see how we might defend the trade-offs manifested in our global order as compatible with justice. And if this order is unjust, then it follows, without appeal to any historical or state-of-nature baseline, that we are harming the global poor—by imposing on them an unjust global order under which the incidence of severe poverty, malnutrition, and premature death is foreseeably much higher than it would be under some feasible alternatives.

6. TO WHAT EXTENT MUST OUR POLICIES GIVE WEIGHT TO THE INTERESTS OF THE GLOBAL POOR?

There are three ways of defending the trade-offs that our governments, often in collusion with corrupt and oppressive leaders in the developing world, have imposed. First we might say that it is permissible for us vigorously to promote our own interests in negotiations about how to fine-tune the various rules of the global order, even when doing so conflicts with the interests of the global poor. With our incomes 200 to 300 times larger than theirs[54] and 799 million living on the brink of starvation (notes 22 and 41), this justification of the status quo is rarely voiced in public. To be sure, it is widely thought that our politicians and diplomats ought to represent the interests of their compatriots. But it is also widely thought that this mandate has its limits: Even if they are able to do so, our representatives should not impose global rules under which we have unfair advantages that add millions of poverty deaths in the developing world. In the examples I have given, it looks like our politicians and diplomats have done exactly that, in our name.

Our second defense avers that appearances are here deceptive, that the decisions reflected in the existing rules do benefit the global poor as well, at least in the long run. But in some important cases, such a defense strains credulity. It is very hard to deny that world poverty is exacerbated by the special prerogatives the rich countries gave themselves under WTO rules to favor their own firms through tariffs, quotas, antidumping duties, subsidies, and export credits. Still, career incentives do produce such denials which, in the more clear-cut cases of unfair rules, often take a weaker form: Instead of claiming that certain prerogatives for the rich countries do not exacerbate poverty, economists merely claim that there are many complicating factors, methodological difficulties, and other imponderabilia so that intellectual honesty precludes our drawing any firm conclusions.[55] If all else fails, we can fall back on the weakest claim: Yes, the fine-tuning of some important rules was indeed worse for the global poor, but it was an honest mistake. When these rules were designed, development economics was less advanced and the relevant officials could not possibly have known that they were serving our interests at the expense of many additional premature deaths from poverty-related causes.

Boilerplate empirical defenses of this kind are easily produced and very well received. And it is quite unlikely that there will ever be a serious inquiry into what our politicians and diplomats and officials in the WTO, IMF, and World Bank knew and should have known during their negotiations of international agreements. The possibility that these respectable gentlemen (very few women there) might be hunger's willing executioners, committing a rather large-scale crime against humanity in our name, will never be taken seriously in the developed world. And yet, nagging doubts remain. If our representatives did make honest mistakes to the detriment of the global poor, should we not at least make up for these mistakes through a real effort at reducing the (unexpectedly) large incidence of severe poverty today?

Similar questions are raised by our third defense, which asserts that the global rules we have imposed are not merely good for us, but also good for global efficiency, productivity, and economic growth. These rules are Pareto-superior to their alternatives—not in the normal sense (better for some and worse for no one), but in this weaker ("Caldor-Hicks") sense: The rules are better for some and worse for others but so that the former can, out of their relative gains, fully compensate the latter for their relative losses. I doubt this argument can succeed for the grandfathering clauses in the WTO Treaty, which still allow us, for many years to come, to favor our firms through tariffs, quotas, antidumping duties, export credits, and huge subsidies. But it may well succeed in other cases such as the TRIPs Agreement. Still, even when it succeeds, there is the nagging question: Given the vast economic inequality between gainers and losers (note 54), is the mere *possibility* of compensation sufficient to vindicate our decision? Or must there not rather be *actual* compensation, so that we may keep only such relative gains as *exceed* their relative losses?

The questions concluding the last two paragraphs indicate more precisely how, with the collapse of the PDPT, conventional discussions of world poverty under the assistance label are misleading. The label is not inaccurate: As affluent people and countries, we surely have positive moral duties to assist persons mired in life-threatening poverty whom we can help at little cost. But the label detracts from weightier, negative duties that also apply to us: We should reduce severe harms we will have caused; and we should not take advantage of injustice at the expense of its victims. These two negative duties apply to us if we (sometimes together with Third World elites) are imposing a global order whose unfairness benefits us while exacerbating severe poverty abroad. We must then at least compensate the global poor. Failing to do this, we would be harming them and profiting from injustice at their expense. And insofar as we do compensate, we are not merely "assisting" the poor abroad, but reducing the impact of unfair rules that bring us unjust gains at their expense. We are not "redistributing" from the rich to the poor, but offsetting an unjust institutional redistribution from the poor to the rich—*re*-redistributing, if you like.

Let me illustrate the special weight these two negative duties are generally thought to have: Imagine, by the side of a country road, an injured child who must be rushed to the hospital if her leg is to be saved. As a competent bystander who ignores her plight, you are subject to moral criticism for failing to assist. But if you are the driver who injured the child in the first place, then more is morally at stake: By leaving the child's needs unattended, you would greatly increase the harm you will have done her. As we judge such inaction of the driver more harshly than that of the bystander, we should judge our own inaction more harshly, too, if we are involved in upholding unjust rules that contribute to severe poverty we ignore.

Imagine further a society in which an aboriginal minority suffers severe discrimination in education and employment, reducing their wages far below those of their compatriots. As an affluent foreigner, you may think that perhaps you ought to do something to assist these people. But if you are profiting from the discrimination (by employing an aboriginal driver at half the wage other drivers receive, for instance), then more is morally at stake: We judge ourselves more harshly for taking advantage of an injustice by pocketing such gains than for failing to spend other assets we have on supporting the poor. As we do so, we should also judge ourselves more harshly insofar as assets we fail to use toward reducing severe poverty abroad constitute gains we derive from the unfairness of a global order that also contributes to the persistence of this poverty.

Negative duties not to support and not to pocket gains from an unfair institutional order that foreseeably contributes to severe deprivations are not only weightier than the positive duty to help relieve such deprivations. They are also much less sensitive to variations in community and distance. Duties to assist are strongest toward the near and dear and weakest toward foreigners in distant lands. But duties not to harm do not fade in this way. Consider again the driver who hits a child and then leaves her unattended by the side of the road. We do not upgrade our moral assessment of him when we learn that he did this far away from his home to a child with whom he had no communal bond of nationality, language, culture, or religion. If the unfairness of the global order we impose causes poverty to persist in the poor countries, then our moral responsibility for the associated deaths and deprivations is not diminished by diversity of nationality and geographical or cultural distance. It might be so diminished, perhaps, if harming foreigners were necessary to save ourselves from a comparable fate. But in the real world, the global poverty problem—though it involves one-third of all human deaths—is quite small in economic terms: Though 2,735 million persons are living below the higher ($2/day) international poverty line, and 42 percent below it on average, their collective shortfall amounts to only 1.1 percent of the incomes of the 955 million people in the high-income economies.[56] Clearly, we could eradicate severe poverty—through a reform of the global order or through other initiatives designed to compensate for its effects on the global poor—without "sacrificing" the fulfillment of our own needs or even mildly serious interests.[57]

It is widely believed in the developed world that we are already spending an inordinate amount on such initiatives. This belief is contradicted by the facts: The high-income countries have reduced their official development assistance (ODA) from 0.33 percent of their combined GNPs in 1990 to 0.22 percent, or $52.3 billion, in 2001.[58] Most ODA is allocated for political effect: Only 23 percent goes to the 49 least developed countries;[59] and only $3.7 billion is spent on basic social services[60]—basic education, basic health, population programs, water supply, and sanitation—far less than the 20 percent agreed to at the 1995 World Summit for Social Development.[61] This is less than 1 percent of the developed countries' "peace dividend"[62] and comes to about $4 per year from each of us citizens of these countries, on average.[63]

When people like us die at a mature age, we can look back on a lifespan in which over a billion human beings, mostly children, have died from poverty-related causes. This massive death toll was and is foreseeable. And it is clear beyond any reasonable doubt that the developed countries could dramatically reduce this continuous death toll and the associated misery at little cost to ourselves (notes 56–57). And yet, very few citizens of the developed countries find these facts disturbing. This widespread unconcern can be explained, in large part, by a false view of why severe poverty persists. Most of us subscribe to the view that the causes of the persistence of severe poverty are indigenous to the countries in which it occurs. I am convinced that, with a better understanding of the role global institutional factors play in the persistence of severe poverty, many would take this problem much more seriously—including my esteemed teacher John Rawls.

NOTES

This essay has been presented at the CUNY Graduate Center, the University of Hong Kong, Soochow University, the University of St. Andrews, Harvard's JFK School, the University of Sheffield, the University of North Carolina, and the Chinese University in Hong Kong. I am grateful to my audiences there, especially to Maria Alvarez, Liz Ashford, Sissila Bok, and Leif Wenar, as well as to Christian Barry, Daniel Bell, Chiara Bottici, and Ling Tong for very helpful written criticisms and suggestions.

1. John Rawls, *The Law of Peoples* (Cambridge MA: Harvard University Press 1999), 37. [§15 and §16 reprinted herein.] For his earlier account, see John Rawls, "The Law of Peoples" in Stephen Shute and Susan Hurley, eds. *On Human Rights* (New York: Basic Books 1993), 55 [reprinted in *Global Justice: Seminal Essays*, 421–60, 431].

2. See Rawls, *The Law of Peoples*, 115–19 [herein 440–43], discussing Charles Beitz, *Political Theory and International Relations* (Princeton: Princeton University Press 1979), [part III of Beitz's book is based on his essay "Justice and International Relations," first published in *Philosophy and Public Affairs* 4: 4, (summer 1975): 360–89, reprinted in *Global Justice: Seminal Essays*, 21–48,] and Thomas W. Pogge, "An Egalitarian Law of Peoples," *Philosophy and Public Affairs* 23 (1994): 195–224 [reprinted in *Global Justice: Seminal Essays*, 461–93].

3. Rawls, *The Law of Peoples*, 32, 63, 69.

4. Ibid., 29, 33, 34–35, 40, 63–67, 69, 115 [herein 439f], 120 [herein 443f]. A society is well-ordered if it has a stable institutional order that is either liberal or decent (ibid., 4 and 63).

5. This feature renders problematic not only Rawls's asserted duty to assist burdened societies, but also his call for "forceful intervention" in the affairs of non-well-ordered societies that internally commit egregious offenses against human rights (ibid., 94 n. 6). Even if such interventions fall short of war (which must not be instigated for reasons other than self-defense—ibid., 37), they may entail considerable risks for the interveners whose representatives would thus not rationally agree to more than a permission so to intervene.

6. Rawls recognizes this problem, in general terms at least, and is concerned to defend his use of an original position "that is fair to peoples and not to individual persons" (ibid., 17 n. 9).

7. See Pogge, "An Egalitarian Law of Peoples," 208–9 [*GJSE* 474–76].

8. See Rawls, *The Law of Peoples*, 106–7 [herein 432f] for the appeal to the just saving principle and ibid., 117–18 [herein 441f], for two invented stories illustrating such unjustified complaints about international inequality.

9. Rawls extensively discusses such societies, exemplified by an imaginary Kazanistan, as ones that liberal peoples should welcome as equal "members in good standing of a Society of Peoples" (ibid., 59).

10. As domestic institutions are to be so adjusted pursuant to the difference

principle. See Thomas W. Pogge, *Realizing Rawls* (Ithaca: Cornell University Press 1989), 252–53.

11. Rawls, *The Law of Peoples*, 108 [herein 433f].

12. Rawls, "The Law of Peoples," 77 [*GJSE* 448]—echoing Michael Walzer: "It is not the sign of some collective derangement or radical incapacity for a political community to produce an authoritarian regime. Indeed, the history, culture, and religion of the community may be such that authoritarian regimes come, as it were, naturally, reflecting a widely shared world view or way of life" (Michael Walzer, "The Moral Standing of States," *Philosophy and Public Affairs* 9: 209–29, at 224-25 [reprinted herein 51–71, at 65]).

13. In fact, this ratio has increased to 40:1, showing that average annual growth in per capita income was 0.7 percent *less* in Africa than in the developed world.

14. See, for instance, the *Economist* cover of December 11, 1999, showing an Indian child in rags with the heading "The Real Losers of Seattle." See also its editorial in the same issue (ibid., 15), its flimsy "The Case for Globalisation," *Economist*, September 23, 2000, 19–20 and 85–87, and the lead editorial "A Question of Justice?" *Economist*, March 11, 2004.

15. *Economist*, September 25, 1999, 89. The three cited studies are: Thomas W. Hertel and Will Martin: "Would Developing Countries Gain from Inclusion of Manufactures in the WTO Negotiations?" (www.gtap.agecon. purdue.edu/resources/download/2868.pdf, 1999); UNCTAD (United Nations Conference on Trade and Development): *Trade and Development Report 1999* (New York: UN Publications, 1999); and J. Michael Finger and Philip Schuler: "Implementation of Uruguay Round Commitments: The Development Challenge," World Bank Research Working Paper 2215 (www-wds.worldbank. org/external/default/WDSContentServer/IW3P/IB/2001/02/10/000094946_ 01013005324822/Rendered/PDF/multi_page.pdf, 1999).

16. World Bank, *World Development Report 2003* (New York: Oxford University Press 2002), 235. Inequalities in wealth are significantly greater than inequalities in income. Well-off persons typically have more net worth than annual income, while the poor typically own less than one annual income. The huge fortunes of the ultrarich have been specially highlighted in recent reports by the United Nations Development Programme (UNDP): "The world's 200 richest people more than doubled their net worth in the four years to 1998, to more than $1 trillion. The assets of the top three billionaires are more than the combined GNP of all least developed countries and their 600 million people" (UNDP, *Human Development Report 1999* [New York: Oxford University Press 1999], 3). "The additional cost of achieving and maintaining universal access to basic education for all, basic health care for all, reproductive health care for all women, adequate food for all and safe water and sanitation for all is ... less than 4% of the combined wealth of the 225 richest people in the world" (UNDP, *Human Development Report 1998* [New York: Oxford University Press 1998], 30).

17. Rawls makes this point himself, quite forcefully, in the domestic context (John Rawls, *Political Liberalism* [New York: Columbia University Press 1993], 267). In the international arena, he vaguely endorses "fair standards of trade" and writes that any "unjustified distributive effects" of cooperative organizations should be corrected (Rawls, *The Law of Peoples*, 43). But he gives no content to these evaluative terms and does not incorporate them into his law of peoples, which is compatible then with the imposition of a skewed global economic order that perpetuates the relative poverty of a large majority of humankind who are collectively unable to reform it by peaceful means (see Thomas W. Pogge, "Rawls on International Justice," *Philosophical Quarterly* 51 (2001): 246–53, at 251–52). Such a global order is unjust even if it also requires the affluent societies to ride to the rescue (pursuant to their duty of assistance) whenever worsening poverty threatens the well-orderedness of any liberal or decent society. This said, the added duty of assistance does make the Society of Peoples Rawls envisions a significant improvement over the status quo. It entails, plausibly I believe, that most rich countries today are immoral or "outlaw states" on account of the severe poverty abroad that they tolerate and, I would add, contribute to. Denmark, Norway, Luxembourg, the Netherlands, and Sweden are possible exceptions—see UNDP, *Human Development Report 2003* (New York: Oxford University Press, 2003), 228 and 290.

18. UNDP, *Human Development Report 1999*, 3, see 38. These ratios compare national average incomes via market exchange rates. The picture is bleak also when one compares the incomes of households worldwide via purchasing power parities: Over a recent five-year period, "world inequality has increased … from a Gini of 62.8 in 1988 to 66.0 in 1993. This represents an increase of 0.6 Gini points per year. This is a very fast increase, faster than the increase experienced by the United States and United Kingdom in the decade of the 1980s. … The bottom 5 percent of the world grew poorer, as their real incomes decreased between 1988 and 1993 by ¼, while the richest quintile grew richer. It gained 12 percent in real terms, that is its income grew more than twice as much as mean world income (5.7%)." Branko Milanovic, "True World Income Distribution, 1988 and 1993: First Calculation Based on Household Surveys Alone," *The Economic Journal* 112 (2002): 51–92, at 88 (www.blackwell-synergy.com/doi/pdf/10.1111/1468-0297.0j673).

19. Peter Singer, "Famine, Affluence and Morality," *Philosophy and Public Affairs* 1 (1972): 229–43 [reprinted herein 1–14]; see also Peter Unger, *Living High and Letting Die: Our Illusion of Innocence* (Oxford: Oxford University Press 1996) [sections 1–3 of chapter 1 and chapter 2 are reprinted herein 325–78].

20. Singer may not regard this reinforcement as regrettable. As a utilitarian, he believes that the stringency of our duty to combat world poverty is unaffected by whether the PDPT is true or false.

21. Shaohua Chen and Martin Ravallion: "How Have the World's Poorest Fared since the 1980s?" *World Bank Research Observer* 19 (2004): 141–69, at 153. (Ravallion and Chen have managed the World Bank's income poverty

assessments for well over a decade. These data are for 2001.) These two poverty lines are defined in terms of a monthly income with the same *purchasing power* as $65.48 and $32.74 had in the US in 1993 (ibid., 147). Today, they correspond to a little more than $1000 and $500 per person per year in the US (www.bls.gov/cpi/home.htm) and to about $240 and $120 per person per year in a typical poor country, where money has much greater purchasing power (Thomas Pogge: *World Poverty and Human Rights: Cosmopolitan Responsibilities and Reforms* [Cambridge: Polity Press, 2002], 97). Those below the higher line fall 42 percent below it on average, and those below the lower line fall 28.4 percent below it on average (Chen and Ravallion: "How Have the World's Poorest Fared since the 1980s?" 152 and 158, dividing the poverty gap index by the headcount index). The former are 44.6 percent of humankind with about 1.21 percent of global income (which, in 2001, was $31,500 billion—World Bank, *World Development Report 2003* [New York: Oxford University Press 2002], 235. The latter are 17.8 percent of humankind with about 0.3 percent of global income.

22. UNDP, *Human Development Report 2003*, 87, 9, 7. Most of those suffering these deprivations are female (ibid. 310–30).

23. UNDP, *Human Development Report 1999*, 22.

24. UNDP, *Human Development Report 1998*, 49.

25. FAO (Food and Agriculture Organization of the United Nations), *The State of Food Insecurity in the World 1999* (www.fao.org/news/1999/img/sofi99-e.pdf), 11.

26. The UN International Labor Organization (ILO) reports that "some 250 million children between the ages of 5 and 14 are working in developing countries—120 million full time, 130 million part time" (www.ilo.org/public/english/standards/ipec/simpoc/stats/4stt.htm). Of these, 170.5 million children are involved in hazardous work and 8.4 million in the "unconditionally worst" forms of child labor, "defined as slavery, trafficking, debt bondage and other forms of forced labour, forced recruitment of children for use in armed conflict, prostitution and pornography, and illicit activities." ILO, *A Future Without Child Labour* (www.ilo.org/dyn/declaris/DECLARATIONWEB.GLOBALREPORTDETAILS?var_language=EN&var_PublicationsID=37&var_ReportType=Report), 9, 11, and 18.

27. For the frequency of specific causes of deaths, see WHO (World Health Organization), *The World Health Report 2004* (Geneva: WHO Publications, 2004), Annex Table 2, also available at www.who.int/whr/2004. About 60 percent of all poverty deaths are children under five. Cf. UNICEF (United Nations Children's Fund), *The State of the World's Children 2005* (New York: UNICEF, 2004), inside front cover. There it is also reported that 640 million children lack adequate shelter, 400 million children lack access to safe water, 270 million children have no access to health services.

28. See G. A. Cohen: *History, Labour, and Freedom* (Oxford: Clarendon

Press 1988), 262–63.

29. It also helped that the US, eager to establish healthy capitalist economies as a counterweight to Soviet influence in the region, allowed the tigers free access to its market even while they maintained high tariffs to protect their own.

30. Some notable recent contributions are David Landes, *The Wealth and Poverty of Nations: Why Some Are So Rich and Some So Poor* (New York: Norton 1998), Jared Diamond, *Guns, Germs, and Steel: The Fates of Human Societies* (New York: Norton 1999), and Lawrence E. Harrison and Samuel P. Huntington, eds., *Culture Matters: How Values Shape Human Progress* (New York: Basic Books 2001).

31. The leftist political coalition responsible for these policies was nevertheless soundly defeated in the last assembly elections, May 10, 2001, gaining only 40 seats out of 140.

32. The *Convention* went into effect in February 1999 and has been widely ratified since (www.oecd.org/department/0,2688,en_2649_34859_1_1_1_1_1,00.html).

33. In the United States, the post-Watergate Congress tried to prevent the bribing of foreign officials through its 1977 Foreign Corrupt Practices Act, passed after the Lockheed Corporation was found to have paid—not a modest sum to some Third World official, but rather—a US$2 million bribe to Prime Minister Kakuei Tanaka of powerful and democratic Japan. Not wanting its firms to be at a disadvantage vis-à-vis their foreign rivals, the US was a major supporter of the *Convention*, as was the non-governmental organization Transparency International, which helped mobilize public support in many OECD countries.

34. "Plenty of laws exist to ban bribery by companies. But big multinationals continue to sidestep them with ease"—so the current situation is summarized in "The Short Arm of the Law," *Economist*, March 2, 2002, 63–65, at 63.

35. As understood by Wesley N. Hohfeld, *Fundamental Legal Conceptions* (New Haven: Yale University Press 1919), a power involves the legally recognized authority to alter the distribution of first-order liberty rights, claim rights and duties. Having *a* power or power*s* in this sense is distinct from having power (i.e., control over physical force and/or means of coercion).

36. See "Going on Down," in *Economist*, June 8, 1996, 46–48. A later update says: "Oil revenues [are] paid directly to the government at the highest level.... The head of state has supreme power and control of all the cash. He depends on nobody and nothing but oil. Patronage and corruption spread downwards from the top" (*Economist*, December 12, 1998, 19). See also www.eia.doe.gov/emeu/cabs/nigeria.html.

37. Because Obasanjo was, and is, a prominent member of the Advisory Council of Transparency International (see note 33), his election in early 1999 had raised great hopes. These hopes were sorely disappointed. Nigeria still ranks

near the bottom of TI's own Corruption Perception Index (www.transparency. org/policy_research/surveys_indices/cpi/2004).

38. This "resource curse" or "Dutch disease" is exemplified by many developing countries which, despite great natural wealth, have achieved little economic growth and poverty reduction over the last decades. Here are the more important resource-rich developing countries with their average annual rates of change in real GDP *per capita* from 1975 to 2001: Nigeria –0.7%, Congo/Zaire –5.2%, Kenya +0.3%, Angola –2.3%, Mozambique +1.8%, Senegal –0.1%, Venezuela –0.9%, Ecuador +0.2%, Saudi Arabia –2.1%, United Arab Emirates –3.7%, Oman +2.3%, Kuwait –0.7%, Bahrain +1.1%, Brunei –2.2%, Indonesia +4.3%, the Philippines +0.1% (UNDP, *Human Development Report 2003*, 278–81; in some cases a somewhat different period was used due to insufficient data). Thus, with the notable exception of Indonesia, the resource-rich developing countries fell well below the annual rate in real per capita growth of their peers and of the developed countries (ibid., 281).

39. "All petrostates or resource-dependent countries in Africa fail to initiate meaningful political reforms.... besides South Africa, transition to democracy has been successful only in resource-poor countries" (Ricky Lam and Leonard Wantchekon, "Dictatorships as a Political Dutch Disease" [www. nyarko.com/wantche1.pdf, 1999], 31). "Our cross-country regression confirms our theoretical insights. We find that a one percentage increase in the size of the natural resource sector [relative to GDP] generates a decrease by half a percentage point in the probability of survival of democratic regimes" (ibid., 35). See also Leonard Wantchekon, "Why Do Resource Dependent Countries Have Authoritarian Governments?" (www.yale.edu/leitner/pdf/1999-11.pdf, 1999).

40. The rulers of resource-rich developing countries have been especially adept at supplementing their income from resource sales by mortgaging their countries' future for their own benefit. As of 1998, Nigeria's foreign debt, run up by its succession of military dictatorships, stood at 79% of GNP. The 1998 ratios of foreign debt to GNP for other large resource-rich countries were: Kenya 61%, Angola 297%, Mozambique 223%, Venezuela 40%, Indonesia 176%, the Philippines 70% (UNDP, *Human Development Report 2000* [New York: Oxford University Press 2000], 219–21). The 1997 ratio for the Congo/Zaire is 232% (UNDP, *Human Development Report 1999*, 195). Needless to say, little of the borrowed funds were channeled into productive investments, e.g., in education and infrastructure, which would augment economic growth and thus tax revenues that could help meet interest and repayment obligations. Much was taken for personal use or expended on "internal security" and the military.

41. See the annual UNDP Reports for the number of undernourished, stuck around 800 million. The incidence of $1/day income poverty is reported to be down 7 percent and $2/day income poverty to be up over 10 percent over the 1987–2001 period (Chen and Ravallion, "How Have the World's

Poorest Fared since the Early 1980s?" 153). Severe flaws in the World Bank's method of calculating these numbers make it likely that the actual extent of severe income poverty is substantially greater. Among these flaws is the use of purchasing power parities based on the prices of all commodities rather than on the prices of basic necessities on which poor households are compelled to concentrate their expenditures. See my "The First UN Millennium Development Goal—A Cause for Celebration?" in *Journal of Human Development* 5 (2004): 377–97, and Sanjay Reddy and Thomas W. Pogge, "How *Not* to Count the Poor" (www.socialanalysis.org, 2003), forthcoming in *Measuring Global Poverty*, ed. Sudhir Anand and Joseph Stiglitz (Oxford: Oxford University Press 2008), for a comprehensive critique.

42. The number of Chinese living below $1/day is reported to have declined by 31 percent, or 97 million, over the period (Chen and Ravallion, "How Have the World's Poorest Fared since the Early 1980s?" 153).

43. Thanks to the end of the Cold War, military expenditures worldwide have declined from 4.7 percent of aggregate GDP in 1985 to 2.9 percent in 1996 (UNDP, *Human Development Report 1998*, 197) and to about 2.6% or $1035 billion in 2004 (yearbook2005.sipri.org/ch8/ch8). This peace dividend was worth $836 billion in 2004.

44. The World Bank Food Index fell from 139.3 in 1980 to 100 in 1990 and then to 90.1 in 2002. These statistics are published by the World Bank's Development Prospects Group. Cf. www.worldbank.org/prospects/gep2004/appendix2.pdf, page 277.

45. See Pogge, *World Poverty and Human Rights*, chapters 6 and 8, for concrete proposals toward modifying the international resource and borrowing privileges and toward reducing the impact of unfair global economic rules through a Global Resources Dividend, respectively.

46. Though it could still be argued that this label is inappropriate insofar as we are beneficiaries, and they are victims, of the historical injustices discussed earlier, such as colonialism.

47. USDA (United States Department of Agriculture), *U.S. Action Plan on Food Security* (www.fas.usda.gov/icd/summit/usactplan.pdf, 1999), p. iii. The US government mentions this fact whilst arguing that the developed countries should *not* follow the FAO proposal to increase development assistance for agriculture by $6 billion annually, that $2.6 billion is ample (ibid., Appendix A).

48. See Pogge, *World Poverty and Human Rights*, 136–39.

49. In 2000, the rich countries spent $245 billion on subsidies to their farmers alone (Martin Wolf, "Broken Promises to the Poor," *Financial Times*, November 21, 2001, 13). In 2002, the US imposed new tariffs against steel imports, with adverse effects in China, Brazil, and Russia, and adopted a $173-billion farm bill that increases subsidies to domestic farmers some 70 percent over current levels and thereby greatly hurts farmers in poor countries. These and many other such examples render somewhat comical the endless polem-

ics for and against free trade and open markets. These debates miss what is happening in the real world: The poor countries are not given access to free trade and open markets. They cannot take advantage even of the entitlements they do have under the slanted rules of the WTO, because they do not have the resources to bring and win cases against the US or EU. Moreover, a poor country would have far more to lose than to gain from imposing retaliatory countertariffs—as winning such a case would entitle them to do—against the US or EU.

50. Where such estimates are seemly, they are readily volunteered. After the terrorist attacks of September 11, 2001, the President of the World Bank publicized his estimate "that tens of thousands more children will die worldwide and some 10 million more people are likely to be living below the poverty line of $1 a day... because the attacks will delay the rich countries' recovery into 2002." (http://web.worldbank.org/WBSITE/EXTERNAL/NEWS/ 0,,contentMDK:20016966~menuPK:34464~pagePK:34370~piPK:34424~ theSitePK:4607,00.html)

51. World Bank, *World Development Report 2003*, 235.

52. The Trade-Related Aspects of Intellectual Property Rights (TRIPs) Treaty was concluded in 1995. For a discussion of its content and impact, see UNDP, *Human Development Report 2001* (New York: Oxford University Press 2001), chapter 5; Carlos Correa, *Intellectual Property Rights, the WTO and Developing Countries: The TRIPs Agreement and Policy Options* (London: Zed Books 2000); Calestous Juma, "Intellectual Property Rights and Globalization: Implications for Developing Countries" (www.ksg.harvard.edu/CID/cidbiotech/dp/discuss4.PDF, 1999); Jayashree Watal, "Access to Essential Medicines in Developing Countries: Does the WTO TRIPS Agreement Hinder It?" (www.ksg.harvard.edu/CID/cidbiotech/dp/discussion8.pdf, 2000); and www.cptech.org/ip/.

53. Such guarantees were part of the initial 1982 version of the Treaty, but the Clinton administration succeeded in renegotiating them out of the Treaty just before the latter came into force in 1996 (Pogge, *World Poverty and Human Rights*, 125–26).

54. In the high-income economies, gross national income per capita is $26,710 on average (World Bank, *World Development Report 2003*, 235), compared to an annual average income of about $139 for persons living below $2/day and of about $86 for those living below $1/day (note 21).

55. Such scruples are selective (see note 50).

56. See note 21. If we covered this entire shortfall, our share of global income would fall from 81.0 to 80.1 percent, from $25,506 to $25,230 billion (World Bank: *World Development Report 2003*, 235).

57. The WHO Commission on Macroeconomics and Health (chaired by Jeffrey Sachs) has sketched how deaths from poverty-related causes could be reduced by 8 million annually at a cost of $62 billion per year. The Commission

proposes that the developed countries pay $27 billion of this cost, leaving $35 billion annually to be contributed by the poor countries (*Economist*, December 22, 2001, 82–83). The high-income countries could afford to pay the full $62 billion, which is under one-quarter percent of their aggregate gross national incomes (World Bank, *World Development Report 2003*, 235).

58. UNDP, *Human Development Report 2003*, 290, down from aggregate ODA of $53.7 billion in 2000 (UNDP, *Human Development Report 2002* [New York: Oxford University Press 2002], 202) and $56.4 billion in 1999 (UNDP, *Human Development Report 2001*, 190). The US has led the decline by reducing ODA from 0.21 to 0.11 percent of GNP in a time of great prosperity culminating in enormous budget surpluses (UNDP, *Human Development Report 2002*, 202). After the invasions of Afghanistan and Iraq, ODA is now growing rapidly through disbursements to these and neighboring states (esp. Pakistan). ODA is reported to have been $58.3 billion for 2002 and $68.5 billion for 2003 (www.oecd.org/document/22/0,2340,en_2649_37413_31504022_1_1_1_37413,00.html).

59. Down from 28 percent in 1990 (UNDP, *Human Development Report 2003*, 290). India, with more poor people than any other country, receives ODA of $1.70 annually for each of its citizens, while dozens of much richer countries receive between $60 and $260 annually per capita (ibid., 290–94).

60. See http://millenniumindicators.un.org/unsd/mi/mi_series_results.asp?rowId=592.

61. "88. Implementation of the Declaration and the Programme of Action in developing countries, in particular in Africa and the least developed countries, will need additional financial resources and more effective development cooperation and assistance. This will require:... (c) Agreeing on a mutual commitment between interested developed and developing country partners to allocate, on average, 20 per cent of ODA and 20 per cent of the national budget, respectively, to basic social programmes" (Programme of Action, Chapter 5, Article 88(c), www.un.org/esa/socdev/wssd/agreements/poach5.htm).

62. See note 43. After the end of the Cold War, the developed countries were able to reduce their military expenditures from 4.1 percent of their combined GDPs in 1985 to 2.2 percent in 1998 (UNDP, *Human Development Report 1998*, 197; UNDP, *Human Development Report 2000*, 217). With their combined GDPs at $25,104 billion in the year 2001 (World Bank, *World Development Report 2003*, 239), their peace dividend in 2001 comes to about $477 billion.

63. Citizens of the high-income countries also give aid through nongovernmental organizations. Each year, such aid amounts to about $7 billion, or $7.60 per citizen (UNDP, *Human Development Report 2003*, 290).

24. ALISON M. JAGGAR

Western feminist theory tacitly encourages a lopsided view of the injustices suffered by non-Western women—and of Westerners' duties toward non-Western women. Jaggar argues that prominent theorists such as Susan Okin and Martha Nussbaum unwittingly imply several misleading theses about injustice suffered by women. These are that, first, local cultural traditions are the primary source of harm to women in poor countries; second, unjust local traditions in non-Western countries are causally independent of Western practices; third, Western cultures are more just in their treatment of women; and as a result, fourth, the role of Western theorists is to expose the injustice of non-Western cultures toward local women. While there may be some truth in these theses, they greatly underemphasize the importance of the Western-dominated global political and economic order in entrenching and perpetuating the poverty that makes women particularly vulnerable to unjust cultural practices. Philosophers would far better serve non-Western women by exploring their own countries' role in supporting that order than by pretending to serve as impartial judges of culture.

"Saving Amina": Global Justice for Women and Intercultural Dialogue

First published in Real World Justice, *ed. Andreas Follesdal and Thomas Pogge (Dordrecht: Springer, 2005), 37–63.*

One of the innumerable electronic petitions flashing across the Internet in the early months of 2003 held special interest for feminists. Carrying the name and logo in Spanish of Amnesty International, the petition asked recipients to "sign" electronically an appeal against the sentence of stoning to death declared against Amina Lawal, a divorced Nigerian woman, who had had a baby outside marriage. In August 2002, an Islamic court in Katsina state in northern Nigeria had convicted Lawal of adultery under Sharia law. The "save Amina" petition collected many thousands of electronic signatures from around the world but in May 2003 it was followed by another e-communication with the subject line, "Please Stop the International Amina Lawal Protest Letter Campaigns." The second e-message was signed by Ayesha Imam and Sindi Medar-Gould, representing two Nigerian human rights organizations supporting Lawal. Imam and Medar-Gould asserted that the "save Amina" petition in fact endangered Lawal and made the task of her Nigerian supporters more difficult, in part because the petition contained a number of factual errors, including a false assertion that execution of the sentence was imminent. They also observed, "There is an unbecoming arrogance in assuming that international human rights organizations or others always know better than those directly involved, and therefore can take actions that fly in the face of their express wishes" (Imam and Medar-Gould 2003).

Electronic petitions have become a popular means by which Western feminists endeavor to "save" women in other countries. A 1998 e-petition on behalf of women in Afghanistan, begun by a student at Brandeis University, garnered so many responses that Brandeis was forced to close the student's mailbox. The petitions often use sensational language to denounce some non-Western culture for its inhumane treatment of women and girls. Worries about non-Western cultural practices are not limited to those in the West who identify as feminists. The popular press regularly runs stories about non-Western practices it finds disturbing, especially when these concern women's sexuality and/or are noticed occurring among immigrant groups. Recent news stories have raised the alarm about arranged marriage, "sexual slavery," dowry murder ("bride-burning"), "honor" killings, genital cutting ("circumcision," "mutilation"), sex-selective abortion, and female infanticide. Newspapers in the United States have also questioned whether female US soldiers, stationed in Saudi Arabia, should be required when off-base to conform to Saudi laws mandating covering their bodies and forbidding them to drive.

The perceived victimization of women by non-Western cultures has now also become a topic within Western philosophy. In this paper, I draw on the work of other feminist scholars to argue that conceiving injustice to poor women in poor countries primarily in terms of their oppression by "illiberal" cultures provides an understanding of the women's situations that is crucially incomplete. This incomplete understanding distorts Western philosophers' comprehension of our moral relationship to women elsewhere in the world and so of our philosophical task. It also impoverishes our assumptions about the intercultural dialogue necessary to promote global justice for women.[1]

1. PHILOSOPHERS SAVING AMINA: TWO INFLUENTIAL PHILOSOPHICAL TREATMENTS OF INJUSTICE TO WOMEN IN POOR COUNTRIES

1.1 THE DEBATE IN WOMEN'S STUDIES

The interdisciplinary literature in women's or feminist studies has discussed the perceived victimization of women in non-Western cultures for at least thirty years. In this academic context, two main positions have been opposed to each other. The first is global radical feminism, a perspective that made its appearance in the early years of second-wave Western feminism. The radical feminists wished to establish that women were a group subjected to a distinct form of oppression and their earliest writings postulated a worldwide women's culture, existing "beneath the surface" of all national, ethnic, and racial cultures and colonized by these "male" cultures (Burris 1973). Global radical feminism asserts the universality of "patriarchal" violence against women and sometimes advocates an ideal of global sisterhood (Morgan 1984).[2] Opposed to this position is postcolonial feminism, which asserts the diversity of women's oppression across the world and emphasizes that this oppression is shaped by many factors, among which past colonialism and continuing neocolonialism are especially important. Postcolonial feminism charges that global feminist criticisms of cultural practices outside the West frequently are forms of "imperial feminism" or "feminist orientalism," often exoticizing and sensationalizing non-Western cultural practices by focusing on their sexual aspects (Amos and Parmar 1984; Apffel-Marglin and Simon 1994). The polarized debate in women's studies has sometimes seemed to suggest that Western feminists who are concerned about the well-being of women across the world are confronted with a choice between colonial interference and callous indifference (Jaggar 2004).

Central to the women's studies debates has been the question of "essentialism," especially as this pertains to many Western feminist representations of "women."[3] Postcolonial feminists argue that universal generalizations about women are essentialist, because they reify gender by treating it as separable from class, ethnicity, race, age, and nationality in ways that the postcolonial critics regard as incoherent and mystifying. "Essentialist" generalizations are always sweeping and treat groups as internally homogeneous, but they are not always universal. For instance, an influential article by Chandra Mohanty challenges the essentialist contrasts between Western women and "the average Third World woman," which she finds implicit in much Western feminist writing. Mohanty argues that this writing represents Western women "as educated, as modern, as having control over their own bodies and sexualities, and the freedom to make their own decisions," while depicting non-Western women as victimized and lacking in agency. She criticizes patronizing Western representations of "the typical Third World woman" that portray this woman as leading "an essentially truncated life based on her feminine gender (read: sexually constrained) and her being 'third world' (read: ignorant, poor, uneducated, tradition-bound, family-oriented, victimized, etc.)" (Mohanty 1991: 56).

1.2 The Debate in Philosophy

In the 1990s, academic debate about the gendered aspects of non-Western cultural practices moved out of the feminist fringe and into the mainstream of Western philosophy. This occurred primarily as a result of bold work by Martha Nussbaum and Susan Okin (Nussbaum 1988, 1990, 1992, 1993, 1995, 1998, 1999, 2000, 2002; Okin 1994, 1995, 1998, 1999, 2002). The recent work of Nussbaum and of Okin diverges in important respects, but the present paper focuses on some parallels between them.[4] In their discussions of poor women in poor countries (and of cultural minority women in rich countries), Nussbaum and Okin both turn away from earlier debates about the universality or otherwise of "patriarchy." They reframe the issues in terms of ongoing philosophical debates between liberalism and communitarianism on the one hand, and liberalism and multiculturalism on the other. Both take as their problem the question of how Western philosophers should respond to non-Western cultural practices perceived as unjust to women and both believe that answering this question requires addressing several current philosophical controversies. These include: moral universalism and cultural relativism; the possibility of "external" as opposed to "internal" social criticism; and the question of whether liberal societies can tolerate illiberal cultural practices within their borders.

Nussbaum and Okin both identify themselves as liberal feminists but both follow the radical feminists in staunchly opposing what they see as the oppression of women in non-Western cultures. They provide new arguments against postcolonial feminists, casting them as relativists who seek to avoid forthright condemnation of injustice to women in developing or Third World countries. They also charge that the antiessentialism advocated by postcolonial feminists rationalizes a disingenuous refusal to acknowledge forms of injustice that are distinctively gendered. Finally, Nussbaum and Okin suggest that women who seem content with unjust cultural practices suffer from adaptive preferences or learned desires for things that are harmful, a phenomenon called "false consciousness" by Western feminists influenced by the Marxist critique of ideology.

Nussbaum's work on this topic draws on Amartya Sen's concept of capabilities, which was developed originally as an alternative to welfarism for measuring international levels of development. Nussbaum has modified the concept of capabilities and uses it to counter "cultural relativism," which she thinks often serves as a pretext for excusing outrageous injustice to women in poor countries. In a spate of books and articles published throughout the 1990s, Nussbaum defends the universal values that she believes are embodied in the capabilities, appealing to these values to condemn cultural practices that subordinate women. An early article provocatively defends "Aristotelian essentialism" against what Nussbaum regards as a "politically correct" antiessentialism that rationalizes "ancient religious taboos, the luxury of the pampered husband, ill health, ignorance, and death" (Nussbaum 1992: 204). In responding to the challenge that many people, including many poor women in poor countries, do not accept the capabilities as universal values, Nussbaum invokes the concept of adaptive preferences.[5] She argues that existing desires and preferences may be corrupted or mistaken when they are adapted to unjust social circumstances; for example, women may sometimes fail to recognize that they are oppressed.[6]

Susan Okin has also been concerned to address the situation of poor women in poor countries. Her analysis draws on her own earlier critique of Western practices of marriage and family, in which she argues persuasively that the traditional division of labor in marriage unjustly disadvantages Western women economically and in other ways (Okin 1989). Okin's analysis of the situation of poor women in poor countries is parallel to her analysis of the situation of Western women: In her view "the problems of other women are 'similar to ours but more so'" (Okin 1994: 8 [herein 237]). Like Nussbaum, Okin challenges feminist antiessentialism, quoting Nussbaum approvingly on this topic.[7] Also like Nussbaum, she worries that "false consciousness" arising from adaptive preferences and internalized oppression limits the usefulness of "interactive" or "dialogic" approaches to justice and advocates an alternative Rawlsian method of hypothetical dialogue in the original position (Okin 1994: 18f [herein 248f]).

Okin's concern about cultural injustice to women emerges again in her contributions to the multiculturalism debate. In the discipline of philosophy, this debate focuses on the question of whether cultural minorities within liberal cultures should enjoy special group rights (Kymlicka 1995). Okin argues that the rights claimed by minority groups may conflict with liberalism's commitment to women's equality, so that a tension exists between multiculturalism and feminism (Okin 1998, 1999). In Okin's view, supporters of multiculturalism have failed to appreciate that illiberal cultural practices are often especially burdensome to women. In addition, she believes that some feminists have paid so much attention to differences among women that they have fallen into cultural relativism, ignoring the fact that "most cultures have as one of their principal aims the control of women by men" (Okin 1999: 13). Okin asks rhetorically, "When a woman from a more patriarchal culture comes to the United States (or some other Western, basically liberal, state), why should she be less protected from male violence than other women are?" (Okin 1999: 20).

1.3 SOME NONLOGICAL IMPLICATIONS OF NUSSBAUM'S AND OKIN'S WORK

Okin and Nussbaum deserve great credit for drawing the attention of mainstream Western philosophers to issues previously neglected by what Thomas Pogge has called the academic justice industry (Pogge 2002: 145). Like all groundbreaking scholarship, Nussbaum's and Okin's work has shaped the subsequent literature in distinctive ways, highlighting some concerns and obscuring others. Specifically, their work has encouraged Western philosophers to understand injustice to non-Western women as a matter of oppression by local cultural traditions. The issues that Nussbaum and Okin raise are crucial to understanding the injustices suffered by non-Western women but the present paper focuses on the issues they have *not* raised, on their omissions and their silences. In other words, I am concerned here with what Cheshire Calhoun would call the nonlogical implications of Nussbaum's and Okin's work in this area, including the moral and political significance of their emphases and their *lacunae* (Calhoun 1988).

In discussing the contributions that care ethics makes to moral theory, Calhoun argues that Western moral philosophy has produced a lopsided ideology of moral life and thought that reflects the moral preoccupations of propertied males and obscures the moral concerns of (among others) many women.[8] Analogously, I argue that Nussbaum's and Okin's representations of the injustices suffered by poor women in poor countries are lopsided, reflecting some preoccupations while obscuring others. Calhoun suggests that the ethics of care, construed as a focus on hitherto neglected aspects of moral life and thought, can help to redress the gendered bias of moral theory. Similarly, I suggest that a focus on certain aspects of the global political economy, hitherto neglected by Western philosophers, can help to present a fuller and fairer understanding of the situations of poor women in poor countries.

My concern is not that Nussbaum and Okin pay excessive attention to the sensationalized sexual issues that preoccupy the popular press. On the contrary, they take the poverty of many non-Western women extremely seriously, recognizing that poverty constrains women's autonomy and makes them vulnerable to a range of other abuses, such as violence, sexual exploitation, and overwork. However, Nussbaum's and Okin's discussions give the impression that female poverty is attributable primarily to local cultural traditions, especially traditions of female seclusion.[9] For example, both treat as exemplary a study by Marty Chen, which explains that many women in India, especially female heads of households, are left destitute because the system of secluding women denies them the right to gainful employment outside the home (Chen 1995).[10]

Nussbaum's and Okin's focus on the injustice of non-Western cultural traditions reinforces several assumptions commonly made in popular Western discussions of the situation of poor women in poor countries. These assumptions are as follows:

1)   A major, perhaps the major, cause of suffering among women in poor countries is unjust treatment in accordance with local cultural traditions—traditions whose injustice is not necessarily recognized by the women involved. Call this the "injustice by culture" thesis.

2)   The unjust local traditions in question may resemble some Western practices but they are causally independent of them. Call this the "autonomy of culture" thesis.

3)   Non-Western cultures are typically more unjust to women than is Western culture. Call this the "West is best for women" thesis.

I doubt that either Nussbaum or Okin would assent to these theses in anything like the simple terms in which I have stated them. Nevertheless, I worry that both philosophers' preoccupation with opposing the perceived injustice of non-Western cultures encourages many Western readers to derive such nonlogical implications from their work. In addition, I worry that Nussbaum's and Okin's work in this area promotes too narrow a view of the task of those Western philosophers who seek to explain injustice to poor women in poor countries. In other words, I am afraid it promotes the view that:

4)   Western philosophy's task is to expose the injustices imposed on women by their local cultures and to challenge philosophical rationalizations of those injustices, many of which rest on mistaken views about essentialism and relativism.

Thesis Four is the philosopher's version of "saving Amina." In the next section of this paper, I critically discuss Theses One to Three; in the following section, I discuss Thesis Four.

2. NON-WESTERN CULTURE AND INJUSTICE TO POOR WOMEN IN POOR COUNTRIES

Assessing claims about cultural injustice requires having some sense of what is meant by the term "culture," which Raymond Williams describes as "one of the two or three most complicated words in the English language" (Williams 1983: 160. Cited by Tomlinson 1991: 6). The 1982 report of a UNESCO conference on cultural policy stated that, in the view of some delegates, "culture permeated the whole social fabric and its role was so preeminent and determining that it might indeed be confused with life itself" (Tomlinson 1991: 5). In most contexts, however, the term "culture" is useful only if it is marked off against other areas of social life, so culture is often distinguished from politics and the economy (Tomlinson 1991: 5). Contemporary philosophical discussions of culture typically accept some version of this distinction. For example, Nancy Fraser contrasts concerns about cultural recognition with concerns about economic redistribution (Fraser 1997). The items on Bikhu Parekh's list of minority cultural practices in Britain all concern marriage, sexuality, dress, diet, educa- tion, body marking, and funeral customs (Parekh 2000: 264f). In Okin's view, "the sphere of personal, sexual, and reproductive life provides a central focus of most cultures... Religious or cultural groups are often particularly concerned with 'personal law'—the laws of marriage, divorce, child custody, division and control of family property, and inheritance" (Okin 1999: 12f).

When culture is equated with dress, diet, sex, and family, it becomes an area of life that has special significance for women. Most of the practices on Parekh's list apply mainly or even exclusively to women and girls and his last item is simply, "Subordinate status of women and all it entails including denial of opportunities for their personal development in some minority communities" (Parekh 2000: 265). Thus, Okin's observation is uncontroversial:

As a rule, then, the defense of "cultural practices" is likely to have much greater impact on the lives of women and girls than those of men and boys, since far more of women's time and energy goes into preserving and maintaining the personal, familial, and reproductive side of life. Obviously, culture is not only about domestic arrangements, but they do provide a major focus of most contemporary cultures. Home is, after all, where much of culture is practiced, preserved, and transmitted to the young. (Okin 1999: 13)

Benhabib writes, "Women and their bodies are the symbolic-cultural site upon which human societies inscript their moral order" (Benhabib 2002: 84). Because women are typically seen as the symbols or bearers of culture, conflicts among cultural groups often are fought on the terrain of women's bodies, sometimes literally in the form of systematic rape.

2.1 THE LIMITS OF INJUSTICE BY CULTURE

The thesis of injustice by culture asserts that local cultural traditions are a major, perhaps the major, source of the injustices suffered by women in poor countries. Is this thesis correct? Certainly it is undeniable that many non-Western cultures are unjust to women. Striking evidence is provided by Amartya Sen's famous calculation that up to 100 million women are "missing" as a result of Asian cultural practices, including both direct violence and systematic neglect (Sen 1990). It also seems indisputable that women in legally multicultural societies tend to suffer disproportionately from religious/cultural law (Shachar 1999, 2000a, 2000b). That injustice to women is inherent in many cultural traditions confirms second-wave feminist arguments that the personal is political and Okin's work on Western marriage and family has made a valuable contribution in drawing mainstream philosophers' attention to such injustices. However, the poverty and associated abuses suffered by poor women in poor countries cannot be understood exclusively in terms of unjust local traditions. To understand such poverty and abuse more fully, it is also necessary to situate these traditions in a broader geopolitical and geo-economic context.

Contemporary processes of economic globalization, regulated by the Western-inspired and Western-imposed principles and policies of neoliberalism, have dramatically increased inequality both among and within countries.[11] Applying neoliberal principles across the world has produced a windfall for some people and a catastrophe for others. Those who have reaped the rewards of neoliberal globalization have belonged mostly to the more privileged classes in the global North or to elite classes in the global South. Those who have been injured by it are mostly people who were already poor and marginalized, in both the developing and the developed worlds.[12] Since women are represented disproportionately among the world's poor and marginalized, neoliberal globalization has been harmful especially to women—although not to all or only women. Women comprise 70 percent of the world's poor and 64 percent of the world's 876 million illiterate people (UNDP 1999). In what follows, I offer a few examples of the impact of neoliberal globalization on poor women in poor countries.

Most poor women in poor countries traditionally made a living in small-scale and subsistence agriculture; even quite recently, 70 percent of the world's farmers were said to be women. However, the impact of neoliberal globalization has made small-scale and subsistence agriculture increasingly unviable. One reason for this is the expansion of export agriculture, typically mandated by programs of structural adjustment, especially in South America and Southeast Asia. Another reason is the refusal on the part of the wealthiest countries to conform to their own neoliberal principles. The United States and the European Union currently spend $350 billion a year on farm subsidies, six times what they spend on aid. As neoliberalism compels poor countries to open their markets, locally grown agricultural products are unable to compete with the heavily subsidized foods dumped by richer countries.

The decline of small-scale and subsistence agriculture has driven many women off the land and into the shantytowns that encircle most major Third World cities. Here the women struggle to survive in the informal economy, which is characterized by low wages or incomes, uncertain employment, and poor working conditions.[13] Many become street vendors or domestic servants. Those who remain landless in the countryside are often forced to work as seasonal, casual, and temporary laborers at lower wages than their male counterparts. Many women are driven into prostitution, accelerating the AIDS epidemic, which ravages the poorest women in the poorest countries.[14]

Neoliberal globalization has also destroyed many traditional industries on which poor women in poor countries once depended.[15] More fortunate women may obtain jobs in newer industries, especially the garment industry, which produces the developing world's main manufactured exports and in which women are the majority of workers. However, conditions in the garment industry are notoriously bad because poor countries, lacking capital, can compete in the global market only by implementing sweatshop conditions. The situation for garment workers in poor countries is worsened by continuing protectionism in the garment industry on the part of the United States and the European Union.

The most obviously gendered consequences of neoliberal globalization are the worldwide cutbacks in social services, also often mandated by programs of structural adjustment. These cutbacks have affected women's economic status even more adversely than men's, because women's responsibility for caring for children and other family members makes them more reliant on such programs. Reductions in social services have forced women to create survival strategies for their families by absorbing these reductions with their own unpaid labor, and more work for women has resulted in higher school dropout rates for girls. In addition, the introduction of school fees in many Southern countries has made education unavailable, especially to girls. Less education and longer hours of domestic work contribute to women's impoverishment by making it harder for them to attain well-paid jobs.[16]

The above examples are not intended to suggest that the poverty and poverty-related abuses that afflict many women in poor countries are caused exclusively by neoliberal globalization. Obviously, these problems result from interaction between factors that are both macro and micro, global and local. It is impossible to explain why women suffer disproportionately from the deleterious consequences of neoliberal globalization without referring to local cultural traditions. For example, if women were not assigned the primary responsibility of caring for children, the sick, and the old, the cutbacks in social services would not affect them disproportionately nor would they find it harder than men to move to the locations of new industries. Only the injustice of cultural tradition seems to account for the fact that, within male-headed families, women and girls frequently receive less of such available resources as food and medical care.[17] Nevertheless, the above examples do show that the poverty of poor women in poor countries cannot be attributed exclusively to the injustice of their local cultures. To suggest this would be to promote a one-sided analysis that ignored the ways in which neoliberal globalization is, among other things, a gendered process that frequently exacerbates inequalities between men and women.[18]

2.2 THE LIMITS OF THE AUTONOMY OF CULTURE

Faced with the evidence of the previous section, Nussbaum and Okin would certainly acknowledge that neoliberal globalization bears considerable responsibility for women's poverty in poor countries and they would surely condemn its injustices. However, they might also observe that injustice in the global economic order simply has not been the focus of their work thus far.[19] Surely, they might say, an author cannot be faulted for choosing to address one topic rather than another, especially if the topic chosen is important and unduly neglected; moreover, if anyone is to be faulted for philosophy's failure to deal with the gendered aspects of the global political economy, why should Nussbaum and Okin be singled out? I agree that it is reasonable for philosophers wishing to address injustice to poor women in poor countries to focus sometimes on local rather than global problems and on cultural rather than economic injustices. However, when discussing issues involving the seeming injustice of non-Western cultures, it is problematic to write as though these cultures are self-contained or autonomous without also noting the ways in which their traditions have been and continue to be shaped by Western interventions.

Theorists of the second wave of Western feminism sometimes inquired whether male dominance had existed in all societies or whether it was introduced to some societies by European colonizers.[20] Whatever the answer to this once hotly debated question, it is indisputable that many supposed cultural traditions in Asia, Latin America, and Africa have been shaped by encounters with Western colonialism. For instance, Veena Oldenburg argues that the practice of dowry murder in India had imperial origins (Oldenburg 2002). Non-Western cultural practices especially affecting women often gain new life as symbols of resistance to Western dominance. In Kenya, for example, "clitoridectomy became a political issue between the Kikuyu and Kenya's white settlers and missionaries, as well as a symbol of the struggle between African nationalists and British colonial power" (Brown 1991: 262). Uma Narayan describes how the supposed "Indian tradition" of *sati* (immolation of widows) was likely "an *effect* of the extensive and prolonged debate that took place over the very issue of its status as tradition. As a result of this debate, *sati* came to acquire, for both British and Indians, and for its supporters as well as its opponents, an 'emblematic status,' becoming a larger-than-life symbol of 'Hindu' and 'Indian' culture...." (Narayan 1997: 65). Today, "marginalized by exposure to an onslaught of conditions of modernity, the market economy, and imperialistic transnational enterprises, distinct cultural groups tend to view themselves as being under pressure to demonstrate their ritual purity and allegiance to traditional high culture" (Obiora 1997, cited in Volpp 2001: 1198n78). This sense of being economically and culturally beleaguered may help to explain the current worldwide flourishing of religious fundamentalisms, defined by Volpp as modern political movements that use religion as a basis for their attempts to win or consolidate power and extend social control (Volpp 2001: 1205n108). Contemporary fundamentalisms all "support the patriarchal family as a central agent of control and see women as embodying the moral and traditional values of the family and the whole community" (Volpp 2001: 1205n108).

Western culture is not only a passive stimulus for gender-conservative reactions by those who have the authority to define "authentic" cultural traditions. In addition, Western powers may reinforce or even impose gender-conservative cultures on non-Western societies by supporting conservative factions of their populations. For most of the twentieth century, for example, British and US governments have supported a Saudi Arabian regime that practices gender apartheid. The Taliban government of Afghanistan, which also practiced gender apartheid, was installed after the US provided extensive training and aid to various mujaheddin forces opposing the then-communist but secular government. President Reagan described the mujaheddin as the moral equivalent of the founding fathers of the United States. Following its overthrow of the Taliban, the United States has installed a weak government in Afghanistan under which women's lives in many ways are even more precarious. The burkha is no longer legally required but most women are still afraid to remove it and they are not safe on the streets. Girls' schools are burned, families threatened for sending girls to school, and three girls recently have been poisoned, apparently for attending school (Bearup 2004). Women are banned from singing on radio and television, and there has been an unprecedented increase in the number of suicides and self-burnings among women. At present, the United States is trying to build an Iraqi government to succeed the Ba'athist regime it has overthrown. Under the Ba'athist regime, whatever its other faults, the conditions of Iraqi women were much better than those of women elsewhere in the region. Today, women are afraid to leave their homes (Sandler 2003) and news media report that the US is seeking political leadership for Iraq among its tribal and religious leaders—few of whom are women or whose priorities include improving the status of women.

Sharp contrasts between Western and non-Western cultures cannot ultimately be sustained. They rely characteristically on what Uma Narayan calls cultural essentialist generalizations, which offer totalizing characterizations of whole cultures, treated as internally homogenous and externally sealed. Typically, such generalizations are quite inconsistent with empirical realities (Narayan 1998). In the Western philosophical literature, it is becoming more common to observe that cultures are internally diverse and often conflict-ridden and that they are not autonomous relative to one another, but it is still unusual to note that they are only partially autonomous relative to political and economic structures. Yet, as the global political economy becomes more integrated, so too do its cultural manifestations. Thus, when multinational corporations exploit women in export-processing zones located in poor countries, it is impossible to say that this practice exclusively reflects either Western or non-Western culture. When Asian governments tempt multinational corporate investment with stereotypes of women workers as tractable, hardworking, dexterous, and sexy, it seems meaningless to ask whether these stereotypes are Western or non-Western or whether the superexploitation and sexual harassment of these women represents Western or non-Western cultural traditions. It seems equally meaningless to attribute the increasing sexualization of women worldwide to either Western or non-Western culture. Many women around the world have been drawn into some aspect of sex work. This includes a multibillion-dollar pornography industry and a worldwide traffic in women, in which the sex workers participate with varying degrees of willingness and coercion. It also includes servicing male workers in large plantations, servicing representatives of transnational corporations, servicing troops around military bases, and servicing United Nations troops and workers. In some parts of Asia and the Caribbean, sex tourism is a mainstay of local economies. Prostitution has become a transnational phenomenon, shaped by global norms of feminine beauty and masculine virility.[21]

In the new global order, local cultures interact and interpenetrate to the point where they often fuse. Some patterns seem discernible, for example, worldwide preferences for women as factory workers, sexual playthings, and domestic servants (Anderson 2000), but these patterns shift and merge in an unending variety of particular combinations. Poor women in poor countries certainly are oppressed by local men whose power is rooted in local cultures, but they are also oppressed by global forces, including the forces of so-called development, which have reshaped local gender and class relations in varying and contradictory ways, simultaneously undermining and reinforcing them (Sen and Grown 1987; Moser 1991; Kabeer 1994). A new but still male-dominant global culture may be emerging, relying on the labor of a new transnational labor force that is feminized, racialized, and sexualized (Kang 2004).

2.3 IS THE WEST BEST FOR WOMEN?

Much of the Western philosophical debate over multiculturalism discusses the relative situations of women in "liberal" and "illiberal" cultures. It tends to equate Western with liberal culture and non-Western with illiberal culture and it usually takes for granted that Western culture is more advanced than non-Western culture. Okin writes, "Many Third World families, it seems, are even worse schools of justice and more successful inculcators of the inequality of the sexes as natural and appropriate than are their developed world equivalents" (Okin 1994: 13 [herein 242]). In her view, "the situation of some poor women in poor countries is different from—as well as distinctly worse than—that of most Western women today. It is more like the situation of the latter in the nineteenth century" (Okin 1994: 15 [herein 245]).

As intercultural interactions accelerate, we have seen that it becomes increasingly problematic to contrast whole cultures with each other. The idealized and unrealistic images of cultures constructed by essentialist generalizations are typically designed to promote political agendas. What Narayan calls the colonialist stance presents Western cultures as dynamic, progressive, and egalitarian while portraying non-Western cultures as backward, barbaric, and patriarchal. Colonialist representations characteristically engage in "culture-blaming," for instance, by treating discrimination and violence against women as intrinsic parts of non-Western but not of Western cultures. While the West historically has blamed non-Western cultures for their backwardness, it has portrayed its own culture as staunchly committed to values like liberty and equality, a "self-perception... untroubled by the fact that Western powers were engaged in slavery and colonization, or that they had resisted granting political and civil rights even to large numbers of Western subjects, including women" (Narayan 1997: 15). Today, as Narayan notes, violence abounds in the United States, yet cross burnings, burnings of black churches, domestic violence murders, and gun deaths are not usually treated as manifestations of United States culture (Narayan 1997: 85). When cultural explanations are offered only for violence against poor women in poor countries, Narayan notes that the effect is to suggest that these women suffer "death by culture," a fate from which Western women seem curiously exempt (Narayan 1997: 84f). Many philosophers continue to write as though Western culture is unambiguously liberal, ignoring Christian fundamentalism's influence on the present United States government, as well as its growth in several former Soviet bloc countries (Grewal and Kaplan 1994: 24). For instance, Parekh treats polygamy as an exclusively Muslim practice, ignoring its existence among Christian groups in the United States. It is true that what Parekh calls the public values of Western societies are mostly liberal (2000: 268–70) but Western cultures certainly are not liberal all the way down—and illiberal values frequently rear above their surfaces.[22]

Although the superiority of Western culture appears self-evident to most Westerners, non-Western women do not all agree. For instance, Western feminists have long criticized non-Western practices of veiling and female seclusion, but Leila Ahmed argues that the social separation of women from men on the Arabian Peninsula creates a space within which women may interact freely with one another and where they resist men's efforts to impose on them an ideology of inferiority and subservience (Ahmed 1982: 530f). Nussbaum and Okin suggest that non-Western women's acceptance of seemingly unjust cultural practices may be due to adaptive preferences or false consciousness. In Okin's view, not only do "many cultures oppress some of their members, in particular women... they are (also) often able to socialize these oppressed members so that they accept without question their designated cultural status" (Okin 1999: 117). To someone like myself, brought up in the British class system, this assertion seems indisputably true. However, raising questions of false consciousness only with respect to non-Western women who defend their cultures could be read as suggesting that these women's moral perceptions are less reliable than the perceptions of Western women whose consciousness is supposedly higher or truer. Such a suggestion reflects a second aspect of the colonialist stance, namely, the "missionary position," which supposes that "only Westerners are capable of naming and challenging patriarchal atrocities committed against Third-World women" (Narayan 1997: 57, 59f). Nussbaum and Okin both recognize explicitly that non-Western women are perfectly capable of criticizing unjust cultural traditions and frequently do precisely that, but their practice of raising questions about adaptive preferences and false consciousness only when confronted by views that oppose their own encourages dismissing those views without considering them seriously. In fact, the question of the superiority of Western culture for women, especially poor women, is not as straightforward as Westerners often assume.

The thesis that the West is best for the poor women of the world is not necessarily true. Even if we set aside deep philosophical questions about how to measure welfare, development, or the quality of life and agree to assess cultures according to their success in preserving poor women's human rights, at least three sets of concerns cast doubt on the West is best thesis.

1) First, it is of course true by definition that liberal cultures give a higher priority than illiberal cultures to protecting civil and political liberties. However, the

ability to exercise these "first generation" human rights can be enjoyed only in a context where "second generation" social and economic rights are also guaranteed. As noted earlier, poverty makes women vulnerable to violations of their civil and political liberties, including assaults on their bodily integrity, and Western societies are very uneven in their willingness to address women's poverty. The feminization of poverty is especially conspicuous in the United States, where women continue to suffer extensive violence. Thus, it must be recognized that the human rights especially of poor women are routinely violated even in liberal Western societies.[23]

2) Second, and turning to poor women in poor countries, it is hard to deny that Western powers are disproportionately responsible for designing, imposing, and enforcing a global economic order that continues to widen the staggering gap between rich and poor countries. Since gender inequality is strongly correlated with poverty, Western countries are disproportionately responsible for creating the conditions that make non-Western women vulnerable to local violations of their rights. It is especially disturbing to wonder how far the prosperity that undergirds Western feminism is causally dependent on non-Western poverty.

3) Third, it must be acknowledged that some of the same Western powers that trumpet democracy and liberalism at home support undemocratic and gender-conservative regimes abroad, fomenting coups, dictatorships, and civil wars (Pogge 2002: 153). Poor women are disproportionately affected by these interventions. They suffer most from the absence of social programs cut to fund military spending and they also suffer most from social chaos. They constitute the majority of war's casualties and 80 percent of the refugees dislocated by war.[24]

These three sets of concerns raise serious questions for the thesis that the West is best for women, especially for the vast majority of the world's poor women.

2.4 CONCLUSION

I do not wish to romanticize non-Western cultures and traditions or to assert that Western culture is intrinsically violent and racist. Such reverse colonialist representations would be as essentialist and distorting as the claim that the West is best for women. In addition, suggesting that neocolonial domination is the cause of all the problems in poor countries would portray the citizens of those countries simply as passive victims, denying their agency and responsibility. My goal has been to challenge the images of both Western and non-Western cultures that are implicit in much of the most influential philosophical discussion on these topics. I do not dispute that non-Western cultures often treat women unjustly, but I have argued that global forces help to shape those cultures, as well as create the larger political and economic contexts in which poor women find themselves.[25] Western powers play a disproportionate role in enforcing an unjust global order, so bringing into question the assumption that, overall, the West is best for poor women in poor countries.

Expanding our understanding of the causes of women's poverty in poor countries requires that Western philosophers also expand our conception of our responsibility toward such women. No longer can we be satisfied to assume that our responsibility as philosophers is limited to employing the tools of our trade to analyze the injustices perpetrated on poor women in the name of non-Western cultural traditions. Once we acknowledge that we share past, present, and future connections with poor women in poor countries, we see that we inhabit with them a shared context of justice. We do not look at their problems as outsiders, from an Archimedean standpoint external to their social world. Our involvement gives us a firmer moral standing for criticizing non-Western cultural practices, provided our criticisms are well informed and, in O'Neill's words, "followable by" members of the society in question (O'Neill 1996). However, it also requires us to investigate how much moral responsibility should be attributed to the citizens of Western countries for the continuation of these practices as well as for the unjust global order that traps many women in poor countries in grinding poverty.

3. RETHINKING GLOBAL JUSTICE FOR WOMEN: WHAT IS ON THE AGENDA OF INTERCULTURAL DIALOGUE?

In Western philosophy classrooms, "cultural abuses" of women have become staple and sometimes titillating examples used to enliven discussion of issues such as moral relativism and the possibility of cross-cultural social criticism. Some Western philosophers address perceived cultural injustice to women by recommending an aggressive cosmopolitanism; others promote a "culturally sensitive" relativism. Increasingly, however, Western philosophers recognize that cultures are neither static nor hermetically sealed and they advocate intercultural dialogue (Parekh 2000; Benhabib 2002).[26] I certainly agree that intercultural dialogues are indispensable and I have previously explored some of their difficulties (Jaggar 1998, 1999). In this section, I wish to suggest some items for inclusion on the agendas of intercultural dialogues among philosophers concerned about global justice, especially justice for poor women in poor countries.

Most obviously, Western philosophers should not regard intercultural dialogues as opportunities for "saving Amina" by proselytizing supposedly Western values or raising consciousness about the injustice of non-Western practices. It is always more pleasant to discuss other people's blind spots and faults than our own, but we need to think more carefully who is Amina and from what or whom does she need saving.

High on the agenda of intercultural dialogue about global justice for poor women in poor countries must be questions about the global basic structure, as well as the justice of those Western government policies that directly affect poor women's lives. Important questions of economic justice include: how to understand "natural" resources, when things like fossil fuels, sunny climates, coral beaches, or strategic locations become resources only within larger systems of production and meaning; how to determine a country's "own" resources, when every country's boundaries have been drawn by force; what is the meaning of "fair" trade, and can trade be free in any meaningful sense when poor nations have no alternative to participating in an economic system in which they become ever poorer. Important topics of political justice include reexamining the Westphalian conception of sovereignty, at a time when the sovereignty of most countries is limited by the rules of world trade and the sovereignty of poor countries is rendered almost meaningless because of their domination by international financial institutions and trade organizations.[27] Although superficially ungendered, these topics in fact are all deeply gendered, most obviously because women suffer disproportionately from economic inequality and political marginalization.

Intercultural dialogue about global justice must also address the problem of militarism. Following and despite the end of the Cold War, arms expenditures rose and wars continued in many non-Western countries, exacerbating and exacerbated by the poverty associated with global neoliberalism. In the late 1990s, "over half the nations of the world still provide higher budgets for the military than for their countries' health needs; 25 countries spend more on defense than on education; and 15 countries devote more funds to military programs than to education and health combined" (Peterson and Runyan 1999: 120). Since 9/11, 2001, arms expenditures have skyrocketed. In today's world, the top arms exporters are the USA, Russia, France, UK, Germany, Netherlands, with the United States accounting for more than 50 percent of sales.[28] The United States also maintains over 200 permanent bases across the world, distorting local economies and employing many thousands of women as prostitutes (Sturdevant 2001). As noted earlier, poor women and their children suffer disproportionately from war and militarism, and the expansion of these raises deep philosophical questions about the meanings of war, peace, and security—especially security for women.[29]

Another set of topics for intercultural dialogue about global justice for women concerns remedial justice, reparation, or compensation for past and continuing wrongs. Do countries that have expropriated resources or fought proxy wars in other countries owe reparations to those countries and, if so, how should these be determined? Should wealthy countries compensate poor countries for the environmental destruction to which they have made a disproportionate contribution not only through militarism, which is the single largest cause of environmental destruction, but also through other destructive practices, including the careless extraction of resources from poor countries, the establishment of factories in poor countries with weak environmental standards, and extravagant patterns of consumption, especially the profligate burning of fossil fuels. The last produces carbon dioxide that causes acid rain and global warming, accompanied by devastating floods and hurricanes and a rise in sea levels that may cause some Southern countries to disappear entirely. Since poor women in poor countries suffer disproportionately from poverty, social chaos, and environmental destruction, they would benefit the most from any system of remedial justice that might be established.

Most of the above topics concern issues of justice among countries. Since such justice is likely to be slow in coming, intercultural dialogue about global justice might also address the question of how in the meantime individual citizens can directly assist Amina Lawal and other poor women in poor countries. Imam and Medar-Gould note that not all victims of human rights violations can become international *causes célèbres* or subjects for letter-writing protests. They suggest that Western feminists who wish to help Lawal contribute to BAOBAB for Women's Human Rights or WRAPA, Women's Rights Advancement and Protection Agency, organizations that they respectively represent. Because money always comes with strings attached, promoting civil society initiatives in poor countries raises questions about the subversion of local democracies. Some critics argue that Northern-funded NGOs are a new form of colonialism, despite using the language of inclusion, empowerment, accountability, and grassroots democracy, because they create dependence on nonelected overseas funders and their locally appointed officials, undermining the development of social programs administered by elected officials accountable to local people.[30] In an integrated global economy, however, nonintervention is no longer an option; our inevitable interventions are only more or less overt and more or less morally informed. Although the foreign funding of women's NGOs has dangers, it is not necessarily imperialistic. Nira Yuval-Davis reports that many NGOs in the global South have been able to survive and resist local pressures through the aid provided from overseas, "as well as the more personal support and solidarity of feminist organizations in other countries." She observes, "it would be a westocentric stereotype to view women associated with NGOs in the South as puppets of western feminism" (Yuval-Davis 1997: 120f).[31]

4. "SAVING AMINA"

The images of Amina Lawal that flashed around the world earlier this year show a beautiful African woman, holding a beautiful baby, looking at first sight like an African madonna. However her head is covered, her eyes downcast, she looks submissive, sad, and scared. Portrayed in bare feet and described as illiterate, she epitomizes the image of the oppressed Third World woman described by Chandra Mohanty. Her image has also been widely regarded as epitomizing the barbarity of Islamic fundamentalism. Such images encourage Western feminists to take up the supposed white man's burden of "saving brown women from brown men" (Spivak 1988: 296).

Challenging the "save Amina" petition and letter-writing campaign, Imam and Medar-Gould write:

> Dominant colonialist discourses and the mainstream international media have presented Islam (and Africa) as the barbaric and savage Other. Please do not buy into this. Accepting stereotypes that present Islam as incompatible with human rights not only perpetuates racism but also confirms the claims of right-wing politico-religious extremists in all of our contexts (Imam and Medar-Gould 2003).

They explain that when protest letters represent negative stereotypes of Islam and Muslims, they inflame local sentiments and may put victims of human rights abuses and their supporters in further danger.

Sensationalized criticisms of non-Western cultures reinforce Western as well as non-Western prejudices, promoting the impression that Western democracies are locked into a life and death "clash of cultures" with militant Islam (Barber 1992; Huntington 1996). Even philosophical criticisms sometimes have consequences outside the academy. Philosophy is often portrayed as an esoteric discipline practiced exclusively in ivory towers, but many moral and political philosophers intend also to influence the "real" world.[32] Philosophical criticism may be a political intervention and may be taken up outside academia in ways that its authors do not necessarily intend (Alcoff 1992). *Nation* columnist Katha Pollitt, upset that militant Islamists had forced the Miss World pageant out of Nigeria, commented, "Not a good week for cultural relativism, on the whole" (Pollitt 2002). Western criticism of non-Western cultural practices is not in principle patronizing or xenophobic, but critics should be aware that our colonial history and current geopolitical situation influence the interpretation and consequences of such criticisms; for instance, opponents of immigration cite non-Western cultural practices as reasons for closing the borders of the United States to immigrants from poor countries.[33] Given this context, Western philosophers need to consider how their criticisms of non-Western cultural practices may be used politically. Amos and Parmar contend that racist British immigration policies were justified partly by invoking feminist opposition to arranged marriage (Amos and Parmar 1984: 11). President G. W. Bush and his wife Laura both rationalized the bombing of Afghanistan by the United States as necessary to save Afghan women from the oppression of the burkha (Bush, G. W. 2002; Bush, L. 2002, cited in Young 2003: 17f).

Philosophers wishing to save Amina and similarly situated women certainly are at liberty to criticize cultural traditions in Nigeria and other countries and such criticisms are often well deserved. However, it behooves us also to ask why these practices have become ensconced as cultural traditions. Nigeria is a country that enjoys huge oil revenues, yet its real per capita GDP declined by 22 percent between 1977 and 1998 (UNDP 2000: 185, cited in Pogge 2002: 235). As we have seen, gender inequality is correlated with poverty and, according to Thomas Pogge, the poverty suffered by most Nigerians is causally linked with the "resource privilege" that the existing international system accords to the de facto rulers of all countries. This encourages military coups, authoritarianism, and corruption in resource-rich countries such as Nigeria, which has been ruled by military strongmen for almost three decades and is listed near the bottom of Transparency International's chart of international corruption. In Pogge's view, "corruption in Nigeria is not just a local phenomenon rooted in tribal culture and traditions, but encouraged and sustained by the international resource privilege"

(112f). In such circumstances, for philosophers to focus exclusively on the injustice of Nigerian cultural practices is to engage in a form of culture blaming that depoliticizes social problems and diverts attention from structural violence against poor populations (Volpp 2000).[34]

In addition to bearing in mind the larger context that sustains many unjust cultural practices in the global South, Western philosophers who criticize those practices should also remember that Southern women are not simply passive victims of their cultures—notwithstanding the images of Amina Lawal. On the contrary, many countries in the global South, including Nigeria, have long-standing women's movements, and Nigerian feminists remain active in struggles to democratize their cultures and to protect women's human rights (Abdullah 1995; Basu 1995). Nigerian women are also active in struggles for justice against Western corporations; for instance, women from Itsekiri, Ijaw, Ilaje, and Urhobos are also currently challenging the activities of Shell Petroleum Development Company in the Niger Delta (Adebayo 2002). These women activists may have a better understanding of their own situation than that possessed by many of the Western philosophers who want to "save" them.

Western philosophers concerned about the plight of poor women in poor countries should not focus exclusively, and perhaps not primarily, on the cultural traditions of those countries. Since gender inequality is correlated so strongly with poverty, perhaps we should begin by asking why so many countries are so poor. To do so would encourage us to reflect on our own contribution to Amina Lawal's plight and this would be a more genuinely liberal approach because it would show more respect for non-Western women's ability to look after their own affairs according to their values and priorities." As citizens and residents of countries that exert disproportionate control over the global order, philosophers in the United States and the European Union bear direct responsibility for how that order affects women elsewhere in the world. Rather than simply blaming Amina Lawal's culture, Western philosophers should begin by taking our own feet off her neck.

NOTES

This paper is dedicated to the memory of Susan Moller Okin, whose work and friendship have been inspirational for me. Susan's dedication to justice for all women was unfailing both in her theoretical writings and in her life commitments. Before her death, Susan read this paper and graciously addressed its challenges.

This essay was initially written for a conference sponsored by the Carnegie Council on "Global Justice and Intercultural Dialogue," held in Shanghai, January 2004, and a slightly different version of it will appear in *Ethics & International Affairs*. The quotation in my title is taken from an article appearing in *Essence* magazine, although the *Essence* article portrays Lawal's Nigerian woman lawyer, Hauwa Ibrahim, rather than Western feminists, as "saving Amina" (Sansoni 2003). The present article develops arguments made in Jaggar 1998, 1999, 2001, 2002a, 2002b, 2002c, and 2004. I would like to thank Abigail Gosselin for her assistance in preparing the paper and participants in the "Global Justice and Intercultural Dialogue" conference, especially Thomas Pogge, for their helpful comments.

1. A note on my terminology: In this paper, "we" refers to philosophers sympathetic to political feminism who work in North America or the European Union. I have in mind primarily citizens but also, to a lesser extent, permanent residents. In speaking of countries' geopolitical and geo-economic locations, feminist scholars have used a variety of terminologies—all problematic in some respects. From the 1970s through the mid-1990s, feminists usually spoke of First, Second and Third Worlds but, by the mid-1990s, the collapse of the Soviet bloc, followed by the expansion of the global market and the establishment of the World Trade Organization, made this tripartite division seem less apt. Nevertheless, some theorists continue to use the term "Third World" as a political designation that also sometimes includes communities of color in North America and the European Union. Other scholars speak of the developed and developing worlds, but this terminology is open to the objection that it suggests a linear and Western-oriented model of development. Since the mid-1990s, my own preference usually has been to speak in terms of the global North and the global South, since this language suggests several contrasts that I find important in the present global political economy. Although I often find the terminology of global North and South provides a useful shorthand, in the present paper I speak mostly of countries that are poor and rich because this terminology is less theory-laden. All the available terminologies have different implications and all suggest binary oppositions that are in various ways objectionable.

2. Mary Daly, for example, contends that women worldwide are subjected to male violence, through such practices as witch-burning, *sati*, footbinding, and "female genital mutilation" (Daly 1978: 109–12). Daly is not isolated in her views. In November 2003, the controversial film "Warrior Marks: Female

Genital Mutilation,"was shown at the University of Colorado at Boulder as part of a weeklong series of events billed as "Breaking the Global Silence: Exposing Violence Against Women." Volpp provides a good overview of the feminist controversy surrounding "Warrior Marks" (Volpp 2001: 1208–9).

3. This debate arose out of concern that the supposedly universal "woman" invoked in much Western feminist writing in fact was a woman privileged along a number of dimensions. For instance, many theorists implicitly imagined her as white, middle-class, heterosexual, able-bodied, and so on. The feminist literature on essentialism discusses how the relationships among various aspects of women's diverse "identities" should be conceptualized (are they additive or multiplicative, analytically separable or not?) and problematizes the whole idea of a universal woman; for example, Carby 1982; Fuss 1989; Spelman 1988; Spivak 1988. The critique of essentialism is now widely accepted within the discipline of women's studies, where the term "essentialist" has become exclusively pejorative. The critique has been extremely valuable in revealing the biases lurking in many Western feminist generalizations about "women," although some theorists worry that denying that any essential characteristics can be attributed to women pulls the theoretical rug from under feminist activism (Martin 1994).

4. Philosophical disagreements between Nussbaum and Okin have recently become more explicit (Okin 2003; Nussbaum 2004).

5. Sen's concept of capabilities was designed in part to address the problem of adaptive preferences; he illustrated this problem by reference to Indian widows, who had learned to disregard their deprivation and bad health (Sen 1995 and elsewhere).

6. More generally, Nussbaum contends that, because preferences may be adaptive, existing desires provide an unreliable guide to justice and the good life, subverting intercultural agreement on universal values. In defending the universality of the capabilities, Nussbaum's earlier work appealed to the Aristotelian method of critically refining the *eudoxa* or reliable beliefs (Nussbaum 1998: 768). More recently, Nussbaum has developed a "non-Platonist substantive good" approach that allows her to postulate the capabilities as universal values even in the absence of expressed consensus (Nussbaum 2000). For critical discussion of this method, see Jaggar 2006.

7. Unlike Nussbaum, however, Okin does not limit herself to rhetorical gestures against antiessentialism. Instead, she argues against the essentialists that sexism can indeed be separated analytically from other categories of oppression, using empirical data to show that attention to gender is comparatively new to justice theories and development studies—and that it matters.

8. For instance, focusing exclusively on people's shared humanity and equal membership in the moral community diverts attention from the ways in which people's basic interests and empirical desires may differ, depending on their social locations. Focusing exclusively on the adult capacity for consistent

and universalizable moral reflection diverts attention from the indispensability of moral motivation, education, and the social availability of morally relevant information. Focusing exclusively on the dangers of egoism and partiality to one's own diverts attention from the dangers of self-sacrifice and devalues the moral significance of special relations (Calhoun 1988).

9. Both Nussbaum and Okin identify their topics as philosophical problems about culture, specifically, cultural relativism and multiculturalism. The term "culture" is also prominent in the titles of their writings about poor women in poor countries; one of Nussbaum's books is titled, *Women, Culture and Development*, and Okin's article analyzing the problems of poor women in poor countries is titled "Gender Inequality and Cultural Differences" [reprinted herein 233–57].

10. Nussbaum (1995: 62 [*GJSE* 497]) regards Chen's study as evidence of the need for her universal capabilities approach. Okin (1994: 15 [herein 245]) refers to Chen's work as evidence for her claims about cultural injustice to women.

11. The principles of neoliberalism include commitments to: free trade (except for the flow of labor); government withdrawal from the social welfare responsibilities assumed over the twentieth century; deregulation of such aspects of social life as wages, working conditions, and environmental protections; bringing all economically exploitable resources into private ownership. Policies justified by these principles have been imposed as conditions of borrowing on poor countries across the world by Western-dominated international financial institutions, such as the World Bank and the International Monetary Fund.

12. In 1960, the countries with the wealthiest fifth of the world's people had per capita incomes 30 times that of the poorest fifth; by 1990, the ratio had doubled to 60 to one; by 1997, it stood at 74 to one. By 1997, the richest 20 percent had captured 86 percent of the world's income, while the poorest 20 percent captured a mere 1 percent. For many—perhaps most—poor people in the world, neoliberal globalization has resulted in their material conditions of life deteriorating not only relative to the more affluent but also even absolutely. In more than 80 countries, per capita incomes are lower than they were a decade ago; in sub-Saharan Africa and some other least-developed countries, per capita incomes are lower than they were in 1970. In developing countries, nearly 1.3 billion people do not have access to clean water, 1 in 7 primary-age schoolchildren are not in school, 840 million people are malnourished, and an estimated 1.3 billion people live on incomes of less than $2 per day. Meanwhile, the assets of the 200 richest people in 1998 were more than the total income of 41 percent of all the world's people.

13. The informal economy is a shadow economy whose operations are not reflected in official records, whose workers typically do not pay taxes, and whose jobs are unregulated by health and safety standards. It covers a wide

range of income-generating activities, including declining handicrafts, small-scale retail trade, petty food production, street vending, domestic work, and prostitution, as well as home-based putting-out systems and contract work. Women predominate in the informal economy.

14. The worst devastation from AIDS occurs in the developing countries, where 93 percent of people with HIV/AIDS lived by the end of 1997, and especially in sub-Saharan Africa, where 80 percent of all deaths occur (UNIFEM 2000). The higher incidence of HIV among people living in the developing world has special significance for women's health, because women comprise a higher percentage of adults living with HIV/AIDS in these areas than they do in the wealthy countries. In sub-Saharan Africa, women account for 55 percent of all new cases of HIV (Nierenberg 2002).

15. The United Nations reports, "Small women-run businesses often can't compete with cheap imported products brought in by trade liberalization. In Africa, many of women's traditional industries such as food processing and basket making are being wiped out" (www.unifem.undp.org/ec_pov.htm).

16. Since women are primarily responsible for caring for children, women's poverty is reflected in disturbing statistics on children's nutritional status, mortality, and health. In many Southern countries the number of children who die before the age of one or five has risen sharply after decades of falling numbers. A new report by the United Nations Children's Fund (UNICEF), the first to measure child poverty scientifically, states that globalized trade and cuts to aid budgets keep a billion children in poverty (Frith 2003). Child poverty is a good indicator of women's poverty.

17. This implies that poverty may be understated even by the United Nations report that women comprise 70 percent of the world's poor, because this report is based on studies of consumption in female-headed compared with male-headed households.

18. Treating the poverty and economic dependence of non-Western women primarily as a matter of cultural constraint disturbingly echoes old Marxist analyses of women's issues as "superstructural" rather than part of the basic economic structure. It also encourages imaging non-Western women as "outside history," stuck in the backwaters of premodernity. (For extended criticism of this view, see Jaggar 1983.) This image continues to affect calculations of the economic contributions of women "at home," which are notoriously undercounted (Dixon-Mueller 1991).

19. In fact, Okin's latest work turns toward issues of political economy (Okin 2003).

20. Somewhat similarly, critics of recent Western-planned development projects have argued that these projects have often reinforced the subordination of women (Boserup 1970; Kabeer 1994; Visvanathan 1997).

21. Media in Europe and North America still portray brown or black women as tantalizing erotic subjects, while in non-European countries white

women are exoticized and eroticized (Kempadoo and Doezema 1998). Connell documents the emergence of a hegemonic transnational business masculinity, institutionally based in multinational corporations and global finance markets (Connell 1998).

22. Earlier this year, Lieutenant General William G. Boykin said of his Muslim opponent, "I knew that my god was bigger than his. I knew that my god was a real god and his was an idol" (Carroll 2003). This remark, offensive to Muslims across the world, including in the United States, suggested that the war on Iraq was after all a religious war or, as President Bush expressed it earlier, a "crusade."

23. On some accounts, for much of the twentieth century women fared better in the erstwhile Second World than in the First World. After the collapse of so-called communism, elites benefited from the privatization and exploitation of hitherto publicly owned resources, but the dismantling of welfare states meant cuts and deterioration in services in health, education, and child care, contributing to deteriorating quality of life for most people. In 7 out of 18 East European countries, life expectancy was lower in 1995 than in 1989 (falling as much as five years since 1987) and enrollment in kindergarten declined dramatically. Women suffered disproportionately from the massive unemployment which followed the collapse of the socialist economies and the decline of social services. They were pushed especially out of high-income and comparatively high-status positions in areas such as public management or universities, and many highly educated women were forced to turn to prostitution, street-vending, or begging.

24. During the twentieth century, civilians rather than soldiers constituted an ever-increasing proportion of the casualties of war. In World War I, 20 percent of the casualties were civilians, but in World War II, 50 percent were civilians. Some 80 percent of the casualties in the Vietnam War were civilians and about 90 percent of the casualties of today's wars are estimated to be civilians.

25. Although women almost everywhere suffer from cultural injustice, this does not mean that we are all victims of a universal patriarchy. Our respective situations, histories, and powers all vary widely, and for this reason our responsibilities also differ.

26. Fifteen years ago, Nussbaum and Sen already challenged sharp dichotomies between "internal" and "external" social criticism, noting the existence of extensive cross-cultural linkages (Nussbaum and Sen 1989).

27. The institutions that govern the global economy are formally democratic but in practice they are heavily influenced by a small group of wealthy countries. At both the World Bank and IMF, the number of votes a country receives is based on how much capital it gives the institution, so rich countries have disproportionate voting power. Each has about 150 members with a Board of Executive Directors with 24 members. Five of these directors are

appointed by five powerful countries: US, UK, France, Germany, and Japan. The President of the World Bank is elected by the Board and traditionally nominated by the US representative, while the managing director of the IMF is traditionally European. The World Trade Organization is also formally democratic in that each of its member countries has one representative who participates in negotiations over trade rules, but democracy within the WTO is limited in practice in many ways. Wealthy countries have far more influence than poor ones, and numerous meetings are restricted to the G-7 group, the most powerful member countries, excluding the less powerful even when decisions directly affect them.

28. India and Pakistan are among the poorest of all countries but India is now the fifth largest importer of major conventional weapons while Pakistan is the twelfth largest. Farrukh Saleem points out that, "When the poverty-ridden East fills (the) West's craving for drugs, there is talk of 'supply control.' (However), (t)he West remains... the largest seller of arms to the East" (Saleem 2003).

29. In addition to the considerations mentioned earlier, women suffer most from militarism's environmental destruction and its promotion of a sexist and violent culture in which men are glorified as warriors while women are either degraded or portrayed as national resources. Rape is a traditional weapon of war, and military activity is usually associated with organized and sometimes forced prostitution.

30. Kalpana Mehta observes that, in India, "NGOs could be said to be running a parallel government in the country, with priorities determined abroad and with no accountability to the people" (quoted in Silliman 1999: 147).

31. Western feminists may also support transnational feminist networks opposing violence against women and promoting their rights, such as the Latin American and Caribbean Women's Health Network, Women Living Under Muslim Laws, and ABANTU for Development (Keck and Sikkink 1998a; Ewig 1999: 83; Yuval-Davis 1997: 121).

32. Nussbaum is one philosopher who is explicit about this (Nussbaum 2000 and elsewhere). That academic writing does indeed have an influence outside academia is shown by politically motivated attacks on ethnic and feminist studies, as well as more recent attacks on postcolonial and Middle Eastern studies.

33. A recent letter to the *Colorado Daily* stated, "First, we need a five year moratorium on all immigration into this country to give us a 'collective break' from the onslaught of foreign languages, diseases being imported, female genital mutilation practiced by Middle Eastern and African muslim immigrants that is barbaric...." (Woolridge 2003).

34. Briggs and Mantini-Briggs describe Venezuelan public health officials blaming cultural practices for high morbidity and mortality from cholera, thereby deflecting charges of institutional corruption, inefficiency, indifference, and genocide (Briggs and Mantini-Briggs 2000, cited in Volpp 2001: 1192n47).

35. "We demand the right to choose and struggle around the issue of family oppression ourselves, within our communities... without white feminists making judgments as to the oppressive nature of arranged marriages" (Amos and Parmar 1984: 15).

REFERENCES

Abdullah, H. (1995) Wifeism and Activism: The Nigerian Women's Movement, in *The Challenge of Local Feminisms: Women's Movements in Global Perspective*. A. Basu, ed. Boulder, CO: Westview Press, pp. 209–25.

Adebayo, S. (2002) N-Delta Women Give Shell 10-Day Ultimatum on Demands (November 20, 2002). www.vanguardngr.com.

Ahmed, L. (1982) Western Ethnocentrism and Perceptions of the Harem. *Feminist Studies* 8: 521–34.

Alcoff, L. M. (1992) The Problem of Speaking for Others. *Cultural Critique* 20: 5–32.

Amos, V., and Parmar, P. (1984) Challenging Imperial Feminism. *Feminist Review* 17: 3–19.

Anderson, B. (2000) *Doing the Dirty Work? The Global Politics of Domestic Labour*. London: Zed Press.

Apffel-Marglin, F., and Simon, S. L. (1994) Feminist Orientalism and Development in: *Feminist Perspectives on Sustainable Development*. W. Harcourt, ed. London: Zed Press, pp. 26–45.

Barber, B. (1992) Jihad vs. MacWorld, *Atlantic Monthly* (March), 53–63.

Basu, A., ed. (1995) *The Challenge of Local Feminisms: Women's Movements in Global Perspective*. Boulder CO: Westview Press.

Bearup, G. (2004) Afghan Schoolgirls Poisoned. *The Guardian Weekly* (May 6–12), p. 4.

Benhabib, S. (2002) *The Claims of Culture: Equality and Diversity in the Global Era*. Princeton and Oxford: Princeton University Press.

Boserup, E. (1970) *Women's Role in Economic Development*. New York: St. Martin's Press.

Briggs, C. L., and Mantini-Briggs, C. (2000) "Bad Mothers" and the Threat to Civil Society: Race, Cultural Reasoning and the Institutionalization of Social Inequality in a Venezuelan Infanticide Trial. *Law and Social Inquiry* 25: 299–302.

Brown, D. L. (1991) Christian Missionaries, Western Feminists, and the Kikuyu Clitoridectomy Controversy in: *The Politics of Culture*. B. Williams, ed. Washington and London: Smithsonian Institution Press, pp. 243–72.

Burris, B. (1973) The Fourth World Manifesto, in *Radical Feminism*. A. Koedt, E. Levine and A. Rapone, eds. New York: Quadrangle, pp. 322–57.

Bush, G. W. (2002) The State of the Union: President Bush's State of the Union Address to Congress and the Nation. *New York Times*, Jan. 20, sec. A, 22, col. 1.

Bush, L. (2002) Mrs. Bush Discusses Status of Afghan Women at U.N.: Remarks by Mrs Laura Bush, March 8, www.whitehouse.gov/news/releases/2002/03/ 20020308-2.html.

Calhoun, C. (1988) Justice, Care, Gender Bias. *Journal of Philosophy* 85: 9.

Carby, H. (1982) White Women Listen, in *The Empire Strikes Back: Race and Racism in 70s Britain*. Centre for Contemporary Cultural Studies, ed. London: Hutchinson, pp. 213–35.

Carroll, J. (2003) Warring with God, *Boston Globe*. Op. Ed., October 21.

Chen, M. (1995) A Matter of Survival: Women's Right to Employment in India and Bangladesh, in Nussbaum and Glover (1995), pp. 37–57.

Connell, R. W. (1998) Masculinities and Globalization. *Men and Masculinities* 1(1):3–23.

Daly, M. (1978) *Gyn/Ecology: The Metaethics of Radical Feminism*. Boston: Beacon Press

Dixon-Mueller, R. (1991) Women in Agriculture: Counting the Labor Force in Developing Countries, in *Beyond Methodology: Feminist Scholarship as Lived Research*. M. M. Fonow and J. A. Cook, eds. Bloomington, IN: Indiana University Press.

Ewig, C. (1999) The Strengths and Limits of the NGO Women's Movement Model: Shaping Nicaragua's Democratic Institutions. *Latin American Research Review* 34(3): 75–102.

Fraser, N. (1997) From Redistribution to Recognition? Dilemmas of Justice in a "Postsocialist" Age, in *Justice Interruptus: Critical Reflections on the "Postsocialist" Condition*. New York and London: Routledge, pp. 11–39.

Frith, M. (2003) Global Trade Keeps a Billion Children in Poverty, Says UNICEF. *The Independent UK*, October 22.

Fuss, D. (1989) *Essentially Speaking: Feminism, Nature and Difference*. New York: Routledge.

Grewal, I., and Kaplan, C. (1994) *Scattered Hegemonies: Postmodernity and Transnational Feminist Practices.* Minneapolis and London: University of Minnesota Press.

Huntington, S. P. (1996) *The Clash of Civilizations and the Remaking of World Order.* New York: Simon & Shuster.

Imam, A., and Medar-Gould, S. (2003) Please Stop the International Lawal Protest Letter Campaigns, May 1.

Jaggar, A. M. (1983) *Feminist Politics and Human Nature.* Totowa, NJ: Rowman & Littlefield.

Jaggar, A. M. (1998) Globalizing Feminist Ethics. *Hypatia* 13(2):7–31. Reprinted in: *Decentering the Center: Philosophy for a Multicultural, Postcolonial, and Feminist World.* U. Narayan and S. Harding, eds. Bloomington IN: Indiana University Press, 2000.

Jaggar, A. M. (1999) Multicultural Democracy. *Journal of Political Philosophy* 7(3):308–329.

Jaggar, A. M. (2001) Is Globalization Good for Women? *Comparative Literature* 53(4):298–314.

Jaggar, A. M. (2002a) A Feminist Critique of the Alleged Southern Debt. *Hypatia* 17(4):119–42.

Jaggar, A. M. (2002b) Vulnerable Women and Neo-Liberal Globalization: Debt Burdens Undermine Women's Health in the Global South, *Theoretical Medicine and Bioethics* 23(6):425–40.

Jaggar, A. M. (2002c) Challenging Women's Global Inequalities: Some Priorities for Western Philosophers, *Philosophical Topics* 30(2):229–53.

Jaggar, A. M. (2004) Western Feminism and Global Responsibility, in *Feminist Interventions in Ethics and Politics.* B. S. Andrew, J. Keller, and L. H. Schwarzman, eds. Lanham, MD: Rowman & Littlefield.

Jaggar, A. M. (2006) "Reasoning About Well-Being: Nussbaum's Methods of Justifying the Capabilities" *Journal of Political Philosophy* 14(3) (September 2006): 301–22.

Kabeer, N. (1994) *Reversed Realities: Gender Hierarchies in Development Thought.* London and New York: Verso.

Kang, H.-R. (2004) Transnational Women's Collectivities as Agents of Global Justice Claims, paper read to American Philosophical Association Pacific Division Meeting, Global Justice Mini-Conference, March.

Keck, M. E., and Sikkink, K. (1998a) Transnational Networks on Violence against Women, in Keck and Sikkink 1998b, pp. 165–99.

Keck, M. E., and Sikkink, K. (1998b) *Activists Beyond Borders: Advocacy Networks in International Politics*. Ithaca, NY: Cornell University Press.

Kempadoo, K., and Doezema, J. (1998) *Global Sex Workers: Rights, Resistance and Redefinition*. New York: Routledge.

Kymlicka, W. (1995) *Multicultural Citizenship: A Liberal Theory of Minority Rights*. Oxford: Clarendon Press and New York: Oxford University Press.

Martin, J. R. (1994) Methodological Essentialism, False Difference, and Other Dangerous Traps. *Signs: Journal of Women in Culture and Society* 19(3):630–57.

Mohanty, C. T. (1991) Under Western Eyes: Feminist Scholarship and Colonial Discourse, in *Third World Women and the Politics of Feminism*. C. T. Mohanty, A. Russo, and L. Torres, eds. Bloomington, IN: Indiana University Press, pp. 51–80.

Morgan, R., ed. (1984) *Sisterhood is Global*. Garden City, NY: Anchor Press/Doubleday.

Moser, C. O. N. (1991) Gender Planning in the Third World: Meeting Practical and Strategic Needs, in *Gender and International Relations*. R. Grant and K. Newland, eds. Bloomington, IN: Indiana University Press, pp. 83–111.

Narayan, U. (1997) *Dislocating Cultures: Identities, Traditions and Third World Feminism*. New York: Routledge.

Narayan, U. (1998) Essence of Culture and a Sense of History: A Feminist Critique of Cultural Essentialism. *Hypatia* 13(2), reprinted in *Decentering the Center: Philosophy for a Multicultural, Postcolonial, and Feminist World*. U. Narayan and S. Harding, eds. Bloomington, IN: Indiana University Press, 2000.

Nierenberg, D. (2002) What's Good for Women is Good for the World. *World Summit Policy Briefs*. Washington, DC: Worldwatch Institute.

Nussbaum, M. C. (1988) Nature Function and Capability: Aristotle on Political Distribution. *Oxford Studies in Ancient Philosophy*. Supplementary Volume, pp. 145–84.

Nussbaum, M. C. (1990) Aristotelian Social Democracy, in *Liberalism and the Good*. R. B. Douglass, G. Mara, and H. Richardson, eds. New York: Routledge, pp. 203–52. German trans. 1999 in *Gerechtigkeit oder das gute Leben*. H. Pauer-Studer, ed. Suhrkamp, Frankfurt, pp. 24–85.

Nussbaum, M. C. (1992) Human Functioning and Social Justice: In Defense of Aristotelian Essentialism. *Political Theory* 20(2):202–46.

Nussbaum, M. C. (1993) Non-Relative Virtues: An Aristotelian Approach, in Nussbaum and Sen 1993, pp. 242–69.

Nussbaum, M. C. (1995) Human Capabilities, Female Human Beings, in Nussbaum and Glover 1995, pp. 61–104 [reprinted in *Global Justice: Seminal Essays*, 495–551].

Nussbaum, M. C. (1998) Public Philosophy and International Feminism. *Ethics* 108:762–96.

Nussbaum, M. C. (1999) *Sex and Social Justice*. New York: Oxford University Press.

Nussbaum, M. C. (2000) *Women and Human Development: The Capabilities Approach*. Cambridge: Cambridge University Press.

Nussbaum, M. C. (2002) Sex, Laws, and Inequality: What India Can Teach the United States. *Daedalus* (winter): 95–106.

Nussbaum, M. C. (2004) On Hearing Women's Voices: A Reply to Susan Okin. *Philosophy and Public Affairs* 32(2): 193–205.

Nussbaum, M. C., and Glover, J., eds. (1995) *Women, Culture, and Development: A Study of Human Capabilities*. Oxford: Clarendon Press.

Nussbaum, M. C., and Sen, A. K. (1989) Internal criticism and Indian Rationalist Traditions, in *Relativism: Interpretation and Confrontation*. M. Krausz, ed. Notre Dame: Notre Dame University Press, pp. 299–325.

Nussbaum, M. C., and Sen, A. K., eds. (1993) *The Quality of Life*, Oxford: Clarendon Press.

Obiora, L. A. (1997) Feminism, Globalization and Culture: After Beijing. *Ind. J. Global Legal Studies* 4:355–406.

Okin, S. M. (1989) *Justice, Gender and the Family*. New York: Basic Books.

Okin, S. M. (1994) Gender Inequality and Cultural Differences. *Political Theory* 22(1) [reprinted herein 233–57].

Okin, S. M. (1995) Response to Jane Flax. *Political Theory* 23(3).

Okin, S. M. (1998) Feminism and Multiculturalism: Some Tensions. *Ethics* 108:661–684.

Okin, S. M. (with respondents) (1999) *Is Multiculturalism Bad for Women?* J. Cohen, M. Howard, and M. C. Nussbaum, eds. Princeton, NJ: Princeton University Press.

Okin, S. M. (2002) "Mistresses of Their Own Destiny": Group Rights, Gender, and Realistic Rights of Exit. *Ethics* 112:205–30.

Okin, S. M. (2003) Poverty, Well-Being, and Gender: What Counts, Who's Heard? *Philosophy and Public Affairs* 31(3):280–316.

Oldenburg, V. T. (2002) *Dowry Murder: The Imperial Origins of a Cultural Crime*. New York: Oxford University Press.

O'Neill, O. (1996) *Towards Justice and Virtue: A Constructive Account of Practical Reasoning.* Cambridge: Cambridge University Press.

Parekh, B. (2000) *Rethinking Multiculturalism: Cultural Diversity and Political Theory.* Cambridge, MA: Harvard University Press.

Peterson, V. S., and Runyan, A. S. (1999) *Global Gender Issues.* Boulder, CO: Westview Press.

Pogge, T. W. (2002) *World Poverty and Human Rights: Cosmopolitan Responsibilities and Reforms.* Cambridge: Polity Press.

Pollitt, K. (2002) As Miss World Turns. *The Nation*, December.

Saleem, F. (2003) *The News International* (Pakistan), www.jang.com.pk/thenews/jan2003daily/12-01-2003/oped/o1.htm, January 15.

Sandler, L. (2003) Women under Siege. *The Nation*, December 29.

Sansoni, S. (2003) Saving Amina. *Essence*, March, pp. 156–59.

Sen, A. K. (1990) More than 100 Million Women are Missing. *New York Review of Books*, December 20.

Sen, A. K. (1995) Gender Inequality and Theories of Justice, in Nussbaum and Glover 1995, pp. 259–73.

Sen, G., and Grown, C. (1987) *Development, Crises and Alternative Visions: Third World Women's Perspectives.* New York: Monthly Review Press.

Shachar, A. (1999) The Paradox of Multicultural Vulnerability: Individual Rights, Identity Groups, and the State, in *Multicultural Questions.* C. Joppke and S. Lukes, eds. New York: Oxford University Press.

Shachar, A. (2000a) On Citizenship and Multicultural Vulnerability. *Political Theory* 28:64–89.

Shachar, A. (2000b) The Puzzle of Interlocking Power Hierarchies: Sharing the Pieces of Jurisdictional Authority. *Harvard Civil Rights–Civil Liberties Law Review* 35(2):387–426.

Silliman, J. (1999) Expanding Civil Society, Shrinking Political Spaces: The Case of Women's Nongovernmental Organizations, in *Dangerous Intersections: Feminist Perspectives on Population, Environment, and Development.* J. Silliman and Y. King, eds. Cambridge, MA: South End Press.

Spelman, E. V. (1988) *Inessential Woman: Problems of Exclusion in Feminist Thought.* Boston, MA: Beacon Press.

Spivak, G. C. (1988) Can the Subaltern Speak?, in *Marxism and the Interpretation of Culture.* C. Nelson and L. Grossberg, eds. Urbana, IL: University of Illinois Press, pp. 271–313.

Sturdevant, S. (2001) Who Benefits? US Military, Prostitution and Base Conversion, in *Frontline Feminisms: Women, War, and Resistance*. M. R. Waller and J. Rycenga, eds. New York and London: Routledge, pp. 141–57.

Tomlinson, J. (1991) *Cultural Imperialism: A Critical Introduction*. Baltimore, MD: Johns Hopkins University Press.

UNDP (1999) Facts and Figures on Poverty. www.undp.org/teams/english/facts.htm.

UNDP (2000) *Human Development Report 2000*. New York: Oxford University Press; also available at www.undp.org/hdr2000/english/HDR2000.html.

UNIFEM (United Nations Development Fund for Women) (2000): *Progress of the World's Women*. UNIFEM, New York.

Visvanathan, N. (1997) Introduction to Part I, in *The Women, Gender and Development Reader*. N. Vivvanathan (Co-Ordinator), L. Duggan, L. Nisonoff, and N. Wiegersma, eds. London: Zed Press.

Volpp, L. (2000) Blaming Culture for Bad Behavior. *Yale Journal of Law and Humanities* 12:89–116.

Volpp, L. (2001) Feminism versus Multiculturalism. *Columbia Law Review* 101(5):1181–1218.

Williams, R. (1983) *Keywords: A Vocabulary of Culture and Society*. 2nd ed. London: Fontana.

Woolridge, F. (2003) Letter to the Editor of the *Colorado Daily*. November 18, p. 10.

Young, I. M. (2003) The Logic of Masculinist Protection: Reflections on the Current Security State. *Signs: Journal of Women in Culture and Society* 29(11):1–25.

Yuval-Davis, N. (1997) *Gender and Nation*. London: Sage Publications.

COMMON INDEX

References in Roman numerals (i, ii, iii…) are to the Common Preface. References in Arabic numerals (1, 2, 3…) are to *Global Justice: Seminal Essays*. References in italic Arabic numerals (*1, 2, 3…*) are to *Global Ethics: Seminal Essays*. This index was composed by Matt Peterson.